FEMALE ACTS IN GREEK TRAGEDY

MARTIN CLASSICAL LECTURES

The Martin Classical Lectures are delivered annually at
Oberlin College through a foundation established by his many
friends in honor of Charles Beebe Martin, for forty-five
years a teacher of classical literature and classical
art at Oberlin.

•

JOHN PERADOTTO, *Man in the Middle Voice: Name and
Narration in the* Odyssey

MARTHA C. NUSSBAUM, *The Therapy of Desire: Theory and
Practice in Hellenistic Ethics*

JOSIAH OBER, *Political Dissent in Democratic Athens:
Intellectual Crisis of Popular Rule*

ANNE CARSON, *Economy of the Unlost (Reading Simonides of
Keos with Paul Celan)*

HELENE P. FOLEY, *Female Acts in Greek Tragedy*

MARK W. EDWARDS, *Sound, Sense, and Rhythm:
Listening to Greek and Latin Poetry*

Helene P. Foley

FEMALE ACTS

IN GREEK TRAGEDY

PRINCETON UNIVERSITY PRESS

PRINCETON AND OXFORD

Copyright © 2001 by Princeton University Press
Published by Princeton University Press, 41 William Street,
Princeton, New Jersey 08540
In the United Kingdom: Princeton University Press, 3 Market Place,
Woodstock, Oxfordshire OX20 1SY
All Rights Reserved

Third printing, and first paperback printing, 2003
Paperback ISBN 0-691-09492-6

The Library of Congress has cataloged the cloth edition of this book as follows

Foley, Helene P., 1942–
Female acts in Greek tragedy / Helene P. Foley.
p.   cm.—(Martin classical lectures)
Includes bibliographical references (p.) and index.
ISBN 0-691-05030-9 (alk. paper)
1. Greek drama (Tragedy)—History and criticism.   2. Women and
literature—Greece.   3. Women in literature.   I. Title.   II. Martin
classical lectures (Unnumbered).   New series.
PA3136 .F65   2001
882'.0109352042—dc21   00-060624

British Library Cataloging-in-Publication Data is available

This book has been composed in Goudy Old Style

Printed on acid-free paper. ∞

www.pupress.princeton.edu

Printed in the United States of America

10   9   8   7   6   5   4   3

For Duncan, Christian, and Froma

Contents

Acknowledgments _____

THIS BOOK has been a long time in the making. So many individual scholars, students, and institutions have in one way or another helped me to formulate and improve my ideas that I have decided to note contributions to individual chapters locally. Nevertheless, some special thanks belong here. The following have at one stage or another read more than one chapter of the book, and I am profoundly grateful to all of them: Duncan Foley, Richard Seaford, and Christian Wolff; the referees for Princeton Press, Mark Griffith and Donald Mastronarde; and the anonymous referee for the Martin Lectures Committee. The intellectual friendship and personal support of Susan Cole, Carolyn Dewald, Simon Goldhill, Frederick Griffiths, Edith Hall, Natalie Kampen, Marilyn Arthur Katz, Rachel Kitzinger, Dirk Obbink, Robin and Catherine Osborne, Sarah Pomeroy, Cynthia Patterson, Daniel Selden, Alan Shapiro, Laura Slatkin, Susan Stephens, Oliver Taplin, Froma Zeitlin, and the late Jack Winkler have also been critical. Brian MacDonald served as an invaluable copyeditor.

I wish to thank the John Solomon Guggenheim Foundation, the National Endowment for the Humanities, and Barnard College, Columbia University, for supporting the writing of this book.

Finally, I am grateful to Oberlin College for inviting me to present the Martin Classical Lectures, for offering me such wonderful hospitality and criticism while I was there, and for permitting me to embed those lectures in a larger study. The lectures themselves dealt exclusively with the issues discussed in part III of the book, but have been changed considerably to fit a new format.

I also wish to thank the following presses and journals for permission to publish revised versions of the following articles or book chapters: to *Classical Antiquity* and the Regents of the University of California for "Medea's Divided Self," *Classical Antiquity* 8.1 (1989), 61–85, now revised as III.5; to Routledge (Taylor and Francis) for "*Anodos* Dramas: Euripides' *Alcestis* and *Helen*," in R. Hexter and D. Selden, eds., *Innovations of Antiquity* (New York, 1992), 133–60, now revised as IV; to Levante Editori and the editors of *Tragedy, Comedy and the Polis* for "The Politics of Tragic Lamentation," in A. H. Sommerstein, S. Halliwell, J. Henderson, and B. Zimmermann, eds., *Tragedy, Comedy and the Polis* (Bari, 1993), 101–43, now revised as I; and to Oxford University Press for "Penelope as Moral Agent," in Beth Cohen, ed., *The Distaff Side: Representing the Female in Homer's Odyssey* (Oxford, 1995), 93–115, now revised as part of III.1, and "Antigone as Moral Agent," in M. S. Silk, ed., *Tragedy and the Tragic: Greek Theatre and Beyond* (Oxford, 1996), 49–73, now revised as III.3.

I dedicate this book to three people whose inspiration has been critical to its formation and development: Christian Wolff, who has not only faithfully criticized my work over the years, but inspired my interest in tragedy in graduate school and helped me through my dissertation; Froma Zeitlin, with whom I have been thinking about these issues and whose work I have admired since shortly after our first publications on women in antiquity; and my husband Duncan Foley, whose ability to stand within Classics due to his knowledge of Latin and Greek, and outside as a scholar in another field, has been as valuable as his daily support, love, and understanding.

Introductory Note and Abbreviations _____

ALL QUOTATIONS and citations from the Greek are from Oxford Classical texts unless otherwise noted. Translations from the Greek are my own if not attributed to others. In general I have Latinized Greek names in order make them more familiar to the nonclassical reader unless doing so would in fact defamiliarize the word (e.g., Core for Kore).

Abbreviations used in the book include the following:

IG   *Inscriptiones Graecae*. Berlin, 1931–.
N²   A. Nauck, ed. *Tragicorum Graecorum Fragmenta*. Leipzig, 1856. Reprint, Hildesheim, 1964.
PMG   D. Page, ed. *Poetae Melici Graeci*. Oxford, 1962. Reprint, 1967.
TrGF   *Tragicorum Graecorum Fragmenta*. Vol. 1, B. Snell, ed., *Tragici Minores*. Vol. 3, S. Radt, ed., *Aeschylus*. Vol. 4, S. Radt, ed., *Sophocles*. Göttingen, 1971, 1985, 1977.
West   M. L. West, ed. *Iambi et Elegi Graeci ante Alexandrum Cantati*. Vols. 1 and 2. Oxford, 1971–72.

FEMALE ACTS IN GREEK TRAGEDY

Introduction _____

What is it about women that interests Mr.
Jacquot? "I was born a man," Mr. Jacquot said,
"and women are a part of humanity that is at once
familiar and very, very strange to me. It's difficult
for a man to ask the question, what is a man. It's
as if the question just doesn't arise. Or as if we
already know the response, and it's not necessarily
amusing. But a woman can ask herself the
question, what is a woman. I try to respond to
that question with the female characters I invent
and the actresses I film. And they always lead me
to further questions."
   (French filmmaker Benoit Jacquot, New York Times, August 2, 1998)

GREEK tragedy was written and performed by men and aimed—perhaps not exclusively if women were present in the theater—at a large, public male audience.[1] Masculine identity and conflicts remain central to the enterprise, but
the texts often explore or query these issues through female characters and the
culturally more marginal positions that they occupy. Such indirection is basic
to the genre as a whole. Tragic plots borrow from the whole repertoire of Greek
myths, often myths about cities other than Athens, and the plays take place in
the remote past. The heroic kings who dominate the cities of Greek tragedies
no more directly reflect the leaders of Athenian democracy than the active and
assertive women who make public choices and determine the outcome of the
plot of so many Greek tragedies resemble their more restricted Athenian counterparts. At the same time, in part through deploying deliberate anachronisms
or overlapping features of the fictional past and the lived present, the tragedies
provoke an implicit dialogue between present and past,[2] and the enduring
fascination of these stories of powerful aristocratic families for a democratic
polis (city-state) requires explanation.

   The study of tragic women is both more limited and in a sense more elusive
than that of tragic men. Tragedy at least makes a pretense of knowing what

---

[1] On the question of women's presence in the theater, see most recently Podlecki 1990, Henderson 1991, and Goldhill 1994. I am of the opinion that a limited number of (perhaps predominantly older or noncitizen) women were present along with metics, foreigners, and slaves, but that
the performances were primarily aimed at citizen men.

[2] See esp. Vernant 1981 and Easterling 1985.

women are and how they should act, and has a repertoire of clichés to draw on in describing them. As a category, women are a "tribe" apparently less differentiated as individuals than men; paradoxically, they are both more embedded in the social system and marginal to its central institutions.[3] Ideally, their speech and action should be severely limited, since they are by nature incapable of full social maturity and independence (see III.1). At the same time, tragedy generically prefers representing situations and behavior that at least initially invert, disrupt, and challenge cultural ideals. Although many female characters in tragedy do not violate popular norms for female behavior, those who take action, and especially those who speak and act publicly and in their own interest, represent the greatest and most puzzling deviation from the cultural norm.

These female interventions would be less puzzling if they could be explained simply as inversions of the norm designed to be cautionary demonstrations of the cultural consequences of stepping out of line. Yet, as we shall see, this is not consistently the case; and even when it is, the repercussions of female speech and action and the ways in which they are represented raise an unexpectedly broad and disconcerting set of questions. For this reason, recent critics, including myself, have hypothesized that female characters are doing double duty in these plays, by representing a fictional female position in the tragic family and city and simultaneously serving as a location from which to explore a series of problematic issues that men prefer to approach indirectly and certainly not through their own persons.[4] In this sense, the female acts investigated in this book are fe(male) acts designed not only by but for men.

Women played a significant role in Athenian culture as reproducers of children, as participants in public and private religious rituals and festivals, and as caretakers within households. Their most important and active tragic interventions tend to reflect these realities, but with a critical difference, since female characters can exercise an independence and a latitude not, at least ideally, permitted to them outside fiction. This book looks first at the tragic representation of women in burial ritual, above all as lamenters of the dead (I), and second, at male and female responses toward and attempts to negotiate the contradictory marriage system that heavily governed Athenian private lives (II and IV). The third and largest part (III, 1–6, the core of the Martin Lectures) deals with ethical interventions by women at different stages of their reproductive lives (as virgin, wife, and mature mother) in the form of choices made or attempts to persuade others to act in their behalf. Each part lays the historical and interpretive groundwork for its own section, but the issues discussed in earlier sections continue to play a role in later ones. Thus, for example, III.2 deals with the *ethics* of women's role as lamenters of the dead in Sophocles' *Elec-*

---

[3] Loraux 1978. In tragedy, however, they can, due to their very marginality, represent a more complex perspective than male characters (Zeitlin 1996: 363).

[4] See esp. Just 1975 and 1989, Gould 1980, Foley 1981, and Zeitlin 1996, esp. 1985a.

tra, and III.4 takes up the challenge made by Clytemnestra to the institution of marriage. Part IV, which addresses Euripides' *Alcestis* and *Helen*, brings together all the themes of the book but with a special focus on marriage.

In the case of each of the major topics discussed in this book we have evidence external to tragedy, especially in prose texts, that these were areas that the culture recognized as not only central but somehow problematic in relation to women. Starting from the archaic period, for example, Athens more than once attempted to control and curtail women's public role in death ritual (I). The emerging city also passed legislation concerning marriage and inheritance and evidence for tensions over and violations of these legal restrictions appears throughout the classical period. For example, Pericles' citizenship law of 451–450 B.C.E, which restricted citizenship to those with two citizen parents, apparently lapsed and was repassed in 403; inheritance law, which aimed to insure the continuity of each household, including those left only with female heirs, met with abuses and controversies that emerge repeatedly in fourth-century court cases (II). Finally, women were not allowed to exercise legal autonomy; hence they normally did not make significant social and economic choices without the supervision of a guardian. Yet philosophers can raise questions about the advisability of women's extreme ethical subordination, and court cases allow us to catch glimpses of women exercising greater autonomy within the household than we might have expected from Athenian ideology (III.6).[5]

The discussion of tragedy in each part of the book takes place in the context of this historical evidence, and permits us better to understand how tragedy deviates from or responds to cultural norms. Thus, as we shall see, tragic lamenters may violate or be forced to conform to the restrictions of the funerary legislation, tragic men and women may escape or implicitly confront the limits of Athenian marriage and inheritance law, and tragic women may make significant and sometimes public choices (commonly but by no means exclusively relating to self-sacrifice or revenge) in the absence of male guardians.[6] Although the plays do not allow their audience to forget the limits imposed on women in real life,[7] the interventions of female characters go beyond being caution-

---

[5] Among the many forms of power, formal or informal, secular or ritual, overt or covert, power exercised singly or jointly, one would expect women to exercise informal, ritual, covert, or shared power in Athens, whether or not this was openly acknowledged.

[6] Hall 1997: 106–9 and McClure 1999 stress that tragic women generally make important decisions in the absence of guardians. Yet we do hear of autonomous decisions, such as Alcestis' choice to sacrifice herself for her husband, that occurred with his knowledge. Moreover, Helen in Euripides' *Helen* first expresses willingness to die and then plans the couple's escape in the presence of her husband Menelaus, and Iphigeneia's choice to sacrifice herself in Euripides' *Iphigeneia at Aulis* is made before Achilles, if not her father.

[7] See Foley 1981: 135, Harder 1993, and Seidensticker 1995. Harder usefully attempts to survey in detail the degree to which Euripidean women conform to gender expectations or go beyond them; even those who attempt to take action are frequently unsuccessful at accomplishing their goals.

ary examples of the dangers of permitting independence to women. Because we have access to the cultural clichés and the expectations that defined women for men, examining their role in tragedy allows us to address a more limited and accessible issue than we would encounter in looking at male roles in the same genre and to begin to define more fully what kind of response tragedy is making to the environment in which it was performed.

Conceptions of Tragic Women

Before returning to a more detailed discussion of the approaches that I adopt in this book, I would like to review briefly scholarly progress on conceptions of tragic women to date. The earliest phases of this investigation were largely historical. Scholars puzzled over a range of apparently contradictory evidence on the subject of Attic women, and especially their seemingly anomalous representation in drama.[8] Leaving aside women's strikingly assertive and even rebellious behavior, the pervasive presence of female characters on the public stage in a society that preferred its own women to have as limited a public reputation as possible was even in antiquity something of a surprise.[9] As early as the second century C.E., the writer Lucian (*De Saltatione* 28) commented that there were more women than men in these plays; Achilles Tatius' *Leucippe and Clitophon* (1.8) remarks on the many plots women have contributed to the tragic stage, as they kill the men they love or hate; only one extant tragedy lacks a woman (Sophocles' *Philoctetes*) and female choruses outnumber their male counterparts in the remaining plays (twenty-one to ten).[10] Moreover, tragedy apparently expands on and often makes more controversial the roles that mythical women played in archaic literature.[11]

By now, the probable relation between life and the tragic stage is better understood; the gap between drama and what we believe to be lived reality exists, but we can envision it on terms that make fiction part of the same social universe.[12] From a generic perspective Greek drama does not directly reflect

---

[8] See esp. Gould 1980, Foley 1981, Blok 1987, Versnel 1987, Rabinowitz 1993, Blundell 1995, Fantham et al. 1994, and Seidensticker 1995, all with earlier bibliography. As A. W. Gomme famously remarked (1925: 4:), "There is, in fact, no literature, no art of any country, in which women are more prominent, more important, more carefully studied and with more interest, than in the tragedy, sculpture, and painting of fifth-century Athens."

[9] On female reputation, see esp. Thucydides 2.46, Gorgias 22 Diels-Kranz, and Lysias 3.6. In court cases witnesses could be summoned to confirm the identity of a respectable wife (Demosthenes 43.29–46 and Isaeus 8.9–10), and the names of living women were mentioned in court only if the orator aimed to cast suspicion on them (Schaps 1975).

[10] See Hall 1997: 105.

[11] Foley 1981: 133.

[12] As Roger Just put it in a pioneering article (1975: 157), woman in drama is a "cultural product" and an "ideological formation" that must be situated "within the semantic field formed by Athenian society."

contemporary life but a remote, imaginary, and aristocratic world that often deliberately inverts or distorts the cultural norm; on the other hand, such inversions testify to an implicit norm, and tragedy often either reminds its audience of or abides by contemporary standards. Thus female characters can be admonished to stay in their place within and keep silent; men express outrage at a female challenge; aberrant women are labeled as masculine.[13] Finally, the Athenian audience must have experienced these female characters in a fashion that grew out of their psychological, political, and social lives.

On the one hand, Attic women were formally excluded from the political and military life of their city; this exclusion was important given the particular significance that Athens' radical democracy placed on participation in public life. They could not attend assemblies, serve on juries, or even speak in court. Nor did they receive the kind of education that would have permitted them to do so.[14] Tragedy, even though it is set in the remote past, largely respects these restrictions with occasional exceptions. Aeschylus' Clytemnestra, for example, is imagined to have exercised power legitimately during her husband's absence at Troy and she later becomes coruler of Argos with Aegisthus; characters like Euripides' foreign Medea or his priestess' daughter Melanippe (*Melanippe Sophe*) lay claim to a remarkable feminine wisdom and many tragic women argue with great rhetorical sophistication.

Although a citizen wife was necessary for the production of legitimate children, women were not registered at birth as citizens in the city's phratries (clans).[15] Their "citizenship" was exercised not politically but religiously. Priestesses of many important cults were citizen women, and the form of female participation undertaken in a range of civic cults could depend on citizenship.[16] Tragic women sometimes seem to confine their horizons strictly to a domestic world, but others clearly view themselves as citizens and even act for their state. Antigone and Ismene clash over exactly these priorities at the beginning of Sophocles' *Antigone* (see III.3). Euripides' sacrificial virgins (III.1) and persuasive mothers (III.6) can pointedly subordinate family to civic concerns. Tragedy thus implicitly adopts a more inclusive and symbolic view of citizenship than those historians who stress a strictly political definition.[17]

[13] See, e.g., Euripides' *Phoenissae* 88–95, 193–201, *Electra* 341–44, *Heracleidae* 474–77; Sophocles' *Antigone* 484–85; and Aeschylus' *Agamemmnon* 11.

[14] Attendance at the theater, at the Homeric recitations at the Panathenaic festivals, and at other festivals that included myth-based songs and dance would have given women, if they attended them, an oral education. Yet knowledge of reading and writing was probably limited (Cole 1981). Xenophon's *Oeconomicus* 7.5–6 suggests that even a girl's domestic education was minimal.

[15] On the question of female citizenship, see esp. Patterson 1986.

[16] See esp. Turner 1983. Osborne 1993 indirectly supports this point.

[17] Osborne 1997 has argued that the growing prominence of women on both white-ground lekythoi (oil flasks) and funerary stelai represents a new emphasis on the importance of the dead to the family circle and testifies to the legitimate citizenship and reproductive capacities of wives and mothers. Sixth-century funerary stelai stressed aristocratic male public achievement.

The respectable, citizen women of the middle and upper middle classes about which our sources provide the majority of the evidence ideally spent their lives indoors or with women in the immediate neighborhood and were primarily oriented to domestic affairs.[18] Even shopping or fetching water was generally done by men or slaves. Yet women also came out of the house frequently to attend religious events and were aware of much that went on in the public world. Tragedy occurs outside the stage building and thus putatively, and sometimes pointedly, stages its women in public or religious spaces. Nevertheless, as Easterling and others have stressed,[19] the plays often treat the spaces before the stage building as in essence domestic and women generally do not stray far from the stage doorway.

As lifelong legal minors, Attic women were meant to make important decisions under the supervision of a guardian (*kurios*), although they could and apparently did exercise influence on family matters concerning adoption and inheritance and may have offered opinions on public affairs (see III.6). Women married young and ideally did not choose their spouses, manage their dowries, divorce without the approval of their kin, or conduct financial transactions over the value of one *medimnos* of barley (enough food to sustain a family for several days). Tragic women, however, frequently make important autonomous decisions, often in the absence of male guardians, and can deliberately flout the authority of their men. Thus tragedy apparently deliberately violates cultural norms, but many of these female decisions (though there are glaring exceptions) involve domestic rather than public life.

Although the gap between tragedy and reality remains critical to evaluating the tragic response to the Attic environment in which it was performed, this focus has ultimately proved to be a less interesting way of getting at the provocative and interesting aspects of tragic women than studies of how the plays use these aspects to think about a range of issues.[20] I outline the major contributions to this second approach briefly here. The remainder of the book also includes contributions made in articles or book chapters that illuminate our understanding of the representation of women in specific Greek tragedies as well as more specialized studies.[21]

Early Greek thought often relied on binary oppositions. In the Pythagorean table of opposites, for example, male is linked with limit, odd, one, resting, straight, light, good, and square and female with unlimited, even, plurality, left,

---

[18] See note 7. Given the limited role of lower-class women and slaves in tragedy, I do not dwell on their status here, except in my discussion of concubines in part II. Poorer women probably participated in agriculture and certainly sold goods at markets. See Aristotle, *Politics* 4.1300a; see also 6.1323a.

[19] See esp. Padel 1990, Easterling 1988, Seidensticker 1995.

[20] See Zeitlin 1996: 1–18, esp. 8, and Foley 1981.

[21] For other important studies, see esp. Loraux 1987 on modes of female death in tragedy and various essays in her 1995a, all of Zeitlin 1996, Harder 1993, and Hall 1997.

curved, dark, bad, and oblong (Aristotle, *Metaphysics* 1.5.986a). Taking a cue from the prominent male-female conflicts and polarizations of Greek tragedy, early work on the conception of women in tragedy explored the significance of the structural equations male : female as culture : nature and male : female as public : private/domestic.[22] My 1981 essay on the conception of women in Athenian drama argued for the relevance of this approach with some substantial qualifications. First, although tragedy can represent women as more closely linked with "nature" or the supernatural than men, both tragic men and women align themselves at various points with what the texts define as nature or culture, mediate between them, or attempt to transcend natural and cultural limits; moreover, the tragic sense of these mutually defined terms does not remain stable over time and is often contested.[23]

Second, it is precisely because neither sex is firmly aligned with household or state that tragic conflicts become so complex and messy and tensions arise both within and between public and private worlds. As I put it then: "Both men and women share an interest in the *oikos* and in the values that help it to survive. But each sex performs for the *oikos* a different function, each requiring different virtues, and acts in separate spaces, one inside, one outside. Each sex also shares an interest in the *polis*, and performs different public functions that help to perpetuate the state, the male political and military functions, which exclude women, the female religious functions. In each sphere the male holds legal authority over the female. When men and women participate in state religious festivals, each sex supports the communal values necessary for the welfare of the state. *Oikos* and *polis* are organized on a comparable and complementary basis, although they differ in scale. . . . What this means is that the simple equation female : *oikos* as male : *polis* does not hold fully on the Greek stage even at the level of an ideal." "Yet occasionally we catch a glimpse of a more complex, reciprocal model" that "helps us to define a norm against which to read the inversions and aberrations of drama."[24]

Too radical a privatization and cultural isolation of the female and what she represents, however, might create an imbalance between the needs, values, and interests of domestic and public spheres.[25] The tragic concern with binary opposition responds in part to the heavy demands that the democratic *polis* put on the male citizen to "subordinate private interests to public, while simultaneously encouraging ambition and competition. The result, drama seems to suggest, is a constant failure of the male to stay within cultural limits. Female characters often make a radical intrusion into the breach, either to expose and challenge this failure, or to heal it with transcendent sacrificial and other reli-

[22] Tragic play with gender categories can often blur any clear definition or opposition, however. See Zeitlin 1996, esp. 15.

[23] Foley 1981: 140–48.

[24] Foley 1981: 153–54, 161.

[25] Foley 1981: 151.

gious gestures.[26] If the female uses religious powers to serve household or state, or to mediate between 'nature' and culture' as these two terms are defined by a specific text, the result can be positive. Otherwise the intrusion of a being ill-equipped for political life can be as dangerous as the disasters that provoked it, the female becomes the locus of oppositions between 'nature' and 'culture,' household and state, and the dramas close with the punishment of the female intruder that implicitly reasserts the cultural norm. The relatively more limited and defined role in which the female is confined by Athenian culture can thus be used to define the more inclusive male role by contrast."[27]

Marilyn A. Katz recently offered a valuable expansion on the structuralist approach, arguing that opposition between the sexes also "operates in the construction of self in tragedy, where the language of sexual difference functions as the mechanism through which individual character is precipitated into existence within the drama."[28] Yet although I stand by the general thrust of the argument that I made in 1981, structuralism by itself remains both too schematic and generalizing to get at the complexity of the language, overt content, and evolution of individual texts and neglects other possible levels of analysis, such as the psychological. Philip Slater, for example, has argued that the powerful, and often threatening, women of Greek drama find their origin in the pathological psychosexual experience of the Athenian male child.[29] The social and political seclusion of the Greek mother makes her alternatively hostile to her more liberated son and seductive to him in the absence of a father rarely at home. The adult male—narcissistic, pedophilic, and obsessively competitive—thus remains uncertain of his sexual identity and abnormally ambivalent toward mature women. This analysis proved valuable in identifying an important set of psychological and sexual tensions in Greek tragedy, but failed to encompass the full range of psychological conflicts portrayed in Greek tragedy or to account for the complex unfolding of its narratives.[30]

Froma Zeitlin developed a far more sophisticated analysis of the ways that "playing the other" on the Greek stage permitted an exploration and expansion of male identity.[31] A form of initiation into the mysteries of what the culture defines as the feminine other—the tensions, complexities, vulnerabilities, irrationalities, and ambiguities that masculine aspiration would prefer to suppress or control—tragedy imagines "a fuller model for the masculine self."[32] "Even when female characters struggle with the conflicts generated by the pe-

---

[26] On the role of the "female intruder" in tragedy, see Shaw 1975 and my response in Foley 1982a.

[27] Foley 1981: 162.

[28] Katz 1994b: 100.

[29] Slater 1968.

[30] See further Foley 1975 and 1981: 137–40 on Slater.

[31] Zeitlin 1996.

[32] Zeitlin 1996: 363.

culiarities of their subordinate social position, their demands for identity and self-esteem are still designed primarily for exploring the male project of self-hood in the larger world. . . . But *functionally*, women are never an end in themselves, and nothing changes for them once they have lived out their drama on stage. Rather, they play the role of catalysts, agents, instruments, blockers, spoilers, destroyers, sometimes helpers or saviors for the male characters.[33] When prominently presented, they may serve as antimodels as well as hidden models for that masculine self and concomitantly, their experience of suffering or their acts that lead them to disaster regularly occur before and precipitate those of men."[34] Thus the male body becomes "feminized" through tragic suffering and madness and more vulnerable to pity or forgiveness; the tragic male confronts and recognizes within himself the powerful secrets that the female brings outside the house; she also controls the tragic plot, manipulating "the duplicities and illusions of the tragic world"[35] and precipitating the activity of forces beyond male control.

Building on Zeitlin's approach, Nancy Rabinowitz, Victoria Wohl, and, most recently, Kirk Ormand made the symbolic exchange of women the starting point for their studies of tragic women.[36] Using a variety of modern theorists, including Lévi-Strauss, Bourdieu, Freud, Foucault, Althusser, Eve Kosofsky Sedwick, Gayle Rubin, and Theresa de Lauretis, and, in Wohl's case, also Lacan, Melanie Klein, and Judith Butler, all three scholars examine how the plays structure audience reaction to impose gender hierarchy, suppress female subjectivity and desire, and legitimate the sex/gender system of the time.[37] As Lévi-Strauss argued, the exchange of women by men establishes culture and defuses hostility among men. Disruptions in the system of exchange entail an attack on male subjectivity, which relies on it, and a demystification of the fundamental system of male bonding, including gift exchange and host-guest relations (*xenia*).[38] In the disrupted world of tragedy the exchange of women begins to dissolve, not cement, social bonds, and men are turned from subjects to objects (above all, dead bodies).[39] For Rabinowitz, there are two basic models of tragic women: the sacrificial and the vindictive. Female sacrificial victims are represented as freely choosing death and fetishized,[40] whereas active female resisters must be punished for their threats to male children. As both Rabinowitz and Wohl argue, father-son or homosocial bonding occurs over the body of the repressed woman, and the fantasy of reproduction without women rears

---

[33] Zeitlin 1996: 347. Griffin 1998: 45–46 completely misreads this passage.

[34] Zeitlin 1996: 347.

[35] Zietlin 1996: 357.

[36] Rabinowitz 1993, Wohl 1998, and Ormand 1999. Ormand stresses (18) that "it is when women are most analogous to objects of economic exchange that marriage becomes least stable."

[37] See esp. Rabinowitz 1993: 14 and Wohl 1998: 179, 182.

[38] Wohl 1998: esp. xxviii, 178, 182.

[39] Wohl 1998: xv.

[40] Rabinowitz 1993: 23 and Wohl 1998: xxviii.

its head more than once on the tragic stage: "The divisive female subject is rejected and reduced; her murdered body becomes the token in the Oedipal identification between father and son, a fetishized gift that binds men to one another."[41] Ormand stresses the failure of marriage in Sophocles to offer women
any sense of fulfillment or completion, whether subjective or objective; virgins
fail to attain marriage, while married women long endlessly for an ever-receding
intimacy or the opportunity for further children.

Both Rabinowitz and Wohl attempt to modify slightly this largely bleak picture of tragic gender relations. Rabinowitz postulates the possibility of a subversive reading by female members of the audience (if they were present), especially through Euripides' perhaps unintentional acknowledgment of female
strength.[42] For Wohl, tragedy reveals the artificiality and violence of the systems that it eventually reaffirms; the eloquent silence of the virgin who has not
yet been exchanged thus becomes a potential site of resistance beyond the
dominant symbolic system.[43]

I conclude with a brief mention of Synnøve des Bouvrie's massive study,
which takes what she calls an anthropological and Aristotelian approach to
understanding the prominent role of women in drama. For des Bouvrie, tragedy does not present "a problem or a discussion of values" or dramatize "alternatives to be reflected upon," but "unarguable truths through a 'symbolic'
medium."[44] "The meaningful level of dramatic action, together with all the
means of rousing the emotions, served the function of marking off the values
and boundaries of social life and charging them with emotion."[45] "Embodying
aspects of the central institutions of Athenian culture [the *oikos*, marriage],
these [tragic] females manifest their 'symbolic nature,' disrupting or corrobo-
rating the complex of values on which these institutions rest, bringing home
their absolute, unquestionable and—then and there—'universal' truth."[46] My
fundamental disagreement above all with the first of these propositions, that
tragedy does not question as well as produce and reinforce Athenian ideology,
has reduced the influence of this book not only in my own work but on those
of others already discussed.[47]

Approaching Female Acts

Greek tragedies are undeniably androcentric and do indeed provide poetic justification for the subordination of women, foreigners, and slaves. The voices
and freedom to act with which drama endows women may in fact, as Zeitlin,

[41] Wohl 1998: 179; see also Rabinowitz 1993: part III.
[42] Rabinowitz 1993: 26–27. See my review of Rabinowitz, Foley 1995c.
[43] Wohl 1998: xv, xvii, xxi–xxii, xxxii, xxxvi–xxxvii, 180, and 182.
[44] Des Bouvrie 1990: 170.
[45] Des Bouvrie 1990: 127.
[46] Des Bouvrie 1990: 325.
[47] For further discussion, see Foley 1995a: esp. 143.

Rabinowitz, Wohl, and Ormand suggest, largely serve this same end despite appearances to the contrary. Ancient viewers, however, seem to have caught a glimpse of the disruptive effects that tragedy's abuse of Athens' far more conservative social mores on gender might have had on its audience. In Aristophanes' *Frogs*, the poet Aeschylus complains that Euripides has made tragedy democratic by allowing his women and slaves to talk as well as the master of the house (949–52). Plutarch (*De Audiendis Poetis* 28a) objects to the highly rhetorical accusations made by Euripides' Phaedra and Helen (in *Trojan Women*), and the Christian writer Origen reports that Euripides was mocked for endowing barbarian women and slave girls with philosophical opinions (*Contra Celsum* 7.36.34–36; see Aristotle, *Poetics* 6.1454a31–33, discussed in III.1). Plato complains of the dangers of the theatrical impersonation of social inferiors such as women and slaves and of feminine emotions (*Republic* 10.605c10–e6). A genre that relies on dialogue and endows characters of subordinate and marginal status with speech and action poses especially difficult problems for interpretation. I share both Wohl's limited optimism that tragedy's demystifications of Athenian institutions can still attract even the most skeptical members of a modern audience and Edith Hall's optimistic argument that tragedy, despite its hierarchical world view, "does its thinking in a form which is vastly more politically advanced than the society which produced" it.[48]

Moreover, nothing requires the modern feminist to identify with tragedy's sometimes rebellious but finally subordinated women, as long as she remains fully conscious of the dynamics that put these characters in their place. Both the male protagonists in Greek tragedy and the male citizens of Athens faced in different ways negotiating conflicts between public and private worlds and identities and creating some coherence between them, challenging the limiting stereotypes of gender roles in order to accommodate to reality, maintaining boundaries and self-control in a competitive and increasingly complex economic and social environment, or balancing the need in a democracy for both egalitarian opportunity and sensitivity and the need for superior leadership. All these problems are now faced by twentieth-century women as well as men, and both women and men can now find themselves in the position of creating and enforcing social and political ideology.

I myself remain more interested in the concerns of Aristophanes, Plutarch, and Origen. Why do women talk (and, I would add, act) so eloquently in tragedy, and what is the function of their masculine rhetoric and philosophizing? In my 1981 article, I closed with an enumeration of unfinished questions. Among these was the question of how the representation of women in drama relates to the social and intellectual issues central to the genre and how it differs in the plays of the three major poets, Aeschylus, Sophocles, and Euripides. *Female Acts* represents a return to those unfinished issues. I wanted to under-

[48] Hall 1997: 125.

stand both how tragic women were used to think about the social order and how they helped men confront intractable social and philosophical problems. The more I studied plays, the more I became convinced that they differ considerably in the way that gender contributes to articulating social and historical issues and that these changing responses are partly to be explained by larger historical shifts precipitated by events such as the Peloponnesian War, and partly a question of the dramaturgy of the different poets in a complex variety of plays. I began by looking at what women argued and did in various plays, and tried to locate their positions both in the plays as a whole and in relation to contemporary historical tensions. Only then did I turn to modern discussions in anthropology, history, or philosophy, both in order to propose possible ways of filling in gaps in our knowledge and/or to put Greek views into some comprehensible and useful relation to our own.

The central areas where women intervene in the tragic action involve death, marriage and inheritance, and the making of difficult ethical choices. Historically, this is not surprising. A society that aimed increasingly over the sixth and fifth centuries to preserve the individual household but subordinate it to the state needed to manage grief. But the privatizing of individual funerals and the self-controlled glorification of the war dead in Athenian public funerals did not necessarily leave enough room for the recognition of suffering and loss involved in individual deaths. This need was likely to have intensified as the losses of the Peloponnesian War were prolonged over a period of nearly thirty years. Tragedy presented a form of public lamentation for individuals that may have obliquely compensated an audience deprived of the full pleasures of expressing grief. Moreover, women historically played the role not only of physically lamenting the dead but of expressing and even acting on views that from Homer on challenged public ideology about death and glory. Tragedy conveniently puts such dissent into female mouths yet, as the century wore on, also made a point of curtailing or limiting it.

As noted earlier, court cases make clear that families sought ways around the restrictions of Greek marriage and inheritance law. Tragedies not only confront some of the contradictions and problems of the marriage and inheritance system and demonstrate their catastrophic repercussions, but offer imaginary escape routes from these same problems and contradictions. In particular, tragic plots involving concubines, unwed mothers, and symbolic remarriages offered a kind of nostalgic return to the less restricted, aristocratic world of Homeric epic. Insofar as these familial issues are implicitly linked with the larger tensions in Attic democracy between the democratic masses and the aristocratic elite whom the masses both feared and relied on for stable leadership, these domestic issues can serve obliquely to illuminate a public set of historical tensions as well.[49]

---

[49] As Zeitlin 1996: 2 puts it: "In such an anthropology of gendered relations, the aesthetic, the social, and the ethical inevitably assumed a political complexion, which brought new insights to bear on the workings of the polis and the making of civic identity."

The overdetermined world of tragedy intensifies the audience's sense that making ethical choices involves the unknowable and the uncontrollable both within and outside the self; yet at the same time divine forces offer the hope of making some kind of larger sense out of human plans and errors. Negotiating public and private priorities in ethical choices is a central problem in tragedy. Equally complicated is the question—a question that I try to show is implicit in the views that clash in a number of plays—of whether public and private morality should operate on the same terms and, if not, what kind of bridge can be created between them. Both Greek popular culture and tragedy in some respects give different social, emotional, and ethical roles to men and women. Choices look different from within a female social role or position than they do for men and may seem to require a different balance between reason and emotion or among other various considerations; they may even demand a different ethical style. Tragedy gives voice to choices or persuasive arguments made from a perspective it defines as female (e.g., those of all three tragic Electras; both tragic Antigones; Euripides' two Iphigeneias; and his Aethra, Hecuba, and Jocasta), or sometimes (as in the case of Aeschylus' Clytemnestra or Euripides' Medea) as androgynous, as well as male. Defining a tragic perspective as gendered entails explicitly drawing attention to a character's female or androgynous status; women more often use the higher emotional register of lyric meter in representing themselves than men; in some cases the specific language, gestures, arguments, or perspectives (including the various ethical modes discussed in III) used by a character are linked to gender.[50] The clash between these voices can change or blur the audience's perspective on larger issues, such as justice or the function of human law, and bring into the forefront neglected or marginalized political and social concerns; the reconciliation between gendered ethical positions, on the other hand, can pave the way to broader social unity.

Due to the complex nature of the topic, I have been forced to restrict the range of my discussion of the representation of tragic women in various ways. I make no pretense to an inclusive study, because all of the issues under consideration play a role in so many tragedies and I aim to locate my discussions in the larger dramatic environment of each text. Yet I do try to make clear why I have emphasized a particular selection of texts. For reasons of both space and theoretical clarity and consistency, I cannot deal with all the possible levels and implications of the questions I explore. Studies such as Edith Hall's *Inventing the Barbarian: Greek Self-Definition through Tragedy*, which treats the role of barbarian women in tragedy, Laura McClure's *Spoken Like a Woman: Speech and Gender in Athenian Drama*, and Joan Connelly's forthcoming study of Greek priestesses also played a role in limiting the scope of this book.[51] In particular, McClure's important study, which appeared too recently for full incor-

---

[50] On language, see McClure 1999.
[51] Hall 1989 and McClure 1999.

poration into this book, isolates speech genres closely identified with women, such as gossip, rhetorical and seductive persuasion, lamentation, and other forms of ritual speech. She then examines how female speech in tragedy on the one hand disrupted, deceived, and seduced and on the other "served as a means of representing the problems of discourse within the democratic polis"[52] and of commenting on the potential of contemporary rhetoric to undermine the power of the aristocratic elite.[53] I have also deliberately acknowledged but excluded from detailed consideration the kind of important psychological or identity issues addressed so extensively by Zeitlin, Rabinowitz, Wohl, and Ormand. The complex roles of gods, myth and ritual, and choruses are included in the discussion at times, but are never—although they deserve to be—the focus of investigation.

Finally, I can do no more than recognize the highly controversial questions of tragic characterization and of the relation between history and tragedy. I try to avoid treating tragic characters with post-nineteenth-century assumptions about dramatic characterization.[54] Greek characters are very much the product of the particular theatrical conventions of the ancient stage: the changeless continuity of the mask; elaborate costumes that do not resemble ordinary dress; the public setting before the stage building; mythical plots and exotic or historically remote locales for action; stylized gesture; the changing media for linguistic expression, such as sung lyric, formal speeches, or dialogue (stichomythia), each with their own conventions and levels of emotional intensity.[55] It is generally difficult to separate Greek characters from the action, from the social roles and expectations of their community, from the effects of the dialogic form of drama, in which each character is defined in interaction with others, and from the rich language and metaphorical systems of the plays.[56] Moreover, due to apparent discontinuities in characterization, some scholars have questioned whether tragic characters can even be said to occupy a coherent position within the dialogue and action of the play.[57] What seems clear is that we cannot treat such characters as individuals with a life offstage, a private and idiosyncratic self, or a subconscious. I have not been able to account for all the forces at play in creating the characters that I discuss—the topic deserves far more study than it has received up to this point—and I have, due to my focus on agency, been forced to confine myself largely to aspects of charac-

---

[52] McCLure 1999: 28.

[53] McClure 1999: 29.

[54] On tragic characterization, see esp. Garton 1957; Jones 1962; Gould 1978; Easterling 1973, 1977b, and 1990; Goldhill 1990; and Gill 1986, 1990b, and 1996.

[55] On these aspects of Greek characterization, see esp. Garton 1957, Jones 1962, Gould 1978, and Goldhill 1990.

[56] See esp. Gould 1978, Goldhill 1990.

[57] See von Wilamowitz 1969, Gould 1978, and the helpful response to these doubts by Goldhill 1990: 112–14 and Easterling 1990: 84, 92–93. See Goldhill 1990: 111 n. 32 for further references.

ter that appear to be less discontinuous and more dependent on the actual motives and rationales offered by the characters themselves in the course of the unfolding action. Moreover, because of the historical and anthropological emphasis of this book, I also give considerably more attention to defining and examining the demands made by a range of social roles (virgin, wife, or mother) on a character's actions than to the influence of chance, fate, and the gods.

Defining agency for characters in Greek tragedy is difficult enough by itself, but the problem is compounded in a context where any independent action by a female, whether in drama or reality, defies ordinary cultural expectations and is potentially problematic or suspect. Moreover, tragedy, as Christopher Gill has stressed, tends in its representation of action and motivation to be ethically and socially exploratory or interrogatory, rather than, as in some philosophical texts, affirmative.[58] Not only tragic choices by women, but tragic choices between two rights or two wrongs are cases in point. Tragic characters may view themselves as undertaking intentional actions for which they may be viewed as responsible and judged accordingly. Yet at other points the character herself, the chorus, or another character may view her action as partly determined, or even in the case of madness entirely determined, by gods, or inherited curses and dispositions, or even separate internal forces within the self (see Euripides' Medea in III.5). On yet other occasions, actions and their causes and motives remain inexplicable; such actions invite empathy, awe, or fear but are dramatically beyond any certain human judgment.[59] Although from this perspective it may be impossible to view a character as autonomous, I have retained the term "autonomous" in my discussion of those passages in which a character sees herself as taking deliberate action for which she is willing to be held accountable,[60] and where she or others see her as adopting the relatively greater social independence of the Greek male.

I consider tragedy's relation to its historical context to be general and oblique rather than topical or allegorical.[61] As an integral part of the city's public and religious life, tragedy can reinforce, justify, or sometimes even articulate the civic life, ideology, social and political roles, and distribution of power in democratic Athens; yet it can also—and this is increasingly the case as the fifth century wore on—raise questions about these same issues. Through its representation of conflict and its agonistic speeches and dialogues, tragedy can negotiate if not resolve critical tensions between public and private life or be-

---

[58] Gill 1990: 18–19.

[59] See esp. Gill 1986, 1990b, and 1996.

[60] Characters generally view themselves as accountable for actions that they recognize to have been partially influenced by divine or other external or warring internal forces. See III.4 and III.5.

[61] On the relation between tragedy and politics, see most recently, two collections of essays, Goff 1995b and Pelling 1997; Griffin 1998, which queries recent treatments of the topic (see also the reply of Seaford 2000); and Saïd 1998, which reviews the issues and contains an up-to-date bibliography. The useful discussion in Pelling 2000, esp. chs. 9–10, reached me too late for inclusion in this book.

tween traditional aristocratic and democratic views, values, and interests, and give us a sense of what problems were of gripping interest to its audience. By representing and referring to rituals and by giving a public voice to those who were normally silent in the political arena but more active in domestic and religious life—women, slaves, foreigners—it can open fresh perspectives on and restore some balance to a civic life and dialogue otherwise dominated by citizen males.

The issues under discussion in this book that tragedy addresses—about death ritual, marriage and inheritance, or ethical choice and argument—are important topics in the literature of both the archaic and classical periods. Tragedy often (and sometimes pointedly) either imitates epic or addresses these issues differently. The form and content of Greek tragedy are above all products of the mythical tradition, the performance context, and a developing and changing set of generic and specifically literary concerns. Yet a knowledge of historical shifts and problems may help to make a particular tragic articulation of or emphasis on a topic to be more comprehensible and more profoundly related to the culture out of which it came.

Part I

THE POLITICS OF TRAGIC LAMENTATION

The naturalizing of lament obliterated the
structured and highly social nature of lament,
which provided a forum both for the woman
lamenter to cry out against her socially designated
status, and for the airing of social grievances.
However, rather than being "unconnected
exclamations of grief," the laments of women
articulated and negotiated the terrain of disrupted
social relationships—raising within this process
recriminations both against the dead and the
relatives of the dead, anger at the felt
abandonment of those left behind, and insecurity
about the future.

(*Mukta 1999: 35 on Colonial India*)

READERS and viewers of Greek tragedy sometimes find their attention wandering during the often lengthy scenes of ritual lamentation in Greek tragedy. My students have almost reached the point of horrified laughter when considering the scene in Euripides' *Bacchae* where Cadmus and Agave apparently lamented each part of the dismembered body of king Pentheus and reconstituted it for proper burial on stage. During these moments of distraction, we tell ourselves that although our own society is uncomfortable with lengthy and elaborate public displays of misery, we must be tolerant of a cultural difference. As readers of Aristotle's *Poetics*, we believe that the pity and fear evoked by the effective tragic plot can be properly elaborated in such lamentation, even if we do not always respond fully to these scenes ourselves.

Yet tragic lamentation does not simply mimic traditional Greek death rites and thus ritualize and to some extent mitigate the horrifying and grievous deaths and cultural disasters of tragedy. A non-Western or rural Mediterranean audience, for example, might well respond differently and I believe more appropriately to the complex variety of scenes revolving around death rites and lamentation in tragedy, instinctively seeing in them a far greater range of purpose and nuance. South Africans or Palestinians, for example, would know that funerals are often political events, opportunities to foment revolution, resistance, or revenge under the cover of one of the few mass events that those in authority do not feel comfortable in suppressing altogether, even if they do their best to control them. A news story on China in the *Guardian* of June 6, 1989, for example, reported that "mock funeral processions were held as a tactic to block the roads and launch a general strike." Singing was forbidden at the funeral of the slain American NAACP director Medgar Evers; but the police ban could not fully silence the six thousand mourners who followed his coffin. In nineteenth- and early twentieth-century India the "consolidating colonial state power . . . attempted to stamp out visible signs of grief (articulated by women) . . . which sought, through this banning to have direct control over forms of community justice, vendetta, and lines of inheritance, all of which could be mediated by lament."[1] This phenomenon was linked to the

An earlier version of this chapter was published as Foley 1993. It was originally designed for a panel on death ritual at the annual meeting of the American Philological Association, Boston, December 1989, and first presented at a symposium at Berkeley in April 1989. I would like to thank Duncan Foley, Christian Wolff, and audiences at Berkeley, Stanford, U.C. Santa Cruz, Cambridge, Oxford, Chicago, Texas, Nottingham, and Johns Hopkins for their responses to earlier drafts, as well as the other members of the APA panel—Ian Morris, Alan Shapiro, the commentator Michael Jameson, and especially Richard Seaford—for everything I learned from their own papers and comments. The following relevant works have been published since this article went to press: Holst-Warhaft 1992 (which profited from my article before its publication), Rehm 1994, Morris 1994, Seaford 1994b, Segal 1994, Jouan 1997, Stears 1998, and van Wees 1999.
[1] Mukta 1999: 26. On a parallel Islamic phenomenon, see Abu-Lughod 1986: 250–1, 198. The similarities with the suppression of lament in Greek state formation are striking.

suppression of everything reminiscent of death and even in extreme (politically motivated) cases with "erasure in the social memory of the dead."[2] Originally confined to an upper-caste, middle-class milieu, it evolved into a broader attempt to replace a traditional "wild" mourning, which nevertheless to this day continues to erupt among the nonelite with a certain amount of social acceptance, with women's subdued devotional readings and singing assemblies during the period of mourning.

In this chapter, I examine some of the ways in which funerary lamentation plays an equally complex and ambivalent role in the politics of Greek tragedy.[3] Our historical sources record various formal attempts from the sixth through the fourth centuries to modify burial practice and attitudes to burial practice in the city-state and, in particular, to place strict controls on the participation of Attic women in death ritual.[4] It should not be surprising, then, that we can see political and social tensions emerging in the way that death ritual and lamentation by women are represented on the tragic stage. Let me begin with a brief review of some important aspects of the historical background and then return to tragedy.

The gradual rise of the city-state in Athens apparently brought with it a deliberate curtailment of death rites. In the early sixth century laws attributed to Solon reportedly inaugurated a process of restriction or reshaping of funeral rites that seems to have continued into the fifth century and beyond.[5] Aristocratic funerals of the archaic period in Greece, as pictured in Homer or vase paintings, were grand public occasions. Lamentation, especially lamentation by women, played a prominent role at every stage: at the wake or *prothesis*, during the *ekphora* in which the body was carried by chariot to the grave site, and at the grave site itself. These lamentations often involved not only family members but hired mourners who were known for their competence in inducing grief. Archaic funerals were an occasion at which the members of aristocratic families or broader groups of kin could gather and display their wealth, power, and generosity to a wider public.

The sixth-century legislation purportedly prohibited above all, to quote Plutarch, "everything disorderly and excessive in women's festivals, processions [*exodoi*] and funeral rites" (*Solon* 21.4, trans. Alexiou 1974).[6] For exam-

---

[2] Mulkta 1999: 27–28.

[3] Caraveli 1986: 171 argues that lament becomes an instrument of social protest in modern Greece at points where the world of women and the larger world intersect.

[4] Garland 1989: 3–5 rightly stresses that the laws were aimed far more at women than men.

[5] For good brief discussions of Greek funerary legislation and funerary rites, see Alexiou 1974: ch. 1, Garland 1985: ch. 3 and 1989, Humphreys 1983a: ch. 5, and Rehm 1994: chs. 1–2. For extensive analysis, see Seaford 1994, esp. ch. 3. As Pomeroy 1997: 101 points out, we cannot be sure, especially given the conservative nature of funeral ritual, how radical a change Solon's reform represented.

[6] See [Demosthenes] 43.62 for further evidence on Solon's funerary laws. We cannot be sure of the reliability of any of these sources, of course. The reforms may have begun considerably later

ple, after the legislation the *prothesis* was to be held indoors or at least in the courtyard of the house. Whereas in the *Iliad* Hector's body was burned after lengthy public lament on the ninth day, Solon apparently restricted the *prothesis* to one day and stipulated that the *ekphora* take place in silence and before dawn. The laws restricted the worth of gifts that could be carried to the tomb and buried with the corpse. Lamentation was permitted at the tomb, but participation, at least on the part of the women, was now limited to close kin (no remoter than first cousins once removed or second cousins). No women under age sixty, other than close relations, could enter the chamber of the deceased or follow the procession to the tomb. Solon, says Plutarch, "forbade laceration of cheeks, singing of set dirges [*pepoiēmena*] and lamentation at other people's tombs" (21.4, trans. Alexiou 1974). At the *ekphora,* women were to keep behind the men. Laws from other Greek city-states—we cannot be sure about Athens—also banned the tearing of women's clothes, the wailing for the corpse at turns in the road, the lamenting for those long dead.

Scholars have speculated that the funerary legislation initially reflected an attempt to curb the power of the aristocracy in Athens and continued at a later period for another set of reasons.[7] Alternatively, Aubrey Cannon suggests that it may be in the interest of those in power to maintain symbolic distinctions among statuses by restraining funerary display once it has been imitated by the lower classes.[8] The privatizing of funerals for individuals and the specific restriction of female participation in death rituals may in any case have served to foster the interests of the state and public unity over those of the family.

Furthermore, funerary rituals may well have provided opportunities for rival aristocratic kin groups to make public displays of emotion that fostered vendettas or consolidated private rather than public interests.[9] Modern anthropolog-

---

than our ancient sources lead us to assume—in the later sixth or even early fifth century, for example.

[7] See esp. Alexiou 1974: 14–23, Humphreys 1983a: 85–90, and Garland: 1985: 21–22 and 1989: 1–8. Funerary legislation was passed in many parts of the Greek world in the late sixth and early fifth centuries. The motives for the legislation may have differed in other cities, but a full understanding of the legislation would require analyzing the factors that made it a Panhellenic as well as a local phenomenon. The motives for restraining funerary rites in the sixth century may well have differed under the Attic democracy.

[8] Cannon 1989 identifies a cross-cultural cyclical pattern of funerary ostentation followed by increasing regulation in the wake of lower-class attempts to blur symbolic distinctions in death rituals. The respondents to his article stressed that a satisfactory explanation must account, as his did not, for all aspects of early Greek funerary practice in the historical context. See also Pearson 1983, who argues that prominent display in death ritual may occur "where changing relations of domination result in status re-ordering and consolidation of new social positions" (112) but diminishes in a stable society.

[9] Alexiou 1974: 21–22 and Garland 1989: 4; Seaford 1989 developed this theme very convincingly and I was indebted to his observations in my original paper; see now his extensive discussion in Seaford 1994: ch. 3. He effectively demonstrates the limitations of the view of Sourvinou-

ical studies in the Mediterranean and elsewhere have documented an intimate relation between lamentation and vendetta.[10] Thus it may be significant that Plutarch in his life of Solon (12) implies a link between the sixth-century legislation and a feud between the followers of Megacles and Cylon.[11] Megacles had massacred Cylon and his fellow conspirators at one of the city's most sacred altars after they had failed in an attempted coup d'etat. The city underwent a military defeat from the Megarians, and seers interpreted various portents as indications of pollution in need of expiation. Solon interposed between the two factions and persuaded the men polluted by the killing of Cylon to submit to a jury trial.[12] After the guilty parties in the family of Megacles were banished, the Athenians summoned Epimenides from Crete to recommend reforms; these reforms included the curtailment of the "barbaric" funerary practices of women. Women may have been targeted for their dominant role in lament, for a loyalty to the household (especially the natal household) that was unmitigated by the compensating civic and military roles offered to men, and because of growing disapproval of public displays of grief by men.[13] (Alternatively, women's growing religious functions in the classical *polis*, including carefully controlled lamentation at public funerals, replaced their more disruptive roles in private burial ritual.) In any case, it is difficult to believe that tragedy would have invented its myths of female lamentation generating vendetta if the practice had not existed in historical memory.[14] Because the

---

Inwood 1983, which explains changes in funerary ritual as the result of shifting views towards death (1994: 79–81).

[10] See, e.g., Alexiou 1974, Black-Michaud 1975, Levine 1982, Caraveli 1986, Seremetakis 1991, and Holst-Warhaft 1992.

[11] Alexiou 1974: 21–22, Garland 1989: 4, and Seaford 1994: ch. 3. As Plutarch's story of the followers of Megacles and Cylon indicates, groups of kin and affiliates such as the Alcmaeonids apparently could cause civic tensions that may have generated the reforms. This does not mean, however, that formal clan vendettas were a significant practice then or later in Attica. On the disputed nature of the aristocratic *genos*, see Pomeroy 1997: 102–3, who argues that Solon's primary motivation for restricting death ritual was sumptuary, and Patterson 1998: 48–50, who stresses that even in the archaic period the *oikos* was the "focus of both sentiment and action" (49). Archaic and classical Greek revenge was the responsibility of family, close relatives, and family friends, not of clans or unilineal descent groups (52–54).

[12] Seaford 1994: 98–99 notes that Dracon's closely contemporary homicide law served to consolidate the move from self-help justice to trial by jury.

[13] On female loyalty to the natal household, see Seaford 1994: 84. On male grief, see my later discussion. Mukta 1999: 39 illuminates a certain irony in the shift from women's loyalty in the performance of lamentation from more extended notions of family and community in prestate society to a more privatized and domestic focus for mourning in colonial India.

[14] Earlier evidence is nonexistent. In Homer, murder is frequently dealt with by exile or compensation. There are significant instances of self-help revenge in the *Odyssey*: Orestes' murder of Aegisthus for killing his father and the plan of the relatives of the dead suitors to avenge their dead by killing Odysseus in *Odyssey* 24. In the latter case male grief certainly stirs the men to action, but the funeral rituals for the suitors, which would have included women, are not described (24.417), and it is not clear who participates in the group mourning before Odysseus' house (24.415–16) prior to the burials.

state did not extensively interfere with family life except where its own interests were at stake, I think we can assume that funerals were potentially a serious challenge to civic harmony.

Yet, although private death rituals were restricted, new forms of public funerary ritual gradually took their place. As Aristotle puts it (*Politics* 6.2.1319b 24–25), in extreme democracies "the private rites of families should be restricted and converted into public ones."[15] At state funerals for the war dead, who were praised and buried collectively, public mourning was permitted, although in a controlled form. In the sixth century tyrants in many Greek cities (we have no certain evidence about Athens) encouraged the establishment of hero cults that gradually replaced aristocratic clan cults or threw them open to a larger public.[16] These cults also involved public lamentation. Tragedy itself may well represent a peculiarly Attic phase of this appropriation of public mourning by state ritual and cults.[17] Indeed, Gail Holst-Warhaft has argued that tragedy deliberately usurps a female art form and makes it its own.[18] Regardless of the original reasons for the funerary legislation and other shifts in funerary practice, however, Athenians of the fifth century would almost certainly have interpreted such changes in death rituals as conforming to and supporting the ideology of the democracy, which appropriated the magnificence of the archaic funeral to glorify its war dead,[19] while minimizing the visibility of all aspects of private life.

We cannot, of course, be sure how well the funerary legislation worked. Probably we are talking about transitions that occurred over a long period of time and were only partially successful in many instances. The continued references to new funerary legislation at various periods and continuing shifts in the archaeological record suggest that Greek society repeatedly reviewed its restrictions on funerary rites and that there were temporary or partial regressions toward the archaic norm. Cicero speaks of a new funerary law restricting the ostentation of tombs and speeches of praise for the private dead that was probably enacted in the late sixth or early fifth century (the *post aliquanto* law, *De Legibus* 2.64–65). From the late sixth to about the last quarter of the fifth century, the archaeological record shows a remarkable absence of pretentious pri-

---

[15] Trans. McKeon 1941. See further Seaford 1994, who notes that hero cult permits the lamentation, intramural burial, the monuments, and the participation by nonkin restricted in the funerary legislation (119).

[16] See further Seaford 1994: ch. 4. Tragedy, like hero cult, permits collective public grieving through the response of its audience (141).

[17] E.g., Cleisthenes of Sicyon transferred the tragic choruses sung in honor of the hero Adrastus to Dionysus (Herodotus 5.67). Loraux 1986: 21 sees lament banished from the Agora and the public funeral to the theater. See further Seaford 1994: ch. 4.

[18] Holst-Warhaft 1992: 157; see also 126, 130. Stears 1998: 118–26 argues that funerals remained a means for the construction and display of female power, however. The correct performance of the rite was critical; the performance of lamentation and burial helped to lay claim to inheritances; lamentation may have served to preserve family history.

[19] Loraux 1986: 19 and 52.

vate monuments that may reflect this legislation; nevertheless private monuments reemerge in the early years of the Peloponnesian War.[20] Hired mourners (in principle limited to the unrelated women over sixty who were permitted at funerals) apparently continued to play some role; Aeschylus' *Choephoroi*
733 can refer to *lupē amisthos* (unhired grief) and in the fourth century Plato's
Laws (7.800e1–3) forbid hired songs at funerals.[21]

The fine arts, however, show a continuous move toward greater reticence in
the representation of funeral rites. Sixth century vases and funerary plaques, as
Alan Shapiro has shown, appropriate Homeric funerary motifs (e.g., funeral
games) to heroize the individual dead; women tear their hair and lacerate their
cheeks with wild archaic abandon.[22] Fifth-century *loutrophoroi* give up these
heroizing motifs and white *lekuthoi* show greater self-control and introspection
emerging in the representation of female grief, as well as a new emphasis on
feminine care of the dead at private tombs. Hans van Wees identifies a growing gender gap and segregation in mourning practices on vases as early as the
late Geometric period (735–700).[23] Only women raise both hands and lacerate their faces.[24] By the mid-seventh century, women monopolize lament and
men appear only in funerary processions. Men do reappear in scenes of lamentation from about 580 on, but they are now intruders from the outside on a fe-
male-dominated *prothesis* held within the house. Finally, the continuity of funerary practice from archaic to modern Greece documented in the works of
Margaret Alexiou, Loring Danforth, and Gail Holst-Warhaft certainly attest
to the persistence of remarkably similar funerary lamentation by women over
a period of nearly two thousand years.

How then does all of this relate to tragedy? Any reader of tragedy knows that
the genre represents behavior that was seemingly discouraged in the practice
of the society that produced these plays. Tragedy is full of the public laceration
of cheeks and the lamentation at other people's tombs supposedly forbidden by
Solon. Revenge and funerary lamentation are intimately related in tragedy, and
women play a public and dominant role in awakening it. To take a familiar ex-

---

[20] It has been argued that this was a response to the neglect of the private dead following the
Athenian plague, or to a need to find positions for unemployed public stoneworkers. Morris 1994,
noting that the reemergence of private monuments at this period is a Panhellenic phenomenon,
thinks that Attic aristocratic monuments absorbed democratic funerary display to highlight civic
leadership. On the monuments, see esp. Clairmont 1970. The monuments reemerge at about the
same period that I find a shift in tragic self-consciousness about the representation of female lamentation (see my subsequent argument).

[21] Garland 1985: 22 cites evidence for a continued desire for a magnificent burial in the classical period. Stears 1998: 117 thinks that the funerary legislation was particularly aimed at hired
mourners, who would have been used only by the wealthiest families.

[22] See Shapiro 1989 with earlier bibliography.

[23] Van Wees 1999. See also Stears 1998: 115.

[24] Men generally stand with one arm to their head (Ahlberg 1971). On black- and red-figure
scenes men enter from the left with both arms raised in greeting (Shapiro 1991).

ample to which I shall return, most of the first half of Aeschylus' *Choephoroi* takes place at the tomb of Agamemnon.[25] There Electra and a chorus of foreign slave women (contrary to the funerary legislation, nonfamily members lamenting at the tomb of one long dead)[26] stir the returning hero Orestes to complete his revenge for his father Agamemnon through their elaborate lamentations at the hero's grave. Did the audience simply view these activities as justified (at least partially) because they were leading to the overthrow of the tyrants Clytemnestra and Aegisthus? Or should we consider the possibility that this *kommos* (a choral lament shared between chorus and actors) was meant to offer a display of precisely those uncontrolled lamentations by women that purportedly led in earlier Greek history to the enactment of the funerary legislation and, more speculatively, to the replacement of vendetta justice by the all male institution of trial by jury?

As noted in the introduction, we do not expect from tragedy any direct reflection of contemporary Athenian social practice. Nevertheless, it can be used to reflect continued tensions in the transition from an aristocratic society to a changing democratic *polis* as well as new tensions within democratic society itself—above all conflicting loyalties between kin and city-state of the kind that the funerary legislation was probably designed to regulate. We know from later funerary legislation (Demetrius of Phaleron) and from the archaeological record that social tensions relating to death ritual continued to be a locus of controversy in Athens. In the case of funerary lamentation, these tensions were not in the mid to later fifth century precisely the same as those that first produced the legislation, and they do not appear in the same form at all periods in which we have evidence from tragedy on the issue. Nevertheless, funerals—especially at periods of social crisis—were very likely to be events at which tensions between public and private interests and emotions emerged in a particularly volatile form.[27] I believe we can see political (and by political I mean issues relating to the *polis*) and social tensions of precisely this sort emerging in the way that death ritual and lamentation are represented on the tragic stage—though it remains to consider precisely why these issues resurface sharply in tragedies that were presented during the Peloponnesian War.

I deliberately restrict my discussion to a limited number of examples in which women, whether choruses or female protagonists, lament in a specifically ritual context, often with the aim of resisting or manipulating the status

---

[25] See now the similar discussions of Seaford 1994 and Holst-Warhaft 1992.

[26] The prohibition of mourning at the tomb of one long dead is in fact explicit only in the late-fifth-century funerary regulations of the priestly clan of the Labyadai at Delphi (Sokolowski 1969: 74c); but the Attic legislation, by prohibiting lament for anyone other than the person being buried and restricting visits to the tombs of nonrelatives except at the time of interment, implies that this Homeric practice (*Iliad* 19.302) was equally unacceptable in Athens.

[27] For the use of death ritual to assert a political point, see Xenophon *Hellenica* 1.7.8, where after Arginusae Theramenes stirred up the assembly by dressing supposed relatives of the dead in mourning garments and close cut hair.

quo or in a fashion that would violate contemporary Attic restrictions on such practices. Thus I do not examine in detail contexts where women borrow some of the language and/or gestures of lament to express sorrow in situations where no ritual (especially death ritual) is being performed (although some of these are mentioned later in the chapter), or where characters are performing what is in essence a conventional private lament (e.g., Agave at the end of Euripides' *Bacchae*). Characters may perhaps significantly use the language of lamentation, however, in the process of taking important action or expressing dramatic resistance in other forms. For example, the Danaids who compose the chorus in Aeschylus' *Suppliants* manipulate suppliant ritual to resist marriage with their cousins, and the Oceanids, the divine chorus in Aeschylus' *Prometheus Bound,* with difficulty persuade their father to permit them to rush precipitously from their modest seclusion and to visit and sympathize with the hero (130–34); finally they choose to share sufferings with the divine rebel at the conclusion of the play.

A full study of this issue would also have to account for tragic representations of men as lamenters of the dead as well. Given our evidence, this second topic is more difficult than the first. In the case of women, we have a body of evidence about cultural attitudes to specific practices involved in female lamentation independent of their representation on the stage. We know that strict lines were drawn on what was acceptable in public and private contexts. Even in this case, however, it is not easy to tell what the audience would have viewed as "normal lamentation," whether normal for the tragic stage, or normal in actual practice. In the case of men, we know considerably less from sources independent of drama about what practices were habitual to male lamentation,[28] although we do know that the public and intense expression of male grief was considerably less acceptable in the classical period than in epic.

A beginning of this shift in attitude can be found in fragments of archaic poetry; a good example is the exhortation to control unmanly grief in the noted fragment of Archilochus (fragment 13 West).[29] Aristotle may be criticizing (certain kinds of?) stage lamentation by men of military age when he remarks on Odysseus' lament (*thrēnos*) in [Timotheus' dithyramb?] *Scylla* as inappropriate (*Poetics* 15.1454a29–30 and 26.1461b29–32). Yet our knowledge is general rather than specific. Thus, when the chorus of Euripides' *Alcestis* repeatedly tries to mute the force of Admetus' lamentations, are we to understand that Admetus is indulging in unmanly or excessive behavior, or is the chorus simply reflecting a topos of funerary lament, where those responding to the grieving kin were meant to offer consolation by urging greater control of grief? Another problem is the age of the male mourner. Older men in tragedy tend to express grief far more intensely than men of military age (Pseudo-Aristotle,

[28] See notes 23 and 24.

[29] See also Theognis 355–60, 441–46 = 1162ab, 989–90. For later philosophical views, see Plato, *Republic* 3.387d1–388d7 and 10.605d7–e1.

Problem 11.62 comments on the shrill voices that they share with women, children, and eunuchs). Finally, the longest and most intense lamentation by tragic males is to be found in Aeschylus' *Persians;* but here the mourners are defeated barbarians, and, as Edith Hall has demonstrated, their lament clearly feminizes them, makes them from the Greek perspective the antitype of the idealized male.[30] Unlike Greek men, Xerxes and the Persian elders tear their beards and their clothes (feminine *peploi*) and beat their flesh. The broader question of Greek male flirtation with orientalizing dress and behavior in both the archaic and classical periods undoubtedly bears on the discussion of tragedy as well (especially because, to Plato's later consternation, male citizens played female and barbarian roles in tragedy, and the tragic dress of actors, at least in the late fifth century, was not typically masculine attire), but is too complex and extensive a topic for discussion here.[31]

Euripides' *Helen*

Let me begin with a tragic incident tangential to the larger historical and ideological issues raised by female lamentation. Euripides' play of 412, *Helen*, begins from the premise, apparently novel to the tragic stage, that Helen of Troy was innocent. Spirited to Egypt by the god Hermes, she spent the Trojan War under the protection of the virtuous king Proteus. The whole war was fought for the phantom or image of Helen that Hera sent to Troy—a fact that Menelaus, when he arrives in Egypt in the early scenes of the play, has a good deal of trouble accepting. Helen's image disappears midplay, however, leaving Menelaus no choice but to accept the innocent Helen as his true bride. The couple's escape from Egypt is jeopardized by king Theoclymenus, the son of the now dead good king Proteus. He wishes to marry Helen himself and has threatened to kill any Greek he finds lurking about his palace. Helen immediately counters Menelaus' suggestions of using force to effect their escape. Impracticality aside, the shipwrecked Menelaus needs a vessel for his return journey. Helen proposes instead that she should pretend she has received news of Menelaus' death at sea. After she has obtained a ship to perform a funeral rite

---

[30] See Holst-Warhaft 1992: 130–33 and Hall 1993, 1996: esp. 168–69, and 1999: 117. (See also the response of Griffith 1998: 48–52.) Hall 1999: 112 notes that "lyric utterance is particularly associated with women" in any case and that most tragic songs were thought to be fundamentally threnodic (113 and n. 85); Theseus in *Hippolytus* and Sophocles' *Ajax* are the only adult men to sing lyrics, and Theseus mixes his with iambic trimeter (117). Griffith 1998: 50 contests Hall, using the example of Orestes' participation in the *kommos* of Aeschylus' *Choephoroi.* Orestes' youth may be critical in this case, however.

[31] Kurke 1992 on the politics of *habrosunē* (oriental luxury appropriated by Greeks) and Bassi 1998 on male role playing offer useful introductions. The bibliography on possible cross-dressing and imitation of Asian practices in Greek vase painting is immense. On these aspects of tragic costume, see, with further bibliography, Foley 2000 and Griffith 1998: 38.

in honor of her reportedly dead husband—a rite she invents for the occasion—
she will, she pretends, surrender herself to a wedding with Theoclymenus. The
dialogue between the spouses runs as follows (1049–56):

> *Helen:* Listen, if a woman can offer clever advice. Though not dead, are you willing
> to be called dead in speech?
> *Menelaus:* A bad omen. But if I gain by it, I'm content. Though not dead, you may
> say I am.
> *Helen:* And in addition I could win pity for you from the unholy king by cutting my
> hair and lamenting in female fashion.
> *Menelaus:* How could this help us? There is something a little old hat about this plot
> [or this proposal, *palaioitēs gar tō(i) logō(i) g' enesti tis*].

Here Menelaus makes a pointedly metatheatrical remark about the triteness
of Helen's plan. If Sophocles' *Electra* was produced before *Helen,* Orestes had
already deceived his enemies by feigning his own death. (He justifies his fears
about dying in speech in a similar fashion, adducing as motives *kerdos* or gain,
and in addition the *kleos* he will achieve by his deeds [*Electra* 59–63].) We do
not know of any examples of the second half of Helen's plot, where a woman
uses funeral lamentation to get what she wants from a man, because in *Electra*
the heroine's lamentation over the urn supposedly containing the ashes of
Orestes is genuine; she is not yet in on her brother's deception.[32] But unless
Euripides is calling attention to the novelty of this device in a decidedly indirect and peculiar fashion, there probably was one or more scenes of this sort in
recent tragedies. Clearly, Menelaus is less sanguine about this second suggestion of his wife—the feigned lamentations. The triteness of the device can
hardly be the whole problem, since the audience for Helen's plot is to be a naive
barbarian (note Theoclymenus' surprised and gullible reaction to the rite for
Menelaus), not an Athenian theatergoer, and the first part of the plan is familiar to the Attic stage. Perhaps we should see Menelaus' reaction in the light
of his repeated suspicions about this new, innocent Helen, suspicions that have
barely begun to be laid to rest even at this point in the play.[33] Situations in
which women approach taking full control of the stage action often create such
uneasiness in a tragic context, and earlier tragedy certainly includes examples
in which women use their authority over ritual to lay traps for their men. Consider Clytemnestra's preparations for the homecoming sacrifices to welcome
Agamemnon returning from Troy in Aeschylus' *Agamemnon,* sacrifices that
lead directly to what the text repeatedly metaphorizes as the sacrifice (and funeral ritual) of her own husband after his entry into the palace.[34] Helen has-
tens to give her husband his own role in the deception of Theoclymenus, and

---

[32] See the discussions of Kannicht 1969, Dale 1967 ad loc., Kitzinger 1991, and part IV.

[33] See Schmiel 1972 on the suicide pact and Menelaus' questioning attitude to Helen in the
two previous scenes.

[34] See Zeitlin 1965 and Seaford 1984a.

Menelaus ultimately joins with gusto in the tears both shed *poiētō(i) tropō(i)* ("in manufactured fashion," 1547) for his dead self.

What this example shows is a self-consciousness about the way tragic women can manipulate the funerary ritual that is their traditional province to deceive gullible men. And in the following scenes the lamenting Helen manages to twist Theoclymenus around her little finger even though—a real theatrical tour de force—she has supposedly marred her famous beauty by cutting her hair, furrowing her cheeks,[35] and stained her face (a changed mask?) with tears. The scene is full of irony and humor, but this display of female power to deceive, a power that this and other plays frequently remind us of, relies as well on a lurking sense of danger. The specter of a lamenting Helen using all the wiles of the deceptive image that destroyed Troy must have left its Greek audience, as it certainly has left some modern critics, uneasy.[36]

Sophocles' *Antigone*

In my second example, we see a female character using lamentation to make a public and politically motivated display of injustice. The scene occurs in Sophocles' *Antigone*. Antigone is leaving to be imprisoned alive in her tomb. She chooses to stage this departure as a lament for herself.[37] She calls attention to the fact that there is no one to mourn for her (*philōn aklautos*, 845–47)—though she herself is dying because of her devotion to performing rites for the dead (869–71, 900–903, 943). She, the *last* of the royal family line (895–96, 940–43), as she insists, will die unwed (814–16, 867, 876–77, 891, 916–18). In this assertion she seems to ignore the existence of her sister Ismene; but then she no longer views Ismene as a family member (see 542–43), even though Ismene had already begun lamenting for the living Antigone in the previous scene (526–30).

Up to a point, we see that Antigone's lamentation has the desired effect on the chorus of old men. They are torn between genuine grief for their princess (they weep at the sight of her, 801–3), and horror at her revolutionary gestures against Creon's edict (872–75, 853–55). Creon, however, has no doubts about his own reaction. Suggesting that Antigone's lamentation is a tactic to delay her departure, he wants to curtail her *aoidai* and *gooi* as quickly as possible (883–85). Antigone's assertive public lamentation for herself contrasts noticeably with the

---

[35] The text seems inconsistent on this point. At 1087–89 Helen says that she will wear black clothing, cut her hair, and furrow her cheeks. At 1186–90 Theoclymenus refers to the change of clothing, the hair, and Helen's tears, and at 1285–86 he expresses concern about the effects of grief on Helen's appearance. Perhaps Helen does not go so far as to furrow her cheeks after all.

[36] See esp. Segal 1971: 606–7, Wolff 1973: 72 and 81–82, and part IV.

[37] While many tragic characters lament their situation, a carefully staged and pointedly isolated self-lamentation in a funereal context is an anomaly.

discreet lamentation that the messenger expects, for example, of Creon's proper (*gnōmēs . . . ouk apeiros*, 1250) wife Eurydice. When, having heard of the death of Haimon, Eurydice exits silently into the palace, the messenger hopes that she has deemed it inappropriate to conduct her lamentation (*gooi*) before the city, but will set her women to bemoaning her private grief inside her house (1246–50; to lament outside would be to commit an error—*hamartanein*).

I suggest that Antigone in this scene is doing more than evoking pity for herself in a fashion that would traditionally, in the case of lament for a virgin, have included a stress on the loss of fulfillment in marriage. First, by lamenting for herself, she exposes Creon's pretense in immuring her alive.[38] She is in fact going to her death, and Creon will effectively deprive her as well as her brother of the burial rites that are her due. Second, Antigone calls on the chorus to witness her mistreatment: "look, rulers of Thebes, upon the last of the royal house, what things I am suffering from what men, for having shown reverence for reverence" (*leussete, Thēbēs hoi koiranidai, tēn basileidōn mounēn loipēn, hoia pros hoiōn andrōn paschō tēn eusebian sebisasa* [940–43], and see also 895–96, *hōn loisthia 'gō kai kakista dē makrō(i) / kateimi*; note the use of the rare word *koiranidai*, "rulers," which seems to attribute a special significance to the chorus as witness to her plight).[39] The Athenian audience would have had no obvious way of interpreting her emphasis that she is the last of her royal line and that Creon is preventing her marriage by his punishment other than through the Attic institution of the *epiklēros*.[40] In Athens, if a man died without sons, it was the responsibility of close male relatives (maternal relatives in the absence, as here, of paternal ones) to ensure that his daughter the *epiklēros* married (ideally to a close relative) and, where possible, produced a male heir for the family line. As Antigone's uncle and guardian, Creon has this responsibility in her case, although he explicitly refuses to recognize Antigone's claims as his sister's child (486–89). Here as elsewhere he ignores family (and, in this case, also state) obligations in favor of what he conceives to be state interests. Creon appropriately pays for his errors with the loss of his own wife and son.

In her departure for death, then, Antigone is hardly, as some have argued, undergoing a moral collapse or a change of heart in the face of impending death. She has already, as Haimon reports, aroused a potentially divisive public sympathy for her burial of her brother. Here she uses lamentation to carry her point assertively in a public context that might otherwise have silenced

---

[38] Creon initially takes the stance that by entombing her alive he will keep his hands pure and the city will not be endangered by pollution (773–76, 885–89).

[39] Trans. Lloyd-Jones 1994.

[40] The text does not refer to the Attic institution of the *epiklēros*, and it would be legitimate to object that my reading is anachronistic. Nevertheless, an audience familiar with the institution would be likely to interpret Antigone's language with their own cultural practice in mind. Ormand 1999: ch. 4 now offers additional support for this interpretation. On the *epiklēros*, see further part II. Antigone's betrothal to the appropriate close relative may partly explain the emphasis on her being the last of her family line.

her speech. She may even be going so far as to suggest that Creon is illegitimately attempting to deprive her future offspring of their rightful leadership of Thebes. The play thus confirms in additional ways (I am thinking of Antigone's initial gesture of burying her brother) the potentially revolutionary force of women's role in rituals performed for the dead.

Aeschylus' *Choephoroi*

I could point to other examples in which a heroine's lamentation in tragedy also serves to express a form of political or social resistance. As I discuss at length in III.2, Sophocles' Electra, for example, uses lamentation to keep alive her father's cause and to stir up others to desire revenge on his behalf.[41] Instead, I turn to examples where lamentation is used to express collective resistance by a female chorus to those in authority, beginning with Aeschylus' *Choephoroi*. In its exploration of human justice, the *Oresteia* offers a mythical version of a historical shift from archaic vendetta justice to trial by jury. When Aeschylus has a lengthy antiphonal lamentation generated by the chorus and Electra reinforce Orestes' determination to take revenge, he presumably develops not only an imaginary but what he believes to be a historical connection between lamentation and revenge. And if for Aeschylus there was a significant connection between lamentation, social protest, and revenge, how would this affect our reading of the *kommos* in this pivotal play of Aeschylus' trilogy?

The *kommos* has provoked a good deal of controversy among scholars about the role that this lamentation plays in Orestes' decision to avenge his father: a determining role, a reinforcing role, or no substantial role at all.[42] The text itself offers no decisive basis for resolving this question. There can be no doubt that Orestes, in obedience to Apollo's command, has returned to Argos in order to carry out his revenge. At the same time, he receives in the scene that includes the *kommos* support for his venture of various kinds, and not simply emotional support. The chorus gives him the opportunity to decode Clytemnestra's dream, and it later facilitates the revenge by helping to deceive Aegisthus. The *kommos* also generates additional motives for Orestes' revenge: the ill treatment of Agamemnon's corpse and of Electra, as well as the full extent of Aegisthus' and Clytemnestra's tyranny. Finally, Orestes participates for the first time in a proper lament for his father, thereby not only propitiating and probably obtaining the help of his father's ghost, but consolidating his claim on his inheritance—an issue with which he is much concerned (275, 301).[43] For by

---

[41] The importance of this aspect of the play was noted by Seaford 1985: 315, n. 2.

[42] For references, see Garvie 1986: esp. 123–25 and Conacher 1974. I agree with those critics who see in Orestes some hesitancy toward committing the crime throughout the play.

[43] Orestes in his opening speech regrets that he has not participated in Agamemnon's burial rite by stretching out his hand to greet the corpse—the male gesture of mourning (8–9). As if in answer to his regret, the black-garbed chorus and Electra arrive with funerary libations.

giving his father his first proper mourning, Orestes makes a claim comparable with what we see in fourth-century law cases, where those who mourn a man strengthen their claim to his property (see Isaeus 4, 6, and 8; Demosthenes 43 and 44).[44] Hence the *kommos* plays an important role in Orestes' revenge, even if we cannot isolate its precise effect on the hero.

For this reason, I am not sure that interpreters have asked the right question about the scene. Should we not rather ask why in *Choephoroi* Aeschylus makes a point of linking Orestes' revenge to the vividly enacted performance of funerary rites by his sister and a group of unrelated oppressed women, whereas in *Eumenides* the Erinyes, representing the female side, are relegated to a symbolic and religious role that ultimately segregates them from an exclusively masculine system of trial by jury?[45] That is, justice (as a legitimate form of revenge) in *Choephoroi* pointedly includes the female (although in contrast to Clytemnestra in *Agamemnon*, the women play not a leading but a supporting role to the male as the actual instrument of justice), whereas in *Eumenides* it excludes her (the Eumenides will serve in the domain of cult as a backup to the autonomous jury trial).[46]

I believe, however, that *Choephoroi* deliberately situates Orestes' ultimate failure to terminate the family vendetta in a context where women traditionally played or were thought to have played a central and perhaps even dangerous role. Lamentation, with its strong generation of emotion, focuses the power and desire to carry through revenge in a communal setting that builds connections between past, present, and future members of the group. Moreover, as the modern Mediterranean evidence has demonstrated, "the dirge is always strongest where the law of vendetta flourishes, as in Sicily or Mani today."[47] To put this another way, Orestes is determined from the start to commit his crime, but the *kommos* creates a social context for his act that subsequently came to be outlawed in classical society along with vendetta justice itself. (We saw earlier how Solon tried to use the institution of a jury trial to resolve the vendetta between the followers of Megacles and Cylon.) As the chorus says

[44] On the connection between lamentation and inheritance, see esp. Alexiou 1974: 19–20 and Humphreys 1983a: 83–84.

[45] On gender roles in vendetta, see III.2.

[46] From a structural perspective, the *kommos* paves the way for the trilogy's resolution, by beginning to heal over the painful rift between the sexes so central to *Agamemnon*, by restoring a relation to the gods perverted by the improper sacrificial rites of *Agamemnon*, and by rebuilding the shattered family group, its gender hierarchies, and its relation to the community. In *Agamemnon*, the chorus of old men attempts to lament the ruler from whose improper funeral rites it is to be excluded as well as hopes for requital; the chorus of *Choephoroi* enacts that lamentation in the second play. Thus, although only members of the royal household lament in *Choephoroi*, the first play has established that their actions represent the desire of the community as a whole.

[47] Alexiou 1974: 22. See also pp. 22, 124–25, and 179 (followed by Seaford 1994 and Holst-Warhaft 1992) on the connection between lament and revenge in *Choephoroi*, and 182, 136, 178, and 182 for relevant comments on the motifs of the *kommos*.

in lines that make lament and revenge inextricable: "the dead one is lamented; the punisher appears; the just lamentation of fathers and begetters seeks
requital [*poinan*] once it has been loudly stirred up [*tarachtheis*]" (327–31).
Tragedy often displays behavior anachronistic to classical society on stage; but
in a play that traces an evolution from a remote archaic world to one that
closely prefigures the institutions of classical Athens, anachronistic behavior
is likely to play, I believe, a more programmatic role in the logic of the drama
than in other plays. From this perspective, vendetta belongs to a world that
does not preserve the same distinctions between the worlds of female and male,
family and state that we find in classical Athens and ultimately in *Eumenides*
itself.

If I am correct, it seems significant that in the *kommos* the chorus and Electra play the dominant role in generating revenge through their lament. As others have suggested, the women of the chorus, dressed in black robes, visually
prefigure the Furies and adopt their role of stimulating vendetta justice. They
are not only unrelated women lamenting at the tomb of a nonrelative long
dead, but deliberately foreign, with their Cissian laments, ripped clothing, torn
cheeks, and pounding of breasts.[48] Because the women share Electra's secret
hatred and her subordinate status, they are eager to overthrow their masters.
There is no doubt, as in the case of Orestes, that their advice leads the uncertain Electra to act on her father's behalf. "How can I ask this of the gods without impiety?" Electra asks. "Surely you can ask them to pay back an enemy with
evil," they reply (122–23, trans. Lloyd-Jones 1993). At the opening of the *kommos* proper, Orestes rather tentatively expresses the wish that a better death
had taken Agamemnon (345–53); but it is Electra who makes the first move
toward revenge (368–71). Angered by her original exclusion from her father's
burial (444–45), she emerges metaphorically in this scene as the child of a wolf
(421; see also 446). The chorus supports Electra by urging action (379—the
text is uncertain here); the chorus names for the first time both the killing of
Clytemnestra and the dread Erinyes (386, 402), and then echoes Electra in
her incendiary depiction of Agamemon's dishonorable burial (especially the
maschalismos [mutilation of the corpse], 429–33, 439–43). The chorus also
formally closes the lament by announcing that because atonement has been
achieved, Orestes must now act (510–13). Yet the choral optimism in *Choephoroi*
ultimately proves to be ill-founded, and Orestes must depart for a different resolution to his difficulties.

In sum, lamentation traditionally allows mourners and, above all, women to
organize their expression of grief, to generate anger, to diffuse a sense of help-

---

[48] Ripped clothing was forbidden in the third-century funerary laws from Gambreion
(Sokolowski 1955: no. 16, 5–6). Although slaves in the royal household, they characterize themselves as alienated from their masters. On the chorus's aggressive role in this scene, and its sudden
loss of confidence at 413–17, see Conacher 1974: 335.

lessness at catastrophic loss, to preserve past memories, and to communicate with the dead. Sophocles' later *Electra* deliberately separates Orestes from the tempting, emotive sphere represented by his sister's lamentation, whereas Aeschylus chose to dramatize Orestes' move to revenge in a far more emotional and ritual context in which women traditionally played the leading role. The fact that both children are more hesitant than the chorus of foreign slaves, although Electra takes up the initiative more quickly, and that this revenge is, in contrast to the standard vendetta, particularly horrific because it is intra-familial, makes the move to an alternative solution seem even more compelling. By contrast, Sophocles shows an Electra attempting and ultimately failing to carry out her Aeschylean role in stirring vendetta through lament. The chorus and Chrysothemis respond but fear to help; Orestes' appearance is long-delayed and he is motivated to act decisively not by Electra but by the pedagogue (see III.2).

Euripides' *Suppliants*

Collective and public lamentation by women can receive a decidedly political response from male rulers. In Euripides' *Suppliants*,[49] for example, the mothers of the seven champions who died at Thebes have come (with their servants) as suppliants to request Athenian support in acquiring for their sons a burial denied by Thebes. Although the lamentation of the women is vociferous and disruptive of the ritual for Demeter that she has herself come to carry out at Eleusis,[50] Queen Aethra feels pity for them and recognizes the force of their supplication. Persuaded by his mother, Theseus eventually accepts their pleas (see III.6). The Theban unwillingness to compromise on the burial issue ultimately leaves Theseus no alternative but to go to war (346–48). He is sure the city will feel the same, and it does. The Athenians win the ensuing battle, but Theseus displays his justice and moderation by halting at the walls of Thebes. We are assured that the war was fought *only* to obtain the bodies and to give them burial (723–25; see also 670–72).

This Theseus proceeds to do. The Argive leader Adrastus is amazed at his

[49] Nicole Loraux is the only critic who has seen the importance of Theseus' attempt to control the Argive burial rites in this play. I owe much to her passing remarks on the topic (see esp. Loraux 1986: 47–49). Mirto 1984, following Loraux, emphasizes the anomalies of Theseus' refusal to permit the mothers to touch their sons. Whitehorne 1986 views the funerary elements in the play largely as a spectacle to be interpreted in relation to the prohibition of the Athenian dead at Delium. Only at one point (70) does his interpretation converge with mine. Rehm 1994: 110–21 now offers a compatible discussion.

[50] See esp. lines 95–97, 103, and 290 and Collard 1975: ad loc., Zuntz 1963: 23, Burian 1985: 130, and Jouan 1997: 219–20 on the potentially unpropitious effects of the women's suppliancy and lamentation in Demeter's sanctuary.

concern; Theseus, a messenger reports, supervises the funerary procedures himself (758–68). He helps to wash and prepare the bodies for burial, covering them and laying them out as in a correctly performed *prothesis*. The anonymous mass of war dead are burned and buried (756–57), but the bodies of the champions are being brought back to receive burial in a family context. Adrastus, who has made a point of asking the messenger about the bodies, begins to lament (769). The messenger objects. Adrastus' laments are useless[51] and make the women weep (770). Adrastus allows his point and affirms that he has been taught to do this by the women (771; earlier he was drawn into a humiliating suppliancy with the women, 163–67).

Nevertheless, when the bodies are carried on stage, Adrastus begins to lead the women in another despairing lament (798–836). Theseus appears and intervenes. In an apparent attempt to replace grief for the dead with admiration (lamentation has already taken place on the battlefield, 837–40), Theseus urges Adrastus to give a funeral oration in praise of the champions, a speech specifically designed to benefit the youth of the city of Athens (842–43).[52] He pointedly instructs Adrastus not to speak about the way each champion died in battle (846–56),[53] for the actual conditions of a battle make such reports impossible. With this display of prohoplite ideology, Euripides may be offering an implicit criticism of Aeschylus' earlier play on this same subject, *Eleusinioi*—at least if it, like *Seven against Thebes*, contained elaborate references to the actions of individual warriors, as did archaic epic in any case.[54] Adrastus gives a funerary oration that has disturbed many interpreters of the play.[55] He praises the champions as models of courage and civic devotion for the young; their examples testify to the fact that courage and manliness are teachable (909–17). In Adrastus' speech, each champion was well educated and grew up to behave in ways that would have been acceptable in a contemporary Athenian youth.[56] Yet in the literary tradition represented above all by Aeschylus'

---

[51] The uselessness of lament is a standard topos—e.g., *Ajax* 852, *Phoenissae* 1762, or *Alcestis* 1079.

[52] The text may also refer to the children of the deceased; see Smith 1966: 169 n. 20, countered by Collard 1975: 2: ad loc. Even if it does not, the sons are present on stage to hear and to be affected by the speech.

[53] The messenger's speech follows this procedure, except that he singles out Theseus for special mention.

[54] Loraux 1986: 406 n. 156 points out that the inadequacy of words to describe action is a theme of the funeral oration, and hence the passage is more than an oblique criticism of Aeschylus.

[55] Collard 1972 and Zuntz 1963: 13–16 see the speech as a sign of Adrastus' rehabilitation (Burian 1985: 219 n. 39 contests Adrastus' rehabilitation). More ambivalent readings are offered by Smith 1966: 162–63, Loraux 1986: 107–8, and Burian 1985: 147.

[56] The rejection of the influence of the Muses in the speech may serve to remind the audience that the champions were educated to courage and control of their appetites, but not to good counsel. Pericles' funeral oration on the other hand celebrates the intellectual as well as the military life of Athens in its role as a school for Hellas.

Seven against Thebes, the champions were largely notable for their hubris and boastful speech. Earlier in Euripides' own play, the champion Capaneus has been singled out for these very faults, for which he died from a lightning bolt of Zeus (494–99; see also 639–40). Is Euripides, as some have argued, parodying the fulsome and unrealistic praise lavished on the war dead in contemporary Athenian funeral orations? Or is Theseus trying to direct Adrastus, as he seems to be elsewhere in the play, to profit from the Athenian example and bring back to Argos a series of lessons about public policy that will prevent the city from repeating its previous acknowledged errors? (Adrastus is said earlier to have rejected a Theban offer to resolve the quarrel between Eteocles and Polyneices by words rather than combat, to have made ill-conceived matches for his daughters, and to have gone to battle with bad omens [739–40 and 133–60].) Finally, Adrastus, once again leaving the mothers aside, neglects to offer the consolation to the bereaved relatives traditional to funeral orations and in fact fails to calm them.[57] Yet after celebrating martial courage at Theseus' request, Adrastus goes on to express a hope that mortals will give up strife and prefer peace to combat (949–54).[58]

Once more criticizing Adrastus, Theseus refuses to allow the mothers of the seven to touch the bodies of their children. The sight of the wounds, he insists, will increase their lamentations (941–47). Adrastus acquiesces and mourns no more on stage, but goes off to participate in an all male cremation ceremony with Theseus and the sons of the champions (the burning and inhumation of the bones from Homer onward [see *Iliad* 24.790–800] seem always to have been a male affair). Deprived of the bodies of their children, the chorus of mothers is forced to accept the new civic attitude voiced earlier in the play by Aethra—that women should always get things done by men (40–41).[59] Nevertheless, the mothers appear unmoved by Adrastus' praise of their sons, and once more begin to lament, if in a slightly less extravagant manner (955–79). After the suicide of Capaneus' wife Evadne, the sons return with the urns containing the ashes of their fathers. In what seems to be a reversal of the tragic norm, the youths, in imitation of their rash fathers, argue for revenge against the more temperate views of the women, a gender otherwise represented in Greek literature as particularly prone to move swiftly from lamentation to wrath and revenge.[60] Commentators have again been left puzzled. Given the emphasis earlier in the play on the misguided expedition of the original seven, and on the importance of peaceful solutions, wherever pos-

---

[57] Of course, Adrastus' speech is not a standard Attic funerary oration. See esp. Collard 1975: ad loc. On the effect of the speech on the chorus, see Jouan 1997: 228.

[58] On the ironic contradictions here, see Smith 1966: 163 and Burian 1985: 149.

[59] Loraux 1986: 49. In contrast to Loraux, I think the mothers continue to resist incorporation into the civic system, especially in their persistent desire to lament their sons publicly.

[60] Loraux 1990: 67. I accept Diggle's 1981 text here, which, in contrast to Collard 1975, gives lines 1145 and 1152 to the grandsons, not the chorus.

sible, to political problems, how are we to feel about this closing return to yet another expedition of revenge?

The play's final lamentation between the mothers and their grandsons is dominated by the grandsons. First, they ignore the mothers' pleas to touch the funerary urns; the mothers *never* touch them, although physical contact with the dead and even the urns containing the ashes of the dead is a very important part of traditional funerary ritual (1160, 1165–67, 1185–88)[61]—recall, for example, Sophocles' Electra (though she is also finally deprived of the urn by Orestes). Athena closes the play by telling Theseus not to surrender the ashes of the dead until the Argives have sworn to avoid war with Athens. She announces that the seven sons will grow up to avenge their fathers at Thebes in an expedition favored by the gods.

In this play, then, Theseus, supported earlier by the messenger, seems to be at pains to take control of the funerary rites for the champions in a striking fashion. In both the archaic funeral and the ordinary private funeral at Athens, women laid out the bodies of the dead and played the dominant role in the *prothesis* and in the lamentation at the grave site. This is what the mothers of the seven clearly expect as they elaborate in detail on their hopes concerning the burial rites in the first scene of the play (16–19, 51–53, 61–62, 68–70, 815–17)—that is, until Theseus intervenes to deprive them of the bodies and to suppress the extravagant lament that they had begun prior to his entrance.

In the case of death rites for the Attic war dead, as opposed to the private funeral, the bodies of the slain were laid out and cremated on the battlefield, a ritual that Theseus has done for the mass of the slain soldiers in this play. Whereas other Greek cities buried the bones of the dead on the battlefield, Athens took pride in its unique custom of bringing them home for public burial.[62] Women clearly played a reduced role in public as opposed to private burial.[63] As we know from Thucydides, each family was allowed to bring gifts to and honor the bones of their kin, which were laid out in tents at a public site. The bones of the dead were divided by tribe and brought in a procession to a public burial site in the Ceramicus. Public lamentation over the bones, a lamentation that included close female relatives of the dead, and then public

[61] Commentators often mistakenly (Mirto 1984 excepted) assume that the mothers embrace the urns. See Smith 1966: 155, Burian 1985: 145. See Shaw 1982: 8 on the theme of lost embraces in the play. Touching the body, and especially the head of the deceased, is shown on vase paintings to be an important part of the burial ritual. See Mirto 1984.

[62] See Loraux 1986: 18. Notice that this practice keeps the remains of the slain out of the public arena, where they might generate the kind of emotional response that Theseus fears here.

[63] As Loraux 1986: 24 puts it, "the Athenian city, which democratized military activity, opening it to every citizen, was, perhaps more than any other polis, a 'men's club.' . . . War was men's business, as were civic funerals." Yet Loraux (24) assumes without evidence that women were excluded from the *ekphora* in the public funeral. Thucydides 2.34 and 2.46 make clear that the women visited the bones of the dead in the tents, marched in the procession (probably with other women), listened to the oration, and lamented at the grave site.

burial were followed by the *epitaphios logos*; this funeral oration usually urged acceptance of death and resigned behavior among the survivors, as well as imitation of the heroic dead by the next generation. The ceremony closed with further public lamentation.

The funeral rites in the second half of *Suppliants* represent a process of transition between a traditional archaic funeral for the individual—*prothesis, ekphora*, praise at the grave, and burial—and those of a state funeral, which includes collective mourning of the dead, controlled funerary behavior, and funeral oration.[64] They resemble neither precisely, however, in the exceptional repression of the female role in the burial, exceptional it seems, even by the standards of public funerals in Athens. Although Athenian rites for the war dead offered a compromise between family and public interests, which nevertheless allowed the latter to dominate,[65] Theseus' procedures outdo that of his descendants by virtually excluding the female kin of the Seven altogether. At the funeral of Hector in *Iliad* 24, male and female roles differ; the men, for example, participate in collective *thrēnoi*, to which the women wail in response (719–22); three female relatives then improvise individual *gooi* to which the women, and finally in Helen's case, the whole people (*dēmos*) responds (723–76).[66] The women, not the men, deliver the final public statements over the body of Hector. In a less formal context, however, both men and women in Homer may on occasion lament in similar ways, voicing similar themes, and expressing grief in a violent and almost suicidal fashion. *Suppliants* apparently reflects its Athenian setting by going to great lengths to differentiate male and female roles in funeral rites, to segregate the men from the women, and to establish masculine and civic control over every part of the ritual. Lamentation itself develops here as elsewhere an explicit association with the feminine (e.g., *Suppliants* 83–85; *Medea* 928; Pollux, *Onomasticon* 6.202), and men, like Adrastus, must be weaned from public expressions of intense grief.[67]

Thus, the play begins with the disorderly women asserting their claims by disrupting the ritual procedures for the festival at Eleusis (97, 290) and proceeds with a series of traditional despairing lamentations by Adrastus and the women, who expect to carry on with the standard aristocratic burials of archaic Greece; it closes by virtually ignoring the mothers altogether. The women's failure to persist in their lament is implicitly anticipated in the opening setting

[64] For the whole topic, see Loraux 1986 and Jouan 1997: esp. 226. See Cicero *De Legibus* 2.64–65 on the law forbidding orations at private graves. The order of the burial rites in *Suppliants*—aborted lament, funeral oration, cremation, more lamentation—is not that of public funeral, because the cremation of the bodies is delayed. As a result, the emotions produced by the contact with the bodies are not contained by the rhetoric of the oration.

[65] Loraux 1986: 24.

[66] The words *thrēnos* and *goos* can be interchangeable in many classical texts. In Homer *gooi* are improvised laments by friends or relatives of the dead person (Alexiou 1974: 13).

[67] See Loraux 1986: 45 and 48 and Reiner 1938: 54–56.

at Demeter's festival, the Proerosia, a festival preliminary to the fall plowing in which offerings are made to insure the future crop.[68] Demeter, the mourning mother par excellence, is petitioned by mourning mothers, whose case is then undertaken by a weeping Aethra.[69] Yet ironically, the lamentation so powerfully associated with the goddess is unpropitious (along with suppliancy) at the Proerosia (and possibly at other sites sacred to Demeter in Athens during classical times),[70] and Aethra soon proves to be an atypical mother in her acceptance of war and Athenian civic ideology. Yet has Theseus succeeded in atticizing traditional death ritual for a new and better cause, or are we instead merely witnessing a return of the repressed in a novel form?

Earlier in the play, Theseus had insisted to the Theban messenger that dread of the corpses of the champions was irrational. As dead men they could hardly overthrow Thebes from the grave or beget children who will avenge them (542–48). Yet this fear of familial revenge, a revenge provoked in this instance by direct contact of the sons with the bodies of their fathers (and Adrastus' oration),[71] is then realized in the expedition of the Epigoni. True, the expedition—which has, according to Athena, divine support (*sun theō(i)*, 1226)—was successful in destroying Thebes with the loss of only one of the champions (Adrastus' son). Furthermore, one purpose of Athenian public funerals was to encourage the young to imitate the valor of their fathers. Yet the play also casts doubts on military solutions as the first line of defense against wrongdoing and on encouraging emotional reactions to the death of family members; youths are advised to attend to the wisdom of the old and mute their courage with good counsel.[72]

---

[68] Conacher 1956: 16 n. 20 is excellent on the importance of the Demetrian setting, which resonates with the play's emphasis on themes relating to both death and fertility or salvation. On the Proerosia, see now Goff 1995a.

[69] The civic Demeter of the classical period thus rejects her own mythic traditions in a cultic context. Further Demetrian motifs may be evoked by the cryptic etiologies offered in Athena's speech ex machina (see Collard 1975: 2: ad loc.).

[70] Andocides 1.110 shows that placing a suppliant's bough in the Eleusinium at Athens during the Mysteries could incur the penalty of death. See Smith 1966: 154. In myth, the Proerosia was established by Delphi in response to a plague in Greece (Lycurgus, fragment 87, Suda II.2420). Athens undertook the festival for all the Greeks, while other cities brought tithes of their crops. An inscription dated to the period of uncertain peace in the Peloponnesian War years (IG I³ 78 = IG I² 76; Meiggs and Lewis 1969: no. 73) indicates an attempt to revive the festival, but donations are required only from Attica and the allies. If the inscription closely predated *Suppliants*, Euripides' choice of setting may have political significance beyond what has been generally recognized.

[71] On this point, see Smith 1966: 160, Burian 1985: 149 and 152, and Fitton 1961: 439.

[72] Note that the grandsons are described as lion cubs in Athena's speech (1222–23). (See Wolff 1979, Shaw 1982: 17, and Smith 1966: 166–67, who notes the possible further reference to *Agamemnon* here.) The same image was earlier associated with the rash violence of Polyneices and Tydeus—the young who promote wars without justice (233). And why should the sons avenge warriors who have been justly punished by Zeus (504–5)? The play repeatedly emphasizes the de-

Nor has Theseus obviously succeeded in suppressing female hysteria in a public context. The funeral oration of Adrastus is immediately followed by the extraordinary suicide of Evadne.[73] Interrupting the renewed lamentation of the chorus, she will imitate her husband's courage by joining him in death. Rejecting lamentation for the pursuit of fame (1015, 1059–63, 1067), she wishes to celebrate a glorious victory "over all women whom the sun sees" (1059–61). With its grotesque mixture of Bacchic (1000–1001) and erotic (1019–30) frenzy and a masculine-style striving for victory (her deed is described as *pantolmon*, 1075), her death might well be viewed as a ghastly imitation of heroic male behavior that pointedly interrupts and distorts the appropriation of male courage in the service of the state by Theseus and Adrastus. Certainly the chorus and Evadne's father Iphis greet the suicide not with admiration but with horror. Evadne's act seemingly embodies a suicidal tendency that Theseus tried to discourage in the earlier lamentation by the women and Adrastus.[74] Finally, her death doubly bereaves her father, who had expected from his daughter a striving to excel in the works of Athena (weaving) and in good sense (*euboulia*, 1062), not an attempt to achieve a masculine-style victory in death. Iphis, after yet another instance of age's failure to persuade the rash young, adopts the suicidal stance earlier abandoned by Adrastus and departs for death by starvation.

Clearly lamentation and death ritual, and controlling the funerary behavior of women in a public context where matters of interstate politics are at stake, are at the heart of what this typically ambiguous Euripidean play is about. If, as many commentators think, the play was presented right after the battle of Delium in 424, in which this first major defeat of the war was temporarily followed by a Boeotian refusal to allow the Athenians to recover and bury their dead, we can explain some aspects of the play as a reaction to recent events, if not the specific concern with women's role in the death rites.[75] Moreover, we continue to find a similar emphasis on the suppression of mourning by women in the later Euripidean play *Iphigeneia in Aulis*, or in Sophocles' *Oedipus at Colonus*. Iphigeneia insists that her mother Clytemnestra not mourn her daughter (1435–50) and Antigone and Ismene are discouraged from lamenting their father's mysterious disappearance into another world (1640–1715). Here suppression of grief is urged because the protagonist is about to become

---

sirability of a complementary relation between youth and age, courage and good counsel. On these points, see esp. Conacher 1956: 25–26, Shaw 1982: 12–15, Burian 1985: 138, and Gamble 1970: 397.

[73] For ironic readings of the Evadne scene, see esp. Smith 1966: 164–66; Burian 1985: 145, 150–52, and 220 n. 53; Shaw 1982: 13–14; and Loraux 1986: 108.

[74] Mirto 1984: 76 and Burian 1985: 145. This tendency to assimilate oneself temporarily to the dead during mourning seems to have been perfectly normal in an earlier period—see Achilles in the *Iliad*. See further Seaford 1994: 86–92, who expands on the ways that the ritual permits mourners to regenerate solidarity in the wake of loss.

[75] I accept Collard's arguments on the dating of the play (1975: 1: 8–14).

or will become a heroic benefactor of society who is not buried in the traditional sense; at the same time the plays highlight women's private pain or anger over the state's appropriation of kin. The fragments of Euripides' *Erechtheus* suggest that Praxithea, who begins in stoic fashion by volunteering to sacrifice her daughter for the city, later seems unable to repress her lamentation when she discovers that she has lost all of her daughters, to say nothing of her husband, in the course of the action.[76]

Theseus' response to female lamentation in this play finds a parallel both in contemporary practice, which aimed to mute and restrain public lamentation by women, and in the attitude of twentieth-century Greek men to their women's lamentations. In rural villages modern Greek women often perform their laments in secret; men, many women, and the church all express ambivalence about these uncanny and terrifying sounds, and the way the lament revives unsettling pain in the hearts of those who perform it.[77] Similarly, Plutarch, in offering consolation to his wife over the death of their child, stresses the need for women to resist extravagant grief and the influence of other women who whet and inflame lamentation without limit (*Moralia* 608b1–610c7). Tragic lamenters are often described, as in this play, with metaphors drawn from Dionysiac cult,[78] which might well reflect, as it does in the case of modern Greek lament, associations between possession and the performance of lamentation.[79] Yet as we know from myths and, above all, from Euripides' *Bacchae*, women's special vulnerability to Dionysiac possession strikes terror into the hearts of men determined to keep women in their place, that is married and inside the house. Moreover, as we are about to see, laments by women are apparently seen in the classical period as fundamentally antithetical to military valor.

Even more important, the themes developed in lamentation are often subtly

---

[76] Fragments 50 and 65 (Pap. Sorb. 2328), Austin 1968. See also Creon's interruption of Antigone's mourning for her mother and brothers in *Phoenissae*. In the latter case, Antigone resists. Plato's *Phaedo* inaugurates the philosophical case against lamentation. See further Loraux 1995b and van Wees 1999.

[77] Caraveli 1986: 169–70 and 185. On the reaction of the early church to the Bacchic lamentations of women, see Alexiou 1974: 29.

[78] Our first literary example is the comparison of the mourning Andromache to a maenad (*Iliad* 22.460, 6.389). See also Aeschylus' *Seven against Thebes* 836 where the lamenting chorus is described as maenadic (*thuias*); the mourning of Euripides' Hecuba for her son Polymestor (*nomon bakcheion, Hecuba* 686–87); or Antigone lamenting her mother and brothers (*bakcha nekuōn, Phoenissae* 1488–89). In *Suppliants*, the Dionysiac element in the mother's lament is suggested by the use of ionic rhythms in the parodos, a meter specifically associated with Dionysiac cult (see Collard 1975: 2: ad loc.). Evadne later becomes a Bacchant who will end in Hades (1000–1001); in a reversal of the Demetrian pattern, the daughter descends permanently to Persephone and marriage in death and rejects reunion with her lamenting father. For further discussion of these motifs, see Seaford 1994: ch. 9.

[79] Caraveli 1986: 179. Laments also become ambivalent because they mediate between antithetical types of experience—life and death, sacred and secular, etc. (178).

at odds with the rhetoric of the public funeral oration and thus with the public ideology of Athens.[80] Laments, like funeral orations, do at times praise the
dead. But, like the mothers here, they stress unrestrainedly the pain of individual loss.[81] By concentrating on the negative effects that death and war itself have on survivors, lamentation can offer a muted reproach of the dead and
of the ambitions of the dead for immortal fame celebrated in funeral oration.
In *Suppliants* the mothers, now childless and thus without a stable identity
(955–79),[82] undermine in their lament the central role of women in the classical city-state by doubting the value of marrying and producing children at all
(786–93, 822–23). In the *Iliad*, the themes expressed in lamentation also subtly
counter the dominant ideology of the poem (see especially the lamentations of
Andromache), which celebrates the immortal *kleos* acquired by the warrior in
battle. But the poet does not problematize this tension in a comparable way.
Instead, when Achilles withdraws from the battle and questions the value of
the noble death, he moves closer to a sphere that has affinities with the language and attitudes expressed in lamentation. His own dramatic displays of
lamentation for Patroclus dramatize his temporary alignment with those, like
women, who are marginal to the culture's centers of power.[83] Yet later it is the
shared lamentation between Priam and Achilles that helps to bring Achilles
back into the cultural mainstream and provides the powerful closure to the
poem. Paradoxically, this lament unites not friends but enemies.[84] The *Iliad*,
then, does not repress the marginal discourse of lament, but appropriates it in
the service of its own plot structure. Theseus, on the other hand, echoes mainstream Athenian ideology in pointedly suppressing the discourse of lamentation in *Suppliants*. At the same time, by emphasizing the potential danger, even
hysteria, in the heroic discourse of courage, and by finally aligning the lamenting mothers with a desire for peace and restraint,[85] the play allows the voice
of lament to counter the dominant discourse of the play, and to provide the
uneasy sense of closure to this "encomium of Athens" noted by so many of the
play's recent critics.[86]

[80] On the the way that lament counters the dominant cultural ethic, see Alexiou 1974: 182,
Caraveli 1986: 181–82, and Holst-Warhaft 1992. On the tension between the motifs of lamentation and those of the funeral oration, see Loraux 1986: 45–47 and 1990: 35 and 82.

[81] See Alexiou 1974: 162 and 184, Loraux 1986: 45, and Caraveli 1986: 181.

[82] Danforth 1982: 136–38 argues that modern Greek women lament in order to continue a relation to their male kin, a relation that gave them an identity in life.

[83] Priam, as an old man, is the other male figure in this poem who laments in a highly emotional fashion. Men in Homer express grief openly and without ambivalence (Monsacré 1984: esp.
137–42).

[84] Seaford 1994: ch. 5 offers a very helpful analysis of the way that the funerary ritual in *Iliad*
23–24 serves to reunite the various social worlds of the poem.

[85] See Loraux 1986: 74 and 108 on the tension between pleas for peace and the rhetoric of the
funeral oration.

[86] The description of the play as an encomium of Athens comes from the hypothesis and pro-

Aeschylus' *Seven against Thebes*

From the *Suppliants* of the mid 420s, I would like to turn finally to a consideration of an earlier drama in which the public lamentation of women plays an equally central role, Aeschylus' *Seven against Thebes* of 467. The play begins with the Theban king Eteocles announcing the ways in which he will carry his city calmly and bravely through the challenge presented by the attack of the seven champions led by his brother Polyneices. After he leaves the stage, the chorus of young, unmarried women enters to embrace statues of the Olympian gods in prayer and supplication. The women express hysterical fears for the safety of the city and name each god in hope of winning his or her protection. Eteocles returns and chastises the women sternly.[87] At first he asserts that women should stay at home; it is the man's task to sacrifice and appeal to the gods in wartime and to take care of what lies outside the house (200–201, 230–32). The women's fears are ill-omened (258) and will undermine the morale of those fighting to defend the city (191–92, 236–38). The women should stop clinging to the statues of the gods (265; see also 185–86) and rely on their human defenders (216–18). If they must pray to the gods—and Eteocles finally does not grudge them this as long as they do so calmly (236) and suppress their hysteria and laments (237–38, 242–43)—they should offer an orderly prayer to the collective gods who defend the city (266–78).[88]

After Eteocles' departure, the women appear quieter and calmer, and pray without wails (279) for the safety of the city to the city's gods collectively rather

vides the basis of Zuntz' 1963 and Collard's 1975 interpretations. For largely ironic readings of the play, see esp. Smith 1966, Fitton 1961: esp. 442, and Gamble 1970. Such critics generally see the play as divided into two parts. The first part praises Athens; the second, focusing on the burial rites, exposes us to the Argive failure to uphold the Athenian ideals. In Aeschylus' *Eleusinioi* the bodies of the slain were recovered by peaceful means. Euripides' choice for a violent solution paves the way for a less ethically satisfying conclusion (Fitton 444). Shaw 1982: 9–11 argues that the example of Theseus' leadership in the earlier scenes is not negated by the concluding scenes with the Argives.

[87] The force of Eteocles' intervention is heightened by the fact that the characters do not generally respond directly to choral odes. See Hutchinson 1985: 75.

[88] For the differences between the male and female gods whom the chorus supplicates as statues and the city gods to whom Eteocles advises it pray, see Benardete 1967. Although Eteocles himself originally prays to both male and female deities, Benardete (esp. 28) views his insistence that chorus ignore the gender of the gods as part of Eteocles' attempt to relegate the family, and above all his own family, to the level of the subpolitical in favor of autochthony and the interests of the city. The state is a ship (and thus an institution without women [see Caldwell 1973: 217]). See also Orwin 1980: 191, Eteocles' "noble dedication to the city is the obverse of his fatal indifference to the family"; "the tragedy of the city is that it both requires and cannot tolerate Eteocles" (196). The reversal begins, argues Vidal-Naquet 1988, with the final three shields, in which the excluded female element begins to dominate (282–92). At 653–55 Eteocles even bursts out into three lines of lamentation himself, then quickly pulls back from weeping that might generate a *goos* (656–57).

than individually; yet they fail in their prayer to follow his instructions precisely. In addition, they evoke a terrible picture of the fate of women and children in a fallen town.[89] Once more they only partially and halfheartedly obey their ruler's request, for they do not suppress ill-omened fear (see 287).[90]

Before turning to the role of the chorus of women as lamenters of the dead Eteocles and Polyneices at the conclusion of this play, let us pause to consider Eteocles' reaction here. Is this, as some have argued, an inappropriate outburst of misogyny from a man who at first deliberately represses his accursed connections to his mortal parents in favor of identifying himself with the autochthonous sown men of Thebes, the patriots who are utterly devoted to the cause of the mother earth who bore them?[91] Or is Eteocles meant to be seen as a model of appropriate masculine behavior in wartime?[92]

The prerogative of Aeschylus' Clytemnestra and Atossa to preside over sacrifices marking victory and defeat is unquestioned[93] in *Agamemnon* and *Persians* (though the former has dubious motives in undertaking the rites); similarly, the older women in Aristophanes' *Lysistrata* easily take over the Acropolis under the pretext of performing sacrifices there. But none of these public sacrifices by women in wartime occur in the context of a city under siege, and the image evoked by the women of the chorus, as they cling des-

---

[89] For these choral departures from Eteocles' instructions, see esp. Benardete 1967: 23–24, where he stresses that the prayer is short-lived; does not include, as Eteocles advises, mention of sacrifices and the propitious *ololugmos*; and dwells far more on potential disaster than on propitious prayer. The chorus acquiesces to Eteocles' commands but does not change its religious views (see Brown 1977: 302 and Gagarin 1976: 155).

[90] They now fear not the danger outside the city but dangers within; hence they break down the boundaries between inside and outside that Eteocles is so insistent to maintain. On this point, see Bacon 1964: 30 and Benardete 1967: 23.

[91] See Benardete 1967: 28–29. The psychological view of Eteocles' misogyny, which stresses the connection between his attitude to both the chorus and women generally and his family vicissitudes, can be found in Méautis 1936: 109, Rose 1956: 13, Dawson 1970: 48, and above all Caldwell 1973.

[92] For a summary of the views of those who defend Eteocles' attitudes as unproblematic and appropriate to the wartime context, see Caldwell 1973: 201–3. Brown 1977 and Gagarin 1976 emphasize that the difference in outlook between Eteocles and the chorus is a central and relatively neglected aspect of the play. For Brown, Eteocles and the women fail to establish communication. The chorus' intuitive and traditional feminine piety, its timidity, and vivid anticipation of suffering clash irreconcilably with the aristocratic courage, ethics, and practicality of the city's defender. Winnington-Ingram 1983: 45–46 suggests that this clash between male and female interests was characteristic of the trilogy as a whole; in the earlier plays, women's dominance in the household threatened the interests of the male Labdacids. For Gagarin, whose overall argument has much in common with Brown's, Eteocles' extreme reaction to the women demonstrates incompetent leadership; he verges on blasphemy in his open criticism of the women's belief in the gods (154–56). The women correctly represent in their ode the pollution and suffering occasioned by war, and the destructive side of military values (158–61). See now also the discussion of Zeitlin 1990. Schaps 1982 gives a good picture of women's actual as opposed to their imaginary behavior in wartime contexts.

[93] Gagarin 1976: 156.

perately to the statues of the gods and attempt to evoke their help rather than that of the mortal defenders of the city, would be likely to remind the audience above all of artistic and literary representations of lamenting women in a fallen city (especially Troy).[94] Hence, in considering this question we might look back to a relatively similar context in *Iliad* 6. There Hector returns to the city to ask some of the women of Troy to pray for the favor of Athena. Hecuba obeys his request. In *Seven against Thebes*, the chorus of women refers to sacred robes and wreathes such as those brought by Hecuba and her women to Athena (101; *Iliad* 6. 87–101 and 270–80). After asking Paris to return to the battlefield, Hector goes home to find his wife Andromache. He discovers that she has left the house with her maidservant and child, lamenting (*gooōsa*, 6.373) like a madwoman (398), hysterical with fear for her husband's safety. Hector meets his wife at the gate by which he will return to the battlefield. He tries to calm her fears, but she is not ultimately convinced. On her return home Andromache generates in her servants a lament for Hector as if he were already dead (6.499–500).

The contexts in the *Iliad* and *Seven against Thebes* are not precisely parallel, in that the public appeal to Athena by Hecuba and the Trojan women is orderly and commanded by the men,[95] whereas Andromache alone displays the hysteria of Aeschylus' chorus. Nevertheless, I think it would be fair to assume on the basis of his prescriptive statements, that Andromache's behavior would be considered ill-omened and inappropriate by Aeschylus' Eteocles; nor would he have commissioned a comparable expedition on the part of the Hecubas of his city, because he believes such rituals to be in wartime the duty of men (200–201, 230–32).[96] Homer's text does not explicitly criticize Andromache's hys-

---

[94] Mortals supplicate images when all hope of human aid is gone (Hutchinson 1985: 74). The epic coloring of the language of the first stasimon reinforces possible associations with the fall of cities. The lament for the fall of cities is an important category in Alexiou's 1974 analysis of Greek lamentation. All loud public outcries of women tend to be linked in the classical Greek mind (Loraux 1986: 36). Although the chorus is not formally lamenting here, the way that the text subtly alludes to traditions in which funerary lament played a central role serves to anticipate and link the role of the disruptive chorus here to its later role in lamenting the brothers. From the perspective of an Eteocles, who equates success with control over language from his first lines (see Cameron 1970: 98–99), the chorus makes the dangers external to the city visible and vividly present through its synaesthetic imagery, which turns sounds into sight (e.g., 103).

[95] See Hutchinson 1985: 74.

[96] Eteocles is in fact only concerned with sacrifices before battle, which will determine whether or not military action is approved by the gods: *andrōn tad' esti, sphagia kai chrēstēria / theoisin erdein polemiōn peirōmenous / son d'au to sigan kai menein eisō domōn*, 230–32). The chorus brings offerings to ask for divine protection for the whole city similar to those brought in *Iliad* 6. Similarly, Eteocles asks the women for a paean and an *ololugmos*. Yet the paean is a male war cry, and the *ololugmos* will greet not a sacrifice (a standard role for women) but the coming war (and perhaps male death in war). On this point, see Vidal-Naquet 1988: 281. The anomalous use of terminology here would suggest that Aeschylus is attempting to characterize Eteocles as extreme in his attitudes toward the women. A similarly violent gesture is Eteocles' threat of death by stoning to the women (199; Vidal-Naquet 280 and Gagarin 1976: 154).

teria or her ill-omened lament for a living husband. Hector's attempt to soothe his wife and return her to her proper place at home is gentle and sensitive. Are we then experiencing in Eteocles' violent reaction, his attempt to silence rather than calm the women, the same Athenian attitude to uncontrolled behavior by women in a public context expressed in the sixth-century and later funerary legislation? In addition to the later evidence of Euripides' *Suppliants*, an incident at Plutarch's *Nicias* 13 could be viewed as supporting Eteocles' views, if not his harsh and repressive behavior, as standard for classical culture. We are told by Plutarch that during the Athenian preparations for the Sicilian expedition, "the women were celebrating . . . the festival of Adonis, and in many places throughout the city little images of the god were laid out for burial, and funeral rites were held about them, with wailing cries of women, so that those who cared anything for such matters were distressed, and feared lest that powerful armament, with all the splendor and vigour that were so manifest in it, should speedily wither away[97] and come to naught." Plutarch's source for this incident may have been comedy, and a very similar passage in Aristophanes' *Lysistrata* (387–96) should perhaps make us reluctant to accept this particular evidence, if not the attitudes it displays, at face value.

Whatever we are to think of this scene in *Seven against Thebes*, however, the tables are eventually turned on the emphatically rational Eteocles. When he discovers that he is to meet his brother at the seventh gate, he becomes impervious to persuasion, irrevocably set on carrying out what he feels to be a destiny lying in wait for him by divine contrivance. The chorus of women tries to dissuade him, asking him to give heed to women for all his dislike (712). It repeatedly urges him to control his emotion and to consider what the polluting act of fratricide will do to the city he was previously so eager to protect (679–82, 694, 718, 734–37). To no avail. Here the chorus becomes the mouthpiece for the interests of the city, while Eteocles is now concerned above all with his family's fate.[98] After Eteocles' departure the chorus brings out all

---

[97] Trans. Perrin [1914] 1982. The image recalls the pots of flowers planted for Adonis that were allowed to wither in the hot sun on the rooftops.

[98] I agree with those like Brown 1977, Gagarin 1976, and Long 1986, in contradiction to earlier critics, that Eteocles does not change his views here. He is still preoccupied with defending the city and still holds a fatalistic view of the gods' relation to humankind, despite his sudden passion to kill his brother. But we interpret these attitudes differently in the changed context at the seventh gate. Similarly, the chorus consistently relies unquestioningly on the gods and is fearful for itself and the city, and its lyrics remain dominated by dochmiacs throughout. But in the second scene with Eteocles both the chorus' emotional meter and its concern with traditional piety read differently in the context of the coming fratricide. The two scenes (on the formal parallels between the two scenes involving Eteocles and the women, see Winnington-Ingram 1983: 33 and Brown 315) have a similar structure, but in the first scene the chorus' emotional piety endangers the city, in the second the danger is posed by Eteocles' fatalism and commitment to aristocratic *aretē* (see Brown 312–17; Gagarin, esp. 159–161). The same issues reemerge over the burial of Polyneices in the disputed section of the play (see Brown 317).

of the terrible family history that Eteocles seemingly tried to ignore in favor of civic concerns in the earlier scenes of the play. It recalls an oracle suggesting that the survival of the city may depend on the extinction of the house of Laius (742–49). Eteocles was apparently not destined to be the exemplary patriot he imagined.

Once Thebes is victorious in the battle, the bodies of the two brothers return to be lamented by the chorus of women. In a notable contrast to Euripides' *Suppliants*, women dominate these burial rites completely. Here the women of the chorus, "daughters of mothers" (792),[99] whose voices and attitudes Eteocles earlier attempted to tame and repress, take over the stage to counter the claims of their former leader. First, their lamentation pointedly blurs the moral distinction between the two brothers that Eteocles was so insistent to make in the shield scene.[100] Both were *poluneikeis*, productive of many quarrels (829–31, 849–50, 940). Yet in his first speech Eteocles had said that if disaster should strike Thebes, one name alone, Eteocles,[101] would be held responsible in the citizens' loud-swelling chants and laments (5–8); the phrasing paradoxically mingles the language of praise and lament (*Eteoklees an eis polus kata ptolin / humnoith' hup' astōn phroimiois polurrothois / oimōgmasin th'*). On the surface the text speaks of the citizens' blame of Eteocles for the disaster; but the use of *humnoith'*, the stress on the name itself (meaning "the man of true fame"), and the choice of the word *oimōgmasin*, which above all connotes lamentation, seem to prefigure the similar mixture of praise and lamentation his corpse later receives from the women. Both Eteocles and Polyneices anticipate a victory celebration (277, 635); but in actuality the Arai (personifications of destructive revenge) utter the cries of victory and Ate (Ruin) erects the trophy (953–60).[102]

Furthermore, although funeral laments, such as those for Hector in *Iliad* 24, traditionally praise the dead and their military prowess, the laments of the chorus of *Seven against Thebes* explicitly criticize the two brothers; both have been wrong and impious (831, 838, 875).[103] "The brothers appear to be praised for their deeds in battle, but in fact their achievement is shown to be both dubious and unimportant" (922–25);[104] their mother, contrary to traditional public lamentation for a dead warrior, was unfortunate in her sons (926–32), and the brothers fulfill the potential of their paternal inheritance (another theme

---

[99] In modern Greece at least, mothers are thought to hand down the style and content of their lamentations to their daughters. See Caraveli 1986.

[100] See Hutchinson 1985: 173 and 961–1004n and Gagarin 1976: 122; Gagarin stresses that only 979–81 and 991–92 make a distinction between the brothers.

[101] Hecht and Bacon 1973: 14–15 argue that Aeschylus plays here on two possible etymologies for the name Eteocles, the "man of true fame" and "the man truly bewept."

[102] Hutchinson 1985: 953–60n.

[103] See also Euripides' *Electra* 907–56 on speaking ill of the dead.

[104] See Hutchinson 1985: xxxviii and ad loc. and Dawson 1970: 111.

of funerary praise) in an ironically aborted and inverted fashion (898–99).[105] As G. O. Hutchinson remarks, "in the final stanza sung by the whole chorus the language of triumph is applied ironically to the disaster inflicted on the house."[106] Laments do, as remarked earlier, traditionally contain reproaches and elements that undermine military praise, but they do so by countering the value of military glory with the sense of loss to the individual. Andromache, for example, reproaches Hector for leaving her a widow and his son an orphan, for grieving his parents and depriving the Trojans of his protection (*Iliad* 22.483, 24.725–26, 22.490, 24.741, 24.729–31). Similarly, the women of the chorus of *Seven* apparently describe themselves as *philoi* of the brothers (909) and claim the grief of the house as their own (1069–70; they are not in fact relatives).[107] Yet their lament lacks features characteristic of lamenting *philoi*: the excited cries, the evocation of the dead person's individuality, the expressions of affection, and the self-pity evoked for the survivors.[108] Described as a *humnon Erinuos* and an *Aida t' echthron paian'* (a hymn to the Erinys and a hateful healing song to Hades, 867–70), the choral song apparently has the form but not the spirit of a more normal lamentation.[109]

Perhaps the choral lamentation here is meant to imply the emergence of a new politics in Thebes, one no longer dominated by the internal squabbles of its destructive royal family;[110] and if so, we must ask ourselves why Aeschylus chose to present the transition in this particular form. For in this play we are told of no one, such as Creon, who might make a hereditary claim to the rule of the city; in the disputed section of the play, the decision concerning the burial of the brothers is made in an assembly by unnamed councilors, *probouloi*, of the people, 1005–6. But whatever way we look at it, the choral lamentation is

---

[105] See Hutchinson 1985: 926nn on the reference to the mother. See also Tucker 1908 on 876–60, 002–05, 000, 922–25, 951–60 and Mellon 1974: 77–79 on the perverted aspects of the lamentation here.

[106] Hutchinson 1985: xxxv; see also 951n and 953–60n.

[107] Here (although the lines belong to the disputed section of the text) the chorus again conflates family and city in a manner contrary to Eteocles' stated practice (not borne out in the event).

[108] Hutchinson 1985: xxxix and 179.

[109] Hutchinson 1985: 180–81; as Mellon 1974: 77 points out, the term *humnos* in a funeral context would normally imply a eulogy of the dead. See *humnoith'* in line 7 discussed earlier. Lines 867–70 belong to a disputed section of the text.

[110] Critics have deemphasized the choral fear of pollution. War itself leads to pollution (344), and the chorus fears that the pollution (681–82; 734–39) of the land caused by the brothers' mutual slaughter will be unending. (See *Agamemnon* 1019–21, *Choephoroi* 48–50 and 66–69, or *Eumenides* 261–63 on the irrevocable consequences of the flow of blood into the earth.) The chorus seems to remain uneasy about the fate of the city even after the Theban victory; and victory is, from a technical point of view, no solution to the problems posed by pollution. Hence, even if the text makes no more explicit mention of this issue after the battle, we cannot assume that the pollution has disappeared. The perverted lamentation may reflect the chorus' anomalous position in undertaking to lament in place of kin those who remain a danger even after death to their beloved city. As Parker 1983: 121 stresses, pollution is a "vehicle through which social disruption is expressed."

on the one hand traditional to archaic rather than contemporary Greek society, in that it allows unrelated women a dominant and public role in mourning the dead, and on the other hand it makes a strong political statement by deliberately undermining the claims made by Thebes' former leader as well as dispraising the dead. Critics have of course been aware of these disconcerting aspects of the concluding choral lamentation of *Seven against Thebes*. But in the light of the attitudes to public expressions of emotion by women found both within the play and in Attic society itself, I do not think that they have fully confronted the challenge that this unusual and even perverted lamentation makes to Eteocles' leadership and to the views that he voiced in the earlier scenes of *Seven against Thebes*.[111] Even without the final disputed scenes, *Seven* from this perspective concludes in a dissonant fashion foreign to what appears to be the case in the other trilogies. Here mourning and death ritual do not perform their traditional function of setting "socially constructed limits on the potentially unlimited, natural expression of grief,"[112] of resolving the irresolvable. Indeed, at moments like this one recalls the final paradox: that tragedy permits male choruses and actors not only to imitate female behavior but to imitate female behavior forbidden to contemporary women in a public context.[113]

The chorus, in keeping with its earlier unease about the undying pollution caused by the mutual fratricide, raises the question of where the brothers will be buried (1002). Indeed, if the original conclusion dropped out, I would speculate that it contained a double burial of the brothers that founded their cult. (The shared cult of the two heroes is mentioned at Pausanias, *Description of Greece* 9.18.3; when sacrifices were made to the two heroes at their tomb, the flame was said to divide in two). The *Oresteia* and probably the Danaid trilogy had etiological conclusions, and as with Euripides, divinities like Athena or Aphrodite could establish cults in order to resolve dilemmas irresolvable on a strictly human level. Because hero cults seem to have been designed to cope with the ambivalent violence and pollution of heroes, the founding of this cult could have resolved the threat of pollution posed to Thebes by the reciprocal fratricide and brought family and city once more into a mutually reinforcing alignment. The distorted and ambivalent lamentation of the chorus would then neatly establish the brothers as appropriate candidates for hero cult.[114]

[111] Among those who give proper stress to the role of the chorus in the play, without directly confronting the perverted choral lamentation, are Finley 1955, Gagarin 1976, Brown 1977, and Orwin 1980. Most critics note the negative turn to the final scenes and the shift of emphasis from the fate of the city to the fate of the family.

[112] Seaford 1985: 320.

[113] See further Zeitlin 1985a. Plato, in his objections to tragedy, later finds such male imitation of lamenting women dangerously feminizing (*Republic* 3.395d; see also 10.603e–604e and 3.387e–389e).

[114] Rosenmeyer 1961: 76 suggests that line 949/50, which describes the bottomless wealth of earth that will lie beneath the bodies of the brothers, hints at the conversion of the burial place

In our disputed manuscript tradition of *Seven against Thebes*,[115] Antigone and Ismene emerge to join the laments of the chorus. A herald enters to announce that a civic council has determined that the noble Eteocles is to be buried, the traitor Polyneices not. This edict thus reasserts the distinction between the brothers denied by the choral ode and the choral lamentation. One half of the chorus joins the cortege following Ismene to the burial of Eteocles, the other joins Antigone in resistance and follows the body of Polyneices. I do not propose to deal here with the arguments about the authenticity of the passage. Critics argue that this scene (or parts of it) was added to *Seven against Thebes* once the popularity of Sophocles' *Antigone* and/or Euripides' *Phoenissae* made some inclusion of Antigone's heroic gesture de rigueur in any production treating this story. Yet it is largely agreed that the interpolator was a remarkably good imitator of Aeschylean style. If, as seems probable, the interpolation was made for an actual revival of Aeschylus in fifth- or fourth-century Athens, however, the interpolator was writing as a member of his culture and for an audience in this culture.[116]

The issues raised by this final scene can thus still be judged as an expression of the tragic politics of lamentation in the classical period. In this passage we find half the chorus disobeying a civic ordinance and legitimizing it as an act of lamentation over which these women were rightfully presiding when the new decree came to their notice. While Antigone ignores the interests of the city, and justifies her action by reference to blood ties over which the city has no rightful jurisdiction, half the chorus supports Antigone because both brothers deserve a public lamentation; Polyneices should not depart "unmourned, his only dirge the lamentation of a sister." (1063–67).[117] Here the women insist on the legitimacy of a public lamentation of the brothers by related and unrelated women forbidden in the funerary legislation. Creon in *Antigone* repeatedly expresses his concern that he not be worsted by a woman. But in Aeschylus' play as we have it, lamentation serves to launch an apparently suc-

---

of the polluted brothers into a sacred and ultimately beneficial spot. He sees the choral lament as a "binding song" to bury the family curse.

[115] See Lloyd-Jones 1959 and Mellon 1974 for earlier bibliography on the authenticity of the final scenes. For other important recent views, see esp. Brown 1976, Dawe 1967 and 1978, and Flintoff 1980.

[116] Both *Phoenissae* and Aristophanes' *Frogs* assume the audience's familiarity with *Seven*, and *Frogs* 868–69 implicitly acknowledges Aeschylean revivals; this suggests the possibility of a fifth-century revival, despite Hutchinson's 1985 doubt that Aeschylus' plays were staged a second time before 386 B.C.E., when the performance of an old play was added to the theatrical contests. Mellon's 1974 comments (11–21) on revivals and interpolations in Aeschylus offer good counterarguments to Hutchinson. From the point of view of civic ideology, the interpretation that I offer here makes it hard to imagine a date at which this interpolation would have been made later than the beginning of the Peloponnesian Wars.

[117] See Orwin 1980: 194–95. Antigone, unlike the chorus, does not attribute the defense of the city to the gods (Orwin 194).

cessful collective female resistance, a resistance whose ultimate result, again in contrast to Sophocles' play (if not Euripides' *Phoenissae*, but here the text is also uncertain), is left disconcertingly open. The choral supporters of Polyneices' burial insist on justifying the rite as a matter of public rather than familial concern. As Orwin agues, they ignore Eteocles' view of the city as a nation of autochthonous warriors; instead their city is designed to protect and preserve a group of families—men, women, and children—descended from the hero Cadmus and the goddess Harmonia. For the chorus, the interests of city and family are coextensive, not in opposition; Polyneices' death is a matter of sorrow to the whole *genea* (house, family, or tribe, 1069–71, *kai gar genea(i)* / *koinon tod'achos, kai polis allōs* / *allot' epainei ta dikaia*), a sentiment that only makes sense if *genea* and *polis* are equated in their minds.[118]

Even allowing for all these textual uncertainties,[119] it is hard to imagine any version of Aeschylus' play being composed or presented at the time of Euripides' *Suppliants*—a period in which a number of other tragedies with an explicitly (or implicitly) Athenian orientation also appeared. Did the Athenian audience simply interpret *Seven against Thebes'* uncomfortable specter of a political rebellion by lamenting women as a specifically Theban phenomenon? As Froma Zeitlin argues, Thebes often served paradigmatically on the tragic stage for the failure to resolve the very cultural tensions that Athens prided itself on mediating or controlling.[120] Or should we conclude that there has been a shift in attitudes from the prewar period in which Aeschylus' play was performed to the wartime context in which Euripides presented *Suppliants*—that Euripides' later play is not only a typically Attic response to the threats imagined to lurk in uncontrolled funerary lamentation but an implicit criticism of earlier tragedy for failing to maintain the proper degree of anachronism on the tragic stage? For just as Euripides' *Suppliants* has Theseus express views perhaps more extreme than contemporary practice reflects, Aeschylus' play permits the archaic-style funerary lamentation of his chorus to move to the outer boundaries of female assertiveness.[121] In support of this point, there do seem to be explicit and possibly critical references to Aeschylus' *Seven against Thebes* in Euripides' *Suppliants*.[122]

---

[118] See Orwin 1980: 195. In his view Eteocles wants to make the city a family that remains primarily a city. The text describes the Thebans throughout as Cadmeians, not Thebans. The chorus defers to Eteocles as leader, but it also twice addresses him as a child (or offspring, *tekos*, 203, and *teknon*, 686), thereby affirming as well his role as a family member.

[119] The loss of the first two plays in the trilogy compounds the difficulties.

[120] See esp. Zeitlin 1986.

[121] In contrast, Brown 1977 sees Aeschylus' chorus as representing feminine timidity and intuitive piety (esp. 305); Zeitlin 1986 seems more accurate in associating the chorus with the Erinys. Note that in other Aeschylean trilogies—in *Eumenides* and *Suppliants* specifically—female choruses are reincorporated into the patriarchal system at the conclusion. Jouan 1997: 232 emphasizes specific ways in which the laments of the chorus of *Suppliants* are more muted (less physical and more pathetic) than those in Aeschylus.

[122] For references, see Fitton 1961: 444 n. 3 and Zuntz 1963: 11 and 12 n. 10.

Sophocles' *Antigone*, usually dated to the late 440s, provocatively uses lament to exacerbate the tensions and contradictions in both the political system (see also III.3) and in the marriage system (a conflict of allegiance between natal and marital family) to be discussed in II.

Furthermore, Nicole Loraux argues that the ideology represented in the classical funeral oration of the kind presented by Pericles and others developed after the late 460s and was a product of Athenian imperialism against other Greek states.[123] This ideology is clearly reflected in *Suppliants*, whereas *Seven against Thebes*, presented in 467, would be too early to be a part of this new historical trend. Finally, *Seven against Thebes* is not the only Aeschylean play in which women collectively use ritual as a context in which to stage social resistance to those in power.[124] We have already mentioned *Choephoroi*. In Aeschylus' *Suppliants*, the daughters of Danaus use not lamentation (although they borrow the language of lament to express their grief) but the ritual of supplication to try to resist marriage to their Egyptian cousins. Their demands endanger the city of Argos, when it finally accepts the obligation to rise to their defense. Furthermore, insofar as we can tell, we rarely find in later tragedy a lamenting chorus of women or a *kommos* dominating the stage action and, in particular, impinging on the political sphere. *The Trojan Women* is an exception, but here the laments—also by barbarians—occur in the context of a fallen city (and a few Greeks actively help the women to conduct the final lament for Astyanax). Sophocles' *Electra* raises important ethical questions about its heroine's use of lamentation to provoke revenge (see III.2, in which I address the dangerous seductive pleasures and attractions of lament as an expressive performance). The solitary lamentation of Euripides' Electra for her plight emphasizes her isolation from the chorus, which is en route to celebrate the festival of Hera. *Helen* and *Iphigeneia among the Taurians* begin with a *kommos*, but in these two plays the lament is for a man only imagined to be dead; similarly, Andromeda's opening lamentation in *Andromeda* proves irrelevant with the arrival of Perseus. In these three plays, the lamentation occurs in a remote, apolitical context and serves to solidify bonds among beleaguered and helpless women. At the concluding lament of *Bacchae* no citizens are present; they are replaced by a foreign chorus who does not share the sentiments of the lamenting protagonists.[125] At the very least the plays of the second half of the fifth century seem to pay considerably greater obeisance to contemporary ideology in the way that lamentation by women is represented on the stage.

In conclusion, then, the Athenian social system seems to have made a concerted effort to control the public behavior of women, especially in relation to

---

[123] See esp. Loraux 1986: 56–69 and 198.

[124] In *Prometheus Bound* and *Eumenides*, female choruses can challenge the Olympian order. The Oceanids finally take Prometheus' side against Zeus and the Erinyes reject Apollo, who claims to represent his father.

[125] For further elaboration of this point, see now Segal 1994.

death ritual. Tragedy, however, allows the politics of the past, whether real or imaginary, to reemerge on stage, and to reenact the sort of social scenarios, including tensions between mass and elite, that may well have led to the earlier funerary legislation. We cannot be sure precisely to what new issues this increasingly self-conscious reproblematizing of funerary lamentation is designed to respond. Clearly, there would be no need to bolster the democratic ideology of the public funeral or for the general emphasis on muting public displays of grief and curtailing funeral monuments that we see in the archaeological and artistic record if there were no opposition to or doubts about these policies. Presumably the strains of the war play an important role here. Threats to the empire are perhaps displaced onto an imaginary plane in terms of the need to exert further control on the public behavior of women. Yet to the degree that all of these plays make public and assertive female funerary behavior serve an important cause or make the male attempt to control and repress it at least partially ambiguous, the plays use traditional motifs from the past to raise questions about similar issues in the democratic society. Above all, these plays demonstrate that lamentation, a ritual form that may well have played a central role in the origins of tragedy, as often divides as unites the stage world in which it is performed.[126] A mourning woman is not simply a producer of pity, but dangerous. Yet the message her lament carries is never fully suppressed.

---

[126] Similarly, Herman 1987 has shown that the dynamics of archaic guest friendship were not fundamentally transformed by Attic democracy. On these aspects of tragedy, see Griffith 1995.

Part II

THE CONTRADICTIONS OF TRAGIC MARRIAGE

Don't look for the functions social practices fulfill,
look for the contradictions they embody.
  (Giddens 1979: 130)

The laws concerning wives are not well
established. For the fortunate man should have
the most wives possible, if his resources permit, so
that he can cast out bad ones from his house, and
happily preserve the one that is good. Now men
look to one wife, risking the greatest danger. For
without testing the ways of their brides men take
them as baggage into their houses.
  (Euripides, Ino, fragment 402N²)

No wall or money or any other thing is as hard to
guard as a woman.
  (Euripides, Danae, fragment 320N²)

But what house among mortals was ever deemed
fortunate without a good wife, even if it was
loaded with luxury.
  (Sophocles, fragment 942 TrGF 4)

THE plots of Attic New Comedy of the fourth century B.C.E. and later generally revolve around the marriages and love affairs of Athenian men. A typical plot recognizes intractable social obstacles to the fulfillment of desire yet can conclude with a young man enabled to marry the girl of his dreams because she turns out after all to be a marriageable citizen daughter, to legitimize the child of a raped (citizen) virgin, or to prolong an affair with a sympathetic concubine (*pallakē*) or *hetaira* (courtesan or prostitute) who has caught his fancy.[1] Although the exact relation of these plots to reality remains controversial, the plays, as J. K. Davies has remarked, show "an intense, even obsessive awareness of the status boundaries separating citizen from foreigner, citizen from slave, well-born from low-born, legitimate from illegitimate, wife from concubine, wealthy man from poor man from beggar."[2] Every contradiction in the Attic marriage system makes its way more or less explicitly into these comedies. The tragedies of the fifth century with which I am concerned in this book also revolve around confronting domestic issues and conflicts, and increasingly so. Euripides, often viewed even in antiquity as a precursor of New Comedy, was famous for his "realistic" treatment of such matters. His characters are wont to make explicit and highly anachronistic remarks about dowry, heiresses, the choice of a proper wife, or the status of slaves and concubines that would not have been out of place in Menander. Those tragedies that have been characterized as "tragic-comic" or "romantic" reach a mixed resolution that both bypasses and recognizes social limitations in a fashion comparable with, if far more ambiguous than, their new comic descendants, yet permit a far more articulate and active role to legitimate wives and daughters.[3]

Yet as always, tragic confrontation with these issues often proves to be far more indirect and oblique. The plays both respond to social and psychological realities and use marriage to address a larger set of social and political issues. In terms of the marriage system itself, the areas that prove to be most problematic are the failure or abuse of the wife's reproductive capacities, since the production of a legitimate male heir for each household was a central goal for the classical Athenian city-state; the potentially divisive power introduced into the household by a wealthy or higher-status wife or an heiress; and the wife's possible division of loyalties between her natal and marital families, and the blurring of boundaries between households that this might produce. Tragedy, as often, makes meaning by collapsing boundaries between private and public worlds; highlights crises and failures in the system; and imagines ways, often

---

[1] See esp. Brown 1990 (with further bibliography) and Plutarch, *Moralia* 712c.

[2] Davies 1977–78: 113.

[3] In New Comedy courtesans or concubines can play an active role in the plot, but respectable women are generally silent and passive.

borrowed from the aristocratic world of epic and archaic literature, of escaping these intractable and contradictory problems. The realities of the marital system were the central factors that shaped Attic women's lives and social identities; at the same time, it is precisely those areas of tension and contradiction in the system that open spaces in which tragic women can, whether constructively or destructively, speak for themselves and take significant action.

Tragic marriage, and especially wedding imagery, has attracted considerable recent interest among scholars.[4] The studies of Nancy Rabinowitz, Victoria Wohl, and Kirk Ormand mentioned in the introduction have explored some of the theoretical aspects of exchange in the representation of marriage in tragedy.[5] My own approach to these questions is more historical and anthropological. Richard Seaford's essay on the structural problems of marriage in Euripides has laid much of the groundwork for further study of tragedy as a whole,[6] and this part begins by expanding considerably on his approach with a more detailed survey of the issues from both a historical and literary perspective. I am particularly interested not only in the way that tragedy responds directly or indirectly to tensions in the marital system but in the areas where it preserves a perhaps surprising silence or highlights issues that appear to play no significant role in actual practice. The discussion in later chapters of the tragic wives Medea and Clytemnestra, as well as the virgins Antigone and Electra, will rely on the reader's awareness of issues relating to the marriage system in classical Athens. In this and in the final part of the book, however, I am interested primarily in exploring in more detail what I would characterize as tragic nostalgia for the aristocratic marital system represented in Homer and some archaic poetry and in particular for the idealized epic marriages of Odysseus and Penelope and Hector and Andromache. In part IV, Euripides' *Alcestis* and *Helen* recreate in a new form the symbolic remarriage of Penelope and Odysseus at the end of the *Odyssey* and a comparably positive, if simultaneously qualified, moral role for the two active wives Alcestis and Helen; here we see a tragic exploration of utopian possibilities that indirectly reveals tensions by deliberately transcending them. From a political perspective these plays reflect an ongoing conflict between "aristocratic" and "democratic" ideals that surfaces in other aspects of tragedy as well,[7] but they also explore additional religious, social, and ethical questions through the marital bond. In the final section of this part I explore the surprisingly prominent role of concubines in tragedy. Those plays in which concubines are major and active presences on stage raise many of the same issues as *Alcestis* and *Helen*, in that these characters are strongly linked with epic models and serve as a positive social and ethical alternative to the

[4] On wedding imagery, see esp. Foley 1985: esp. 65–102 (and part IV in this book), Seaford 1987, and Rehm 1994.

[5] Rabinowitz 1993, Wohl 1998, and Ormand 1999.

[6] Seaford 1990a. See also Ormand 1999.

[7] See esp. Griffith 1995 and, on the topic generally, Ober 1989.

often-problematic tragic wife. In other plays, concubines inadvertently disrupt marital or political stability, thus revealing in the process contradictions in the marital system and becoming the cause of violence that dangerously links public and private spheres.

Before turning to the tragedies, however, I review what we know of the legal, social, and economic issues that might condition tragedy's complex response to the Athenian marital system. After framing the discussion by situating Attic marriage cross-culturally, I turn to major aspects of the marital system that were potentially problematic from an economic or legal perspective, especially dowry and inheritance. Reproduction of the household leads naturally to a brief consideration of attitudes to divorce and adultery. Both the relation between households established by marriage and dowry and the complex workings of bilateral inheritance created an ambiguous role for women, who were often placed in a difficult role mediating between two families. The transition from the marital system represented in Homeric epic to that in classical Athens is important to this discussion because it also reveals possible areas of tension that inevitably emerge in such historical transitions. In particular, Athens curtailed marriage patterns that had been practiced by aristocratic families in the archaic period, and the aftereffects of this transition clearly leave their mark on the tragic imagination. Finally, I attempt to locate the marital system in relation to the city-state as a whole, by examining the legislation created to control aspects of the system, and the potential tensions between public and private interests that appear to have emerged during this process.

Marriage in Classical Athens

The system of marriage and inheritance that obtained in classical Athens is typical of settled and generally literate Eurasian societies with an advanced agricultural economy and complex political systems. (I stress this point, because it makes the Athenian situation more accessible to insights gained from studies of comparable societies.) As the anthropologist Jack Goody has argued,[8] advanced agriculture, especially the use of the plow, permits individuals to produce more than they can consume. This development results in a growing concentration of wealth and social stratification based on different styles of life, a population increase with an accompanying scarcity of land and a growth in land value, and a tendency to wish to retain resources in the basic productive and reproductive unit, the family. Population increase releases societies from the need to create military alliances through marriage outside the

[8] Goody in Goody and Tambiah 1973 and Goody 1976, criticized by Leach 1982: 180–81. Ortner 1996: 108–9 (this essay was originally published in Ortner and Whitehead 1981: 359–409) cautions that many aspects of the social organization of hierarchical societies predate the introduction of advanced agriculture.

social group (exogamy), and permits the more desirable option of marriage within the social group (endogamy).[9]

Such societies generally practice a system of inheritance that Goody calls "diverging devolution," a vertical transmission of property that permits a family to maintain its wealth, honor, and status by including children of both sexes (bilateral inheritance). This system of inheritance favors the male, but privileges female descendants over collateral males, even in the same agnatic lineage; women also serve as residual heiresses when a man has no sons. They are generally provided with a dowry when married away. The dowry, a form of premortem inheritance to the woman, permits her to maintain her former standard of living, to protect the interests of herself and her natal family in the marriage, and to attract a husband (if not to control this inheritance herself).[10] Women in advanced agricultural societies do not plow and hence make a relatively lower contribution to agricultural work than in the case of shifting (hoe) cultivation; slaves or hired laborers help to release women from agricultural work as well. They thus become more economically dependent on men, more isolated in a domestic sphere (where they perform domestic work, especially weaving, and childcare), and are valued above all for their reproductive rather than productive capacities (barren women thus become increasingly vulnerable).[11]

Dowries, which may well reflect this new economic reality, can be a severe drain on the family resources, especially where (as in Greece) property (above all, land) is divided equally among the sons. Hence such societies generally practice monogamy and call public attention to the transition to marriage with more elaborate wedding ceremonies. Concubinage, a secondary "additional union with a partner of a different, indeed lower, status,"[12] most frequently occurs where the original marriage has not produced (especially male) children. Children tend to marry individuals with the same social and economic status, and the society as a whole tends to endogamy (marriage within the society, especially with friends and relations). In Goody's view, the system of diverging devolution (especially dowry) is "the main mechanism by which familial status was maintained in an economically differentiated society."[13] Diverging devolution permits continuity in familial wealth, security in old age, and the maintenance of family status after death. This system of inheritance leads to an increased social control over marriage, namely, arranged marriage, a system

---

[9] As Vernant 1980a: 60 puts this point: "As soon as it no longer proved advantageous to exchange women" and transmit prestige and wealth, "one keeps them for oneself."

[10] Ortner 1996: 106–9 criticizes Goody and Tambiah for not making a sufficient distinction between dowry and female inheritance in hierarchical societies, and explains dowry as an attempt to keep women within the status group from which they came.

[11] Here Goody 1976 draws on Boserup 1970.

[12] Goody 1976: 46.

[13] Goody 1976: 19.

whose advantages may be more apparent to parents than spouses. Greater restrictions on courtship and female premarital sex and adultery limit conflicting claims on an estate.[14] Marriages are generally patrilocal. The need to return the dowry with a bride often serves to discourage divorce.

The Marital System in Greek Epic

Some of the conditions that produce this kind of system of marriage and inheritance in classical Athens are already visible in the archaic Greek society represented in the poetry of Homer or Hesiod. A shift to settled agriculture, including the use of the plow, as the basis of the economy that was accompanied by increasing economic stratification began at least in the Dark Ages and is clearly present in Homer.[15] Yet as the Greek city-state developed its own military forces, laws, and institutions, powerful families no longer had to rely on making alliances through (largely exogamous) marriage to protect their interests and survival as in Homer;[16] moreover, because such alliances helped to establish tyranny and were perceived to enhance the authority of individual aristocratic families at the expense of the welfare of the community as a whole, they became increasingly suspect in democratic Athens. In addition to taking responsibility for defense, the emerging city began to introduce legislation that regulated family life and, above all, systems of inheritance in its own interest. Because these changes in the matrimonial system profoundly affected the lives of women and the cultural ideology about gender roles and left a legacy of unresolved tensions and contradictions in tragedy as well as in reality,[17] it is important to examine this transition briefly.

Aristocratic marriage in Homer generally entailed an exchange of gifts at marriage. The groom won his wife by offering *hedna* or *eedna* (ideally cattle) to the bride's father; at marriage the groom received with his bride valuable gifts (*dōra* or *keimēlia*, generally movable property). The bride then became a member of her husband's family and produced heirs exclusively for it. In an alter-

---

[14] Goody 1976: 14.

[15] Morris 1986: 112. One might argue that pastoralism plays a proportionally greater role than advanced agriculture in the Homeric economy, especially in the *Odyssey*'s Ithaca. As discussed later, Homeric brides were "purchased" with gifts, not married with a cash dowry.

[16] See Seaford 1994: 211. Guest friendships continued to play a far more important role in aristocratic personal and political strategies than marriage, however. On the influence of the development of the city-state on these transitions, see Gernet 1937: 396–98, Leduc 1992: 256, and Seaford 1994: 209.

[17] Vernant 1980a: 45. As he argues, marriage in the fifth and fourth centuries "cannot itself be understood properly unless account is taken of the historical background from which, it is true, it marked a departure, but from which, at the same time, it inherited a number of characteristics."

native and less common form of Homeric marriage, the bride's father gave the bride to the groom with possessions (generally including a house or land), but the groom offered no gifts. Such marriages were matrilocal and linked with an authoritative role for the wife (e.g., Helen, Arete).[18] Both forms of marriage created the expectation of an exchange of military and social support among the linked families. As Jean-Pierre Vernant puts it, Homeric marriage thus created "links of union or dependence, of acquiring prestige or confirming vassaldom. In this interchange the women play the role of precious objects."[19]

Dowry

By the early seventh century B.C.E. at the latest, what Vernant and J. M. Modrzejewski characterize as a radical change or inversion has taken place in the Attic matrimonial system—at least as far as the privileged classes whose lives are documented in our sources are concerned.[20] The bride now brought with her a dowry (*proix*) that won her a husband of comparable status, provided for her maintenance throughout her life (ideally to the standard to which she had been accustomed before her marriage), and protected the interests of the woman and her natal family within the marriage.[21] The Attic woman only had title to her dowry, because her husband had the right to administer and use it without her consent.[22] A woman's dowry was inherited by her sons (occasion-

[18] See Leduc 1992: 249. On Homeric marriage, see also Finley 1978, Lacey 1966 and 1968, with the responses of Snodgrass 1974 and Morris 1986, who defends Lacey and Finley against the views of Snodgrass.

[19] Vernant 1980: 49.

[20] Vernant 1980: 56 and Modrzejewski 1981. Gernet saw the development of the city-state as the critical factor here (Gernet 1937: 396–98; Vernant 1980a: 57). Morris 1986 sees the transition as less radical; stressing the critical role of economic determinants, he characterizes Homeric marriage as a form of diverging devolution and argues that the marriage patterns of Homeric aristocrats were probably atypical of the society as a whole. Hence a period of overlapping matrimonial systems would have been resolved in favor of the nonaristocratic, later mode. Patterson 1998 also downplays the notion of a radical shift between Homeric and especially Hesiodic marriage and inheritance patterns. A better understanding of how civic military authority developed during this period and how systems of inheritance and the establishment of dowries articulate with the development of the city-state is clearly critical to clarifying these issues. De Ste Croix 1981: 102 argues that depriving women of direct inheritance in Athens helped to prevent the accumulation of property by the rich (as in Sparta).

[21] Wolff 1944: 62 asserts that the dowry also secured for the bride's children a share in the estate of their maternal family, because descendants of daughters could inherit. Legal procedures (*dikē proikos, dikē sitou*) could be used to ensure that the dowry was properly used; the interest was 18 percent on nonrepaid dowry (61). Witnesses to the delivery of a dowry or to a marriage were therefore desirable.

[22] Wolff 1944: 53.

ally it was used to dower daughters)[23] and had to be returned to her family in the case of her death without children or divorce (probably even in the case of adultery); recovery of the dowry did not always prove to be easy in reality, however, particularly if the woman or her family instituted a divorce.[24] Because the dowry generally consisted in money and movable goods,[25] the husband could gain the equivalent of an interest-free loan to enhance the family property.[26] The dowry became a sign of the wife's affiliation with two kinship groups, and "had the force of a legitimation, testifying that the daughter had truly been settled by her *oikos* in the family of her spouse."[27] At the same time, protection of the dowry remained a continuing obligation for her natal family, and reinforced bonds between sons, sisters, and mothers. Dowries were not obligatory but a matter of honor.[28] Although a dowry, which generally represented 5 to 20 percent of a paternal estate, could put considerable strain on a family's resources and made careful family planning critical, a dowerless girl was an undesirable marriage prospect.[29] Furthermore, the absence of a dowry could be used as circumstantial evidence that a marriage by *enguē* (betrothal) had not taken place.[30]

In tragedy, disillusioned spouses of both sexes refer to dowry with the language of the marketplace. "First we have to buy a husband at a steep price, / then take a master for our bodies," says Euripides' Medea (*Medea* 232–34). Or

[23] See Leduc 1992: 279. This puts the daughter largely in the father's camp, but because the dowry could include material goods such as clothing, jewelry, or furniture, families could use the mother's dowry for her daughter. See Cox 1998: 74 and 103.

[24] Harrison 1968: 55–56. If the woman's husband died, her sons had to provide for their mother during her lifetime from the dowry. On recovering the dowry in cases of divorce, see Cohn-Haft 1995: 11 n. 40. Dowries were sometimes confiscated, perhaps illegally, to pay a husband's debts (Cox 1998: 74).

[25] Land was sometimes used as a security for the dowry.

[26] Leduc 1992: 278ff. She stresses (281) that although in rural societies dowries often represented "immobilized, unproductive wealth," in Athens marriage could be the ancient equivalent of an investment bank merger; this made it obligatory for a father to find a husband whose fortune corresponded to the size of the daughter's dowry (282). Seaford 1994: 216–17 stresses the possible dangers accompanying such accumulation of monetary wealth, in contrast to gifts. As Ortner 1996: 109 points out, a dowry in land would alienate a critical source of maintenance from a woman's natal family.

[27] Vernant 1980a: 46; see also Leduc 1992: 278. Ideally, it also gave her a stake in her new household (Harrison 1968: 45).

[28] Lacey 1968: 88–90 and 109.

[29] See Schaps 1979: 75, 78–79, including examples of extravagant dowries.

[30] See Isaeus 3.39. On the complexities of defining the institution of *enguē*, which cannot be captured by the English term "betrothal," see Harrison 1968: 1–9, 48–52 and Patterson 1991: 49–51. The verb *enguan* means "put into the hand," "pledge," or "entrust." At *enguē* the girl's male guardian formally pledged the woman to a man for the creation of legitimate (and after 451/50 B.C.E citizen) children; a specific dowry was normally promised at this time. *Enguē* was a nonbinding private contract; witnesses were not required, but advisable in case questions over legitimacy of children arose later.

as a character in Sophocles' *Tereus* laments: "But when we have reached maturity and can understand, / we are thrust out and sold / away from the gods of our fathers and our parents, / some to foreigners, some to barbarians, / some to joyless houses, some full of reproach. / And finally, once a single night has united us, / we have to praise our lot and pretend that all is well" (fragment 524 N[2] = 583 *TrGF* 4, 6–12; see also Euripides, *Electra* 1090). Relinquishing the gods of the paternal household or foreign marriage was not required of Attic brides, however.[31] In Euripides' *Phaethon*, the title character [?] laments that "although he is a free man, he is a slave to his marriage-bed, for he has sold his body for a dowry" (fragment 775; see also *Phrixus*, POxy 2685, fragment i.10–23, and Alexis, fragment 150 Kassel-Austin).[32] In his *Captive Melanippe*, "Men who make a marriage above their rank, or marry wealth, do not know how to marry. The wife's sway in the house enslaves the husband, and he is no longer free. Imported wealth coming from marriage with a woman brings no benefit; for divorces are not easy" (fragment 502 N[2]).[33] Similarly, in Euripides' *Electra*, Aegisthus, by marrying the higher-status Clytemnestra, has become her man and of less account, rather than the reverse (931, 937).[34] A character in a later New Comedy by Menander implies that a rich heiress might be able to pressure her husband into getting rid of his mistress.[35]

This tragic language significantly suggests, on the one hand, a kind of debasement of the aristocratic gift exchange in which marriage played a central part in Homer and, on the other, a threatening curtailment of the central democratic rights to masculine freedom (including bodily autonomy) and equality. Not surprisingly, then, fourth-century philosophical texts took considerable interest in reform in these matters. Xenophon favors treating the dowry as the maternal contribution to the combined household assets (*Oeconomicus* 7.13, 7.30).[36] Plato advocates abolishing the dowry to avoid arrogance (*hubris*) among women and less slavery, subservience, and lack of freedom among married men (*Laws* 6.774c). At *Laws* 6.773a he advocates for the benefit of the

---

[31] Pomeroy 1997: 70–71 stresses that daughters were not severed from natal household gods; nor is there evidence that they were formally inculcated into the cults of the marital household, as has generally been supposed. If she is right, this is another example of a woman's retaining formal bonds with the natal household.

[32] Trans. Collard in Collard, Cropp, and Lee 1995. Age can apparently also prove problematic for a husband's autonomy. "Children are a trouble to an old man. He pays (the penalty) who marries late. For a wife lords it over an elderly bridegroom" (Euripides, *Phoenix* 804 N[2], trans. Webster 1967).

[33] Trans. Cropp in Collard, Cropp, and Lee 1995. The fragment may alternatively be from *Melanippe Sophe*.

[34] See also Euripides, fragment 214.

[35] Menander, *Plokion* fragment 333. The husband is forced to conceal the mistress from his despotic wife.

[36] Court cases also assume that spouses will ordinarily try to make a marriage work. Cox 1998: 72.

state neither shunning poverty nor actively pursuing wealth, but allying oneself with a family of moderate means in marriage.[37]

Inheritance and Divorce

Diverging devolution became the Attic norm; the system was male-oriented
but not strictly agnatic, since inheritance was possible through the female line.
The predetermined order of succession in the *anchisteia* (the circle of close kin
who could inherit a man's property in the absence of direct descendants), for
example, places sisters of the deceased and their descendants second in the line
of succession after brothers and their descendants; maternal relatives followed
paternal relatives in the sequence.[38] In practice, however, especially in the case
of conflicts between father and sons or brothers, men might attempt to circumvent the laws by turning to female agnates or even the matriline for heirs,
though these choices were often challenged by the kin group.[39]

The vocabulary used suggests that the bride was no longer, as in Homeric
marriage, the valuable gift in an aristocratic exchange of gifts and services but
was the object of an economic contract between two men.[40] The bride was
"lent" in marriage to her husband for the "plowing of legitimate children"
(*paidōn ep' arotōi gnēsiōn*, Menander, *Dyscolus* 842; see also Menander *Perikeiromene* 1013–14) but retained throughout her life a relation with her natal
family and could be reclaimed to produce an heir for it. The language used for
the transaction (*ekdidonai, ekdosis*) elsewhere entailed handing over for a limited purpose, such as letting on lease or hiring a slave. As Julius Wolff puts it,
"the woman's separation from her original family never became complete," and
"the aim of the *enguē* [betrothal] was to entrust rather than to alienate the object."[41] Not surprisingly, the bonds between father and daughter and brother
and sister in tragedy (and New Comedy) tend to be both strong and positively
characterized.[42] By contrast, a quotation such as the following from Euripides'

---

[37] Dowries were in proportion to the expected patrimony of the husband (Schaps 1979: 75;
Isaeus 11.40). On the need to marry a social equal and to keep the dowry in proportion to the husband's patrimony, see Lacey 1968: 69 and Foxhall 1989: 34.

[38] For succession in the *anchisteia*, see Harrison 1968: 144–49. Through marriage a man could
thus move closer to a source of wealth (Just 1989: 87).

[39] Cox 1998: xvi–xvii, 8, 36, 128–29, and 209. Because women married young, sisters often
married before brothers and secured a beneficial alliance for the brother; the brother's additional
concern for the sister's dowry and children often served to create a close sibling bond (114–16).
A man's relations with his mother's brother could also be close (116).

[40] Wolff 1944: 53.

[41] Wolff 1944: 47 and 53. The marriage unfolded in several stages: the pledging of the bride,
the handing over of the bride to the husband (*ekdosis*) in a formal ceremony (*gamos*), and cohab-
itation (*sunoikein*).

[42] Pomeroy 1997: 127 notes that married women are often buried with their father's name on
graves.

lost *Danae* expresses, at least as far as a daughter is concerned, a partial reality that more closely reflects the hopes of a woman's marital family: "A woman, leaving her paternal home, belongs not to her parents but to her husband. But the *male* kind remains permanently in the house as a defender of the paternal gods and tombs" (fragment 318 N²).[43]

In principle, divorce was for these same reasons relatively easy in Athens, although the dowry, social custom, and family politics probably served as a serious deterrent in many cases.[44] Women could initiate a divorce with the help of their families but had to appear in person to register a divorce with the archon.[45] Men could simply send a blameless woman back to her natal family, but in order to avoid offending her family they often arranged another marriage for her in the process of doing so. A father might dissolve a marriage (*aphairesis*) if his daughter was being mistreated, if her dowry was mismanaged, or if he felt that a better match could be made.[46]

Heiresses

Furthermore, as Harrison argues, "in principle, the Athenian system was endogamic, as can be seen very clearly in the laws relating to *epiklēroi*."[47] In contrast to Homeric marriage, if a man died intestate, the *epiklēros*, a daughter without brothers, was adjudicated by a process called *epidikasia* along with her father's estate to her closest surviving male relative, defined according to the law of intestate succession.[48] The adjudication took place even if the *epiklēros* was already married (Isaeus 3.64), but perhaps not if she had already produced male children.[49] The system of bilateral inheritance makes it clear that the in-

[43] Trans. Seaford 1990a.

[44] On divorce, see generally Harrison 1968: 30–32 and Cohn-Haft 1995, who offers a cautious review of the evidence and argues that families probably did not easily resort to divorce in practice.

[45] The purpose of this may have been to protect the woman's reputation and preserve her marriageability (Cohn-Haft 1995).

[46] For possible examples of real or threatened *aphairesis*, see Menander, *Epitrepontes* 657–59, 714–15, and 1063–67; the Didot Papyrus; Plautus' *Stichus*, based on a Greek *Adelphoi*; and Demosthenes 41.4. For a discussion, see Scafuro 1997: 307–8, Katz 1992: 702–3, and Cohn-Haft 1995, who questions the validity of some of these examples. *Aphairesis* is not a legal term; the father relied on his strong moral authority to reclaim his daughter (Scafuro 1997: 308). For a father's intent in making a marriage, see Euripides' *Electra* 1018.

[47] Harrison 1968: 21–22.

[48] If more than one daughter survived, the estate was divided equally among them, as with sons.

[49] Harrison 1968: 301–11. The only legal action that a young citizen undergoing military service could pursue in Aristotle's time was to claim an *epiklēros* and her estate (*Athenaion Politeia* 42). In the case of a woman of the poorest class of citizens at Athens (the *thessa*), if her closest kin did not wish to marry the *epiklēros*, "the law provides her a sufficient dowry, if nature has given her even a moderate appearance" ([Demosthenes] 59.113). Cox 1998: 95 says that *epiklēroi* unmarried at the time of their father's death are rare in our sources; when close kin refused to marry the

stitution of the *epiklēros* was designed above all to produce heirs for a man's household, but the household was not necessarily defined patrilineally.[50] As the orator Isaeus states, men nearing death take action to prevent their *oikoi* from becoming extinct (Isaeus 7.30; see further Isaeus 2.15, 6.5; Demosthenes 43.84). Demographically speaking, the epiklerate was an important institution, since it is estimated that about 40 percent of marriages did not produce sons to assure the patriline (20 percent of marriages produced no sons, and another 20 percent no children at all).[51] The *oikos* was in this respect a fundamentally unstable institution, requiring complex legal support (including the alternative of adoption of male or occasionally female heirs) to ensure, or sometimes inadvertently to jeopardize, its reproduction;[52] families must have frequently been tempted to defy or circumvent both inheritance and citizenship laws.

As in the case of dowry, the economic influence that the *epiklēros* could wield through her property, particularly when it was substantial, created tensions within the marriage, and enhanced the pressure (often fulfilled in reality) to marry within a narrower range of kin, friends, and people of similar wealth. Aristotle, after comparing the normal *oikos* to an aristocracy, adds that "sometimes wives rule because they are *epiklēroi*; their rule is not according to virtue, but by wealth and power, as in oligarchies."[53] He even cites a case of civil war emerging out of a conflict over (rich) *epiklēroi* (*Politics* 5.1304a).

New Comedy also made the wealthy *epiklēros* a target along with the richly dowered wife and the wife of higher social status. One fragment from the New Comic poet Menander complains of a "witch" of an *epiklēros* who is "an outright boss of the house and the fields and everything." Another Menandrian

---

epiklēros, her children by an outsider could face difficulties in claiming the paternal inheritance (99).

[50] Attic law did not require the adoption of the *epiklēros*' son by his maternal grandfather, and he was thus potentially heir to two households. Hence Schaps 1979 argues that the institution must have been designed instead to insure that the unprotected *epiklēros* got a husband (40–41). Clearly, insuring a woman's marriage was felt to be important (see Isaeus 2.7–8 and 8.36 on the significance of motherhood to women). Yet Katz 1992: 700 argues that the needs of the *epiklēros* in relation to marriage would be better served by specifying an attractive dowry. More important, in the cultural view, as noted already, the institution did function (regardless of these potential contradictions) to protect the survival of the household and the family cults. Furthermore, even if two households were sometimes amalgamated in practice, the son of the *epiklēros* was less likely than anyone else to neglect either the property or the cults of his maternal grandfather (implied in Plutarch, *Solon* 20). For additional objections to Schaps, see Todd 1993: 230 and Fisher 1981. Katz 1992 aims like Gernet 1921 to define not the purpose of the epiklerate but its function (699) in promoting endogamy (700–701). In her view, the *epiklēros*, who was adjudicated first to a living paternal uncle, is symbolically assimilated to the father's wife. While true in principle, the institution promoted endogamy, but not necessarily in the paternal line.

[51] Goody 1976: 86–98 and app. 2, Pomeroy 1997: 122, and Patterson 1998: 255 n. 59.

[52] On the adoption of female heirs, see Cox 1997 and Pomeroy 1997: 122. On the instability on the household, see Roy 1999: esp. 12.

[53] *Nicomachean Ethics* 8.1161a1–3; trans. adapted from Schaps 1979: 37.

character announces that "Whoever sets his heart on marrying a rich *epiklēros* is either paying the penalty of the gods' anger, or else wants to be miserable and be called lucky."[54] (Marriages with *epiklēroi* may have been matrilocal and the *epiklēros* may have exercised considerable authority over her inheritance during her son's minority.)[55] On the other hand, Menander's *Aspis* expresses sympathy for an *epiklēros* who has been adjudicated to a greedy uncle, rather than married to the young man to whom she had been previously engaged; the vulnerability of real *epiklēroi* is well attested in Attic court cases.[56] The tragic response to the *epiklēros* is less pointed and explicit, but not insignificant, as we have already seen in the case of Antigone in part I (see also Electra in III.2).

Adultery

As would be predictable from Goody's model, Attic law and society publicly regulated chastity, adultery, and wifely fertility in order to control major threats to the marital system. In Athens the legitimate wife (or the *epiklēros*) became the sole producer of heirs for the household. "She whom her father or her homopatric brother or her grandfather on her father's side gives by *enguē* to be a lawful wife, from her the children shall be legitimate" (Demosthenes 46.18).[57] Because legitimacy came to be required for citizenship, adultery became a public as well as a private offense (as in Homer).[58] Laws concerning adultery required the husband to divorce his wife under penalty of *atimia* (loss of civic rights), and he was permitted to kill an adulterer caught in the act. The legal requirement for divorce probably reflects disincentives such as the need to return the wife's dowry or shame at cuckoldry (Aristotle, *Rhetoric* 1.1373a36–37).[59] The Attic wife received lesser penalties for adultery than in many ancient societies, in that she could not be put to death;[60] instead she was barred from participation in public religious activities (the equivalent of *atimia* or dis-

[54] Fragment 334 Koerte = 403 Kock; fragment 582 Koerte = 585 Kock. See Schaps 1979: 36–37 for these translations and other examples.

[55] I owe this latter point to Cynthia Patterson. Fourth-century material may, of course, introduce new perspectives, despite the overlap with Euripides. On the *epiklēros* in New Comedy, where the institution is exploited to effect marriages of sentiment, see Scafuro 1997: 284 and 293–305.

[56] Humphreys 1983a: 5 and 1995: 104. See also Aristophanes, *Wasps* 583–86.

[57] Trans. Just 1989. See Menander, *Perikeiromene* 435–36 for the enactment of an *enguē*; see also *Dyscolus* 842–43.

[58] Lacey 1968: 113. See also Ogden 1996: ch. 3. Cohen 1991: 124 thinks that laws on adultery did not aim at regulating sexual practice but at curtailing public violence and disorder by preventing feuds and by regulating self-help justice. There was also a penalty against the procuring of a free boy or woman (Harrison 1968: 37).

[59] See also Cohen 1991: 130 on the possibilities of profiting from adultery by ransom or prostitution.

[60] Cohen 1991: 124, Todd 1993: 279. Patterson 1998: 130 links the limitation on the adulteress' punishment to general restrictions on the physical punishment of Athenian citizens. Women could be tried in Athens only for homicide.

enfranchisement for men)[61] and sometimes, but not always, remained at home unmarried (see Hypereides, *Lycophron* 1.12–13). According to the orator Aeschines (1.183), however, being deprived of getting dressed up for festivals made "life not worth living" for such women.[62]

Mediating Marital Relations

In the Homeric system of marriage, the aristocratic bride (we do not know what forms of marriage were practiced by ordinary people at this period) often married out of her community and was incorporated into her husband's family to maintain her husband's property and produce children; she could even become a structural "daughter" to her husband.[63] The Homeric wife could wield considerable informal authority in her husband's interest and may have mediated among families linked by marriage to consolidate alliances. In Homeric exogamous marriages there was presumably less chance or motivation for daily conflict of loyalties between natal and marital family; hence it is not surprising that such conflicts are a far more important aspect of tragedy than of epic.[64]

In comparison with the Homeric bride, the Attic wife remained to some extent a marginal and even suspect outsider in her marital family.[65] Her interests could be represented by a number of male guardians (*kurioi*) ranging from her husband or son to a male member of her natal family;[66] this diffusion of authority again opened possibilities for conflict and instability, perhaps even initiated in some cases by the woman herself.[67] Young and Wilmott can cite "al-

[61] Todd 1993: 279 and [Demosthenes] 59.87. Aeschines 1.183 notes a fear that adulterous women might corrupt others.

[62] Although some Homeric brides or aristocratic woman in the sixth and fifth centuries may occasionally have exercised some choice of husbands (Helen, Elpinice [see Plutarch, *Cimon* 4.7]), we do not know of such cases in classical Athens. In New Comedy, young men fall in love with future spouses. At Menander, *Aspis* 258–73, Chaireas is in love with a girl with whom he was brought up. See also Demosthenes 40.27. Lacey 1968: 108 gives examples of women who resisted male plans for their marriages.

[63] Leduc 1992: 245 and 253 argues that in oblique marriages the older groom belongs to the generation preceding that of the bride and occupies the position of father or uncle. In her view Penelope may have assumed the structural role of daughter to her husband and consanguine sister to her son.

[64] For examples, see Seaford 1990a and 1994: 211 and, more generally, Foxhall 1989: 34, who stresses that Attic women had a stake in two households, especially before children. A mistreated Homeric bride could presumably be avenged by her natal family, or play a diplomatic role in maintaining alliances among families, but we do not hear of any woman returned to her family, avenged, or playing a mediating role between natal and marital families as we do in Attic drama.

[65] Seaford 1990a: 152 correctly notes that "the wife may be in an ambiguous position between her family of origin and her family by marriage." Yet it is important to stress the degree to which this tension is built into the system.

[66] See Wolff 1944: 72 on wide-ranging identity of the *kurios*.

[67] Gould 1980: 43.

most a universal rule that when married life is insecure, the wife turns for support to her family of origin, so that a weak marriage tie produces a strong blood tie."[68]

Although tragedy tends to exploit these very instabilities and tensions, various forces also brought kin linked by marriage together. Again in contrast to the Homeric world, Attic marriage alliances seem to have played relatively little role in Athenian politics.[69] Yet marriage served a more complex function than simply promoting the economic and social status of the couple and their linked families. (Once again, these speculations reflect the bias of our sources, which are concerned with wealthier families.) Certainly, evidence from court cases shows that the bride's family, who may have had fewer conflicting interests in matters of inheritance, frequently offered active legal support to her husband, support sometimes more reliable and extensive than that from his own family. The bride's family also maintained an active interest in her children.[70] Families apparently often remained close even when women married outside their demes.[71] Inscriptional (especially grave stele) and legal evidence make clear that Attic women could actively maintain positive relations between and within their natal and marital families, especially between children and stepchildren, or between brothers and brothers-in-law.[72]

Marriages among close kin (the *anchisteia*) or close friends were typical among the wealthiest families and could thus alleviate potential tensions. Not to seek a husband from among kin could be viewed in court cases as evidence of bad family relations (Isaeus 7.11–12) and required a family to forgo the advantage of substantial knowledge of the prospective spouse.[73] As the orator Isocrates put it, "Yet to whom would one more willingly give one's daughter in marriage than to those from whom one thought it appropriate to take one's own wife?" (19.46) Alternatively, as Cheryl Anne Cox has shown, families could balance marriages outside the kin group with retreats to endogamous marriage, especially in times of crisis. Rural marriages tended to be more endogamous, with neighbors also playing a critical role, whereas urban marriages were more heterogamous.[74]

[68] Young and Wilmott [1957] 1972: 158.

[69] "Neither family ties, nor favors to cousins, nor hereditary offices, nor marriage alliances, in short, the stuff of 'politics' in many a monarchy, tyranny, or aristocracy, were fundamental issues in Athens" (Strauss 1993: 214). The structure of the *polis* made such alliances unnecessary or undesirable (Seaford 1994: 211).

[70] On court cases, see Humphreys 1986: esp. 88. Witnesses tend to come predominantly from the nuclear family with affines playing an important role in the circle of kin identified. See Isaeus 8.15–17 for close relations between a maternal grandfather and his daughter's sons.

[71] Osborne 1985: 133. A woman's children could be brought back to marry in her original deme, however (Cox 1998: 66).

[72] Humphreys 1986: esp. 70, 73, 77, and 90. Cox 1998: xvi, 211–12 sees this as an area in family life open to important female influence.

[73] For evidence concerning marriage with a narrow range of kin, see Thompson 1967. For sources on motivations for marriage, see Schaps 1979: 74 with notes.

[74] Cox 1998: esp. 10, 28, 31, and 34. Marriage patterns reflect the bias in inheritance law more

In short, diverging devolution created in Athens what Claudine Leduc calls a system of "overlapping" (rather than "discrete") households linked by bilateral inheritance and cemented by dowry.[75] This blurring of boundaries between households in Attic marriage practices could have both positive and negative repercussions. On the domestic front, Cox argues that the guardianship of minors and women, remarriage, and the absence of men from the household on military or other business had precisely this effect, especially as concerns the use of household property.[76] On the broader civic level, Attic marriage occasionally served to consolidate deme relations, but more often the preference for marriage with close kin and within a certain social stratum to gain prestige (Andocides 1.119, Demosthenes 44.10) meant that marriages linked families at some geographical distance.[77] Indeed, Stephen Todd argues that the transfer of property through women "will have tended to break up the association between deme membership (hereditary in the male line) and landed property within the demes."[78] If the shift to marriage with dowry and bilateral inheritance began for economic reasons, as Goody suggests, it certainly not only disrupted patrilineage by blurring the distinction between paternal and maternal lines, but served to cement relations among families throughout Attic territory.[79] Here, as elsewhere, marriage thus promoted, for better or worse, the interests of state as well as family.

Attic Marriage and the *Polis*

As in the case of lamentation, the early Attic statesman Solon was thought to have been the first to formulate and/or consolidate changes in the matrimonial and inheritance systems that were enforced for all citizens and residents of the city-state. Solon attempted to insure the survival of the individual household, to regulate its structure and autonomy, and to turn a society of households and kin groups into a political state.[80] As Richard Seaford puts it, "once

---

than in the case of transmitting property (31). She points out (31) that only 19 percent of marriages were endogamous, a low percentage for agrarian societies with kinship inmarriage.

[75] Leduc 1992: 239, 243, and 289. In discrete households, such as we find in Homer, inheritance is unilineal and the mobile partner is incorporated into the household of his or her spouse.

[76] Cox 1998: 166. Remarriage could lead to disputes over property.

[77] Osborne 1985: ch. 7 shows that intrademe marriages were rare except in demes where strong pressures threatened to diffuse deme identity (Sounion, Rhamnous). Because both local and family bonds were strong in Attica, local solidarity could sometimes be in conflict with kinship when kin lived outside the deme (152). On the other hand, Cox 1988 shows that a family could consolidate its interests in the deme into which its women married by marrying more than one kinswoman into the same deme, or consolidate estates outside the deme of origin through marriage.

[78] Todd 1993: 219. One could say the same for phratry and tribe.

[79] Gernet 1937: 396–98 attributes the shift to dowry to the formation of the city-state.

[80] Seaford 1994: 216 after Vernant 1980a. Parallel reform regulated death ritual (see part I).

a means of reciprocity between [noble] families, marriage tends instead to become a means for the polis to make permanent its identity through reproduction."[81] After a period of intensive unrest in seventh-century Attica, provoked largely by economic inequities and the exile or enslavement of citizens for debt, Solon's civic and legal reforms aimed to stabilize the society by outlawing debt bondage (Aristotle, *Athenaion Politeia* 12.4) and by permitting political participation to all members of four economically based groups (including those without land). Quantity, not quality, of wealth served as his criterion, and households in each group were given the same legal status. Although he did not redistribute property, Solon apparently aimed to prevent the consolidation of households and the resulting accumulation of wealth through inheritance laws (*Solon* 20; see also Plato, *Laws* 6.773a–d).[82] Thus he mandated that an adopted son had to give up claims to inherit from his natal family and curtailed the bridal trousseau (*phernē*).[83] The right of the childless citizen to perpetuate his *oikos* now took precedence over the right of his collaterals to inherit his property.

In aiming to narrow and delimit the circle of those entitled to inherit, Solon's laws formalized or created the institution of the *epiklēros* (Aristotle, *Athenaion Politeia* 9.2; Plutarch, *Solon* 20), including a requirement that her husband have intercourse with her three times a month (*Solon* 20.3); he also insured inferior inheritance rights to bastards, and prescribed selling unmarried girls who were seduced into slavery (*Solon* 22–23). Institutionalizing the *epiklēros* and permitting adoption to the heirless man (see Isaeus 3.68 and 9.7) replaced partly or entirely the reproduction of heirs through concubines common in Homer.[84] Although Solon's reforms seem to have been largely successful in stabilizing the distribution of wealth and property in Athens, these changes in inheritance law continued to produce tensions that resurface in fourth-century court cases concerning inheritance.[85] Even at the time Solon's

---

Wolff 1944: 90 sees the reforms as responding to the need to protect the *oikos* from individualistic tendencies promoted by the extension of franchise (93). He notes that in Rome there was considerably less interference in family matters concerning heiresses, orphans, and the family unit. Roy 1999 stresses the ways that the *polis'* legislation failed to protect the *oikos*.

[81] Seaford 1994: 306.

[82] For later rhetoric against attempts to be in possession of more than one *oikos* or *klēros*, see Demosthenes 44.28 and 42.21; Isaeus 7.45 and 11. 47.

[83] Seaford 1994: 210. Although most scholars think that *phernē* should be interpreted here as trousseau (e.g., Wolff 1944: 58), Leduc 1992: 285 interprets it as a poetic word for dowry, including land. If the *phernē* that Solon curtailed included dowry, then he aimed to increase intermarriage among economic groups and to equalize the status of households (Leduc 289). If *phernē* is trousseau, then he aimed to prohibit divisive displays of wealth. Some sources attribute the law on dowering the poor *epiklēros* to Solon (Harrison 1968: 1: 46).

[84] Seaford 1994: 209. Ogden 1996 argues that Solon's laws entirely excluded all *nothoi* from inheritance.

[85] Just 1989: 92 sees these tensions reflected in the law preventing an adopted son from adopting in turn.

legislation reportedly produced *stasis* (civil conflict); Aristotle (*Athenaion Politeia* 13.2) tells us that the immediate object of the strife was the eponymous archon who administered the law concerning family and property.

Under the democracy, the needs of the demes for male citizens to provide military service, hold offices, provide liturgies, and carry out religious functions would have helped to perpetuate the Solonian policy of preserving individual households.[86] Later reforms gradually refined or stabilized criteria for legitimacy and created new criteria for citizenship. This process culminated in the citizenship law of Pericles in 451/0 B.C.E., which restricted citizenship to those born of two Athenian parents. Pericles' law also prevented aristocrats from making alliances with foreigners through marriage, although they continued to maintain relations through *xenia* (guest friendship).[87] There is little evidence that this exogamous marriage pattern was common in Athens beyond the sixth century in any case, however, and marriages between citizens and foreign residents within Athens may have offered a more immediate threat.[88] Overall, Cynthia Patterson seems more convincing in arguing that Pericles' law was above all the result of a need to consolidate a specifically Athenian identity in its growing empire.[89]

Yet at every stage reforms of laws relating to citizenship reportedly involved inclusions as well as exclusions. Solon extended citizenship to those in exile from their homeland and those who came to Athens with their whole household and practiced a trade (Plutarch, *Solon* 24); the sixth-century tyrant Peisistratus was supported by "those not pure in family" (Aristotle, *Athenaion Politeia* 13.5);[90] the democratic reformer Cleisthenes expanded the citizen body to include foreigners and resident slaves (Aristotle, *Politics* 1275b37); Athens gave the right of intermarriage to the Euboeans, and extended citizenship to Plataeans, Samians, and those who manned the ships at Arginusae in 406

[86] Lacey 1968: 94–96. For the *polis* as a collection of *oikoi*, see Aristotle, *Politics* 1.1252b.

[87] Herman 1987. Athenian aristocrats apparently became increasingly careful to avoid foreign marriages, and to insist that their relations with guest friends could serve the interest of the state. The democracy downplayed the claims of kinship and stressed the legal equality of citizens.

[88] See Patterson 1981: 99, Morris 1986: 112, and Osborne 1997: 7 (Sicilian tyrants were an exception). Diverging devolution encourages marriage between families of equal wealth, a criterion many upwardly mobile metics could have met. Ogden 1996: 66, who also reviews the evidence, thinks that the citizenship law was motivated by the Athenian ideology of autochthony.

[89] The law may have halted an increase in the citizen population as well (Patterson 1981: 102; Osborne 1997: 5–6 is more skeptical on this point). Patterson dismisses arguments that the law was designed to prevent debasement of the population or to provide husbands for Attic women. See also Boeghold 1994, who argues for the important role played by the scarcity of land and problems of inheritance in the legislation. On defining Athenian identity in the context of empire, including the promotion of the myth of Athenian autochthony, see also Osborne 1997: 9–11.

[90] Ogden 1996: esp. 44–46, 58, and 64 believes that those impure in family are people whose mothers were foreign. His overall argument is that public hostility to this group goes back far earlier than Pericles' citizenzhip law and remains the central target for civic regulation.

B.C.E. as well as to individuals who had benefited the city-state. Even after Pericles' law (probably in the last quarter of the fifth century), Diogenes Laertius (*Vitae Philosophorum* 2.26) reports that "the Athenians, on account of the scarcity of men, passed a vote with a view to increasing the citizen population, that a man might marry [*gamein*] one Athenian woman but have children [*paidopoieisthai*] by another" (whether this second woman had to be a citizen or not is unclear from the grammar of the sentence).[91] A law passed in the archonship of Eukleides put an end to this lapse by reinstating Pericles' law, although it specified that those born of non-Athenian mothers before 403/2 B.C.E. were not to lose their citizenship. Sometime before 340 B.C.E. it became punishable even to cohabit with a noncitizen.[92] Yet lawcourt cases also make clear that citizenship remained a constant bone of contention in the fourth century. Wolff argued that the refining of criteria for citizenship reflected a democratic policy that was relaxed under oligarchy, because the reinstatement of Pericles' law in 403/2 did coincide with a restoration of the democracy after an oligarchic regime.[93] Clearly, Athenian endogamy and exclusivity were hard to maintain in a context where war, empire, resident foreigners, and conflict between mass and elite created a series of conflicting pressures for inclusion or exclusion in the citizen body.

Attic law also defined rights and obligations within the *oikos* and provided some legal redress (which was frequently ineffective) in case of exploitative or incompetent *oikos* heads.[94] The eponymous archon, for example, was charged with the oversight of heiresses, orphans, and widows claiming to be pregnant by their late spouses. Any citizen could initiate a suit (*eisangelia*) on behalf of a wronged orphan or heiress. Similarly, close kin were required to prosecute homicides, and Solonian law deprived men who beat their fathers and mothers or failed to support them in old age of the right to speak in the assembly (Aeschines 1.28).

Nevertheless, one should not overemphasize the interference of the state in the private life of classical Athens and the public control of the "traffic in women." First, although the state regulated access to citizenship and inheritance (all cases were formally adjudicated with the exception of direct inheritance by sons)[95] and viewed interference with the correct succession within

---

[91] Trans. Just 1989. See also Athenaeus 13.555d–556a; Aulus Gellius 15.20.6. The decree was probably prompted by a shortage of manpower. See MacDowell 1978: 89–90, Harrison 1968: 1: 13–17, Just 1989: 52–55, Patterson 1990: 55, and Ogden 1996: 72–72.

[92] [Demosthenes] 59.16. This may mean only that a man could not cohabit with (*sunoikein*) a concubine to produce legitimate children (see Just 1989: 62–63), since there is evidence that men continued to live with concubines at this period (Wolff 1944: 67).

[93] Wolff 1944: 86. See Patterson 1981: 103 and 107 on how the citizenship law protected democratic privileges.

[94] See Humphreys 1983a: 5; the lawcourts thus "became a theatre for the expression of what may perhaps be called the ideology of the *oikos*."

[95] Just 1989: 32.

oikoi as a threat to itself, the state was clearly less interested in regulating marriage than in defining the status of sons.[96] As Roger Just points out, laws governing the *epiklēros* were the only positive marriage rules in Athens,[97] and marriage laws remained general rather than specific.[98] *Enguē*, for example, was not a legal requirement for marriage but for legitimacy.[99] Furthermore, in reality, as court cases show, both the privacy and protection that marked women's lives and the (potential) ease of divorce often made marriages and legitimacy difficult to certify.[100] Unlike men, wives and daughters were not formally listed in phratry registers.[101] Betrothals (*enguē, enguēsis*) and especially weddings (*gamos*) often included witnesses, because, as Demosthenes puts it, men are "entrusting to the care of others the lives of our sisters and daughters, for whom we seek the greatest possible security" (30.21).[102] A man could celebrate (and was required in some cases to celebrate) his marriage by offering the feast of the *gamēlia* to his fellow demesman (the bride was not present); in the fourth century he might announce the birth of daughters (Isaeus 3.70–71). If the daughter of the Corinthian prostitute Neaira could become the wife of the archon basileus ([Demosthenes] 59) and play an important role in a civic festival, other noncitizen women could have slipped (and did slip) more easily than men through the net designed to exclude their children from citizenship.[103]

Second, Athenian democracy prided itself in creating and maintaining a private sphere, including freedom of speech, association, and life-style, that was ideally out of the reach of formal public interference.[104] Virginia Hunter has recently demonstrated the role of unofficial mechanisms of social control such as private arbitration, neighborhood gossip, and shame in regulating social behavior in Athens.[105] Lin Foxhall argues that political institutions did not in fact supersede those of the household in classical Athens, but that the household sometimes maintained separate spheres of activity, sometimes was in conflict with the state, and sometimes civic and household interests were inter-

[96] Wolff 1944: 75.

[97] Just 1989: 79. Lacey 1968: 30 notes that all legal cases affecting family are public, not private.

[98] Todd 1993: 212.

[99] Harrison 1968: 1: 5–8.

[100] See Sealey 1990: 14 on problems involved in proving the status of a man's mother.

[101] For a recent discussion of the evidence, see Ogden 1996: 113–15. Other gestures to demonstrate the legitimacy of wives were entertaining the wives of fellow demesmen at the Thesmophoria (Isaeus 3.80) and tending to a wife's visibly located tomb (Isaeus 6.64–65 and Ogden 1996: 87–88).

[102] Trans. Murray 1988. Ogden 1996: 84–85 notes, however, that weddings are never used as evidence for marriage in forensic speeches, whereas the *gamēlia* is.

[103] Ogden 1996: 115.

[104] Cohen 1991: 220–34. This applied less to those who played active leadership roles in the democracy; their lives were often exposed and criticized in public orations by rivals and political enemies.

[105] Hunter 1994.

twined in a productive tension because the bonds to both were strong.[106] Indeed, fourth-century philosophers like Aristotle criticized democracy for leaving private life too unregulated, allowing *anarchia* among slaves, women, and children (*Politics* 6.1319b30; see also Plato, *Republic* 8.563b). In Aristotle's view, uncontrolled private lives can lead to revolutions; hence the well-governed state should inspect private life more closely (2.1269b–70a, 4.1299b19, 4.1300a5–10, 6.1323a). He wants all aspects of marriage regulated to produce civic harmony (*koinōnia*): age, choice of partners, manner and time of intercourse, and so forth (7.1334b29–1336a). Plato proposes similar reforms to scrutinize and regulate private life and marriage in both the *Republic* and the *Laws*.

Although we should not exaggerate the extent to which Athenian society conformed to legal expectations,[107] we can generalize tentatively about some of the important effects that the civic shaping of the matrimonial system had on women's lives. As a closed group of citizens linked by kinship, bilateral inheritance, and religion, Athens included women.[108] Marriage was the major means of integrating women into the civic community, and it served a critical role in preserving the cohesion of the community. At the same time, as Roger Just argues, "In narrowly oligarchic, aristocratic, or monarchic states, women who belonged to the elite have often wielded considerable power, even if illegitimately; on the other hand, since the bulk of the population, whether male or female, possessed no political rights, 'politics' was not something which in general distinguished men from women. . . . the access that every adult male had to the offices and honours of the state sharply distinguished the citizen's life from that of his wife or daughter."[109] Democracy meant that politically speaking women were lumped with other outsiders, such as metics or slaves, who were officially subject to rule by the "men's club."[110] The centrality of political and military life to the male citizen made women's exclusion from it more critical to their definition.[111] Female citizenship above all consisted in the capacity to bear citizens;[112] male guardians thus closely regulated their sexual lives. The *epiklēros* is a prime example of legally enforced female passivity. Or, as Andrew Stewart puts it, "women now increasingly fitted into the city's signifying space in a most awkward way."[113]

[106] Foxhall 1989: 43, who challenges Humphreys 1978: 201 and 1986: 91. See similarly Strauss 1993: 12. Patterson 1998: esp. 66–69 takes a similar view.

[107] Foxhall 1989: 25, Patterson 1990: 70, and Cohen 1991.

[108] Just 1989: 23.

[109] Just 1989: 22. The system fostered security for women at the expense of making her a legal minor. Here we can contrast Sparta or Dorian Crete, where a woman remained "mistress of her person and her portion" (Leduc 1992: 239).

[110] Just 1989: 23. On the "men's club," see Vidal-Naquet 1981b: 188.

[111] Just 1989: 25.

[112] Sealey 1990: 14.

[113] Stewart 1995: 85.

More generally, as Christine Gailey argues in her cross-cultural study of the effects of state formation on women, the creation of a civil sphere produces a situation where people can be considered and ranked hierarchically solely in terms of their sex, in contrast to defining men or women primarily in relation to age, life experience, or kin position, as in prestate kinship societies. The ideological effort required to maintain this division or structure by gender as "natural" promotes an ideology of essentialism, or even a systematic formulation of female inferiority.[114] Civic authority sharpens gender hierarchy in that "social power and control over labor, resources, and products" were more firmly "associated with masculinity."[115] In her view, conflicts between kin and civil authority also serve to further subordinate family to state and to consolidate gender hierarchy by increasingly curtailing traditional female roles in acting and mediating for and among kin.[116] Women are then only permitted public authority by shifting their allegiance and reproductive potential to the state.[117] Tragedy certainly exploits gender differences and conflicts far more than Homeric epic. Moreover, Gailey's argument concerning the allegiance of women to the *polis* suggests new perspectives on apparent conflicts between public and private interests such as those represented in plays like Sophocles' *Antigone* as well as on several of the tragic mothers in Euripides (see III.3 and III.6).

Sally Humphreys makes a similar point to Gailey's when she argues that Athens effaced local communities that had once mediated between *oikos* and *polis* and weakened bonds of kinship in ways that probably reinforced female isolation and dependence in a fashion reflected in tragedy.[118] Sharpening the division of social life according to sex (men interacted with men, women with women) in her view also heightened gender hierarchy.[119] Moreover, with the exception of Pericles' citizenship law, family law apparently remained largely unchanged (and difficult to interpret) in Athens between Solon's time and the fourth century despite radical social change in the city as a whole.[120] This was bound in Humphrey's view to lead to conflicts between legal regulations and shifting sentiment (e.g., the severing of relations with his natural parents by an adopted child, or the prohibition against marriage between matrilateral half-siblings).[121]

---

[114] Gailey 1987a and b. On the second point, see Ortner 1996.

[115] Gailey 1987b: 32. Advanced agriculture had already estranged women from critical economic roles as well.

[116] Gailey 1987b: 60.

[117] Gailey 1987b: 52–53.

[118] Humphreys 1983a: 9 and 62.

[119] Humphreys 1983a: 59.

[120] Humphreys 1983a: 8. Roy 1999: 3 qualifies Humphreys' point. In particular, descent from the mother became more important.

[121] Humphreys 1983a: 7.

Marriage in Tragedy

Euripides' *Medea*, in a passage to be discussed shortly, offers a direct response to the most complex fifth-century philosophical discussion of marriage that emerges in a fragment of the sophist Antiphon (fragment 49 Diels-Kranz, trans. Freeman 1971):

> For marriage is a great contest for mankind. If the woman turns out to be incompatible, what can one do about the disaster? Divorce is difficult: it means to make enemies of friends, who have the same thoughts, the same breath, and had been valued and had regarded one with esteem. And it is hard if one gets such a possession, that is, if when thinking to get pleasure, one brings home pain. However, not to speak of malevolence: let us assume the utmost compatibility. What is pleasanter to a man than a wife after his own heart? What is sweeter, especially to a young man? But in the very pleasure lies near at hand the pain; pleasures do not come alone, but are attended by grief and troubles. Olympic and Pythian victories and all pleasures are apt to be won by great pains. Honors, prizes, delights, which God has given to men, depend necessarily on great toils and exertions. For my part, if I had another body which was as much trouble to me as I am to myself, I could not live, so great is the trouble I give myself for the sake of health, the acquisition of a livelihood, and for fame, respectability, glory and a good reputation. What then, if I acquired another body which was as much trouble? Is it not clear that a wife, if she is to his mind, gives her husband no less cause for love and pain than he does to himself, for the health of two bodies, the acquisition of two livelihoods, and for respectability and honour? Suppose children are born: then all is full of anxiety, and the youthful spring goes out of the mind, and the countenance is no longer the same.

This discussion brilliantly expresses the threat of marriage and a wife to a man's very conception of himself. His troublesome quest for economic and social identity, including the support of like-minded friends, among whom a wife's relatives are critically included, are compromised at best by another body whose close identification with himself (even as a mere possession) can compromise each of the goals outlined by Antiphon. Tragic heroes in Euripides can wish that children could be bought or acquired at temples—anywhere but from a wife.[122] For Antiphon, a wife is necessary for reproduction, but even a good wife cannot ensure good and healthy children; and her very potential as child producer is intimately tied to old age and mortality. One might add, extrapolating from other classical sources, that taking into one's house another body over which one cannot exercise the same highly prized self-control that a classical citizen expected of himself (indeed a body who was neither trained to maintain or perhaps even capable of maintaining such self-control or aspira-

---

[122] *Hippolytus* 616–68 and *Medea* 569–75.

tions) compounds the problem (see III.1). It is precisely to these kinds of broader issues about marriage that tragedy responds.

Indeed, Euripides' Medea offers the following female perspective on Antiphon's argument (Medea 230–51):

> Of all beings who breathe and have intelligence,
> we women are the most miserable creatures,
> First we have to buy a husband at a steep price,
> then take a master for our bodies.
> This second evil is worse than the first, but
> the greatest contest turns on whether we get a bad
> husband or a good one. Divorce is not respectable
> for a woman and she cannot deny her husband.
> Confronting new customs and rules,
> she needs to be a prophet, unless she has learned
> at home how best to manage her bedmate.
> If we work things out well and the husband
> lives with us without resisting his yoke,
> life is enviable. Otherwise it is better to die.
> A man when he is tired of being with those inside
> goes out and relieves his heart of boredom,
> or turns to some friend or contemporary.
> But we have to look to one person only.
> They say we have a life secure from danger
> living at home, while they wield their spears in battle.
> They are mistaken! I would rather stand three
> times beside a shield than give birth once.

The wife problematically "buys" an unknown master, a foreign, claustrophobic, and isolated environment in the house, and the often life-threatening pains of reproduction. Her only potential consolation is a manageable husband—a goal that may put her in direct conflict with the desire of Antiphon's husband to manage himself and his possessions to suit a different set of interests. Indeed, both the surprisingly active terms—buying, taking, managing, working out—in which Medea describes dealing with the wife's circumscribed existence and lack of control and her critique of the institution from a female perspective prepares the audience for Medea's surprising expectation of a more reciprocal partnership from her spouse. Marriage was normally to involve the protection of the subordinate woman's safety, modesty, and economic well-being (including preserving her dowry and managing financial affairs responsibly) in exchange for her maintaining chastity and producing and raising children. Yet Medea's assumption that she is entitled to a moral recognition as wife comparable with that normally offered by men to male friends leads inevitably to a tragic conflict (see III.5). Aeschylus' adulterous Clytemnestra (see III.4) also refuses in different respects to confine her actions and thinking within the limits expected of the conventional wife and challenges traditional patterns of inheritance and marriage.

As was mentioned earlier, court cases offer many examples where family rivalries and crises lead men to try to circumvent citizenship and inheritance laws and where circumstances leave room for the informal mediation by and influence of women. We do see male quarrels over inheritance in tragedy (e.g., Eteocles and Polyneices, the Theban brothers whose feud over the kingship is partly provoked by their father Oedipus' curse) and the occasional female mediator, such as Jocasta, who fails to resolve the quarrel between the brothers in Euripides' *Phoinissae* and successfully diffuses the quarrel between her husband Oedipus and her brother Creon in *Oedipus Rex*. Nevertheless, the tragic failure to highlight what must have been in reality a critical role for women in uniting two linked households may reflect the kind of civic deemphasis on such kinship roles suggested by Gailey; certainly tragedy does, as she predicted, give public authority to women when they shift allegiance from family to state (see III.6).

Yet the myths on which Greek tragedies are based are products of earlier eras. The way that poets adapt them to tragedy both responds, sometimes in highly anachronistic ways, to the tensions identified earlier in the marital system of classical Athens and goes beyond them to offer philosophical critiques and to imagine alternatives unlikely to be practiced in reality. Predictably Euripides' plays, which often elaborate myths that highlight issues relating to marriage, respond most directly to domestic realities.[123] His characters are as attuned as Antiphon to the threats, dangers, and unstable pleasures involved in marriage. As one of his characters proclaims in a notorious fragment: "The hatred women incur is very hurtful. Those who have fallen are a disgrace to those who have not; the bad ones share their censure with the good. And with regard to marriage men think that women are entirely corrupt [lit., that women think nothing healthy]."[124] Another fragment preserves the regretful remark that "a wife is the hardest thing of all to fight against" (*Oedipus*, 544 N^2, trans. Webster 1967). In the context of the play, however, this line may have more positive connotations than at first appears, for in fragment 543 N^2 Oedipus apparently argues that losing a self-controlled (*sōphrōn*) wife is worse than losing children, fatherland, and money; for children and wife have great power over a man.

The tragic response to the contemporary marital system is wide-ranging, but those issues that affect the reproduction of legitimate children and the unity of the household receive more attention than others. Sometimes tragedy directly responds to democratic ideology concerning marriage. For example, although the mythical marriages of epic and archaic poetry are largely exoga-

[123] On marriage in Euripides generally, see Seaford 1990a.
[124] Euripides, *Melanippe Desmotis*, fragment 493, trans. Cropp in Collard, Cropp, and Lee, 1995.

mous, tragic representations of the same myths occasionally explicitly favor endogamous marriage within the boundaries of a particular *polis* or kinship group that would potentially reduce either civic tensions or those between natal and marital family.[125] Several Euripides plays directly question marrying daughters to foreigners (Euripides' *Temenus, Archelaus, Andromeda, Ion,* and *Suppliants,* 220–25, 132–61).[126] An extreme example is offered in Euripides' *Aeolus,* where the son of Aeolus, Macareus, succeeds in arguing for incestuous marriage among all of his siblings in order to legitimize his own illicit passion for his sister Canake.[127] By contrast, Aeschylus' Danaid trilogy, which antedated Pericles' citizenship law, seems preoccupied with a different set of issues. Whether the plays actually aim to reject endogamy has been a matter of considerable controversy.[128] The trilogy revolves around the resistance to marriage with their first cousins of the Egyptian daughters of Danaus; after forty-nine of the fifty kill their husbands on their wedding night, the daughters are probably absorbed into Argos and married to Greeks.

Discussions of other criteria for choosing a spouse are pervasive in Euripides, however, and largely reflect or respond to contemporary popular wisdom that marriages between spouses of comparable wealth and stable heritage are the most desirable. Some fragments discussing wealth, birth, and status have been cited earlier. In what appears to be a debate over marriage in Euripides' *Antigone,* it is argued in various fragments "that a beautiful woman is no good unless she has sense (fragment 212 N^2); beauty is as surfeiting as rich food (fragment 213 N^2); marriage partners should be equal (fragment 214 N^2); good women have good children (fragment 215 N^2)."[129] Other fragments counter that "children need not be like their parents (fragment 167 N^2)"; one's "parentage may be irregular but this does not affect" one's character (fragment 168 N^2); "a man can have no better possession than a sympathetic wife (fragment 164 N^2)."[130] Similarly, in one of Euripides' Melanippe plays, someone argues that "for mortals it is best to obtain moderate unions, moderate marriages accompanied by temperance" (fragment 503).[131] In Euripides' *Andromeda* the barbarian king Cepheus rejects Perseus as a spouse for his daughter Andromeda, even though he has just rescued her from death with divine help, on the grounds that he is a pauper and a bastard (fragment 141 N^2). More fantastic is a debate in Euripides' *Meleager.* Meleager's desire to marry the huntress Ata-

---

[125] See my subsequent discussion and Seaford 1994: 211–12. In Euripides' and perhaps Sophocles' *Oenomaus* (Hippodameia and Pelops) a father creates virtually impossible obstacles to his daughter's marriage.

[126] For discussion, see Seaford 1990a: 154–58.

[127] P.Oxy. 2457, fragments 20 and 22 N^2.

[128] See Seaford 1987: 110–19 (with further bibliography), who interprets the Danaids' resistance to marriage as a heightened form of that expressed in marriage songs and rituals.

[129] Webster 1967: 183.

[130] Ibid.

[131] Trans. Cropp in Collard, Cropp, and Lee 1995.

lanta is rejected on the grounds that a reversal, in which men weave and women take to war, would be disastrous (fragment 522 N²). Atalanta apparently counters with, "if I were to marry (and may that never happen!) my children would be better than the children of women who spend all day in the house" (fragment 525 N²).[132] These last two plays reflect in part a youthful desire to choose a marriage partner or to marry for love that becomes central in Attic New Comedy.[133]

Equally central are the tragic tensions that reflect a classical marriage system in which the daughter is, at least potentially, never fully transferred, as apparently in epic, to her marital family. As noted earlier, daughters could be reclaimed as *epiklēroi* to produce children for their natal families; the daughter's heirs remain potentially implicated in lineages on both sides; and, in practical terms, the bride's natal and marital families could remain close, allowing the wife a potential role both as mediator and unifier of families and as a source of divisiveness. This failure of complete transferal of the bride takes several forms that are reflected in tragedy. A wife's higher social status or substantial dowry may from the perspective of the groom's family permit her or her male relatives undue influence in the marital dialogue (Euripides' *Electra*, *Andromache*, *Phrixus* [POxy 2685, fragment i.10–23], *Phaethon*, fragment 775, and one of the Melanippe plays, fragment 502 cited earlier). Her natal family may wish to retrieve her for another marriage (a resisting Hyrnetho in Euripides' *Temenidae*), or the wife may otherwise maintain a decided and problematic preference for her marital over her natal family (Euripides' *Suppliants* [Evadne], *Protesilaus* [Laodameia], *Oedipus* [Jocasta], *Alkmaion in Psophis* [Arsinoe]), or the reverse (Meleager [Althaea], *Alcmene*, *Andromache* [Hermione], *Melanippe Desmotis* [Siris]).[134] Imagery derived from the wedding ceremony that effects the bride's transferal is pervasive in tragedy and perhaps reflects, in its continued perversion and inversion, the inability of the rite to enforce a stable transition from one household to another.

The need to produce legitimate heirs for each citizen family in Athens emerges in the tragic emphasis on the problems posed by (especially) female adultery, which generally occurs in the absence of the husband, and thus reinforces the need for assiduous male guardianship (Clytemnestra in plays by all three major poets; Euripides' *Sthenoboia*, Aerope in *Cretan Women*, Pasiphae [with a bull] in *Cretans*).[135] The disconcerting questioning by women like

[132] Trans. Webster 1967: 235.

[133] Brown 1993 argues that this tendency reflects historical reality. See also Wiles 1989.

[134] Seaford 1990a: 166–68. The Didot papyrus (Page 1970: 185–87) may represent a fragment from either tragedy (Euripides?) or New Comedy.

[135] Phaedra in Euripides' first *Hippolytus* and (probably) Astydameia in his *Peleus* attempted to seduce a young man and then falsely accused him to conceal their attempt. Sophocles also wrote a *Phaedra* whose contents are unknown. On the absence of husbands in cases of tragic adultery, see Hall 1997: 108.

Aeschylus' Clytemnestra of the double standard in sexual fidelity also finds a place on the tragic stage, however (see III.4). In the Athenian view, adultery caused division in the household by disrupting the bond of *philia* (affection and friendship) between husband and wife: "When a wife is deprived of like-mindedness [*homonoia*] with her husband, life is henceforth unlivable" (Stobaeus, *Florilegium* 68.35 from Lycurgus, *Against Lycophron*; see also Xenophon, *Hiero* 3.3).[136] As Cynthia Patterson points out, tragedy makes a point of linking adultery, such as that of Clytemnestra's, with public death and violence as well as corruption of the entire household; by contrast, Attic oratory stresses the public danger of the adulterer, who is generally characterized as an unmanly male (*moichos*).[137] Tragic adultery thus provokes a *stasis* (civil conflict) that extends directly from *oikos* to *polis*, and tragic action exploits the critical importance of marriage as the central link between public and private worlds.

As disrupters of easy succession and challengers to the boundaries between households, wicked stepmothers were as problematic on stage as they very probably were in life. Unfortunately, this important theme is not developed in extant tragedy, although we know of its importance from tragic fragments (Euripides' *Aegeus* [Medea], *Ino*, *Phrixus* B [Ino], *Melanippe Desmotis* [Siris], *Antiope* [Dirce], Creusa in *Ion*; Ino may have played a role in Sophocles' *Athamas* and *Phrixus* and Aeschylus' *Athamas*; Tyro was mistreated by her stepmother Sidero in Sophocles' *Tyro*).[138] In Euripides' *Alcestis* we get a brief mention of the dangers posed by tragedy's otherwise often literally murderous stepmothers (as Creusa threatens briefly to be in *Ion*) in the heroine's request to Admetus that he not remarry and threaten her children, and especially her daughter, with possible mistreatment from a stepmother who might destroy her stepdaughter's reputation and chances of marriage (304–16).

Childless marriages (e.g., Euripides' *Ion*, *Andromache*, *Melanippe Desmotis* [Siris]) or *epiklēroi* pose major problems in tragedy. This last group includes the numerous daughters without brothers of tragedy who are impregnated out of wedlock by a god or mortal and initially or permanently rejected by their natal families, often with their children.[139] By contrast with later New Comedy, where, as Adele Scafuro has shown,[140] the raped girl's story is believed and her awkward dilemma discreetly resolved by private reconciliation among concerned bourgeois families in a fashion that may reflect contemporary behavior

[136] See further Patterson 1998: 125, 164, and 172.

[137] Patterson 1998: 140–72. Tragic adulterers like Aegisthus (Aeschylus' *Agamemnon*, Euripides' *Electra*) are also represented as effeminate.

[138] See further Seaford 1990a: 170–71.

[139] The pattern in myth and tragedy has been well analyzed by Burkert 1979 (who dubs it the "girl's tragedy") and Scafuro 1990; for a discussion of this motif in Euripides, see Seaford 1990a: 159–61 and Collard, Cropp, and Lee 1995: 245–46. On the legal aspects of rape in Athens, see esp. Scafuro 1990 and Cohen 1991, both with earlier bibliography.

[140] 1997: esp. 227. Scafuro stresses the willingness in New Comedy to forgive rape as a product of love or drunken folly.

or aspiration, the tragic victim is disbelieved and punished and often (unlike the later silent and passive New Comic heroine) actively attempts to defend her children on stage. Yet the exposed or rejected bastard sons of the tragic heroine are always reinstated as rulers of a city, sometimes their own (Euripides' *Alope, Danae, Melanippe Sophe,* and Creusa in *Ion*).[141] Indeed, as Burkert puts it, this mythical pattern often serves as a necessary "prelude to the emergence of a hero."[142] Despite the suffering of the heroine and her pointedly noble offspring, divine insemination can permit in the end a return to de facto endogamy; the daughter's family does not have to give her in marriage to another or introduce a man from another family into their own household in order to produce heirs. This plot, in contrast to the arguments of Aeschylus' *Eumenides,* for example, also permits the mother to be the primary human parent, as she seeks to protect her offspring, and often becomes the object of a much desired recognition and reunion with and even homage by her sons.[143] Thus Euripides' Ion wishes to have access to freedom of speech, a critical political right, through his mother (589–92).

Such plots perhaps respond as well to the vulnerability of the *epiklēros,* who must produce heirs for her father's household in situations that could become threatening, in myth as well as in reality.[144] Although the status of both Sophocles' Antigone (I) and Electra (III.2) as *epiklēroi* plays an implicit role in the action, our only complete tragedy in this category is *Ion,* which makes this significant group of plays hard to evaluate in any depth.[145] The play stresses the immediate intuitive bond between Creusa, the heir to the autochthonous Attic line of Erectheus, and her unrecognized son Ion, who was fathered and rescued by the god Apollo after she exposed him. Creusa's foreign husband Xuthus is tricked into believing that Ion is his son and accepting him as his heir; in response, she temporarily attempts to play the role of murderous stepmother. In the end, however, an emotional recognition between Ion and Creusa establishes Ion's Athenian identity. Although the truth of Ion's parentage must remain secret, Xuthus is not accorded full tragic status, and Ion's bond

[141] The children in Euripides' *Antiope* and Auge in Sophocles' *Tyro* (I and II), inherit other kingdoms rather than that of their maternal grandfather; so will the offspring of Aeschylus' Io (*Prometheus Bound*). Among other unwed mothers, the children of Hypsipyle and Jason are united with their mother at the close of Euripides' *Hypsipyle;* Achilles marries Deidameia, mother of Neoptolemus, after he rapes her in Euripides' *Skyrioi.* Sophocles' *Creusa, Danae,* and *Hipponous* probably also dealt with unwed mothers; the story of Auge may have received some mention in his four plays on the Telephus myth (*Aleadae, Mysioi, Telephus,* and *Eurypylus*) or in Aeschylus' *Mysioi.* Aeschylus' *Women of Aetna* probably belongs in this category as well.

[142] Burkert 1979: 6–7.

[143] It also contrasts with plots that stress hostile mother-son relations.

[144] Court cases clearly demonstrate the family conflicts that result from competition over a rich *epiklēros,* or the exploitation and abuse of *epiklēroi* who lack a *kurios* properly concerned with their interests. See Lacey 1968: 141–45.

[145] Unlike other *epiklēroi* in tragedy, Creusa's secret pregnancy is never publicly revealed; hence she has not and will not leave her family in any case. Her husband, Xuthus, is a foreigner imported to marry and protect the brotherless daughter.

with his mother remains primary for the audience.[146] Finally, according to Scafuro, Euripides in this play breaks a taboo by permitting Creusa to voice her shame and pain over the divine rape.[147]

In Homer, the children of an unmarried mother were apparently dependent on her family; Eudorus son of Polymele was raised in his maternal grandfather's house (*Iliad* 16.180–92; see also *Iliad* 6.23–24).[148] By Attic standards, the children of such illegitimate unions had no claim to their paternal inheritance from Solon's time on and their mothers were a source of familial embarrassment. Hence the insistent concern of tragedy to reinstate such children as legitimate heirs clearly contradicts political and social reality.[149] In "Family Romances," Freud argues that such myths appeal to the male imagination because they permit the fantasy of a higher-status father who will ensure an extraordinary destiny for his illegitimate or lower-status son.[150] Other possible reasons for the popularity of this plot will be become clearer in our examination of the closely related question of concubines and their offspring.

Tragic Concubines

In the remainder of this chapter, I consider the often strikingly positive and in any case prominent role of concubines in tragedy. Although the Attic *polis* gradually limited the ability of concubines to produce legitimate heirs for their male consorts, tragic concubines seem quite consistently to adopt the roles played by the faithful wives and concubines of epic and threaten to displace, directly or by implication, their legitimately married but problematic sisters; where they serve as critical but silent (Iole in Sophocles' *Trachiniae*) or even invisible (Cassandra in Euripides' *Hecuba*) presences, they cause major disruptions in the domestic or civic arena in a fashion that comments indirectly on contemporary tensions. The concubines' illegitimate offspring, like the sons of tragic unwed mothers, are pointedly noble and often become, against reality in classical Athens, kings and progenitors of dynasties. Yet the focus in these plays tends to be as much or more on the concubine or her conflict with the hero's wife than on the status of her sons.[151] Because a number of plays featuring con-

---

[146] For further valuable discussion of *Ion*, see esp. Loraux 1993: 184–236, Scafuro 1990, Zeitlin 1996: 285–349, and Rabinowitz 1993: 189–222.

[147] Scafuro 1990. Cassandra in Aeschylus' *Agamemnon* is the only other character in extant tragedy openly to discuss divine rape.

[148] See Patterson 1990: 50.

[149] Tragedy includes many passages on the relation between birth, status, and virtue (see Patterson 1990: 65) that reflect contemporary sophistic arguments (see Antiphon the Sophist, *On Truth*, fragment 44B, Diels-Kranz).

[150] Freud [1908] 1909.

[151] Ogden 1996: esp. 194–211 recognizes Euripides' fascination with these domestic disputes, although he fails to note the equally central tensions produced by stepmothers. Other plays, such as Euripides' *Medea* or *Hippolytus*, deal with the potential rivalry between bastard and legitimate sons.

cubines are extant, they give us an opportunity to examine a broader tragic attraction to the mothers of illegitimate children in (especially Euripidean) tragedy than do the fragments. When they are major protagonists in the plays (Tecmessa in Sophocles' *Ajax*, Cassandra in Aeschylus' *Agamemnon*, and Andromache in Euripides' *Andromache*), these concubines can anticipate the important role of the courtesan or concubine with the heart of gold in New Comedy, but once again the bourgeois bias of the later genre illuminates by its difference the backward-looking, aristocratic emphasis of the comparable tragic figures.

Whereas Homeric husbands could produce children with rights of inheritance from concubines (*pallakai*), the rights of Attic bastards (*nothoi*) to inherit or to win citizenship and of men to keep concubines for producing children were increasingly curtailed throughout the period of Athenian state formation until they were eliminated altogether.[152] In Homer, the children of purchased slave women or women bought or won in war such as Teucer (*Iliad* 8.283–84), Menelaus' son Megapenthes (*Odyssey* 4.10–14), or Odysseus in one of his lying tales (*Odyssey* 14.200–210) are free, recognized by their fathers, and referred to by their father's name (patronymic). They could be brought up with legitimate (*gnēsioi*) children and treated as secondary and inferior heirs,[153] while their mothers apparently resided in the hero's household. On occasion, however, the epics note a wife's resentment of this arrangement. At *Iliad* 5.70–71, Theano is said to have performed a special favor for (*charizomenē*) her husband in raising her husband Antenor's bastard son. Phoenix' mother resents being displaced by her husband Amyntor's concubine and causes a family feud (*Iliad* 9.449–52). Clytemnestra kills Agamemnon's concubine Cassandra (*Odyssey* 11.421–23). Odysseus' father Laertes, on the other hand, avoids the anger of his wife by not sleeping with the slave Eurycleia (*Odyssey* 1.433).

In Athens, Dracon's pre-Solonian (721 B.C.E.) homicide law (Demosthenes 23.53) specified penalities for those caught in adultery with a man's wife (*damar*), mother, daughter, or *pallakē* (concubine) whom he kept for procreating free children, and even in the early fifth century the lines between wives and concubines remained blurry. Solon was apparently the first to codify or define the disabilities of illegitimate offspring or *nothoi* in relation to inheritance (although he may have permitted them to inherit in the absence of legitimate children), perhaps in order to curb aristocratic excess and promote the integrity and solidarity of individual *oikoi*. (I follow Cynthia Patterson in defining a *nothos/nothē* as the child of a mixed or unequal union who nevertheless retained a socially recognized relation to his or her father at the margins of

---

[152] See Ogden 1996 for the most extensive discussion. He controversially dates the exclusion of all bastards from citizenship to Solon's legislation.

[153] Odysseus claims that he did not inherit equally with his legitimate siblings (*Odyssey* 14.203–10). If, as in the case of Megapenthes, the father has no male heirs, the Homeric bastard son may perhaps acquire full inheritance rights (Patterson 1990: 50 n. 40).

Athenian society.)[154] Solon may have discouraged concubinage as an aristo-cratic flaunting of wealth and as potentially disruptive of family solidarity.[155] Although Athenian men commonly had sexual relations with a range of women including slaves, *hetairai* (courtesans), and *pornai* (prostitutes), after Pericles' citizenship legislation of 451/0 (repassed in 403) they could probably produce legitimate children only from citizen wives. The children of foreign or noncitizen concubines were certainly deprived of rights of inheritance and cit-izenship, and scholars arguing that the bastard children of citizen (rather than foreign) concubines had full inheritance rights in Attica at all periods remain in the minority.[156] By 403 a law, the product either of the lapse or temporary revocation of Pericles' citizenship law, denied *anchisteia*, familial rights of in-heritance, to the *nothos* (Demosthenes 43.51, Isaeus 6.47).[157] Although, as mentioned earlier, there may have been a decree passed sometime during the Peloponnesian War that temporarily permitted a man to marry one citizen woman and create legitimate children as well from another woman, all con-cubines who appear on stage in tragedy are noble foreign women captured and enslaved in war. Hence, although the possibility of such temporary loopholes is less directly relevant for our discussion here, the contemporary situation in Athens, which perhaps included loss of deme records or witnesses to marriages during the war, may have made it easier and more desirable to defy the citi-zenship law.[158]

Although there is little evidence of Athenian men who have wives and con-cubines at the same time, concubines continued to serve as an alternative to a legitimate wife in some cases. The author of *Against Neaira* presumably re-sponds to social reality when he defines the role of courtesans, concubines, and wives in fourth-century Athens as follows: "We have *hetairai* for pleasure, *pal-lakai* to care for our daily bodily needs, and *gunaikes* to bear us legitimate chil-dren and to be a trustworthy guardian of affairs in our households" ([Demos-thenes] 59.122).[159] In the fifth century, Pericles took up with the foreign woman Aspasia after a divorce. (See also Philoneos in Antiphon 1, *Against the Stepmother*, Euctemon in Isaeus 6, Demeas in Menander's *Samia*). Although the children of concubines had no rights to inheritance, the women themselves may have had access to their lover's wealth.[160] All tragic instances of a ménage

[154] See Patterson 1990: 41, 55, and 64 (contra Ogden 1996: 15–17).

[155] Patterson 1990: 51.

[156] See Ogden 1996 and Carey 1995: 416–17, esp. n. 33, in contrast to others such as Patter-son 1990 (with full bibliography).

[157] Patterson 1990: esp. 41 and 51. *Nothoi* may have maintained informal claims to family and community membership. Solon also excused *nothoi* from supporting their parents.

[158] See Ogden 1996: 76.

[159] The passage probably does not aim at excluding the wife from the first two functions.

[160] Cox 1998: xviii. Isaeus 3.39 also says that those who gave a woman to another man as a *pal-lakē* or concubine came to an agreement as to what would be given with her. Demosthenes 48.53 complains of the ruinous effects on Olympiodorus of an *hetaira* whom he purchased, freed, and now keeps in his house.

à trois, with wife and concubine living in the same house, prove disastrous, and it seems unlikely that the practice was considered socially desirable (see also Athenaeus, *Deipnosophists* 13.556b–557b). Our evidence concerning etiquette in these matters, however, makes it difficult to distinguish, here as elsewhere, between *pallakai* and *hetairai*. Lysias refused out of respect for his wife to lodge his Corinthian *hetaira* in his house when he brought her to Athens ([Demosthenes] 59.22), and Alcibiades' wife Hipparete sought a divorce when he brought courtesans home ([Andocides] 4.14; Plutarch, *Alcibiades* 8.3).[161] Alcibiades' insistence on rearing the son of a captive Melian concubine as a part of his household is noted with disapproval by Andocides because he produced a child with an enemy, who will now be divided in his loyalties (4.22; see also Plutarch, *Alcibiades* 16).[162] [Demosthenes'] remark, then, probably indicates both the continuities among the three roles and the importance of respecting the boundaries among them.

Despite their loss of status in the classical period, however, the largely silent and anonymous concubines of epic and their bastard children can play far more important roles in the same or similar myths in tragedy. Despite her status, for example, the tragic concubine often sets herself apart from the majority of tragic wives through the perfection with which she enacts the role of marital partner (from the male perspective). Evocation of epic models can play a critical role in the creation of these dramatic characters, precisely because the epic wife both belongs more fully to her partner and tends to adhere voluntarily to social ideals. Sophocles' spear-bride Tecmessa, for example, resembles in part the other loving slave concubines of the *Iliad* such as Achilles' Briseis, but also, in her famous attempt to persuade Ajax not to abandon his family and commit suicide, adapts the words of Hector's virtuous wife Andromache (493–524; *Iliad* 6.407–38).[163] Like these epic predecessors, Tecmessa also takes center stage with her heartfelt laments over a dead hero (937–73; *Iliad* 19.282–300, 24.723–45), a gesture that implicitly reinforces her claim as mother of Ajax' only male heir.[164] The *Iliad*'s Andromache and Briseis are wellborn and noble

---

[161] The two passages stress that these women were both slave and free, native and foreign. The distinction suggests that the kind of mistresses introduced into the household may be important in judging a man's behavior.

[162] Hipparete was apprehended by Alcibiades on her way to register a divorce with the archon, in part because he did not wish to lose her outrageously large dowry. In Hellenistic papyri, a husband may agree as part of a premarital contract not to bring home another wife or maintain a concubine or little boyfriend (Pomeroy 1984: 88).

[163] See Kirkwood 1965 and Easterling 1984. For a discussion of the speech, see Gill 1996: 119–23 and 208–14.

[164] Lamentation expresses a claim to be a dead person's inheritor or dependent. Ormand 1996 and 1999: 119–23 argues ingeniously that the chorus would expect what turns out to be a mute Tecmessa to lament the body of Ajax; while I agree that the audience did not know she was played by a mute actor until Odysseus appears, Tecmessa does in fact include most of the standard elements of wifely lament at 937–73, and hence the audience may not expect any further lament from her until Ajax' funeral takes place.

in character, but without family or city; their loyalty is not divided between natal and marital family. Due to her status, the wellborn Tecmessa also totally and unambiguously identifies herself with the fate of her partner and his household (203–4, 392–93, 791; at 896 she describes her loss in terms that suggest a sacked city, *diapeporthēmai*). Both his life and his death seem extensions of her own, and she has no wish to go on living without him (392–93).

Like Briseis, Tecmessa has come to care for the captor who destroyed her city and family (490–91), and the slave's freely given affection and loyalty seem eventually to produce at least some response in her master (210–11, 807–8).[165] Her only leverage on Ajax, aside from a shared concern and forethought for the welfare of their son, is the pleasure and *charis* (favor, 520–22) she gave to her master.[166] Both the chorus and Tecmessa attempt to rely on Ajax' history of normal spousal affection for her (*sterxas anechei*, 212; *charis*, 808), and although the harsh and brutal Ajax is, in contrast to Hector, initially unresponsive to Tecmessa, he eventually expresses (in my view genuine) pity for her plight as his future widow (*chēra*; see 650–53).[167] Thus Tecmessa implictly gains a symbolic recognition as "wife" for which the *Iliad*'s Briseis futilely longed.[168]

Tecmessa's unquestioning obedience—her willingness to fall silent on command, or to go inside and pray (529, 684–86 followed by her exit)—reflects contemporary popular wisdom, as the play makes clear: "he spoke a few hackneyed words to me, 'woman, silence ornaments a woman's beauty'" (292–93, quoted at Aristotle, *Politics* 1.1260a). Yet the play also trusts her to pursue a number of independent actions that demonstrate her devotion to the continuity of Ajax' household, such as removing the child Eurysaces from the reach of his deranged father and attempting to deflect her partner from abandoning his family to danger through suicide. Although Tecmessa fails to persuade Ajax to live, her pleas, her sense of vulnerability, and her lamentations are echoed by the chorus of loyal sailors, and she takes an active role in directing the effort to find and save Ajax and to protect his dead body (by covering it).[169] Un-

[165] Synodinou 1987: 100 attributes this identification with the master as characteristic of slaves. It could, however, be articulated as a goal in actual marriages. See Brown 1993. Plutarch, *Moralia* 712c, describes good *hetairai* as those as *anterōsai*, loving in return.

[166] This locates Tecmessa within an aristocratic gift economy.

[167] Despite Synodinou 1987: 103, *stergein* rather than *eran* is a perfectly proper term for what a husband should feel for a wife. See *Trachiniae* 577. For further bibliography on the question of Ajax' feelings for Tecmessa, see Synodinou 1987: 102 n. 27. Ormand 1999: 111 and 116 argues that Ajax ignores Tecmessa and treats her simply as a link to his son. In my own view, his initially harsh response to Tecmessa and his silence over her future (568–77) is more probably a question of his character and his impossible situation, not of her status as slave and concubine.

[168] Ormand 1996: 50–51 and 1999: 112–19 argues that in her speech to Ajax, Tecmessa, by borrowing from the legitimate wife Andromache, insinuates herself into a wifely role that she does not possess but consolidates after Ajax' death.

[169] See Synodinou 1987: 105.

usually for such scenes in tragedy, the chorus makes no attempt to restrain her grief over the body, but pointedly empathizes with it (940–43).

This exceptional and respectful (see esp. 210–12, 331) bond between concubine and her spouse's male followers serves once again to emphasize her "wifely" perfection. By blurring the boundaries between slave, concubine, and wife, Tecmessa articulates dramatically a perhaps normally repressed fantasy of the Athenian aristocratic husband. As a character in Euripides' *Oedipus* similarly avers (fragment 545 N[2]): "the modest wife is the slave of her husband, the immodest wife in her folly despises her consort" (see also Andromache's speech in Euripides' *Andromache*, discussed shortly).[170]

Finally, *Ajax* implicitly recognizes the disability of bastards in Attic society, but does not respect the limits of Pericles' citizenship law. The bastard Eurysaces is treated as Ajax' legitimate heir and Tecmessa's status as a barbarian is unimportant to her claims as Ajax' all but legitimate wife. This is not surprising, because distinguished Athenians claimed descent from Eurysaces, after he supposedly made over Salamis to Athens and settled on the Attic mainland at Melite (Plutarch, *Solon* 10; Ajax himself was the eponymous hero of one of the ten tribes in Athens). The inferior social position of Ajax' bastard brother Teucer is stressed by Agamemnon, who treats him as an illegitimate, barbarian slave (1259–63). In response, Teucer defines himself as an "*aristos* from two *aristoi*" (most noble from two noble parents, 1304). Against expectation, he comes as close as possible to fulfilling Ajax' seemingly impractical hopes that he will take his place as protector of family and friends, and his nobility contrasts pointedly with that of the other legitimately born Greek chiefs.[171] Elsewhere, Euripides' Hippolytus, Theseus' bastard son by an Amazon queen, and his Ion, bastard son of the Athenian queen Creusa, demonstrate equal nobility of nature despite their birth. Because tragedy is perfectly capable of departing from Homeric social codes, it seems unlikely that these prominent noble bastards represent simply an innocent reflection of the myths of earlier eras, but raise implicit questions about contemporary Athenian policy and social reality.

In Aeschylus' *Agamemnon*, we learn few details of the relation between Agamemnon and his slave concubine Cassandra, but in the course of the play she gradually fills the structural role of proper "wife" abandoned by Clytemnestra. Clytemnestra herself, exulting over the entwined bodies of the dead Agamemnon and Cassandra, mocks her rival as not only the sharer of his bed (*koinolektros*, 1441) but as his faithful bedmate (*pistē xuneunos*, 1442). She clearly means to imply that Cassandra has threatened to double or replace her (see III.4). Although Clytemnestra's interpretation of Cassandra may be self-serving and distorted, the play has subtly prepared us for viewing this relation

---

[170] Trans. Webster 1967.

[171] See Patterson 1990: 63 and on Ajax, Ormand 1996: 47–48 and 1999: 105–110 and 123.

between slave and master as more than merely functional. In Euripides' *Trojan Women*, Cassandra explictly treats her future relation with Agamemnon as a "marriage"; in *Agamemnon* she probably is veiled (at 1178–79, her prophecy is suggestively described as like a veiled bride looking out), and her arrival by Agamemnon's side in a carriage may suggest a bridal procession.[172] Agamemnon, who describes Cassandra as a "chosen flower out of much wealth and a gift of the army" (954–55), outrageously makes a point of publicly requesting good treatment for his mistress from Clytemnestra, after he has resisted, then grudgingly given way to his wife.[173] More generally, the language used both in tragedy and in reality of brides and concubines repeatedly overlaps, making them potentially interchangeable. *Lektra*, a word that describes both wife and concubine, also applies to the marriage bed and the "marriage" itself. Both wives and concubines are repeatedly described as sharing a bed (*eunē*) with their partners.[174] In fact, there was, as Aristotle pointed out, no word to denote the (legitimate) union of a man and woman: *anōnumon gar hē gunaikos kai andros suzeuxis* (*Politics* 1.1253b).

On her side, it is Cassandra who pointedly makes a monster of Clytemnestra as adulterous wife (*Agamemnon* 1125–29, 1228–38, 1319). Identified as a (here voluntary) bride/sacrificial victim with Agamemnon's innocent daughter Iphigeneia,[175] Cassandra becomes, like the Homeric wife, not only spouse but structural daughter to her protector. Indeed, as Victoria Wohl has stressed, Cassandra completely assimilates herself to a male point of view and paves the way dramatically for the forgiveness of Agamemnon by his children in *Choephoroi*.[176] She departs from the stage offering in advance for both Agamemnon and herself the lament of which his legitimate wife will later deprive him (as with Tecmessa, this implicitly claims a status above that of slave concubine for herself) and imagines Orestes as their future avenger (1305, 1313–14; 1280–84, 1323–26). Orestes is certainly not bound by Greek custom to act for the barbarian concubine Cassandra as he is for his father, and he does not mention her in *Choephoroi*. Cassandra's assimilation of herself to Agamemnon in this respect is thus unusual and striking. Here, as elsewhere, the barbarian slave concubine, with her repeated reminders of proper wifely etiquette and her demonstrated loyalty to the patriline, becomes a foil whose presence highlights the inappropriate and destructive behavior of the unfaithful wife

[172] The prophetic garb that she strips off at the end of this scene may or may not have complemented this image.

[173] It is hard to judge cultural attitudes to Agamemnon's behavior. Certainly Clytemnestra and other tragic wives find it unacceptable, and attempting to establish a household with "two wives" meets, as noted earlier, with consistent resistance and disaster in tragedy.

[174] See my subsequent examples.

[175] Wohl 1998: 110.

[176] Wohl 1998: 110–16. The play's ultimate female commodity (111), Cassandra even excludes Iphigeneia and Helen from her visions of the house (112).

and demands pity and sympathy for her plight from the audience onstage (the chorus) and off.

Although in Euripides' *Trojan Women* the maddened Cassandra, devoted as a virgin daughter to her natal family, is depicted as reveling in the revenge that her "marriage" to Agamemnon will ultimately bring (353–405),[177] in his *Hecuba* she has become to the besotted Agamemnon a new Chryseis, the slave mistress whom Agamemnon prefers to his wife at *Iliad* 1.113–15. Early in the play, the chorus tells us that in the army's debate over whether Hecuba's daughter Polyxena should be sacrificed to the demands of the ghost of Achilles, Agamemnon defended Hecuba's interests, constant to or upholding (*anechōn*) the *lektra* of the prophetic madwoman (120–22). By contrast, the two Attic sons of Theseus argue against putting Cassandra's bed before Achilles' spear (127–29)—that is, his service to the army. Agamemnon's devotion to Cassandra continues to prove embarrassing to him. Hecuba later pleads with Agamemnon for help in avenging herself on the barbarian king, Polymestor, who treacherously killed her last son, Polydorus. When arguments from justice appear ineffective (he threatens to withdraw from her suppliancy, 812), she turns to what she describes as a point perhaps foreign to the argument, Aphrodite the goddess of sexual passion (824–25), and asks whether Cassandra will receive from Agamemnon *charis* (reciprocity) for her nights of love and her desirable embraces in bed (*en eunē(i) philtatōn aspasmatōn*, 828–30; recall Tecmessa's similar if more discreet plea).[178] If so, Agamemnon should treat the murdered Trojan boy as a relative by marriage (*kedestēn*, 834). At this point, Agamemnon wishes to avoid seeming to have plotted the killing of an ally for the sake of Cassandra (854–56). But he offers tacit support for the queen's own revenge and gives a judgment in her favor in the play's final "trial scene." Clearly, his barbarian slave concubine has won from Agamemnon the affection and loyalty due a legitimate wife. Hence it is not surprising that the play closes with a prophecy of his death and that of Cassandra at the hands of Clytemnestra (1275–81).

In this play, both the desire of Achilles' ghost for the sacrifice of the virgin Polyxena and Agamemnon's for Cassandra invades the political arena in a divisive fashion that recalls the quarrel between the two heroes over concubines at the opening of the *Iliad* and thus creates a sense of inevitable repetition of violence. Agamemnon's conflict between the mass of the army and his private allegiance to his barbarian mistress and her family clearly does not reflect con-

[177] In Euripides' *Phoenix*, the slave concubine of Phoenix' old father, who has decided not to remarry, attempts to seduce the son. But she is the only known wicked concubine in tragedy. Medea is treated as concubine by Jason in Euripides' *Medea*, but she rejects this interpretation of her role; this early play (438 B.C.E.) may be responding to the plight of foreign wives in Athens after Pericles' citizenship law.

[178] At 831–32 Hecuba adds that "the greatest reciprocal pleasure for men is from darkness and night magic (*philtrōn*)."

temporary social reality in Athens. Yet Attic aristocrats had relations that involved serious private commitments with *xenoi* (guest friends), both Greek and barbarian, in other parts of the Mediterranean. Such *xenoi* could become positively linked with Athens through the diplomatic efforts of these same aristocrats, but the practice of maintaining such relations remained suspicious to the democratic masses.[179] To the degree that the conflicts of this play may indirectly reflect some of these tensions, the choice to represent them as heavily colored by sex, violence, and an incompatibility between individual and public justice may be significant (see III.6).

Sophocles' *Women of Trachis* collapses the boundaries between wife and concubine to terrifying and disastrous effect. The silent spear-bride Iole, for whom the violent Heracles sacked a city, is at first singled out as a noble (*gennaia*) and sensitive (*phronein*) anonymous victim by his wife Deianeira from a procession of captive female slaves (307–13).[180] Iole is a younger double of herself, as each incurred suffering due to their beauty (465, 523–28). Yet when the queen learns the truth about Iole, she cannot share her bed with a more youthful woman sure to displace her in Heracles' affections as something more than slave concubine.[181] Deianeira's destruction of her husband with a robe smeared with what she believes to be a love potion, but is actually blood from a centaur who tried to rape her mixed with the deadly poison of Heracles' arrows, is ultimately represented as a tragic error (*ouch hekousia*, 1123) committed with good intentions (*chrēsta mōmēne*, 1136) by her initially angry son, Hyllus.[182]

What seems most important here is that by tactlessly introducing a concubine into the household (the messenger Lichas expects Deianeira to be upset and thus lies about his master's intentions, 479–83) and by losing control over his own erotic desire, Heracles has introduced illegitimate *erōs* and hence moral chaos into his household.[183] The self-control of the proper Greek wife depends on the moderation of erotic feeling for her spouse. Wives are not expected to have the knowledge and self-control to make important independent decisions in the absence of a guardian or, ideally, to have interests that divide

[179] Herman 1987.

[180] Wohl 1998: esp. 34, 38, and 40 stresses how she projects her own feelings through imagining Iole's.

[181] Iole's father refused Heracles' request for Iole as a *kruphion lechos* (360). Heracles did not send her home without forethought (*aphrontistōs*, 366) or as a slave (367), but as a *damar* (428–29), an archaic word for wife or concubine. The chorus echoes Deianeira's views on the intolerability of the shared marriage (841–44). On the bridal imagery in this play, see Seaford 1986.

[182] In justifying his mother's error, Hyllus even refers to the love charm as a *stergēma* (1138), a term that downplays its erotic force. Faraone 1994 argues from ancient evidence on aphrodisiacs that Deianeira knows that the centaur's blood contains poison but believes that in small doses it will serve as an aphrodisiac and make Heracles pliable to her demands.

[183] Segal 1992: 86 notes that he has also destroyed Iole's *oikos* and violated male patterns of proper exchange.

them from a spouse.[184] Deianeira has lived a life of endless anxiety, isolated from her family and fatherland, and forced, due to Heracles' long absences, to raise her family without male guidance. Her mistaken choice is thus ironically the almost inevitable result of her long adherence to wifely virtue, and Hyllus ultimately sees Heracles as the one with the distorted moral imagination: "Alas, to be angry with a sick man is wrong; but who could bear to see you thinking as you are" (*oimoi. to men nosounti thumousthai kakon, / to d'hōd' horan phronounta tis pot' an pheroi*, 1230–31).[185]

It is from this perspective that we should evaluate Deianeira's controversial choice to act.[186] She has over the years tolerated Heracles' many love affairs without reproach (460–62); she repeatedly attempts to adhere to the standards of perfect wifely self-control, eschewing anger against her "sick" husband (438–48, 543–44, 552–53; Hyllus echoes her at 1230–31) and moving reluctantly to action (582–87; earlier she asks Hyllus to act for her in finding out the whereabouts of Heracles). Although women's reliance on the advice of other women is repeatedly criticized in tragedy, Deianeira's attempt to consult the chorus of women here appears more as a desperate effort to find an appropriate substitute for the male authority that has betrayed her interests, since she explicitly rejects evil daring as inappropriate for a wife (582–83).

Yet, although Deinaeira does not intend to destroy her husband and takes full responsibility for her action, her feelings in the scene leading up to her decision are mixed and her arguments contradictory.[187] She is bitter over her husband's unjust return for her years of stressful housekeeping (541–42) and perhaps oversteps wifely limits in admitting to an active desire (*erōs* and *pothos*) for her husband (441–44, 630–32; the use of the love charm itself suggests the same intense desire) as opposed to proper moderate and self-controlled spousal affection (*stergein*, 577). Despite her awareness of *erōs* and potential anger in herself, and her knowledge that she has not tested the "love charm" (590–91), she fails until it is too late to see the full implications of the centaur's "gift." At the same time, her final words referring to the act suggest lingering moral qualms: "for in darkness, even if what you do is shameful, you will never be put

---

[184] Wohl 1998: esp. 17–28 argues that Deianeira's failed attempt to participate in the male territory of contest and gift exchange both questions the economy of heroism and justifies female exclusion from it. Segal 1992: 79 thinks that Deianeira appropriates a male role in the marriage ceremony by sending a procession with gifts to Heracles. Lawrence 1978 traces Deianeira's disastrous move from a passive to an active reception of knowledge. Ormand 1999 argues that Deianeira thinks that she is a subject in her own marriage only to discover at 707–10 that she is simply an intermediary in homosocial relations among men (37–38, 48, 51, 54–56). Marriage is doomed to be an incomplete experience for Deianeira (44, 59); any subjective assertion on a wife's part, even the desire to be desired, is dangerous and disruptive (50, 57, and 59).

[185] Trans. Lloyd-Jones 1994.

[186] The two most recent articles on Deianeira's choice, Ryzman 1991 and Gasti 1993, refer to the earlier bibliography.

[187] See Ryzman 1991 and Gasti 1993 for detailed analysis.

to shame" (*hōs skotō(i)* / *k'an aischra prassē(i)s, oupot' aischchunē(i) pesē(i)*, 596–97).[188]

Deianeira grotesquely imagines her future as one of two objects of embrace for Heracles under one blanket (539–40); he will now be her *posis* (legitimate husband) and Iole's *anēr* (man, 550–51). The image reflects the degree to which Heracles has unbound her imagination and the result is a highly sexual suicide in which Deianeira retires to her marriage bed, loosens her dress, and plunges a sword into her side.[189] She is soon joined by her lamenting son Hyllus, who lies by his mother's side embracing and kissing her (936–42). Such nearly incestuous results of the father's attempt to double his marriage recur in the final scene, where Heracles demands that the woman who has lain at his side (1224–26) marry his son.[190] Despite Hyllus' revulsion at marrying both an enemy and a woman responsible for both of his parents' deaths (1233–37) and Iole's status as concubine, this inherently noble woman will apparently become the legitimate ancestor of a noble and important dynasty.[191] Once again, Pericles' citizenship law leaves no mark on the resolution of this play. Indeed, as critics have argued, Heracles' autocratic gesture represents in part a brutal attempt to restore the institution (marriage) that he shattered by the introduction of Iole into his household.[192]

Among all of tragedy's noble concubines, however, the heroine of Euripides' *Andromache* plays the most complex role. As the protagonist of a *nostos* (return-to-home) drama,[193] Andromache borrows her character both from her own epic role as virtuous wife in the *Iliad* and from that of the waiting Penelope attempting to preserve her single son from disaster in the absence of her husband (elsewhere in the tradition, Andromache had three children by Neoptolemus).[194] Her links with epic are underlined even in the meter of her opening lament, a rare tragic solo in a meter closely linked to hexameter, elegiacs (103–16).[195] Although a beleaguered slave threatened with death in the early scenes of the play, Andromache eventually upstages Helen's daughter Hermione as "wife," and dominates in her debate scenes with Hermione and Menelaus through her greater rhetorical skill, her longer speeches, and her

[188] Trans. Lloyd-Jones 1994. Both Gasti 1993 and Ryzman 1991 comment on the similarity of these words to the sophist Antiphon's *On Truth*, fragment 44A10–20 Diels-Kranz.

[189] See Loraux 1987: 54–55 and Wohl 1998: 35–36 and 48–49.

[190] The poisoned robe also clings to Heracles' body like a monstrous embrace. Segal 1992: 83 sees the union with Iole as both incestuous and endogamous.

[191] Segal 1994a convincingly disputes the view of MacKinnon 1971 that Heracles is not establishing legitimate marriage here. See Wohl 1998: 4–15 and 38 on Hyllus' Oedipal self-sacrifice in agreeing to marry Iole.

[192] See, above all, Segal 1975 and 1992, MacKinnon 1971: 34, and Wohl 1998: 10–13.

[193] As Lloyd 1994: 3 points out, women tend to play a major role in such plots.

[194] See Gantz 1993: 689 on postwar myths about Andromache.

[195] See Lloyd 1994: ad loc.

traditional female virtues.[196] She is defended and released from death and bondage by the aged Peleus, threatens in the disgraced Hermione's view to become mistress to her slave (860, 927–28), and is finally sent off by the goddess Thetis to marry a fellow Trojan survivor, Helenus, in Molossia, where her son by Neoptolemus will rule a dynasty. The play's debates and conclusion come close to explicitly recognizing the limits of Pericles' citizenship law (199–202, 655–59, 1246–49). Andromache's bastard and half-barbarian son cannot and does not become the heir of his father in Phthia. Yet Euripides goes out of his way to make Andromache the dominant (wise) female voice in this multi-character and episodic drama, and her bastard child superior to noble offspring (636–38).

The play emphasizes repeatedly Andromache's symbolic claims to be a more legitimate "wife" to her master than Hermione. In the opening scenes we find Andromache a suppliant at the monument sacred to the sea goddess Thetis. This Thetideion is revered by the family as a symbol (hermēneuma, 46) of her marriage to Peleus. Under this sign of marriage, which she literally embraces under stress later in the play (114–16), Andromache recalls her ideal marriage to Hector.[197] Once given in marriage as a richly dowered, child-producing (paidopoios, 4) bride from a free and noble family, she is now only a slave spear-bride who has shared her master's bed and produced a son against her will. She is under threat from Neoptolemus' barren wife Hermione, daughter of Helen and Menelaus, who accuses her of alienating her husband's affections and using poisons to make Hermione infertile (32–35, 155–58, 355–60). Andromache denies both accusations. Yet her later arguments show that the contrast between herself and Hermione is, despite this denial, a potential source of divisiveness in this marriage with two brides. Andromache does not comment directly on her relationship with Neoptolemus—she was an unwilling bed partner, and apparently he left her bed on his marriage with Hermione (30)[198]—but it is clear that she nevertheless relies on him for protection of herself and her son, and even expresses respect for his heroism (see 75–76, 268, 339–44, 414–18). Hermione, by contrast, has repeatedly emphasized her superior social status and contrives plans against her husband's interests in his absence.

In her speech to Hermione (205–31), Andromache even goes beyond being the play's eloquent advocate for conformity to the standards of a proper wife.[199] She argues that a wife maintains her husband's affections by virtuous

---

[196] See Lloyd 1994: ad loc. and 1992: 51–54.

[197] Kyriakou 1997: 9 thinks that Euripides has Andromache suppress her premarital family history in order to suggest that her marriage has absorbed her whole existence.

[198] Here I disagree with Kovacs 1980: 15–18.

[199] On the sophistication of this speech and its reflection of past values, see McClure 1999: 176–82.

behavior rather than wealth and beauty.[200] The conformable wife does not set her own family above her husband's, quarrel with her spouse over erotic matters, and try to control his behavior. Andromache claims that she even went so far as to assist in the errant Hector's love affairs and nursed his bastards. Hermione, who in her youthful injustice flaunts both her dowry and her heritage and broadcasts her frustration over erotic matters (209–12, 240), is bound to alienate a spouse. Andromache claims that her age, nationality, and slave status make Hermione's accusations against her an absurdity (192–202). Yet if wifely virtues (*aretai*, 208) are the key love charm (*philtron*, 207) that holds a bed partner, her virtuous presence and fertility logically pose a challenge to Hermione. It should be noted here that in Euripides' *Trojan Women* Andromache makes very similar arguments on wifely virtue (643–74). She claims that she worked hard in the household, stayed inside (against her desires), segregated herself from other women and kept her own sound mind as a teacher, remained quiet and calm in Hector's presence, knew when it was right for each marital partner to have his or her own way, and aims now to preserve his memory after his death.

In *Andromache*, epic nobility thus becomes identified with an extreme (even active) wifely tolerance that was never required in Homer, whereas Hermione's and Menelaus' far more contemporary views are defined as Spartan and excessive. The anachronistic invasion of contemporary Attic realities concerning marriage and dowry (370–77, 668–77, 904–5) throughout the play reinforces this effect. Menelaus' treatment of the helpless slave Andromache as a serious threat and of her half-Greek, bastard son as a future enemy—a respectable fear in archaic myth—appears outrageous in a context where the slave woman's child had no chance to inherit the kingdom.[201] Hermione and Menelaus make a spirited case for the problematic dependence of a wife on the success of her marriage (370–73, 668–77, 904–5), and Hermione announces that her dowry grants her the female equivalent of a citizen's free speech (*eleutherostomein*, 153). Yet she later recants her earlier stance and wishes that she had avoided other women and relied in a subdued and conventional fashion on the security of her marital status (938–42).[202] By contrast, Andromache's very dependence and subservience as slave concubine additionally and ironically reinforce her ideal wifely behavior and self-control and permit her to assert herself both actively and articulately without violating the limits of the role of the

---

[200] The following fragment from Euripides' *Oedipus* (909 N²) makes a similar argument: "Not beauty but excellence is the standard; the good woman who is in love with her husband knows modesty; she will believe him beautiful if he is ugly," etc. (trans. Webster 1967).

[201] See 326–29, 519–22, and 650–51. Although lines 714 and 720 suggest that Peleus intends to bring up the child in noble fashion as his own, the play never even implies that he can become heir to the kingdom.

[202] She is at this moment, however, standing outdoors in a position that sets her up for a move to an adulterous relationship at Orestes' arrival (McClure 1999: 195).

ideal "wife."[203] Moreover, Menelaus and Peleus demonstrate the disastrous effects of divided *kureia* (guardianship) over Hermione (558, *kuriou;* 580, *kuriōteros*), and the former abuses his status as relative by marriage when he uses his license to share goods in common to destroy Neoptolemus' property (his son and concubine) in his absence. Indeed, Peleus' agreement that the marital bond does potentially entail such license, including the father-in-law's continuing *kureia* over his daughter in the absence of her husband, introduces evidence for additional stresses in the Attic marriage system for which we do not have direct evidence in court cases.[204]

In *Andromache*, character, heritage, nationality, and past actions are pointedly viewed as central determinants to the success or failure of a marriage. This emphasis allows the poet to use marriage to comment on a larger set of political and social issues. Hermione displays the lack of self-control of her mother Helen (229–31, 619–23) and ends up running away from her husband with his future murderer.[205] Menelaus once again pursues a quarrel generated by uncontrolled female behavior to absurd lengths and fails to keep proper watch on his women (361–63). Peleus complains that Menelaus left his uncontrolled wife unguarded and she went reveling in Bacchic fashion (*exekōmasen*, 603) to another land with Paris. He goes so far as to blame Menelaus for the death of his son and the losses of the Trojan War (610–15). In his view, Menelaus should have rejected his wife, even paid not to take her back, rather than stir up conflict over her (605–9).

In addition, according to Peleus, Spartan customs—women's bare thighs, loose robes, and participation in running races and wrestling—undermined Helen's and Hermione's character and their proper female self-control (595–601).[206] According to Aristotle, who disapproves of the practice, at Sparta whomever a man leaves as his executor bestows an *epiklēros* upon whomever he chooses (*Politics* 2.1270a28–29).[207] Menelaus also reflects these far too casual procedures in marrying off his brotherless daughter. He initially promised Hermione to her first cousin Orestes (by Attic standards an appropriate choice for an *epiklēros*), then gave her to the outsider Neoptolemus in exchange for

---

[203] Fantham 1986: 268–69 remarks that she is "a better mate to the son of her husband's killer than his lawful wife." Conacher 1967: 177 comments that "this switch in the conventional characterization of mistress and lawful wife is no mean achievement."

[204] This passage confirms the suspicion of Cohn-Haft 1995: 7, esp. n. 28, that in the absence of a husband, the father-in-law would often take over as *kurios* of his married daughter (see Demosthenes 50.24).

[205] On such repetitions of the past in the play, see esp. Lloyd 1994: 5 and Kyriakou 1997: 24, who notes that, Andromache excepted, these characters reproduce the past and fail to learn from it. On the telling use of patronymics, which reinforce such characterization, see Philippo 1995.

[206] See McClure 1999: 188 and 193 on the dangers of this masculinizing Spartan education.

[207] Spartan women could inherit property, were apparently less supervised than Attic women, and were known for their public sayings, including criticisms of men. They are constantly criticized by Attic writers. See my subsequent discussion.

services in war. Orestes' matricide has prevented him from marrying out of the close family,[208] and hence Neoptolemus incurs his fatal enmity.

By contrast, the Trojans and Phthians are associated not only with ideal marriages, but with aristocratic morality, heroic superiority in battle, and a refusal to privilege the distinction between barbarians and Greeks as opposed to a Spartan expediency based on wealth and power.[209] The remoteness of the play's setting suggests a world apart from contemporary corruption under the sign of a divine-mortal marriage once blessed by the gods that echoes the isolation from external forces proposed for the ideal wife; Peleus is celebrated in Pindaric style by the chorus for his aristocratic nobility (766–801), yet also proves himself suitable to a broader form of leadership by defending democratic achievement in battle (693–705). Euripides has even inflated Peleus' heroic credentials. Earlier myth puts him on board the Argo and at Heracles' conquest of Troy; but here he, with thematic appropriateness, has defended the institution of marriage by fighting with the Lapiths against the centaurs (790–801). At 723–26 Peleus unexpectedly defends his bastard grandson as noble and promises to bring him up as an enemy to Sparta in epic fashion. Finally, although Neoptolemus made a critical error in blaming Apollo for his father's death (52–55, 1194–96)—an error he has gone to Delphi to try to rectify—he too is otherwise represented as heroic.

The Phthians and Trojans not only observe standards of heroic behavior but, despite repeated reversals in circumstance,[210] maintain a consistent character under pressure. Peleus remains a just ruler of his country despite his advanced age and manages to intimidate the younger Menelaus into a quick retreat. His surprising effectiveness is underlined by his anomalous victory in his debate with Menelaus that is quickly put into action.[211] Andromache risks speaking in a fashion true to herself despite her circumstance (186–91). When faced with a choice between her own and her son's death, she chooses her son; her noble reasoning echoes that of other sacrificial victims in tragedy (404–20).[212] (In fact, however, most sacrificial victims are virgins. Only Alcestis makes a comparable sacrifice, but in a play that did not occupy a tragic slot at the festival.)[213] Even Andromache's fellow Trojan slave heroically risks her life for her mistress and remains a steadfast friend in adversity (86–90); by contrast,

[208] Keeping the marriage of an *epiklēros* or a disgraced relative within the family are Attic preferences as well. See Humphreys 1983a: 25.

[209] On the contrast in morality, see esp. Boulter 1966 and Lee 1975. Aldrich 1961: 71 comments on Menelaus' habitual misuse of traditional aphorisms.

[210] Andromache, as at Troy, nearly loses her son, and actually loses Neoptolemus. Peleus is once again bereaved of a male heir.

[211] See Lloyd 1994: ad loc. and 1992: 51–54. Normally Euripidean debates fail to affect the action.

[212] See Lloyd 1994: ad loc. with further bibliography.

[213] *Alcestis* was performed as a fourth play—a slot normally occupied by satyr drama.

Hermione's nurse at first criticizes her mistress' behavior, then reinforces her pretentions (866–75).

In this play, then, marriage becomes a central philosophical concern.[214] Justice in house and city are repeatedly and explicitly linked. Corrupted character, disruption of marriage bonds, and female strife have historical effects of almost Senecan proportions.[215] The strife of the goddesses over beauty generates Paris' abduction of the beautiful Helen and the Trojan war (274–92); gossiping women lead Hermione into her quarrel with Andromache and her husband (929–53); Orestes' attempt to win back his promised bride kills Neoptolemus. The sickness (*nosos*) begun at Troy comes home to roost in Greece (1044–46). However virtuous or desirable, concubines destabilize an already contradictory situation. The divisions produced by two "wives" in one household are compared to the disaster produced in ships, cities, or artistic endeavors in which more than one person shares responsibility for decision making (465–85). Peleus' loss of son and grandson leads to his abandoning his leadership in Phthia (1222–25). He views Neoptolemus' inappropriate marriage to the wealthy daughter of a bad mother and a less than heroic, self-serving father as the *archē kakōn* (beginning of evils; 620–23, 1186–93, 1279–83). Like Peleus, Aristotle also sees undisciplined and wealthy Spartan women as a key factor in their city's decline (*Politics* 2.1269b7–1270b13) and Plato's *Republic* defines the governance of an individual's soul as intimately connected to familial and political structures.[216]

Euripides also anticipates later philosophic concerns over the divisive effects of unequal marriage or disproportionate dowry on the overall political health of a state as well as with the role of imitation.[217] The play ultimately divides by marriage the villains and the virtuous,[218] thus creating three well-matched marriages among social equals that prevents future violence and political conflict, even if it does not ensure the future of Phthia or Sparta. The plot's pairings of like mortal characters may also reflect the Attic preference for endogamy, although similarity in character, wealth, and nationality predomi-

---

[214] On double marriage in *Andromache*, see 177–80, 465–70, 486–90, and 909; on polygamy in Thrace, 215–19; on the need to compromise over double marriage, 423–24, 232–33; and on criticism of Hermione's excessive reaction to the double marriage, 866–68, 938–42. On double marriage in Euripides' *Electra*, see 1032–34.

The following critics emphasize this aspect of the play: Aldrich 1961: 67–68, Garzya 1951, Steidle 1968, and, above all, Storey 1989. Both Aldrich and Stevens 1971 stress the interconnection between domestic harmony and the disastrous effects of war.

[215] In the stoic-influenced drama of Seneca, the state of the individual soul at centers of power reverberates worldwide. See McClure 1999: 162–64, 203 on the broadly divisive effects of female speech in this play and its links with the male slander of Orestes (198–200).

[216] On the speech of Spartan women and its effects, see his *Republic* 8.549c–e and 8.551a.

[217] On dowry in *Andromache*, see 147–53, 209–12, and 639–41.

[218] Conacher 1967: 173.

nates.[219] Thus the misguided Hermione will presumably wed her first cousin, the polluted Orestes, and the noble Andromache will be returned to a royal Trojan brother of the dead husband to whom she has remained devoted.[220] Thetis' willingness to honor the *charis* (favor) of her bed (*eunē*, 1253) with Peleus will transform him into a divine spouse in her father's sea dwelling and reunite Peleus with Achilles, while his half-Greek great-grandson will preserve the memory of the family greatness on earth.[221]

One of Euripides' two Melanippe plays pointedly raises the dangers posed by marriage to a bad woman for the whole female sex, because other women will imitate her: "This is the source of women's corruption; some men when they find a woman is bad do not do away with her, either protecting children or because of kinship; then this wrongdoing seeps gradually into many women and advances, and so in the end the virtue they had is vanished (fragment 497 N²).[222] Peleus anticipates the play's resolution in arguing that Menelaus should have sent Helen back to Sparta. Andromache's efforts to propagate an admittedly extreme and unrealistic model of the virtuous wife in the end fails to spawn serious imitation. The chastened Hermione, who repeatedly abused her husband whether present or absent, briefly accepts the ideal presented by Andromache only to revert to an irresponsible departure with Orestes.

Euripides' obsessive concern with marriage and domestic unrest anticipates but differs critically from New Comedy.[223] In New Comedy the plight or undue influence of the *epiklēros* and the wife of higher wealth or status than her spouse became central topics. Ensuring the marriage of unwed (citizen) mothers and the legitimacy of their children was equally popular. The comedy of Menander in particular seems to have made attractive heroines out of virtuous courtesans and concubines, who often prove to be better than their detractors and can be treated with the respect due to wives.[224] Tragedy, however, constantly makes marriage a metaphor for civic life and explores public conflicts through private quarrels. The tensions between two wives become a form of domestic *stasis* that reverberates in the larger social and political world. A similar reasoning appears in Aristotle, who argues that "even trivial disputes [in this case a love

[219] King Tharpys of Molossos had recently visited Athens and been accorded citizenship. Hence the stress on the concluding Molossian dynasty may not be accidental. A scholiast at *Andromache* 445 also says that the play was not given its initial performance at Athens. See Easterling 1994: esp. 79 on such performances outside of Athens and Hall 1989 on Greek attitudes to Trojans.

[220] For the case that a mute Andromache was present on stage to hear these final words, see esp. Golder 1983 (critiqued by McClure 1999: 159 n. 6).

[221] Storey 1989: 20 notes a possible irony here in Peleus' return to Thetis' father's residence.

[222] Trans. Cropp in Collard, Cropp, and Lee 1995.

[223] See the scholiast at *Andromache* 32, trans. Aldrich 1961: 11–12: "The mutual suspicions of women, their rivalry and abuse, and other elements that make up a comedy, every last one of these is included in this play."

[224] See Henry 1985.

quarrel in Syracuse] are critical when they occur at centers of power" and that "conflicts among prominent people generally affect the whole community" (*Politics* 5.1303b19–20, 31–32). Similarly, the famous Athenian tyrannicides, Harmodius and Aristogeiton, were propelled into action by a slight to Harmodius' sister from the tyrant Hipparchus (Thucydides 6.56.1; Aristotle, *Athenaion Politeia* 18.2).

Concubines take center stage in Homeric epic only in the absence of wives due to war, and epic wives, who generally live at a substantial distance from their natal families, do not face the conflicts of loyalty between natal and marital family presented to their tragic counterparts. Tragedy, very likely in response to contemporary tensions, highlights such conflicts. Foreign concubines play a far more substantial role in tragedy than one might have expected on the basis of both epic and contemporary social reality. Their presence introduces conflicts among public and private priorities and within households, where they activate wives to defend their interests. They remain, especially in their characterization, linked to a past Homeric and aristocratic world in which their power to reproduce children for a man's household could still at a pinch resolve problems of succession. Concubines (Tecmessa, Andromache, Aeschylus' Cassandra) can demonstrate their loyalty by being permitted to take action and speak persuasively on stage, where their gestures are praised or tolerated without suspicion by male characters. Yet their dependent social and economic status forces them into the role of compliant wife that is so often rejected or compromised by their legitimately married rivals. Freely chosen, private sexual partners, they are not to be confused with a man's own social, economic, and political body in the fashion that Antiphon found so threatening in a wife. Above all, the loyal and noble concubine brings into play the fantasy of a world in which wives are fully a man's property and echo their desires and aspirations (the ideal like-mindedness or *homophrosunē* of the epic husband and wife) and inheritance remains under paternal control (see III.1).

Along with those tragic plots that legitimize the children of unwed mothers, these plays reflect the tensions of a marital system that gave the Attic wife a different and potentially divisive economic and social influence in her marriage and maintained her ties to her natal family as well as required her reproductive capacities to insure citizen heirs. Euripides' special concern with these issues perhaps reflects the tensions over marriage, inheritance, and citizenship that may have intensified during the Peloponnesian War as well as continuing tensions between aristocratic aspirations and the democracy. While there is considerable evidence that aristocrats largely tolerated and even internalized to a substantial extent the ideology of the democratic *polis* in the course of the classical period,[225] the city's family legislation had not originally been in their

[225] Humphreys 1983a: 29. As Morris 1986: 112–14 points out, aristocrats exclusively may have practiced this form of marriage even in the Homeric period.

interest. Even before Pericles' law, these aristocrats had apparently lost interest in turning foreign marital (and even other personal) alliances exclusively to their personal advantage, and the democracy was hostile to their doing so. The popular tragic plots discussed in this part may reflect traces of suppressed aristocratic resistance in the realm of the imaginary to that sacrifice or at least a persistence of aristocratic values that resonated with the inability shared by an even wider group of citizens to maintain control over the patriline. Only the wealthy could afford easy access to women in all three of Demosthenes' categories (*hetaira*, concubine, and wife), and the law and custom of the *polis* made it virtually impossible to unify, possess, and control them under one roof. Yet these plots can predate (*Ajax*, *Oresteia*) as well as follow Pericles' citizenship law, and thus cannot be tied exclusively to the issues emerging from this legislation. Moreover, the role of concubines can be used to express a range of broader political and social tensions including those between Sparta and Athens (*Andromache*) or barbarians and Greeks (*Hecuba*).

Antiphon, however, perhaps best expresses the fundamental terrors presented by marriage for the male spectator of tragedy: the fear of introducing into intimacy another even more vulnerable and less self-controlled being who may be an incompatible partner and the producer of children of uncertain health and character and who has rights to resources of her own as well as deep ties to others who can be offended by and take action on her behalf. Finally, and especially in her husband's absence, this woman can speak, act, and make choices from a position that may or may not conform to her spouse's interests. When Hermione claims that her dowry gives her (if only in the household) the male citizen's right of free speech (*Andromache* 153), her abuse of this right does not deprive her and other female tragic players of a major role in what Antiphon calls the marital "contest."

Part III

WOMEN AS MORAL AGENTS IN GREEK TRAGEDY

Child, I want to instruct you. When you are a child, think childish thoughts and no more; in maidenhood, have the mores of a maiden; but when you fall under the cloak of a well-born husband [. . .] and leave other subtle contrivances to men.

    (*Euripides*, Peliades, *fragment 603N²*)

Learn how to change the color of your actual thoughts for your husband like an octopus on a rock.

    (*Sophocles*, Iphigeneia, *fragment 307 TrGF 4*)

Whoever lumps all women together and blames them in speech is gauche and unwise. Of the many women that exist, you will find one bad, and another like this one who has a noble temper.

    (*Euripides*, Protesilaus, *fragment 657N²*)

I know young men who are no better than women at resisting Aphrodite's attacks on their immature minds. But their male status helps them out.

    (*Euripides*, Hippolytus 967–70)

III.1

Virgins, Wives, and Mothers; Penelope as Paradigm

IN THE *Poetics*, Aristotle defines tragic character in relation to tragic choice. In drama, character, Aristotle argues, reveals a *prohairesis* or a process of undertaking commitment in which a person chooses to act or to abstain from action in circumstances where the choice is not obvious (*Poetics* 6.1450b8–10).[1] What I would like to begin to explore in this part of the book is the representation of the making and enacting of difficult moral choices—if not necessarily difficult choices in precisely the Aristotelian sense—by female characters in Greek tragedy, and to examine the complex interrelation between female moral capacity and female social role that conditions, and is articulated in, such choices.

Female characters in tragedy often, and seemingly more often than male characters, violate Aristotle's assumptions about what they should be like. In Aristotle's view tragic characters should be good; elsewhere he endows women with sufficient virtue to maintain *sōphrosunē* (self-control, chastity), to fulfill their function in the household, and to obey their men. Yet Euripides' Medea makes a deliberate choice to kill her children (*Poetics* 14.1453b suggests that this is less effective dramaturgy than a tragic choice made in ignorance). They should be traditional and consistent—unlike Euripides' Iphigeneia at Aulis, who undergoes, in Aristotle's view, an unconvincing and unmotivated change of heart (*Poetics* 15.1454a31–33). Or, perhaps, like Antigone, whose rationale for risking her life to bury her brother rather than a husband or child is described by Aristotle in his *Rhetoric* as *apiston* (not credible).[2] They should be appropriate—female characters should not be manly or clever like Euripides' philosophical Melanippe. Melanippe's speech seems to have contained a knowledge of science and philosophy unsuitable for a woman (*Poetics* 15.1454a29–31; on these points he is later echoed by Plutarch, *De Audiendis Poetis* 28a, and Origen, *Contra Celsum* 7.36.34–36). Presumably Aristotle disapproves of behavior in a tragic character that he would have disapproved and/

---

[1] The formulation here is special to drama; elsewhere *prohairesis* reveals *ēthos* for Aristotle. Here I accept the view of Chamberlain 1984 that *prohairesis* entails a process of choosing a course of action and sustaining commitment to that course of action. Halliwell 1986: 151 argues that *prohairesis* is a matter of conscious desire and intention, a deliberate moral choice. See further Schütrumpf 1970 and Gill 1984.

[2] 3.16.9.1417a. Elsewhere, however, he cites Antigone's reference to the unwritten laws with approval (*Rhetoric* 1.15.1375a30–b2; cf. 1.13.2.1373b). See further below.

or found to lack verisimilitude in a real woman. Very likely this standard of verisimilitude played an important role in theatrical representations generally; in Plato's *Ion,* a rhapsode argues to Socrates that he knows "the kind of thing . . . that a man would say, and a woman would say, and a slave and a free man, a subject and a ruler—the suitable thing for each" (*Ion* 540b).[3]

The case of Melanippe makes clear the depth of Aristotle's potential difficulties with female tragic figures, for to eliminate manly or clever heroines would be to purge much of Euripides, to say nothing of Aeschylus' brilliant and androgynous Clytemnestra. For Aristotle, ethical choice plays a critical role in generating tragic action and in producing tragic catharsis.[4] Aristotle argues that an audience cannot experience a sympathetic moral affinity with characters who stand at an ethical extreme; his own relatively traditional views on women severely limit the cases in which female ethical choices could be categorized as good and appropriate.[5] Autonomous actions by women on the tragic stage thus pose a special set of problems for the philosophical defense of tragedy and for understanding the quality of emotional response produced by tragedy in the predominantly or exclusively male audience for which the plays were designed.[6]

A closer look at Aristotle's assumptions about women as moral agents indicates why one cannot generalize so easily, for example, from Oedipus to Antigone. In his *Politics* and *Ethics,* Aristotle defends the view that women are by nature morally inferior to men.[7] Woman's natural function is to reproduce the species and care for the daily needs of her household and her virtues make her good for this function;[8] man's function is to live a life in the *polis* that offers him opportunities for rational activity, higher learning, leisure, and the exercise of the virtues suitable for such political activities. Men are good absolutely, women are good for their function. A woman's capacity for moral deliberation is without authority or not operative (*akuros, Politics* 1.5.1260a13), hence she benefits from the protection and supervision of a *kurios* or guardian.

---

[3] Trans. Cooper in Hamilton and Cairns 1961.

[4] Ethical choices do in fact play a central role in Greek epic and tragedy and attempts to understand characterization in epic or tragedy from the naturalistic or psychological perspective more congenial to our own age have on the whole proved less successful than more formal modes of analysis. See further the introduction to this book.

[5] Halliwell 1986: 154 and 158–59 tends to dismiss these problems of status too readily.

[6] I am not assuming here that a Greek audience would have viewed tragic and contemporary women in the same terms, but its expectations concerning tragic character are virtually impossible to recreate. See further the end of the introduction.

[7] These views are largely represented in the *Politics* and the *Nicomachean Ethics*. See also *Poetics* 15.1454a19–21 and *Rhetoric* 1.9.22–23.1367a16–18. For a discussion, see esp. Okin 1979: ch. 4 and the extensive bibliography cited in Ward 1996.

[8] In this case it is the female's function in the household to preserve, the male's to acquire (*Politics* 3.1277b24–25); here she can exercise some independence (*Nicomachean Ethics* 8.5.1160b33–35). Removing women from their proper sphere, as Plato proposes in his *Republic,* would in Aristotle's view leave an impossible gap in the domestic world (*Politics* 2.2.14.1264b1–3).

"A wife is more compassionate than a husband, more given to tears . . . more jealous and complaining, more apt to scold and strike. The female is also more dispirited and despondent than the male, more shameless and lying, is readier to deceive and has a longer memory. She is also more wakeful, more afraid of action, and in general less inclined to move than the male and takes less nour-ishment" (*History of Animals* 9.1.608b8–15).[9] Women's virtues fit them to be ruled, men's to rule (*Politics* 1.2.1254b14–15; cf. *Eudemian Ethics* 7.1237a). Man, as a naturally superior being thus has a permanent constitutional rule (*politikōs*) over the naturally inferior and less mature woman (*Politics* 1.5.1259a39–b41). Friendship between husband and wife similarly reflects a relation between ruler and ruled (*Nicomachean Ethics* 8.10–11.1160b33–1161a25) in which the husband receives a greater proportion of affection due to superior merit (*Nicomachean Ethics* 8.7.1158b12–28). Both sexes can display, for example, the virtues *sōphrosunē* (self-control) or courage, and female excellence includes industrious habits, free from servility (*Politics* 3.2.1277b20–25, *Rhetoric* 1.5.6.1361a). Yet the virtues of women differ in kind and not in degree from those of men (*Politics* 1.5.1260a21–24).[10] As free citi-zens, women must be educated to be virtuous (*Politics* 1.5.1260b15–21), but they have need only of right opinion, not of a genuine practical wisdom. Aris-totle thus quotes with approval the popular view that "silence brings glory to woman" (*Politics* 1.5.1260a29–31).[11]

Aristotle's assumption that women are fundamentally different as moral agents from men is not idiosyncratic but derives from popular perceptions in force in the fifth as well as the fourth century. Plato and some provocative pas-sages from drama to the contrary, most Athenian writers assume that any nonreligious public activity performed by a woman violates the silence, invis-ibility, and moral dependence appropriate to a virtuous wife. Of course, this as-sumption could not be applied in the same terms to poorer citizen women, since they had to work outside the household in the fields and markets, and the views discussed here derive largely from middle- to upper-class sources in relation to women of their own social status. As noted in the introduction, despite their important informal influence on family affairs, Attic women were in most cir-cumstances legally not permitted to undertake significant actions without the supervision of a *kurios* or guardian. Attic law, beginning with Solon (Plutarch, *Solon* 21.3), equates the persuasion of a woman with other deleterious influ-ences on a man's reason such as sickness or drugs. Indeed, popular culture often viewed women as incapable—physically as well as socially—of making au-tonomous moral decisions. The following offers a selective survey of some of the important cultural views and expectations about women as moral agents in Greek literature from Homer to Aristotle, expectations that clearly condi-

[9] Trans. Balme 1991.
[10] On female courage, see *History of Animals* 9.608a33–34.
[11] For a defense of Aristotle, see esp. Sparshott 1985.

tioned the assumptions of the tragic poets, even though literary representations of women often do not reflect either social reality or such popular conceptions in any direct or unquestioned fashion.

From the archaic through the classical periods, Greek tradition represents sharply conflicting views about the capacity of women to act as mature moral agents. As we shall see in the section in this chapter on Penelope, the Homeric epics and some Homeric Hymns do not differentiate between the capacities of men and women for moral action, although the sexes may, due to their different social roles, exercise these capacities in different ways. The archaic misogynistic poets like Hesiod and Semonides, on the other hand, define female nature as fundamentally different from and inferior to that of men. For Hesiod the race of women is created separately from that of men. In his *Theogony*, women are merely an economic drain on the household (they are "bellies" and "drones," as well as partners in evil, 592–602); a good (*kednē*) wife can upon occasion suit a man's thoughts (*arēruian prapidessi*, 608). But the first woman created in Hesiod's *Works and Days* has a doglike mind and thievish nature fit for lies and tricky words (77–78). It is thus not surprising that Pandora foolishly opens the fatal jar containing all human ills and diseases (94–95). For Semonides of Amorgos, different tribes of women descend from animals, sea or earth, and each reflects the amoral or immoral characteristics of her origin. Zeus, he says, "made women's minds separately" (7.1–2 West); their appetites are ill-controlled. Semonides' fox woman cannot distinguish good from bad (7–11; see also the amoral earth woman, 22–23); the weasel woman steals from neighbors (55). His sea woman "thinks two things" (27), whimsically changing from pleasant to hostile regardless of circumstances; when hostile, she fails to distinguish between friends and enemies (28–36). Only the sexless bee woman, who devotes herself to a family isolated from outside influences (especially other women and their gossip, 90–91) transcends the subcultural nature of her sex. And the bee woman, the poet suggests, may be a wishful figment of the male imagination (108–11).

The philosophical tradition of the fifth and fourth centuries is equally and similarly divided about the moral capacities of woman. In Plato's *Meno*, Socrates makes a point of arguing that the capacity for virtue (*aretē*) of a man and woman are the same (*Meno* 72d–73c). Despite a generally low opinion of his female contemporaries and their moral character,[12] Plato in the *Republic* views women's lesser physical capacity as unrelated to their mental and moral potential and argues that some women of his guardian class will rule as philosopher kings (*Republic* 5.454d–456a). He suggests that all irrational and immoral human behavior is due first and foremost to a lack of knowledge and adequate

[12] See, e.g., his disparagement of "womanish" behavior at *Republic* 5.469d; the nagging mother of the timocratic youths (*Republic* 8.549c–d); and women's susceptibility to democracy (8. 557c); *Timaeus* 42b, 90e; *Laws* 8.836e. Plato also agrees with Aristotle that as a class women are generally morally inferior to men (*Republic* 5.455 and *Laws* 6.781b), and more superstitious and subject to emotions (*Laws* 10.909e–910b).

training, but that women are additionally crippled in becoming mature moral agents by their confinement to private life in the family (and thus he proposes to abolish the family in his ruling class). Even in the second best state described in the *Laws*, trained women are still thought to have sufficient courage for military service and the capacity to serve as state supervisors of marriage (7.804e–805a and 813c–814c, 8.833c–834d, 7.794b–c, 11.932b–c). On the other hand, Plato thinks that theatrical impersonation of inferiors like women or slaves is morally harmful (*Republic* 3.395d–e), as is the representation of "womanish" emotions (*Republic* 10.605c10–e6).

Another Socratic disciple, the philosophical and historical writer Xenophon, advocates in his treatise on household management, the *Oeconomicus*, training a wife to become ruler or "queen bee" in her household (7.17, 7.33–34). In his view a woman shares with a man an equal capacity for *sōphrosunē* and *enkrateia*, self-control, and for learning and retaining civilized precepts (7.14–15, 7.26–27). A woman is by nature less courageous than a man and more affectionate to newborns; but these qualities are not serious moral handicaps, for they suit her for the social role she is designed to play of protecting and caring for what is inside the house (7.21–22, 7.24–25). A woman's more fearful nature, for example, is well adapted to the necessary vigilance a housewife must display for her property, whereas the male's greater courage is required for his natural role in protecting the household from without and supplying it with raw materials (7.25). The wife who serves as Xenophon's case in point arrives at her husband's house at fifteen with little more than a training in self-control of her appetites, having seen, heard, and spoken as little as possible (7.5–6). If properly educated by her husband she can be left fully in control of her sphere (9.16, 7.41–42). Acting as a physical and moral guardian (a *nomophulax*) of her household, she is to train servants and mete out praise and blame, justice and honor to her domestic subjects (9.15). Once so educated, she will possess *aretē* (and a nearly masculine mind) and win honor for herself (7.43,10.1). Here Xenophon, like Plato, is critical of the neglect of female education apparently typical in contemporary society (there are few people with whom Socrates' interlocutor in this dialogue speaks [seriously] less often than his wife [3.12]); yet he is optimistic about the capacity of a well-trained woman to operate virtuously within a strictly defined sphere. At the same time, he continues to have fundamental reservations about women's responsibility as moral agents. If there is a fault in a horse or a sheep, he says, we blame the groom or the herdsman. If there is a fault in a woman, it may be right to hold her responsible, whereas there is no doubt in a man's case (3.11). Elsewhere, a spectator at Xenophon's *Symposium* 2.9 who is admiring a clever girl juggler, remarks that "woman's nature happens to be no worse than a man's, though it is deficient in judgment [*gnōmē*] and strength."

In the view of Aristotle and the Greek medical writers (whose treatises date from the fifth century on), however, female biology alone condemns women to a subordinate role in culture and a reduced moral capacity. Throughout his works Aristotle views female anatomy and generative capacity as linked with her mental, emotional, and moral capacities. Both Aristotle and the medical texts agree that a woman's body is more porous than a man's. For Aristotle, her blood, like that of old and sick people, is thicker than that of the male, her teeth are fewer and less effective, her muscles weaker, her brain smaller and with fewer sutures to allow it to breathe.[13] Females are products of a weaker sperm (*History of Animals* 7.1.582a30); the birth of a female child results from a "natural mutilation" and "the female is as it were a defective male" (*Generation of Animals* 4.767b6–9, 4.775a15–16). The female fetus moves later and causes a more difficult pregnancy (*History of Animals* 7.4.584a12–17). After birth, she develops more quickly than the male, a sign of her lesser perfection (*Generation of Animals* 4.6.775a20–22).

The medical writers of the Hippocratic corpus demonstrate an intimate connection between women's physical and mental health.[14] The healthy adult woman is pregnant, menstruating, or lactating. Dysmenorrheal women, virgins, and widows are subject to a variety of mental and physical disorders. The womb, when it is not weighted with child or wet with semen, can migrate to various parts of the body, causing in the women hysterical symptoms, a lust for wandering, or even madness. Before menstruation, virgins may experience suffocation and depression from the pressure of the unreleased menstrual blood. They may choke themselves or leap spontaneously into wells. In this case, doctors propose marriage and sexual intercourse as the appropriate cure. Such biological conceptions of women's bodies as unstable and penetrable clearly reinforce or perhaps even derive from popular views that women are more susceptible than men not only to erotic desire, but also to madness, prophecy, demonic possession, and pain. As the chorus of women laments in Euripides' *Hippolytus*, woman's body dooms her to helplessness by its *dustropos harmonia*, its ill-turned unity (161–64).

Drama itself is full of gnomic statements that echo the popular view that women are by nature deceptive (Euripides, *Danae*, fragment 321 N[2]), unpredictable (Sophocles, fragment 811 TrGF 4), irrational (Euripides, *Ino*, fragment 400 N[2]), superstitious (Menander, *Dyscolus* 407–18; Aristophanes, *Wealth* 641–747), credulous (Aeschylus, *Agamemnon* 274–77, 483–87), or cowardly (Aeschylus, *Seven against Thebes* 236–63; Sophocles, *Electra* 997–98, Euripides, *Medea* 263–64; Euripides, *Auge*, fragment 276 N[2]), although these views can be partially undercut by the larger context in which they occur. The repeatedly fearful (736, 785–86) chorus of Danaids in Aeschylus' *Suppliants*, for example, remarks that "women are nothing alone, no Ares is in them"

---

[13] On blood, see *History of Animals* 3.19.521a22–24; on muscles, *Parts of Animals* 2.2.648a9; on teeth, *History of Animals* 2.3.501b19–21 and *Parts of Animals* 3.661b34–36; on the brain, *Parts of Animals* 2.7.653a37–b1, 653b2, and 653a27–29; on her general physical inferiority, *History of Animals* 4.11.538b7–13.

[14] On women in the Hippocratic corpus, see esp. Dean-Jones 1994, King 1983 and 1998, and Hanson 1990 with further bibliography.

(749).[15] Yet, in fact, they are willing to commit suicide and commit murder in order to avoid marrying their Egyptian cousins. Gossip among women is said to be a danger to female moral stability (Euripides, *Andromache* 943–53, *Phoenissae* 198–201); Euripides' Hippolytus even emphasizes the danger of any female speech at all (*Hippolytus* 645–50). Susceptibility to *erōs* is in particular a common female ill.[16]

Theseus in Euripides' *Suppliants*, argues that "much that is wise comes from the female sex too" (293); but most virtuous tragic women offer suggestions apologetically (Euripides, *Helen* 1049, *Suppliants* 293–300). Moreover, "a wife is always less than her husband even if the basest man marries a noble woman" (Euripides, *Oedipus* 546 N^2, trans. Webster 1967; see also Euripides, fragments 319 N^2 and 401 N^2). More generally, Euripides' Medea laments that women are fundamentally incapable of doing good (407–9). Tragic women are also "remarkably fertile in invention" (Euripides, *Iphigeneia among the Taurians* 1032), and, when crossed (especially in love), expert at taking revenge (Euripides, *Medea* 263–66, *Andromache* 911, and *Ion* 843–46), as well as deceptive workers of ill who will not keep their word (Aristophanes, *Ecclesiazusae* 238, *Lysistrata* 12, and *Thesmophoriazusae* 290; Alexis, fragment 146 Koch = 150 Kassel-Austin, 10–11; see also Democritus B273). They are also far more prone to the extravagant expression of grief (Euripides, *Andromache* 93–95, and *Helen* 991–92), pity (Sophocles, *Ajax* 650–52, and *Trachiniae* 1071–75; Euripides, *Heracles* 536, *Iphigeneia among the Taurians* 1054, *Medea* 928, and *Orestes* 1022), and volatile temperament (Euripides, *Medea* 909, and Alexis, fragment 146 Koch = 150 Kassel-Austin, 5–6; see also the orator Aeschines 2.179).

Even defenders of the race of women in tragedy, like Euripides' Melanippe, base their defense of their sex on women's useful actions in the domestic and religious spheres, not on their demonstration of effective moral autonomy (Euripides, Page 1962, *Greek Literary Papyri* 13.1–25). To the degree that Greek women are ethical, then, they seem, like Semonides' tribes of women, to have in practice as many moralities as there are individuals or types of women, even though there is only one ideal toward which each should aim, that of the possibly nonexistent bee woman. Female virtues are to a great extent more passive than active, more negative than positive, and for these reasons hard to define beyond simple obedience to the dictates of men and society. (Real women receive public praise for virtue almost exclusively on grave epitaphs.) At the same time, given women's natural, social, and political disabilities, their limited education except in the sphere of religion, and their isolation from daily contact with men, female moral autonomy becomes unpredictable and threatening.

Given these popular assumptions about women as moral agents, it is not surprising that when tragedy (to say nothing of epic and comedy) gives moral autonomy to assertive female characters like Antigone, Medea, Phaedra, or

---

[15] Trans. Benardete 1967.

[16] Euripides, *Trojan Women* 665–68, fragment 323 N^2 (*Danae*), *Hippolytus* 967–70, and *Medea* 569–75; see also Hesiod fragment 275 Merkelbach-West (see Solmsen 1970).

Clytemnestra, it simultaneously and often anachronistically reminds the audience of what is expected of Attic women in everyday life.[17] Tragedy does confirm the prejudices and fears of its audience about independent female actions and attitudes. Women's reputed incapacity for self-control, their vulnerability to desire, their naive ethical misjudgments, their passionate responses to victimization, their desire for autonomy and reputation at others' expense, and their social incapacities are all characteristics men feared in themselves and preferred to explore in women. A few examples of such disastrous female ethical choices in tragedy serve to make the point. In Euripides' *Hippolytus*, Phaedra falls prey to a love for her stepson Hippolytus and, in fear for her reputation after her nurse has revealed her secret, eventually punishes his impassioned and misogynistic rejection of her by committing suicide and leaving behind a tablet accusing him of rape. Here the heroine makes clear that her problems are compounded by the leisure and lack of positive activity that leave a virtuous wife vulnerable to and unable to master *erōs*, and by the lengths to which male suspicions of women can drive them (383–418). In Sophocles' *Trachiniae*, Deianeira's ignorance of *erōs* leads her to make a critical error; she tries to win back her husband Heracles' love from a young mistress by smearing his robes with what she believes to be a love potion but is in fact the poisonous blood of a centaur that destroys the hero. In short, female moral incapacity is represented as socially constructed as well as "natural" to her sex.

Yet, as noted in the introduction, tragedy does not simply aim to prove that all the negative stereotypes are true or to enforce cultural ideals. Here as elsewhere Greek male writers are using fictional women to think in a challenging fashion.[18] When tragic poets choose to allow an entire action to turn on the moral decision of a woman or to show women taking or urging significant moral positions in a public context, they apparently make at least a partial break from a cultural ideal and use female characters to explore ambiguous and often dangerous moral frontiers. Indeed, it is precisely because women are ethically speaking a marked category that they offer unusual dramatic opportunities. (Here men would be the unmarked category, just as song is marked speech in comparison to ordinary prose.)[19] Insofar as women in tragedy and epic are moral agents with a difference, they reveal in a positive sense important social and ethical alternatives and in a negative sense the social consequences of actions undertaken from a marginal, morally questionable, or socially resistant position.

By stressing the centrality of ethical choice to tragedy, Aristotle's *Poetics* made the case for the philosophical value of tragedy against Plato in his *Re-*

[17] See Harder 1993 and Seidensticker 1995.

[18] See further, the introduction and Foley 1981, Just 1989, Gould 1980, Zeitlin 1985a, and Hall 1997.

[19] For further discussion of the linguistic categories marked and unmarked, see Nagy 1990: esp. 30–34.

public. Recent examinations of tragic ethics and tragic choice by scholars like Martha Nussbaum, Mary Whitlock Blundell, Bernard Williams, Alistair McIntyre, and Chistopher Gill have also made a powerful case that tragedy does indeed have an important contribution to make to philosophy.[20] Although I have benefited immensely both from their studies and the earlier discussions by Bruno Snell, Arthur Adkins, and others to which they respond, in this book I approach tragic ethics with a different set of questions.[21] Despite recent studies showing that gender is often critical to both argument and characterization in Greek literature, these earlier studies of ethical choice in Greek epic and tragedy have paid only passing attention to the gender of the agent. This has been both a critical omission and a lost opportunity.

My interest in the female moral agent has nevertheless led me to share several presuppositions with the post-Kantian position on ethics adopted by McIntyre, Williams, and Gill, a position to which Aristotle's ethical approach has proved highly relevant.[22] Because these issues have been extensively discussed by Gill, I offer only a brief summary here. McIntyre, Williams, and Gill agree that "ethical life can be properly understood as inhering in the fullest possible participation in the roles and practices of the community; and that the ethical (or moral) quality of this response does not depend on an autonomous act of self-binding to universal principles [the Kantian position]. They . . . accommodate, in different ways, the idea that such participation is properly associated with full psychological engagement (involving interrelated reasoning, emotion, and desire); and this is again different from the kind of rationality, and abstraction from personal inclinations, associated by Kant with the moral response."[23] This position is critical to understanding the representation of ethical positions and actions taken by female characters who were created by male authors in tragedy because women are depicted as sub- or superhuman unless they remain embedded in a social role that normally does not accommodate full autonomy. As we saw earlier, Aristotle's standards for female virtue are for this reason not the same as those for men, and in these assumptions he is largely representative. Although female characters in tragedy offer reasoned

---

[20] Nussbaum 1986, Blundell 1989, Williams 1993, McIntyre 1985, and Gill 1996.

[21] Snell 1960 and Adkins 1960.

[22] See Gill 1996: 8, 43–44, 68, and 71–72 on Aristotle's recognition of the central importance of ethical dispositions developed within a specific community and on his conception of "deliberate desire," which is described in my subsequent discussion of Achtenberg 1996. "Aristotle's account of ethical virtue presupposes that a human life is normally lived within a nexus of interpersonal and communal relationships. But he defines virtue not simply in terms of the fact of such participation but rather by reference to the quality of the participation, and the quality of character which underlies this. . . . for any person at any one time, there is *a* response which is appropriate for her to make, given her location in a nexus of relationships" (Gill 71).

[23] Gill 1996: 68; see also 63. This view is accompanied by a rejection of Cartesian models of the mind and of subjective and individualist conceptions of the person, in favor of what Gill calls the objective-participant conception of the person (1996: esp. 11–12, 35, 42).

justifications for their positions, emotion and desire can play a proportionally greater role in the representation of ethical positions adopted by women, again in conformity with social stereotypes and with the real demands that were placed on women in the social world in which they lived.

Finally, because female behavior in Athens was more closely scrutinized, controlled, and criticized than that of their male counterparts, women are probably more vulnerable than men to the dictates of "shame culture." In general, shame culture can reinforce the kind of "virtue ethics" endorsed by Williams, McIntyre, and Gill because it is a highly interactive ethical mode.[24] I strongly endorse the view of Bernard Williams, however, that shame culture ethics are not more primitive than those of guilt culture. "In not isolating a privileged conception of moral guilt, and in placing under a broader conception of shame the social and psychological structures that were near to what we call 'guilt,' the Greeks, once again, displayed realism, and truthfulness, and a beneficent neglect."[25] According to Williams, shame cultures do not depend exclusively on face-to-face interaction; nor do *aidōs* (shame) and *nemesis* (retribution) simply enforce communal prejudices. Instead the shame culture agent internalizes an other who is the locus of genuine social and ethical expectations.[26] Moreover, as Gill shows, Greek ethics tend to be defined and implemented as part of a social dialogue or debate that keeps an individual in communication with his or her community; this holds true even when an individual is deliberating by himself or herself.[27] Although, for example, Euripides' Phaedra is induced to commit a crime because of her fears for her reputation, the internalization of the other can provide a positive as well as a compromising limit to autonomy. At the same time, the other internalized by female tragic characters may not, perhaps due to their different social roles and experiences, always correspond to that internalized by men. When it appears to be absent, as in the case of a "shameless" woman like Aeschylus' Clytemnestra, the absence is telling.

Women in tragedy can nevertheless take ethical stances that either prove to be superior to those of men in particular instances or appropriate but different from those of men due to the constraints of their social role or status. Unlike philosophy, which aims at establishing standards for virtuous behavior, tragedy remains fascinated with flawed, mistaken, and partially appropriate ethical behavior,[28] and with the issues that the cultural system and the dominant morality sacrifice or devalue. Female characters can serve to represent such positions.

---

[24] Williams 1993: 81–84. As he points out, shame cultures are not just concerned with success, as Adkins 1960 argued. This is an important consideration, since female agents are normally confined to exercising what Adkins calls the quiet virtues.

[25] Williams 1993: 95.

[26] Williams 1993: 82, 98, and 100.

[27] Gill 1996: 15.

[28] Fate and divine influences may play a role in these errors as well.

Like the female characters of tragedy, tragic choruses are by convention not expected to act—hence they are most frequently old men or women. Nevertheless, choruses occasionally do act and in any case make an important contribution to our understanding of the ethics of tragedy and to the evaluation of actions, responses, and themes in the plays; moreover, female choruses do not necessarily react in the same way or deploy the same traditional wisdom as male choruses. In Attic democracy, men must understand the role of followers as well as leaders and exercise ethical judgment in that role, as well as evaluate present actions and choices in relation to the past and the mysterious divine world. Both the culture and drama can place women in the role of followers, but the action of tragedy often propels them to abandon this role, whether to good or bad effect.

I am interested here in establishing the range and complexity of the ethics of tragedy in relation to its larger social context rather than in how these ethics conform to expectations generated either by contemporary and later Greek philosophers, or by later Western philosophy, although how tragic ethics contributes to our own contemporary interests in these matters inevitably plays a role. Because I adopt an anthropological or social and historical approach to tragedy, I examine female moral agents in tragedy through three different social statuses given to women at different times in their life cycle: virgin, wife, and mother.[29] Each of the three roles involves meeting a different set of social expectations, and entails acting under the influence of different emotional and social commitments. This study examines ethical stances and choices adopted by virgins (III.2 and III.3), choices made by wives who act in the absence of a male guardian (III.4 and III.5), and instances where virtuous, older mothers try to persuade men to take action on their behalf (III.6). In each case, the social position from which the woman acts conditions her perspective on the situation that she faces and the significant choices open to her. In each case a woman accustomed to operate, with the exception of religious roles, within the realm of the family makes choices that have larger public and political implications. By bringing to this larger arena a set of considerations or an alternative mode of ethical decision making that is not always thought to belong there, they require the audience to reconsider public morality. Because women are ideally not supposed to take action for themselves, their choices occur in extreme circumstances and from a position that is even more circumscribed by social expectations and responsibilities than those undertaken by men (see II). By experimenting with what one might call alternative moralities, tragedy ap-

---

[29] In so far as I have been able to ascertain, there are no important anthropological studies specifically addressed to ethical systems cross-culturally. There are, however, closely related studies of emotions. See M. Z. Rosaldo 1980 and especially Lutz 1988; the latter provides extensive bibliography and pointedly includes gender issues. Lutz' study affirms the inseparability of emotion and ethical choice among the Ifaluk, as well as the critical role of particular contexts, social role and status, and social responsibility in cultural decision making.

proaches moral choice from a far less universalizing perspective than philosophy, and in this sense becomes a richer source for modern philosophical scholarship that is engaged in exploring ethics from a post-Kantian "virtue ethics" or feminist perspective.

In III.3, for example, I consider Antigone's ethical mode in relation to the ethics of care developed by feminist sociologist Carol Gilligan.[30] More important, Deborah Achtenberg has recently argued that feminist philosophers should look to Aristotle's discussion of male ethical practice and development as an inspiration to moving beyond both current clashes among virtue ethicists, rule-based ethicists, and feminists advocating an ethics of care and beyond simplistic dichotomizing of reason and emotion, connectedness and separateness.[31] Aristotelian ethics recognizes the importance of a rich emotional and intellectual response to particulars in the making of ethical decisions. It relies not only on the acquisition of knowledge but on appropriate emotional development. For Aristotle, ethical choice does not involve the suppression of emotion by reason; reason and emotion should be in harmony, not in conflict. For Aristotle, choice is "deliberate desire for things that are in our power. For when as a result of deliberation we have decided, we desire in accord with our deliberation" (*Nicomachean Ethics* 3.3.1113a10–12). Virtue is a mean with respect to both actions and emotions; when we choose to do what is fitting and appropriate in a particular case, our actions lie in a mean between deficiency and excess. In the case of courage, deficiency would be cowardice, excess recklessness.

In Aristotle's view, emotions are a form of perception or cognition, and virtues are controlled dispositions to experience emotions. A person who pities, for example, perceives someone else experiencing undeserved suffering (*Rhetoric* 2.8.1385b13–14). Emotions, which are types of pleasure and pain, involve the perception of particulars as good or bad. "To be pleased or pained is to activate the perceptual means toward what is good or bad as such." (*De Anima* 3.1.431a10–11). These aspects of Aristotle's theory find a receptive audience among virtue ethicists and proponents of an ethics of care, who insist with Aristotle that we cannot specify how to act in advance of making a particular decision, that moral growth can only be completed in relation to others, and that virtue involves the awareness of the value of particulars, "where value is a kind of relatedness in which one thing, person, or state of affairs is not replaced, destroyed, or harmed by another, but is enabled to flourish and grow."[32] For Aristotle, appropriate action, aiming at the mean, entails the pursuit of what is good in the situation and for the person. "Cognition of value has both a universal and a particular component since we can know the gen-

---

[30] Gilligan 1982.

[31] Achtenberg 1997. Greek translations in this and the next paragraph are Achtenberg's.

[32] Achtenberg 1997: 112.

eral concept of value without knowing how it will show up in particular circumstances."[33]

This approach is valuable for evaluating ethical choice, and especially female ethical choice, in tragedy because tragic decisions tend to be made in unpredictable, highly specific, and extreme contexts. Emotion, principle, and perception nearly always play important roles in tragic choice, and response to the suffering of others is critical. The choices taken by one character strongly affect the lives of others, even to the point of destroying another's capacity for humanity. The greater embeddedness of the female agent in social expectations, constraints, and realities and her (sometimes) more limited vision and knowledge of public affairs can be used to reflect the human condition in tragedy, where characters often face circumstances beyond human control.

In short, Aristotelian and other later philosophical arguments will not necessarily help us to understand the tragic representation of ethics directly, but they can help us to judge its broader significance. They permit us to evaluate the failure of characters like the lovesick Phaedra, for example, to move beyond seeing her reason in irresolvable conflict with her passion, or like Creon, who cannot understand that even choices undertaken in the interest of the state entail a greater sensitivity to particulars and to human relationships than he permits himself and that choices made from different social positions and situations may require a different kind of ethical response. Similarly, Sophocles' Electra thinks and argues from a position of deep personal engagement with the specific problems that she faces, whereas Orestes' stance is—at least initially—distanced and abstract (III.2). Characters in tragedy whose choices or positions are accorded respect in the plays—among these we can include Alcestis, Helen (IV), and two of the tragic mothers discussed in III.6—tend to operate with reason and emotion in harmony, and deliberate with a greater sensitivity to the claims of both particulars and general principles than others. Aethra in *Suppliants*, for example, urges her son Theseus to defend the mothers of the seven against Thebes in their quest to bury their sons out of pity for the mothers, concern for her son's reputation, and a sense of the political and religious principles at stake. She willingly puts aside her maternal fears for her son in favor of protecting his reputation as a leader.

This chapter does not aim to make a comprehensive study of female moral agents in tragedy and deliberately excludes from discussion a number of female choices worthy of consideration, largely because proper evaluations of these decisions would require establishing a much broader context: choices by divinities, priestesses and prophetesses, slaves and other lower-class characters, and choruses. Divinities have a level of power, knowledge, and incomprehensibility that makes them both inaccessible to analysis by human ethical standards and less interesting for an investigation of female agency. Priestesses and

---

[33] Achtenberg 1997: 117.

prophetesses such as Cassandra, Theonoe in Euripides' *Helen*, and Iphigeneia in *Iphigeneia among the Taurians* face choices conditioned not only by human social and ethical standards but by divine and ritual necessities and religious roles. Of the two important slave nurses in extant tragedy, the nurse in Aeschylus' *Choephoroi* simply follows the instructions of the chorus of women and misleads Aegisthus.[34] The nurse in *Hippolytus*, who attempts to persuade and finally acts for her mistress, clearly makes a significant ethical intervention and offers ignoble, sophistic advice apparently suitable to her status—a status whose dimensions also need detailed consideration beyond the scope of this book.[35]

Finally, although choruses largely avoid taking action, some choruses do make important choices or take active ethical roles. One half of the chorus of women in Aeschylus' *Seven against Thebes* chooses to resist the assembly's edict and bury Polyneices (see part I). The (divine) chorus of Oceanids in Aeschylus' *Prometheus Bound* chooses to visit the hero with their father Oceanus' reluctant approval (128–35) and finally courageously decides to remain with him and share his punishment at the end of the play (1063–70). The fifty Danaids in Aeschylus' *Suppliants* repeatedly choose—although in a fashion that fits a conventional female role—to obey their father and stay within the bounds of proper female behavior (see esp. 195–203, 724–25). The chorus of Aeschylus' *Choephoroi* urges Orestes and Electra to act (see I). The chorus of Sophocles' *Women of Trachis* does not dissuade Deianeira from making her catastrophic error of judgment (723–28), whereas the chorus of Euripides' *Medea* urges the heroine not to kill her children (811–18). Choruses actively approve or disapprove the arguments and choices of the protagonists; for example, the chorus of women in *Hippolytus* praises Phaedra and disapproves the arguments of the nurse (482–85). Various Euripidean choruses abide by a promise of silence made to the heroine (*Hippolytus* 710–14, *Medea* 266, *Helen* 1385–89, *Iphigeneia among the Taurians* 1056–77). For example, Iphigeneia supplicates the chorus at some length, and the chorus not only complies but runs considerable risks on her behalf by attempting to deceive the king and a messenger. It barely escapes punishment by being rescued en masse by Athena for its just judgment (*gnōmēs dikaias hounek'*, 1469; see 1431–34, 1467–69). Again, however, close analysis of these choices would have to be made in the context of the complex role of the chorus in tragedy, including its tendency to give voice to conventional wisdom.

While some important female characters in tragedy make no autonomous rational choices (e.g., the helpless Trojan captives in Euripides' *Trojan Women* or the maddened Agave in Euripides' *Bacchae*), others were excluded because

[34] One manuscript attributes the role of the figure who resists the vengeful Theoclymenus at the end of Euripides' *Helen* to the chorus. If so, the choral leader (?) makes a significant and courageous ethical intervention.

[35] For a discussion, see most recently McClure 1999: 135–41.

the plays do not elaborate in sufficient detail on their decisions (e.g., Creusa in *Ion*, who is persuaded to try to poison her son by a male slave). Still others, such as Euripides' sacrificial virgins or Sophocles' Deianeira and Euripides' Phaedra have already been accorded careful study by others.[36]

Virgins

Tragic virgins are faced with making and defending difficult ethical choices in a fashion different from the more experienced married women in tragedy in part because they encounter a different set of social constraints and responsibilities. Situated in a marginal position between a sheltered youth and married life, they are emotionally and morally linked primarily with their natal families, but the forces propelling them to marriage also come powerfully into play. Unmarried youths of either sex have not yet been inculcated into adult roles or fully educated; hence they are thought to be less civilized (untamed), more idealistic, and more susceptible to an uncritical acceptance of adult rhetoric.[37] Although the circumstances differ in each case, these tragic virgins often make a conscious choice to forgo marriage and sacrifice their lives for family, state, or nation. In the following chapters, I examine the choices made by Sophocles' Electra and Antigone. Euripides' plays, in which the sacrificial virgin becomes something of a stock figure,[38] serve only to introduce the social constraints surrounding this figure, to offer an example of how male and female tragic characters of a comparable age make ethical decisions differently in a very similar situation, and to analyze why this difference is significant.

A brief look at a situation where a young man and woman in tragedy are faced with precisely the same ethical choice helps to clarify this point. Euripides wrote several tragedies involving the voluntary sacrifice of an unmarried young man or woman (see also *Heracleidae*, *Hecuba*, the fragmentary *Erectheus* and *Phrixus*). In both Euripides' *Iphigeneia at Aulis* and *Phoenissae*, a prophet asserts that the sacrifice of Iphigeneia and Menoeceus will make possible in the first case the Greek expedition to Troy, and in the second Thebes' victory against the army of Polyneices. Both young people choose to accept the sacrifice, and in each case their motives are the same: patriotism or Panhellenism. Nevertheless, they imagine the decision in different, and I would say characteristically different, terms. Menoeceus is the last of the sown men of Thebes, the autochthonous warriors who were born from and are willing to die for their mother earth. Menoeceus has to deceive his father, who is trying to save his son's life, in order to kill himself. He does not wish to be branded a coward, and

[36] On Deianeira, see part II; on Phaedra, see most recently McClure 1999: 112–57 with full bibliography; on voluntary sacrificial action, see note 38.

[37] See the appendix to III.3 for further discussion of youthful character.

[38] For further bibliography, see Foley 1985: 65 n. 1 and O'Connor-Visser 1987.

although too young to fight, he will symbolically join the Theban soldiers in dying for his land. His patriotism, his devotion above all to the collective interest, is, he argues, a model all cities should follow (990–1018). In short, Menoeceus acts on a moral principle and deliberately devalues (although he recognizes, 1003) the cost of his act to his own family.

By contrast, Iphigeneia, who in fact can only choose whether to die willingly or unwillingly, acts (as a woman should) in obedience to her father's words, not in his despite.[39] She is apparently converted to accepting the sacrifice by her father's appeal to the freedom of Greece and by an inescapable passion for war in the Greek army. Before Agamemnon's speech she sees her sacrifice in strictly personal terms as a father's betrayal of a daughter to death for an adulterous aunt Helen. Glory means nothing to her in comparison with life. She tries to save herself by invoking her relationship to her father (1211–52). Her mother Clytemnestra retains this view of the situation, which reflects the private, familial context in which mother and daughter have been hitherto confined. Nevertheless, following Agamemnon's speech and the entrance of the heroic Achilles, who is willing to die in her defense, Iphigeneia comes to accept her father's appeal to an abstract impersonal cause and to a glorious death (1368–1401). Yet unlike Menoeceus, she views her sacrifice not as the equivalent of military service to his country but as a marriage to Greece, the equivalent of children. She will save her father and Achilles from the wrath of the army and Greek women from rape; she will obey the goddess Artemis' commands and keep the barbarians subservient to Greece. The life of many women is in her view not worth that of one man. She departs refusing the mourning of her mother, offering greeting to her siblings, and urging Clytemnestra to forgive her father and preserve the unity of the family (1436–56). Aristotle, who saw Iphigeneia's sudden shift to patriotism as unmotivated, no doubt failed to notice that Iphigeneia's moral imagination has not changed fundamentally. Unlike Menoeceus, a junior patriot from the first, she changes her mind under unbearable pressure from men with authority around her. When she surrenders to her father's words, she envisions her sacrifice as an extension of the commitment to family, father, and marriage (though here her commitment is ambivalent) that has characterized her from the start. Like the bride she has imagined herself to be, she tries to unite Achilles with her father as well as the factions in the Greek army.

This is not simply a case, to paraphrase Jean-Pierre Vernant, of marriage being to a Greek woman as war is to a man.[40] Whereas Menoeceus defends his patriotic choice strictly in public and civic terms, Iphigeneia remains equally concerned with the divisive effects her sacrifice may have on her family. Leaving aside all the complex ironies created by the contexts in which Euripides'

[39] On Iphigeneia's decision, see further Siegel 1980, Foley 1985: ch. 2, and Gibert 1995: 202–54, all with further bibliography.
[40] Vernant 1980b: 23.

heroic sacrificial victims act,[41] the attraction of these figures to the poet seems to me to derive in part from their struggle, which is self-conscious and explicit in the case of the female tragic virgins, to bridge the gap between public and private worlds typically opened when society demands violent sacrifice from its citizens. In *Iphigeneia at Aulis*, Agamemnon and Menelaus have engaged in a futile struggle from the beginning of the play over the choice to sacrifice a daughter/niece for Troy. The despairing Agamemnon finally abandons the struggle to necessity; he cannot control the army. Only Iphigeneia is able to imagine this sacrifice in terms that make it morally intelligible and even finally acceptable to herself. Overall, Iphigeneia's ethical mode, like that of his other virgins, serves, as a woman's should by the terms of popular morality, the interest of father, family, and society. Her moral imagination is conditioned by her place in the reproductive cycle, as she moves from a primary and deeply emotional engagement in her natal family and in cults suitable for young women toward a larger set of relatively unfamiliar and more abstract marital and religious responsibilities.

Sophocles' Antigone and Electra (in contrast to their less heroic sisters, Ismene and Chrysothemis) also, when faced with an extreme situation, devalue marriage in favor of another priority, in this case obligations to kin. Both are, or briefly believe they are (Electra), brotherless daughters (*epiklēroi*), who thus by classical standards have an obligation to produce children for their *oikos*. Although their status as virgins complicates and conditions their choices, the stances adopted by Electra and Antigone are considerably more developed and challenged by conflicting viewpoints than those of Euripides' sacrificial virgins.[42] In particular, each deploys moralities that differ from those of the male characters.

Wives

As discussed in part II, Attic wives are under the supervision of their husbands, although their natal families may remain invested in their behavior and continue to make claims on them. Emotionally and ethically, they may also be divided between their loyalties to natal or marital family. Although they retain some autonomy and moral influence in the sphere of the household or in religious cults, they do not normally make important decisions for themselves. In tragedy, nearly all critical independent decisions by wives are made in the absence of their husbands or other male supervision.[43] The autonomous decision

---

[41] For my own views on this issue, see Foley 1985: 65–105.

[42] Other important tragic virgins in addition to Euripides' sacrificial virgins include Antigone and Ismene in Sophocles' *Oedipus at Colonus* and Aeschylus' *Seven against Thebes*, Antigone in Euripides' *Phoenissae*, and Electra in Euripides' *Electra* (see III.4) and *Orestes*.

[43] See Hall 1997 and McClure 1999. See also Hermione in Euripides' *Andromache*, the women of Thebes in his *Bacchae*.

to sacrifice oneself for husband or family is an important exception (Alcestis, Andromache in *Andromache*, and Megara in Euripides' *Heracles*). Decisions by tragic wives often have, whether intentionally or not, devastating consequences. Moreover, the consequences—adultery, suicide, the deaths of husbands or children—can reverberate out to corrupt the city as a whole, for, as Aristotle says in his *Politics*, "even the smallest disputes are important when they occur at centers of power . . . conflicts between well-known people generally affect the whole community" (5.2.1303b19–20, 31–32). I have already briefly mentioned the examples of Phaedra in *Hippolytus* and Deianeira in *Women of Trachis* (II); the decisions of the suicidal Evadne in Euripides' *Suppliants* (I) and nearly homicidal Creusa in Euripides' *Ion* (II) are equally unfortunate if more limited in their consequences. In this part of the book I limit myself to two critical choices. Clytemnestra defends her choice to take a lover and plan her husband's murder in revenge for the sacrifice of her daughter Iphigeneia while her husband Agamemnon was at war in both Aeschylus' *Oresteia* and Euripides' *Electra* (III.4); Medea chooses to avenge herself on Jason, the husband who abandoned her, by killing both his new wife and her own children in Euripides' *Medea* (III.5).

Choices made by tragic wives are not always negative, however. Megara in Euripides' *Heracles* argues in seemingly admirable terms with her father-in-law Amphitryon about how to deal with the threat of unjust death for themselves and her children, and decides to act in what she thinks would be a proper imitation of her husband. Moreover, as we shall see in the case of Alcestis or Helen (IV), the positive paradigm against which Alcestis, Helen, Deianeira, and Clytemnestra are explicitly measured is the *Odyssey*'s Penelope.[44] (The virtuous concubines such as Sophocles' Tecmessa and Euripides' Andromache discussed in part II are similarly linked with the *Iliad*'s ideal wife, Andromache.) Hence the remainder of this chapter is devoted to exploring this paradigm as background for my discussions of tragic wives and the ways in which they deviate from or approach an epic ideal.

Penelope

The central moral decision on which the action of the *Odyssey* turns is Penelope's.[45] She must decide whether to stay in Odysseus' house and continue to guard it and wait for her husband's return, or to marry one of the suitors. Yet she must make this decision in ignorance as to Odysseus' identity; that is, she

---

[44] Laodameia, who refuses to remarry in Euripides' *Protesilaus*, may be another example.

[45] A version of this discussion was originally published as Foley 1995b. A part of it was also presented at Vassar College, spring 1992. I wish to thank the audiences at Oberlin, Bard, and Vassar, and at a conference on Women in Antiquity in St. Hilda's College, Oxford in September 1993, as well as Richard Seaford and Laura Slatkin, for their comments on an earlier draft.

does not know who the beggar is and hence whether Odysseus is alive or dead. Thus, as in Aristotle's exemplary tragedy *Oedipus Rex*, Penelope's choice entails the tragic dilemma of a person faced with the need to act without critical knowledge of the circumstances. We need to examine the complex interrelation between female moral capacity and female social role that conditions and is articulated in Penelope's critical choice, to speculate briefly on why the poem gives that central decision to a woman, and to consider how the world of the *Odyssey* prefigures and even sets the standards for popular classical Athenian assumptions about women as moral agents. In contrast to tragedy the *Odyssey*'s women *are*, on the surface at least, endowed with the same moral *capacities* as men. Both men and women are praised for *eidos*, physical appearance, *megethos*, stature, and *phrenas endon eisas*, a balanced capacity for thought and feeling within (18.249 of Penelope, 11.337 of Odysseus, etc.). The same formulas are used to describe the way that they reason about questions of strategy or moral dilemmas.[46] The *thumos* (heart) of both sexes can deliberate, be divided,[47] and then decide in a rational fashion that one alternative is better than another. Both can subdue emotion through reason or bring desire into line with rational goals. Both Penelope and Odysseus are singled out for their ability to be hardhearted and enduring in the face of suffering. Homeric women are expected to display moral responsibility in their own sphere of the household and to enforce moral standards, such as those relating to hospitality, in the absence of their menfolk.

More important, both sexes can publicly demonstrate *aretē* (excellence or virtue) and achieve *kleos* (fame), for their actions, although they exercise their capacities for virtue in different contexts and achieve fame by different routes.[48] Odysseus wins *kleos* for his skills in battle and counsel in the Trojan War (9.20, which includes his reputation for *dolos* [trickery]; 16.241; see also 8.74), for his role as king (1.344, 4.726, 4.816), and ultimately for his journey and his revenge against the suitors (implied by the *kleos* of Telemachus' journey, 1.95 and 3.78, and the *kleos* won by Orestes and others for revenge, 1.298 and 3.204). Penelope wins praise for her *kleos aretēs* from the shade of the dead Agamemnon in book 24 (196–97). Men will sing songs of praise for her because she remembered Odysseus (*hōs eu memnēt' Oduseos*, 195). Although Agamemnon means here to celebrate Penelope's chastity (198, *echephroni Pēnelopeiē(i)*, and 194, *agathai phrenes*), the explicit emphasis on her remembering Odysseus has far larger implications in the poem. Moreover, the role of

---

[46] One exception, addressed later, is that Penelope does not have any moral soliloquies. See Russo 1968: 28–94 on the way that the *Odyssey*'s typical scenes of deliberation depart in certain respects from those in the *Iliad*; in particular, decisions in the *Odyssey* are only exceptionally resolved by divine intervention.

[47] See, e.g., 16.73 and 19.524 of Penelope, 9. 299–306 and 20.9–13 of Odysseus.

[48] As Naerebout 1987: 123–25 points out, however, Homeric women tend to be recognized more for their reproductive than productive capacities, and for passive rather than active virtues.

women as actual or implied audiences for the poem itself indicates that the praise and blame accorded female behavior in the poems is designed to further their own socialization in the Homeric world.[49]

In the second book (116–28) the suitor Antinous argues that Penelope knows in her *thumos* (heart) that Athena endowed her with the knowledge of beautiful works (weaving), *phrenas esthlas* (good sense), and *kerdea* (clever counsels), such as no other Achaean woman had before—not Tyro, Alcmene, or Mycene. No other woman was capable of *homoia noēmata* (similar ideas). For this, says Antinous, she is at this very moment winning *kleos*. As the suitor Eurymachus later adds, the suitors thus sensibly compete for Penelope on account of her *aretē* instead of marrying other women (2.205–7). Penelope herself thinks that she will win *kleos* or good report for her correct treatment of guests, and she chastises Telemachus for permitting the mistreatment of the beggar Odysseus (18.215–25). As she says at 19.325–26 to Odysseus, disguised as a beggar, "How shall you know if I excel other women in mind [*noos*] and thoughtful good sense [*epiphrona mētin*]," if a beggar sits unwashed in the halls? In praising men for their good sense (19.349–52), or in chastising the suitors for their violation of hospitality or their mode of wooing in Odysseus' house (16.409–33, 21.331–33), Penelope repeatedly shows that she shares the value system of her men (see also the chastising of the immoral maidservant, Melantho, 19.91–95). In recognition of her capacity for moral responsibility, Odysseus entrusted the care of his household, his son, and his parents to Penelope on his departure for Troy (18.266).[50] Most important, in Odysseus' mind the ideal couple shares the same mental outlook (6.180–85). *Homophrosunē* (like-mindedness) is the quality most to be desired in a marriage. A husband and wife *homophroneonte noēmasin* (like-minded in their thoughts) are a grief to foes and delight to well-wishers.

Although women in the *Odyssey* (even Clytemnestra and Helen) are generally viewed as ethically responsible for their actions,[51] they do not have the same degree of moral autonomy and self-sufficient virtue as men. All characters in Homer are subject to social constraints and divine intervention. Yet although women's ethical capacities are apparently the same, they are notably less free to ignore moral pressures from others or to define themselves and to act apart from their families, and there are many fewer areas in which they can make an independent show of virtue.[52] Penelope's beauty and *aretē*, she twice

---

[49] See Doherty 1991 and 1992.

[50] It is also said that Odysseus left Mentor to oversee his *oikos* (2.226); but Mentor has apparently not exercised whatever authority he may have in this circumstance. As the assembly in book 2 makes clear, the community is in general helpless to oppose the suitors.

[51] For a discussion, see Katz 1991, on both Clytemnestra and Helen. For female responsibility in tragedy, see III.4.

[52] Adkins 1960: 37 remarks that *aretē* in Homeric women is defined by men and entails the "quiet" or cooperative virtues (see also Naerebout 1987: 124–25). Because they are not called on to defend the household, they do not need competitive virtues. "As a result, Homeric women may be effectively censured for actions which Homeric heroes have a strong claim to be allowed to per-

repeats, were destroyed on Odysseus' departure for Troy (18.251–53, 19.124–26; see also 18.180–81). Similarly, Zeus takes away half the *aretē* of a man on the day of his slavery (17.322–24). If Odysseus were to return, Penelope's *kleos* would, she says, be greater and better and she would give the stranger Theoclymenus or the disguised Odysseus many gifts (17.163–65, 19.309–11; Helen gives them in the presence of Menelaus). In short, Penelope is not fully herself without her husband. A woman must also defer to the master of her household. In book 1 (345–59), for example, Telemachus for the first time attempts to claim authority (*kratos*) over his house, and tells Penelope to leave the choice of themes for song at the banquet to himself. Although the theme of the Achaeans' return from Troy is wounding to Penelope, Telemachus finds it appropriate. Penelope should go within; speech will now be a care to men. The amazed Penelope returns in silence to her quarters and lays the wise saying of her son to her heart. Virtually the same thing happens when Telemachus reclaims Odysseus' bow from Penelope in book 21 (343–53).

Finally, the poem continually expresses doubt that even wives of basically good character, when unsupervised by a husband or his surrogate, will make decisions in the interests of their marital family. Before Penelope makes her decision in book 19, both Helen and Clytemnestra have served as examples of what happens when wives make decisions in the absence of their husbands; in book 15 (20–23), when Athena appears in a dream to Telemachus, she warns Telemachus about the *thumos* (physical source of decisions) in the breast of a woman (see III.5). She tends to forget her previous marriage and children when she weds another (yet Penelope asserts at 19.581 that this will never be the case with herself). Overall, women are vulnerable to seduction in the absence of their husbands, and endowed with deceptive intelligence that can be used to destroy them if they decide on another man.

As the recent and formidable studies of Sheila Murnaghan, J. J. Winkler, Nancy Felson-Rubin, and Marilyn A. Katz among others have argued, the narrative context in which Penelope acts has made both her decision to establish the contest for her hand and her behavior leading up to that decision appear ambivalent, opaque, and/or contradictory to critics from antiquity on.[53] The books of Katz and Rubin make clear that these problems deserve a book-length discussion; it is neither possible nor desirable for me to go over the same ground

---

form." The women of the *Odyssey* are self-conscious about such public opinion. Nausikaa seeks to compromise between her social obligations to the shipwrecked Odysseus and her reputation; she would chastise an unwed girl who consorted with men (6.286). Public opinion is a factor in Penelope's decision concerning remarriage (16.75, 19.527), and the people criticize her when they think she has chosen to do so (23.149–51).

[53] Murnaghan 1986a, 1987, Winkler 1990a, Felson-Rubin 1988 and 1994, and Katz 1991. Except for a few brief notes on critical issues, in this essay I refer the reader to the extensive discussion of these questions in Katz and Felson-Rubin 1994. My own focus on Penelope as a moral agent leads me to adopt a different interpretation of Penelope's decision to establish the contest of the bow from that of these recent critics.

in detail once more in this chapter. Instead, I take the position, at the risk of oversimplification, that although the text does not give us full access to Penelope's thoughts and feelings, her well-articulated dilemma and her stated reasons for establishing the contest make it possible to judge and make ethical sense of her decision. Books 1 and 2 of the poem examine Penelope's dilemma from the perspective of the goddess Athena disguised as Mentes, the suitors, and Telemachus. Books 18 and 19 at last give us Penelope's own views on the issue. Finally, Penelope reluctantly makes a decision to set up the contest of the bow for her hand, ironically in the presence of Odysseus disguised as a beggar. My discussion stresses the moment at which Penelope chooses to act, to establish the contest for the bow.[54]

Because we see her situation first through the eyes of others, the text emphasizes from the start the social constraints that Penelope faces. In book 1 (274–78), Athena, disguised as Mentes, gives advice to Telemachus. He should let the suitors depart. If Penelope's *thumos* bids her marry, let her go back to the halls of her powerful father. Her family will prepare a feast and make ready gifts that should go with a *philē pais* (beloved daughter). Shortly afterward, Athena offers a second piece of advice on the same issue. She urges Telemachus to find out if Odysseus is dead. If he is, Telemachus should heap up a mound for his father, perform over it appropriate funeral rites, and give his mother to a husband (1.289–92). While Odysseus lives, Athena advises Telemachus to let Penelope choose to return to her father's house and to remarry. If he is dead, she advises Telemachus to act for her.

At 2.50–54, Telemachus complains to the assembled Ithacans that the suitors beset an unwilling Penelope with their wooing and shrink from going to her father Icarius so that he might provide her with marriage gifts (see II) and give her to whomever he wishes. Not so, replies Antinous the suitor. Penelope, not the Achaeans, is to blame in this case, for she knows wiles beyond others and has been deceiving the suitors for almost four years (85–110). Send her back to her father, he advises Telemachus, and command (*anōchthi*) her to marry whom her father bids and whoever is pleasing to her. Penelope knows, Antinous says, how superior she is to other women. And the *noos* (intelligence) that the gods are putting in her breast will bring great *kleos* to her, but want of livelihood to Telemachus. Thus Antinous concludes, the suitors will wait until Penelope marries the suitor whom she wishes (2.113–14, 116–28). Telemachus replies that he will not thrust from the house the mother who bore and reared him. If he willingly (*hekōn*) sent his mother away, he would have to compensate her father, Icarius, for many gifts and suffer retribution from him; his mother would invoke the hateful Erinyes (spirits of revenge) on her departure;

[54] As was said earlier, by Aristotelian standards at least, character (*ēthos*) reveals *prohairesis*, the sort of thing a person chooses or avoids in circumstances where the choice (and the resulting commitment to carry through on the choice) is not obvious; speeches in which the speaker does not commit himself or herself or avoid something convey no character (*Poetics* 6.1450b8–10).

and there would be *nemesis* (moral disapproval) from men (2.130–37). Eury-machus, another suitor, then again urges Telemachus to command (*anōgetō*) his mother to return to her father for marriage and wedding gifts. Until then, the suitors will compete for her on account of her *aretē* (2.195–207). Tele-machus, defeated, asks for a ship. If he finds his father is dead, he will give his mother to a husband (220–23). In book 15 (16–23), Athena warns Tele-machus in a dream that Penelope's father and brothers bid (*kelontai*) her wed Eurymachus, because he has surpassed the other suitors with his gifts and has now increased them. Athena advises Telemachus to look to his possessions, since Penelope may decide to marry and take Telemachus' goods with her.[55] (This dream does not correspond to what the audience hears elsewhere about Penelope in Telemachus' absence.) In book 20 (341–44), Telemachus reiter-ates to the suitors the point he made in book 2. Insisting that Odysseus is now dead (although he now knows that he is not), he bids (*keleuō*) Penelope marry whomever she wishes, offers to provide gifts, but is ashamed to force her to de-part unwillingly from the house.[56]

The text thus identifies the factors conditioning Penelope's decision in a somewhat confusing fashion. Sometimes the choice to remarry is said to be Penelope's alone; sometimes it lies in the hands of her son or father; sometimes the decision is a joint one in which Penelope will decide in conjunction with her son or father. After his return to Ithaca, Telemachus is willing to play a more active role by urging Penelope to remarry if Odysseus is dead, but he is consistently unwilling, even though the delay continually threatens first his livelihood and then his life, to force her to leave the house and remarry; Odysseus' parting instructions to Penelope reported at 18.257–70 also place the choice to remarry in Penelope's hands.

I am avoiding the use of the later term *kurios* or guardian to describe the au-thority that male figures have over women in this context, because these pas-sages raise considerable doubt about the exact parameters involved in male guardianship of a wife in the *Odyssey*.[57] Fathers generally arrange first mar-riages for their virgin daughters in Homeric epic, although even here (as in the case of Helen and her suitors) the daughter's preference may play a role; this is an option in Penelope's case. Yet Telemachus suggests that a wife or widow can invoke strong sanctions against being forced to remarry against her will. Clearly, Penelope cannot create the economic conditions of a proper marriage, like the preparation of a wedding feast or the presentation of wedding gifts; and male relatives can play a major role in urging her to make a choice, even a par-ticular choice. So her decision is not fully her own. Nevertheless, despite minor

[55] For further discussion of this passage, see Murnaghan 1994.

[56] This last speech comes after Penelope has decided on the contest, but it is clear from what Penelope says in book 19 that Telemachus has made similar statements to her earlier.

[57] For further discussion, see Finley 1955, Lacey 1966, Vernant 1980a, Mossé 1981, Morris 1986, Naerebout 1987, and Katz 1991.

inconsistencies, it appears that her preference plays an essential role in the process, a role sufficiently important that she can delay the marriage and even incur from the suitors a mixture of public calumny and grudging praise for her crafty behavior. After book 2, because no one claims the authority to force her to remarry, Penelope is apparently left free to choose if and when she will do so. In book 19, she herself does (after acquiring the approval of Odysseus in disguise) make the decision to set up the contest with the bow for her hand. Thus the *Odyssey* gives its audience the opportunity to observe a mature female moral agent making a critical and independent ethical decision.

When the poem returns to the issue of Penelope's marriage in books 18 and 19, the focus is on Penelope, and we discover that she views her dilemma more or less in the fashion that Telemachus has reported to Eumaeus and Odysseus in book 16 (73–77). Here Telemachus says that Penelope's heart is divided over whether to stay with him and respect her husband's bed and the voice of the people or to follow the best of the Achaeans who offers the most gifts of wooing.

In book 18 (257–70) Penelope reports to the suitors, Telemachus, and the disguised Odysseus on Odysseus' parting instructions to her as he left for Troy. Odysseus put his right hand on her wrist, in a gesture that echoes the initial appropriation of a bride by a husband in marriage. Uncertain as to whether he would survive the war, Odysseus entrusted the care of the household to her and bid her wed whomever she might wish and leave when her son is bearded. Penelope asserts that all that Odysseus predicted is being brought to pass. She thus represents the timing of her remarriage as powerfully conditioned by Odysseus' parting instructions.[58]

Before the suitors, whom she then provokes into offering new gifts of wooing, Penelope mentions only one reason why she must soon remarry. In book 19 (124–61), Penelope describes her dilemma more fully to the disguised Odysseus. The suitors have discovered her deception with the web; she can no longer unweave each night the shroud she was weaving for Odysseus' father Laertes. Now she cannot escape marriage or devise a new trick; her parents press her to act, her son frets, the suitors are devouring Telemachus' livelihood, and Telemachus is a man. Later in book 19 (524–34), Penelope gives the beggar a precise statement of her moral quandary. She says that her heart is divided over whether to stay by her son, guard the house, revere the bed of her husband, and respect public opinion (for this important influence, see also 16.75 and 23.149–51), or to marry (literally, follow a husband). Her child, who previously would not permit her to marry, is now grown and vexed over his loss of livelihood. She then tells Odysseus about a dream in which her pet geese are slain by an eagle who goes on to say that he is Odysseus (19.535–53). Odysseus

---

[58] Doherty 1995 stresses the unreliability of female narrators in the *Odyssey*; but here Penelope's story is told before the teller, and he does not question it.

affirms the dream. Penelope doubts his interpretation; in her view the dream was a false one. But, she laments, the day is coming that will divide her from the house of Odysseus and she decides to appoint the contest for her hand with the bow. Later, when she gets the bow from the storeroom, she weeps (21.55–60). She also wishes to die and dreams of Odysseus as he looked when he left for Troy (20.61–90; see also 18.202–5). Although she clearly regrets her decision to remarry, Telemachus' maturity, the threat to both his livelihood and his life, make it imperative for Penelope to act.

In book 19, then, Penelope gradually arrives at the point where she is willing to make (at least in her own view) a socially responsible decision to move toward remarriage—in contrast to expectations that the poem generates about the behavior of wives (like Clytemnestra) in the absence of their husbands, who generally surrender to seduction.[59] In full recognition of the suffering it will bring her, she moves to subordinate her own desires to the needs of her son and the parting instructions of her husband. Yet critics have argued that because Penelope has received repeated signs that Odysseus' return is imminent, her decision to remarry is both ill-timed and an inadvertent betrayal of her husband, who is in fact alive and present without her knowledge.[60] Her behavior has also been categorized as intuitive, irrational, passive, contradictory, indicative of a moral collapse, and even unintelligent.[61] Nevertheless, it should be stressed again that critics' questions about the decision have, often by their own admission, arisen above all from the narrative context in which her choice is made.

In my concern with the nature of Penelope's moral choice, I wish to stress the following points. First, she is facing a dilemma that she defines clearly and rationally. Penelope's moral stance is in itself, as both the poem and Aristotle

[59] See above all Helen, Clytemnestra, and the behavior of the unfaithful maidservants.

[60] See Katz 1991: 93–113 for a summary of previous views.

[61] Those critics who view Penelope as unintelligent think that she ought to have recognized Odysseus. (I am here rejecting the views of critics like Harsh 1950 and Winkler 1990a who argue ingeniously that Penelope has recognized Odysseus.) Critics such as Amory 1963 and Russo 1982, who think that Penelope has subconsciously recognized Odysseus, view her as a positive example of feminine intuition. Those who view her as irrational object to her resistance to the signs indicating an imminent return for Odysseus. For a full summary of earlier views, see Katz 1991, Murnaghan 1987, and Felson-Rubin 1994. These last three critics, in different ways, view the constraints of the narrative as responsible for Penelope's multivalence in the eyes of the reader. I agree with Katz 1991: 92–93 that the audience's knowledge of Penelope's moral dilemma as reported by Telemachus in book 16 helps to give coherence to the scene in book 18. Penelope has no character beyond what the poem gives her, hence we cannot fill in the gaps in her motivation. Yet a divided self can still in a strictly limited sense be psychologically and characterologically coherent (see Gill 1996), and the narrative has established the terms by which an audience, and particularly an audience whose expectations are shaped by the conventions of oral narrative, can and (despite textual ambiguities) inevitably will construct a plausible agent from Penelope (for this position, see Felson-Rubin 1994).

make clear, intelligible, commendable, and appropriate to her role as wife. As in Aristotle's [*Oeconomica*] and *Politics*, the Homeric wife's virtue apparently consists in her ability to obey with intelligence and self-control the instructions of her husband, even when he is absent. Indeed, the pseudo-Aristotelian *Oeconomica* 3.1 asserts that Penelope not only fits the wifely ideal that has just been defined in these terms, but adds that she won the opportunity for acquiring fame by proving herself faithful (like Alcestis) to her husband in adverse circumstances. The *Odyssey* repeatedly acknowledges Penelope's virtue and casts no *explicit* doubts on her action. Even Agamemnon in the underworld of book 11 (444–46) thinks Penelope is an exception to the general danger of women's infidelity; Odysseus' mother (11.177–83) and Athena (13.379–81) earlier affirm her fidelity; at 20.33–35, shortly after Penelope's decision, Athena again affirms the worth of Odysseus' wife and child. Finally, the shade of Agamemnon praises Penelope in book 24. Later Greek tradition simply makes Penelope the paradigm of the virtuous wife.

The disguised Odysseus twice endorses Penelope's decision to abandon her customary retirement and approach the suitors. In book 18 he approves Penelope's showing herself to the suitors (18. 281–83) and winning wedding gifts while her mind intended other things (see overall 18.158–303; also 2.87–92 and 13.379–81, where Antinous and Athena interpret her intentions in other contexts in the same terms);[62] in book 19 he approves her choice for the contest for her hand.[63] Given Telemachus' situation and Odysseus' instructions re-

[62] Does the text at the same time represent Odysseus as repeatedly deceived by Penelope? In book 18, it is clear, as critics have pointed out, that Penelope's motives for appearing before the suitors are not quite as clear-cut as Odysseus imagines. Athena intends her to excite the suitors and win greater honor from her husband and son. Penelope herself resists the impulse Athena instills in her. She laughs *achreion* (pointlessly, 163) as she tries to explain the sudden urge to show herself to her wooers, though they are hateful to her. Eurynome interprets Penelope's move here as one toward remarriage; yet Penelope refuses to beautify herself as Eurynome suggests, denies her beauty, and wishes for death. She says she wants to warn Telemachus and she actually does chastise him over the treatment of the beggar (at 16.409–33 Penelope similarly decides to appear before the suitors and chastise them because of her fear for Telemachus). Showing herself to the suitors is no decision to remarry, although it prepares for her later moves to do so; in book 19, she represents herself as still struggling with the decision in the terms that Telemachus laid out in book 16, where he represents Penelope as continually divided between staying and remarrying. In book 18, Penelope acts the part of a prospective bride, but her mind is still divided over the gesture (she is also still playing the mother to Telemachus). Hence, she can be said to be intending simultaneously things other than those that are apparent to the suitors, and Odysseus is not incorrect in interpreting her actions in the light of what he has heard from Athena and Telemachus. Furthermore, because Penelope represents the move toward remarriage in the light of Odysseus' original instructions, and denies her beauty even as it is melting the suitors, he has no reason to be other than delighted with her actions. He knows that the suitors' gifts will remain his and that Penelope is attempting to be faithful to his intentions. For extensive discussion of this scene, see especially Katz 1991, Emlyn-Jones 1984, and Felson-Rubin 1994 with full bibliography.

[63] The ambivalence that Penelope shows in the dream with the geese (19.535–81, she weeps over their slaughter) goes unregistered. Katz 1991: 119 sees Odysseus' approval as a patriarchal maneuver that denies Penelope a set of meanings and interests separate from those of her spouse and

ported by Penelope in book 19, both to remarry and not to remarry are potentially acts of moral fidelity to Odysseus.[64] Because of her ignorance of both Odysseus' identity and his fate, the critical problem for Penelope is the timing of the decision, not the decision to remarry itself.[65] Let us turn briefly, then, to the issue of timing and circumstances.

Penelope could not in conscience have continued to delay her remarriage much longer. After Telemachus returns from his journey and recognizes Odysseus, he demonstrates his ability to take charge of the household for the first time; pretending that he thinks that Odysseus is dead, he takes a more active role in encouraging Penelope to remarry (see esp. 19.159–61, 19.530–34, 20.339–44); at the same time, he is under threat from the suitors. In book 19, where she begins to move explicitly toward the decision to remarry, Penelope consistently expresses pessimism about Odysseus' return and rejects the signs and dreams that presage it (19.257–60, 313–16, 560–68; 20.87–90; 23.59–68).[66] Even when she has reliable evidence from Eurycleia of Odysseus' return in book 23, Penelope refuses to recognize her husband until she has tested his knowledge of their bed. Here she apologizes to Odysseus for her insistence on

---

makes the couple appear more compatible than they are. At the same time, in her view, feminist readings like Felson-Rubin's (1988) give Penelope an autonomy that the text does not support. In my view both Penelope and Odysseus subscribe to a patriarchal ideology; the text makes a point of giving Penelope the autonomy to make a nevertheless severely circumscribed choice; in judging Penelope as a moral agent, what is important is what action she takes and the role that reason and emotion play in a choice made in a specific context. (See Murnaghan 1995 on the male-dominated ideology of the poem.)

[64] Thornton 1970: 109–10 and 113 argues that Penelope's choice is appropriately conditioned by Odysseus' instructions, although her overall discussion does not come to terms with the full complexity of the circumstances.

[65] See, e.g., Katz 1991: 148, who argues that Telemachus' coming of age on the one hand legitimates the decision to remarry; yet in the light of the surrounding narrative the decision also becomes a form of (unintentional) betrayal (153; Murnaghan 1987, Felson-Rubin 1988 and 1994, and others take a similar position) that is only forestalled by Odysseus' interpretation of Penelope's choice as faithfulness (147). It is true that Penelope comes close to inadvertent adultery; but in my view this does not make her morally suspect. As long as we accept her lack of trust in the portents as rational, her behavior is not incoherent.

[66] The earlier portents to which Penelope reacts are as follows. In book 17, Telemachus reports on the account of Proteus to Menelaus. The news rouses the heart in Penelope's breast (17.150). Theoclymenus says Odysseus is already there and planning evil for the suitors (17.157–59). Penelope wishes it might come to pass (17.163). At the end of book 17, Penelope hopes Odysseus might arrive and avenge the violence of the suitors (17.539–40). Telemachus sneezes. Penelope interprets the sneeze as a sign the suitors will meet their fate (17.545–47). The text repeatedly stresses that Penelope wishes to believe in the portents, but resists that wish, either at once, or by the time we next return to her in the text. Her momentary optimism in book 17 does give way to the desire (which puzzles Penelope herself) to approach the suitors in book 18. Yet the continuing dilemma as defined by Telemachus in book 16 has not evaporated in book 18; nor has there been any direct sign of Odysseus' return. I endorse the view of Emlyn-Jones 1984: 3 that, by and large, Penelope's skepticism rarely wavers, "only occasionally straying into the optative in the face of a particularly convincing prediction." Moreover, it "enables the poet to exploit dramatic irony" (5).

testing to the last.[67] She was always afraid, she tells him, lest some man would come and beguile her with his words; for there are many men who plan such evils (23.215–17). Earlier she remarks to the disguised Odysseus in a similar vein that she pays no attention to strangers, suppliants, and heralds (19.134–35). The swineherd Eumaeus, who apparently receives a positive appraisal for being equally cautious, tells us in book 14 that Penelope repeatedly questions beggars, but that no wanderer with reports about Odysseus could persuade his wife and son (122–28). In a poem that registers with admiration an equal wariness in Odysseus himself (see esp. 13.330–38), is Penelope's skepticism, a vigilance that logically increases as the temptation to give way to hope becomes more pressing, really as contradictory as many critics would have it?[68] Or does the timing of Penelope's choice seems questionable only from the perspective of a privileged access to the truth?

In my view Odysseus' approval of Penelope's choice to establish the contest is perfectly intelligible. Logistically, it creates the opportunity (heretofore missing) for him to take on the suitors; and it is a contest in which he knows he has a chance of success. It has been argued that the plot simply demands from Odysseus a reaction that does not account for the full complexities of the situation. Yet, from an ethical perspective, in a context where Odysseus has chosen to test his wife rather than reveal his identity, he observes her following his own previous instructions (reported by Penelope in his presence) and maintaining a heroic and crafty defense against seductive evidence to hope and delay. From this perspective, Penelope's choice is less dubious or irrational than tragic (by Aristotle's standards): the dilemma of a good person attempting to act correctly without full and in this case critical knowledge of the circumstances (Odysseus' identity and fate). As in tragedy, the consequences of both alternatives are unavoidably at least partially and potentially negative.[69] For

---

[67] Penelope's final decision about whether to test Odysseus or fall into his arms (23.85–87) parallels Odysseus' concerning Laertes in 24. Both decisions have raised questions in the minds of readers (see Katz 1994a on the poem's recognition scenes as a whole); but the poem seems overall to offer a positive appraisal of seemingly hardhearted caution. See Athena on Odysseus' exceptional caution at 13.330–38. Eurycleia displays hardness of heart over Odysseus' secret about the scar (hard as stone or iron, 19.494). At 19.209–12 Odysseus pities Penelope, but refuses to lament as she does—his lids are of horn or iron. Although Penelope is criticized for her hardness of heart in book 23 (72, 97, 103), she gives a good explanation for her resistance during the recognition.

[68] See Zeitlin 1995 on how Penelope's bed trick also serves to test the heroine as well as Odysseus; Penelope here proves that she never gives in too easily.

[69] In the *Poetics*, ignorance concerning the identity of a relative (or of one's own identity) is the typical tragic error. This is part of the issue here. But in the *Nicomachean Ethics* (3.1.1110b–1111a), when Aristotle is discussing by what standards one may treat an act as voluntary (blameworthy) or involuntary (to be pitied and forgiven), he broadens the ways in which an agent may be considered ignorant of his or her interests. One may be ignorant concerning the agent (one's own identity), the act, the thing or person affected by the act, the instrument, the effect of the action, and the manner. In 2.7.11–12.1108b, when discussing the emotions that moral agents feel, he argues that time, occasion, purpose, and manner are critical. It seems likely that Aristotle would have wanted these broader standards to apply to tragic ignorance as well.

Aristotle, tragic irony of the kind created in this scene appropriately evokes pity and fear.[70] One could even argue that it is precisely by proposing to establish the contest for her hand with such evident regret that Penelope passes the test of the faithful wife.

Telemachus, complaining that his house is overrun with enemies who waste his livelihood, remarks that his mother neither refuses hateful marriage nor is able to make an end (16.121–28). The poem might have rescued Penelope from a decision by having Odysseus return and dispose of the suitors while she still delayed, or it could have staged an earlier recognition between husband and wife (this is what the suitor Amphimedon imagines actually occurred in 24.120–90). Yet in my view Penelope's fidelity to Odysseus would be far less effectively demonstrated if the poem had simply taken the painful choice out of her hands. After the recognition in book 23, Penelope raises the puzzling exemplum of Helen in relation to herself; it is certainly possible to interpret this exemplum as a recognition by Penelope that she inadvertently flirted with adultery in setting up the contest of the bow.[71] And public opinion has apparently always been on the side of waiting, although the public is neither privy to the complex events within the palace nor able to defend Telemachus. Insofar as the text does endow Penelope with desire (e.g., her sudden urge—produced by Athena and resisted by Penelope—to show herself to the suitors in book 18) and ambivalence (her weeping over the geese slaughtered by the eagle Odysseus in her dream in book 19) and offers general warnings about women's vulnerability to seduction, Penelope's acceptance of the less palatable choice in book 19 demonstrates—however ironic the scene given the audience's knowledge of the truth—a greater moral fidelity to her spouse.[72]

Finally, although Penelope's distress makes it clear that she views the contest with the bow as the critical step on a path toward remarriage, the narrative indicates that her choice of a contest of skill and strength leaves open, in a fashion characteristic of Penelope, several possibilities. The suitors may demonstrate that none of them is the equal of Odysseus; although Penelope

[70] One might argue—from the perspective of critics who think that the narrative denies coherence to Penelope's actions and feelings—that tragic irony is blurred in this case because clear lines between what the character and the audience know do not exist. But from a strictly ethical perspective, I have tried to demonstrate that this is not the case.

[71] On the complex issues raised by Penelope's use of Helen as an exemplum in this scene, see esp. Katz 1991, Murnaghan 1987, Felson-Rubin 1994, and Fredricksmeyer 1997, with further bibliography.

[72] The text clearly takes a risk, given these cultural preconceptions, on giving Penelope what amounts to sexual autonomy. At the same time, by *acting* Penelope becomes a far more convincing example of the faithful wife. The fact that Penelope's desire for marriage (and/or the disguised Odysseus) is gradually reawakened in books 18–23 at the same time that she resists it does not compromise her as a moral agent. Desire is a legitimate part of the ethical process in the views of most Greeks, including Aristotle, as long as it serves the dictates of reason. Indeed, knowing that Penelope has complex emotions of grief and desire simply makes her decision to suppress her own wishes more impressive.

has put her fate into male hands by establishing the contest, she has at least tried to insure that the victor will be like her former husband. The contest with the bow has the potential to serve, like the web, as a tricky device to delay the remarriage. The text has led us to expect that Penelope would choose to marry the suitor who offered the most gifts of wooing, as her family advised; the surprise choice of the contest may thus suggest that Penelope has delay in mind. If all the signs and portents prove reliable, Odysseus will return and Penelope will not have to abide by the consequences of her choice. The beggar insists that Odysseus himself will be there before the suitors have shot the arrow through the iron (19.585–87), and Penelope acknowledges, even after her choice, how pleasurable this outcome would be to her (19.587–90). In addition, the audience knows at the time Penelope makes her decision that she will be rescued from her suffering (and hence that her decision will have no negative consequences).

The *Odyssey* ultimately locates significant action within a social context that threatens to destroy the household of Odysseus from many angles. Ithaca does not readily submit to the returning Odysseus' authority. Odysseus' men have been destroyed during the journey home in large part over their refusal to listen to and obey Odysseus; the suitors persistently violate the laws of hospitality. Both groups submit too readily to their appetites. Telemachus cannot imitate Orestes in avenging his father and he could not in book 2 mobilize public opinion for his just cause in any effective fashion; Odysseus' subjects seem to have forgotten his paternal form of kingship, his fairness and gentleness. Even when the suitors recall Odysseus' generous leadership, it has no effect on their actions. At 16.442–47, for example, Eurymachus recalls Odysseus' hospitality to himself as a child and promises to protect Telemachus for this reason; but he is lying. At 16.424–33 Penelope reminds Antinous, to no effect, of how Odysseus saved his father's house (see also 4.687–95 where Penelope chastises Medon, and by extension the suitors, for not remembering Odysseus as king). The poem predicates survival on intelligence and social cooperation within the family group. Even Odysseus cannot achieve his return without his son, wife, and servants. In making the action turn on Penelope's decision, the poem seems to privilege and celebrate the importance and even the heroism of social responsibility in a moral agent as well as the contingencies that make taking moral responsibility problematic.[73] In Penelope's domestic world on Ithaca there is no legitimate room either for the wrath, withdrawal, or honor

---

[73] Murnaghan 1987: 128–29, 134, and 146 rightly stresses that the plot makes Penelope far more vulnerable to contingency and less able to control her circumstances than the disguised Odysseus. In her view Penelope is "defeated . . . by the incompatibility between her fidelity to her husband and her social position"; hence she forces "us to acknowledge the element of chance that turns the contest of the bow into Odysseus' triumph" (1986a: 113). Because I view Penelope's final decision as an act of loyalty to Odysseus, I find her choice less disturbing. Nevertheless, I agree with both Murnaghan and Felson-Rubin 1988 and 1994 that Penelope's ignorance is central to our understanding and judgment of her situation and actions in books 18–23.

from Zeus alone temporarily espoused by Achilles in the *Iliad* or for the freely chosen immortal obscurity offered by Calypso to Odysseus. The forces driving her to remarry leave little place for self-interest, for the near godlike freedom to shape a human destiny offered to the two Homeric heroes. She can only attempt to serve her son's interests and to obey her husband's parting instructions. The potentially notorious *kleos* that Penelope won during the period of wooing, which threatened to destroy Telemachus' livelihood, becomes the permanent *kleos* won by her devotion to her husband, a *kleos* that now enhances the household of Odysseus. (See her point that *kleos* can be achieved by being *amumōn*, blameless, at 19.332–34.)

A poem that urges the value of conformity to certain basic social norms like hospitality in an Ithaca represented as either indifferent to them or afraid to act on them needs to make its case in a subtle fashion. As in later Greek literature, the *Odyssey* deploys to its advantage a female figure, whom no listener could imagine escaping from social encumberment without great damage to her family and to the reputation of all women (see *Odyssey* 24.199–202). Penelope's sophisticated moral choice thus forms a key part of the *Odyssey*'s emphasis on ethical norms such as justice, and on the quieter values that promote social cohesion. In book 19, the disguised Odysseus compares Penelope to a king whose benevolence brings fertility and order to his kingdom. I suggest that Penelope's ethical behavior in part prefigures that of the restored Ithaca in a context where the paternal king Odysseus cannot as yet display his full character as leader. As was mentioned earlier, in book 24 Penelope is awarded *kleos* in part for remembering her husband (*hōs eu memnēt' Oduseos*, 195); and she elsewhere insists that, even if she remarries, she will, unlike other women who tend to forget their previous marriage and children (15.20–23), remember Odysseus' house in her dreams (19.581). In remembering Odysseus and reminding others to conform to the standards that he once enforced—and we should recall how important a theme memory is in the poem as a whole— the beleaguered Penelope continues to live by the standards of that vanished kingdom, and through her actions we can begin to glimpse what it might be. The reestablishing of order in the household—a smaller institution in which roles and responsibilities are relatively well defined—can be symbolically extended to the fragmented and ill-defined public arena. The poem can also stress through Penelope the heroism of social responsibility without compromising to the same degree the greater autonomy of its hero Odysseus. Odysseus' ethical responsibilities as king are in partial conflict with his ambitions to win fame and to protect his household as hero and avenger, roles that involve in each case a dramatic destruction of his male subjects. Penelope's choice allows the returning Odysseus to retain both the heroism he won as an individual for his journey and his revenge and his future fame as a just and benevolent king.

When major Homeric characters deliberate, reasoning generally provides the basis for a course of action to be taken in a specific case. In the majority of cases, the choice to be made is narrowly strategic: how best to survive in a situation of war or danger, and how best to win a desired goal (e.g., honor).[74] The most elaborate decision of this kind is faced by Odysseus at the beginning of book 20. First, he debates whether to punish the unfaithful maidservants immediately or to delay the punishment to a more strategic moment; then he turns to worrying over how to punish the suitors or to escape from the consequences if he does kill them. Sometimes, although rarely in the *Odyssey*, gods intervene to influence the choice.[75] Odysseus' choice to leave Calypso and Achilles' choice about whether to return to battle are unusual, because the hero has already been told the major outlines of his fate. Penelope's critical and elaborated choice has been incomprehensibly neglected in the general literature on Homeric decision making.[76] Penelope makes a fully conscious and independent decision that entails rejecting hope and desire for obedience to social responsibilities; there is no question of divine intervention in the critical moments in book 19 (or 23; in 18 Athena intervenes, and Penelope resists).[77] Certainly, the question of contingency is notably operational in this instance. Indeed, if I am correct, Penelope's decision best prefigures those singled out by Aristotle as particularly effective on the tragic stage and thus gives an as-yet-unrecognized depth to Homeric philosophy.[78] Most important, by forcing Penelope to make a choice so conditioned by both critical responsibilities and uncertainties, the epic takes a leap into a complex moral territory that it normally avoids (Achilles' complex decision in *Iliad* 9 is a very different matter).[79]

[74] For examples, see Sharples 1983, Gaskin 1990, and Gill 1996: esp. 73–93. The implications of these decisions may, as in the case of Achilles' choice in *Iliad* 9, entail larger issues concerning the quality of a hero's life.

[75] Athena intervenes in a decision-making scene only in this instance. See further Russo 1968: 292–93 and Gill 1996.

[76] The debate, inaugurated by Snell 1960: 1–22 and Voigt 1933 (see also Fraenkel 1975, Adkins 1960), has concentrated largely on the nature of the Homeric moral agent, and whether such agents can be understood to act as integrated beings (see most recently Sharples 1983, Gaskin 1990, Williams 1993, and Gill 1996). Most of the more detailed discussion has justifiably centered on Achilles in *Iliad* 9 (the bibliography is too extensive to cite here). Williams recognizes that the case of Penelope is more complex and hence decides not to address her decision in detail (1993: 48). It is surprising that Nussbaum 1986 did not turn to Penelope in a study that makes the problem of moral contingency in Greek literature a central concern.

[77] As Murnaghan 1995 points out, Homeric characters rarely resist divine suggestion. Penelope's defiance of convention in this respect may serve to underline her self-control. Unconscious forces may, as critics have argued, play a role in Penelope's decision, but this does not undermine my point.

[78] Gaskin 1990: 14 thinks that Penelope comes close to tragic *amēchania* (helplessness) in 4.787–94, where she debates over the threat to Telemachus' life by the suitors. He argues that most decisions in epic lack the complexity of the tragic dilemmas facing an Agamemnon or Orestes. "While Achilles' decision in the *Iliad* to avenge his friend is to be sure tragic, it is so in a different and much simpler sense than Agamemnon's. . . . Achilles has no difficulty reaching his decision; he faces no insoluble moral dilemma, with disaster threatening him on either side of the choice. All that is required of him is courage, and that is a virtue which he can unproblematically supply" (14). By these standards, Penelope's decision to approach remarriage is more deeply tragic.

[79] Williams 1993: 41–42 notes that duty in the modern sense has not been thought to play a

In my discussion, I have also tried to emphasize the ways in which the *Odyssey* defines and makes use of subtle differences between men and women as moral agents. Decisions by Homeric male as well as female characters are always heavily determined by communal standards. Moreover, as a result of the formulaic nature of oral epic, all characters tend to deliberate about moral issues in virtually the same terms. Although I agree with recent critics of Bruno Snell such as Bernard Williams that Homeric characters are convincing moral agents, they are not ethical individuals in a post-Kantian sense.[80] Nevertheless, even when men and women share the same values and moral capacities and deliberate about ethical issues in the same fashion, as they do here, they act under different constraints and with different priorities. Relatively speaking, for example, Penelope operates more fully than any male character in the poem within a web of relationships and responsibilities from which she neither can nor wishes to withdraw. This is not simply the result of a distinction between public and private worlds, since in the household of a king no such clear boundaries can be consistently drawn. Penelope's actions can affect and be celebrated by the world beyond her household, and thus have public implications; yet her choices, unlike those of a male hero, are limited to defending her present household and those within it or committing herself to follow another husband. Sex roles, then, are critical to defining gender differences in moral agency in this poem. Penelope makes a choice to sacrifice her own desires in establishing the contest with the bow and she is placed in a paralyzing position in which she can take no action that is without negative consequences.[81]

Positive actions by women in Greek literature (whether virgins or wives like Alcestis) typically involve such sacrifice and self control. Penelope is apparently the only character in either of the two Homeric epics who faces a choice between two responsibilities to others; and it may be significant from this perspective that she is never, like the male heroes, permitted an ethical soliloquy, but always debates her alternatives in dialogue with other characters. There are no discussions comparable with those in *Odyssey* 2 about Penelope's remarriage over whether a male agent has or should have the autonomy to make a critical decision. Similarly, Clytemnestra's betrayal of Agamemnon is said in

---

role in Homeric decision making (see also Gill 1996). The term does not occur in Homeric vocabulary, but Penelope's choice perhaps comes closer than any other Homeric decision to invoking what we might call duty as a basis for her choice. Hector, whose representation is so closely linked with that of his city, is the male character most similar to Penelope. In his decision about whether to stay outside the walls and fight Achilles or retreat into the city, as his parents wish him to, Hector weighs the taunts of those who will accuse him of ruining his people by his mistaken strategies if he goes into the city and his fear that Achilles would not negotiate with him against risking death with glory (*Iliad* 22.98–130). Even here, however, Hector's own honor as a warrior ultimately takes precedence over his responsibility to protect his city or at least to delay its fall.

[80] Williams 1993: esp. 21–29 is the most recent of the critics of Snell (see also Gill 1996).

[81] In the view of Gilligan 1982: 82 as moral agents, women tend toward self-sacrifice, and are often "suspended in a paralysis of initiative with respect to action and thought."

Odyssey 24 to tarnish the reputation of *all* women, even those who, like Penelope, act appropriately (*kai hē k'euergos eē(i)sin*, 199–202); the *kleos* of a Homeric hero does not depend in part on the presence or actions of another person as does Penelope's (17.163–65, 19.309–11). Penelope wins *kleos* as wife, as a person powerless to act except in relation to another, not as a powerful warrior-leader defending his reputation.

Nevertheless, the particular limits under which a female agent in Homer is ideally meant to operate make giving Penelope moral autonomy in this instance an attractive opportunity to the *Odyssey* poet.[82] On the one hand, her social role makes it dangerous for a woman to claim full moral autonomy. Furthermore, feminization, or a breakdown in gender boundaries, is a fate repeatedly feared by the typical male hero; warriors taunt their opponents by associating them with women; the bodies of male heroes, lying helpless and without armor on the battlefield, are viewed as feminized;[83] Hector in *Iliad* 6 insists on sex role differences between men and women as a defense against Andromache's plea that he adopt a more defensive role in the battle (490–93). On the other hand, choices made from a marginal, relatively powerless position can also serve to set a new moral direction for the dominant male agents of Homeric poetry.[84] Because Penelope shares Odysseus' values and is both constrained and willing in a situation of hopeless uncertainty to sacrifice her own needs for the benefit of others, her female difference contributes to rather than undermines the social order. Indeed, it is this willingness to abide by the social standards of her world that ultimately separates her from Odysseus' disruptive enemies, the suitors, and makes her the figure for a future order in which respect for such standards will be the basis for a community united under the leadership of her husband.[85] Insofar as tragic choices of the kind identified and praised by Aristotle are symptomatic of a social world in which obligations to promote civic welfare have acquired a greater ideological interest and resonance, it is not surprising that the *Odyssey*'s most nearly tragic choice is made by a character whose social role is defined so pointedly in terms of responsibilities.

Penelope's paradigmatic choice has particular resonance for tragedy, and not

---

[82] For a recent general discussion of sexual ideology in the *Odyssey*, see Wohl 1993.

[83] See Vermeule 1979: esp. 101–3 and 105.

[84] The role played by the marginal figure Thersites in the *Iliad* also serves to reshape our perspective on the ethics of Homeric heroes. In tragedy also, female experience can be educative to the male. See, e.g., part IV, for Penelope and Odysseus serving as a paradigm in this respect for Helen and Menelaus in Euripides' *Helen,* as well as Zeitlin 1985b, on Phaedra and Hippolytus. In its use of reverse similes, which often assimilate male and female experiences, the *Odyssey* similarly plays with dissolving gender role boundaries. See further Foley 1978.

[85] Insofar as the Homeric epics reflect the early stages of the development of the Greek city-state, this attitude prefigures the later commitment of the citizen to the *polis*.

only because tragedy holds her up as an implicit example, but rarely trusts its women to imitate her. Tragic wives typically make important choices, as did Penelope, in the absence of their spouses. They too face maximal constraints in reaching a decision, including uncertainty, ignorance, and the limitations and responsibilities imposed by their social roles. As with Penelope, any choice that they make, even choices that serve husband and family, is also potentially dangerous to masculine interests. Cultural memory and reputation often play a critical role in female choice, as does the potential for divided loyalties between households. Female choices in tragedy also tend to have implications for the public as well as the private sector and to serve as a means to explore indirectly masculine choice in circumstances that would compromise male identity.

Mothers

Distinguishing between mothers and wives may seem arbitrary, because the actions of tragic wives usually affect children as well as spouses. Yet there is a small class of tragic women who act and speak persuasively above all in relation to children. Their husbands are absent or unimportant to the stances that they adopt, but they do not betray the family group. As older women for whom *erōs*, reproduction, and pressures from the natal family are no longer a direct concern, their vision can unusually encompass the needs of both family and state. They are unconventional in their bold assertion of their views to men, but conventional in their attempt to persuade men to act on their advice, rather than taking matters into their own hands. Because they raise issues that men can recognize as of positive importance in public affairs, the stances taken by these tragic women indirectly offer a complex commentary on contemporary Athenian affairs. Their role is not surprising, because mothers of this age—postmenopausal women or widows—often have a cultural authority different from wives of childbearing age in an enormous range of traditional societies; and we observe a few traces of older women's exercise of authority in Attic court cases from the fourth century B.C.E. (see the introduction, II, and III.6). My discussion centers on women in Euripides—Aethra in *Suppliants*, Jocasta in *Phoenissae*, and the more ambivalent figure of the Trojan Hecuba in *Hecuba*. Among other persuasive older mothers in tragedy, the Persian queen Atossa in Aeschylus' *Persians* consults the male chorus on how to respond to her frightening dream. On its advice, she prays to the gods and sacrifices to the dead, including her dead husband Darius, and then questions the newly arrived Persian messenger. Later she leaves the stage to follow Darius' instructions to offer Xerxes new robes and soothing words. Despite her august status, she plays a largely traditional female role in following male instructions and performing religious duties, and is thus less interesting for consideration here than those who take active persuasive stands.[86] Jocasta in Sophocles' *Oedipus Rex* plays an important mediating role as wife and sister rather than mother. Alcmena in Euripides' *Heracleidae*, who does fit the category under discussion, controversially takes and defends revenge against her tormentor Eurystheus; in doing so she both defends her family and jeopardizes its future.[87]

---

[86] There are a number of non-Greek examples of persuasive mothers in Herodotus (see Dewald 1981).

[87] See Burnett 1998: 142–57 with further bibliography and Falkner 1989. Falkner suggests that her androgynous character, her informal authority, and her wrath are related to her advanced age.

III.2

Sacrificial Virgins: The Ethics of Lamentation in Sophocles' *Electra*

IN SOPHOCLES' *Electra* Orestes, Electra, and Chrysothemis all accept the necessity and justice of taking revenge for their father Agamemnon's murder by Clytemnestra and Aegisthus, but each has reacted differently to the difficult situation in which the siblings find themselves at the opening of the play. Orestes has spent his life preparing to return from exile to Argos and to enact the revenge. As unmarried women, Electra and Chrysothemis wait at home for Orestes to take action on their behalf. Chrysothemis has chosen to accommodate herself to her oppressors, whereas Electra has chosen a strategy of open resistance. Critics have already identified and discussed marked differences in male and female ethos in this play. Thomas Woodard, for example, has argued that "Orestes and Electra embody two contrasting moral tempers and moral codes";[1] in his view, Orestes' stance toward the revenge displays moral detachment, Electra's moral immediacy.[2] Or, as George Gellie puts it, "Man and woman, action and word, immediacy and timelessness, thought and feeling, deception and truth, intrigue and tragedy, are the obvious black and white pieces of this stage game."[3] The contrast between Orestes' and Electra's different ways of thinking, speaking, and acting[4] is pointedly dramatized in the prologue and in the following scene between Electra and the chorus of women, and reemerges in the recognition scene between the siblings and the revenge that closes the play. In the scenes that frame the drama, Orestes and the pedagogue reject Electra's expressive verbal response to taking revenge in favor of a stress on action, and in the final scene Electra subsumes herself to Orestes

I wish to thank audiences at Oberlin and Cambridge, and Richard Seaford and Christian Wolff for comments on an earlier draft.

[1] Woodard 1964: 164; see also 165. He sees this contrast as rooted in the social differentiation of men and women in fifth-century Athens.

[2] Woodard 1964: 168. He also contrasts Orestes' active virtue and Electra's "inner *aretē*" (167). Bowra 1944: 248, defines the contrast as one beween abstract right and intimate knowledge and feeling. In Sheppard's view (1918: 82), justice is a personal experience for Electra; for Orestes it is a distant event. For Burnett 1998: esp. 120, 130, and 141 the contrast is between the male who is passionless, divinely inspired, forward-looking, unfree, and effective, and the female, who is passionate, backward-looking, wholly free, and incapable of effective action.

[3] Gellie 1972: 116.

[4] See Kitzinger 1991: 301.

and agrees to make her speech serve action alone. Yet, although the play as a whole inflicts increasing pain and deception on Electra, and finally subdues and even to some extent silences (even while it rescues) her, the central scenes that frame the deceptive speech of the pedagogue about the supposed death of Orestes give her the dominant moral voice in the play. The play thus gives its most important and emotionally powerful role to a character whom it seemingly aims to contain or transform.

Electra has often left its audience uncertain about the justice of the revenge undertaken. At the conclusion, no furies appear to pursue Orestes for his matricide as in Aeschylus; he undergoes no trial for his crime, nor expresses any doubts or regrets.[5] Does the play present a clean and heroic revenge without further repercussions, to be praised and held up as an exemplum for male behavior as the Odyssey does in the case of Orestes?[6] If so, why is Electra the central character? Or do we in the process of the drama come to evaluate the crime as just, but also shameful and terrible,[7] and perhaps likely to entail repercussions in the future?[8] For reasons that will become clearer, I am not sure that

[5] In addition, the death of Aegisthus rather than Clytemnestra serves as a climax to the play.

[6] For many critics, there is no question that the revenge is as just, uncomplicated, and affirmative as the final lines of the play assert. For summaries of past views, see Woodard 1965: 233 n. 98, Kells 1973: 2–3, and Segal 1966: 474–75 and 1981: 461 n. 2. Typical views are as follows. "It is arguable that . . . [Orestes'] pursuit of his mission, unclouded by passion, represents an objective, rational, divine confirmation of the rightness of Electra's position" (Blundell 1989: 182). Bowra 1944: 231 argues that the play demonstrates how Orestes could commit matricide without being a monster; there is no snake in Clytemnestra's dream (223). In a conflict between the duty to take vengeance and piety toward a mother, revenge must come first (227). Jebb [1924] 1962: xl thinks that Clytemnestra forfeited all moral claims to her children's loyalty; Stevens 1978 stresses that Clytemnestra and Aegisthus are clear villains and that the plot deemphasizes the matricide. Linforth 1963: 120–21 argues that Orestes must appear guiltless to preserve the central focus on Electra. Burnett 1998 argues that "with divine help a mortal can mix rectitude with remembering passion in an untainted approach to a physical act"; yet the play "leaves its audience with the simple conviction that no human achievement will ever be perfectly clean" (141).

[7] Many critics adopt this divided opinion. On the outcome as shameful or terrible but just, see Minadeo 1967: 140, McDevitt 1983: 3, and Alexanderson 1966: 87. Segal 1966: 475 thinks the outcome of the plot is good, but the means by which it has been achieved questionable. Blundell argues that the justice of the talio is acceptable in principle (149), but it is "rooted in passion and therefore raise[s] profound questions about the rationality of moral action and the relationship of moral justification to the emotions" (1989: 1). Electra and Clytemnestra both cite the principle help friends, harm enemies; they cannot both be right (162). Many critics argue that although the revenge is divinely sanctioned, Orestes becomes an unwitting agent in the destruction of Electra.

[8] Those who argue that the play hints at a negative aftermath point to the several mentions of Furies in the text, to Electra's role as victim and agent of the Furies, and to the prediction of further trouble for the house of Pelops by Aegisthus at 1498–1500. (See esp. Winnington-Ingram 1980: 218–28.) McDevitt 1983: esp. 9 elaborates on the link between Pelops' ominous chariot race and the pedagogue's lie about Orestes. Alexanderson 1966: 94–95 counters that Aegisthus' warning comes too late and is immediately dismissed. Segal 1966: 477, 480 stresses the movement in the play from light to darkness, from outside to inside, from linearity to hints of a renewed circularity (1981: 251). He doubts that so much suffering can be undone (1981: esp. 262 and 290).

these are the right questions to ask about this play.[9] Nevertheless, looking more
closely at the way in which the drama defines, authorizes, and/or undercuts its
two central, different, and pointedly gendered voices can help to lay the basis
for interpreting its controversial ethics. My approach to these questions, which
have already received considerable attention from critics, entails an attempt
to define the ethical stances of the central characters more closely than before
in relation to the cultural contexts out of which they emerge. *Electra* is particularly difficult to interpret because the text does not offer us any easy way to
evaluate its representation of a system of vendetta justice that is anachronistic
in practice for its original (and its twentieth-century) audience, for whom civic
justice has at least formally superseded the self-help justice of earlier eras. We
must be careful, however, not to ignore the fact that vendetta is for those who
practice it often the only formal system of justice available, or, if available, the
possibility of the lawcourt is a despised alternative; vendetta has its own ethical codes and includes carefully defined roles for each sex. An anthropological
approach to the ethics of revenge tragedy can help us to uncover the particular coloring that Sophocles gives to the action and to the significant choices
made or defended in this play.

Let us begin with the way that the opening scenes define and contrast the
voices and strategies of Orestes and Electra. The pedagogue defines the public
space into which he enters with Orestes and Pylades as symbolic of the city of
Argos. He draws attention to the grove of Io, to the agora of Apollo the Wolf
God, to the famous shrine of Hera, to Mycenae rich in gold, and to the destructive house of Pelops (4–10).[10] The ensuing dialogue seems to match the
imagined civic setting framed by the shrines of important deities, above all
Apollo in a guise that suits his promotion of revenge;[11] it is pragmatic, eco-
nomical, and dispassionate. The pedagogue, using language with military overtones, asserts that Orestes must follow in the footsteps of his father the general
at Troy (1–2). The question here is not whether to enact the revenge, but

---

[9] A number of critics have adopted a version of this stance. Jebb [1924] 1962: xli thought that
Sophocles was not interested in the ethical and legal aspects of the story, but offered a Homeric
style narrative. Kirkwood 1958: 166, for example, suggests that "the guilt, if it is guilt, is Orestes',
the play Electra's. Sophocles does not mean to give a solution to the moral problem insofar as it
pertains to Orestes. What we should expect to find in the play is a clear indication of the effect of
the moral question on Electra." (See similarly Schein 1982: 78 and Horsley 1980: 19, 21, 25, and
27.) Whitman 1951: esp. 160 and Erbse 1978: 293 argue that the play focuses on neither myth nor
matricide, but on the spiritual greatness or endurance of Electra. Gellie 1972: 106 argues that the
play seems to be looking at matricide "from some other angle than that of divine or human justice"; at the conclusion "we may hover between 'how elegant a plot' and 'how terrible an experience.'" De Wet 1977: 35 thinks that the play does not illuminate justice, but questions late-fifth-
century values (see also Segal 1966: 535).

[10] Segal 1981: 250 makes a point of contrasting this outer civic world with the inner world of
Electra, who is confined within the house.

[11] Here Apollo is *Lukeios*, or wolflike. See Burkert 1985: 145.

how.[12] Orestes has been raised from childhood by the pedagogue to accomplish this mission (11–14); the Delphic oracle has advised him to proceed by stealth and without force of arms (shields and an army, 35–37). In order to reappropriate his inheritance, restore his house, and win glory, Orestes makes a proposition to Pylades and the pedagogue. The two young men will fulfill the oracle's instructions and pour libations and place locks of hair at the tomb of Agamemnon (51–53). The pedagogue will enter the palace first, with a story that Orestes is dead; he may even offer an oath to that effect (47–50). Orestes and Pylades will follow with an urn containing the supposed ashes of Orestes (54–58). By dying in speech (*logō(i)*), Orestes will be saved in reality (*ergoisi*) (59–60). Regardless of method, the aim is fame (60) and fortune (71); the result will be a divinely inspired justice (*endikous sphagas*, 37). Language must serve action; the conspirators must develop the right plan for the right moment (*kairos*, 22, 31).

This prologue is interrupted by a cry of lament from within the place by Electra (77). Orestes hesitates. Should he wait and hear these laments (*goōn*, 80–81)? The military overtones of the language have already implicitly excluded women from participation in the revenge, and the pedagogue thus responds predictably with a firm no (82).[13] They must follow Apollo's instructions; this will bring *nikē* and *kratos* (success and power, 82–85). For an audience familiar with Aeschylus' *Choephoroi*, Sophocles' play has just pointedly refused to recreate the famous opening scene at the tomb of Agamemnon, in which Agamemnon's son and daughter first recognize each other, then go on to offer prayers and laments at his tomb and to invoke the dead hero's ghost along with the chorus of women. In *Electra*, male and female will instead pursue different paths until the final scenes bring them back together.[14]

For Electra too, the question is not whether to avenge her father, but how. While waiting within the palace for Orestes to take action for her (117), Electra has kept alive her father's cause in speech. Like Penelope in the *Odyssey*, who spends the years waiting for Odysseus and lamenting for her absent husband, Electra fiercely refuses to forget the past (146, 342, 346); she freezes time

[12] Despite Sheppard 1927a (elaborated by Kells 1973), Orestes, as many later critics have stressed (e.g., Bowra 1944: 217, Winnington-Ingram 1980: 216, Horsley 1980: 20, Alexanderson 1966: 81, and Segal 1981: 280), assumes that Apollo has authorized his act (see lines 36 and 82–83). Skeptics counter that Orestes' assumption is not based on Apollo's words and that Apolline oracles are notoriously ambiguous. The potentially problematic lines 1424–25—all's well in the house, if Apollo gave his oracle well—can be interpreted as a sign of certainty as well as doubt (see further Alexanderson 1966: 92).

[13] Sandbach 1977 attributes these lines to Orestes. I follow the traditional reading. The refusal to listen to Electra stands in either case.

[14] Burnett 1998: esp. 120, 127, 131, and 141 argues that the two are separated so that the orientations that each represents (the pure impulse to revenge untainted by its goal and divinely inspired duty) can be analyzed separately until the two are united; she underestimates the complexity and acknowledged impurity of Electra's position, however.

and blurs the division between day and night, past and present, with her end-less lamentations.[15] This behavior has won her a wretched life in the palace and support and maternal concern from the chorus of women, who join her after her opening monologue.[16] She is dressed in rags, excluded from the family table and from marriage and children, and forced to observe her mother reveling in the fruits of adultery and celebrating her past crime. Electra's continual lamentations have so provoked Aegisthus and Clytemnestra that they confine her within as much as possible; indeed, we soon learn from Chrysothemis that Aegisthus is threatening to incarcerate her altogether on his return to the palace (378–84).

This fear is understandable, when we see the effect of Electra's words and lamentations on the chorus. Electra's prayer to the gods for help is answered by the entrance of a chorus eager to console the heroine (*paramuthion*, 130).[17] The women of the chorus share Electra's hatred of the tyrants and accept as legitimate her desire for revenge (126–27), but they think it better to leave matters to time and Zeus. They begin the scene resisting or attempting to calm Electra's extreme behavior. Yet the women soon draw closer, sharing her horror at the past crimes (193–200, echoed by Electra in 201–12), and her hopes for revenge (160–63).[18] By the conclusion of the *kommos* (shared lamentation between chorus and characters), they even agree to defer to Electra if their advice is not good (251–53). From then on, both choral odes and choral interventions are tightly linked with the action and above all with the concerns of the heroine.[19] In contrast to the crisp opening male dialogue in iambic trimeters, the intense initial exchange between Electra and the chorus is sung in lyric meters. The visual contrast is equally powerful. The young men—whose dress must be normal if they are to carry out their strategy—hope for heroic recognition. Electra's cropped hair and perhaps even her mask mark her dedication to a life of pain and lamentation for the dead.[20]

The burden of her grief is threatening to become too great even for the resistant heroine (119–20, 186). Responding to choral questioning of her ex-

---

[15] On the continuous nature of Electra's laments, see 104, 122, 141, 148, 218, and 231–32; for the extension of grief over night and day, see 92 and 259. In *Odyssey* 19.521–23 the ceaselessly lamenting Penelope compares herself to a nightingale, as Electra does here. For further parallels with Penelope, see Davidson 1988: 15. On the static and circular nature of Electra's laments, see further Woodard 1965: 196–97, Segal 1981: 265, Seaford 1985, and Kitzinger 1991: 304–5.

[16] The chorus refers to itself as mother at 234 and addresses Electra as *pai*, child (121).

[17] Gardiner 1987: 143.

[18] I agree with Gardiner 1987: 143–45 that the chorus urges moderation here (*ta metria*, 140, see also 177; avoidance of *perissa*, 155), above all to keep Electra from endangering herself and a cause that they support in principle.

[19] Segal 1966: 544. Ierulli 1993 and Harder 1995: 26–27 both stress the chorus' gradual conversion to Electra's point of view.

[20] See Seale 1980: 59 and Winnington-Ingram 1980: 230 n. 45, who thinks that Electra's mask remains sorrowful to the end, and thus undercuts the "happy" ending.

cessive behavior, Electra is quite aware of the ambivalent moral position in which she finds herself.[21] If she does not lament and the murderers do not pay the penalty for their crime, she will betray *aidōs* (shame or reverence) and *eusebeia* (piety) and her noble birth (245–50, 257; see the choral confirmation of Electra's *eusebeia* at 464). Yet her piety toward her father has required perverted behavior toward her mother.[22] Electra is ashamed (*aischunomai*, 254; see also 606–7, 616) that she has been forced (256, 620) to do such terrible things (*deina*, 221, 223; *kaka*, 308–9, *aischra*, 621; *aikōs*, 216); she knows that her disposition is extreme (222), that her behavior could be interpreted as mad (*aluein*, 135; for *atē*, see 215, 224, 235), and that she betrays with her aggressive behavior the quintessential female virtue of *sōphrosunē* (self-control, chastity, discretion).[23] In such circumstances it is not possible to be self-controlled or pious (*sōphronein* or *eusebein*, 307–8; see also the ironic *phronein kakōs*, 345); piety toward a mother who is an unjust murderess and unmaternal to her children cannot take precedence over piety to her father. From a spatial point of view, the action increasingly forces Electra to come and stay outside—where women and, above all, unmarried virgins do not belong—to pursue her cause (see 516).[24] In contrast to Orestes, who aims with a precise plan at the *kairos*, for Electra timely wisdom (*phronounti kairia*, 228) is hard to formulate. From her mother's perspective, Electra has shamed her *philoi* (close relatives, 518) and committed *hubris* (violence) in speech (522, 613); she drinks her mother's life blood like a Fury (785–86).

In the following scene, we learn that Chrysothemis has responded differently to her female inability to exact revenge with her own hands.[25] She accepts the justice of Electra's position (333–34, 338), but thinks that her response is not sensible (*phronein*, 394; *aboulia*, 398, 429). Good sense entails collaboration and self-protection, a pursuit of material comfort and an avoidance of suffering.[26] She herself wishes paradoxically to win freedom by obeying those in power (339–40). This does not suit Electra's character (*tropous*, 397). In Electra's view, Chrysothemis forgets their father and cares for her mother (341–42); she does not think for herself (344). She hates in words, but lives with her killers and betrays her friends (357–58). In a remarkable redefinition of the term, Electra argues (365) that if Chrysothemis were *sōphrōn*, she would not

---

[21] This does not mean that Electra doubts the need for revenge, which supersedes any hesitations she may have about murdering and castigating her mother. See Alexanderson 1966: 98.

[22] Blundell 1989: 170 and Segal 1966: 499–500.

[23] Aeschylus' Electra prays to be *sōphronesteron polu* than her mother (*Choephoroi* 140); she also has doubts about whether to take revenge on Clytemnestra (see Winnington-Ingram 1980: 239–40), as the chorus does not. Similarly, his Orestes acts out of fear of the oracle ("even if I lack belief the deed must be done," 298) and later hesitates to kill his mother.

[24] Goldhill 1994: 354.

[25] See further Blundell 1989: 161 and Kirkwood 1958: 102 and 240, for whom this scene expresses a conflict between justice and expediency.

[26] See Kirkwood 1958: 240.

want the *timē* (status, 364) that she has. *Sōphrosunē* is in this speech no longer a matter of female discretion, self-control, and obedience to her guardians, but of an active piety, courage, and even self-respect (the chorus echoes her at 465, *sōphronēseis*).[27] Despite her female inability to act except in words, Electra sees herself as avenging her father (*timōroumenēs*, 349; *timōroumenoi*, 399). Not to do so would demonstrate cowardice and betrayal (351, 367–68). Clearly, Electra's position has pushed her beyond the boundaries of the submissiveness normally expected of females to the point that she comes close to defining female virtue as entailing independent thought and activity rather than obedience. In this way she prepares the audience for her later adoption of a plan of action once she believes that Orestes is dead. As she did earlier with the chorus, Electra in this scene ultimately wins her sister to a temporary and partial acceptance of her view of things. She sends Chrysothemis to Agamemnon's tomb to make prayers and offerings on their own behalf, not to follow Clytemnestra's commands.

In these early scenes, Electra practices through her aggressive lamentation what I shall call an ethics of vendetta.[28] Lamentation has a particular function to play in the jural system of cultures that practice feuds or vendetta justice; it aims to provoke revenge through the awakening of shared pain, through the blurring of boundaries between past and present injustice, between the living and the dead. In a fashion traditional to the function of lamentation both in ancient and modern Greek culture, Electra keeps alive the cause of the dead Agamemnon, awakens the citizens' longing for the return of Orestes,[29] and makes them witnesses to her own view of the past. The women of the chorus are significantly called *politides*, female citizens (1227); when Electra stirs them to lament, she violates contemporary Athenian strictures against women lamenting with nonkin.[30] Like a Fury, she tortures Clytemnestra, making her fearful and defensive. Her verbal control of the stage increases throughout the first half of the play; Clytemnestra is afraid, for example, to pray openly to Apollo.[31] Electra's stance can only result in completed revenge when the male avenger responds to her words; but in the meantime, she persuades the chorus to join at least partially in her lament, she stirs the timid Chrysothemis to undertake an important religious mission, and she successfully puts her mother "on trial" for her crime.[32] In this *agōn* (debate), she deflates Clytemnestra's

[27] North 1966: 55 and Blundell 1989: 159.

[28] For Woodard 1964: 180, lamentation and rebuke make up Electra's ethos.

[29] As Gardiner 1987: 163 argues, a chorus of female citizens symbolizes "the spirit of the nation without implying any actual participation of women in the political realm of the state."

[30] For further discussion, see Foley 1993 and part I. Note, however, that Sophocles' chorus consists of local women, not foreign slaves as in Aeschylus. On the civic status of the chorus, see Ierulli 1993: 218 and Harder 1995: 24.

[31] On Electra's control of the stage here, see Seale 1980: 63.

[32] See Woodard 1964: 181, who goes so far as to say that the "persuasive force of her arguments contains her moral supremacy."

claim to justice (*ou dikē(i)*, 561) by demonstrating that her mother's real motive for killing Agamemnon was not Iphigeneia but her lover Aegisthus; Clytemnestra's later unmaternal behavior to her children further confirms this point.[33]

Lamentation is traditionally performed as an antiphonal dialogue between single lamenters and a chorus of other lamenting women. This is the case whether we are speaking of Greek tragedy and epic or the modern Greek village. As modern studies of rural Greece by Seremetakis and others have shown, lament thus creates social unity through the force of shared emotion, shared moral inference, and shared memory.[34] Lament facilitates the "production/reception of jural discourse, and . . . the cultural construction of truth."[35] It helps to create a collective oral history, a narrative tradition.[36] Lamentation also serves as a form of sociopolitical resistance[37] and organizes the relation of women to male-dominated institutions.[38] Among the Mani in the southern Peloponnesus, for example, there are "two kin-based institutions that assumed those political-legal functions currently assumed by the state: the *yerondikí*, the all-male council, and the *kláma*, the women's mourning ceremony."[39] The two institutions can both complement and oppose each other. The male council has a formal legitimacy, and the kláma has indirect political and jural power, but it is also more ritualized and public, since the men are often forced to seek justice by guile.[40] The same jural and political issues are confronted by both institutions: revenge code killings, inheritance, marital relations, and kin obligations. But they are subject to "different valuation."[41] "In Maniat society, men traditionally manage violence through physical action. Women, in contrast, manage violence with language and sound. Men do display violence linguistically, but their verbal power is dependent on the capacity to perform physical violence. Women's acoustic-linguistic violence has no external authorizing referent," except perhaps the dead themselves. Yet the laments of women can "kill a person with language (*lóyia*)."[42]

In the modern context, women's lamentations provoke complex and ambivalent reactions. On the one hand, these lamentations have no formal legitimacy and can express views that counter dominant cultural ideologies.

[33] She also asserts that Agamemnon had no choice about killing Iphigeneia, since the fleet could neither remain at Aulis nor leave unless the sacrifice was performed.

[34] Seremetakis 1991: 4–5.

[35] Seremetakis 1991: 100, 4–5, 120.

[36] Seremetakis 1991: 105, 120.

[37] Seremetakis 1991: 4.

[38] Seremetakis 1991: 100.

[39] Seremetakis 1991: 126.

[40] Ibid. Unmarried men are generally made responsible for carrying out the revenge (38–39).

[41] Seremetakis 1991: 126.

[42] Seremetakis 118. On women's role in generating male revenge through lament, see also Vlavianos 1924: 63 and Tetzlaff 1965: 153.

They often marginalize men, who can be relegated to the periphery of a group of mourning women; here men maintain an inhibited silence or speak "rationally," whereas the women "scream the dead."[43] Yet men can also admire, critically appraise, and even (as in the case of Greek tragedy) appropriate lament.[44] This grudging fascination may in part result from the fact that lament often demonstrates women's dependence on men for status and freedom and can directly serve a patriarchal agenda. Above all, in cases of feud, women's loyalty tends to rest with their natal families, especially their brothers. Women can provoke revenge among resisting men (here invective plays a role)[45] and raise children to undertake revenge on murdered kin. Because they normally neither perform the killings nor are objects of vendetta themselves, women retain a freedom of speech not permitted to the men who exact revenge.[46] They can keep a clan group functioning, whereas men have to go into hiding or exile.

In Sophocles' play, Electra has attempted to play a role similar to that played by women in the modern context. Her status too, depends on a dead father and brother. After acting as mother to Orestes (1143–48), she sent him off to exile with the pedagogue and has kept in continual touch with him, stirring him to return and take revenge (319–22). Despite her resistant behavior, Electra has up to the play's opening been permitted the freedom of speech necessary to keep Orestes' and her father's cause alive among those outside the palace. She, not Orestes, has whenever possible engaged in a public struggle to keep a silenced community united against the usurpers.

Although modern anthropological evidence often proves anachronistic in the case of ancient texts, I shall argue here that the close similarity to Aeschylus' and Sophocles' representation of vendetta in the Orestes myth and the exceptional continuity in traditions concerning death ritual and lamentation in Greece can make this later evidence illuminating. Most important, it is difficult to make sense of these aspects of Greek tragedy without assuming that the original audience brought to the plays not only contemporary experience of lamentation and death ritual but a cultural memory (one that Athenians themselves clearly believed to be genuine) of those aspects of the tradition that had been curtailed by law. In the Odyssey, the hero takes a justified revenge with continuous divine support from Athena. The relatives of the slain suitors in Odyssey 24.433–35 fear dishonor if they do not immediately take action on behalf of their relatives. In the same book, the shades of the dead suitors also think (mistakenly) that Penelope has been a conscious coconspirator in

---

[43] Seremetakis 100, 11, and 167. The pain expressed in lament opens the group to the outside in a fashion not permitted elsewhere (116).

[44] The church disapproves yet tolerates lament (Caraveli 1986 and Alexiou 1974); for literary appropriations, especially Ritsos' famous *Epitaphios*, see Holst-Warhaft 1992: ch. 6.

[45] Seremetakis 1991: 39.

[46] For exceptions, see ibid.

Odysseus' revenge.[47] Although even in Homer there are alternatives to re-solving quarrels by self-help justice, it is clear, as Anne Burnett argues, that the civic community's power to punish is "a borrowed version of each man's in-grained right to retaliate" and that revenge is "an honorable imperative essen-tial to the preservation of order."[48] Even the anger that provokes revenge can, according to Aristotle, align suitably with reason, honor, and justice.[49] The popularity of revenge in tragedy must be evaluated from this perspective.

The ideologies of revenge developed in *Electra* were still operative in con-temporary Attic contexts, moreover, although almost exclusively exercised in and not outside of the lawcourts.[50] Plaintiffs frequently use words denoting re-venge to describe the result that they wish to achieve against their opponents. To give one example particularly relevant to the situation in this play, Lysias' *Against Agoratus* (39–42) tells the story of a group of condemned men who sent for their female relatives or wives in prison. One, Dionysodorus, sent for his wife. He had charged his brother and brother-in-law with executing vengeance on Agoratus, whom he held responsible for his death. Yet he also charged his wife, whom he believed to be pregnant, with raising a male child, if she bore one, to avenge his father. The anthropologist Renato Rosaldo has shown that although headhunting by the Ilongot tribes was over a period of time finally fully outlawed by the Philippine government, they remained obsessed with keeping the tradition and its songs and stories alive—in part because they were not fully satisfied with the new ways of defining the achievement of man-hood.[51] In the agonistic and competitive society of classical Athens, cultural memories of feud and revenge would logically have been both attractive and productive of ambivalence. Permitting women a major role in dramatic vendetta may well have served to reinforce that ambivalence for the audience, and explains why the cultural memory preserved and elaborated their now-outlawed roles.

In tragedy we see this kind of traditional vendetta justice operating in the initial scenes of Aeschylus' *Choephoroi*, where Aeschylus wishes to represent Greek culture prior to the institution of trial by jury. Aeschylus' play opens with the exiled Orestes making a furtive offering at the tomb of his father. He pro-

[47] See Burnett 1998: 38–42 on Odysseus' revenge in the *Odyssey*.

[48] Burnett 1998: 64 and 6.

[49] Burnett 1998: 8; see also xvi–xvii and 33.

[50] For historical evidence, see Bowra 1944: 219–22 and 259 and Burnett 1998: 52–56 and the important recent discussions of Herman 1993, 1994, and 1995, Cohen 1995, and Allen 2000. On the duties to take vengeance for those murdered, see esp. Demosthenes 47.72, Antiphon 1.2–4, 21–22, and Plato, *Laws* 9.871a–c. Demosthenes 23.74, however, says justifiable homicides were tried in the Delphinium because Orestes' acquittal by the gods had shown that murder could be just. Charges to take revenge (in war) are also given in myth; at the end of Euripides' *Suppliants*, for example, Athena charges the sons of the seven murdered champions at Thebes to avenge their fathers when they reach adulthood.

[51] Rosaldo 1980.

nounces a prayer to Hermes, appeals to his father's ghost, and regrets that he was not able to participate in his burial; yet, unlike Sophocles' Orestes, he will soon assuage that loss with lament. Dressed in black, Electra and the chorus of women enter to perform libations at the tomb. Just as Orestes is instructed in Sophocles' play by the pedagogue, the youthful Electra is instructed by the older women of the chorus (85–164), who are characterized from the first as eternal lamenters (24–31, esp. 26, *di'aiōnos*; also 81–83).[52] The chorus urges Electra to use libations and prayer to summon gods and her father to accomplish the necessary revenge on the murderers of Agamemnon. After a recognition between Electra and Orestes, the young men join in prayer and lament with the women. In contrast to Sophocles' play, both male and females join in the lyric. The scene stresses the similarity between brother and sister, not gender differences; brother and sister have the same hair and feet, and presumably similar masks as well, if Orestes is still beardless. The chorus stirs the children to express pain, anger, and loss in their lamentation (275, Orestes is *tauroumenon*, made bull-like, by the loss of his status and possessions; 299–301, 348–49). Electra and the chorus urge Orestes to act (512–13) by recalling the perverted burial of Agamemnon and the servile life that Electra has been forced to live in the palace (418–19, 429–33, 439–50, 491–95).[53]

According to Seremetakis, in the modern contexts, hearing and seeing "do not have the *passive* or purely receptive implications that" such terms have in English, but imply "an *active* role in the production of juridical discourse. . . . The act of hearing carries the value of the soloist's discourse. Hearing in the antiphonic relation is not external to speech but metonymical to it. *Hearing is the doubling of the other's discourse.*"[54] Similarly, in *Choephoroi* the words of the women pierce Orestes' ear like an arrow (380–81; see also 451–52). When the entire *kommos* is over, Orestes turns to action, the deceptive plan authorized by Apollo that will be necessary to accomplish the revenge (555–84). From then on, the chorus actively assists in the revenge by directing the nurse to tell Aegisthus to return to the palace alone (770–82) and by deceiving Aegisthus (848–50). In short, as can be the case in rural Greece today, Aeschylus' men and women act in concert to achieve revenge. The lamenting women take the lead in creating shared memory and social and familial unity, in stirring or confirming the courage and desire to act, and in linking the worlds of the dead and the living through ritual; the men then use deception to perform the deed, with the verbal assistance of the women, who can openly deceive because they are not by cultural standards normally expected to take violent action themselves.

---

[52] On the teacher-pupil relation among lamenters in the modern context, see Holst-Warhaft 1992: 72.

[53] The exact distribution of lines in this scene remains uncertain. See Garvie 1986.

[54] See Seremetakis 1991: 104. Perhaps tragic lament also doubles its discourse in the mind of its audience.

Sophocles' play also represents a world in which vendetta serves as the only system of justice. Yet whereas the chorus in *Choephoroi* acts in concert with both children and takes the lead in fomenting the revenge, the Sophoclean chorus initially tries to calm Electra, to divert her from immoderate lamentation and anger. Despite its desire for revenge and for Orestes' return, the chorus is only gradually and reluctantly drawn into active participation in Electra's grief and resistance. Although this attempt by the chorus to calm the mourner's grief is conventional in both ancient and modern lamentation,[55] the play stresses the problematic side of Electra's obsessive grieving. In the chorus' view, prayers to Agamemnon's ghost are useless (137–39), and Electra's grief is only destroying the heroine herself (141). As we saw earlier, the authority of lamentation depends on the vitality of the dead and the past in the minds of the performers.[56] Whereas lamentation traditionally helps the mourner to reorder her life, and to transfer her pain to a group, to an object of blame, or even to a landscape outside herself, Electra is trapped in unending lamentation (123) and liminality, unable to exact revenge for her father or to perform her social duty and desire to marry and produce children.[57] In her isolation she lacks "the strength to balance the counterweight of sorrow" (119–20). What is ordinarily a temporary identification with the dead has become for Electra a living death.[58]

In Sophocles' play, Electra begins her lament alone. The anomalous position of the heroine's lament is made striking, not only because Orestes turns away from her lament and his Aeschylean role at the end of the prologue, but because a lyric solo by a major character between prologue and the entrance of the chorus is unusual in Greek drama.[59] Something similar can happen in modern contexts, when a dead person lacks a sufficient number of relatives and friends to receive a proper lamentation. Seremetakis cites the case of a Maniat niece who exhausted herself mourning her aunt alone for seven hours in order

---

[55] In the modern context, another singer or the chorus will take over to reintegrate the mourner into a supportive and caring group and rescue her from self-inflicted violence. The intervention is often made at a lower pitch, and can sound somewhat like a lullaby (Serematakis 1991: 119; see also Holst-Warhaft 1992: 29). Male onlookers can also intervene to revive overwhelmed mourners (Serematakis 1991: 111). A tragic chorus will typically attempt to reintegrate mourners gently into normal existence by reminding them that they are not the only ones to have lost loved ones, that one must set a limit to grief, etc. See the choral response to Electra's lament over the report of Orestes' death and the urn supposedly containing Orestes' ashes (860, 1171–73), or the choral response to Admetus in Euripides' *Alcestis* (416–19, 890–94, 903–11, 931–34; see also part IV).

[56] Notice that when Chrysothemis invokes the dead Agamemnon's presence on her return from his tomb, Electra, who now thinks that Orestes is dead, loses her earlier faith in the power of the dead (883–84; see the chorus' earlier skepticism at 137–39).

[57] Seaford 1985 stresses Electra's liminality (319) and her inability to be detached from identification with the dead and reintegrated into the life of the living, due to Clytemnestra's monthly insults to Agamemnon (316–18). See also Holst-Warhaft 1992: 73.

[58] Segal 1966.

[59] Seale 1980: 59.

to protect the dead woman from a "silent death."[60] As the play evolves, however, the chorus begins to share the heroine's grief and enters into an active conspiracy with Electra, inquiring after Orestes and urging Chrysothemis to adopt her sister's plan at Agamemnon's tomb; it participates in two more *kommoi* with Electra, one after the pedagogue's announcement of Orestes' death, and one during the murder of Clytemnestra. It bravely regrets in Clytemnestra's presence the downfall of the house (764–65). It celebrates Electra's plan to undertake the revenge once she believes Orestes is dead. Electra may even remain onstage to hear the final words of the chorus, which mark the release of the house from suffering.[61] The play reconstitutes for the isolated Electra a chorus that, despite occasional criticisms and calls to moderation, hears and responds to her lament in a traditional fashion and becomes fully identified with the heroine.[62] In the modern context, one might say that a *kláma* had been constituted.

In Aeschlyus' *Choephoroi*, female lamentation works in conjunction with male action and a deceptive strategy legitimized by the authority of Apollo. Only in *Eumenides* is justice or revenge taken out of the realm of vendetta, in which both male and female have played their prescribed roles, and put into the hands of the all-male jury. In this trilogy, the unity of male and female serves to legitimize Orestes' matricide and to prepare for the final compromise where a separate role is established for the female deities, the Eumenides, in cult.[63] By contrast, in Sophocles' play the ethics of female lamentation and male action are not (at least initially) represented as complementary aspects of the system of justice but as potentially in conflict; Orestes looks only to men (and Apollo) to form and achieve his goals.[64] Elements that productively united male and female in Aeschylus are repeatedly frustrated. In Aeschylus' play the chorus and Electra offer Clytemnestra's dream for interpretation to Orestes; in Sophocles' play Electra is unable to offer the good omen (of male fertility) to Orestes. Both Electra and the chorus accept the dream as a positive portent, yet it goes uninterpreted except by the audience. The lock of Orestes' hair and the libations on the tomb of Agamemnon do not lead as in Aeschylus to a recognition. Most important, when the recognition between brother and sister finally occurs, Orestes tries to silence Electra. In both the first scene and after the recognition, success requires delay and cutting short hearing his sister's words and pain. Orestes draws back from hearing about the evils perpetrated by Clytemnestra and Aegisthus that played an important role in Aeschylus' *kommos* (1288–91); the need to take immediate action (*kairos*, 1292) overrides all.

---

[60] Seremetakis 1991: 101.

[61] Segal 1981: 250, on the other hand, thinks she follows her brother after a brief delay into the darkening house.

[62] Here I tend to agree with Gardiner 1987: esp. 146–47, 151–52, and 154.

[63] The Erinyes have no place in court, but they remain supportive of the formal jural system.

[64] This means that the women no longer share Orestes' direct claim to divine authority.

The contrast with the system of vendetta justice represented in Aeschylus and with Aeschylus' own play seems deliberate. Indeed, Sophocles' text seems to draw attention to its refusal to follow the Aeschylean pattern.[65] At the same time, from a contemporary Athenian perspective, Sophocles' choice to complicate and problematize the role played by female lamentation and invective in vendetta reflects a contemporary trend in tragedy. In part I, I argue that plays in the later years of the fifth century often undercut or question tragic women who lament in ways that were deliberately curtailed by Athenian funerary legislation that began as early as the sixth century. Sophocles' play frees Orestes' act from the ambiguous associations (including with vendetta) that female lamentation had developed for the fifth-century audience. Orestes thus appears, to use the words of the text, as a purifier (*kathartēs*, 70), stripped, unlike Homer's avenging Odysseus or Aeschylus' Orestes, of emotion and explicit ethical ambiguity. He never, as in Aeschylus, debates over killing his mother. Clytemnestra's final appeal from within the palace for pity from her son meets with silence (1410–11), rather than, as in Aeschylus, momentary paralysis and consternation. Orestes uses military language designed for attacks on enemies unselfconsciously against those who are also relatives. Here, as in the *Odyssey* and in Aeschylus' *Choephoroi*, lying and deception are authorized by divinity and serve in an apparently unexamined fashion the positive cause of restoring the social order.[66] The delay in the recognition between Orestes and Electra in Sophocles' play makes the need for action increasingly compelling.[67] Yet in both *Choephoroi* and in Homer, grief, anger, and memory play a critical role in stirring men to enact revenge and in making it possible; Penelope's lamenta-

[65] Many critics have noted probable references to Aeschylus in the play. The delay and curtailment of the recognition, Orestes' resistance to listening to Electra lament and past family crimes both initially and after the recognition acquire more dramatic force from the implicit contrast. Euripides' nearly contemporary plays *Electra* and *Orestes* come close to parody in their explicit citation of Aeschylus. Hence, contrary to some critics (see esp. Stevens 1978: 112), I think both poets assumed knowledge of Aeschylus in at least part of their audience, probably because of a recent revival. Nevertheless, the audience would not need to be familiar with Aeschylus' play to respond to Sophocles' different treatment of gender roles in vendetta, which is presumably based on cultural tradition.

[66] Vidal-Naquet 1981a: esp. 160–61 and more generally 1986: part II have explained Orestes' use of deception as behavior to be expected in ephebes that would not be tolerated in an adult warrior. A number of critics have argued that the Sophocles who produced the *Philoctetes* would not have meant Orestes' use of deception and willingness to lie on oath as admirable behavior (Schein 1982: 71, Segal 1966: 475, and Blundell 1989: 173); Clytemnestra and Aegisthus are condemned for their use of *dolos* (124, 197, 279: see Horsley 1980: 21). Yet *Philoctetes* does not involve a case of vendetta; Apollo mandates Orestes' use of deception in both Aeschylus' and Sophocles' plays; and deception is a standard and indeed necessary part of revenge plots, because circumstances, in both the ancient and modern contexts, do not permit an open use of force. See further Davidson 1988: 51 on the *Odyssey* and its appropriation by Sophocles. On the further complication of Orestes' willingness to lie under oath, see Blundell 1989: 173 n. 83, Segal 1966: 483, and Sheppard 1927a: 5.

[67] Woodard 1964 repeatedly stresses this point.

tion and her other attempts to keep Odysseus' memory alive, for example, make a critical contribution to the epic (see esp. *Odyssey* 24.195).[68] The question remains whether both Orestes' refusal to allow emotion or lament to play the same kind of significant role in his revenge (unusual by the standards of epic and Aeschylus) and the unnecessary pain that his deception causes Electra[69] require his audience to respond critically to what is largely a remarkably uncomplicated enactment of a standard male role in vendetta.

Critics have identified as central to an interpretation of *Electra* a contrast between the "rational" and pragmatic Orestes, representative of action, and the emotional, intuitive, even (self-consciously) irrational Electra, representative of *logos* detached from the performance of a physical deed of violence.[70] Despite Electra's insistence that she has chosen, in contrast to Chrysothemis, not to act in a typically feminine fashion, and that her nature suited her to take direct action from the start (1023), her expressive mode of behavior is often categorized as simply "feminine."[71] I hope that I have shown that this contrast between Electra and Orestes is best understood and evaluated within the economy of an ethics of vendetta, however.[72] Both Electra and Orestes are socially

[68] For examples, see Davidson 1988: 54. Although Odysseus too does not entrust Penelope with a direct role in the revenge by delaying his recognition with her and refuses to show that he is moved by her tears, her plan to create the contest with the bow makes it possible.

[69] See esp. Kells 1973: 10, Segal 1981: 273, and Schein 1982: 73. Orestes does not expect that pain would result from his deception (*lupei*, 59; see 822, 1170). Orestes does, of course, respond to Electra's grief; but rather than motivate him to act directly, it temporarily distracts him from action.

[70] On the relation between *logos* and *ergon* in the play, see esp. Woodard 1964 and Minadeo 1967. In Woodard's extensive argument, Sophocles dramatizes certain large issues through the duality expressed by Orestes and Electra. The play moves dialectically toward a unity between *logos* and *ergon* in the reunion of Electra and Orestes. Male and female are in his view unnaturally separated in the play (1965: 218). Electra comes to recognize the need for action and breaks out from her subjective world through Orestes (169). Her passion and hate serve the action (170). Orestes recognizes the inadequacy of his reasonable point of view; he feels pity and gives up his deception. Justice is meaningless without *logos* (1965: 218), and the revenge is held back "until . . . proven emotionally" (1965: 217). Minadeo 1967 thinks the play contrasts the rational and the irrational (120) and the *logos* of Apollo with the *ergon* of men. Along similar lines, Reinhardt 1979 sees a contrast between emotion and action (137–39). Minadeo 1967: 119–122, Segal 1966: 532, and Kitzinger 1991: 304–5 n. 23 criticize and modify Woodard. Kitzinger points out that Electra views speech as action (see also Blundell 1989: 157; yet see Woodard 1964: 178 and 181); in her view there is no concluding unity of speech and action, only speech as action and action without speech. Electra understands the need for action from the start. Segal 1966: 532 argues that *logos* in the service of *ergon* degenerates, deceives, and causes pain as the play evolves.

[71] E.g., Segal 1966: 539 sees Electra's passion (in contrast to Orestes' adherence to principle and justice in the abstract) as "deeply feminine" and hence suspect in Greek eyes. Woodard 1964: 165–67 and 198 develops a contrast between the emotional, intuitive, unambitious, private, and imaginative Electra and the calculating, rational, publicly oriented, materialistic, and analytic Orestes; these personalities are in his view typical of their respective sexes.

[72] Here I also disagree, for example, with psychological interpretations that view Electra as traumatized (e.g., Linforth 1963: 116).

constructed as characters in a clearly identifiable tradition. In the case of lament, words and body, emotion and principle, speak as one.[73] Lament is tactile; the lamenter touches the body of the dead—or, as later in this play, the urn supposedly containing the ashes and bones—and inflicts pain on herself. Lamentation actively seeks justice through pain and the creation of shared values and memories; it aims quite consciously to arouse anger, even hatred. What makes Sophocles' Electra extreme is not the form and content of her ethical stance, but the ferocity with which she pursues her goals under duress and her ability to endure continually the pain that a lamenter must express to fulfill her function; her partially self-imposed isolation from a fragmented and oppressed community; and the situation in which she finds herself, where she must live with, pour invective on, and desire to take revenge on murderers who include her own kin. To the degree that the heroine's pain and language become futile in *Electra* (in contrast to *Choephoroi*), it is because the play makes lamentation and the whole female role in vendetta irrelevant to, and even a possible impediment to, Orestes' success.[74]

In the early scenes with the chorus, Chrysothemis and Clytemnestra put Electra's resolve to resist to the test. The lack of overt action permits us to examine and consider her position in detail. Electra's moral dilemma changes, however, when she thinks that Orestes is dead. There is now no male family member to take revenge for Agamemnon. First, Electra determines never to return to her life within the house (817–19). Then she proposes to Chrysothemis that they kill Aegisthus themselves.[75] The sisters will act to win feminine goals: marriage, wealth, and children (958–72). Yet Electra also expects a recognition normally accorded to male heroes. She and Chrysothemis will acquire *logōn . . . eukleian* (a heroic reputation, 973). Who of the townspeople and resident aliens (*astōn* and *xenōn*), she asks, won't greet the sisters with

---

[73] See further Seremetakis 1991: 121.

[74] Many critics see Electra's speech as sterile or futile, unable to accomplish decisions or actions (Minadeo 1967: 121 and 123 and Segal 1981: 250 and 274); Gellie 1972: 108 and 117 contrasts words for the sake of action and words for words' sake. Swart 1984: 27 thinks that Electra's verbal defeat of Clytemnestra makes the need for action more urgent.

[75] Electra only mentions killing Aegisthus, not her mother, in this speech, and the audience has no reason not to take her at her word. After what she has said earlier about the shame produced in her by her hostile relation to her mother, she could hardly represent the killing of her mother as glorious. Gellie 1972: 119 (see also Linforth 1963: 103) explains Electra's silence on Clytemnestra by arguing that killing Aegisthus is the difficult and therefore heroic task; Clytemnestra is an easy victim. It gives Electra a chance to show reckless courage (Alexanderson 1966: 88). Moreover, women are not usually the object of vendetta (although Clytemnestra's collaboration with Aegisthus has put her in this anomalous position). Gardiner 1987: 165 argues that the mention of Aegisthus sets up conflict between personal danger and self-preservation, whereas mentioning Clytemnestra would raise a moral issue. Others interpret Electra's silence on her mother as part of a ruse to win over Chrysothemis or as an unwillingness to face the horror of matricide (Kirkwood 1942: 90, Letters 1953: 259, and Johansen 1964: 21).

praise when they see them, relatives who saved their paternal household and did not spare their lives to slaughter well-placed enemies (975–80)? She claims that people will treat them as *philoi* (friends or relatives), reverence them (*philein, sebein,* 981), and honor them with feasts. The whole city will respect their *andreia* (courage suited to a man, 982–83). The sisters must work with their dead father and brother (986–87). For the well born, she argues, it is *aischron* (shameful) to live *aischrōs* (shamefully, 989).

Both the chorus and Chrysothemis question Electra's proposal. The plan is unlikely to work; this is a case for forethought (*promēthia,* 990, 1036, *pronoia,* 1015). "You are a woman, not a man, less strong in hand than your enemies," says Chrysothemis (997–98; see also 1014).[76] It won't help, she argues, to free us to win a noble reputation and to die ignobly (1005–6). Do not destroy us and wipe out our whole *genos* (clan, 1009–10). Chrysothemis finally does not deny the justice of Electra's position, but she departs from the play refusing to pursue a justice that brings harm (1042). The chorus, on the other hand, after attempting to restrain Electra, closes the scene with an ode that praises Electra's heroic sacrifice. For her choice to revere her father, to live a life of lament and solitude, she should be pronounced *eupatris* (1081, well fathered), the wise and best child who risks death to destroy a double Erinys (1074–89). The chorus prays that Electra will live superior to her enemies, in power (*cheiri*) and in wealth (1090–92), "in regard to the laws which originated as greatest, here winning the first prize by reason of your pious devotion to Zeus" (1095–97, Kells' literal translation [1973]). Critics have tended to side with Chrysothemis in this scene. Electra's stance here is in their view extreme, foolish, unfeminine, and futile; it is fortunate that Orestes' return precludes further folly.[77] This interpretation does not give sufficient weight to the remarkable shift in choral attitude from doubt to the highest praise for the heroine's choice.

In my view, this scene is once again best interpreted in terms of the ethics of vendetta and lamentation that have characterized Electra from the start. It seems not unlikely that in classical Attica, as in the modern rural Mediterranean, it was popularly perceived to be the function of a surviving daughter (at least in myth and in the cultural imagination if no longer in reality) to act in the absence of all supporting male relatives and the possibility for future ones (another brother).[78] The modern cases most frequently concern revenge, and here the daughter may choose to take on symbolically the characteristics of a

---

[76] Jones 1962: 145 and Dover 1974: 100 also stress the anomaly of Electra's decision as a woman here. Segal 1981: 254 and 259 thinks there is a role reversal for both sexes. Orestes ends by going into the house while Electra waits without; he "battles with women," like Aegisthus (302).

[77] See Woodard 1964: 189 or Gellie 1972: 120, who thinks that Electra is "riding on a cloud of words again" and has no concrete plan of action.

[78] De Wet 1977: 29 also views Electra's choice as a matter of duty, arguing (36) that during the Peloponnesian War many women would have been faced with making important choices without the supervision of a *kurios* or guardian. See part II on the institution of the *epiklēros*.

male member of her family and risk becoming an object of vendetta herself. To quote from a study of Corsican blood revenge:

> It is important to stress that while vendetta was both a right and an obligation for men, for women only the former was the case. Only if they wished to undergo the hazards of vendetta would they be placed at direct risk by it. In practice, however, women would become directly involved in the accomplishing of vendetta only if there were no male relatives . . . or if such male relatives declared themselves unwilling to assume responsibility for vendetta. In such cases, either the daughter, or more usually, the sister of the victim would take on the male role of realizing vengeance; having assumed this clearly male function, she would then be fully entitled to all the privileges enjoyed traditionally by males in Corsican society; that is, she would be honoured because of the restoration of clan repute achieved by her. . . . In undertaking the task of revenge she would at the same time expose herself to dangers identical to those suffered by the males. . . . Once she had committed herself to taking a direct part in vengeance procedures, she was counted by the enemy clans amongst the potential victims of vengeance, especially when there were no males remaining to her family.[79]

Gail Holst-Warhaft cites similar cases among the Mani of southern Greece. A woman named Parsaki is celebrated in a well-known Maniat lament for poisoning her husband, brother-in-law, and father-in-law in revenge for their treacherous killing of her only brother. Her parents welcome her home after the crime. "'You did well,' says her mother. 'May you eat and drink [your inheritance] with the new husband you'll find.'"[80] In another lament a mother encourages her daughter Vyeniki to avenge her murdered brother: "'Now, black Vyeniki / woman, become a man. / Buckle up and arm yourself . . . so our Ligoris will be avenged.'"[81] At the same time, in the course of the lament the mother wavers; fearing for her daughter's life, she reminds her that she is a female child. Albanian mountain women who chose to remain unmarried vir-

---

[79] Deliyanni 1985: 95–96. See III.3 and Foley 1996: 55–57 for my discussion of Antigone's choice in *Antigone* in light of this same passage. *I would like to thank Richard Seaford for giving me access to Deliyanni's manuscript, and for calling my attention to the relevance of this passage for interpreting Electra.* See also the similar conclusions of Wilson 1988: 211–23. He quotes a lament by a Corsican woman, Maria-Felice: "Of so large a family / You leave only a sister, / Without first cousins, / Poor, orphaned, and unarmed, / But to accomplish your vengeance / Rest assured that she alone suffices" (219–20). On Montenegrin women, who receive more respect than men if they undertake a revenge that is not viewed in their case as an obligation, see Boehm 1984: 46–47 and 55–56. On gender role reversals in vendetta and lamentation generally, see Seremetakis 1991: 222.

[80] Holst-Warhaft 1992: 81; see further 77–84. She notes (47) that Maniat women frequently demonstrate a stronger allegiance to blood kin than to the husband's family.

[81] Holst-Warhaft 1992: 85–86.

gins could in early-twentieth-century Albania take on the role and the privileges of their brothers, dress in male clothes and carry arms, and, in the absence of male relatives, enact revenge for their family.[82]

Electra proposes to win honor and in this case also marriage in precisely the fashion of these later sisters by taking revenge on Aegisthus when she thinks that Orestes is dead. (Note that Antigone, as discussed in the next chapter, must give up marriage to bury her brother.) By contrast, the more conventional Chrysothemis, who does not share Electra's *phusis* (nature, 1023), refuses to run the risks involved, to exercise what is for the Corsican daughter or sister a right rather than an obligation. The chorus' shift to praising Electra, once it has failed to dissuade her, reflects an attitude not dissimilar to the kind of public recognition that Haimon reports Antigone has won for her attempt to serve the gods below and the unwritten laws in burying her brother. (In *Electra*, however, only women give Electra public recognition. Orestes is not enthusiastic about the presence of the war god in women [1243–44]. On Antigone, see III.3.) Like the mother of Vyeniki, the chorus initially attempts to dissuade Electra, yet finally celebrates her heroic female action.

In an Athens that prided itself on avenging murders in the lawcourts, such cultural scenarios concerning vendetta had no doubt receded to the realm of myth and popular tradition. Yet when Electra chooses to adopt not only her brother's role but his typically masculine ambitions for public recognition, I think she is meant to be viewed as making a culturally prescribed female choice of the kind discussed in modern ethnographies.[83] And as long as we set this story of revenge in a cultural context where recourse to other forms of public justice are unavailable, Electra's choice is a noble and ethical one, which emerges logically from her earlier resistance through lament.[84] Her proposal has all the heroic simplicity of the pedagogue's imagined vision of Orestes at Delphi. (Orestes in *Choephoroi* is similarly willing to die if he succeeds in his revenge [438]). Electra thus nearly upstages Orestes as avenging hero, even if her vision of successful revenge may (as in the case of Orestes) seem overly simplistic in comparison with her earlier perception of the issues and her previous

[82] Durham [1909] 1987: 35, 57, 63, 80, and 173 and Cozzi 1910.

[83] Historical examples of autonomous actions taken by Athenian women, other than priestesses, are lacking altogether. In addition, there is no solid evidence of historical vendetta in classical Athens (see Cohen 1995 and Herman 1994 and 1995), although Thucydides' passage on the Corcyrean revolution seems to imply outbreaks of personal revenge (3.84–86), and revenge is cited as a motive for action in court cases; the passage in Plutarch's *Solon* (12) on Megacles and Cylon is probably an archaic instance (see part I). Whatever the historical reality in Athens or the modern Mediterranean, Sophocles' virgin daughters or sisters take or propose to take autonomous action only in a limited range of circumstances.

[84] In a similar vein, Whitman 1951: 167 argues that "tragic tlemosyne in reality is only arete hindered and made impotent by circumstance, but surviving in time." In his view "character, choice, and will are the action" in this play (171).

struggles. Moreover, should Electra survive,[85] her choice will allow her to fulfill her private obligations to her family, including the chance to marry and prolong the family line that is the critical obligation of all virgins, but especially
those without brothers (epiklēroi).[86] In the process, she can also win public
recognition for an act that liberates her city from tyranny (the chorus is there
to underline the public implications of her act).[87]

As Bernard Knox above all has argued, Sophocles' intransigent heroes are
similar in temperament and ambition.[88] Yet gender plays a more critical role
in defining the heroic temper than Knox allows. Both in choosing to resist the
murderers through lamentation and accepting a life of suffering and in choosing to undertake a heroic action defined in masculine terms after Orestes' supposed death, Electra acts within a set of specifically female constraints and
opportunities. Electra's late recognition of Orestes and the deception that prevents her from correctly interpreting the signs of Orestes' presence at Agamemnon's tomb give her a legitimate opportunity to demonstrate for the first time
in tragedy her own ability to make a heroic and risky choice. This choice, the
only ethical choice undertaken in the course of the drama, is particularly significant in a play that increasingly emphasizes the need for action. Even
Chrysothemis, once she has agreed to do Electra's bidding at the tomb, asserts
that in such circumstances it is not reasonable to dispute what is just, but rather
to hasten to do it (466–67).[89]

The choral celebration of Electra's choice to act and its prayer for her success are immediately followed by the entrance of the disguised Orestes.[90] The
urn distracts Electra from her heroic plan and soon makes it unnecessary. In-

[85] Kitzinger 1991: 320–22, pointing especially to the linguistic ambiguity of 984–85, suggests
that Electra is deliberately concealing from Chrysothemis the strong likelihood that her plan will
lead to death (see also Alexanderson 1966: 88, who disputes Johansen 1964: 22 on this point).
Hence her language becomes, like Orestes', a means to an end rather than a vehicle of truth (see
also Segal 1981: 284). In the scene as a whole, the risk of death comes out clearly (see 1080, 1321),
and I do not see that anyone is under any serious misapprehension. Rather, Electra affirms the
heroic potential of the inevitably risky matricide.

[86] Sorum 1982: 209–11 thinks that when tragic women act out of place and reject marriage,
they threaten family continuity. This is true, but the many celebrated sacrificial virgins in tragedy,
especially in Euripides, make clear that there were causes that, at least in fiction, arguably took
precedence over family continuity. Electra, unlike Sophocles' Antigone, has no choice to marry
in this case. On Electra as epiklēros, see now Ormand 1999: 62 and 72–75. He notes that it is in
this scene that she first expresses concern over the loss of the sisters' paternal inheritance.

[87] I agree with Juffras 1991 that Electra imagines winning the kind of recognition accorded the
Athenian tyrannicides, Harmodius and Aristogeiton. Yet one must go a step further and recognize
that noting this similarity does not fully explain a woman's adoption of this kind of traditionally
male role.

[88] Knox 1966.

[89] Chrysothemis does not accept Electra's claim that her lament and resistance are a form of
action (331).

[90] Similarly, Clytemnestra's prayer to Apollo is followed by the appearance of the pedagogue,
who apparently fulfills her wish. (See among others, Horsley 1980: 23.)

stead, she continues her role as mourner by turning to perform proper lamentation for her supposedly dead brother (1146–70).[91] Electra's lament is traditional in content: she laments for herself as well as for the dead person, assimilates herself to the state of the dead beloved, regrets her inability to give him a proper burial and the waste of her previous nurture of the dead man, recalls her past relation to Orestes, and stresses her dependence on her brother for status. Yet the lament is performed not in lyrics but almost exclusively in iambic trimeters;[92] the chorus responds in a muted fashion, simply reminding Electra that others have lost loved ones to death (1171–73); the irony of this lament over the empty urn contrasts starkly with Electra's previous role as heroic avenger. As Seremetakis remarks of Maniat lament, the presence of a solo mourner with no "help" from a chorus is "a dramatic sign of deritualization."[93]

Now abandoned even by Chrysothemis, Electra's helplessness in the face of unending pain may be expressed here even in the unlyrical form of her lament. She cannot stir others to act or share her pain, and her speech no longer has the power to terrorize. She must rely entirely on herself. Orestes, presumably for strategic reasons, permits Electra to engage in this perhaps ill-omened (since Orestes is alive) lament (1211).[94] Yet even though the authority of Electra's lament is partially undercut by her deception, her grief apparently has at first the predictably powerful effect on Orestes. He sees and knows the situation for the first time from Electra's perspective and nearly loses control over his tongue (1174–75).[95] His strategy of deception has caused pain to a *philos*, and both the present and past humiliations of Electra win pity from her brother (1199)—her ill-kept body, her lack of proper nurture and masculine defense, her ill treatment by her mother that borders on slavery, all the pains of living with the murderers of her father (1177, 1179–87, 1190–92, 1193–98). He defines her sufferings as his own (1201). Ecstatic, Electra bursts into lyric, and almost lures Orestes into her own camp, although he does not join in her song. The chorus shares Electra's emotion with tears of joy (1230–31).

Whereas Aeschylus brings Orestes and Electra together in a lament that acquires communal dimensions through the participation of the chorus, Orestes in these final scenes, despite his initial and significant moments of wavering,

[91] Here she sees herself as once again countering her mother's mockery of the dead (804–7). In fact, however, both Clytemnestra and Aegisthus plan to give Orestes a proper burial.

[92] There are a few anapests (1160–62). Gardiner 1987: 153 notes that here the ever hopeful chorus is brought to despair; "the poet dissolves the conspiracy of women, so that Electra appears deprived of all possibility of help."

[93] Seremetakis 1991: 101.

[94] Orestes intervenes once he ascertains that the chorus is trustworthy.

[95] There is considerable critical division on Orestes' response to Electra in this scene. For example, Bowra 1944: 249–50 thinks that Orestes must abandon his superficial understanding and know the true nature of his task before doing it. Woodard 1964: 190 thinks that Orestes recognizes here the inadequacy of his previous reasonable point of view. By contrast, Gellie 1972: 122 stresses what he sees as the "deadness" of Orestes' response to Electra in this scene.

struggles to detach himself from a traditional pattern of vendetta that gives free rein to the female voice and the passions generated by lament.[96] Despite her appropriately female willingness to leave the initiative to Orestes once again, Electra, unlike Aeschylus' mature chorus of women, must be repeatedly silenced in the interests of success (see 1236, 1259, 1296–97, 1322, 1353, 1364). Her lament may also be dangerously seductive to the hearer. Men wish for a proper burial by their womenfolk in tragedy (e.g., Euripides' *Iphigeneia among the Taurians* 700–705). Grief traditionally has its pleasures throughout Greek literature, and tragedy licensed its actors and choruses to perform forbidden female behavior in its scenes of lamentation. In the modern context at least, Palamas' "Death of a Brave Lad" presents the story of a dying young man whose passionate last wish is to hear his mother's full lament for himself before he dies.[97]

In Aeschylus' play the chorus from the start underlines Orestes' pleas for silence and caution (233–34, 265–67) and actively supports him in his deception. Eventually, Sophocles' Orestes and the pedagogue win Electra to their cause, and she adopts this Aeschylean role of female supporter of male intrigue. During the death of Clytemnestra, Electra first silences the chorus (1399), then joins it in a *kommos*. She pleads with Orestes, who is inside the house, to enact a death for Clytemnestra that perfectly matches the double blow she inflicted on Agamemnon: "If you have the strength, strike twice," Electra cries (1415).[98] Here she echoes the Aeschylean chorus, which looked forward to raising a triumphant cry, *ololugmos*, over the dead Aegisthus and Clytemnestra (386–89).[99] Sophocles' chorus plays a supporting role to the heroine, first heralding, then finding no fault with the revenge (1423). It warns of Aegisthus' approach, orders the men inside, and advises Electra to deceive Aegisthus with soothing words. Electra not only helps to deceive Aegisthus (1448–65) but refuses him a final chance to delay his death in speech (1483–84).[100]

---

[96] Some critics envision Electra's hope of enacting independent revenge as futile, because she is not yet schooled in the masculine strategies of action. Gellie 1972: 124 argues that Electra has no gift for action, since her feelings "swamp her brains." In his view, her return inside the palace with Orestes raises the possibility that she will participate in the crime (126); instead she returns outside to continue speaking. In fact, Electra proves effective at deception in the Aegisthus scene, although her lies express truth to those who know it. Furthermore, the chorus does not finally judge Electra on the viability of her plan, but on the heroic nobility of her choice.

[97] Holst-Warhaft 1992: 173–77.

[98] See Johansen 1964: 26 on the perfect reciprocity here. Note that Electra, unlike her mother, plays no active role in the crime.

[99] Gardiner 1987: 156–57 rightly stresses the choral complicity here. As she points out that since only nine of the twenty-four lines of the *kommos* are in lyric meters, the tone here is not particularly heightened or irrational.

[100] Electra's behavior in this final scene is often interpreted as a sign of her dehumanization. Gellie 1972: 122 and 130 argues that the tragedy of this play is not in the plot, but in the warping of Electra's capacity to feel, her loving nature. Electra, noble in the realm of *logos,* becomes immersed in the violence of *ergon*; the triumph of deceptive *logos* destroys all civilized distinctions between "loved one and enemy, man and beast, living and dead, nobility and evil." (Segal 1981:

We know from the start of the play that Electra's grief and suffering will soon be assuaged by Orestes' arrival.[101] Yet in the first half of the play this irony does not make Electra's speech less powerful. She is increasingly persuasive to the chorus and Chrysothemis; she undermines her mother's claim to have killed Agamemnon in justice. As other critics, but above all Rachel Kitzinger, have pointed out, Electra's speech in the second half of the play loses some of its authority in the eyes of the internal if not necessarily of the actual audience.[102] Once deceived by the pedagogue, her activities become increasing futile or detached from reality. Clytemnestra no longer fears Electra, and hence she cannot "kill her with language" for her crime; Chrysothemis will not share her heroic plan; Electra fruitlessly laments a brother who is not dead; and Orestes, despite his initial sympathy, sees his sister's words as uncontrolled and inopportune emotional outbursts that endanger the successful execution of the revenge.[103] By putting the traditional male and female roles in vendetta in conflict with each other, the play in a sense fragments and disrupts the coherence of the system of vendetta justice presented by Aeschylus. Female lament plays no role in motivating, directing, or compromising Orestes' action, even though it produces powerful emotions in him. Yet Orestes is forced by Electra's pain to offer his sister and the chorus a role, however limited, in what was initially planned as an all male adventure. In the public funerals of Athens, men curtailed the earlier female role in death ritual and muted private grief in favor of a celebration of masculine *kleos* in war.[104] Yet women were included in the rit-

---

285–86). Electra's cry to strike again shows "that it is to this that daughterly devotion has reduced an admirable woman" (Gellie 1972: 127). The final scene contrasts Orestes' quiet efficiency with Electra's ruthlessness, above all manifest in her desire to deprive Aegisthus of proper burial (Gellie 1972: 128). She insists on silencing Aegisthus as she herself had been silenced by Orestes (Alexanderson 1966: 94–95 counters that whereas Clytemnestra gets to defend herself, Aegisthus does not because he is guilty and a dangerous speaker). Electra's final "primitive and unreflecting" rage sacrifices in the final scenes completeness of character and subtlety and entails a loss of the play's main themes (Kirkwood 1958: 168). For a rebuttal, see esp. Gardiner 1987: 164–75. She argues that in contrast to Euripides, Sophocles shows how a woman could be involved in a revenge and not be a monster (173).

[101] On the use of tragic irony here, see Gellie 1972: 120 and Stevens 1978: 118.

[102] Kitzinger 1991: 301–2, 305, 316–17, 320, and 327 argues that Electra dominates the play up until the pedagogue's speech and is victorious in each encounter with others. After the lie, Electra must act under an illusion. It is possible that dramatic irony could nevertheless increase an audience's sympathy and respect for Electra, however.

[103] As Gardiner 1987: 156 stresses, we have been shown that this is a real threat. Many critics see Electra as silenced and marginalized in this final scene (see esp. Minadeo 1967: 118 and Kitzinger 1991: 325). Segal 1981: 253 and 257 thinks that the protagonists become isolated from each other, with a hint of a barrier between them. Ormand 1999: 77–78 argues that the play offers her no ending; she remains unmarried, childless, and literally outside the house of Agamemnon. Yet Seale 1980: 75 argues that from the perspective of the staging that Electra takes command here; Alexanderson 1966: 89 n. 76 asserts that Electra is unchanged, but liberated to show hate and joy.

[104] Note that in Sophocles' play the chorus invokes the war god as Orestes enters to kill his mother (1384–85).

ual and collectively lamented the war dead. Philosophy (especially Plato) later shut out mourning from an important ethical role altogether. Sophocles' concluding scene reluctantly includes the female; she still plays a traditional role in fomenting and celebrating revenge, but on strictly masculine terms.

Orestes' actions gain authority by creating—to the degree possible—dramatic closure.[105] Yet the play also gives Electra a powerful voice before making her the servant of Orestes' plan. No audience can depart without remembering the lamentations to which Orestes tries to close his ears, nor the chorus' open admiration for Electra and its celebration of her choice. The conclusion cannot eliminate the complex struggles represented in the central scenes of the play. Orestes' revenge is so clinical that it virtually precludes the pity and fear Aristotle expects from a tragic audience.[106] Through Electra, we witness the painful history of the house, the effort to maintain a moral integrity in a situation where, because one is a woman, one normally cannot and should not act (except, to a limited degree, through words). Living with the problems of endlessly pursuing justice in a social context that perverts all possibility for normal behavior or action, and inflicting it impersonally from without, are not the same things.[107] Electra pursues justice with a self-consciousness not displayed by Orestes,[108] who claims Apollo's authority both for the deed and his method

[105] Some elements in the final scene militate against closure—above all hints of the future sufferings of the house, or Electra's possible refusal to give Aegisthus proper burial. See notes 8 and 9. Furthermore, for many critics Orestes remains "an unrealized character," who is not a "prime mover" because he has a mentor (Gellie 1972: 106–8). For Seale 1980: 57, 66, and 77 Orestes' revenge is not heroic; his crimes are hidden in the darkness of the palace. Kells 1973: 12 labels him a Spartan and links him to the Athenian oligarchs.

[106] Whitman 1951: 155 locates tragedy in this play in the character and experience of Electra, above all in her heroic suffering and endurance; Orestes simply plays the supporting role of "dispassionate and divinely sent adjutant" or deus ex machina (171). Similarly, Segal 1966: 539 argues that through Electra the "myth rises from the level of sordid intrigue . . . to heroic action." "The artifice needs action without moral second thoughts; the tragedy is to be found in Electra's sensibilities" (Gellie 1972: 115–16). The male story involves recognition, intrigue, and practical success by "two-dimensional manipulators"; Electra's story involves a movement from hatred to love to hatred (130). Sheppard 1918: 85 (see also 88) sees Electra as self-conscious until she abandons herself to Orestes, then tragic. Seale 1980: 79 thinks that Electra gives the tragedy its meaning. Kitzinger 1991 asserts that Electra represents human justice, Orestes divine justice that can have no real meaning to humans (327). Up to the pedagogue's speech, Electra "creates an understanding of human justice as the expression of a harmony between feeling, thought, language, and action" (301). After the pedagogue's lie, her vision no longer constitutes a measure of "reality"; she becomes an object of pity and her feelings are extraneous to the action (319). She subsumes her will into Orestes and ceases to be the primary interpreter or performer of the action. Orestes cannot replace her, for action without *logos* is not human justice. The loss of Electra's speech is the heart of the tragedy (302).

[107] De Wet 1977: 27 interprets the play as about living with the powerful or tyranny.

[108] Knox 1964: 38 characterizes Electra as "the most self-analytical of all Sophoclean heroes." See further Sheppard 1918: 84–86, Bowra 1944: esp. 240–42, Johansen 1964: 13, Winnington-Ingram 1980: 225, and Blundell 1989: 170. Kirkwood 1958: 166 concludes that there is no moral issue concerning Orestes' revenge in this play; all moral questions arise in relation to Electra. She is "a soul tormented by the fullness of its knowledge of what the situation means" (167).

of acting. By contrast, Electra recognizes that her lament, invective, and desire for revenge combine piety toward her father with impiety toward her mother.

Electra and Chrysothemis not only disagree with each other on how to handle the ethical dilemma before them, but they live with Clytemnestra's own claim to justice. When Electra puts Clytemnestra on trial, the trial that we witness is not enacted in the larger, impersonal theater of the Aeschylean Areopagus, where gods act as prosecutors, support defendants, and instruct the jury of male citizens, and where Orestes' defense is based on a divine mandate. In *Electra* the trial of Clytemnestra takes place within the family and among women; character, motive, and social necessities play a major and complicating role.[109] For Electra, not even her victory in the trial can obscure her impiety toward her unmaternal mother (her violation of the nurture and filial devotion to her parent expected of any adult daughter), nor the way in which Clytemnestra's crime has begun to assimilate her daughter to the one she hates (607–9; cf. 559).[110] She feels the pain that she inflicts on the murderers;[111] she herself has become to Clytemnestra the Fury who is officially absent from this play.

Anthony Long argues that the emphasis in this *agōn* on character and motive, on the personal and particular over the appeal to general principles, is typical of early Attic oratory.[112] Yet character, motive, and particulars also play a role in court cases preserved from fourth-century Athens. The justice of Orestes' revenge is nowhere questioned in the play, and it has the authority of

[109] See further, Kitzinger 1991: 312–15. Many critics have noted that it is during the trial scene that potential contradictions in Electra's claim to justice appear. See esp. Woodard 1964: 184–86, Segal 1981: 271, and Blundell 1989: 162–73. Yet as Blundell 1989: 75 points out, "in the strictest sense the talio requires no consideration of motive."

[110] Winnington-Ingram 1980: 246. Johansen 1964 (followed by Kamerbeek 1974: 17–20) thinks that Electra's tragedy lies in her own sense of moral degradation arising from her obsessive hatred of her mother and constant scenes of recrimination, which reduce her to her mother's level. Her final deterioration of character is incurable. It is too late for Electra to escape her past (Segal 1966: 507); her victory is her tragedy (485). "There are tragedies worse than death, as even the weak Chrysothemis knew (1107–08)" (Sheppard 1927a: 9). Kells 1973: 10–11 sees her destroyed to the point of madness. Alexanderson 1966: 98 views these interpretations as anachronistic. Stevens 1978: 119 similarly argues that fifth-century Athens would have found successful revenges satisfying. As I have argued, expressing hatred and passion and urging on punishment are a traditional (see Aeschylus) part of the female role in revenge scenarios of the kind that Electra has been promoting from the start. Nevertheless, it remains difficult to evaluate this behavior in the complex context of the play as a whole and especially the final scenes. For the larger problem of evaluating revenge in Greek tragedy, see with further bibliography Saïd 1981, Mossman 1995, and Burnett 1998.

[111] Electra asserts that those who take revenge may also suffer it (580–83); it has been argued that she lives out her own assertion in advance of the deed. Electra "has made a terrible choice, and the choice has become part of her" (Gellie 1972: 130). Evil has left a deep brand on Electra; "the whole characterization of Electra shows how Clytemnestra's crime breeds its own punishment in hatred and revenge" (Bowra 1944: 260).

[112] Long 1968: 158–59.

Apollo. Yet the play asks an audience who has served on Attic (or twentieth-century) juries to confront the celebration of an impersonal revenge envisioned in terms more familiar in myth, epic, or the outlawed justice of the vendetta than in contemporary life. The role played by female lamentation and invective in vendetta is messy, personal, angry, excessive, even dangerous. The pursuit of justice is for Electra equally messy—even Orestes is finally drawn into it to some extent—and her self-consciousness must be particularly pointed in a situation where the audience has already replaced vendetta with civic justice, yet continues to share the sentiments on which the earlier system was based. Thus, however one interprets the final act of revenge, the play's central focus on the female pursuit of justice through lamentation complicates the simpler and cleaner vision of a heroic revenge exacted by Orestes and momentarily planned by Electra herself. The audience is free to hear and respond to everything that both Clytemnestra's crime and the delayed recognition and the deception inflicts on Electra, as well as the opportunities for heroic choice that it offers her. Action may lead to a restoration of social order and to material success, but perhaps it is only from the perspective of those who cannot act but only speak that we can come to understand the profoundly contradictory nature of pursuing revenge.

We cannot explain why Sophocles chose to represent the problem of Orestes' and Electra's revenge in these terms. Yet if this play was presented after the oligarchic revolution of 411 B.C.E.,[113] many Athenians must have recently experienced just this frustrating inability to act in a situation that demanded it or had recourse to self-help justice in the absence of confidence in the legal system. In the modern context, the Holocaust has taught us that it was not enough to end the Second World War with a clean and "just" victory over the patently guilty. If we do not remember those who resisted or collaborated, and the pain of those whose lives were destroyed, we will not avoid repeating those crimes. Lamentation gave the role of remembering the often inglorious details to Greek women and, by extension, to the tragedy that incorporates it, and its relation to action in this play remains problematic to the end. The same function was performed in practice by public oratory, which also raised anger and vengeful feelings in the mind of its audience and could at times stir men to intemperate political and military choices (one thinks of the punishment of the generals at Arginusae); and in court cases and on *defixiones* (curse tablets) men could indulge in their own form of "killing enemies with words." As David Cohen puts it, "one can also read the *Oresteia* as a monument not to the end of feud, but to its incorporation into the world of the polis . . . disputes of the elites are henceforth subject to the judgment of public institutions."[114] Yet in

---

[113] The date of this play is unknown. Kamerbeek 1974: 6, e.g., dates it between the mid-420s and 409, with a preference for the later date. For a later date, see also Owen 1936 and Rehrenboeck 1988. For an earlier date, see Burkert 1990.

[114] Cohen 1995: 16–17.

Electra, this brand of masculine rhetorical persuasion is relatively restrained, and Orestes apparently wins a heroic success without immediate repercussions. Instead, the heroine—perhaps as a scapegoat—plays out the full range of female roles traditional in vendetta to the audience if not to her brother; she pays a great price to give the revenge emotional authority. In this play the female lamenting voice is restrained, brutalized (inadvertently by Orestes, and by the play deliberately), questioned, partially undercut, put in its place, but nevertheless takes on itself the role of articulating and engaging the audience in the complex ethics of lamentation and vendetta.

III.3

Sacrificial Virgins: Antigone as Moral Agent

IN THE preceding chapter on Sophocles' *Electra*, I explored the implications of the ethical differences represented in the stances of Orestes and Electra in the context of roles and traditions relating to vendetta. As son and virgin daughter excluded from their proper inheritance by an unjust tyranny, however, neither character faces a serious question of divided allegiance in their quest to avenge their father, Agamemnon. By contrast, the situation faced by both Antigone and Creon apparently requires a choice between important responsibilities. In a fashion comparable with Euripides' sacrificial virgins, Antigone sacrifices marriage for the larger cause of burying her brother and serving the unwritten laws and, in addition, challenges a civic decree. Creon cannot stand by his decree without leaving his nephew unburied and preventing the marriage of his son to his brotherless niece.[1] The choices made by each are clearly shaped by their social roles as virgin daughter and statesman. In my discussion here, I confine myself to examining the way that Sophocles' Antigone offers an alternative mode of ethical reasoning to that adopted by Creon. The play exploits this contrast in ethical mode both to make the case for and to raise questions about the moral positions adopted by each character. Here we see that the tragic representation of ethical choice differs from and in some ways goes beyond that of contemporary and later Greek philosophy. The gendering of ethical positions permits the public exploration of moral complexities that would not otherwise have been possible.

Sophocles' *Antigone* makes clear from the start that Antigone and Creon speak in different moral voices, even if they are not precisely representative of their respective genders, as we know from the conflicting views offered by Ismene and Haimon. "There is nothing in your words that is pleasing to me, and

This chapter appeared in an abbreviated form in Silk 1996. An earlier version was first presented at a symposium in honor of Helen North at Swarthmore College. I would like to thank audiences at Oberlin, Vassar, Cincinnati, Wellesley, University of Iowa, Trinity College, Hartford, Minneapolis, CUNY graduate center, and King's College, London, and Christopher Gill, Rachel Kitzinger, Page du Bois, Richard Seaford, Michael Trapp, and Christian Wolff for comments on an earlier draft.

[1] Although *Antigone* as a whole elaborates on issues relating to the *polis* and does not specify obligations to the *anchisteia* in the text, it seems likely (contra Konstan 1996: 91, although we have no definite evidence) that an Athenian audience would have assumed that close relatives had a cultural, if not legal, responsibility to bury their own. (Creon does acknowledge kin obligations at 486–89, however.)

may there never be! And my words are also not pleasing to you," says Antigone to Creon (499–501). "Are you not ashamed," says Creon to Antigone, "to think differently from these men (the Thebans and the chorus)?" (510). As many critics have pointed out, Antigone and Creon use the same moral vocabulary in subtly different ways—the words *philos* (friend) and *echthros* (enemy), for example, develop different connotations in the context in which each character employs them.[2] What has received considerably less detailed attention is their fundamentally different mode of making ethical decisions.[3] The following discussion will stress in particular those parts of the play in which Antigone and Creon explain and defend their actions and the moral style that each adopts in doing so.[4]

I shall begin with Antigone. Each of Antigone's three explanations and defenses of her choice to bury Polyneices in the play, although fundamentally the same in content, are aimed precisely at the different audiences she is addressing: Ismene, Creon, and finally the chorus. Antigone's motive for action is throughout a deeply felt personal responsibility both to bury blood relatives in the same household, and to honor the gods below with their due. Initially treating her sister as another self in the first scene, Antigone leads up to her request for help from Ismene by evoking familial bonds and common experiences—

---

[2] On the different languages of Antigone and Creon, see Reinhardt 1979: 79 and 87, Goheen 1951: 17, Knox 1964: 80, Dalfen 1977, Hester 1980, Kitzinger 1976, Porter 1987: 61, and Goldhill 1986: ch. 4. On a similar contrast in the use of *sebas* and *timē*, see Kitzinger 56.

[3] The bibliography on *Antigone* is so voluminous that any discussion will consist largely of deploying the same chess pieces to play a new game. I have attempted here to cite literature that influenced my own thinking or the most recent or well-developed version of a particular position. Griffith 1999, Tyrrell and Bennett 1998, and Bollack 1999 reached me too late for inclusion in this book. For a summary of the bibliography on major questions in the play, see Hester 1971. Philosophical discussions of the play range from Hegel to the recent, stimulating analyses of Steiner 1986, Nussbaum 1986, Oudemans and Lardinois 1987 (with full bibliography), and Blundell 1989. Nussbaum and Oudemans and Lardinois argue that both Antigone and Creon take a position that does not stand up to the test of events. Nussbaum argues (see esp. 51–52) that both attempt to close off tensions and simplify their commitments and involvements, social and emotional— although Antigone is more correct and morally superior. Oudemans and Lardinois, after offering a convincing critique of Hegel, adopt a modified Hegelian position (e.g., in their version the play offers no synthesis following its thesis and antithesis); by the end of the play the audience sees that all the characters have ironically destroyed what they set out to save (182–83) and each undergoes a reversal in the course of the action (187–201). Blundell, in a thoughtful study of the friends-enemies ethic in Sophocles, offers a far fuller discussion of Creon than Antigone.

[4] Aristotle in the *Rhetoric* describes style (*lexis*) as being ethical or emotional. Ethical style relates to such features as age, sex, country of origin, or degree of education. Forms of expression, such as maxims or narrative, may be used "emotionally" to reflect anger and so forth. (See, e.g., 2. 21.1395a23–24, 3.7.1408a10–b20, 3.16.1417a16–b10, 3.17.1418a12–21, and Gill 1984: 155.) My own discussion develops on different lines but includes the notion that gender and the use of maxims play a role in creating ethical style in Sophocles. Aristotle argues that the use of maxims is especially appropriate to mature, educated speakers. In *Antigone* (not in tragedy generally), male characters are especially given to gnomic generalizations.

shared suffering and dishonor. She takes it for granted that they have the same assumptions about the need to bury Polyneices (she is correct in this assumption; see Ismene at 65–67) and thus she does not try at first to justify her position, but only to stir her sister to act. To Ismene she argues that to perform the act will demonstrate her (and her sister's) noble heritage (37–38), and to fail to perform it would be an act of betrayal (46). Only when Ismene refuses to join her does she attempt to justify her proposal. She asserts that hers will be a noble death (72, 96–97). She will lie *philē* (beloved or loving) to her *philos* (*philou meta*) Polyneices (73).[5] Antigone will commit a holy crime (74) and *please* those whom she ought to *please* (89), because there is more time to *please* those below than those here (74–75).[6] Finally, Antigone will not dishonor the things due to the gods (*ta tōn theōn entima*, 77). In comparison with that in her next two scenes, Antigone's language here is narrowly focused to evoke close *philia* in what is staged as a private, familial context (see her terms of affection, her use of the dual, and the frequent possessives that personalize the burial issue).[7]

After Antigone is caught burying her brother, Creon questions her disobedience to the edict. She begins by responding directly to his query. She defends her disobedience by citing Zeus and the unwritten laws (or customs) and the rites due to the gods below. From the unwritten laws Antigone turns to her motives, both social and emotional, for acting. As in the first scene, honor, a principled responsibility to gods and family, and personal pain are given equal weight in her self-defense. She says that she fears not men's *phronēma* (attitude), but penalties from the gods if she does not act (458–60). The painful evils that beset her life (the loss of mother, father, and brothers) make death a gain in her eyes (461–64). By contrast, if she had left her mother's son unburied, she would have grieved (466–68). She expects to win glory for her gesture (502–4). Once again, Antigone's language pointedly personalizes the burial issue. She says that Creon made the edict for Antigone and Ismene (32, see also 45); it is not for Creon to keep her from her own (48). In neither of these first two scenes does Antigone generalize her case beyond the need to act, once

---

[5] In this line she employs language drawn from both the sphere of *erōs* and reciprocal social commitment. See Winnington-Ingram 1980: 129.

[6] For additional language referring to pleasure and pain, see also 4–6, 465–68, 499–501, 551, 857–71, and 1165–71. Ismene's initial replies responsively echo Antigone's evocation of shared pain and pleasure, happiness and unhappiness. References to pleasure and pain also appear in the language of the guard. Creon does not cite such motives for action, although political opposition (318, 573) and, at the conclusion, his own personal suffering (1271–76, 1288–89, 1336) eventually cause him pain.

[7] On the narrowness of her use of these terms, see Goldhill 1986: esp. 90–91, where he contrasts Ismene's inclusion of the interests of the city in her responses. For repeated references to herself in relation to others and to terms of endearment, see, e.g., 81, *adelphō(i) philtatō(i)*, 1, 32, 45. When challenged, however, she makes assertive use of the first person (32, 45, 48, 70, 71, 80, 95). See 70–77 and the first part of her dialogue with Creon.

Ismene has demurred, in this *particular* situation. Tiresias, not Antigone, universalizes the issue by raising the question of burying the other slain enemies (1080–83).[8] Antigone's language in this *agōn* with Creon more closely matches the public context in which she speaks; it lacks the marks of intimacy, the appeal to shared familial experience displayed in the first scene. Yet the same combination of public and private concerns, of principle and emotional commitment, is used to explain and justify her actions in this specific context.

In a final—and, I believe, authentic[9]—speech in which she defends her burial of her brother to the chorus (904–20), Antigone says that she would not have acted against the citizens to bury a husband or a child, who are replaceable. This last justification for her action comes as Antigone departs for death regretting both the loss of marriage and children and the loss of lamentation for her own death that her courageous act has precluded.[10] In burying Polyneices she has not only ignored the claims of the city in favor of familial bonds, but has implicitly foregone marital bonds for those with blood relations.[11] A virgin daughter had a primary responsibility to her family and its hearth before her marriage, and continued to have a responsibility to that family even after she was lent in marriage to another family (see part II). Hence Antigone was faced with two conflicting responsibilities to her natal family, burying her brother or marrying to preserve a soon-to-be extinguished line. Arranging and completing marriage was a male responsibility. Creon, as Antigone's guardian, abandons his responsibility to ensure her marriage. Thus, like Antigone, Creon has made a choice between two important priorities; Haimon similarly re-

---

[8] These lines have been bracketed by many editors, above all on the grounds that the other warriors have played no role in the action until now.

[9] For an excellent defense with full bibliography, see Neuberg 1990: esp. 59–62.

[10] Murnaghan 1986b: 195 and 198, Neuberg 1990: esp. 70, and Blundell 1989: 135 all see this speech as arising from Antigone's preoccupation with marriage. The marriage to Haimon is raised for the first time by Ismene at 568, where Creon responds by asserting the replaceability of spouses (569). In Neuberg's view, replaceability characterizes "for Antigone the difference between the blood-family and the marriage-family" (69).

[11] Antigone has been criticized for abandoning her responsibility to marry and procreate, although the text nowhere questions her choice on this basis. In this she lives up to her name, "instead of or opposed to generation." (See Murnaghan 1986b: 207, Sorum 1982: 206–7, Segal 1981: 189–90, Goldhill 1986: 102, Sourvinou-Inwood 1989a: 140, and Oudemans and Lardinois 1987: 177. Seaford 1988 and 1990b addresses the larger implications of such failures to marry in Greek myth; and Ormand 1999: ch. 4 now stresses the double bind in which she finds herself as sister and *epiklēros*.) This speech makes clear that Antigone is aware of what she has sacrificed, but nevertheless remains committed to her original choice and expects her family's approval for her act in the world below. Antigone risked death and hence loss of marriage from the start, of course; yet as Neuberg 1990: 75 argues, Antigone's argument now reflects the choice forced on her by Creon's punishment. To have chosen marriage would have been to dishonor her blood kin, not to act would be to disobey divine laws for a mortal decree. See further Segal 1981: 189. Oudemans and Lardinois' 1987: 167 claim that Antigone has broken her ties to her family by disobeying her guardian has no basis in the text.

sponds to Creon's request that he not value marriage above his father (637–38). Antigone's final attempt at self-defense is addressed to and introduced by a lyric dialogue with the chorus that, despite the public context, reopens the possibility of a more intimate and sympathetic communication among characters than was possible in her first confrontation with Creon. Only when Creon interrupts this lyric exchange does Antigone begin a self-defense in iambic trimeters.[12]

Antigone apparently turns to this final, formal argument because, as far as she knows, everyone has failed to accept or to understand her position, despite her repeated efforts to justify it in other terms.[13] Even Ismene, who finally wants to die with her, to the end thinks Antigone did the wrong thing (555–57). Earlier, Antigone tells Creon that her act would be pleasing to the elders of the chorus (as representative of the people of Thebes) if they were not afraid to speak in front of him (504–5, 509.) Antigone's initial use of the lyric mode with the chorus suggests that, as in the first scene with Ismene, she hopes to involve them emotionally in shared values and in the past suffering of her family. Here she has them fully engaged in a dialogue for the first time.[14] Yet, contrary to her earlier expectation, they do not approve her act (873–75). Although they begin the scene unable to contain their tears at the sight of Antigone (801–5), the elders do not respond with lamentation to her complaints that she is going to her death unwed and unlamented. Indeed, she feels mocked by them (839–41).

In contrast to Creon, for whose edict she shows little respect from the start, the elders of the chorus (and the city [842–43], to which Antigone appeals once she thinks that the chorus has failed to respond to her) are a source of authority for her. In this final scene Antigone elicits a response from them as citizens and witnesses to her plight (806, 937–44), and addresses them respectfully (koiranidai, 940). Thus it makes sense that Antigone first explicitly recognizes the opposition of the city to her act (bia(i) politōn, 907) in this speech, as she refused to do with Ismene or Creon earlier; earlier she concentrated on resisting Creon's edict, which, unlike Ismene, she apparently did not equate with the will of the city, because she thought that the chorus was on

---

[12] Cropp 1997: esp. 148–52 provides an excellent analysis of the rhetoric of the speech, which he agrees is aimed at persuading the chorus and the city (see his 139 for other views). The first part of the speech addresses the dead in Antigone's family and demonstrates the justice of her act in terms of kinship obligations. I would add that it continues the lament with political implications staged for the chorus earlier in the scene (see I). The second part addresses those with good sense among the living (enlightened citizens), and the third the implications of her act in the eyes of the gods.

[13] See further Winnington-Ingram 1980: 141 and Webster 1969: 99. On her isolation here, see Linforth 1961: 224.

[14] Although his exit is not marked in the text, it is possible that Creon is not on stage for the first part of Antigone's scene with the chorus; her words are aimed at the chorus and Creon does not speak until he interrupts their lyric exchange at 883.

her side.[15] (Her assumption is not implausible, since the citizens cited by Haimon do take this view.)

The qualifications that Antigone offers concerning her act in this last speech about her brother are not, as many have argued, inconsistent with the position she has taken at any point in the play;[16] at all times the personal commitments to bury her brother (specifically her brother) and to give the gods their due are her primary motives for action. What differs is the way that she presents her case to a different audience in a different context.[17] Antigone does not in this speech deny the universal validity of the unwritten laws concerning the dead in making clear that *she* would only have risked her life, ignored her obligation and desire to marry and prolong her family line, and disobeyed the citizens for a last brother who had no other family member to bury him. She simply wants to make the chorus understand that, as the last survivor of the doomed Labdacids, she would only have *acted* to bury her brother. Knowing what is right on the level of general principle apparently does not require a woman in her position to act on this knowledge in all instances and irrespective of context. Throughout the play she defends an action undertaken in a specific, emotionally concrete instance; the loss of this irreplaceable and known brother to whom she has a deep personal and familial commitment at this time and place has made her willing to accept death and eager to please the dead and to act for the gods below (notice her pathetic stress at 897–99 on her hopes to be welcome to those below).[18] The whole force of the argument in this last speech develops the contrast between a concrete basis for action and alternatives that

[15] Antigone has been criticized for ignoring the interests of the city both by characters inside the play and generations of critics. The views of Knox 1964: esp. 75–76 and 83 are typical. For exceptions, see Blundell 1989: 146, Lane and Lane 1986, Whitman 1951: 85–88, who sees Antigone as the ideal citizen, and Bennett and Tyrrell 1990, who think Antigone's words and acts reflect typical themes in public, democratic rhetoric.

[16] For exceptions, see Blundell 1989: 133, Neuberg 1990: 63, and Linforth 1961: 203. I do not think Antigone undergoes a reversal in this last scene (for the fullest case for reversal, see Oudemans and Lardinois 1987: 187–93 and Rohdich 1980; see also Knox 1964: 103–10). She expresses pain over the loss of marriage, the unexpectedly horrifying punishment of a living death, and the seeming indifference of the gods and everyone else to her conception of justice, but she never doubts the correctness of her action; she was prepared for immediate death and soon acquires it (see Winnington-Ingram 1980: 139).

[17] She also, as Neuberg 1990: 72–75 points out, speaks to different thematic concerns. Her speech to Creon asserts that death is better than disobeying divine laws in favor of mortal laws. The second speech implictly maintains that joining her family in Hades is better than dishonoring blood kin for marriage.

[18] As Neuberg 1990: 69 stresses, Antigone "describes what she *has* done; and this is all that matters. She *didn't* fail to bury a dead husband, or a dead brother when she had another brother living, and her parents *are* dead, so it is we who construct irrelevant hypotheses if we worry about this; 'such was my *nomos* in burying you' is not the same as 'such would have been my *nomos* regardless of the situation.'" See also Bowra 1944: 95. By contrast, Gellie 1972: 48 sees Antigone's reliance on this contrast between brother and hypothetical husband and wife as "pathetic," even though he concedes that there are cultural parallels for such positions in "the primitive thinking of many peoples" (47); Kitto 1969: 130 calls the argument on replaceability a "frigid sophism."

would not at this point impel her to act. In short, she would not have challenged the state for a set of relations that are hypothetical to a virgin.[19]

Sophocles is thought to have borrowed in this speech from Herodotus (3.119), where the wife of Intaphrenes was given the opportunity to *save* the life of husband, child, or brother; she chose the brother, because she could not get another. The adaptation of this story in Antigone's case has been criticized as ill-conceived, because Antigone has no husband and child and chooses to die in a suicidal fashion for a dead brother rather than to save a living one.[20] Herodotus' passage contains an implied criticism of Intaphrenes' wife; the Persian king Darius, astonished that she does not prefer husband or son, saves both her brother and her eldest son.[21] Antigone's decision is in my view more, not less, defensible and comprehensible, precisely because she does not choose a brother over a family to whom she now has real social obligations as a wife. As the last of her family line (see part I), Antigone is by implication obliged to marry (895–96, 940–43); in arguing that she could get another husband and child if she lost either, she also implies that her first priority would have been to bear children for her natal (rather than a marital) family. Both Creon's initial decree and his punishment give her no choice but to act as virgin and member of her natal family; but she tragically cannot fulfill both obligations to that family.

In this last speech, Antigone also responds implicitly to the full range of constraints on her action articulated in the play as a whole.[22] From the first scene,

[19] Although Antigone, unlike many classical Athenian brides, knew her fiancé Haimon and is, according to Ismene, well suited to him (570), she now thinks that Creon has reneged on that marriage. (Ismene may mean that the couple are well suited personally, that the match is socially appropriate, or both.) Hence, although the loss of the marriage to Haimon makes her lament particularly poignant to the hearer, both an actual husband and child are once more only hypothetical in her case.

[20] E.g., Blundell 1989: 134. Hester 1971: 36, on the other hand, argues that Antigone's emotional state and the fact that she has no husband or child makes her argument "natural." Mackay 1962: 171 argues that Antigone did not have a social commitment to a husband and child, because they belonged to a different family, with whom a wife is less than fully identified (see also Murnaghan 1986b: 201). In the same vein, Murnaghan 198 thinks that ties of blood are instinctive, whereas the role of husband is abstract and instituted by society; Cropp 1997: 150 similarly argues that as earlier with the unwritten laws, Antigone poses natural laws against man-made ones. Winnington-Ingram 1980: 143–45 stresses that this speech must be interpreted in the light of the audience's knowledge that Antigone was betrothed; Murnaghan 1986b: 206 similarly thinks that Antigone's childlessness makes the paradigm more pathetic. Bremmer 1997: 97 cites parallels from the literature of India and Persia (see also Visser 1986 and Holst-Warhaft 1992: 163). No anthropologist with whom I have discussed this passage finds Antigone's argument surprising.

[21] See Murnaghan 1986b: 202–3 and Zellner 1996–97: 316, who stresses the critical importance of postmortem existence to Antigone here. Plutarch, *Moralia* 481e, approves the wife's choice.

[22] Sourvinou-Inwood 1989a and 1990 has attempted to make a particularly damning case against Antigone as a "bad woman." She acts outside the house, disobeys her guardian, attempts to bury a relative without male supervision, betrays her responsibility to marry and procreate, and assumes on no justifiable basis that her views are correct. For my response, see Foley 1995a.

when she admits to Ismene that she will only perform the burial to the degree she can (91), Antigone shows, along with her rash defiance and her unwillingness to tolerate disagreement from a loved one, an ability to recognize both her limits and the difficulties of communicating her position to others.[23] She is well aware that some will agree with Ismene and Creon, and think her reasoning a case of ill-judgment and folly (95, 469–70). Both have asserted that women should not act against men and the city—in short, that they should not in this situation, as in the popular view in Athens, be independent moral agents at all. More immediately, the chorus has expressly disapproved of both her act and her temperament.

Antigone's speech to the chorus, and by extension to the city, relies on the point that there is no other family member left to perform obligations for her blood kin (Ismene would not act, Creon has denied his responsibility to kin, and her parents and brothers are dead). As I argued in my discussion of Sophocles' Electra, it seems not unlikely that in classical Attica, as in the modern rural Mediterranean, a surviving daughter could be imagined to take appropriate action in the absence of all supporting male relatives and the possibility for future ones (another brother);[24] here myth, popular tradition, and tragedy undoubtedly posed choices that the classical *polis* was designed to make unnecessary in reality. The modern cases most frequently concern revenge, in which the daughter may choose to take on symbolically the characteristics of a male member of her family and risk becoming an object of vendetta herself. Electra proposes to win honor in precisely this fashion by taking revenge on Aegisthus when she thinks that Orestes is dead in Sophocles' play (III.2). In matters relating to burial, however, the same options seem to obtain both among the Mani and in Sophocles as for revenge. "In an act of daring that was repeated in villages all over Greece during the German Occupation, . . . [the Maniat woman Costantina Dimaronga] and two other women risked execution by burying their cousin and a group of fellow resistance fighters killed in the battle of Verga-Armyrou."[25] Dimaronga's later lament for her cousin expressed pride in her action and anger at those who refused to help or collaborated with the Germans.

As Christiane Sourvinou-Inwood has pointed out, initiating the burial ceremony and interring the body are normally male tasks in ancient Greece (women do pour libations and lament but under male supervision).[26] Yet, in

---

[23] Sophoclean heroes are, as Knox 1964 argues, generally impervious to appeal. Antigone, who exhibits the typical Sophoclean heroic temper, does not back down; but she does in this last speech make a serious attempt to explain her position to the community. See Blundell 1989: 146 on Antigone's greater willingness than Creon's to recognize competing claims of *nomos*, justice, and institutions (for her, that of the *polis*).

[24] Here I disagree with Lane and Lane 1986: esp. 163–67 who argue that Antigone pursues honor and acts out of total disregard for the limits of gender.

[25] Holst-Warhaft 1992: 91–92.

[26] Sourvinou-Inwood 1989a.

Oedipus at Colonus (1410–13), Polyneices—a male character—urges his sisters to bury him by predicting that they will win praise (*epainos*) if they do so. Although Antigone's actions clearly run counter to normal expectations about female action (as Ismene or, in *Electra*, Chrysothemis makes clear), the views of the citizens cited by Haimon, who pronounce her act to be worthy of the highest praise, a praise she incurs specifically as a woman (694), must be culturally comprehensible to the play's audience.[27] Antigone's adoption of goals that would normally be appropriate to men, such as the pursuit of honor for her action, would from this perspective be understood as part of a special situation that encourages the daughter to act in the interests of her family in the absence of a male relative who is willing to do so—even to the point of a seemingly suicidal heroic death. Although Creon expresses outrage that he is challenged by a woman and even calls Antigone a slave (479), his insistence both on treating his young and virginal ward as a moral agent responsible under penalty of law for her act and on meting out (at least initially) the prescribed punishment of death by stoning even for a woman makes sense in a context where a woman has chosen to act (at least in part) as an honorary male. This hypothesis would also explain why Antigone implies (911–12) that she would not have acted if her parents had been alive, and why Antigone must try to persuade Ismene to act in a case where both sisters agree that Polyneices should in principle be buried. In insisting that there was only *one* case in which her action is in her own view fully justifiable, Antigone's speech probably capitalizes on cultural presuppositions about exceptional circumstances in which women could be expected to act autonomously.

To put this another way, in this play a young, unmarried princess (we should not forget that although Antigone is a woman, her affairs have public as well as private importance)[28] wins praise from a substantial portion of the city as the last member of her family willing to act in that family's interest, although she defies men and the state to bury her brother; as was mentioned earlier, even the chorus, which is known for its devotion to the past rulers of Thebes and pointedly disapproves of her disobedience, recognizes (unlike Creon) a certain piety in the attempted burial (872) and honor in her mode of death (817–18, 836–38). If such a woman had insisted, especially in the face of the opposition expressed by Ismene, Creon, and the chorus, on her need to act for the full range of hypothetical marital relations to whom she might by public and male standards be obligated by the unwritten laws, Antigone would I think have become a cultural monstrosity rather than a subversive yet admirable anomaly.

Many critics have found what they characterize as Antigone's highly con-

---

[27] Van Erp Taalman Kip 1996: 521–24 has offered a highly convincing argument against those who think that Haimon is inventing this popular support for Antigone.

[28] Blundell 1989: 148.

textualized and contingent mode of moral argument in this passage intolerable.[29] Their Antigone is a woman who should consistently have been willing to sustain a universal commitment to the gods' laws in all instances, or at the very least to all members of her natal and (hypothetical) marital family, and not risked death exclusively for a dead brother in one context. Other critics have been far too quick to label Antigone as merely intuitive, emotional, primitive, inconsistent, and illogical; or they fail to accord her ethical framework the precise attention that it deserves.[30] We need to examine the assumptions of Antigone's critics, and even of her admirers.

Creon's mode of moral and political deliberation, to be discussed shortly, is more familiar to us; yet we should not permit its familiarity to distort our judgment of his behavior in Sophocles' play. Nor should we assume that the stance developed for Antigone throughout this play is anything but an equally serious ethical mode that operates on different terms from those adopted by other characters. These less familiar terms have required careful attention to define. It is important to accept the possibility that gender can be a critical factor in defining moral action in Greek culture and literature. General principles dictate the behavior of both Antigone and Creon, but moral problems arise for each in a contextual framework that eludes an exclusive reliance on abstract reasoning. This is especially the case where the culture does not normally permit adult moral autonomy to the female agent—as Ismene and Creon make clear, women's virtues are traditionally exercised through obedience to men in authority—and defines her above all in relation to the family context in which

---

[29] Contextuality and contingency differ; contextuality can include the localized application of general principles, whereas contingency may not.

[30] As Goheen 1951: 94 remarks, Antigone's "way of knowing is usually thought less acceptable than Creon's." For Antigone as intuitive and instinctive, see, e.g., Murnaghan 1986b: 195, Goheen 1951: 82, and Knox 1964: 116, who sees Antigone as the embodiment of love and intuition; for her illogical thought processes and her emotional piety, see esp. Goheen 1951: 76–79, 98, Waldock [1951] 1966: 229, who argues that when Antigone turns from instinct to logic at 904 the result is clumsy, or Norwood 1948: 139, who claims that Antigone has no reason only instinct. Kitto 1969: 131 argues that Antigone's *instinct* was right, and Creon's *judgment* wrong (my emphasis). Kirkwood 1958: 165 argues that Antigone acted "from instinctive feeling rather than reasoned principles. To find logical justification for intuitions is by no means easy." Levy 1963: esp. 138 and 144 tries to make the case that Antigone combines reason and instinct. Critics often attribute a serious religious force to Antigone's supposed intuition (e.g., Reinhardt 1979: 76–77); from this perspective the drama pits religious against political priorities. Antigone's certainty about the unwritten laws and the gods below does seem to be derived from a kind of religious intuition. Yet there are religious and political dimensions on both sides of the conflict (see, e.g., Knox 1964: 75), and to adopt a religious stance or a defense of unwritten laws does not require an "intuitive" mode of deliberation. (See the passage from Aristotle's *Rhetoric* 1.15.1375a–b on Antigone's citation of the unwritten laws discussed later.) Even adherence to the unwritten laws is a matter of education and politics as much as intuition. Similarly, the commitment to a brother can also be understood as both a social obligation for a virgin and a matter of self-interest, because a living brother was often the family member most likely to defend a married woman's interests if she faced difficulties in her new family. See Bremmer 1997: 95–98 on brother-sister relations in Athens.

she is normally inextricably embedded. In Antigone's view, the unwritten laws do require family members to bury their kin. Virgin daughters are apparently last in the hierarchy of those who should undertake this obligation, and the last to undertake risks on behalf of the family, perhaps above all because these risks conflict with their cultural role of producing the next generation. To accept Antigone's argument that there are only specific circumstances in which a virgin daughter should contemplate taking autonomous action in life-threatening circumstances requires her audience to understand that her heroic action cannot serve in any simple sense as a timeless, gender-free model for civil disobedience. At the same time, it does not diminish her heroism and her moral audacity. Within the context of a Mediterranean morality that offers to a woman specific exceptional opportunities to win honor by acting on behalf of the natal family, Antigone's choice to accept a challenge that requires her death still defines her as heroic.

What has been called inconsistency, despite that fact that Antigone remains committed both to the same principles (the unwritten laws) and to her act of disobedience throughout, has been shown to derive from her attempt to persuade or to explain her position to three different audiences at three different stages in the narrative of her attempted burial. The fact that each scene attempts a justification of the same act underlines the role that each audience and each context plays. With Ismene, Antigone, using language adapted to this private context, above all tries to evoke family bonds and shared goals and experiences to persuade her sister to act. With Creon, fully recognizing the public and generalizing mode of reasoning adopted by her opponent, she begins with a general principle already stated to Ismene, her religious motive for having taken action, and only then moves on to personal motives. Here her style adjusts to the public context in which she defends an act already undertaken. With the chorus, she first engages in lyric mode in an apparent attempt to win open sympathy for her position, then uses an argument in iambic trimeter to make clear that acting against the city *was* a concern for her; to the chorus she stresses her role as the "last" member of their royal family. In trying after an apparently blanket rejection to make her act understandable in this broader civic context, she shows that she has sacrificed other priorities such as marriage to act and that she is not attempting to generalize her stance in an absurd fashion for a woman. In sum, Antigone adopts a range of styles, each suited to a different private or public context and to her interlocutor, to convey a consistent position that repeatedly insists on giving equal weight to concerns of justice and familial responsibility.[31]

[31] Antigone's insistence in this speech that the burial coincides with the gods' will proves correct, and Ismene, Haimon, Eurydice, and Creon come to share, as she requests (927–28), her pain over the loss of loved ones and (if they survive) to face the living death that Antigone seemed so extreme in claiming as a motive for action in the first scene. Eurydice dies on the altar of Zeus Herkeios, the very god whom Creon neglected; Creon also becomes suppliant to his rejected son

Although her emotional motives are always firmly linked to rational ones,[32] Antigone refuses to hierarchize the reasons that impel her to act. As moral agent she unashamedly constructs the concrete other for whom she acts in relationship, rather than (like Creon) creating an objective distance between self and other.[33] If Antigone has difficulty communicating persuasively with her audiences both inside and outside the play, it may be because there is no ready traditional vocabulary or recognized procedure for a female moral agent in classical Athens, or it may be because Antigone's situation requires her to abandon one set of traditional female obligations (to marry and to obey her guardian) to pursue another. Despite her willingness to adopt styles of argument suitable to her interlocutors, the concreteness of Antigone's language, her repeated references to pleasure and pain as a motive for action, her infrequent use of generalization, and her pointedly narrow use of terms such as *philos* and *echthros* throughout these scenes[34] have all served in the eyes of critics (and of some in the play) to create a sense of stark moral isolation, of a person struggling to communicate in a form that is not fully accessible to her audience, a form that seems to an Ismene or Creon the product of folly or even madness, yet to Haimon and others in the city a heroic act. Nevertheless, if we abandon the assumption that there is a form of deliberate moral reasoning that requires action regardless of circumstance and the identity of the agent either in Greek society or in this play, Antigone's act develops a generally unacknowledged coherence.

Whereas Antigone's ethics derive from a dual responsibility to the unwritten laws and the gods below and to family relations and care for others, Creon's derive exclusively from a commitment to general principles as the major determinant of moral action that is entirely familiar in later Western tradition. In his view the interests of the city-state are primary and enemies to the state should not be buried. He identifies his and even the gods' interest with that of the city. In contrast to Antigone, emotions and the calculus of pleasure and pain are not cited as supporting motives for Creon's actions. Creon is sure that his principles are best for *all* situations, whereas Antigone, although the unwritten laws play a critical role in her decision, develops her position out of her own familial experience and in the specific context of the burial of her brother. Creon will count no one as a *philos* who does not accept his views about the *polis* and its priorities (182–83, 187–90, 209–10).[35] Blood and marital rela-

---

(1230). See Oudemans and Lardinois 1987: 195. For tragic examples in which male characters are "educated" by experiencing the suffering of tragic women, see Zeitlin 1985b and my part IV.

[32] Nor is this a case of passion setting goals that reason defends (see Blundell 1989: 141 on this tendency among the characters of the play).

[33] Creon does evoke his relationship to Haimon, but does not treat him accordingly.

[34] Antigone herself seems to use *philos*, *echthros*, and related terms for relatives, even if for other characters they have the broader meaning advocated by Konstan 1996.

[35] On this position as exemplary of democratic ideology in Athens, see esp. Sourvinou-Inwood

tionships and the responsibilities they entail are of secondary importance to him, and easily expendable when the interests of city and family (apparently) come into conflict. "She is my sister's child," he says "but were she child of closer kin than any at my hearth, she and her sister should not so escape their death and doom" (486–89). He will leave his nephew unburied because he fought against Thebes, condemn his nieces to death, and threaten to kill Haimon's bride before his very eyes.[36] Creon defines the self in relationship to others in a hierarchical and contractual fashion. Sons should obey fathers and prospective wives are interchangeable. If Haimon cannot marry Antigone, Creon asserts, there are other furrows for his plow (569). Yet wives are not interchangeable for the same reasons that a husband and child are to Antigone. He has experienced these relations, and as a male leader he is in a position to choose (for others and himself) among alternatives concerning them. Unlike Antigone, Creon will not permit past personal experience to explain or color his judgment.

Creon insists that one cannot know the soul, thought, and judgment of a *man* (*andros*) unless he shows his practice of government and law (175–77).[37] Although this statement proves ironically true in his own case, it also means that moral knowledge of women or slaves or even perhaps the passive citizenry is fundamentally impossible. No wonder Creon cannot trust any judgment but his own (see 736)—except, finally, that of the chorus, which has demonstrated political loyalty to the ruling house of Thebes in the past, and Tiresias, who has been proved right before. In contrast to Antigone, Creon does not adjust his style of speaking to his interlocutors or to changing contexts; consistent with the ethical stance he has adopted, he presents his case in a public, iambic mode until he reviews his actions in his final lyric laments.

The way that Creon deploys gnomic truths makes his moral range particularly clear.[38] He approaches every dilemma that requires judgment through de-

---

1989a and Blundell 1989: 117. Oudemans and Lardinois 1987: 164 argue that Creon is thus tragically forced to suppress the claims of family. In favoring *polis* over family, he also avoids the accusation of nepotism (174). For my own views, see Foley 1995a.

[36] See Blundell 1989: 118–19, Linforth 1961: 189, and Knox 1964: 88.

[37] See also Aristotle, *Poetics* 6.1450b6–10.

[38] On Creon's gnomic language, see Wolf 1910: 48–53 and 126–31 (see 49 n. 1 on the disjointed quality of his gnomic utterances), Winnington-Ingram 1980: 120 and 126, Gellie 1972: 33, Reinhardt 1979: 73, and Kitzinger 1976. Critics (see esp. Sourvinou-Inwood 1989a and Calder 1968) have argued in Creon's defense that the generalizations and choices that he adopts reflect standard cultural assumptions. Women should obey men, the interests of the city should take priority, generals had extraordinary powers to put people to death in war (Calder 1968: 393), and so forth. Yet the dramatic action exposes problems in the enforcement of these generalizations in this particular case. For example, the obedience that Creon expects from son and citizens is perfectly conventional (Calder 399), nevertheless, as Blundell 1989: 125 points out, a good ruler should also, as Haimon's argument presupposes, attempt to promote civic *homonoia*. See also Winnington-Ingram 1980: 120. Kitzinger 1976: 122–25 and 144–50 argues that each of Creon's generalizations masks other motives and concerns, such as his fear of conspiracy and dissent and his ambition.

scriptive and prescriptive generalizations about money, human types, and the behavior expected from such types; his speeches contain 25 such generalizations in 350 lines in contrast to 2 for Antigone in 212 lines.[39] Such assumptions about human types and human society may be reasonable in themselves and even necessary where public decisions must be undertaken without full and reliable knowledge of the circumstances and the characters of those involved in a particular situation. Creon's first speech makes a case for the value of the generalizing mode in a public context. Yet, as is the case with Antigone, his views are immediately put to the test in the following scenes. Because Creon (unlike Antigone) creates the full positive case for his action in this first speech and the play ultimately exposes the error in his initial stance on Polyneices' burial, subsequent scenes serve to reveal the limitations of his position and his ethical mode.[40] Thus, where human beings and situations defy his expectations and prove not to be interchangeable, Creon repeatedly fails to register their actual character. To put this another way, in contrast to the moral agent defined by Aristotle in his *Nicomachean Ethics*, Creon proves deaf to the knowledge of particulars—of place, time, manner, and persons, for example—essential to successful practical reasoning.[41] In short, he does not effectively correlate general principles and specific situations (*Nicomachean Ethics* 6.9). By contrast, Haimon uses generalization in a fashion that is far more responsive to the circumstances than his father. Whereas Aristotle argues that *aisthēsis*, *orexis*, and *dianoia* (perception, desire, and thought) all play a critical role in this process, Creon does not acknowledge that emotion (in alliance with reason) and perception (or intuition) are as critical to proper moral deliberation as reason.[42]

Unsurprisingly, then, in a sequence of scenes, Creon misjudges and/or fails to respond appropriately to the actions and motives of the guard, Tiresias, Antigone, Ismene, and even to his own son, who, as a young man, should from Creon's perspective accept his father's views without question. His errors are often understandable, but the repetition cannot fail to affect the audience's view of Creon's judgment nevertheless.[43] The guard, like others of his type,

---

[39] The statistics are from Kitzinger 1976: 144. The number of generalizations is highest in the scene with Haimon, his closest male relative.

[40] Parker stresses that Greeks generally recognized the obligation to bury a potential source of pollution (44) and that prolonged public exposure of a corpse is overall shocking and not the practice of Greek states. The content of Creon's decree, which did not correspond to the usual treatment of traitors (Parker 1983: 47), would thus have disturbed the audience from the outset. Polyneices is not in any case called a traitor in the play, but an enemy (Parker 48). See further Brown 1987: 6 and Foley 1995b. Matters of content do not prevent an audience from observing in a critical fashion the way that each character presents an argument, however.

[41] Nussbaum 1986: 80 argues that Tiresias and Haimon, who favor flexibility and responsiveness to the world and its complexities, express an Aristotelian sensibility. The exercise of practical wisdom often entails situations where principles can only serve as guidelines.

[42] Seale 1982: 86 argues that Creon only trusts what is visible and empirically verifiable. In contrast to Creon, the chorus unhesitatingly reacts to events emotionally as well as rationally (e.g., it weeps for Antigone).

[43] Critics (e.g., Oudemans and Lardinois 1987: 198–99 and Sourvinou-Inwood 1989a) who de-

must in Creon's view be venal; in fact, as the guard himself remarks, Creon's judgment is in error here (323).[44] Creon initially makes another error of judgment with Tiresias, whereas the chorus puts faith in its past experience of Tiresias' reliability (1091–94). Even more telling are Creon's misinterpretations of his close relatives—people whom he presumably ought to know. Creon originally sees the two very different sisters that the audience has observed in the first scene as indistinguishable. He misreads Ismene's distraught appearance within the palace as a sign of guilt (489–92).[45] The chorus, when Ismene appears, immediately interprets her tears correctly as *philadelpha* (loving toward her sister, 527); later it persuades Creon to renege on his error (770). Creon sees *erōs* as motivating Haimon when Haimon asserts his devotion to Creon's interests, then fatally misjudges both the intensity of Haimon's devotion to Antigone and the girl's unwillingness to live immured in a cave.[46] The chorus, by contrast, takes Haimon seriously; they see merit in both Haimon's and Creon's positions and worry over the implications of Haimon's stormy exit. Creon refuses to credit the possibility of a divine role in the first of the two attempted burials of Polyneices, despite hints of supernatural happenings at the site that awe the watchman and the chorus (278–303). Ignoring the chorus' advice and the order of Tiresias' words, he buries Polyneices before going to rescue Antigone. The disastrous outcome was no doubt unavoidable, but the reversal of priorities is indicative of the judgment that created it nevertheless.

Haimon reveals that Creon's devotion to the state is becoming simply a rigid commitment to his own self-interest and detrimental to civic *homonoia*.[47] Creon ignores the possibility of a conflict between family and state (and among his own family obligations), although we might have expected him to defend himself on these points each time the dilemma arises on stage in his case.[48]

---

fend Creon by arguing that men cannot know cosmic law (see Tiresias on the error common to all mortals, 1024; also 1160) and that his mistake concerning the burial was unavoidable do not account for Creon's repeated errors of judgment throughout the play. On Creon's limitations, see esp. Goheen 1951: 75 and 83, Knox 1964, Winnington-Ingram 1980: 120–28, and especially Roisman 1996, whose study of Creon as an authoritarian personality now overlaps in a number of details with my own.

[44] See Gellie 1972: 35 and Leinieks 1962: 65.

[45] See Linforth 1961: 206 and Gellie 1972: 40. Seale 1982: 93, noting the legal coloring of 493–94, argues that Creon summons Ismene as if she were a witness in a lawcourt (rather than a niece). Women did not testify in person in Attic courts, however.

[46] See Seale 1982: 99.

[47] See further Blundell 1989: 125 and Foley 1995a. Sourvinou-Inwood 1989a: 145 argues that Haimon here ignores the problem of anarchy and disobedience repeatedly stressed by Creon. Yet a ruler who is responsive to his city and serious about maintaining civic harmony and consensus will not destroy civic order by changing his mind. Creon repeatedly aims to repress dissent rather than to create consensus. As Reinhardt 1979: 86 puts it: Creon "thinks himself equal to the *polis* and his judgment equal to *nomos*."

[48] Blundell 1989: 122 and Nussbaum 1986: 55. On his scorn of family ties, even to the extent of dismissing Zeus Herkeios (486–89), and—with an ironical pun on Haimon's name—Zeus *xun-*

Collapsing the differences between public and private worlds, Creon thinks a man *chrēstos* in his household is also *chrēstos* in the city (661–62). Here he refuses to consider differences in the two institutions that may require from those representing their interests a different mode of ethical reasoning.[49] Furthermore, as critics have pointed out, by these very standards Creon demonstrates his shortcomings as a leader, because he repeatedly betrays household obligations (and in so doing also civic obligations, since Polyneices' body pollutes the city).[50] Nor is Creon ultimately willing to look at decision making in dialogic terms; he aims to enforce his will, not to examine and reexamine his choices in context or, like Antigone and Haimon, to adapt his language and argument to his interlocutors.

When Tiresias frightens Creon into changing his mind, he collapses and asks the chorus to make his decision for him (1099).[51] And in his final laments, where he adopts the lyric mode for the first time in the play, he stresses in particular the failure of his deliberation and judgment: the errors of his ill-thinking mind (*phrenōn dusphronōn hamartēmata*, 1261), his unfortunate plans (*ō moi emōn anolba bouleumatōn*, 1265), and the death of his son through his poor deliberations (*ethanes, apeluthēs emais oude saisi dusbouliais*, 1268–69).[52] Creon's own words (and Tiresias and the chorus agree with this evaluation) thus raise fundamental questions about the way that he has chosen to deploy the mode of deliberation that he defined and adopted in his first speech. In fact, after the scene with Tiresias he recognizes at first only the validity of the traditional usages (1113–14) that he rejected in Antigone's argument;[53] it takes the loss of his family to bring home to him the full range of his limitations.[54]

Haimon, on the other hand, attempts a genuine if tragically hopeless mediation between Creon's and Antigone's modes of morality. Like Antigone, Haimon tries to frame his position to communicate with his interlocutor. Like Creon, he uses gnomic generalizations. Haimon cites Antigone's position on the gods below (749) and the glory of her deed (693–98),[55] but he uses other

---

aimon (658–59), see respectively Blundell 1989: 118–119 and Oudemans and Lardinois 1987: 181.

[49] See further Goldhill 1986: 99 and Blundell 1989: 120. Creon asks for Haimon's loyalty as a son, not as a citizen; hence he contradicts his own principles, by having recourse to the authority of the very blood bonds—and even to authority of unwritten laws that traditionally require honoring parents—that he generally devalues. He has also inherited power through kinship bonds (174). (See Neuberg 1990: 71.)

[50] Blundell 1989: 122.

[51] See Linforth 1961: 237 and Roisman 1996: 36–37.

[52] See Cropp 1997: 143 on the play's language of deliberation generally.

[53] See further Goldhill 1986: 103–4.

[54] Even at this point, because he does not bring back Antigone's body with him, he leaves the question of her own proper burial puzzlingly open. See Calder 1968: 403 and Seale 1982: 107. As Porter 1987: 61 remarks, Creon's separation of the bodies of Haimon and Antigone echoes his initial attempt to divide the two dead brothers.

[55] On this echoing of Antigone, see Brown 1987 on line 745. Haimon is not simply urging ex-

popular wisdom to argue that Creon should be flexible in this instance and bend to the concrete fact of a popular feeling in favor of Antigone. Although Creon denies that public decisions should be influenced by family relationships, Haimon insists on his care for and relationship to Creon as his father.[56] "Father, I am yours," he says (635). Reasoning as both son and member of the *polis*, he thinks that Creon's own welfare will be served by listening to those who care for him. The father-son relation should be reciprocal to the extent that fathers should hear and consider their sons' advice (or even, by implication, women's advice) when it is good. Public decisions should be reached and reevaluated in a dialogic, not monologic fashion. While assenting to Creon's view that the interests of the state are primary and that a son should obey his father (635–38), Haimon argues for a more nuanced view of the city and its governance that is attentive to context (e.g., the attitude of the community, the identity of the perpetrator, and the nobility of her act). Haimon's speech makes clear that Creon's mode of generalizing moral reasoning could, if all his principles were correct and deployed in a fashion responsive to context and productive of civic *homonoia,* provide a satisfactory basis for public morality— even if it will always be vulnerable to chance and human ignorance.[57]

Haimon's speech is critical because up to this point the play has dramatized a clash between modes of deliberation derived from very different social positions and circumstances. Creon seems to assume that "the wider the system administered to, the less contextual specific interpretations can be."[58] Haimon, however, takes a position (a position partially approved by the chorus) that even on the level of the *polis,* perception, the bonds of kinship, and a sensitivity to context and motivation can, if deployed in the interest of the city, play as critical a role in public decision making as reason and principle.[59] Like Athena, who casts her vote for Orestes in Aeschylus' *Eumenides* because of who she is (the motherless daughter of Zeus), Haimon is not ashamed to urge a position on his father and ruler because he is his son. Justice, even civic justice, can be no more detached entirely from the person (or the family) and the circumstance than Haimon in a private context can find another furrow for his plow or Creon can find another wife and son. Pericles implies something sim-

---

pediency here. He would not have been persuasive to Creon if he had directly supported Antigone's position.

[56] As Blundell 1989: 122 remarks, Haimon only rejects Creon when he has threatened to kill Antigone before his eyes.

[57] Leaving aside the issue of the burial, many of Creon's gnomic generalizations may well hold up in the right contexts.

[58] Porter 1991: 148. As she stresses, "the emphasis of women's moral agency reflects their historical involvement in small groups" (148). Yet just habits can be learned in the family, even if the formal claims of justice are less operative there (162).

[59] As Broughton 1983: 614 argues, "while justice requires abstraction, it is intended as the abstract form that caring takes on when respect is maintained and responsibility assumed for those we do not know personally."

ilar when he asserts in the Thucydidean funeral oration (2.44.3–4) that those who do not have children to hazard cannot offer fair and impartial counsel to the *polis*. Dinarchus, *Against Demosthenes* 71, says that a rhetor or a *stratēgos*, in order to get the people's confidence, must observe the laws in begetting children. Both apparently refer to an archaic law (cited at Aristotle, *Athenaion Politeia* 4.2) that required an archon or a hipparch to have a child over ten. In *Against Ctesiphon* 77–78, Aeschines argues that Demosthenes is not fit to be a political leader, because he put on white clothes, sacrificed, and took part in public affairs only seven days after the death of his only daughter. Such a bad father, he argues, could never be a good political leader. Those who do not feel proper affection for those most closely related to them will never value nonkin as they should. Those depraved in private life can never properly direct public affairs.[60]

Creon himself adopts a position consistent with these views when he argues that a man not *chrēstos* in his household cannot be *chrēstos* in the city (661–62), but he fails to put it into practice.[61] At the very least, a certain tact was felt to be appropriate where civic and personal interests came into conflict in Athens. Aeschines also criticizes Demosthenes for personally torturing a suspected spy who had formerly entertained him; Demosthenes caused an outcry in the assembly by saying that "he rated the city's salt above the table of hospitality" (2.22, 3.224–25). Presumably Aeschines means that Demosthenes should have upheld the national interest but not so actively.[62] When Aeschines remarks (3.194–96) that in the good old days men would even indict their own friends for illegal procedures, he implies that such behavior may be a thing of the past.

Before concluding, I would like to consider the conflict between Antigone and Creon in the light of questions raised by the cognitive moral psychologist Carol Gilligan. Gilligan's work challenged the theories of Lawrence Kohlberg, who had identified a series of stages in human moral development.[63] Gilligan,

---

[60] See also Aeschines 1.28–40 and Lysias 31.21–23. A man could be disqualified from office for maltreatment or neglect of parents, squandering his inheritance, failing in his military service, or prostituting himself. On related issues, see Leinieks 1962: 78 and 85, where he argues that Antigone displays the kind of family affection on which the prosperity of cities is based.

[61] Leinieks 1962. See further Musurillo 1967: 54, Knox 1964: 11, and Bowra 1944: 77 on Creon's abandonment of his familial obligations. Griffith 1998: 67–72 comments on the difficulties of equating *oikos* and *polis*, especially in a democracy.

[62] Dover 1974: 302. See Dover 302–6 for examples of the importance of subordinating personal needs to those of the state, however.

[63] Gilligan 1982. See also Gilligan 1983; Gilligan, Ward, and Taylor 1988; and Kohlberg 1981 and 1984. In 1984 Kohlberg redefined his position and argued that he was measuring justice reasoning, not moral maturity; justice ideally entails a resolution of competing claims through the impartial application of abstract and universal principles to the situation at hand. Women tend to be arrested at stage three of Kohlberg's six stages. This stage involves mutual role taking and concern with the approval of others and is linked by Kohlberg to the institution of the family.

initially puzzled by the failure of women to achieve high scores on Kohlberg's tests of moral maturity, came to argue that there is empirical evidence that more than one equally valid mode of moral reasoning and moral agency operates in our society. Those who adopt the second mode, what Gilligan calls a different voice, are often, although by no means exclusively, women. Women's attraction to this second mode of moral agency derives in part from their personal rather than positional orientation to other people from the earliest childhood. Whereas masculinity is defined by separation (from the mother) and threatened by intimacy, feminine identity develops through continued attachment and is threatened by separation.[64] For Gilligan, moral problems arise often for women "from conflicting responsibilities rather than from competing rights and requires for their resolution a mode of thinking that is contextual and narrative rather than formal and abstract."[65] In her view the morality of responsibility and care differs from the impartial morality of rights, equality, and justice often practiced by men, and especially by those acting in public contexts, in its emphasis on connection rather than separation, in its consideration of the relationship rather than the autonomous individual as primary. The moral self is radically particularized, and achieving knowledge of the other concrete persons toward whom we act is a complex and difficult moral task. Moral deliberation in this case is not simply a question of impartially weighing competing claims but of sustaining connections, expressing emotions appropriate to the relationship and the situation, and including those who require care. The appropriate action for a particular individual to take is not necessarily the right action for anyone to take in that situation.

The morality of care and responsibility does not in Gilligan's view encompass all morality or replace a morality based on impartiality, impersonality, formal rationality, and universal principle, but it remains in dialogue with it. "Through the tension between the universality of rights and the particularity of responsibility, between the abstract concept of justice as fairness and the more contextual understanding of care in relationships, these ethics keep one another alive and inform each other at critical points. In this sense, the concept of morality sustains a dialectical tension between justice and care, aspiring toward the ideal of a world more caring and more just."[66] Gilligan's data in

---

[64] Here Gilligan relies on the work of Chodorow 1978 and her predecessors. Girls continue to identify and live in daily intimacy with their mothers or female caretakers even after the oedipal transition, whereas boys, who generally grow up with less intimate contact with their fathers, develop masculine identity through relations with peers and by distancing themselves from the mother.

[65] Gilligan 1982: 19.

[66] Gilligan 1983: 47. See also Gilligan in Gilligan, Ward, and Taylor 1988: 4–19. As Porter 1991: 156 points out, Gilligan initially tended to ignore women who (like Antigone) use abstract principles and men who (like all of the characters in this play) give a high priority in moral deliberation to social responsibility. Attachment and connection may be felt for units larger than the nuclear family.

fact show that female subjects do not necessarily ignore considerations of justice in making ethical decisions, but issues relating to care and responsibility tend to predominate or to weigh more heavily with them than with male subjects. At the same time, she does not make clear how the complex dialogue between the two ethical modes might work in practice, and how the tensions between them might be resolved.[67]

I do not have the space here either to do justice to Gilligan's theories, or to contend with the legitimate problems that they have raised. Although she has offered a valuable challenge to post-Kantian ethical discourse, Gilligan's standards have provoked a good deal of controversy in themselves for being, among other things, essentialist, ahistorical, or insensitive to issues of class, status, age, or cultural difference.[68] Nor does she sufficiently account for the possibility that the ethical positions women adopt—actually or prescriptively—are socially constructed by the communities in which they live. The historically and socially constructed expectations for both women and men in classical Athens

---

[67] The best defense of the significance of Gilligan's work for ethical theory is Blum 1988. He, too, however, does not show how moral theory could bridge the gap between these two ethical modes.

[68] For representative critiques of Gilligan, see esp. Porter 1991: ch. 6, Nails 1983, Moody-Adams 1991, and Tronto 1993: 61–97. Porter argues that styles of moral deliberation derive not from essential differences among people, but from socialization and social opportunities (see esp. 142). The data do not consistently report gender differences in cognitive moral development, and educational, class, ethnic, and economic differences may be equally telling explanatory factors; the new and old paradigms may not be concerned with explaining the same phenomena at all. (See Kohlberg 1984, Addelson 1987: 105, and Tronto 1993: 82–84.) Although there is a growing recognition that there may empirically be two (or more) different kinds of moral orientation, and that considerations of care play an important role in moral deliberation, it is not clear that these moral orientations are in fact gender related (see Kohlberg 1984). Moody-Adams 1991 criticizes Gilligan for reproducing in the long run Kohlberg's unwillingness to allow for diversity of moral discourse, by confining her considerations largely to a single alternate possibility instead of exploring the empirical practice of moral reasoning more widely. The care orientation identified by Gilligan may well be the function of setting and dilemma, of private and familial contexts in which certain obligations are presupposed (Kohlberg 1984). Gilligan's attempt to argue that her different voice is the product of a separate track of moral development, or even to articulate precisely the nature and field of operation of that voice, has been hampered both by the highly contextually based nature of this morality and, as Gilligan herself recognizes, by the lack of a traditional moral vocabulary to articulate the nature of these decision-making processes. Kohlberg 1984 takes on the question of two possible tracks of moral development, if not precisely in these terms. See further Porter 1991: ch. 6. Critics have also attacked Gilligan because her arguments are conservative and vulnerable to supporting limiting stereotypes of women, biological determinism, and hierarchizing of differences in moral reasoning. See, e.g., Nails 1983 and Moody-Adams 1991. Tronto 1993: 63 and 91 argues that Gilligan's "theory functions as an account of partial privilege in our society, not as an account of an alternative way to conceive of morality. . . . Gendered morality helps to preserve the distribution of power and privilege." Although these aspects of Gilligan's research make it potentially useful for examining gender issues relating to morality in a society in which such gender-based stereotypes obtained, tragic discourse does not reflect everyday speech and in particular, standard female speech.

differ from our own and what we know of Greek views on moral agency do not correspond to the post-Kantian ethical expectations of Kohlberg. Athenians neither deliberated in terms of competing rights (both Antigone and Creon act out of a sense of responsibility to the family and the unwritten laws or to the *polis*) nor acted as modern ethical individuals. Antigone is a literary character constructed by a male author, and neither the myth-based plots nor the formalized poetic language of tragedy reflects the cultural context in which it was produced in any simple fashion.

In short, although I am contending that male writers of classical Greece recognized and mobilized for their own ends ethical differences between the sexes, I would not argue that the different voices of tragic women correspond to Gilligan's standards. Antigone acts in part on a sense of responsibility and care for her brother, and contextual and narrative thinking plays a role in motivating and justifying her act. Antigone claims that it is her nature to join in love and not in hate (523). Like Gilligan, she takes the stance that appropriate *actions* are not necessarily universal or generalizable. Yet the combative, even confrontational temperament (*autognōtos orga*, 875) and autonomy (*autonomos*, 821) that prove so problematic in the eyes of the chorus, and her assured allegiance to justice in the form of the unwritten laws and to the gods below make Antigone unlike Gilligan's typical female moral agent.[69] Ismene, especially in the choice that she makes in her final scene (to be discussed), or Iphigeneia in Euripides' *Iphigeneia at Aulis*, whose moral stance is initially defined entirely by her role within a family until her final conversion to patriotic principle, come closer to fitting both Gilligan's model and traditional Greek expectations of the female than Antigone, whom the play represents (like Electra) both as extreme and even at times masculine in her assertiveness, yet also defined by female status, limits, and priorities.

In contrast to Gilligan's different voice, Antigone sees no contradiction between a deeply felt commitment to general moral rules and to familial responsibility, between the dictates of pleasure, pain, and experience and a rational adherence to the unwritten laws and the gods below.[70] Antigone's flexible moral style, despite her unflagging, even obsessive devotion to principle, her struggle to defend familial concerns in a public context, and her self-consciousness about the way that gender-specific social roles condition moral

[69] In considering the possibility of a feminist morality, Porter 1991 argues that love and justice need not be antagonistic virtues (161). "If one could show formal operational thinking within typical 'feminine paradigms,' then one could demonstrate that Kohlberg's claim of moral inferiority is merely an experimental artifact" (145). Antigone's ethical reasoning takes us toward this goal by a different route.

[70] On the unwritten laws as sanctioned by the *polis* and central to its interest, rather than marginal to it, see Creon at 1113, Blundell 1989: 128, and Knox 1964: 96–97. At Xenophon, *Memorabilia* 4.4.19–24, Socrates suggests that the transgressors of man-made laws may escape punishment, but not those of divine law. Oudemans and Lardinois 1987: 174 argue, unconvincingly in my view, that because Creon identifies king, country, and gods, his edict is not strictly human.

choice give her a different voice that must be defined on terms that go beyond Gilligan's current formulations.[71] The play articulates its different and gendered ethical voices in a fashion unlike that of Kohlberg and Gilligan, and shows in practice what amounts to an attempt by Antigone to bridge the morality of care and justice that fails to convince Creon as advocate of a principled, impartial morality, even when championed in a more palatable form by Haimon. By staging on slightly different terms the necessary and tension-filled dialectic that Gilligan argues must eventually take place between different moral modes, it can perhaps open new perspectives on the modern debate. What this argument owes to Gilligan, who served as a catalyst for my own thinking, is a critical strategy. For just as Gilligan has argued in a twentieth-century context that Kohlberg's assumptions about ethical maturity may have been distorted by adopting the practice of a male elite as normative or by being insensitive to the range of contexts in which ethical choices are confronted and to the differences among moral agents, I have argued that the examination of the ethical stance of the characters in *Antigone* as a whole has been overly conditioned by a set of anachronistic assumptions about what constitutes a valid mode of moral reasoning.

We cannot be sure what range of views Greeks of the 440s might have had about modes of moral deliberation. The age of sophistry and philosophy was at an early stage on these questions. If Sicilian rhetoric and Protagoras had begun to influence Athens in the 450s, *Antigone* would have been composed at a period of new self-consciousness about differing modes of discourse and ethical argument. Insofar as we can tell, however, neither the later sophistic debates nor philosophy aimed at describing different moral modes that might be suited to resolving different kinds of ethical issues in different contexts.[72] Sophists such as Antiphon enjoyed pitting two arguments against each other so that each undercut and revealed the weaknesses of the other; but these arguments are not expressed in different ethical modes or attached to the specificities of social role and situation in the fashion of this play. Antigone and Haimon both deliberate with an Aristotelian sensitivity to the specific situation, but Aristotle aims at establishing a generalizable ethical system, not staging a clash between valid modes of argument that, despite their strengths, each prove tragically unequal to the full range of public and private contexts in which humans must deliberate and to the questions they face.

Sophocles rarely shows the enthusiastic receptivity to contemporary rhetoric and philosophy that we find in his younger contemporary Euripides; if anything, he is probably more influenced at this stage of his career by Homeric debates (recall the clash of positions between Achilles and his friends in *Iliad* 9,

---

[71] Antigone's stance also reflects, however, a female inexperience in undertaking public roles required, in Creon's view, of leaders.

[72] I am grateful to Michael Trapp's discussion of these issues in his comment on Foley 1996.

where Achilles struggles to introduce a new level of complexity into an argument that otherwise unfolds in conventional terms).[73] In this play Sophocles nevertheless mobilized remarkably sophisticated and subtle differences in characterization and ethical mode to explore difficult moral issues. Due to the very specific context that it is designed to serve, Antigone's moral difference in the end does not provide a generalizable model of ethical deliberation (and cannot do so since virgins face strictly limited legitimate choices), but raises questions about and exposes contradictions in Creon's mode of morality, and hence indirectly problematizes, as tragedy often does, Athenian civic values and discourse.[74] By emphasizing the importance of the unwritten laws in the public sphere, the play refuses to confine Antigone and her ethics to the world of the *oikos* from which they largely derive. Even if it does not go so far as to challenge the relative assessment of justice and care in public morality, it shows the dangers of relying exclusively on universal principle and rigid impartiality.[75]

Indeed, whereas Ismene initially permits the city and its leader to override her responsibility to her dead brother (and living sister), Antigone attempted to define her responsibility to gods, brother, and city as one. Under the pressure of circumstances, Ismene finally chooses to share Antigone's deed for personal more than principled reasons.[76] Life now means nothing to her without Antigone (548), and she wishes to share in her troubles and to take responsibility for the burial (see her fruitless use of the dual at 558). She becomes wild and laments her sister. Ismene bases her reversal not on devotion to the unwritten laws as well as to *philia*, but on her fears of being totally abandoned by those she loves. The guard, who echoes the language of pleasure and pain used by the sisters, but not in conjunction with principle, similarly serves like Ismene as a foil for Antigone; despite some sympathy for Antigone, he is simply concerned with his own survival.[77] Both characters highlight Antigone's more courageous ethical stance, which involves adhering to a general principle in a fashion highly sensitive to personal motivation and context.[78]

Haimon's mediating speech brings some of Antigone's concerns into play in the context of a justice-oriented morality explicitly attentive from the first to the interests of the *polis* and hints at a possible and better mode of public de-

---

[73] See Gill 1996 with earlier bibliography.

[74] See esp. Vernant 1981.

[75] Most unwritten laws affirm behavior sanctioned in the family. Yet I disagree with those critics who see Antigone as consistently aligned with the natural, the supernatural, and the private and criticize her for devaluing human institutions (e.g., Murnaghan 1986b: 200–201).

[76] Linforth 1961: 211 argues that Ismene is not concerned with helping Antigone here, but only with her own loss. I disagree with those critics who see Ismene as a reconciler of conflicts (Jens 1967: 297) or a figure of ideal prudence (Rohdich 1980: 31).

[77] See Nussbaum 1986: 53 on the guard's form of practical deliberation.

[78] In the first scene Ismene defers on principle to the authority of Creon's decree, but she does not view women as capable of making independent choices to act.

liberation. Both Haimon and Antigone's last speech aim to make her seemingly antisocial female rebellion an intelligible stance that citizens can consider appropriate and even praise. The disapproving male chorus nevertheless
feels pity for Antigone, and Tiresias shows that the interests of family and city
are not at odds in this particular situation (and, in fact, the public rhetoric of
the funeral oration celebrated Athens' willingness to defend the burial of the
seven at Thebes on the grounds of traditional usages).[79] Indeed, the play seems
to suggest that both justice and care should ideally play a role in both public
and private ethics. Xenophon's *Oeconomicus* 9.14–16 makes a comparable
point by arguing that a wife must imitate the public sphere in enacting a judicial function in the household.

The play itself, again in a fashion typical of Theban tragedy, is not optimistic
about the possibility of establishing this better mode of public deliberation.[80]
In the end Antigone, Creon, and Haimon are all accused of being irrational;
each turns on those they profess to care for; each in turn fails to persuade
the other.[81] (For a brief discussion of what critics have viewed as flaws in
Antigone's character and behavior, see the appendix to this chapter.) Yet the
fact that all the major characters end up experiencing and surrendering to the
devastating effects of the loss of family bonds seems to raise questions as well
about the morality of the city (both the city of Thebes and the city of Athens,
which also privileged in its public rhetoric the concerns of city over that of the
oikos).[82] The interdependence of citizens central to civic morality fails here to
replace the bonds of kin. A *polis* that denies such attachment, that legislates to
isolate the family too heavy-handedly, may endanger its mode of deliberation
and even its existence. Aristotle himself seems to be concerned with closely
related issues, when he criticizes the watery *philia* that Plato's ideal republic
will inevitably create by eliminating familial bonds. And in the *Rhetoric*
(1.15.1375a–b; cf. 1373b) he cites with seeming approval the fact that
Antigone justifies her disobedience to Creon's *nomos* by referring to the unwritten laws: "it is the part of a better man to make use of and abide by the un-

---

[79] On this issue, see Bennett and Tyrrell 1990 and Foley 1995a.

[80] On Thebes as a tragic anti-Athens, see esp. Zeitlin 1986.

[81] On the effects of passion on Haimon, Ismene, and Eurydice, see Blundell 1989: 138–39 and
Oudemans and Lardinois 1987: 180–84. Antigone does not appear to be much influenced by *erōs*,
although she may, as Winnington-Ingram 1980: 129 argues, harbor erotic feelings for her dead
brother. I do not agree with those critics (Nussbaum 1986: 64, Neuberg 1990: 71, or des Bouvrie
1990: 169) who argue that Antigone is motivated not by strong feeling but by an abstract commitment to kin.

[82] See Sorum 1982: esp. 201–202. She reads the play as a response to the Athenians' appropriation of blood relationships and the household. Sorum argues that when women are compelled
to defend the family, tensions and a skepticism about the family's traditional juridical and religious
role are revealed (210). Antigone's apolitical conception of the family is subversive to civic ideology (205).

written rather than the written law" (trans. Freese [1926] 1967). Such laws are constant and based on nature, whereas written law (Creon's decree belongs at least in Aristotle's view on this side of the opposition being developed here, even if it is a proclamation), because it varies with time and place, may fail in specific contexts to accord with justice.[83] Haimon's position similarly implies that moral rules (such as the unwritten laws defended by Antigone) have less need to be sensitive to context than moral principles such as those on which Creon bases his stance, and that public rhetoric and public morality need not be based on a rigid refusal to give familial feeling, experience, and responsibility their due. Indeed, one might argue that respect for the unwritten laws is precisely the way that a public morality can begin to balance considerations of care against those of justice.

I would not suggest that the tragic virgins discussed in this and the preceding chapter are in any way typical either of the genre itself or of the real women of classical Athens. Tragedy deliberately creates extreme situations and demands unusually problematic choices. Furthermore, from the perspective of earlier Greek literature, some aspects of the moral stance adopted by Antigone are arguably at least as familiar as that of Creon. Like Antigone, the equally irascible Achilles responds in a different fashion to each of his addressees in *Iliad* 9 and unashamedly cites emotional commitment as well as social generalizations in reaching decisions. Creon in principle rejects an aristocratic autonomy in favor of the state, and his first speech certainly contains democratic topoi that give priority to civic over familial interests. Yet we cannot therefore argue that Antigone simply adopts an archaic aristocratic and heroic stance, because the balance between justice and care and the more limited social autonomy of the female agent clearly distinguish her from Achilles. Instead, I hope I have demonstrated that considering how moral agency is articulated in relation to gender in this play permits us to understand the strikingly new ethical frontiers that tragedy is attempting to explore.

Appendix: Antigone's Moral Character

This appendix briefly weighs objections made to Antigone's act and to her ethical character and purported inconsistencies. As we saw, Creon in his devotion to principle cannot imagine contexts in which the interest of the state could legitimately give way to the concerns of individuals or groups of citizens or that

---

[83] See III.6 for further discussion. Knox 1964: 96–99 argues that Antigone is speaking of usages of the gods, not universal laws, just by nature; nor is she contrasting written and unwritten laws. Yet the *polis* passed funerary laws and restricted the burial of the enemies of the state, whereas Attic funerary topoi treated these burial rites as age old and Panhellenic. Hence the general contrast that Aristotle identifies would have been familiar.

there are areas that the state (especially a state that becomes equated with the judgment of one man) should not or cannot control as it wishes. Antigone, on the other hand, has been thought to display some of the limits of an ethical stance that relies too heavily on personal bonds.[84] Creon, Ismene, and the chorus see Antigone as subversive to the civic order, and both Creon and Ismene accuse Antigone of moral myopia. Antigone will not be caught betraying (*prodous'*, 46) her brother, but her brother's attack on his country means nothing to her (see Creon at 512–20).[85] In Creon's view she privileges the interests and justice of the gods below over those of the gods of the city.[86] We have seen that Antigone is not unresponsive to the concerns of the city, although she does not equate those concerns with Creon's decree. Certainly, Antigone's ethical mode neither derives from nor suits public deliberations by the city's leaders in any general sense, and it would be hard to disagree on the limitations of her stance—although it may be the most appropriate one available for her situation.[87] The dramatic action, however, treats Creon's and Antigone's ethical modes in an entirely different fashion. Creon's moral and personal limits are revealed as he is tested in making judgments (in accordance with his own words at 175–77). The principles for which he acts through his decree are admirable if deployed correctly, and no doubt Demosthenes cites Creon's first speech with approval for that reason (19.247 on *Antigone* 175–90). Although Antigone indeed threatens the civic order with her act and ensures its disastrous conclusion by her intransigence, it is Creon who acts destructively to the city in aiming to serve it. His decree pollutes the land and exposes it to new dangers; his punishment of Antigone divides the city; Tiresias announces that he made the wrong decision from the start.[88] Indeed, it is the principles defended by Antigone that ultimately prove to be of public as well as private importance.

Although claiming to be devoted to the care of her family, to be acting in the interests of love and not from hate (523), Antigone has been criticized for refusing to listen to and then quickly turning on the last remaining member of

[84] Some of Antigone's assumptions seem to be culturally anomalous. She denies the persistence of enmity beyond the grave, a convention in epic or even in Sophocles' *Ajax*, while expecting welcome from her relatives in Hades. See Winnington-Ingram 1980: 132 and Blundell 1989: 114.

[85] For a condemnation of Antigone for ignoring city for family, see Knox 1964: 82–83 and 90. Blundell 1989: 113 argues that Polyneices, like Ismene, has forfeited his claim to kinship by engaging in fratricide; the poet does not have Antigone mention that the two brothers were equally responsible for the war (145).

[86] In the view of Sourvinou-Inwood 1989a, she also claims here a knowledge of the unknowable.

[87] On Antigone's narrow and contradictory use of terms such as *philia*, see Goldhill 1986: esp. 97.

[88] Leinieks 1962: 84 argues that Creon teaches city-protecting sentiments, but destroys both city and family.

her family.[89] Antigone, faced with a conflict between two blood relations, defines away Ismene's relation to herself. She will not care for a loved one (*philēn*) loving (*philousan*) in words only (543).[90] Just as for Creon all brides are interchangeable and no one will count as his *philos* who does not give the *polis* the highest priority, for Antigone loved ones must be willing to offer unquestioning and *active* support to kin. Moreover, we see Antigone's model of kinship expressed by brothers toward brothers in fourth-century lawcourt cases, with comparable dilemmas occurring when a brother fails to play his expected role as another self.[91] In other words, the unquestioning and active devotion that Antigone has to her brother is, in the private contexts at stake in these lawsuits, as axiomatic as is Creon's commitment to the state in the context of public action. If a brother who fails to aid a brother can no longer be defined as true kin, the principle can be extended to sisters on the tragic stage. In practice, then, Greek audiences apparently could accept ethical reasoning in one context that proved problematic in another.

Aristotle argues that an audience cannot experience a sympathetic moral affinity with characters who stand at an ethical extreme. Yet the complex problems faced by poets in constructing a morally intelligible female agent who can evoke pity and fear in a predominantly or exclusively male audience are generally greater than Aristotle recognizes. Extreme situations demand extreme choices that do not leave psychological room for sympathetic and tolerant attention to the views of others. Yet those who stress Antigone's harshness toward Ismene must consider first the consequences of passively acquiescing to Ismene's initial objections or accepting her proposed self-sacrifice.[92] Ismene's initial stance leaves no room for mediation, since it denies action to Antigone and burial to Polyneices; indeed, her refusal made it impossible for Antigone to lift the body and hence to complete the rites successfully.[93] It is no accident

[89] Although Ismene is still alive, Antigone describes herself as the last of her family line (895–96, 940–43); hence she evokes the institution of the *epiklēros*, the brotherless "heiress" who must produce an heir for her natal family. Where two brotherless daughters survive their father, both are normally considered to be *epiklēroi*. (See further part I, where I argue that Antigone here attempts to dramatize Creon's failure to marry her off as the last of her family line and to permit her the lament that is her due.) As Neuberg 1990: 71 notes, however, it was Creon's edict that causes this division.

[90] On this point, see Kitzinger 1976: 51. Kin ties are not simply natural and unalterable for Antigone, and marital ties institutional, as some have argued (Murnaghan 1986b: 198).

[91] Golden 1990: 115–19 and Bremmer 1997: 88–94.

[92] As Whitman 1951: 89 remarks, the chorus, in criticizing Antigone, "has failed to reckon with the moral destruction Antigone would have met had she obeyed the decree." Easterling 1990: 93 rightly cautions against detaching the motives offered by each character from the larger context of the play.

[93] Creon may have undone the rites by having the dust removed from the body. Oudemans and Lardinois 1987 argue that if the rites had been fully successful, Polyneices would not have continued to pollute the city. At 904, Antigone says that she paid due honor to the corpse. By this standard, her gesture was not totally worthless. Yet Brown 1987: 9 argues that her attempt not only fails but destroys three people.

that Ismene's words anticipate those of Creon, and to the end she will not acknowledge that Antigone acted appropriately.[94] Finally, Ismene feels emotionally rejected by her sister, but Antigone's reaction is more complicated
than outright rejection. In the first scene, she threatens (in two conditional
clauses, 86–87, 93–94) to "hate" Ismene in *words*, but her refusal of Ismene's
complicity helps preserve her sister's life.[95] Nor does she wish Ismene's death.
"My dying is enough," she says (547); Ismene's survival is a favor to herself
(552–53). She also here confesses pain at "mocking" her sister (551).

Let me turn finally to the much-debated question of Antigone's fierce and
passionate temperament, which has been thought to compromise her ethical
position. In contrast to Ismene, who initially expresses the views of a perfectly
socialized woman,[96] Antigone's wildness and rawness is conventionally characteristic not only of the Labdacids, but of young and unmarried girls, of females who are not under the control of a male, and even of young men.[97] In
the *Rhetoric* (2.12.1389b), Aristotle finds characteristic of the young a concern
with honor, an intense devotion to friends that ignores expediency, optimism,
excess, and a sense of omniscience. Although he undoubtedly has young men
in mind here, female virgins in myth and drama conventionally share many
more characteristics with their male counterparts than do married women. In
Xenophon's *Oeconomicus*, Socrates' interlocutor tries to train his wife to a
proper understanding of her commitments to her marital household only after
he has "tamed" her (7.10). Mythical virgins who reject marriage characteristically head for the wilds sacred to Artemis or become wandering maenads for
Dionysus. In the Hippocratic *On Virgins*, unmarried girls are said to develop a
death wish and leap into wells. Antigone's passionate devotion to her dead
brother is similarly extreme, if culturally comprehensible.[98] Funerary legisla-

[94] The scholiast even finds Ismene's change of mind so halfhearted that no one would believe it.

[95] "*Dikē* will not permit" sharing the blame (538). By Antigone's active standards of *philia*,
Winnington-Ingram 1980: 134–35 is wrong to assert that Antigone's threat that she and Polyneices will hate Ismene is an example of the *sunechthein* in which she tells Creon she will not join.

[96] Weinstock 1937: 125.

[97] Sophocles' virgins (contrast the concubines/wives Tecmessa in Sophocles' *Ajax* and
Deianeira in *Women of Trachis*) can be very like his heroes in temperament. On the heroic or masculine characteristics of Antigone, see esp. Whitman 1951, Knox 1964, and Pomeroy 1975. On
the characteristics of virgins in myth and drama, see further Seaford 1988 and 1990b and Goldhill 1990: 103–4. In Antigone's case the same characteristics are attributed to her Labdacid heritage. Oudemans and Lardinois 1987: 173 argue that Antigone tends to deny the dangerous implications of this heritage. Johnson 1997, perhaps anachronistically, argues that Antigone's
abnormal oedipal attachment to her father and brother explains her rejection of Ismene and her
indifference to Haimon.

[98] The morality of care has been popularly linked with self-sacrifice in the Western tradition;
it could be argued that the spirit in which Antigone's act is undertaken reveals that her mode of
morality contains within it the potential danger of entering too far into the needs of others and
thus failing to protect the survival and integrity of the self (see Gilligan 1983: 74, Tormey 1976,
and Porter 1987: 153–54). Brown 1987: 8 argues that most Greeks would have felt obligated to
bury the dead, but not to the point of dying to satisfy their obligation, or of disobeying authority.
See the chorus at 220: "only a fool desires to die."

tion in Athens from the early sixth century aimed precisely to control women's participation in death ritual and their public displays of incendiary emotion. Antigone shows herself to be characteristically dangerous in this respect; in addition, she stirs up dissension among the people and attempts to carry out alone a rite that she would normally—by Attic convention at least—have conducted in the context of male kin.[99] Antigone's disruptive character and emotions are thus predictable for one in her exceptional situation, yet they do not in fact lead her to a moral error in this instance, even if they put off Creon and the chorus and guarantee tragic suffering. This suggests that the play does not necessarily conform to later philosophical views on the moderate temperament and education that are consistently necessary to proper ethical deliberation in every case.[100]

---

[99] For further discussion of Antigone's attempt to create dissension, see part I and Foley 1993. On the last point, see Sourvinou-Inwood 1989a: 139–40.

[100] See, however, Aristotle's views on anger mentioned in III.2.

III.4

Tragic Wives: Clytemnestras

THE MOST INFAMOUS of Greek stage wives is Clytemnestra. Combining the
treacherous murder of her husband with adultery, she embodies the greatest
threats to the cultural system of which a wife is capable; her crime, performed
in revenge for a child, then divides her from her remaining children, and thus
brings her maternal role into question as well. Yet in plays by all three famous
Greek poets, Aeschylus' *Oresteia*, Sophocles' *Electra*, and Euripides' *Electra*,
Clytemnestra takes center stage to defend her crimes and her "just" reasons
for undertaking them at some length and with ambiguous results. In all three
plays, gender issues play an explicit and critical role in Clytemnestra's defense
and the judgment that her claims evoke. Yet these are formulated differently
in each play. The rare opportunity to compare versions of the same scene enables us to examine more fully both the nature of female moral agency and
the cultural issues at stake in representing it on the tragic stage. In each play,
women's comparable moral choices also contrast dramatically with those
made by men.

This chapter looks closely at the relevant defense scenes in both Aeschylus'
Agamemnon and Euripides' *Electra*.[1] Aeschylus' Clytemnestra resists being
judged simply as a female or domestic agent, but ultimately fails in her attempt
at resistance, whereas Euripides' queen envisions her choice entirely from
within a traditional female role and is judged accordingly. The context in
which each heroine speaks and acts—explicitly public or largely domestic—
conditions strongly the representation of her actions and choices.[2] In each
case, social, philosophical, and moral questions are so intertwined that we can
only evaluate the ethics of these scenes by considering these issues in conjunction with each other. These plays testify to the impossibility of imagining

I would like to thank Rick Griffiths and Christian Wolff for their response to a very early draft
of this chapter and audiences at Oxford, Berkeley, and the Center for Hellenic Studies for their
comments.

[1] Although Sophocles' play also stresses gender issues in a fashion already discussed in III.2, the
debate between Clytemnestra and Electra itself raises these issues less directly and centers so
strongly on Electra that it is of less interest for this chapter, although it will be mentioned for comparative purposes at various points. In any case, the debate operates on entirely different terms because Electra claims that Agamemnon had no choice about sacrificing Iphigeneia, because the
army could neither go home from Aulis nor depart for Troy unless Artemis was appeased for his
killing of her sacred deer.

[2] Although all scenes are played outside the stage building in Greek theater, various dramatic
clues can help to establish a more domestic or public tone for a scene. See Easterling 1988.

a Greek wife and mother as a moral agent acting autonomously and in her own interest, regardless of the claims made by the various Clytemnestras themselves. Yet, especially in Aeschylus, the terms in which this case against female justice is represented are not what a modern audience might have expected.

Aeschylus' Clytemnestra

Three times in the *Oresteia*, an avenger stands triumphant over the bodies of his or her enemies and defends the murders to a shocked chorus. In *Agamemnon*, Clytemnestra's defense of her killing of Agamemnon (and, indirectly, Cassandra) is followed immediately by that of Aegisthus. In *Choephoroi*, Orestes offers the first of two defenses of his killing of Clytemnestra and, to a lesser extent, Aegisthus. All three defenses are represented in language that suggests a trial and hence prefigure the proceedings that finally occur in Orestes' formal civic trial by jury at the Areopagus in Athens.[3] The scene between Clytemnestra and the chorus is by far the longest and most complex. In the case of both Clytemnestra and Orestes, the chorus is left in a state of perplexity. The chorus of elders in *Agamemnon* is not won over by the queen, but it admits that Clytemnestra's case is hard to judge (1561). The chorus of women in *Choephoroi* has supported Orestes as liberator of the city of Argos from tyranny (1046–47) and as the loyal avenger of his father (1051); he is in the chorus' view a noble victor (1052). Yet the women are appalled by the visual impact of the dead bodies and confused by the sudden appearance of the to-them-invisible Furies. Their final words clearly incapsulate their uncertainty about Orestes: "and now thirdly has there come from somewhere a deliverer—or shall I say a doom?" (*Choephoroi* 1073–74, trans. Lloyd-Jones [1979] 1993). The chorus of *Agamemnon* expresses no doubt in its condemnation of Aegisthus. He deserves to be pelted to death by stones and cursed by the people (1615–16); as a man who let a woman act for him, he is unworthy to rule Argos. Yet they cannot contend with his superior force.

These three scenes also occur in a closely similar theatrical context. Each avenger stands over or near the dead bodies of the slain. Clytemnestra's victims lie side by side, Agamemnon still draped with the netlike robes in which he was trapped in his bath. Orestes, standing over the bodies of a second set of illegitimate lovers, displays these same robes. Each scene echoes the other in its language and concerns, yet each is critically different. The audience is clearly meant to compare and, like the chorus, to judge them.

It is not difficult to demonstrate that the text presents Clytemnestra's "trial"

---

[3] III.5 on *Medea* makes the case that the choice to take revenge is in the Greek context viewed as a serious ethical responsibility, although in the real world of Athens revenge must be taken only in the lawcourts. The amount of dramatic time devoted to Orestes' decision to obey Apollo and kill his mother and avenge his father should make this point for the trilogy as well.

before the chorus of elders in subtly different terms than the nevertheless pointedly similar defenses of Aegisthus and of Orestes in *Choephoroi*. What is far more complex is to explain and evaluate these differences and their implications concerning the moral agency of the sexes. Indeed, depending on how we interpret the notoriously difficult passage, *Agamemnon* 1497–1504, it could be argued that Clytemnestra is not an autonomous moral agent at all. If in these lines Clytemnestra attempts to avoid responsibility for her crime by claiming that it was not she but the Alastor or avenging spirit of the household who killed Agamemnon by taking her form (though I do not think we should interpret the text this way), then she cannot be judged as an agent comparable with Aeschylean male characters. Although the range of an individual's moral activity in Aeschylus is frequently limited by forces outside the individual's control, and a god may pervert the course of a person's thinking without that person displaying outward signs of such possession, there are no other cases where the issue of a character's responsibility for his or her actions could be interpreted as questioned because a daimonic force acted in the character's shape.[4]

What makes the moral dilemma posed by Clytemnestra different? Precisely, I would argue, because she is a woman. The *Oresteia* evolves dramatically as a male-female conflict and tensions between the genders are explicit throughout.[5] This scene offers the climactic female challenge to a masculine system of justice, language, and ethics. Clytemnestra asks to be judged as a public autonomous actor on the same terms as a male leader about to take over the throne, but the chorus refuses to respond to the queen on her terms. They visualize her as a mad irrational housewife who has killed her husband. In their view, the heroic king Agamemnon has not only been killed unjustly but has been killed *by a woman*; they cannot conceive how this can represent justice from Zeus (although they believe it must). Clytemnestra repeatedly undercuts the chorus' attempts to reflect on and comprehend the crime by envisioning and formulating the issues from a different perspective that is clearly condi-

---

[4] In the *Oresteia*, Orestes is directed to act by Apollo's oracle, and Agamemnon's choice to kill Iphigeneia may be partially determined by unspecified external forces such as hereditary guilt, *atē* (divinely inflicted blindness or destruction), excess of wealth and power, or prophecies interpreted as divine commands. Eteocles in the *Seven against Thebes* may be influenced by a Fury or his father's curse in his choice to kill his brother. The decision to commit a crime or the performance of bad deeds can also pervert an individual's ethical reasoning; this seems to be the case with Agamemnon after or as he chooses to kill Iphigeneia. Both Clytemnestra and Agamemnon are said to become all daring, *pantotolmos*, after they commit crimes (221, 1237). The bibliography on Agamemnon's choice and the forces that influence ethical choice in Aeschylus is immense. See, with further bibliography, especially Dodds 1990, Dover 1973, Doyle 1984, Edwards 1977, Fisher 1992: 283–86, Gantz 1982, Hammond 1965, Lesky 1966, Nussbaum 1986, Peradotto 1969, and Rosenmeyer 1982: 257–308.

[5] On male-female conflict in the *Oresteia*, see esp. Zeitlin 1978 (rev. 1996), Gagarin 1976: 87–110, and Winnington-Ingram 1983: 101–31.

tioned by her social role as woman, albeit an unusually androgynous one.[6] At the same time, she uses her ability to mimic and appropriate masculine and public language to serve what from the choral perspective would be a regime that entirely undercuts the cultural status quo. She implicitly remakes the rules of marriage and inheritance, reverses traditional sexual mores, and publicly expresses a female sexual pleasure in her triumph. Although her defense is in some respects remarkably powerful, her attempt to respond to choral concerns ultimately leads her to undercut her own case, especially her claim to be acting as a fully autonomous agent. The evolution of her conflict with the chorus thus sets the stage for a process of refeminization that is displayed in the final scene with Aegisthus and for Clytemnestra's later confrontation with and decisive defeat by Orestes in *Choephoroi*. Before turning to Clytemnestra's defense, however, I consider in more detail the important differences between her defense and those of Orestes and Aegisthus, and then turn to a brief survey of the way in which Clytemnestra has deployed language prior to this scene.

The Case against Clytemnestra

Orestes' defense, although it by no means resolves his case or establishes a certain claim to justice, is presented in terms that invite a different judgment of his crime than of Clytemnestra's. Politically, he is a liberator of a city oppressed by tyrants and is openly supported by Electra and the chorus, whereas Clytemnestra and Aegisthus use their act of vengeance to appropriate Agamemnon's wealth and to establish their rule over an unwilling city. While Clytemnestra, at least initially, gloats over her "victory" with language thick with sexual innuendo and perverted ritual,[7] Orestes simply tries to argue the justice of his case. (We should recall here, however, that erotic pleasure in violence or revenge is ascribed to Agamemnon and/or the army over the sacrifice of his daughter and to the Greek army in its conquest of Troy [215–17, 341 with 827–28]).[8] Although Clytemnestra explicitly views herself as put "on trial" (judged) by the chorus (1412, 1420–21), Orestes' language is more frequently colored by sober legal overtones, and he tries to make his case not only by impugning Clytemnestra's character but with visual proof—the

[6] As Betensky 1978: 13 describes Clytemnestra more generally: "As much as Achilles or Ajax or Antigone, she finds that society's values do not fit her; she can change her circumstances, but not . . . prevent the consequences." See further Fraenkel 1962 on 1401; Clytemnestra "rejects the application to her of accepted ideas as to what is womanly."

[7] See esp. Zeitlin 1965, Vickers 1973: 381–82, and O'Daly 1985: 8–12; on the perverted sympotic imagery here, see Macleod 1983: 26 n. 29; on Clytemnestra's *hubris*, see Fisher 1992: esp. 291; and on her sexual innuendo, see Pulleyn 1997.

[8] On the pleasures involved in revenge, see *Iliad* 18.108–10, Aristotle, *Rhetoric* 1.11.8–13.1370b, and Cohen 1995: 66–68.

bloodstained robe.[9] The step between *Choephoroi* and the decorum of the law-court is smaller. Orestes, like the litigants in the Areopagus according to Aristotle, sticks to the point (*eis to pragma*).[10] He can claim explicit divine authorization for his act that takes precedence over his own human motivation; his reluctance to kill his mother is pointedly staged for the audience and the killing requires a surprise intervention by the heretofore silent Pylades. Clytemnestra also claims divine support for her action, ranging from Zeus, Ate, the Erinys, and the *daimōn* of the house to her daughter's Dike, but the claim receives neither certain external confirmation after the fact nor the validation of prophecy in advance.[11] Whereas the elders of the chorus view the triumphant Clytemnestra as mad and out of control from the start—the blood they see in her eyes also drips from the eyes of the Furies (*Agamemnon* 1428, *Choephoroi* 1058, *Eumenides* 54)—the women of the chorus in *Choephoroi* are shocked and puzzled by Orestes' madness.[12] They cannot see the Furies and at first doubt their reality (*Eumenides* confirms their reality by bringing them on stage); they wonder if it is simply the temporary effect of the blood on Orestes' mind (1055–56) and expect Apollo to purify Orestes successfully. Furthermore, whereas the source of Clytemnestra's supposed "madness" remains threateningly obscure, Orestes' is imposed from the outside and has been predicted by his mother, who has threatened Orestes with maternal Furies (*Choephoroi* 912, 924). Even after the appearance of the Furies, Orestes' claim to justice remains sober, consistent, and unchanged, whereas Clytemnestra's stance has been interpreted as changing and inconsistent.

Finally, and perhaps most importantly, we do not see Clytemnestra make her choice for vengeance but only defend it after the fact. Although the chorus views a wife's killing of her husband as a crime requiring exile or death, Clytemnestra does not represent herself as struggling to choose between avenging her daughter and committing a crime against her husband, the legitimate king of Argos, and the father of her children. By contrast, we see Orestes' struggle between two highly overdetermined courses of action. (The same is true of Agamemnon in his deliberations, reported by the chorus, over the sacrifice of Iphigeneia, 205–27.) Killing his mother is mandated by Apollo and by his obligations to avenge his father, whose Furies will pursue him if Orestes does not act; yet to do so requires matricide. Right clashes with right, wrong with wrong. Several Aeschylean male heroes make difficult moral choices on

[9] Cohen 1995: 84 notes that in many modern cultures that practice vendetta it is mothers who keep a piece of bloodstained cloth to stimulate their children to enact revenge.

[10] Aristotle's *Rhetoric* 1.1.5.1354a18 says that at the Areopagus litigants could not speak *exō tou pragmatos*, off the point.

[11] Calchas' prophecy at 150–55 does hint at Agamemnon's murder, but it remains unclear whether it forms part of Artemis' divine plan.

[12] On Greek views of madness in tragedy, see most recently Padel 1992 and 1995.

stage;[13] the very dramatic ellipsis of choice for Clytemnestra may well significantly undermine her status as a serious moral agent. With all these strikes against her (although, of course, we have not yet seen Orestes when we hear Clytemnestra's defense), it may seem surprising that the dialogue between Clytemnestra and the elders leaves them so puzzled about her act.

Nevertheless, the contrast between her defense and Aegisthus' has quite the opposite effect. By the standards of vendetta justice, Aegisthus would seem to have almost as good a case as Clytemnestra (even, in the view of Denys Page, a better case).[14] He is taking revenge on Agamemnon for his father Atreus' crime against the children of Thyestes. His father presumably had as legitimate a claim to the throne as that of Atreus. In contrast to Clytemnestra's hyperbolic and metaphorical language, his defense is relatively circumspect and to the point. He alone planned what he views as a just crime and takes responsibility for it. His action was strictly voluntary (*hekōn*, 1613). He claims the gods support his act (1578–79), and he has dutifully fulfilled his father's curse (1601–2). Although the chorus accuses him of inappropriately displaying his triumph over the dead man (*Aigisth,' hubrizein en kakoisin ou sebō*, 1612),[15] Clytemnestra's language in fact expresses triumph far more extravagantly. Despite his sober claim to justice, the elders of the chorus at once condemn Aegisthus to death by stoning and the people's curses, and, until Clytemnestra intervenes, they do not back down even when threatened with force. It is enough for them (and here they echo contemporary Attic legal standards) that he planned the crime *hekōn*; they look forward to the avenging Orestes' return.[16]

As in actual court cases, character clearly plays an important role in the chorus' judgment here. Aegisthus is characterized, as many commentators have shown, by the crude language of a swaggering bully who will prop up his rule by using Agamemnon's wealth.[17] In the chorus' view his claim to the throne is undermined by his cowardice and lack of masculinity: he is a "woman," an adulterer, and a stay at home who let a woman kill a returning general and pollute the country and its gods. Aegisthus' assertion that trickery is a woman's

---

[13] Eteocles in *Seven against Thebes* and Pelasgus in *Suppliants*.

[14] Denniston and Page 1957: ad loc. In fact, enmity could be inherited even in classical Athens (see Lysias 14.40 and Demosthenes 21.49 on *patrikos echthros*), but it was meant to be played out nonviolently or in the lawcourts.

[15] I retain the manuscript reading *hubrizein* here. As Fisher 1992: 271 and 283 points out, this is the only place in the *Oresteia* where the term *hubris* is used to condemn the actions of a character on stage.

[16] See note 44.

[17] See the commentaries of Denniston and Page 1957 and Fraenkel 1962. Goldhill 1984a: 95–96 comments on Aegisthus' lack of skill with words; whereas Aegisthus relies on clichés, Clytemnestra uses clichés self-consciously to make a pun. As Conacher 1987: 55 points out, he shows little awareness, in contrast to Clytemnestra, of the current dangers of the *talio*. Like Clytemnestra he suppresses the role of adultery in the crimes of the house.

role and that he was a suspect enemy, and therefore could not challenge Agamemnon directly (1636–37), cuts no ice with the chorus. If anything, Aegisthus' appearance seems to restore a sense of moral clarity to the chorus and mute the powerful confusion unleashed by its encounter with Clytemnestra. Yet many of the issues raised in this last scene with Aegisthus appeared in the scene with Clytemnestra. Clytemnestra also lays claim to the crime (planning as well as executing it) and the chorus at first has no doubts about her appropriate punishment; she too triumphs inappropriately over the body. She too announces that she will rule if her forces (Aegisthus) prove stronger (1421–25). When she describes her killing of Cassandra, her language descends to provocative crudity (1440–47).[18] If anything, the case against her character is far richer than that made against Aegisthus'. Yet the chorus finally concludes that the defense presented by Clytemnestra, which it views as an exchange of mutual recriminations (*oneidos hēkei tod' ant' oneidous*, 1560), is difficult to judge (*dusmacha d'esti krinai*, 1561).

Clytemnestra's Language

The *Oresteia* repeatedly raises doubts about women's moral capacity and stability in a fashion that echoes standard views in classical Athens and Clytemnestra repeatedly challenges the chorus' doubts about the authority of female speech. The chorus claims to respect Clytemnestra's *kratos* (political power) in the absence of her husband (258–60) and once concedes that she speaks *kat' andra sōphron' euphronōs legeis* (sensibly like a self-controlled man, 351), but it clearly expects women to be more readily influenced than men by dreams or by indirect and hence unreliable evidence—perishable rumors as opposed to solid visual appearances. In its view a woman's mind (literally, her boundary) or her ordinance (*horos*) is too easily persuaded or too persuasive— the sentence is almost impossible to translate (485–87).[19] Clytemnestra objects that the chorus blames (*emōmēsō*, 277) her *phrenas* (mind) as if she were a young child; later she gloats over its error in upbraiding (*eniptōn*) her for a premature celebration of the Greek victory based on the fire signals (590–92; she is responding to the chorus' words at 479–84). The tone of Clytemnestra's verbs here suggests continuous tension over this question of female competence and the truth of female speech.

In the trilogy, even talking to women is viewed as fundamentally different from talking to men. When Orestes arrives at the palace in *Choephoroi*, he thinks it would be better for a man in authority to respond to his knock rather than the mistress of the house: "For the respect [*aidōs*] owed a woman in con-

---

[18] See O'Daly 1985: esp. 15 on her violent, vivid, and coarse language.

[19] See Denniston and Page 1957: ad loc.

versation makes one's words obscure; a man speaks confidently to a man and signifies an open, sure sign" (665–67, trans. Lloyd-Jones [1979] 1993, modified; see also *Agamemnon* 351 and *Choephoroi* 735 and 849–50). Nevertheless, Clytemnestra appears at the door to greet him; she is clearly the one in charge of this house, despite her lip service to a properly subordinate female role and her deference to Aegisthus as ruler. It is she who also closes *Agamemnon*, tactfully ushering Aegisthus away from his fruitless confrontation with the chorus while asserting that he and she, ruling the house together (the dual form *kratounte*, 1673), will set things right. Although neither Orestes nor the chorus of elders seems reluctant to challenge Clytemnestra, and she may be arguably viewed as forfeiting a normal woman's role by her brazen indifference to shame (*ouk epaischunthēsomai*; 1372, *aischros*, 614; *aischunoumai*, 856) and female limits, the language of these two scenes with the queen remains far more complex and even obscure than the choral confrontation with Aegisthus. Her exceptional persuasive powers and her challenging and famously ambiguous speech do indeed make her difficult to argue with.[20]

Moreover, as other scholars have shown in some detail,[21] Clytemnestra frequently demonstrates her ability to disconcert and undermine the chorus and Agamemnon with the persuasive power of her speech. As noted earlier, the chorus is inclined against accepting the evidence of the beacons that Troy has been captured. It is impressed by Clytemnestra's speech (317–19) and entirely unaware that she has framed her description to bring the fires of Troy's destruction metaphorically to rest on the house of Atreus.[22] By the end of Clytemnestra's next uncannily prophetic speech,[23] which envisions the fall of

[20] Goldhill 1984a: 85, 89, and 91 contrasts Clytemnestra's ambiguous speech with Cassandra's desire for accurate language and prophetic clarity. Clytemnestra is quite capable of prophetic clarity and accuracy, however, as we see in her speech where she imagines what might have happened during the fall of Troy.

[21] See esp. Neustadt 1929, Betensky 1978, Goldhill 1984a, Sevieri 1991, and McClure 1997a and 1997b. For Clytemnestra, speech becomes action. Goldhill 89 comments on her ability to preempt choral deliberation and asserts that her willingness to reverse her earlier deceptive position and speak to the moment hints at her lack of sexual control and her perversion of the boundaries of ritual and nature.

[22] On this speech, see esp. Betensky 1978, Goldhill 1984a, and McClure 1999: 74–75.

[23] Critics from Neustadt 1929: 254–61 on have noted the suggestive combination of truth and deception in her speeches. Sevieri 1991: esp. 13–14, 19, and 29 stresses that Clytemnestra is the only character in the play with the conscious knowledge to take effective action. Thalmann 1985: 226 in his discussion of 611–614 comments on her "self-conscious, and almost a mocking, use of verbal ambiguity" and her excess of meaning. She suggests her willingness to conform to a typical female role and at the same time reveals her adultery and her murder plans. Clytemnestra repeatedly challenges the conventions associated with messenger speeches. Her own messenger speech is, according to Goldhill, untransparent and hypocritical (1984a: 53); see also Vickers 1973: 358 on the "polyvalent" aspects of this speech. She usurps a choral role by announcing the entrance of the messenger (489–98), then rejects hearing his message in favor of learning directly from Agamemnon. Clytemnestra does not need to hear from others to be prophetic. See Taplin 1977: 229–302 on how her entrance and exit in this scene reflect this mastery.

Troy and expresses her fears that desire (erōs, 341) has led the army to destroy what they should not and offend the gods, the chorus praises the speech for its masculine good sense and is willing to offer thanks to the gods (351–54). Clytemnestra, however, has just pointedly called the same speech that of a woman (348). Indeed, Michael Gagarin argues that her description represents a female perspective on the fall of Troy by emphasizing the plight of the defeated survivors, whereas the messenger stresses the suffering of the Greek army and the joy of victory.[24] The effect of this speech has worn off by the end of the next choral stasimon, where the chorus begins once again to doubt female speech and the validity of the beacon signs (475–87). Clytemnestra's words are confirmed by the herald, however.

After Agamemnon's return, Clytemnestra's masterly duplicitous address to the elders in his presence reveals her murder plan under the guise of a list of female sufferings in the absence of a husband at war, and offers her the opportunity to spread the purple tapestries before the king's chariot under cover of fulsome, orientalizing praise of her husband (895–913). As Stephen Halliwell remarks of this speech, "it derives a crucial part of its eerie resonance from the way in which, at its very opening, it seems to confound public and private, political and personal, by mixing a sense of an official occasion with the professions of an ostensibly faithful wife."[25] She flouts the norms of shame by announcing her virtue to the city, not privately to her husband. The "image of female isolation and psychological vulnerability" that she projects in this speech "sits uneasily alongside the rhetorical boldness, indeed bravura, with which she now dominates the formal occasion of the king's return."[26] Above all, she combines masterful public rhetoric with deliberate untruth in a pointedly civic context (as she later chillingly admits, she has exploited the rhetorical formula of speaking to the occasion or the kairos [kairiōs eirēmenōn, 1372]).[27] As the Attic orator Demosthenes puts it, "there is no greater harm that anyone could cause you than by speaking falsely. For how could those whose political life is grounded in speeches be politically secure if these speeches are not true?" (19.184)[28] Indeed, Halliwell wants to see in Clytemnestra's usurpation of "male" rhetoric, style of deliberation, and action a reflection of Athenian ambivalence about rhetoric itself.[29]

Finally, in a brief thirteen-line dialogue (931–43), Clytemnestra persuades Agamemnon to walk on the tapestries against his better judgment. She dis-

[24] Gagarin 1976: 93–94.

[25] Halliwell 1997: 132.

[26] Ibid. As Denniston and Page 1957: ad loc. note, she here speaks like a person defending herself against a charge that has yet to be made.

[27] The word also implies speaking diplomatically or to produce a desired result. Thalmann 1985: 228 notes that in her speech after the murder Clytemnestra now uses multivalence of language to reveal truth rather than to express and conceal it simultaneously.

[28] Trans. Halliwell 1997: 121.

[29] Halliwell 1997: 134.

concertingly introduces a series of hypothetical circumstances in which someone would walk on the tapestries and ends by getting her husband both to do
so and to agree to her "victory" in this contest (as her future sacrificial victim,
he must walk voluntarily to his demise).[30] As he exits, her prayer to Zeus asks,
from the perspective of the audience, for support in accomplishing his murder (973–74).[31] The house of Atreus is, as the watchman puts it in the first
speech of the play, indeed ruled by the expectant heart of a woman with the
deliberative capacities of a man (*androboulon*, 11). Among other things, Clytemnestra has in the tapestry scene implicitly made a public demonstration of
Agamemnon's unfitness to rule and of his corruption by the Trojan experience;
her earlier speech about the army at Troy is confirmed by Agamemnon's own
description of the army's behavior at the city's fall (821–28) and hence taints
him with impiety.[32]

Laura McClure appropriately stresses Clytemnestra's bilingualism in these
early scenes, her ability to offer epic boasts, sure proofs, and public addresses in
masculine style and to play the role of a woman, whose speech, like that of Cassandra, is characterized by ritual language, deferential gnomes that reinforce
traditional female roles, prayer, and even silence.[33] For example, in her opening speech to Agamemnon, she pretends to be vulnerable to rumor and dreams
in typical female fashion, having earlier denied any such weakness to the chorus (274).[34] In her triumphant speech over the dead body of her husband,
Clytemnestra frighteningly mixes male and female language and perspectives.
Here she is no longer hiding the truth, and her "true" character emerges. Her
revenge is a masculine contest against enemies seeming to be friends (1374–
81)—yet her first weapon is a net, not the sword. She compares her third blow
to the third libation poured (always by men) to Zeus (now Zeus of the dead)
at a banquet or male symposium (1385–87) and goes on to conclude:

[30] On her use of potentials and negatives that do not prove a positive statement, see Goldhill
1984a: 77; for a range of other interpretations of this complex scene, see, with further bibliography, Buxton 1982: 106–8, Goheen 1955, Easterling 1973, Gundert 1960, Judet de la Combe
1989–90, Konishi 1989a and b, Jones 1962, Meridor 1987, Sevieri 1991, Pucci 1994: 96–99,
Simpson 1977, Vickers 1973: 367–70, and Winnington-Ingram 1983: 106–7. Headlam (Thomson [and Headlam] 1966) on 931 comments on "an undertone of strife between the two wills"
stressed by the repetition of the first-person pronoun (*emoi, egō, eme*). Wohl 1998: 104 argues that
Agamemnon is unable to resist Clytemnestra's eroticization of him, as well as her "interpellation
of him as an illegitimate and impossible creature." On Clytemnestra's language of victory, see Bonnafé 1989: 154.

[31] See Goldhill 1984b, Lebeck 1971: 72–73, and McClure 1997a.

[32] Clytemnestra then announces that she too would have vowed to tread on robes if she could
have secured thereby Agamemnon's return (963–65), and goes on to repeat his act by destroying
a valuable cloth from the household herself. She stains the "net" in which she captures Agamemnon with his own blood. Wohl 1998: 105 argues that Clytemnestra's debased economic language
characterizes her as a dispensable, bad aristocrat.

[33] McClure 1997b: 115–16 and 1999: 71–80. See also Sevieri 1991: 14, 20, and 27–29.

[34] McClure 1997b: 120 and 1999: 79.

And if one could pour over a corpse libation of a fitting liquid,
It would be just to pour this, no, more than just!
Such a mixing bowl of evils, sprung from the curse, did he
Fill up in the house and return himself to drain!
(1395–98)[35]

Yet this perverted banquet is also a perverted fertility ritual-birth-sexual climax as well as a (from this perspective legitimate) claim to cosmic justice, in which the avenging Clytemnestra symbolically becomes the earth's crops ecstatically renewed by the moisture of the king's blood (1388–92). Because she views this claim as legitimate, she even invites the chorus to rejoice with her (1394).

Having established Clytemnestra's disconcertingly androgynous mastery of language, let us now turn to an examination of Clytemnestra's defense of her killing of Agamemnon to the chorus. My analysis is detailed because this complex scene has received insufficient attention and discussions have tended to leap too quickly to generalization about its evolution and arguments.[36]

Clytemnestra's Apology[37]

After Clytemnestra's initial speech over the dead body, the chorus' first reaction is to object to her bold language (*thaumazomen sou glōssan, hōs thrasustomos*, 1399),[38] and her inappropriate boasts over the body of a man/her husband (*ep' andri kompazeis logon*, 1400).[39] As we saw, they will make the same objection to Aegisthus; from Homer onward it was considered inappropriate to boast over the body of a dead man (*Odyssey* 22.412, Archilochus fragment 134 West; see also Euripides, *Electra* 900–956), although of course epic warriors do so nevertheless. The chorus domesticates this traditional wisdom to fit

---

[35] Trans. Lloyd-Jones [1979] 1993.

[36] The most extensive and valuable analysis is that of Neuberg 1991. For other useful discussions of the scene, see O'Daly 1985, Konishi 1989b: 124–33, Vickers 1973: 382–85, and Winnington-Ingram 1983: 108–12. Vickers argues that the final scenes progressively undermine Clytemnestra and Aegisthus (although the process begins with the Cassandra scene). Konishi argues that Clytemnestra's goal here is to suppress the elders' attack (124); once the elders realize they cannot blame Clytemnestra, they attack Helen (127).

[37] In Greek, an apology (*apologia*) is a defense speech.

[38] On the tongue as a weapon in this trilogy, see esp. *Choephoroi* 309–10 and Cassandra on Clytemnestra's deceptive bitch's tongue (1228–30).

[39] Even to engage in argument with a woman nevertheless implies offering a sort of grudging equality to her. In Euripides' *Iphigeneia at Aulis*, Agamemnon tells Clytemnestra that she has spoken well, but that it is indecent for him to engage in argument with women (829–30); in *Agamemnon*, the king tells Clytemnestra in the tapestry scene that it is not a woman's part to desire [verbal] battle (940). In actual lawcourt cases, one does not duel verbally with inferiors (Cohen 1995: 79).

a different context. The implication seems to be that in its view this outrageously bold woman, who is not entitled by her sex to such boasts in any case, is boasting over the one man she ought above all to have respected, her domestic partner.[40]

Clytemnestra, who, like Euripides' Medea, has been perverting through excess the language and ideology appropriate to a heroic male warrior,[41] interprets these words of the chorus as trying her like a mindless woman (*peirasthe mou gunaikos hōs aphrasmonos*, 1401). In insisting that she speaks with a fearless heart (*atrestō(i) kardia(i)*, 1402) to those knowing (*pros eidotas*), and that the corpse is the work of her right (masculine) hand (1405), a worker of justice (*dikaias tektonos*, 1406), she seems to be objecting to the chorus' domestication of the situation and its refusal to understand her act from her own perspective. She asks to be praised or blamed (1403) by putative equals on the terms she describes: that is, as a heroic and just (male-style) avenger, not as a woman using speech inappropriate to her sex about her husband. It is surprising that she thinks the first alternative—praise—possible for the chorus. Agamemnon has already stressed that such public praise is traditionally part of an exchange among men (914–17). In short, Clytemnestra demands to be treated on the same terms as an autonomous, masculine agent, even though she will repeatedly fail in this scene to adopt a standard masculine perspective on the events that have occurred.

The chorus now bursts into a lyric mode in which it remains for the remainder of the scene (1407–11). This spectacle of a group of men in an epirrhematic scene singing, while a female character speaks, is anomalous in tragedy, and must serve to contrast Clytemnestra's assertive claims to justice with the response of an increasingly disconcerted chorus.[42] The elders of the chorus cannot accept Clytemnestra's representation of herself on heroic terms. They pointedly address her as woman/wife (*gunai*, 1407). They wonder what transforming drug she has consumed.[43] But they do now direct their attention to her act and treat her as liable to civic punishment for it. They propose banishment. This is not the normal punishment for deliberate, premeditated homicide in Athens, although it is a punishment for involuntary homicide.[44]

[40] For the choral emphasis on Clytemnestra's crime against her *husband*, see Neuberg 1991: esp. 60–61. McClure 1997b: 119 stresses the masculinity of such boasting.

[41] Bonnafé 1989 offers the most detailed examination of Clytemnestra's appropriation and perversion of heroic language in the play (see also Winnington-Ingram 1983); she sees Clytemnestra as assimilating herself to a male role in order to replace Agamemnon.

[42] In the Cassandra scene, the reverse is at first the case. Cassandra finally draws the chorus into the lyric mode at 1119; at 1178, she inaugurates a shift to iambic trimeter.

[43] See Winnington-Ingram 1983: 108 n. 42. The elders of the chorus are "still preoccupied with the fact that a woman (*ō gunai*) has done it—a phenomenon they can only ascribe to drugs." Similarly, Vickers 1973: 283 speaks of the chorus' persistent failure to believe that a woman has done it.

[44] Voluntary homicides were tried at the Areopagus court, whereas unintentional homicides were tried at the Palladion and with different penalties. Planning a murder, as Aegisthus claims

The elders do prescribe the normal death penalty at once for the male Aegisthus, who is represented as acting deliberately and voluntarily. Thus their choice of punishment for Clytemnestra may suggest that they still resist her claim to have planned and performed the act deliberately. Clytemnestra will, they assert, also be cursed by the people and citiless (*apopolis*, 1410).

In response to the choral shift in tone, Clytemnestra, ready mimic of a range of public discourses, now abandons heroic language and female claims to cosmic justice for the diction of the courtroom. (We should recall here that women did not represent themselves in court.) Using legal language, Clytemnestra recognizes this as a judgment, but a harsh one (*dikazeis*, 1412; *epēkoos d'emōn / ergōn dikastēs trachus ei*, 1420–21).[45] Yet, as in the tapestry scene, she shifts the interpretive context for the chorus' traditional response to homicide. The elders have in her view not established themselves as just judges, because whereas they propose this punishment for her, they did not do so in the case of Agamemnon's heinous crime against Iphigeneia, who was the product of her labor, and a charm (*epōidon*)[46] against Thracian winds (1417–18). This whole formulation is unsettling in numerous ways. Her term for the banishment that the chorus proposed, *andrēlatein* (literally, drive out a man, 1419), by implication fits the male Agamemnon better than herself.[47] The chorus has expressed unease about the sacrifice of Iphigeneia and indeed the whole Trojan War itself, but it did not earlier view Agamemnon's choice as actionable in a civic context. For Clytemnestra, Iphigeneia is viewed, in contrast to standard patriarchal views, as *her* child by right of her birth pains, outrageously expropriated by her father for a cause here trivialized as mere magic. The public concerns that the chorus views as involved in Agamemnon's choice—Paris' violation of Zeus' laws of hospitality, the will of the army—play no role in her representation of the event. Finally, Clytemnestra hints that she is not a helpless woman, but has the force to rule the city against its will.

The chorus replies to this unsettling challenge not by responding to its content but by labeling it as an outrageous display of boldness (*megalomētis*, 1426; *periphrona d'elakes*, 1427), representative of a madness literally visible in the blood fleck in her eyes (1427–28). Bereft of *philoi* (friends or relatives), Clytemnestra is in its view no longer simply ripe for exile but for the violent infliction of the *talio* (*tumma tummati*, 1429–30).

Clytemnestra, in contrast to the chorus, always responds directly and point-

---

that he has done, was treated as voluntary homicide. See MacDowell 1963: 46–47, 60–62, and 110–22, and 1978: 114–15 and 120. At the Areopagus, however, litigants claimed to be innocent; those who admitted guilt simply received their punishment outright.

[45] Fraenkel 1962 on 1418 comments that "the first half of this speech, 1412–18, is couched in a single rather elaborate period. Clytemnestra pleads her cause like an advocate in court." Gantz 1983: esp. 68 argues that the chorus prefigures the jurors of Eumenides, but cannot respond effectively to establish judicial control of violence.

[46] Fraenkel 1962: ad loc. thinks that the word has a "deprecatory flavor" in this context.

[47] Goldhill 1984a: 91 and Winnington-Ingram 1983: 111 n. 53.

edly, if on different terms, to what the chorus says in this scene.[48] She shows that she is not bereft of *philoi*, although her *philoi* are not blood relatives. Such reliance on support from outside the immediate family would normally be characteristic of men rather than women. Reinvoking the power of her oaths as well as the justice of her child,[49] and the Ate and Erinys for whom she slew Agamemnon, Clytemnestra patiently explains that her confidence is not representative of insanity, but derives from Aegisthus, who protects her, lights *her* hearth, and has proved loyal and well disposed to her (as Agamemnon has not, 1434–37).[50] (The image of "lighting one's hearth" probably has sexual connotations as well; see *Choephoroi* 629–30.)[51]

She then further castigates Agamemnon's corpse by complaining of his adultery—literally his polluting outrage (*gunaikos tēsde ho lumantērios*, 1438) against either herself or Cassandra—with women at Troy and with his current sexually aggressive and trustworthy concubine (*pistē xuneunos*, 1442, i.e., she displays wifelike devotion).[52] She describes Cassandra as a lover, *philētōr* (1446), a term usually reserved for men. Here Clytemnestra may attribute to Cassandra her own active sexuality, since her death is said to add relish to the queen's own bed (1446–47). As discussed in part II, importing a concubine

[48] See esp. Kranz 1919: 315 (reprint, 1967: 22) on the close correspondence here between choral challenges and Clytemnestra's answers. He argues that this represents a survival from the epirrhematic composition of drama in its early stages. O'Daly 1985: 17 notes that Clytemnestra agrees twice with the chorus, whereas the elders never reply to details from her speeches or echo her words, as she does theirs. Thus, "the invitation to an *agōn* (1421–25) is never fully taken up." He also comments on the contrast between the chorus' fear and grief and the actor's more rhetorically articulated and argued sentences (2).

[49] Daube 1939: 181–82 remarks on Clytemnestra's blasphemous travesty in linking oath and sacrifice.

[50] In Athens marriage is confirmed in large part by the couple's residing together (*sunoikein*). See part II. We know little of gender roles in relation to the kindling of the hearth fire. Tending the hearth may normally have been the task of a virgin daughter or a wife after her incorporation into her husband's household (Vernant 1969: 135–36), but the rekindling of a hearth by a new master may have been a different matter. (Sacrificing at the hearth was a male task. See Fraenkel 1962 on 1435.) At Argos, for example, the fire at the hearth of those recently bereaved is extinguished as polluted and rekindled from the house of others (Plutarch, *Quaestiones Graecae* 296F). Vernant (139–42) argues that the masculine Clytemnestra here gives Aegisthus the role normally performed by the wife, although this interpretation does not accord with her treatment elsewhere of Aegisthus as husband. Pulleyn 1997: 566 n. 9 argues that by calling the hearth her own, Clytemnestra demotes Aegisthus from dominant male to attendant. Whatever the proper procedures, Clytemnestra is probably changing and/or perverting them here.

[51] See Clytemnestra's dream of Agamemnon's royal scepter in Sophocles' *Electra*, which sprouts when thrust into the hearth (Vernant 1969: 140), and Artemidorus' *Interpretation of Dreams* 1.74, where the hearth signifies life and the wife of the dreamer, and the lighting of the hearth the begetting of children. See also Wohl 1998: 103 and Pulleyn 1997.

[52] See Winnington-Ingram 1983: 109 and Vickers 1973: 385. Konishi 1989b: 128 sees Clytemnestra's implicit comparison of Aegisthus' devotion to herself with Cassandra's to Agamemnon as part of Clytemnestra's attempt to deflect criticism of her adultery.

into a household presided over by a wife was frowned upon in Athens (see, e.g., Sophocles' *Women of Trachis*; Clytemnestra in Euripides' *Electra* makes a similar argument at 1030–38).[53] Yet David Daube notes that from a legal point of view *lumantērios* should apply to Aegisthus, not Agamemnon; unlike Aegisthus, Agamemnon is not culpable by Attic law for his adultery.[54] Clytemnestra's own "adultery" is swept aside in her blithe treatment of Aegisthus as someone who already is and acts as her husband—he protects her, treats her as a *philos*, and lights her hearth—whereas she attributes to Agamemnon's inappropriate liaisons with women the culpability normally accorded unfaithful wives. In one blow, both the sexual double standard and the masculine right to make marriages have fallen.

The chorus, once again failing to respond directly to Clytemnestra's arguments, now seems to shift course from directly condemning the queen.[55] Presumably, the reality of Aegisthus' power has undermined the elders' ability to serve as effective judges.[56] They wish for painless death because Agamemnon, now viewed as their kindest protector in contrast to their previous criticism of the king, has suffered at the hands of a woman/his wife (*gunaikos*, 1453, 1454). In searching to explain this horrifying unnatural event, they turn to the mad (*paranous*) Helen, who alone (*mia*) destroyed many at Troy and caused strife in her husband's house (1455–61).

Clytemnestra now shifts into another more intense register in a move from spoken iambic trimeter to anapests in recitative. This shift seems to reflect both increasing frustration and a new approach to communicating with the elders of the chorus.[57] Apparently she is now willing to respond to their desire to look at the crime in broader perspective. She tells the elders not to be suicidal and not to blame Helen alone as a man-destroyer (1462–67). In short, she refuses to allow them to rely on the traditional poetic cliché they have been bandy-

[53] See Headlam (Thomson [and Headlam] 1966) ad loc.: "perhaps by the active word she wishes to imply that the woman was the seducer." See also O'Daly 1985: 14–15 on *paropsōnēma* (relish).

[54] Daube 1939: 182.

[55] Neuberg 1991: 59 argues—in my view, convincingly—that the chorus' shift represents an attempt to understand and acquire moral perspective on Agamemnon's death. In his view, the chorus wants to understand why, if Zeus is just, Agamemnon had to die and how his death relates to the Trojan war and the family history. Similarly, O'Daly 1985: 16 and Conacher 1974: 329 define the transition as an exploration of the act's ethical and religious dimensions.

[56] In contrast to critics like Vickers 1973 or Konishi 1989b, I think we cannot assume here that Clytemnestra has persuaded the chorus of the justice of her position. O'Daly 1985: 16 by contrast thinks that the chorus wants to imagine Clytemnestra as both agent and victim (of drugs, madness, the *talio*, the *daimōn*).

[57] Hall 1999: 115 suggests that such anapests permit a grand declamatory manner more suitable than lyric for masculinized females (see also Pintacuda 1978: 114 and 171–73); lyrics would normally be expected of female relatives in a context where others are beginning to lament. The generalization concerning masculinization may hold true in most cases, but in this scene the shift also corresponds to an increasingly defensive posture for Clytemnestra.

ing about, especially in the second stasimon, which finds the root of all ills in women and their adultery.[58] Clytemnestra's term man destroyer, *androleteira* (1465), implicitly assimilates Helen to Amazons. It literalizes and makes absurd the chorus' claim that Helen could actually kill many men (perhaps in unspoken contrast to the deed of the heroic, androgynous Clytemnestra herself). Yet in a sense it deprives the chorus of a sort of consolation, for the man-destroying Amazon can at least offer, according to Apollo in *Eumenides*, a death more noble than that inflicted by a deceptive wife (627–28).[59]

The chorus then stops blaming Helen on these terms but will not let women off the hook. It turns to the *daimōn* (the evil spirit) of the house, which is (again unnaturally) exercising power through women (*kratos t'isopsuchon ek gunaikōn . . . kratuneis*, 1470–71). The borders between Clytemnestra and the *daimōn* seem to collapse in the choral image of a (carrion-eating) raven standing over the corpse and singing tunelessly (1472–74); the participle describing the crowlike figure, *statheis* or an elided *statheis'*, might be either male (the *daimōn*) or female (Clytemnestra), but the visual image evokes Clytemnestra's posture on stage. Like that of the *daimōn*, her hymn/language is discordant/out-of-cultural bounds (*eknomōs/humnon humnein epeuchetai*, 1473–74).

Clytemnestra, turning on the chorus a touch of its own previous condescension to herself, now commends the chorus for straightening its judgment (*ōrthōsas . . . gnōmēn*, 1475). By calling the *daimōn* thrice-fattened (*tripachunton*, 1476), she paves the way for making a connection between the current crime against Agamemnon and two earlier ones.[60] In her mind, the two earlier crimes would logically be the death of Thyestes' children and Iphigeneia; if so, Clytemnestra implicitly remakes inheritance law by integrating her daughter into the direct lineage of the royal house (usually considered male, especially when the daughter has a brother). By contrast, at the end of *Choephoroi* the chorus sees the three storms encountered by the royal house in strictly patrilineal terms as the death of Thyestes' children, Agamemnon's murder, and the Furies' attack on Orestes, which prevents him from assuming the throne.

The elders of the chorus are outraged by what they interpret as Clytemnes-

---

[58] See also Cassandra on the *prōtarchon atēn* (the initiatory blindness or disaster, 1192) of the household, Thyestes' adultery with Atreus' wife. Goldhill 1984a: 95 n. 46 argues that Clytemnestra's later reference to the remote ancestor Pleisthenes (1569) implicitly challenges Cassandra's claim.

[59] The chorus may pick up on a contrast between the two adulterous sisters in its reply, as it calls them *diphuioisi*, two in nature (1468). Clytemnestra has earlier suggested that that she herself is a worthy heroic opponent to her man.

[60] Note the earlier claim that her third strike on Agamemnon was performed as a libation to Zeus. As Conacher 1987: 52 points out, by invoking the endless flow of blood caused by the *daimōn*, she unconsciously condemns herself; Vickers 1973: 384 thinks she has found "the perfect metaphor for her situation, unaware though she is."

tra's *praise* of the *daimōn* (*aineis*, 1482; *ainon*, 1483).[61] Again, her language, which might be viewed as reveling in the *daimōn*'s bloodthirsty habits (*erōs haimatoloichos*, 1478), strikes the elders as challenging their sense of propriety (although the modern reader might not be likely to interpret Clytemnestra's language here as praise). The elders now turn to Zeus for consolation, as they did in their prayer in the parodos (1485–88). Zeus must be the cause of all. Yet this turn to Zeus and by implication to his justice apparently does not console them, for they at once revert to their despair over the mode of the ignoble (*aneleutheron*, 1494) death of their king, trapped in the web of a spider, the victim of deceit and a two-edged weapon (wielded by implication by the unheroic female, 1492–96).[62] How can they properly lament the victim of such a fate (1489–91)? For violent death outside the battlefield deprives a hero of the most honorable forms of burial ritual (see *Choephoroi* 345–71).

Interpreting Clytemnestra's next shocking response has provoked a storm of controversy.

αὐχεῖς εἶναι τόδε τοὔργον ἐμόν
μὴ δ᾽ ἐπιλεχθῇς
Ἀγαμεμνονίαν εἶναι μ᾽ ἄλοχον.
φανταζόμενος δὲ γυναικὶ νεκροῦ
τοῦδε ὁ παλαιὸς δριμὺς ἀλάστωρ
Ἀτρέως χαλεποῦ θοινατῆρος
τόνδ᾽ ἀπέτεισεν,
τέλεον νεαροῖς ἐπιθύσας.

aucheis einai tode tourgon emon.
mē d'epilechthē(i)s
Agamemnonian einai m'alochon.
phantazomenos de gunaiki nekrou
toud'ho palaios drimus alastōr
Atreōs chalepou thoinatēros
tond'apeteisen,
teleon nearois epithusas.
(1497–1504)

Eduard Fraenkel translates these lines as follows:

Thou art confident that this deed is mine, . . . [he brackets 1498] that I am Agamemnon's wife. But appearing in the shape of this dead man's wife, the ancient fierce spirit

---

[61] On *aineis* and *ainon* here, see Fraenkel 1962: ad loc. It is possible to interpret these words less provocatively, as "you tell of" rather than "praise" and "tale" rather than "eulogy." But this accords less well with the choral outrage and Clytemnestra's own repeatedly disconcerting language in this scene.

[62] At 1332–42, the chorus is already appalled at the prospect of the victorious and divinely honored Agamemnon dying for those who died before.

[Alastor] that takes vengeance for the misdeed of the cruel feaster Atreus has now rendered this full grown man as payment to the young, a crowning sacrifice.

From the perspective of those who adopt this or similar translations, Clytemnestra now asserts that the killing of Agamemnon is not actually her deed, but that of the Alastor of the house (the *daimōn* in avenging mode), who has in her form taken a full-grown sacrificial victim (Agamemnon) in payment for the young (the children of Thyestes and possibly as well Iphigeneia).[63] In the view of many scholars, this speech represents an attempt to avoid responsibility for the crime that is immediately challenged by the chorus and denies Clytemnestra full moral agency and intent.[64] Yet as others have pointed out, and I shall not reproduce the extensive arguments here, this claim would be inconsistent with Clytemnestra's assertion of "responsibility" for the crime both before and after this passage.[65] Fraenkel himself is loath to interpret these words as a denial of responsibility on Clytemnestra's part; he views this speech as a momentary lapse.[66]

[63] Denniston and Page 1957: 208 interpret as follows: "Clytemnestra is not saying . . . that it was not her hand which did the deed, but only that the Alastor worked *through* her; there was only one person engaged—the Alastor embodied in Clytemnestra."

[64] Daube 1939: 190 (and 186) argued that Clytemnestra here makes a deliberate attempt to shift the legal responsibility for Agamemnon's death from herself and to protect herself from punishment. If so, as Neuberg 1991: 47 points out, she does not succeed in her aim. Among others, Adkins 1960: ch. 6, Conacher 1974: 326–28 and 1987: 52, Hommel 1974, Konishi 1989b: 130, O'Daly 1985, Rosenmeyer 1982: 240, Vickers 1973: 385, and Winnington-Ingram 1983: 112 also view Clytemnestra as attempting to avoid responsibility for her crime. Vickers interprets her claim as an inconsistent excuse that is depicted as deliberately feeble. Rosenmeyer 298 (see also 271) raises the difficulty of understanding causality in such Aeschylean claims: "it seems as if talk about the curse or the demon of the house is likely to come in at a point when agents, sufferers, or for that matter, bystanders sense a need for unusually emphatic formulations. It answers psychological needs rather than strictly etiological considerations."

[65] Neuberg 1991 reviews previous arguments and makes an eloquent case that interpreting this passage as an attempt to transfer responsibility for the crime from Clytemnestra makes no sense dramatically, philosophically, and thematically. He argues that human responsibility in the face of divine interference in human events is not an issue for characters in the *Oresteia* and not the point of the drama (51). For Clytemnestra's assertions of responsibility for her deliberate and premeditated crime, see 1377, 1380, 1404–6, 1421, 1497, 1551–53, and 1567–76; *Choephoroi* 887–91. She also continues to fear punishment for her crime.

[66] For Fraenkel 1962: ad loc., Clytemnestra is "not making excuses for herself: she means what she says." Clytemnestra experiences a moment of realization in which "the deed now appears to her so frightful that *at least at this moment* [my emphasis], she is convinced that . . . the Alastor . . . borrowed her shape." See the criticism of Page 1957: ad loc.: "there is nothing in the text to suggest that Clytemnestra is suddenly aware of the horror of her deed, and looking around for an excuse or explanation." In general, previous approaches to this passage with the exception of Neuberg 1991 cannot explain why Clytemnestra would make this possibly contradictory and (to the chorus) unconvincing speech at all. Neuberg 1991: 53 argues that Clytemnestra asks the chorus not to take into account that she is Agamemnon's wife and adduces a divinity of vengeance to support this point, because this is not relevant to the justice of the case; she wants to be labeled avenger, not wife (62). As he points out (53 n. 19), other commentators have inadequately ex-

Alternatively, Hugh Lloyd-Jones [1979] 1993 translates 1497–1502 as follows (the alternatives in brackets are also possible):

You aver that the deed is mine.
But do not [don't even] consider [take into account][67]
that I am Agamemnon's consort!
But manifesting himself to[68] this dead man's wife [woman]
the ancient savage avenger
of Atreus, the cruel banqueter, . .

For the remaining lines I would retain Fraenkel's translation. Difficult as the passage is, this translation in my view best fits the extant text, the normal lexical range of the vocabulary, and the dramatic context as a whole.[69] The choice is not critical to the main thrust of my argument, however, because I take the position that neither translation in fact implies that Clytemnestra is denying responsibility for her act; nor is responsibility the central issue at stake.

If we look carefully at Clytemnestra's previous claims in this scene, we know that she calls Agamemnon her *posis* or legitimate husband (1405) only in the

---

plained *Agamemnonian einai m'alochon*, "I am Agamemnon's wife." Conacher 1987: 51–52 sees the apparent shift as part of Clytemnestra's attempt to blame Agamemnon rather than Helen; this could be an element in the text, but does not fully explain it.

[67] The scholiast probably misinterprets 1498–99, *mēd' epilechthē(i)s / Agamemnonian einai m'alochon* as *me nomize eme einai, phēsin, alochon tou Agamemnonos*, or "do not think that I am Agamemnon's wife." The aorist passive *epilechthē(i)s* can be deponent, and normally means "consider" or "take into account." *Mēde* as a connective meaning "and" or "but . . . not" requires a preceding negative or the equivalent and is according to Fraenkel 1962 unexampled in the sense required for this passage. To take it as a nonconnective, "not . . . even" puts in his view too much emphasis on the following verb. Neuberg 1991: 62 by contrast argues for the translation "Don't even take into account." Other commentators (Conacher 1974: 325 n.2 and 1987: 73 n. 92) have thought either that Fraenkel may overemphasize the problems here or adopt, as does Page's Oxford text, Scaliger's emendation *tē(i)d' epilechthē(i)s* (the translation would then be: "[You] considering in the following way that . . . ").

[68] As Fraenkel admits, the rare word *phantazomenos* with the dative normally means "make manifest to," "become visible," "appear" (sometimes like a dream [Herodotus 7.15]) not "liken oneself to" or "appear in the shape of."

[69] At *Persians* 354, an *alastōr* appears (*phaneis*) from somewhere to the Persians. A Greek man comes from the Athenian forces and deceives Xerxes. This Greek may serve as the instrument of the *daimōn*, just as women do in the chorus' view at *Agamemnon* 1470, but the text does not assert that it acts in his shape. A closer parallel, perhaps influenced by this passage, occurs at Euripides' *Electra* (979), when Orestes, questioning the justice of Apollo's oracle, wonders whether an *alastōr* could have likened himself to (*apeikastheis*) the god; at *Orestes* 1668–69 the hero similarly fears that an *alastōr*'s voice speaks through Apollo. Divine beings disguise themselves as mortals to deceive humans from epic on. They also appear to mortals and often tell them how to act. A human slayer can also be described as an *alastōr* (*Eumenides* 236). Overall, the tradition does not strongly favor any one interpretation of the passage. For further bibliography, see Fraenkel 1962: ad loc.

context of proclaiming her heroic act of justice over his corpse.[70] She already viewed Aegisthus as her de facto spouse (he has lit her fire and proved himself a steadfast protector); hence she does not wish her legal relation to the corpse to be taken into serious account in determining the justice of the case.[71] Indeed, at 1374–75, she went so far as to categorize Agamemnon as an *echthros*, enemy, though he seemed a *philos*, friend or relative (*echthrois . . . philois / dokousin einai*); this also implicitly denies the moral force of her marital relation to him. So far, then, Lloyd-Jones' translation makes sense in context. Despite the chorus' plaints, Agamemnon's status as her husband was not a deterrent factor in her choice to take revenge for her child and should not constitute an important consideration for the chorus. Moreover, Clytemnestra herself, as she twice says, explicitly acts to avenge her *daughter* and claims justice for her deed on that basis. It is logical for Clytemnestra to take on the earlier crimes of the house of Atreus against the children of Thyestes, as she does here, only as Aegisthus' consort, because this is the crime that he (not she) must by the logic of vendetta avenge.[72] As wife of Agamemon or mother of Iphigeneia, she would not normally treat Thyestes' children as kin to be avenged.[73] Moreover, she earlier viewed other deities besides the Alastor (Ate, Erinys) as in some sense participants in the crime as well.

The appearance of the Alastor to the woman (wife) of the corpse, or alternatively the Alastor's action in her form, represents in my view a daimonic incarnation of Clytemnestra's relation to Aegisthus.[74] Aegisthus lays claim to the crime and asserts that he enacted the murder through Clytemnestra and put her up to it. Cassandra had earlier prepared the audience, if not the chorus, which cannot understand her, to interpret the murder on these terms. At 1217–22 Cassandra has her second vision of the children of Thyestes, who in her view continually haunt the house. She asserts that because of the children (lit. *ek tonde*, for this reason, 1223) a cowardly lion, who frequents a bed that the audience knows to be Clytemnestra's, is plotting penalties for Agamem-

---

[70] At 1405, she perhaps implies in her use of *posis* her right as wife to avenge Agamemnon's abuse of his role as husband. She also refers to him as *posis* elsewhere when addressing the chorus (600, 604), but in these earlier speeches she is playing the proper wife, not representing her real views. In the tapestry scene, she exploits the ambiguity of her situation by using the more general term *anēr*, man or husband (867, 896; the term *philanoras tropous*, husband or man-loving ways (865), in particular, hints, unbeknownst to her internal audience, at her adultery).

[71] See note 50.

[72] As Fraenkel 1962: ad loc. notes, without seeing the significance of the point, "that is really Aegisthus' justification, not her own."

[73] See Winnington-Ingram 1983: 112 n. 57. He disagrees with Daube 1939: 192, who claimed that Clytemnestra acquired the curse by marriage. Daube's claim runs counter to everything we know about a wife's legal and social position in Athens. See part II.

[74] Winnington-Ingram 1983: 113 n. 60 suggests in passing something similar when he notes that "Aegisthus is, in one aspect, the *alastōr* embodied (and truly *patrothen*)." My point applies only to the murder of Agamemnon; elsewhere in this final scene the *daimōn* is treated as external and now hostile to both Clytemnestra and Aegisthus (1569, 1660).

non. In her view it is Aegisthus who plots punishment for Thyestes' children, and Aegisthus' own later words echo the image of exacting payment for their deaths (*cheiros patrōias ektinonta mēchanas*, 1582) that Clytemnestra uses of the Alastor (*apeteisen*, 1503). By contrast, in Cassandra's prophecy Clytemnestra, like the treacherous Ate (1230) to whom Clytemnestra later says she sacrificed her child, will bring the murder to pass; the female is slayer of the male (1231) and a monstrous mother is at war with her own *philoi* or relatives (*thuousan Haidou mēter' aspondon t'Are / philois pneousan*, 1235–36). At 1108 Cassandra also prefigures the chorus' horror at Clytemnestra's treatment of her legitimate husband (*homodemnion posin*).

To repeat, Clytemnestra's representation of her act outside this passage suggests strongly that she does not refer to the Alastor in order to deny that she performed the deed or that she may be liable to punishment for it. She relies on Aegisthus to avoid civic punishment for the crime (at least for the immediate future); yet she did it and will soon try to make a deal with the *daimōn* to appease it with wealth and to deflect it from her house (1568–76). Nevertheless, Aegisthus also had a role, as yet unknown to the chorus, in planning and instigating the crime. Indeed, he soon claims to be its sole planner despite Clytemnestra's initial claim to premeditating it (*emoi d'agōn hod' ouk aphrontistos palai*, 1377). At this point in the scene, the elders of the chorus are also not interested in punishment for Clytemnestra's crime, but in making sense of the humiliating justice offered by Clytemnestra to their king. As noted earlier, Clytemnestra repeatedly responds directly and pointedly to choral concerns throughout the scene, although she does not interpret the issues in the same terms.[75] Here she reacts to the elders' concern over Zeus' justice, Agamemnon's ignominious death by a woman/wife, and the difficulty of lamenting the king as the hero they want him to be. She is after all planning to rule over them as subjects, and, despite her seeming lack of concern over their attitude to the crime and her exchange of reproaches, she has throughout the play also aimed to persuade them of her just authority and status, not simply to inflict it, as does Aegisthus. The elders themselves imagine a *daimōn* that attacks the house and the two brothers Agamemnon and Menelaus as exercising power humiliatingly through *women*. Clytemnestra aims here primarily to establish that the *daimōn* is male, that his cause is (also?) patriarchal (involving male children and the royal line),[76] and that the murder is connected to and even derives from crimes

---

[75] O'Daly 1985: 17 argues that from the moment Clytemnestra shifts to anapests, she and the chorus enter into a process of mutual correction. Clytemnestra criticizes its interpretation of Helen's role; the chorus then turns to the *daimōn* instead; Clytemnestra makes the *daimōn* responsible for the crime, and the chorus modifies Clytemnestra's claim. My disagreement with this analysis overall will be clear, but from the start, the turn to the *daimōn* that works through women does not involve an abandonment of the Helen thesis.

[76] Clytemnestra may include Iphigeneia in this formulation, since she has implictly integrated her daughter into the royal line.

in the male line (see the chorus' term *patrothen* at 1507). Her act is, by implication, not just the act of a woman to avenge her daughter, and thus easier for the chorus to envision as a product of Zeus' justice.

Just as the elders of the chorus earlier misunderstand Clytemnestra's confidence in her power to ignore their condemnation because she had not yet mentioned Aegisthus, here they do not yet see (because they have not yet heard) the connection of her claim about the *daimōn* to Aegisthus. Who shall be *witness*, they say, that Clytemnestra is *anaitios* (1505) in relation to the murder? The word *anaitios* is hard to translate and its implications here are uncertain; possibilities range from "guiltless," "blameless," to "not the origin or cause of."[77] No alternative can be ruled out here, given the uncertainty of the context, but the problem also lies partially in the difference between Greek notions of liability or responsibility and our own.[78] In a somewhat similar situation at *Iliad* 19.86–144, for example, Agamemnon claims that he was not *aitios* for his actions toward Achilles because he was in an abnormal state of mind (under the influence of *atē*, moral blindness, sent by the gods); nevertheless, he did the deed and is willing to make up for it. The cause or origin of his action and his intentions do not lose their importance, but, as Bernard Williams puts it, "there is an authority exercised by what one has done. . . . As the Greeks understood, the responsibilities we have to recognize extend in many ways beyond our normal purposes and what we intentionally do."[79]

In *Eumenides*, Orestes admits that he did the murder, although he leaves it to Apollo to argue whether his act was just. Apollo says that he will be Orestes' witness (*marturēsōn*, 576) and advocate/fellow pleader (*xundikēsōn*, 579), as well as accept *aitia* for instigating the matricide (*aitian d'echō* / *tēs toude mētros*

---

[77] The one other use of the term *anaitios* in the trilogy is not decisive. The women in the chorus of *Choephoroi*, when they hear Aegisthus' death cry, propose standing aside so they will appear *tond' anaitiai kakon*, not *aitiai* for these evils (8/3). They did not perform the act, so it cannot be attributed to them, as is the case with Clytemnestra. But they could be blamed for assisting in the crime by deceiving Aegisthus.

[78] Neuberg 1991: 68 wants to interpret these lines not in terms of responsibility, but censure. In his view the chorus here refuses to withdraw censure: "How could anyone possibly attest that you are not to be censured for this murder?" In other words, the chorus will not give up considering that she is a wife who killed her husband but will now grant her the role that she claims as avenger. This ingenious interpretation cannot explain why the chorus grants her this avenging role now, rather than earlier, when she made her case about Iphigeneia. It also depends on suppressing other possible meanings of the word *anaitios* in a fashion hard to do in a passage this ambiguous. See Neuberg's interesting appendix on *aitios* (65–68) in the trilogy; he makes a good case that it does not mean responsible in the modern sense, but focuses entirely on connotations of blame or censure (the word's earliest meaning in Greek literature), rather than the causal implications of the word (see also *Agamemnon* 811). The two, as in the *Oresteia*, are often hard to separate. At *Antigone* 1183, to give another example, the chorus accuses Creon of being *aitios* for Haimon's death. Here Creon is apparently interpreted as both cause of and to blame for his son's suicide. On the causal and initiatory aspects of the term, see Williams 1993: 58–61.

[79] Williams 1993: 69 and 74. Thus, at *Odyssey* 22.154–56 Telemachus takes the blame for having unintentionally left the door to the storeroom open and thus permitting the suitors access to weapons.

tou phonou, 579–80).[80] In *Eumenides*, the Furies accuse Apollo of sharing *aitia* (*metaitios*, 199) for instigating Orestes' crime and his actions following it or even being entirely *aitios* for Orestes' actions (*panaitios*, 200) due to his prophecy.[81] Yet in the Furies' eyes Apollo's position as *aitios* does not exempt Orestes from punishment for the matricide that he performed[82] and half of the jury agrees with them. Apollo's role as *aitios* nevertheless makes possible Orestes' claim to *justice* for his action. Clytemnestra's claim about the Alastor could be interpreted on comparable terms. Clytemnestra does not deny that she performed the deed and answers for it, but the *daimōn*'s role makes it more *just*. At the same time, Greek women normally obeyed the commands of a male guardian. Ironically, once Clytemnestra has introduced a *male* instigator/co-performer for her crime, she begins to undermine in a male-dominated world her earlier claim to the role of a just, autonomous (masculine), heroic avenger, and implicitly to adopt a secondary female role.[83]

At *Agamemnon* 1505–6, the chorus may on one level be responding to Clytemnestra on her own terms and asking for *evidence* that she is not the most authoritative blameworthy originator or instigator of the slaughter. At 1507–8, the elders for the first time in the scene partially echo Clytemnestra's claim and her violent language about the crime and concede that the Alastor *from the father* (*patrothen*) might be a *sullēptōr* (accomplice or assistant) in Agamemnon's murder. They further stress the masculinity of this violent, bloody daimonic force by relating it to old, black Ares (1509–12). The ambiguity of the term *anaitios* keeps open the possibility that the elders are responding to Clytemnestra's claim on different terms from her own, and concerned exclusively with guilt or blame, but in fact their concession and their continued focus on the humiliating nature of the king's death that immediately follows (1513–20 =

---

[80] Zeus is *panaitios* at *Agamemnon* 1486. At *Choephoroi* 1031, Orestes says that Apollo told him that if he killed Clytemnestra he would be *ektos aitias kakēs*. Apollo's statement in *Eumenides* apparently clarifies this cryptic phrase. Orestes did the deed and is liable for it, but it was just. On these two passages, see further Neuberg 1991: 55 and n. 24, and 58. He thinks that Apollo intervenes not to diminish Orestes' liability or agency, but to break the moral deadlock by overvaluing his role as father avenger in comparison to his crime as mother killer.

[81] Neuberg 1991: 67–68 thinks that the *aitios* words here refer not to the crime, but to the Furies' presence in Apollo's sanctuary. The following conversation indicates, however, that they are referring to the whole chain of events, from the prophecy instigating the murder to Orestes' presence in the sanctuary. When applied to mortals, as by the chorus here, such terms may have slightly different implications. At *Choephoroi* 134, for example, Electra calls Aegisthus *metaitios* of (sharing *aitia* for) the murder. At *Agamemnon* 811 the king calls the gods *metaitious* in his return—they shared in it, and, presuming that he is being suitably pious, he would attribute the authoritative role to the gods in enabling his return home. On *metaitios* in Sophocles' *Trachiniae*, see Holt 1995.

[82] Neuberg 1991: 67.

[83] Something similar can be argued in relation to male leaders and followers. In Thucydides, for example, the leaders who initiate an alliance are *aitioi*, not the allies who follow them (3.55.1, 3.55.4). Sophocles' *Electra* also argues that her mother killed Agamemnon unjustly under the influence of persuasion from a bad man (561–62), but this does not absolve her from punishment. For his Electra, the crime against the husband is also the central issue (558–59).

1489–96) makes this less likely. The old men of the chorus had already spoken of the *daimōn* working through women, envisioned it in terms indistinguishable from Clytemnestra (1470–74), and interpreted the blood flecks in Clytemnestra's eyes as a sign of some uncanny divine visitation; Cassandra had prepared them to accept connections among different crimes in the house of Atreus. It cannot be simply the evidence of a *daimōn* at work that stirs them to oppose Clytemnestra's words here, or the possibility that multiple factors can help to make sense of the justice of the crime—they raised both possibilities themselves.[84] Certainly, they have been repeatedly distrustful of the persuasive force of a woman's words in contrast to what they can witness visually or hear directly from men; Apollo in *Eumenides* bears witness, the Alastor does not— although Aegisthus soon will.

Apparently the elders of the chorus are not fully convinced by Clytemnestra that the death of Agamemnon can be categorized as an act deriving from and representing male as well as female concerns and hence just on a different basis than a woman's deliberate and premeditated killing of her husband for her daughter would be by itself; the term *sullēptōr* implicitly refuses to establish a hierarchy in Clytemnestra's relation to the *daimōn* (indeed, insofar as the term *sullēptōr* is interpreted as "assistant," they are still attributing the primary role in the murder to Clytemnestra). Even when Aegisthus appears, they do not accept the act as his because he planned it. In their view a woman did it and, in so doing, brought pollution to the land and the gods (1643–46). Aegisthus is in their eyes a "woman," and hence the deed is now doubly a woman's. Even if the crime is influenced or partly determined by a daimonic force representing the male line, the chorus' concern about the king's death at his wife's hands is not resolved and they repeat once more their despairing words over that humiliating event (1513–20).

Clytemnestra's fragmentary response to the chorus at 1521–29 once again poses serious interpretive problems. But it is clear that she is (in my view once again) responding to the chorus' concern that Agamemnon has died an *aneleutheron* death (1494), one not suitable for a free (*eleutheros*) man. The following attempts a literal translation of the text of 1521–29, including West's version of a missing line after 1521:

> οὔτ᾿ ἀνελεύθερον οἶμαι θάνατον
> τῷδε γενέσθαι
> [δόλιόν τε λαχεῖν μόρον οὐκ ἀδίκως]
> οὐδὲ γὰρ οὗτος δολίαν ἄτην
> οἴκοισιν ἔθηκ᾿·
> ἀλλ᾿ ἐμὸν ἐκ τοῦδ᾿ ἔρνος ἀερθὲν
> τὴν πολυκλαύτην
> Ἰφιγένειαν . . .

---

[84] Denniston and Page 1957: ad loc. remark: "The chorus refuse to accept wholly the plea which they themselves had suggested (1468–74), that Clytemnestra is the instrument of divine justice."

ἀνάξια δράσας
ἄξια πάσχων μηδὲν ἐν Ἅιδου
μεγαλαυχείτω, ξιφοδηλήτῳ
θανάτῳ τείσας ἅπερ ἦρξεν.

out' aneleutheron oimai thanaton
tō(i)de genesthai
[dolion te lachein moron ouk adikōs]
oude gar houtos dolian atēn
oikoisin ethēk';
all'emon ek toud'emos aerthen
tēn poluklautēn
Iphigeneian . . .
          anaxia drasas
axia paschōn mēden en Haidou
megalaucheitō, xiphodēlētō(i)
thanatō(i) teisas haper ērxen

I do not think his death was unsuitable for a free man
[and he met a treacherous fate not unjustly].[85]
Did this man not bring guileful destruction on the house?
But my sprout raised up from this man,
the much lamented Iphigeneia . . . . [text may be missing here]
Having performed unworthy deeds, suffering worthy retribution,[86]
let him offer no boast in Hades,
having paid for what he did with death by a sword.

Throughout the play, the *talio* is worked out in terms of an exact reciprocity of deaths. In *Choephoroi*, Clytemnestra understands that she will die by a trick, just as she killed by a trick (887–88). Reciprocity is evoked here in 1527: Agamemnon unworthily killed Iphigeneia with a sword, thus he worthily died by one (*anaxia drasas, axia paschōn*). (Of course, she does not mention that he died by the sword wrapped in a net and naked in a bathtub.) I believe, with scholars such as Thomson-Headlam, Lloyd-Jones, and Martin West, that Clytemnestra must be saying in this passage that Agamemnon justly died by a trick because he killed her "sprout" Iphigeneia by a trick.[87] Hence 1523–24 must be a question, not a statement: "Did this man not bring guileful destruc-

[85] Most commentators agree that a line is missing after 1521. West 1990: 222–23, following the views of Groeneboom 1944 and Denniston and Page 1957, defends his own conjecture, *dolion te lachein moron ouk adikōs*. This suits the logic of the passage up to this point.

[86] West's 1991 text has "performing worthy" rather than "unworthy" deeds.

[87] At 1525 Clytemnestra describes Iphigeneia as *aerthen* from Agamemnon; Fraenkel 1962 translates this as "my offspring that I conceived from him," whereas Pearson 1930 translates the passage as "my branch begotten of him, her whom I upreared." Lloyd-Jones [1979] 1993, "my child *raised up* [my emphasis] from him," perhaps best preserves the ambiguity of the text and Clytemnestra's attempt to establish her "ownership" of Iphigeneia by both nature and nurture throughout this scene.

tion on the house?" It is true that neither Clytemnestra or anyone else has mentioned the version of the myth in which Agamemnon deceived Clytemnestra and Iphigeneia with the promise of marriage to Achilles (rather than a sacrifice) at Aulis, and that if she is raising it obliquely here, as Fraenkel objects, she has thrown away a good argument.[88] But we need not take her reference to guile as so specific. Agamemnon presumably did not tell Clytemnestra why Iphigeneia was brought to Aulis. His deception of her need not have taken the form of a promise of marriage and therefore needs no elaboration at this point. If this interpretation of the passage is correct, however, Clytemnestra (unless she is being ironic) does not interpret tricky death by a woman on the same terms as the chorus. Having failed in her last argument, she now reverts to arguing that the gender of the killer is irrelevant. To receive what he gave, regardless of the actor and the mode of death, is in Clytemnestra's view suitable for a free man as a logical part of vendetta (and, in fact, Orestes uses trickery to serve vendetta justice apparently without sacrifice of status both in *Choephoroi* and in Sophocles' *Electra*).[89] Hence even as a woman, Clytemnestra implies, she has inflicted a worthy death. Yet though the death is appropriate to his status, Agamemnon cannot boast of it in Hades (1527–28).[90]

The elders of the chorus are put totally at a loss by Clytemnestra's reply (*amēchanō phrontidos sterētheis*, 1530). They envision the house as falling in a rain of blood (1533–34; the image has strong associations of political turmoil), while Moira whets her blade for a new crime. This implies that they accept political reality and realize that Orestes' revenge will offer the only possible, but potentially disastrous, resolution to the situation. They now turn to more practical issues about Agamemnon's burial. Clytemnestra's (mis)interpretation of an appropriate death for Agamemnon raises new fears, just as her language has rejected their traditional assumptions about appropriate behavior. Once again, they wish they had died before seeing their king in his lowly bath (1538–40). They begin to grasp that not only a proper lamentation but even a proper burial is out of their hands, as they cannot imagine his own house, in the form of Clytemnestra, providing a ceremony worthy of Agamemnon's great deeds. How could his murderer offer in sincerity proper lament and funereal praise—a male job in any case (1541–50)? They are correct. Clytemnestra plans to exclude the outsiders[91] appropriate to the burial of a noble king, thus making his funeral, as in the fifth-century funerary legislation, a private and familial mat-

---

[88] Fraenkel 1962: ad loc.

[89] It has been argued that trickery of this sort is appropriate to a young man rather than an adult warrior. See Vidal-Naquet 1972.

[90] Clytemnestra seems to object to applying military standards for masculine death here.

[91] Conducting funerals was a privilege of the deceased's closest relations (see Thomson [and Headlam] 1966 on 1551–53). West 1990: 224 convincingly defends Auratus' reading *exoikōn* (outsiders) over *ex oikōn*, "those from the household." At *Choephoroi* 431–32, Electra complains that her mother buried her father "without citizens and laments." The humiliating lack of public recognition in the king's funeral parallels his humiliating death by a woman.

ter. In Greek funerals, men inhumed the dead body, women mourned it. Presiding over a burial was a claim to inherit a man's wealth and household.
Clytemnestra will bury Agamemnon with the hand that killed him but offer
no lament (1552–54). Agamemnon's only "mourner" will greet him in
Hades—his sacrificed daughter, Iphigeneia.

At this point the elders of the chorus declare the case hard to judge (1561).
Clytemnestra answers and perverts/reinterprets each of their concerns (oneidos ekei tod' ant' oneidous, 1560). All they can see is the talio in action, and they
cling to their faith that these events still represent the justice of Zeus. They
implicitly accept Clytemnestra's view that the whole race is involved in (glued
to, 1566) this disaster for the future as well as in the past. (Although they do
not mention Orestes explicitly here, his obligation to avenge his father will
threaten the royal line once again.)

That Clytemnestra takes the choral response on the one hand as a concession of sorts on the question of justice and on the other as a challenge difficult
to meet is shown in her forthcoming and even uncertain reply. On this point,
she announces, the chorus has offered a true prophecy (1567–68).[92] Earlier in
the play, Clytemnestra spoke of the household wealth as inexhaustible and
planned to exploit it to serve her own power. Now she appears less confident, as the chorus brings home forcefully the logic of the talio, which even
Aegisthus' strength may not ward off. But she hopes to make a deal with the
daimōn of the house—a house that, as the house of the Pleisthenids (1569),
pointedly includes Aegisthus—and tolerate the family suffering by swearing to
forgo all but a small proportion of the wealth that she now controls as leader of
the house and to purify the house from mutual slaughter (1568–76).[93] Buying
the goodwill of any divinity (a coarse way of describing religious ritual, oath, or
prayer), is, as experience should have taught her, a highly uncertain process.

To sum up and consolidate the discussion so far, the scene between the chorus and Clytemnestra is above all about interpreting her crime as justice from
Zeus, and Clytemnestra and the chorus repeatedly interpret the situation differently. Curiously enough, what we see if we look closely at this scene, is that
the chorus has far less interest in Clytemnestra's own justifications for her crime
than in expressing despair at the humiliating mode of death Agamemnon has
received from his wife/a woman and the related problem of mourning him
properly. Clytemnestra may see herself on trial, and she works hard to unsettle
all the chorus' traditional assumptions and to make it accept Agamemnon's
death as a deliberate and autonomous act of justice (and hence her future rule
over them). Yet the chorus cannot, somehow, categorize death from a woman
as justice or respond to her formulation of the issues, in large part because to
do so challenges Agamemnon's status as hero, and because Clytemnestra

[92] Prophetic statements could apply to past, present, and/or future. See further O'Daly 1985:
10.
[93] Eteocles in Aeschylus' Seven against Thebes also believes he can escape his family curse until
he meets his brother at the seventh gate.

nowhere recognizes seriously his claim as husband to escape death from his wife. Her refusal to see the public side of the question, to envision her crime as a choice between two claims, one domestic (revenge for her own child and, to a lesser extent, the insult to her status as wife, which is challenged by Cassandra's presence), and one public (involving the traditional claims of marriage, kingship, and military prowess), also undermines for the chorus her seriousness as a moral agent and as a claimant to justice.

In the chorus' view Clytemnestra as woman/wife offers inappropriate vaunting words over the body of her husband. The elders do not accept her heroic vision of her act but categorize it as madness, possibly drug-induced; indeed, they repeatedly view her through the traditional cultural presuppositions about women, that they are prone to irrationality, shamelessness, and lack of control. Everywhere they look they see more mad women and irrational forces at work bringing humiliation to men: Helen, the *daimōn* working through women. It is a mark of their confusion that the chorus finally seems to concede that Zeus' justice is at work even with Clytemnestra—a woman—as the perpetrator. Yet it is ironically exactly at this moment when Clytemnestra faces the possibility that the cycle of revenge may make her its next victim, and Aegisthus appears on stage to lay claim to the deed (and the Alastor's motives) himself.

Because Clytemnestra had made her argument in terms that destabilize the elders' application of their traditional views to this situation and force them to abandon their attempt to establish through lament Agamemnon's superior status as husband, beloved king, and heroic general, his death is humiliatingly engulfed in the house with its family crimes and made to seem just in ways that they prefer not to recognize. The principle that the elders wish to establish— that Clytemnestra had in avenging her daughter not killed just a man but a husband and king—for the moment loses its force.[94] Indeed, she has undercut all their assumptions about female autonomy and liability for action, female decorum (especially sexual decorum), marriage, inheritance, adultery, royal succession, and burial. Their tendency to *chercher la femme* as the origin of the house's disasters has been dealt a telling blow. At the same time, Clytemnestra, through her dialogue with the chorus, moves from defining herself as an independent heroic agent to confessing her reliance on Aegisthus' power to representing her act as inspired by (or even in essence enacted by) an external, daimonic force that uncannily resembles Aegisthus. In this sense she gradually reassumes the role of "wife," in which a woman is meant to follow the guidance of her *kurios* or guardian and not to make choices on her own and ironically allows the father's cause (even if it is Thyestes' cause and not Agamemnon's) nearly to supersede the crime committed against her daughter (who from now on virtually disappears from the text).

Later in the scene with Aegisthus, Clytemnestra's behavior further suggests a process of refeminization, although playing the wife remains more role than

[94] On this point, see esp. Neuberg 1991 and O'Daly 1985: 8 n. 30.

reality for Clytemnestra to the end, and she certainly maintains authority more effectively than Aegisthus in this scene.[95] Once the bloodthirsty avenger, she now wants no more bloodshed (1656); the harvest of Agamemnon's blood (1390–92) is now in her view an unhappy one (*dustēnon theros*, 1655); she represents herself and Aegisthus as struck by the heavy hoof of the *daimōn* (1660). Now she mediates between the chorus and Aegisthus and even in her final lines echoes her new spouse's own crude words in wifely fashion as she adopts his description of the elders' language as the "barkings" of a dog (1672; see Aegisthus at 1631). When she closes her attempted mediation with "such is the speech of a woman, if any deem it worthy to heed it" (1661), the words ring differently from her earlier challenges to the chorus on the subject of female speech in that they apparently accommodate without deliberate deception to a traditional female social role.[96]

The scene in *Agamemnon* has ultimately made it impossible for a woman to be a true agent of justice, even if she committed and is liable to be punished for the act. The stichomythia (dialogue) between Orestes and Clytemnestra in *Choephoroi* reestablishes the values whose loss the chorus lamented and, whether directly or obliquely, overturns Clytemnestra's stance point by point in preparation for the final trial.[97] Orestes is not intimidated by his mother's verbal facility, and it is he, rather than she, who constantly destabilizes his opponent's arguments,[98] often through an appeal to the traditional values and arguments that Clytemnestra had undercut or redefined in the first play; in-

[95] The shift from certainty to doubt and unease on the part of both Clytemnestra and the chorus in this scene is typical of the play as a whole (see Goldhill 1984a: 146). Many scholars see a gradual shift in Clytemnestra's behavior in the scene (Page is an exception). For a summary of earlier views, see O'Daly 1985: 5. He himself wishes to define this shift not in terms of psychological change, but in terms of thematic shifts (6). Fraenkel 1962 identifies a gradual change in her soul that begins with her first mention of Aegisthus at 1431–35. Taplin 1977: 327–28 stresses her gradual recognition that the *talio* will apply to her. Dodds 1960 sees Clytemnestra as undergoing a permanent change at the end of this play. Michelini 1979: 155 notes Clytemnestra's shift from spendthrift in the speech about the wealth of the house that closes the tapestry scene to making a deal with the *daimōn* for a small portion of the royal possessions. She explains Clytemnestra's apparent shift as based on a change of status to ruler of Argos and consort of Aegisthus (158). Vickers 1973: 387 thinks that Clytemnestra here dwindles from superhuman to normal stature, from avenger to peacemaker. Rosenmeyer 1982: 240 sees a transformation of Clytemnestra into a woman: "The man-woman, now depressingly all woman, contemplates peace, but sees her new role *within* the social structure, with Aegisthus as the new king, thrust peace out of her reach"; he thinks Clytemnestra demonstrates a new "incapacity for action." Thalmann 1985: 230 argues that Clytemnestra's language is reduced to straightforward prayers and wishes; now that her plot is known, the magnificent ambiguity of her earlier speeches is no longer possible.

[96] By contrast to most critics, Lloyd-Jones [1979] 1993: ad loc. interprets these words as ironic.

[97] This does not mean that Orestes' own case is simple. For a good summary of the complexities of his position and character, see Fisher 1992: 292–95.

[98] Goldhill 1984a: 168 comments that Clytemnestra is now "on the receiving end of the capabilities of language to go beyond its user." The chorus also now uses the power of its speech (848–50) in Orestes' cause and deliberately deceives Aegisthus.

deed, ironically, he even forces her to appeal to these once despised traditions herself.

Clytemnestra's first words in her encounter with Orestes evoke *Agamemnon*. She at once recognizes the *talio* at work in the reciprocal exchange of deceit: she will die by a trick just as she killed through deception (888). It is now Orestes, not Clytemnestra, who uses sacrificial vocabulary of his act (904, *sphaxai*).[99] Ever the hero in action, Clytemnestra calls for an ax as she enters into another monstrous contest for victory, now with her son (889–90).[100] Yet Orestes undermines her heroic claims on a new level. In deciding, with Pylades' reminder, to respect Apollo's oracle, Orestes piously transfers the victory in this struggle (*nikan*, 903) to the gods. This appeal to the gods also permits Orestes to resolve a conflict concerning *aidōs*. Already a pious son, he hesitates to fail in respect and reverence (*aidesthō*, 899) toward his mother, whereas Clytemnestra, who so often appeared indifferent to or even flaunted her lack of *aidōs* in *Agamemnon*, is forced to appeal to this very virtue as she displays her maternal breast to Orestes (*aidesai*, 896).[101] In a second appeal to traditional wisdom, Clytemnestra makes a maternal claim to nurture in old age as a return for her raising of Orestes that is countered on two levels: Orestes could not live with a mother who had killed his father, and she has "sold" her son into slavery in a fashion unworthy of a man with a free (*eleutherou*, 915) father.[102] Agamemnon's adultery (one of Clytemnestra's justifications for her act in *Agamemnon*) is in Orestes' reply explicitly no worse than her own (917–18). The Moira (the "order of things" personified) that was part instigator/justifier of Clytemnestra's crime (*paraitia*, 910), now by the same logic partly justifies her own death.[103] The daimonic force of Clytemnestra's curses is effectively canceled for an Orestes trapped between the Furies of his father and those of his mother once she is dead (the parental curses, *genethlious aras*, to whom Clytemnestra appeals at 912 as her own apply also, as Orestes at once insists, to the father's curses). In Orestes' later speech over the bodies, Clytemnestra

---

[99] See Garvie 1986: ad loc. in response to Zeitlin.

[100] Clytemnestra remains concerned with the heroic code even as a ghost in *Eumenides* (McClure 1997b: 124).

[101] At 917 Orestes again turns *aidōs* against Clytemnestra, when he refuses to mention the price for which he was sold (her adultery), thereby preserving his own *aidōs* while in fact making his point just as strongly or even more emphatically (see Goldhill 1984a: 181 n. 151).

[102] Electra makes a similar accusation earlier (132–34): Clytemnestra sold her into slavery and got Aegisthus in return. Clytemnestra's counterclaim again forces her to appeal to the *xenia* (host-guest relationship) that she previously abused.

[103] At 923 Orestes says that it is really Clytemnestra who is killing herself, not Orestes. Naturally he is not abjuring responsiblity here but engaging in the kind of subversive wordplay earlier used by Clytemnestra. Similarly, Clytemnestra suggests the she is being forced to lament at a tomb in vain (926). She presumably means her words fall on deaf ears and that she is about to encounter herself the kind of corrupted burial accorded Agamemnon, but Orestes takes the tomb to be that of his father, at which the impious Clytemnestra will appeal in vain (927). Her symbolic recourse to lament, given her refusal to perform her proper function for Agamemnon, is once again ironic.

see also 919, which again stresses the *ponos* or labor of the father in contrast to the activity of those *inside*). It is now the father who is the provider of a nurture (*trephei*) that is often the mother's special province (*eutraphes gala*, 898).[109] The dialogue clearly sets up Apollo's argument in *Eumenides*, which attempts to create a hierarchy of father, husband, and king over mother and of public over domestic.[110] As Winnington-Ingram remarks of *Eumenides*, "there is thus a certain irony in justifying the matricide on the grounds that Clytemnestra the woman had killed Agamemnon the man, and this is further brought out by the description of Agamemnon (637) as 'all-worshipful' (*pantosemnos*), when he had been so humiliated, and as an 'admiral of the fleet.'"[111] In *Choephoroi*, the socially constructed marriage bond begins to gain equal and effective weight with bonds among kin. Indeed, Orestes closes his defense speech to the chorus with the ringing wish that he would rather die childless than have such a mate to share his house (1005–6). The chorus now categorizes the three storms to shake the house of Atreus as the death of Thyestes' children, the death of Agamemnon, and Orestes' recent crime, which threatens the royal succession (1065–74). All these stress the paternal line; gone are the claims of the female child, Iphigeneia.[112]

In her defense scene with the chorus, *Agamemnon* thus makes a case against Clytemnestra that is linked in more ways than are generally recognized with the arguments of the following plays. I have argued that the complex ethical case against Clytemnestra involves far more than dismissing her claim to justice due to Agamemnon's killing of Iphigeneia because of her crazed and outrageous language and behavior, her uncontrolled sexuality, her ambitions to tyranny, or her deceptive manipulations of language—as if this were not enough. As a rebel, Clytemnestra represents a larger challenge to the cultural order than the chorus can encompass with its traditional views about women's instability and deceptiveness. Clytemnestra is allowed to articulate in detail a positive as well as a negative case[113] that challenges male assumptions about her act and makes the chorus' traditional wisdom hard to apply. Indeed, after *Agamemnon*, the trilogy moves gradually toward asserting the familiar male-dominated order, while at the same time drastically simplifying or ignoring many of the questions raised in Clytemnestra's apology. However outrageously,

[109] Clytemnestra does not accept Orestes' claim. She insists on her nurture, but now sees that she has raised a snake (*ethrepsamēn*, 928). Orestes cannot avoid the monstrosity that he accuses her of embodying.

[110] See Gagarin 1976: 99.

[111] Winnington-Ingram 1983: 122.

[112] As Goldhill 1984a: 205 remarks, Thyestes' adultery, Troy, Helen, and Menelaus are also left unmentioned.

[113] It is difficult to calculate how much or what aspects of Clytemnestra's arguments convince the chorus or would have been convincing to the ancient audience, but the scene is surely pointless if her arguments are completely meaningless. Here I disagree with consistently negative assessments of Clytemnestra in this scene, such as that of O'Daly 1985.

is once more the unnatural monster that Cassandra pronounced her to be, epitome of daring (*tolmēs*) and an unjust spirit (*ekdikou phronēmatos*, 996) she and Aegisthus are now described pointedly as tyrants and sackers (*[thētoras*, 974) of Orestes' house.

Most important, however, by entirely ignoring both Clytemnestra's m: justification for her own act, the sacrifice of Iphigeneia, and the links betwe Agamemnon's death and the crime of Atreus against the children of Thyest *Choephoroi* redefines Clytemnestra's act and highlights the monstrosity of t: wife's crime against her husband that so disturbed to no avail the chorus *Agamemnon*. The reference to Moira as a contributing factor in her crime (91(may obliquely hint at Clytemnestra's earlier argument on this point in th Alastor passage but is no longer dramatically forceful; Aegisthus is dismisse as a mere adulterer, who has encountered the standard legal penalty.[1(Clytemnestra's adultery brings her now a suitable death at the side of her lovei her attempt to name Aegisthus as heroic—*philtat' Aigisthou bia*, 893, is epi: language—is similarly undercut.[106] The status and honor of the father, whicl has been gradually restored in this play through his children's response to him as hero and his reception of the sincere lamentation and praise denied to him by Clytemnestra, now takes precedence over the concerns of the mother. The chorus strongly reasserts the traditional standards of female and especially wifely behavior. In particular, the chorus' ode on the infamous transgressions of women closes with the recollection of "plots contrived by a woman against a warrior husband treated like an enemy. I honor the hearth of the house un- fired [by passion] and a woman's unventuresome spirit" (626–30).[107]

Orestes refuses to permit Clytemnestra to categorize Agamemnon (or, later, her children) as enemy, not *philos* and husband (*hon de chrēn philein stugeis*, 907). Her children are not exclusively hers but also her husband's, and ironi- cally she can no longer defend herself through her own relation to her children as she did before.[108] The sufferings of a wife in war, which Clytemnestra pit- ted against those of male warriors at such length in her speech to Agamemnon and the chorus in the tapestry scene, are now trivialized by Orestes, who will not accept an equivalence between the one who sits at home and the toil of the husband in the public world (*trephei de g'andros mochthos hēmenas esō*, 921;

[104] On making Clytemnestra into a monster in the *Oresteia*, see esp. Zeitlin 1978, Betensky 1978: 21, Rabinowitz 1981, and Moreau 1985: 171–74.

[105] In fact, however, self-help justice, in the form of murder against an adulterer, was permit- ted only in the case of a couple caught in flagrante delicto. MacDowell 1978: 124–25. If the adul- terer was condemned in a trial, any penalty short of bloodshed was permissible.

[106] Orestes now mocks Clytemnestra's sexuality as she did Agamemnon's. Line 895 suggests ei- ther that Clytemnestra will not betray Aegisthus because they will both be dead, or that she will not have an opportunity to betray another husband.

[107] See Garvie 1986: ad loc.

[108] Even the witness to whom Orestes here appeals concerning the justice of his crime, Helios, is a father (985–86).

Clytemnestra had asked the chorus to see the world from the perspective of those excluded from or subordinated by major parts of the cultural system and to imagine the implications both of including it and allowing moral agency to women. Why should a mother tolerate what the chorus itself describes as the horrific, perverted, and unwilling sacrifice of her daughter for a cause in which Clytemnestra disbelieves and about which she has not been consulted?[114] Why does this society not include the possibility of bringing Agamemnon formally to justice for it? Is the cultural hierarchy that subordinates private to public concerns consistently legitimate? Should such concerns be treated as separable? Why should Helen be blamed for the Trojan War when we have heard from Cassandra about male transgressions that inaugurated it and heard Clytemnestra describe the army's own abuses there.[115] There is more than one perspective on such questions, just as the voices and destinies of conquerors and captives in the war differ (Clytemnestra at 321–25). Why should Clytemnestra accept a marriage made by others in which her husband has become an enemy to herself, when she can choose a spouse who protects her interests and pleases her? Why should she tolerate a concubine, a sexual display of Agamemnon's prowess, whereas her own liaison with Aegisthus is defined as impious adultery and her own desires must be concealed and suppressed in accord with feminine *aidōs*? Why should a just revenge performed by a woman be a priori illegitimate? Why should the roles in death ritual be divided rigidly among the two sexes, so that performing the ritual accords legal authority only to one party? Why should a woman so familiar with male rhetoric, with a legitimate claim through Aegisthus to the throne, not wield power with him over Argos? Clytemnestra's monstrosity cannot entirely silence the fundamental moral imbalance in the culture's ethical system that she reveals.

At the same time, her own arguments and situation finally collapse on her. Her self-defense cannot bridge public and private worlds, or move beyond house and kin, just as the Furies, her representatives in *Eumenides*, pursue victims who murder kin, but claim to have no interest in social bonds constructed among nonkin or in the welfare of cities that depend on those bonds. Clytemnestra in some ways effectively challenges cultural hierarchies in speech, but because she does rely on male support to make her claims effective in reality, the claims of husbands, fathers, and, in their wake, children return to destroy her. She herself is finally forced to rely on the very ethical princi-

---

[114] See Wohl 1998: esp. 71–81 on Agamemon's abuse of the cultural exchange of women by hoarding his most valuable gift (*agalma*) and virtually raping his daughter. Whereas critics of *Antigone* constantly blame the heroine for abandoning her marriage, Wohl is the first critic to ask similar questions (in this case far more central in the text) of Agamemnon.

[115] Wohl 1998: 81–91 and 98–99 argues that the play defetishizes Helen and reveals her as a commodity rather than an *agalma*. Male abuse of the exchange of women objectifies women and destroys male subjects who normally acquire identity as exchangers in this system (96). These male abuses of the system are then projected onto Clytemnestra (102).

ples—such as *aidōs*—that she was willing to undercut in the service of her own claims to justice.

The anthropologist Joan Bamberger's argument about "myths of matriarchy" has been applied to the *Oresteia* by Froma Zeitlin and others.[116] For Bamberger, this cross-cultural category of myth justifies women's subordinate status by imagining that women once wielded cultural power over men but lost this authority through their own errors and abuses. As Bamberger notes, the mythical case against women must be *moral*, because there is no other obvious natural reason why, for example, heredity should be patrilineal when the maternal line is more reliably verifiable. Aeschylus' case against Clytemnestra is clearly moral, but its dimensions are far more complex than in Bamberger's South American myths.[117] Like trials in Athens itself, the *Oresteia*'s scenes of judgment are not primarily about who committed an act, or even so much what should be done about the offense, but about the implications of the case for the community, the city, and its leadership.[118] Clytemnestra has access to public power, but her power can never be wielded for the benefit of the community, because this scene has demonstrated that any autonomous action by a woman threatens irrevocably the status of its men and that women—even a boundary-crossing woman like Clytemnestra—cannot maintain in reality either social or moral independence.

Clytemnestra in Euripides' *Electra*

A shift in setting and characterization changes dramatically the issues at stake in Clytemnestra's claim to justice over the murder of her husband. In both Sophocles' and Euripides' *Electra*, the debate over Clytemnestra's crime and her stage "trial" are conducted by her virgin daughter Electra in the presence of a female chorus. Orestes never speaks directly to his mother or confronts the full power of her body and speech until he enacts the deed. The shift to a confrontation among women in itself domesticates an occasion that is as well pointedly isolated from the public sphere by Euripides. Euripides' play is set outside the city in a country house where Electra lives with the poor but noble farmer to whom she has been given in marriage by Aegisthus. Aegisthus, fearing that she might produce children who would avenge Agamemnon, first planned to kill Electra, but was persuaded by Clytemnestra to take a less violent course. Electra is painfully conscious of her loss of status and her isolation from the palace. The chorus is a group of country women on their way to a fes-

---

[116] Bamberger 1975 and Zeitlin 1978.

[117] Aeschylus' plot pattern also does not conform to Bamberger's, because the *Oresteia* does not imagine that women ever ruled men, but only that mythical queens had more access to political authority than Attic women.

[118] See Dover 1974: 158 and 292.

tival of Hera in holiday dress; they know little of the goings on in the city, though they are eager to be informed.

Because both Electra and Clytemnestra repeatedly evoke standards for female behavior that apply to contemporary Attic women, the audience is invited to judge their words and arguments by these standards. We learn that Electra is wife in name only to her husband, who has respected her higher birth and refused to collaborate in humiliating her. In exchange, Electra is attempting to play the role of proper wife. In a speech to her husband, which gives the wife responsibility for matters within the house, and the husband for those without (74–77), Electra expresses a cliché developed with philosophical elaboration in Xenophon's fourth-century treatise on household management, the *Oeconomicus* (7.17–32). When Orestes and Pylades arrive at her door, she runs from unfamiliar men like a proper chaste woman; her husband is later concerned to find her speaking, like an improper wife, to strangers (343–44). When Orestes goes off to try his luck against Aegisthus, Electra keeps a sword ready; as an exaggerately chaste woman, she will not allow her body to be outraged if Orestes is defeated (695–98).

Clytemnestra is equally represented not as an Aeschylean androgynous, persuasive rebel, but as a conventional wife and even to some extent a genuinely concerned mother; Electra is sure that she will come when her daughter asks for help after (supposedly) giving birth to a son and Clytemnestra is willing to listen patiently to her angry daughter. Clytemnestra is highly concerned about public opinion and pleasing her spouse in the manner of a traditional wife (60–64, 265, 1138), and active only to the point of wifely mediation. On this occasion, Clytemnestra did not accompany Aegisthus to his sacrifice, but delays her appearance due to a fear of censure from the people (642–45). Like the proper Attic woman, she tries to get men to act for her; Aegisthus shared in the killing of Agamemnon, a task she would apparently not have undertaken alone (the crime deployed her trickery, but relied on his hand, 9–10 and 163). Clytemnestra has produced children for Aegisthus, and thus finds herself in a position of divided loyalties vis-à-vis her children. Bowing unlike her Aeschylean counterpart to common cultural clichés about women, she admits that women as a group are foolish (*mōron*, 1035), thus raising the possibility of her own unreliability as an adult moral agent (despite remaining liable to punishment for her crime).

Clytemnestra's concern for her reputation also forms the proem of her defense speech to Electra. She asks to be judged on the facts, not on the bitter speech that her bad reputation as a woman has forced her to adopt (1013–17). Instead of taking the unusual step of castigating Agamemnon for appropriating an Iphigeneia who is *hers* by right of birth pangs (Sophocles, *Electra* 536; see also *Agamemnon* 1417–18, 1525), Clytemnestra conventionally evokes her own *father's* rights.[119] Tyndareus, she argues, did not give her to Agamemnon

---

[119] Attic women were "lent" in marriage to their husbands to produce children. See part II.

to bear children for death (1018–19). Agamemnon betrayed this trust by using the ruse of marriage to Achilles to take Iphigeneia in person from the house. She claims that the sacrifice of her child to defend a city against capture, to help the house, or to save many with the life of one would have been pardonable (1024–26). Yet her child was only sacrificed because of Menelaus' failure to discipline his lecherous wife (1027–29). The unconventional mothers Aethra and Praxithea discussed in III.6 and Euripides' Iphigeneia are by contrast willing to entertain a broader and less defensive model of warfare.

Even so, she asserts, despite Agamemnon's injustice to her, she would not have *acted* if Agamemnon had not imported a second "wife" into the household (1030–34). A husband's error in rejecting his wife for a crazed seer is, she claims, apt to produce imitation (1036–38). Men, who are thus the real cause (*aitioi*) of women's taking lovers, always escape a bad reputation while their wives are publicly blamed (1039–40). In sum, Clytemnestra asserts that as a proper woman she acted only when outrageously wronged, and then in imitation of her husband. She took the only route possible (the *poreusimon* or passable road, 1046, which again depicts Clytemnestra as follower in another's tracks). Agamemnon's friends would not have helped her, so she was forced to turn to his male enemy to defend her interests (1046–48). If Menelaus had been abducted and she had killed Orestes to save him (an almost absurdly hypothetical example), she would have been subject to punishment from Agamemnon; why should the case not be the same for her husband (1041–45)?

Clytemnestra sees Electra as a child who has always had more affinity for her father; she will pardon her angry words for this reason (1102–5). Still maternal, she is willing to help Electra carry out the necessary rituals for the newly born child despite the pressing sense of obligation to her husband characteristically expressed in her final words on stage (1138, *dei gar kai posei dounai charin*). She does recognize the claims that her children Electra and Orestes have on her, but she is afraid to act on them (1114–15). And she finally admits that her previous actions give her no pleasure (1105–6). Her sudden shift to regret for her excessive anger against her husband (*orgēn posei*, 1110) and her past plans echoes, perhaps deliberately, the famous monologue of Medea discussed in III.5 (*oimoi talaina tōn emōn bouleumatōn*, 1109; *Medea* 1079). By contrast to Medea, Euripides' unheroic and conventional wife finally confirms her somewhat appealing moral inadequacy with a feminine inability to stand by her convictions.

The choral response to her speech expresses a judgment also founded on the standards demanded of a proper wife. In their view, Clytemnestra invoked just arguments, but her justice is shameful (*aischrōs*, 1051); women should go along with their husbands in everything (*panta sungchōrein posei*, 1052) if they have any sense (*phrenērēs*, 1053); anyone who does not share this view does not count in their eyes (1053–54). Later, however, they modify this judgment slightly by recognizing not only her unholy deeds, but the suffering that led to them (*schetlia men epathes, anosia d'eirgasō . . . eunetan*, 1170–71). Overall then, Clytemnestra domesticates the defense of her revenge and is judged primarily as a conventional wife. Iphigeneia is less important to her than her status as wife (jeopardized by Cassandra). She views herself as buffeted between loyalties to two families but helpless to take decisive action entirely on her own.

Electra, who has more of the Aeschylean Clytemnestra in her, is less conventional despite her lip service to her female role, but equally limited in her moral imagination to domestic and sexual issues. Adherence to proper female behavior and Clytemnestra's mistreatment of herself and Orestes are the two things on her mind. In her speech over the remains of Aegisthus, Electra stresses not his crime against her father, which receives a passing mention (914–15), but his marriage to her mother. Spouting conventions, Electra extrapolates on the dangers of marrying a wife who has already been unfaithful to her husband, the contagious impiety of a bad marriage, and the humiliating inequality of the couple. Aegisthus is in her view Clytemnestra's "wife," and his children are known by their mother's name; he has married above his station, and his possessions are no compensation for his weak nature and loss of status (931–37). (Despite her claims, however, there is no evidence that Clytemnestra has been unfaithful to Aegisthus; indeed, it appears that the handsome Aegisthus is the womanizer [945–48].)

The same concerns appear in Electra's debate with Clytemnestra. In Electra's eyes the good looks of Helen and her mother concealed their identical nature (1062–64). Wives, Electra implies, do have a choice, if only to adhere to the opportunities convention offers. Helen may have been abducted, but she was willing (1065). A proper wife does not tend to her beauty or display her face in her husband's absence—especially right after he has left for war (1069–75). Distinction won by proper behavior (1080, *kalōs sōphronein;* here the quintessential wifely virtue of *sōphrosunē* is evoked) was open to Clytemnestra, and all the more important to attain given the contrast with Helen (1083–85). Finally, Clytemnestra used Agamemnon's money as a dowry and bought a husband instead of settling it on her innocent children as convention (and Attic law) expected (1088–90).

Electra's final lines, which pronounce on the folly of marrying a bad woman for her wealth and birth, and favor the humble but virtuous union (1097–99), have generally been bracketed as spurious for destroying the parallelism between Clytemnestra's speech and her own. Just as Clytemnestra closes by asking Electra to show how her father died unjustly (1049–50), Electra should in the view of these scholars close the speech with her determination to exact the *talio* and enact justice herself (1093–96). I remain uncertain. Justice has not been the central issue on Electra's mind, and the final shift away from it preserved in the text as we have it is in keeping with her characterization and the thrust of this scene, which is less about justice than proper female behavior.[120]

---

[120] At *Choephoroi* 1005–6, Orestes, in preparation for the arguments offered in *Eumenides,* also closes his speech with his views of the marriage to be avoided.

In his book on the Euripidean *agōn* (formal debate), Michael Lloyd argues that the debate between Electra and Clytemnestra in this play is the first among the poet's extant plays to present a balanced debate between two characters who are both rhetorically expert and who both present plausible arguments.[121] He sees this as related thematically to the uncertainty raised by the play as a whole over the justice of the crime.[122] The *agōn* also concludes abnormally for Euripides with a concession to Electra by her mother (1105–10), rather than ending intractably in a quarrel.[123] Furthermore, it should be stressed that neither Clytemnestra nor Electra is definitely a reliable speaker or witness. Clytemnestra is vague about when her adultery with Aegisthus began, but she implies that it began after Agamemnon's return. Electra implies that Clytemnestra was at least open to adultery even before the sacrifice of Iphigeneia. Although she claims to have been a firsthand witness of Clytemnestra's actions, she earlier said that she was too young to have woven a sampler for Orestes before his departure (538–39). Such inconsistencies among the views represented by various characters (there are a number of others)[124] create an atmosphere where innuendo takes precedence over facts, and subjectivity clashes with subjectivity. Rhetorical expertise blurs rather than clarifies the central issues, and especially the question of justice. In a woman's world, which is limited both by the moral stature of the contestants as women (they are uncontrolled, changeable, and so forth), and by the moral expectations required of women—that they be virtuous followers—the issue of justice in a more abstract and principled sense gets lost.

In *Electra*, the *justice* of the matricide is faced more directly in a scene between Electra and Orestes, as well as after the crime takes place. Lloyd argues that in her dialogue with her brother over the matricide Electra uses the arguments of Aeschylus' Orestes, whereas Orestes uses those of his Clytemnestra.[125] In fact, both children have a more limited perspective than their Aeschylean counterparts. In this dialogue Orestes remains possessed with the problem of killing his mother and doubts Apollo's oracle. He first catches sight of Clytemnestra at the conclusion of Electra's tirade over Aegisthus. He sees the mother who bore him (964) and would feel pity at the sight of her body (967–69, a hint that the mother's presence might affect him even more powerfully than in Aeschylus; later he drops his weapon when she supplicates him (1214–17) and cannot look at her while he kills her [1221–23]).[126] He accuses

---

[121] Lloyd 1992: 55, 70.

[122] Lloyd 1992: 70.

[123] Lloyd 1992: 69.

[124] Goldhill 1986: 253.

[125] Lloyd 1992: 60. He stresses the separation of the *agōn* from the process of deciding to carry through with the matricide (59). Burnett 1998: 238 more aptly suggests that Electra here plays the role of a verbose Pylades.

[126] This second gesture echoes the reference linking Orestes to Perseus' conquest of the gorgon at *Choephoroi* 835–37.

Apollo of *amathia* (971, moral ignorance) in relation to his command, and wonders if an Alastor (a covert reference to the *Agamemnon* passage discussed earlier?) spoke in the god's form (*ar' aut' alastōr eip' apeikastheis theōi*, 979).[127] Electra doubts that an Alastor would sit on the holy tripod (980), and impatiently interprets Orestes' doubts as cowardice (982). Orestes exits prepared to do dreadful things because it is god's will but is conscious of the bitterness it will produce (985–87).

Electra, by contrast, remains focused on the pious duty of performing the revenge and is surprised at Orestes' sudden pity. Unlike Orestes, she does not anticipate her later reaction to the matricide. Modeling herself at first on Aeschylus' Clytemnestra, she cannot sustain the role. She wants to take a bloodthirsty delight in her act and insists on planning a ruse to lure her mother herself.[128] She uses sacrificial language to introduce the crime (1141–44) and sees in Clytemnestra someone making her way nicely into the (Aeschylean) net (965); she also wishes her mother to be killed in the same trap that she prepared for Agamemnon (983–84). She aggressively pushes Orestes into action and puts her hand on the fatal sword with her brother (1224–25). Despite this display of vengeful passion, she lacks the complexity and fierce consistency of Aeschylus' heroine. Immediately after the crime she (like her mother in this play) comes to a different view of her behavior. Recognizing her blameworthiness and liability to penalties (*aitia d'egō*, 1182), she regrets her anger against the one who bore her (1183–84). Her mother was at once both friend/relative and not (*phila(i) te kou phila(i)*, 1230). The chorus accuses her of not thinking (*phronousa*, 1204) holy thoughts and doing dreadful things to her unwilling brother (*deina d'ergasō . . . kasignēton ou thelonta*, 1204–5). From its perspective, Electra exerted an inappropriate persuasive influence on Orestes.

Orestes' doubts about his act are confirmed after the crime and he receives a punishment that both formally exonerates and permanently exiles him. Helen's divine brother Castor announces from the machine that Clytemnestra's punishment was just, but that the children did not work justice (*dikaia men nun hēd' echei, su d'ouchi dra(i)s*, 1244). Castor prefers silence on the subject of his lord Apollo (1245–46); though Apollo is wise, he did not prophesy wisely to Orestes (1246). Castor closes the play by reaffirming that although *moira* and *anangkē* (necessity) were leading to this outcome, Apollo's prophecies were unwise (*asophoi*, 1301–2). Castor attributes the bloody crime to Apollo (*Phoibō(i) tēnd' anathēsō / praxin phonian*, 1296–97) and at once exonerates the children of pollution for the crime (1294), whereas Aeschylus' Orestes was not freed from pollution until after a period of wanderings and rituals, including

---

[127] This suggests that Euripides might have interpreted the *Agamemnon* passage along Fraenkel's lines.

[128] To show her mettle, she says she would not only endure to have Orestes commit the crime but would kill to share directly in the blood (278–81).

Apollo's rite at Delphi.[129] The god is apparently not only instigator of the crime but also in a sense commits the act (1297) and bears a greater share of the blame (*aitian*, 1266) for it than in Aeschylus. Orestes will go into exile hounded by the Keres, be tried in Athens and acquitted by the equal and incorruptible votes of the jury, and found a new city in Arcadia (1265–66, 1273–74). Although exiled, Orestes remains worthy of both happiness (1291) and civic leadership.[130]

Electra, too, was apparently fated to share in the family *atē* (1305–7). She first asks to be included in the discourse about Moira and necessity with Castor (1295), then inquires about what decrees of Apollo ordained that she should slay her mother (1303–4). Castor assures her that the siblings share both actions and fate (1305–6). In contrast to Sophocles' and Aeschylus' Electra, then, Euripides' heroine shares in the act, the planning, and the punishment for the crime. Yet Electra's punishment—to be properly married within her own class to Pylades and even further socially isolated from her home by exile—symbolically reasserts social control over the family's uncontrolled women and deprives them of further significant public action. Marriage will be the central concern for the new couple (*toisde melēsei gamos*, 1342), and with husband and home (*posis . . . kai domos*), Electra will suffer nothing pitiable (*oiktra*) except exile (1311–13).

Neither Orestes nor Electra displays the authority and insight into the broader issues at stake in the revenge articulated by Aeschylus' Orestes or the conviction of Sophocles' siblings, who appear certain of the proper culturally determined roles assigned to them. It would be difficult to argue that two defined moral modes clash here as in Sophocles' *Electra* or *Antigone*.[131] Euripides' Orestes is no hero in contrast to his Sophoclean counterpart; immature, uncertain, and tentative, he allows his old servant and Electra to plan his revenge for him. He does not, like Aeschylus' hero, attempt to locate his crime in a civic context or argue for the value of gender hierarchy in the family. Yet the play pointedly contrasts Orestes' male foresight and moral sensitivity about committing the matricide with Electra's unpitying anger and impulsive eagerness to act.[132] Orestes implicitly recognizes clashing principles—the wrong of committing matricide over the need to obey a possibly unjust divine command

---

[129] At the same time he cannot step on the earth of Argos due to the matricide (1250–51).

[130] To Electra and Orestes, Castor's prophecies seem an inadequate consolation for separation and exile (1307–10, 1314–15). Orestes (shockingly?) requests from Electra the dirge normally sung at the tomb of the dead (1325–26).

[131] Lloyd 1992: 60 thinks that the decision to follow through with the matricide would be blurred and trivialized by introducing Clytemnestra's responsibility and motivation—though this is hardly the case in *Choephoroi*. Euripides' and Sophocles' motives for separating the *agōn* from Orestes' discussion of his choice are uncertain, but they are likely to have been more complex than Lloyd allows in the case of Euripides.

[132] This gender difference is anticipated even in the scene where Electra rejects an Aeschylean recognition scene with her brother by denying the Aeschylean evidence of their fraternal identity—identical hair and footprints (508–46).

and avenge his father—and he maintains this stance throughout. By contrast, Electra does not think in terms of conflicting rights and wrongs, engages in no moral struggle, and seems more concerned with her own injuries than justice. Unlike Orestes, she only develops doubts once she has helped enact the murder.[133] While stirring the male to revenge is a culturally prescribed role for women in vendetta, Electra undertakes to spur Orestes on from a position that lacks the developed self-consciousness and sense of a cultural mission that we see in Sophocles' heroine. Thus, although the play raises serious doubts about the performance of the matricide on both human and divine levels, these doubts remain more fully linked to Electra. Electra's punishment, which returns her to a proper (and hence inactive) female role, her own change of heart, and the chorus' consistent disapproval of both her (and not Orestes') actions and her deleterious influence on her brother make this clear.

This contrast between the siblings both prepares for the play's refusal to pronounce clearly on the justice of the matricide and may offer the first level of explanation for why Euripides has chosen to represent the debate over Clytemnestra's crime as an *agōn* between two women in a pointedly noncivic and domestic setting where contemporary standards of female and especially wifely behavior are repeatedly invoked. The play clearly does not aim simply to show that the morally limited female is exclusively responsible for the injustice of these crimes; both men and gods have also played questionable roles. Justice simply does not look the same from the perspective of those who have lived intimately with the domestic repercussions of crimes, and other issues, such as female status, may even take precedence over it.[134] Within families, issues are always dangerously ambiguous and transgressions are contagious (1038–39, 921–24). (This last point also plays an even more important role in the mother-daughter debate in Sophocles' play—see *Electra* 608–9 and 616–21.) We cannot decide between Clytemnestra's and Electra's contradictory claims, in part because we will never know the truth about Clytemnestra's adultery. Both mother and daughter themselves modify their original responses to their own actions. Euripides' Orestes lacks the direction of Sophocles' pedagogue and the active support of his aristocratic companion Pylades as in Aeschylus, but his noble birth preserves a certain independent moral potential in him; in his case, justice can be (perhaps arbitrarily) determined on different terms in a public court, an arena unavailable to Electra or her mother.

Both Euripides and Sophocles (see III.2 on *Electra*) apparently preferred to isolate in different ways their chief male protagonist from full entanglement in Clytemnestra's claim to justice; both Orestes are pointedly motivated by gods,

---

[133] Burnett 1998: 236 remarks that in the case of Aegisthus, "the honey-sweet pleasures of revenge—the triumph, the retrospective summation, and the insults offered to the enemy—all are handed over to Electra."

[134] Burnett 1998: 237 argues that Electra kills her mother more over her loss of status than for her father's sake. Thury 1985 and Harder 1995 both emphasize the corrosive effect of circumstances (especially poverty) on Electra's judgment and moral integrity.

whereas the female characters confront the corrosive uncertainties of revenge on a more direct and personal level. Euripides' female characters aspire to proper femininity and become actors in their own lives only when confronted by male abuse and, in Electra's case, through a radical disruption of the normal female passage to adulthood. By contrast, Aeschylus' androgynous and outrageous Clytemnestra claims full ethical adulthood, even if, as a woman, she finally fails to exercise and maintain it. Euripides' women differ as moral agents from both men and Aeschylus' queen not only because of the social constraints under which they operate but because they demonstrably lack the experience of wielding power and participating in public life. Their rhetoric may be skillful, but they do not attempt to exercise it in the larger civic context, to mix private and public realms, or to use it to claim civil authority as does Aeschylus' heroine. Instead, rhetoric serves to dramatize the indeterminacy of decisions undertaken in a disrupted household and exclusively in the private realm.[135]

As recent studies have argued, Attic juries generally were not equipped to investigate the facts involved in legal claims. The Areopagus apparently was a partial if probably very limited exception.[136] On the one hand, as in Aeschylus, the real issue for a jury was the implications of the crime for the city; moral assessment of the quality of both the act and the actor was equally central.[137] His Clytemnestra's defense, and the trilogy as a whole, focus strongly on this aspect of her own and others' crimes. The trial of *Eumenides* to a large extent subsumes the confusions generated within the domestic environment and shifts the audience's attention to a broader set of public and civic issues. The interpretative challenge offered in Euripides' irresolvable debates also echoes that encountered in the Attic experience of adversarial rhetoric. Yet Euripides isolates his protagonists from the civic environment and turns our attention to determining justice in a far more intractable context, where disparities and contradictions are rampant and hearers will never know the "truth"; where no certain criterion for judgment exists, even a divine one; where the emotional realities of domestic life are as important as legal ones; and where female persuasion is as powerful as male action.

[135] Lawcourt speeches tend by contrast to claim that only friends and relatives know the truth of a situation (Demosthenes 48.40).

[136] Wallace [1985] 1989: 121–22.

[137] Cohen 1995: 190.

III.5

Tragic Wives: Medea's Divided Self

LIKE CLYTEMNESTRA in the absence of her husband Agamemnon, Euripides' Medea becomes in essence a woman without a *kurios* or guardian. She has irrevocably severed bonds with her natal family and her homeland, her husband Jason has married the Corinthian princess and deserted his family, and finally, she faces imminent exile from Corinth. Yet despite her apparent helplessness, Medea has no effective opponents in this play but herself. The play becomes a laboratory in which the audience can observe a mature woman attempt to make and carry out a critical decision about avenging her wrongs in a context where her husband refuses to treat her as a rational peer or to recognize her grievances against him. This choice is made both outside the confines of either the natal or marital households that normally define the space in which a woman lives, and outside the confines of a city in which she is in any sense a citizen.[1] A normal Greek woman had no model of full social and ethical autonomy available to herself. The decision to avenge her wrongs presents no problems for Medea; she borrows heroic masculine ethical standards to articulate her choice and stereotypically feminine duplicity and magic permit her to achieve her goals. In effecting her revenge, her major problem is at first how to carry out her plans given the tools available to her. Yet this revenge comes to seem in her view to require the killing of her own children.

Although eloquent about the wrongs marriage and society inflict on women, Medea struggles to find an ethical voice that can articulate her maternal concerns and her female self-interest, despite her husband's view that she has no serious cultural need for her children, because the boys were born (at least originally) to reproduce the paternal line and are supported by their father (565, 460–62). Aeschylus' Clytemnestra claimed ownership of her daughter Iphi-

A version of this chapter was originally published as Foley 1989. I wish to thank discerning audiences at Delphi, Connecticut College, Lehigh, Emory, Oberlin, and CUNY Graduate Center, as well as Michael Jameson and the anonymous referees for *Classical Antiquity*, for their comments and questions on earlier versions of that article. The following works were unavailable to me until after the completion or publication of the original article: Rickert 1987, Stanton 1987, Gill 1987 and 1996, Gredley 1987, Gellie 1988, Barlow 1989 and 1995, McDermott 1989, Michelini 1989, Newton 1989, Ohlander 1989, Rehm 1989, Schein 1990, Seidensticker 1990, Williamson 1985 (rev. 1990), Boedeker 1991 and 1997, Galis 1992, Rabinowitz 1993, Friedrich 1993, Gibert 1995, Worthington 1990, Sfyoeras 1995, Segal 1996, Dillon 1997, and Burnett 1998.

[1] Friedrich 1993 stresses Medea's lack of grounding in the ethics of *oikos* and *polis*, and Rabinowitz 1993: 128 and 138 her dangerous independence of male protection and supervision.

geneia; Medea seems finally able only to achieve her goals by disowning her sons and the maternal commitment that blocks her autonomy, thus accepting the permanent suffering that she inflicts on herself. This chapter examines closely the implications of Medea's self-division in the context of the gender relations developed in the play as a whole.

Self-Division in Medea's Monologue

Debate over Medea's famous monologue (1021–80), in which the heroine argues with herself over her plan to kill her children, began in antiquity.[2] In this century Bruno Snell revived the Platonic interpretation of Galen, who saw in the monologue a psychological struggle between reason and passion.[3] Snell argued that the speech provoked Socrates to formulate his famous dictum that virtue is knowledge. W. M. Fortenbaugh instead asserted that the passage anticipated Aristotle's concept of a bipartite soul.[4] Most recently, Christopher Gill made a case for the perceptiveness of the Stoic Chrysippus' interpretation of lines 1078–80 of the monologue, which demonstrates a psychological division "not so much within the person, and between psychological elements, but rather a division between the person as he is at this moment and as he might be, if he exercised his full potentiality for human reason. At any one moment, the person functions (in one sense rationally) as a whole; even if his functioning is (as he himself may recognize) a kind of malfunctioning."[5] From Homer onward, characters in Greek literature often seem to recognize in themselves some form of struggle between different parts of their being. Recall, for example, Achilles' famous lines in *Iliad* 9 (645–46, trans. Lattimore 1951, modified), "All that you have said seems spoken after my own mind [*thumon*] / But my heart [*kradiē*] is swollen with anger [*cholō(i)*]." Among tragedians, Euripides is notable for exploiting such moments of internal division.[6] Nevertheless, especially given our limited knowledge of intellectual debates about ethical decision making contemporary to *Medea* (431 B.C.E.), we should probably be wary

---

[2] See Gill 1983 and 1996 and Dillon 1997 on Chrysippus' and Galen's views (Dillon includes additional views from antiquity), and Dihle 1977: esp. 5–11, on how later philosophy and drama produced a misreading of *Medea* as a tragedy of passion, although not all ancient interpreters discussed the dynamics of Medea's speech in these terms.

[3] See Snell 1948: 126, 1964: 52–60, and 1960: esp. 126. Among many others who have explored this view, see esp. Dirlmeier 1960: 31–32 and Walsh 1973: 16–22. Voigtländer 1957: esp. 236–37, in contesting Müller's 1951 claim that 1078–80 are the work of a Platonic interpolator, makes a strong argument that the passage in no way directly reflects Platonic or Socratic ethics, although the concluding lines may have been influenced by contemporary Socratic thought.

[4] Fortenbaugh 1970. Christmann 1962: 137–45 also describes Medea's struggle in terms that anticipate Aristotelian practical ethical reasoning.

[5] Gill 1983: 140.

[6] See Gibert 1995.

of both ancient and modern attempts to impose on the passage an anachronistic philosophical reading.

Alternatively, Anne Burnett and Albrecht Dihle saw the forces debating
within Medea as gendered:[7] that is, the monologue presents a conflict between
what the audience would have read as a masculine, heroic, and public self and
a feminine, maternal self.[8] The masculine heroic self requires the killing of the
children and the maternal self defends them. The masculine self wins. As Burnett put it, Medea's internal "dialogue is held between a part of herself called
thumos (1056, 1079), or sometimes *kardia* (1042, 1242), and another part that
is *mētēr* (1038; cf. 1247, etc.). Psychologically speaking it is a struggle between
Medea's masculine, honor-oriented self and her feminine, hearth-oriented
self."[9] Bernard Knox, Elizabeth Bongie, Christian Wolff, and Dihle have all offered readings of the play that support, directly or indirectly, this passing remark of Burnett's.[10] Yet, in fact, this perspective has played virtually no role in
philological discussions and close readings of the monologue itself.[11] By advocating this second position on the internal conflict displayed in the monologue
I intend to confront in more detail than have previous critics the implications
of assuming that the forces debating in Medea have as it were two genders. In
a larger sense, I hope to consider what point Euripides is making to his predominantly or exclusively male audience about the masculine ethics and masculine heroism adopted by his heroine, and why he chose a barbarian woman

[7] Dihle 1977: esp. 29 accepts Burnett's (1973) assumption in order to bolster his own argument
that in the monologue Medea's maternal love temporarily defeats her masculine warrior code.
Rickert 1987, McDermott 1989: 56, and Seidensticker 1990 adopt similar positions. Burnett 1998
now sees the conflict as one between a cowardly maternal desire to spare and a courageous pro-
gram of vengeance.

[8] Interpreters generally view the monologue as a struggle (with a foregone conclusion) between, on the one side, Medea's (sometimes heroic) passion for revenge and, on the other side,
her maternal emotions or her rational deliberations in defense of saving the children. Yet many
critics still assume that this conflict serves primarily to illustrate a philosophical point concerning the relation between passion and reason in ethical decisions. Voigtländer, following Müller
1951 (who nevertheless speaks [70] of a duty for revenge), argues that the speech shows an amoral
struggle between two emotions, one favoring revenge, the other maternal love; in her self-division Medea makes a typically tragic protest against the nature of the world that requires the revenge and hence her own misfortune. This interpretation has been effectively contested by
Christmann 1962: 65–82.

[9] Burnett 1973: 22. Knox 1977: 201 takes a position similar to Burnett's when he argues that
"in this great scene the grim heroic resolve triumphs not over an outside adversary or advisor but
over the deepest maternal feelings of the hero herself." See also Barlow 1989 and 1995.

[10] Wolff 1982: 238–39 briefly considers the implications of adopting this interpretation of
Medea's two selves. Knox 1977 and Bongie 1977, by making the case for Medea's masculine and
heroic side (see also Maddalena 1963), offer strong indirect support for this interpretation as well.
(Even in antiquity, Epictetus speaks of Medea as exemplifying an error committed by a soul of great
vigor [2.17.19–22]). The antipsychological reading of Schlesinger 1966: 26–53, esp. 30, laid the
groundwork for all these essays.

[11] The exception is Dihle 1977.

to make his dramatic statement. Before turning to a more extended discussion of my own position, however, I would like to make the case for my reading of the monologue through addressing the prevailing counterargument that reads the speech as a clash in some form or other between reason and passion.[12]

Reason versus Passion?

Those who read the monologue as a struggle between reason and passion view Medea's story as a tragedy of sexual jealousy. In the famous closing lines of her monologue (1078–80), the irrational passion for revenge (*thumos*) provoked by Jason's sexual betrayal is seen in their view to be at war with her rational *bouleumata* (deliberations/plans); passion wins. In my view, this is the Roman dramatist Seneca's Medea, not Euripides'.[13] Seneca's Medea does allow her passion to subdue her reason. Euripides' Medea, whenever she explains her decisions, is proud of her intelligence and unashamed of the complex emotional and rational motives that she has for her actions; throughout the planning of her revenge, passion and reason explicitly operate in concert.[14] Medea is quite capable of recognizing that emotion can lead her to make critical errors. At 485 (see also 800–802) she complains that she was more eager (*prothumos*) than wise when she allowed her love for Jason to lead her to commit crimes against her family and to depart from her homeland. She also knows that decisions can be arrived at through a suppression of passion by reason (although she uses no technical terms to this effect), but she never makes this a goal in her own decision making. This is partly because the control or devaluation of emotions by rational deliberation is an ethical mode that she associates with the despised Jason. Thus at 598–99 Medea rejects Jason's practical rationalization for the marriage with the princess on the grounds that she wants no happiness won with pain.[15]

---

[12] See Dihle 1977: esp. 28–29 n. 18, for a summary of those views, including his own, that contest the standard passion-versus-reason reading of the speech; Zwierlein 1978, Lloyd-Jones 1980, Gill 1983, Kovacs 1986, and Rickert 1987 have recently taken a similar position. My own objections come closest to those of Dihle 1977, despite my disagreement with his overall argument.

[13] Neophron's Medea, in a play that may well have predated Euripides' version, also represented herself as overcome by madness (Neophron fragment 2 N² or *TrGF* 15.2; see Michelini 1989: 128).

[14] In this respect I disagree with Fortenbaugh 1970, who makes the most extensive proto-Aristotelian reading of the passage. Fortenbaugh argues that Medea often engages in Aristotelian practical ethical reasoning, in means-ends deliberation. But with Medea it is not, as in Aristotelian practical reasoning, a simple case of emotion proposes, reason disposes. She is motivated from the start in her revenge plans by justice and intellect as well. Medea does not reason against emotion in wanting to spare the children, or reason about emotion (Fortenbaugh 238n) in the monologue. As Dihle 1977: 28–29 points out, one cannot distinguish in Medea Aristotle's two forms of ethical reasoning, practical planning, and the moral control of emotion through reason.

[15] In deciding to kill the children, however, she does deliberately choose to inflict pain on herself.

Jason claims to Medea that he has not been motivated by desire in his decision to marry the princess (556); he has considered (*bebouleumai*, 567) his actions and their consequences and so can claim to be *sophos* (548) in the plans he has made. In her second interview with Jason, Medea pretends to apologize for her anger (*orgas*, 870; see also 883) and lack of good sense (882, 885). She has engaged in discussion with herself (*logon*, 872; *bebouleumai*, 893) and decided to give up her anger (*thumou*, 879). Having considered her children's welfare and her impending friendless exile, she says she has come to a better understanding. Jason, pronouncing Medea's anger understandable, is delighted that after reflection Medea has accepted the superior plan (his own: *boulēn*, 913). But this is all playacting on Medea's part; she cleverly mimics Jason's own mode of ethical reasoning and feigns female subservience only in order to deceive her adversary. Although she is in full control of her reason throughout,[16] Medea never elsewhere indulges in such bloodless decision making; indeed, she aims in her revenge precisely to make Jason feel the emotions he once rejected (1360, 1370).

As would be expected in a debate that pits a maternal Medea against an avenging Medea (rather than reason against passion), there are rational as well as emotional or counterrational considerations on both sides of Medea's internal conflict concerning the children. On the one hand, Medea first rationally reflects that killing the children will bring punishment to herself as well as to Jason and will destroy her own future (1021–39); the sight of the children with their breathtaking childish beauty and innocence then reawakens vivid maternal feelings (1040–43). Yet to the Medea who advocates revenge these maternal arguments instantly appear "soft" (1052; at 776 such soft words are associated by Medea with female subservience and deceptiveness); insofar as they violate from this opposing perspective her self-interest and reputation, the arguments of the mother are in Medea's view counterrational. On the other hand, we come to Medea's monologue with an accumulated knowledge of all her motives for revenge, both rational and irrational, although in the speeches in which she addresses her revenge plans she stresses the rational motives for her act.[17]

We have, of course, been told repeatedly from the beginning of the play that Medea is enraged at Jason's erotic betrayal of her, and in the closing scene she eloquently defends being motivated in her revenge by *erōs*, or, more precisely, *lechos* (marriage bed or marriage), which represents a broader set of social issues for a woman than mere desire: "Do you think this [*lechos*], then, a trivial pain for a woman?" (1368; see also 265–66, 1354).[18] Justice is an even more important motive (see 26, 160, 165, 578, 580, 582, 1352–53). Medea has sac-

---

[16] See *manthanō* in 1078. Despite the nurse's fears of Medea's heroic, almost bestial wrath, the Medea we see on stage never seems close to *mania* or irrationality.

[17] See Bongie 1977: 42 and 44, on Medea's first scene with Jason, and Dihle 1977: 14–16.

[18] See now Burnett 1998: 194–95.

rificed her homeland for Jason; she has incurred many enemies in order to help her husband (483–87, 506–8). Jason has made his plans without thinking of the welfare of either Medea or the children. He has thus in Medea's view wronged his friends, while she has kept her side of the bargain by giving him heirs (470, 696, 698; 489–91). Above all, Jason broke his oath to Medea, an oath sworn by the gods (20–23, 161, 439, 492, 1392);[19] Medea is for this reason quite certain that the gods will support her punishment of Jason. And the final surprising appearance of the chariot of the sun seems to prove her right.[20]

Medea does not need to review all these concerns in the monologue for them to be present in the minds of the audience. Here she stresses the need to take revenge regardless of the personal costs involved, and to avoid being mocked by her enemies. This argument has its own rationality as well, although some recent critics assume the contrary. In his commentary on the passage Alan Elliott, for example, asserts that "Here as in 797, Medea is concerned not so much that her treatment has been unjust, but that her enemies may have the chance to laugh at her. Moral principle plays no part in her revenge."[21] This is taking the speech out of the context developed for it in the play as a whole, for the line is a shorthand reference to a position Medea has developed in detail earlier in the play. A Greek hero traditionally wished above all to do good to his friends and harm to his enemies. (The desire to avoid the laughter of enemies is a logical extension of this shame-culture position.) That this remained a dominant Greek ethical position as well as a major, even the major, principle of social organization in the archaic and classical periods is made clear in the first book of Plato's *Republic* (1.332a–b), where it is adopted quite sincerely as a definition and apparently the standard popular definition of justice.[22] A failure to win honor and defend his self-worth made a hero a fool in the eyes of his enemies.

Medea has evoked this standard for her actions at several earlier points in the text. She succinctly explicates the conception of the self that compels her to complete her revenge: "Let no one think me of no account or powerless, nor a quiet stay-at-home. Quite the contrary: consider me hard on my enemies and to my friends kindly. That sort of person has the life of greatest glory."[23] In a world without trial by jury, without justice for women and foreigners (Jason is *xeinapatou*, 1392; see Medea's speech at 230–51), revenge, however necessary and justified from one point of view, may in its wake bring death and other dev-

---

[19] On the importance of Jason's breaking of the oath, see esp. Burnett 1973 and 1998: 197–205 and Flory 1978.

[20] Helios is a god of oaths; the violation of oaths often entails the destruction of progeny (see Rickert 1987: 109 and 112).

[21] Elliott 1969: 94. See also Voigtländer 1957: 223.

[22] Müller 1951: 70 makes a similar point, but then contradicts himself by arguing that the monologue pits two emotions against each other. See also McDermott 1989: 55.

[23] Lines 807–10, trans. Wolff 1982: 238.

astating consequences for the revenger. The *Iliad* does not treat the *motives* for Achilles' wrath as irrational (though, as with Medea, the principles governing his wrath conflict with those governing relations between *philoi*); instead the poem emphasizes the devastating effects of this (initially) justified wrath on Achilles' friends and its unforeseen consequences for the hero himself. As in the case of Achilles, Medea's pursuit of her code tragically seems to require the injury of friends as well as foes. To characterize a revenge so carefully motivated throughout the early scenes of the *Medea* as merely the product of irrationality flies in the face of the entire Greek heroic code.[24] Nevertheless, unlike Achilles, Medea fully anticipates how painful the emotional consequences of her revenge will be on herself as a woman.[25]

Thumos and *Bouleumata*

The case for reading the monologue as a debate between passion and reason rests above all on retaining lines 1078–80 of the text and on interpreting these three lines as a summation of the struggle in which Medea engages throughout the speech. (Readers may prefer to move directly past this detailed discussion of the text to the next section.) Several scholars have in fact bracketed lines 1056–80 of the monologue;[26] many others have felt pressed to defend or explain them. Although deleting all or part of 1056–80 eliminates some serious difficulties in the passage, arguments can be made for retaining the text as we have it.[27] Tempting as it would have been for an actor to enlarge this remarkable speech, it is in my view too easy to assume, especially given Euripides' complex and contradictory dramaturgy, that the textual difficulties here are due to an interpolator's incompetence. Hence, while remaining uneasy about aspects of the passage, I base my argument almost entirely on Murray's Oxford text,[28]

[24] See Dihle's emphasis (1977: 14–16) on Medea's warrior code as a product of her powerful intellect. As he points out, to equate this code exclusively with emotion would have shocked a Greek audience. For women's exclusion from this code, see my subsequent discussion.

[25] See Schlesinger 1966: 53, who nevertheless thinks that Medea does not at first realize the consequences of her action. I think rather (see 791 for her initial awareness of the pain her crime will bring) that she does not anticipate how powerfully her maternity will contest her determination for revenge.

[26] Bergk 1884: 3: 512 n. 140, Jachmann 1936: 193 n. 1, Müller 1951, Reeve 1972, and Zwierlein 1978. On the strength of Reeve's arguments, Diggle brackets the passage in his 1984 Oxford text. Voigtländer 1957 (emphasizing [224–25] the dramatic richness of the contested lines) and Steidle 1968 defend the passage at some length, while Lloyd-Jones 1980 and Kovacs 1986, contesting Reeve and Zwierlein, propose briefer deletions (see my note 96). For other recent summaries of the controversy, see Christmann 1962: 125–46 and Lesky 1983: 226–27.

[27] Seidensticker 1990 makes a particularly telling case.

[28] Murray [1902] 1963; one exception is noted later. Even the almost universally bracketed 1062–63 can be viewed as contributing to the argument of the passage, although see note 96.

although my overall interpretation of the nature of the forces contending within Medea in the speech does not, in fact, depend on retaining the disputed lines.

Although there are three important arguments for deletion of 1056–80 (see the appendix to this chapter for a brief discussion of the other two), only the third, the authenticity and the interpretation of lines 1078–80, is relevant to my discussion here. The debate centers on the translation of line 1079: *thumos de kreissōn tōn emōn bouleumatōn.*[29] Several translations claim to resolve the difficulties posed by the text. Philosophically oriented scholars often translate the line, "My passion is stronger than my rational deliberations/plans [concerning murder of the children]." The proponents of this translation variously interpret *bouleumata* as deliberations provoked by Medea's maternal emotions; rational plans to save the children; or general and rational deliberations on the evils of her plan or on the negative effects her passionate emotion for revenge have on her reason.[30] Both the logic of the monologue itself, which brings the maternal Medea into conflict with the avenging Medea, and Medea's previous habits of deliberation make translating *bouleumata* as "rational plans to save the children" the most viable of these alternatives. *Bouleumata*, both in this play and elsewhere in Euripides, are generally specific plans, rational deliberations directed to a practical goal, rather than ethical meditations about what is virtuous or bad.[31] Medea's deliberations, except when she is pretending otherwise to Jason, consistently involve considering how to put into effect specific plans proposed to her by her emotions, her heroic code, her sense of what is good for herself, and her sense of injustice (usually in combination). Even in this passage, she deliberates not over the morality of the crime or its violation of her own ethical code (the injustice of harm to *philoi*) but about whether to put into action a rescue plan that will save her from pain and bring her practical advantages and pleasure in the future. She previously viewed the deed as unholy (796; see also 1383), but this knowledge did not deter her; in the monologue she gives divine

[29] The grammar of these lines is not in question. I return later to further discussion of lines 1078 and 1080.

[30] For a recent summary of this range of interpretations, see Dihle 1977: 27–29 n. 18.

[31] For arguments in favor of this position, see esp. Diller 1966: 274–75. Christmann 1962: 137–45, Lesky 1983: 227, and Dihle 1977: 28–29. In their support, it should be emphasized that every other use of *bouleumata* and *bouleuō* in *Medea* refers to a precise plan or change of plans: at 372, 769, 772, 1044, and 1048 *bouleumata* refers to Medea's revenge plans, at 270 to Creon's plans to exile Medea, and at 449 and 886 to the plans of Jason and Creon for a new marriage; 402, *bouleuousa* refers to Medea's plans; 893, *bebouleumai* to Medea's false change of plans; 317, *bouleuē(i)s* to Creon's fear of Medea's evil plans; 37, *bouleusē(i)* to the nurse's similar fear; 567, *bebouleumai*, to Jason's plans concerning his marriage to the princess; and 874, *bouleuousin*, to Jason's plans for Medea. Christmann 1962: 65–82, who argues for an opposition between the rational plans of the mother and emotional self-destructive revenge, makes the case that 1079 thus translated can form a proper climax to the struggle between mother and avenger in the monologue.

authority to the murder by describing it as a sacrifice (1054).[32] Earlier in the play Medea says explicitly that women do not have the resources to do good (*esthla*), but are of every evil the cleverest of contrivers (407–9). In the monologue she observes self-consciously that she is being led by her *thumos* to a choice with bad consequences for herself. In addition, she has earlier mocked Jason for his rejection of emotion in favor of the dictates of reason.[33]

The most important argument against translating *bouleumata* as "plans to save the children," however, is that the word is used emphatically to refer to "revenge plans" twice in this speech as well as elsewhere (along with related words) in the play.[34] This consideration led Hans Diller to suggest the attractive alternative "Meine Leidenschaft Herr über meine Pläne ist," or "My passion *is master of* my plans."[35] In this reading Medea knows (*manthanō*, 1078) that she is about to do herself harm (*kaka*), but her *thumos* triumphantly insists on putting into action her plans of revenge.[36] Yet one could object that Diller's translation of *kreissōn* as "is master of" or "controls" is far less intuitively obvious than the comparative use of the word, "stronger than." Could the hearer easily suppress the common meaning of this word?[37]

---

[32] For a discussion of Medea's use of the rhetoric of sacrifice and self-pity to make the murder of the children appear to herself inevitable, see Pucci 1980: ch. 4. As Pucci stresses, Medea sometimes equates her "I" with maternal feelings, sometimes with her revenge. At other times she sees the "I" under pressure from separate forces inside herself, like *thumos*. Pucci's argument confirms from another perspective that Medea is not here determined by her passion but chooses finally to side with her *thumos*.

[33] Christmann 1962 argues strongly against Snell's Socratic reading of the passage by arguing that *kaka* in 1078 means what is bad for Medea, in the sense that the murder is to her practical disadvantage as a mother and as a human being who seeks pleasure rather than pain. This interpretation makes the meaning of *kakos* throughout the passage consistent and consolidates the argument made by others that *kaka* here does not mean morally evil. Lloyd-Jones 1980: 57 dismisses the problem of a possible inconsistency in the use of *kakos* here.

[34] See 372, 769, 772, 1044, and 1048. Dihle 1977: 27–29 (with bibliography) consolidates the case for this extremely telling point. The word would have been ringing in the audience's ears, and in this dramatic context the term cannot be considered neutral (contra Lloyd-Jones 1980: 58). The argument that *bouleumata ta prosthen* at 1044–45 implies an imposing set of plans to save the children is very weak from the dramatic perspective of a listener; furthermore, as Voigtländer 1957: 226 recognizes, *bouleumata* in Euripides refers far more frequently to destructive than positive plans.

[35] Diller 1966: 367 and Walsh 1973: 19, defended by Steidle 1968: 165 and Rohdich 1968: 64.

[36] Diller 1966: 366 also argues that since at 1060–63 Medea has rejected the notion of saving the children, at 1079 she can hardly view these plans as viable. In his favor, note that she does not speak of rescuing them after 1058 but only bemoans her loss (1071–75).

[37] Lesky 1983: 227 (citing, following Kessel 1973: 103 n. 21, *Medea* 965) and Reeve 1972: 59 n. 2 (citing Euripides fragment 718 N², but not giving full credit to Diller's [1966] whole argument) are reluctant to accept Diller's parallels (*Medea* 443–45, *Bacchae* 880, and later philosophical passages) as sufficient evidence. Stanton 1987 (with further lexical support), Gill 1996: 223, and Segal 1996: 24 support Diller's views. I view Diller's translation of *kreissōn* as both possible and preferable, and problematic only because it is the more obscure alternative.

A third reading, proposed by A. Dihle (and now seconded in a modified form by A. P. Burnett), interprets *thumos* as the maternal love that proves stronger than Medea's revenge plans; this interpretation poses even more substantial difficulties.[38] Neither in this play nor elsewhere in Euripides is *thumos* equated with anything like maternal love.[39] The *thumos* to which Medea appeals at 1056 is capable of hearing the arguments for sparing the children and being cheered by them (1057–58). But the request to the *thumos* to spare the chil-

[38] Scholars have rejected the translation for 1079 "My passion is stronger than my revenge plans," although it is grammatically correct, because this would mean that Medea has decided to save her children. Yet this is basically the argument of Dihle 1977. Dihle's essay makes many brilliant points, but I cannot accept his ingenious but ultimately unconvincing reading of 1079. The arguments that he makes for reading *bouleumata* as revenge plans should hold as well for interpreting *thumos*. *Thumos* in the *Medea* is elsewhere said most often to be affected by *erōs* (8, 640) and anger (879, 1152), and this is even more the case with related words (e.g., *oxuthumos*, 319; *thumoumenēn*, 271) Medea's feelings in this passage are not consistently against her revenge plan (Dihle 16)—they waver back and forth—and her plan is not quite so intellectually motivated as Dihle suggests. Dihle admits Medea's actions are overdetermined, that she cannot spare the children. Hence his reading makes Medea's decision to save the children unrealistic and irrational, when she elsewhere seems highly realistic. Dihle also argues that his view makes sense of the chorus immediately following the speech, where the chorus speaks, not of the horror of killing the children, as elsewhere, but of the burdens of maternity. (See also the similar argument of Burnett 1998: 287 on this point.) Yet there are other possible interpretations of this chorus (Buttrey 1958: 9, for example, sees it as a lament for Jason, not Medea, and I offer another shortly). See further the arguments of Zwierlein 1978: 35–37 n. 24c against Dihle's interpretation.

[39] Burnett's ingenious reading (1998) equates a passionate maternal pity with cowardice; hence the impulse to spare that concludes the monologue is not the equivalent of a decision, but an irrational (irrational above all because she cannot take the children) surrender to the children's vivid physical presence (283) that leaves her in a state of irresolution. It seems surprising then that immediately following the next choral ode a Medea who has given way to maternal pity revels in the gory details of the deaths of the Corinthian princess and her father that will ensure the children's demise and then without further explanation reverses herself and kills the children in order to spare them from vengeance from the Corinthians. As I have argued, Medea's maternal voice has offered the heroine rational arguments to spare the children, and it cannot be equated simply with cowardice or irrationality. (Burnett [210] apparently dismisses as deceptive the first part of Medea's speech that offers these arguments, because in her view the pedagogue is still on stage at this point, even though Medea has told him to go inside [*Medea* 1019–20].) Just before lines 1078–80, Medea urges the children to leave and refuses to look at them (1076–77); this hardly seems like a prelude to a final surrender to maternal pity (at 1053 the same gesture is linked with the impulse for revenge). Translating 1078 as "Certainly I understand what I mean to do is cowardly" puts Burnett in the position of claiming, with little evidence, that *dran* (do) can describe the abandonment of a plan (281). Moreover, the Homeric monologues where heroes make decisions on the battlefield that, as Burnett points out (212, 285), serve as a model for this passage to some extent end in a reassertion of courage, not cowardice. To conclude the monologue with a gnomic statement in which cowardice or irrational pity (rather than aggressive emotions like anger) "is the cause of men's greatest sufferings" is also anomalous; heroic men simply do not make such decisions in equivalent contexts and women, who might be expected to do so, rarely debate choices in Greek literature in any case. It is true that other characters, like Iphigeneia in Euripides' *Iphigeneia among the Taurians* do shift from vengeance to pity, but the shift in such cases is good and not harmful to friends.

dren makes it clear that *thumos* is also capable of sacrificing them; *thumos* is thus equated at 1056 not with maternal love but with a capacity in Medea that presently favors the revenge (and will do so in 1079), but might be persuaded to spare because the children will bring it pleasure. Yet Dihle's discussion should make us wary of being too reductive in translating *thumos* simply as passion for revenge and a capacity for the irrational.[40] In both archaic poetry and Euripides, *thumos* can be virtually equated with *erōs* or anger, but it is also a more general term used to describe a force (e.g., courage) that directs the self to action. The Homeric *thumos* can be affected by a vast range of feelings, from anger and *erōs* to pity and reverence, but it can also make rational decisions (e.g., *Iliad* 1.193 or 2.5; *Odyssey* 14.490)[41] or, as in the passage from *Iliad* 9 quoted earlier, even feel itself in tension with a *kradiē* swollen with anger. In this sense it is most commonly a capacity in the self, particularly vulnerable to the persuasion of strong emotions, but not in essence irrational; when a character addresses his *thumos* in internal dialogue, it even comes close to representing what we might call a self.

A study of the term *thumos* in Euripides indicates a range of meaning comparable with that found in epic, if somewhat narrower.[42] The Euripidean *thumos* is the seat of emotion, of instinct, and even of deliberation and is subject to a range of emotions from anger, grief, and *erōs* to pity, hope, or pride. Medea is twice said to be struck in the *thumos* by *erōs* (8, 639) and a cloud of grief has fastened on her great *thumos* (108). Medea pretends to Jason that she will give up *thumos* (anger, 879), and Jason asks the princess to give up hers (1152). Similarly, Heracles is supplicated by Amphitryon to check the *thumos* of wild lion (a mixture of suicidal grief and anger, *Heracles* 1211). A *thumos* elsewhere can be violent for revenge (*Heracleidae* 925); Hecuba avoids the vengeful *thumos* of the blinded Polymestor (*Hecuba* 1055); Aphrodite gratifies her *thumos* in destroying Hippolytus (*Hippolytus* 1328). An angry person breathes out *thumos* (*Bacchae* 620, *Iphigeneia at Aulis* 125, *Phoenissae* 454). Theseus advises those who have been wronged to bear the injustice moderately in their *thumos* (*Suppliant Women* 556). The chorus thinks that Medea's *thumos* will pity her sup-

---

[40] See Dihle 1977: 30. Schlesinger 1966: 29 reduces *thumos* to "lebenskraft" or "vitalität." Dihle argues effectively against earlier translations and for Medea's powerful and controlling intellect, but then settles once again on equating *thumos* with emotion.

[41] See Diller 1966: 364–65 on decisions made by the Homeric *thumos*; Medea's case is anomalous here because, in contrast to Homer, her *thumos* directs her to a choice described as bad. In the case of decisions made by the archaic *thumos*, reason can act in concert with emotion (e.g., *Odyssey* 20.10). Nevertheless, as Gill 1987: 28 points out, although Homeric *thumos* can be treated virtually as a person with a range of emotions, it is rarely treated as an agent who performs and refrains from deliberate actions.

[42] Previous discussions have looked more narrowly at *thumos* in *Medea* or in archaic poetry, where the acts influenced by *thumos*, as here, are associated with courage (see 1042, 1051, 1242) or anger. My discussion here omits lines too difficult to categorize precisely: several fragments and *Hippolytus* 1087. See now Burnett 1998: 211 and 277 with further bibliography; she interprets *thumos* as "a vital, breathy, chest-located organ that can translate impulse into physical action" (211).

plicating children (865). Elsewhere a chorus can wish for a *thumos* untouched by grief (*Hippolytus* 1114). In more unusual cases, the grieving Electra's *thumos* is not stirred by festive jewelry (*Electra* 176); Peleus' *thumos* is prophetic in anticipating the news of Neoptolemus' death (*promantis*, *Andromache* 1072); Creon's preference for a son-in-law is located in his *thumos* (*Medea* 310).

A *thumos* under the influence of or the seat of emotions or instincts can be viewed positively or negatively. Hope may negatively influence the *thumos* (*Suppliants* 480); a grieving *thumos* has no stability (fragment 1039 N²). *Thumos* can be classified as a bad thing with *axunesia* (want of understanding, fragment 257 N²). A wise man does not have a *thumos* that thinks like a woman (*gunaikophrōn*, fragment 362.34 N²). Yet *thumos* (anger) can under the proper supervision be a valuable quality in the people (*Orestes* 702). Achilles' proud *thumos* is uplifted at the thought of rescuing Iphigeneia from her death (*Iphigeneia at Aulis* 919). Heracles' *thumos* warned him not to carouse in Admetus' house (*Alcestis* 829). Electra's *thumos* shows the capacity to deliberate when it is persuaded by the tokens offered by the old man of Orestes' identity (*Electra* 578).

Prior to the monologue, Medea's *thumos* is said by characters other than herself to be affected by anger, grief, and *erōs*, and, in the imagination of the chorus, it will soon be affected by pity. In the monologue she first asks it to listen to the reasons for sparing the children (1056–57). The use of *ge* to reinforce *su* in 1056 is especially telling:[43] "Do not [*mē dēta*], *thume*, do not you of all people [*mē su ge*] do these things [*ergasē(i) tade*]." A *thumos* that can impel Medea either to kill or to spare, and to hear the reasons on both sides for so doing, is apparently capable, like the Homeric *thumos*, of some sort of deliberate choice, even if, by 1079, the *thumos* is finally set (and was probably from the start irrevocably set) on doing things to Medea's harm (*kaka*). Hence it is better to categorize *thumos* in the monologue not as "irrational passion" or "rage" but as a capacity located in Medea that directs her to act, a "heart" that can (or at least pretends to itself that it can) choose to side either with the arguments of the revenger or the arguments of the mother (although it is predisposed to the former).

Passion *and* Reason

In view of all the above considerations, let us now return to the problem of interpreting 1078–80:

καὶ μανθάνω μὲν οἷα τολμήσω κακά.
θυμὸς δὲ κρείσσων τῶν ἐμῶν βουλευμάτων.
ὅσπερ μεγίστων αἴτιος κακῶν βροτοῖς.

---

[43] On this point, see Dihle 1977: 14. It could perhaps be disputed whether *ge* should be strictly attached to *su* or rather to the combination *mē su*, making the prohibition more forceful, as probably in Sophocles' *Oedipus at Colonus* 1441 or Euripides' *Phoenissae* 532, among the passages cited by Denniston 1975: 122.

kai manthanō men hoia tolmēsō kaka,
thumos de kreissōn tōn emōn bouleumatōn.
hosper megistōn aitios kakōn brotois.

The following (expanded) translation might best capture the implications of
these lines in the context of this play and this monologue: "I understand what
sort of bad things I am about to do [or, suffer],[44] but my heart-determined-on-
revenge is master over my [revenge] plans,[45] a[n avenging] heart that is generally the greatest cause of bad consequences for mortals." I wish in particular to
preserve in this rather awkward translation both the combination of reason and
passion operating in Medea's *thumos* at this climactic moment (her revenge is
motivated by rational heroic principles as well as avenging anger) and the transition that Medea's *thumos* has undergone in this passage. Medea's *thumos* presumably begins the monologue determined on revenge; at 1056–58 she gives
it arguments for sparing the children, apparently appealing to its capacity, well
known to herself, for a rational pity (*su ge*). At 1059–64 these arguments are
rejected through an appeal to the counterarguments for revenge. The *thumos*
Medea addresses at 1056 could *not* be categorized in a general fashion (*hosper*,
1080) as "the greatest cause of bad consequences for mortals." But by 1079 the
thumos is irrevocably set on revenge, and it is this avenging *thumos* that, however justified from one perspective, predictably creates, as it has from Achilles
onward in Greek poetry, negative consequences.

By suppressing any moral opposition between passion and reason, this translation of 1079 would make a proper and predictable climax to a deliberation
by the Medea we have come to know both in the speech and throughout the
play (see my subsequent discussion), whereas to read the speech as a victory of
passion over reason would be anomalous, producing a Medea who resembles
Jason (who is concerned with the ill effects of passion on reason) more than
herself.[46] In the latter case, the audience would surprisingly confront in the

---

[44] This line consciously underlines the defeat of the maternal by the heroic Medea. I have accepted here Kovacs' argument (1986: 351–52) for printing *tolmēsō* (the reading in all the manu-
scripts except L) for *dran mellō*, "I am about to do"; *tolmēsō* can be understood in an active or a passive sense.

[45] Although I here adopt Diller's 1966 reading of *kreissōn* and *bouleumata*, his translation of *thumos* as "passion" leads him to support Snell's 1960 reading of the speech as a battle between reason and passion. Diller 1966: 358 sees here a tragic tension between the goddess in Medea who ac-
complishes a just revenge and the woman who is painfully aware of the senselessness of her act.

[46] Christmann 1962: 143 argues effectively against an anachronistic philosophical reading of
the monologue, yet ends by taking a closely similar position himself. According to Gill's 1983
analysis, Chrysippus cites *Medea* 1078–80 to illustrate his account of *pathos*: "Medea, on the other
hand, was not persuaded by any reasoning to kill her children; quite the contrary, so far as reasoning goes, she says that she understands how evil the acts are that she is about to perform, but
her anger is stronger than her deliberations; that is, her affection (*pathos*) has not been made to
submit and does not follow reason as it would a master, but throws off the reins and departs and
disobeys the command" (4.2.27 [372K], Gill 140). In Gill's subtle account of Chrysippus' reasoning on this point, the Stoic view comes far closer than a Platonic or Aristotelian reading to cap-

monologue the victory of an irrational masculine imperative over a rational maternity. By suppressing altogether the claims of her maternal side, this interpretation of 1079 confirms our sense that Medea's choice for revenge has been inevitable from the start, that her self-debate aims finally not at persuading herself to save the children (a plan in any case abandoned after 1058) but at making the crime seem inevitable to herself.

Plato in the *Republic* sees *thumos* as a capacity in the soul, like anger, that can ally with reason or with the appetites (4.439e–441c).[47] Euripides' own sense of *thumos* is much more easily understood in the light of epic; Medea's *thumos*, like that of epic characters, is not so much a part of her soul as it is a capacity in herself that can reason (in a practical sense) as well as feel. In Medea's case, the *thumos* that rules her plans, if we read it in the context of the motives for her revenge offered throughout the play, unites jealousy, anger, and courage with justice and a rational principle of heroic action that has consistently operated for Medea: that of harming enemies and helping friends. This is true within the speech itself but is even more obviously true when we consider the speech in the light of the dramatic action up to this point.

In sum, I would not wish to deny Euripides' interest in what later became explicitly philosophical problems.[48] Furthermore, no philological argument can suppress the ambiguities present in language, and all possible readings of 1079 must be present at some level in the consciousness of the hearer. If the closing lines of this speech are genuine, an audience cannot but see reflected in their ambiguity the overdetermination of Medea's thoughts, emotions, and actions throughout the play. We may even recall here Jason's preference for

---

turing the dynamics of the monologue: in particular, Medea's self-division "between two possible (complete) selves" (Gill 142), the fundamentally rational nature of all human impulses (in the sense that they involve judgments that a certain goal is desirable), and Medea's *deliberate* rejection of the rational arguments of the mother in herself. Yet it anachronistically ignores the fact that for Medea her motives for revenge are not simply irrational. By her own standards she does not have an "irrational and unnatural" (cf. 4.2.8 [368K], Gill 140) impulse to kill her children; she wants to take revenge on her enemies and save face before them, and she convinces herself that killing the children is necessary to attain this goal.

[47] See the discussion of Rickert 1987: 99–100 and Gill 1996: 233–34, who argues that Greek philosophy generally views psychoethical conflict as a matter of two conflicting sets of beliefs accompanied by reason and emotion rather than a conflict between reason and passion. Both Gill and Seidensticker 1990: 97–98 support interpreting Medea's self-division in these terms. Rickert argues that Medea, although recognizing that it is better not to kill the children, genuinely thinks that her act of vengeance is the best choice and has good reasons for thinking so. Hence her monologue represents a tragic conflict of values, not an instance of *akrasia*, where an agent recognizes one thing to be best but does another under the influence of internal forces such as *thumos* or pleasure (103, 105–6, 114). "In fact, the hero's *thumos* and its principles are so uncompromising that it may be difficult to find one who is truly akratic" (117). Michelini 1989: 133, however, thinks that Medea suppresses her maternal feelings and thus does not make a clear choice between two options.

[48] See fragments 220, 572, 840 N².

plans that purportedly subordinate emotion to reason (though, given the nature of these plans, his preferred mode of decision making appears dubious). Yet what seems more certain than any one authoritative translation of 1079 (for scholarly controversy has demonstrated that this is impossible) is that the speech as a whole represents a clash between two positions in which reason and emotion unite on either side of the argument. And it is precisely this inseparable combination of rationality and irrationality, passion and intelligence, in Medea's determination for revenge that makes it so very terrifying and, I think, far more tragic than a philosophical defeat of reason by passion.[49]

Gender and Self-Division

Through a careful dramatic orchestration of the relation between the two engendered sides of Medea that is echoed in the conflict between male and female characters,[50] the earlier scenes of *Medea* prepare for the climactic display of self-division in the monologue. (By contrast, the play does not prepare the audience to confront in the monologue a conflict between passion and reason or between two emotions.) The first scene provides disturbing hints about the contradictory aspects of Medea's character.[51] On the one hand, Medea seems suicidal, a helpless, feminine victim of her husband's desertion. She has sacrificed everything for Jason. This is the side of Medea that moves and impresses the chorus of women. On the other hand, the nurse, as she expresses her fears about the dangerous temperament of the proud and wrathful heroine, anticipates in her language Medea's own heroic view of herself. Her nature is royal (119–21; see Medea at 403–6); she is self-willed (*authadous*, 104; see Medea at 1028), high-spirited, and hard to check (*megalosplanchnos* and *duskatapaustos*, 109) and, in her anger against the injustice (26) and dishonor (20, 33) done to her, may turn against her own *philoi* (95).[52] From the moment of her first appearance on stage, Medea's female side is in this play not taken for granted but carefully defined through the relationship she creates with the chorus.[53] Her heroic, masculine side only emerges explicitly in the speeches (364–

---

[49] Gill 1983: 142–43 comments on the horrifying way that Medea's rationality "deliberately intensifies, by arguments and exhortation, her own desire to carry out her revenge" (142) and on the way that she passively distances herself from her crime in announcing the final subjection of her maternal side to her *thumos*.

[50] See Schlesinger's emphasis (1966: 45) on the pervasive conflict between male and female worlds in the play and Williamson 1985 (rev. 1990) on gender and space.

[51] On tragic characterization, see part I.

[52] See my earlier discussion of Medea's motives for revenge—injustice, dishonor, mistreatment of *philoi*.

[53] There seem to be two reasons for this. First, the play can win sympathy for Medea as victimized woman before revealing the full range of her differences from her own sex; second, Eu-

409, 764–810) where Medea announces her revenge plans, although it is implied to a lesser degree in her first and final forthright encounters with Jason.

At her first entrance Medea makes an appeal to the chorus as fellow married women by describing her own situation in terms of the difficult life of all women and their potential for becoming victims of a male order (230–51). With this speech Medea obtains the silence of the chorus and—surprisingly, given her myth—establishes a strong association between herself and the ordinary housewife in a Greek city. The women of the chorus approve her revenge on Jason (267) and even tacitly consent to the destruction of members of their own royal family, although they do not wish to be tortured by *erōs* like Medea but desire for themselves a moderate Aphrodite appropriate to a proper wife (635–41). For them, Medea's eloquence and just complaints against Jason and Creon represent a reversal of poetry's silencing of women through the centuries and its maligning of them as sexually unfaithful (410–30). The women of the chorus only break with Medea, see her as other than themselves and unlike women, when she determines to include the killing of the children in her revenge on Jason. The protection of children from harm is such an intimate part of the self-interest of mothers (the women repeatedly remind Medea of the negative effects that the crime will have on herself: see esp. 818, 996–97, and 1261 on the waste of Medea's efforts in rearing her children), that they can think of only one example of a woman who killed her children, Ino, and she (unlike Medea) was mad when she committed her crime and followed the murder by suicide (1282–89).[54]

The case for Medea as an ill-treated female victim is tellingly built up in the early scenes of the play where she adopts traditionally "feminine" weapons in her self-defense. Both Creon's gesture of immediate exile for a woman who has nowhere to go and Jason's indifference to it seem extraordinarily callous, as the shocked reaction of King Aegeus to Medea's plight later confirms (701–7; see also the nurse at 82–84 and the chorus at 576–78). The egotistical Jason has clearly given little thought to his family's welfare, despite his belated protests to the contrary, and his callous behavior in his first scene with Medea cannot but call attention to her beleaguered situation. Creon is aware of Medea's unusual intelligence and her capacity for anger, but Medea deceives him into a temporary reprieve by using the weapons of the weak: supplication (338) and an appeal to her children's welfare (340–47). Medea also gives up trying to persuade Jason honestly. Instead, she successfully feigns being the helpless woman,

---

ripides must confront the mythological tradition, which often envisioned Medea as a witch with magic powers. See, however, Knox 1977: 204 and 212–13 for the ways that Euripides plays down Medea's supernatural powers here, at least until the concluding scene. Rohdich 1968: 47–55 overemphasizes the degree to which Medea has become merely a woman in this play. Barlow's 1989 argument has some similarities to my own.

[54] As Visser 1986: 158 points out, women kill their children in Greek myth elsewhere only to avenge their kin.

given to tears and irrationality, who will now for the good of her children accept, as a proper woman should, her husband's superiority and guidance. This feminine role playing, which in the second scene with Jason does have some basis in Medea's feeling for the children, dupes even her own husband, who should (like the nurse) have known better.

These early scenes of the play, by building a powerful case for male exploitation of women and Medea's entrapment in a female role, may temporarily distract the audience from the initial contradictory view of a dangerous Medea presented above all by the nurse in the first scene. Increasingly, however, the text emphasizes Medea's distance from her carefully contrived appearance of solidarity with her fellow women, as she uses her "femininity," the desire for children, and even her own maternal love to manipulate and deceive not only Creon and Jason but even her supporter Aegeus. Furthermore, as several critics have pointed out, her eloquent first speech on the wrongs of women deceptively applies only in part to herself.[55] For Medea is far from the passive victim of marriage and masculine brutality that she claims to be. Unlike the typical housewife, she did not in fact need the dowry she complains of to the chorus (232–34); she chose her own husband and has won him by her ruthless deeds. Indeed, she often seems to envision herself, contrary to Greek practice, as an equal or even the dominant partner in the marriage. Note Medea's use of the feminine active participle *gamousa*, at 606 (women normally marry in the middle, not the active voice); she speaks of her gift to the princess as *phernas*, or dowry (956). In her view the choice of a husband is an *agōn*, a contest (235). The clasping of right hands that confirmed Medea's marriage to Jason is a gesture typical of the affirmation of bonds between men;[56] in the standard marriage the man grasps the woman's wrist in a gesture of domination. Medea speaks of reconciliation with Jason as if it were a truce between two cities (898).

Extraordinarily intelligent (*sophē*), Medea can sing an answer to the other sex (426–27). She is not, as the chorus continues to believe (1290–92), motivated only by betrayal in bed (265–66). Medea is also responsible for Jason's fame (476–82; she even, probably contrary to the better-known tradition, kills the dragon herself, 480–82), as he himself indirectly admits when he says that she should be consoled for what has happened to her because if she had not come to Greece *she* would not have been famous (see 536–41). Medea would prefer battle to childbirth (250–51), and Euripides uses the language of athletic contest to describe her struggles against Jason (44–45, 765, 366–67, 403, 1245). Despite her own denial (407–9), Medea, though a woman, has the capacity actively to do good, as the Corinthians and Aegeus know.[57] We are told by the nurse that Medea won the favor of the Corinthians (11–12, probably

[55] See esp. Pucci 1980: 64–69, Bongie 1977: 36, and Easterling 1977a: 182.

[56] Flory 1978: 70–71.

[57] Easterling 1977a: 179 emphasizes that Aegeus treats Medea as a respectable religious authority.

by averting a famine [see the scholiast at Pindar *Olympian* 13.74; in some versions of her myth, Medea even ruled Corinth for a while]);[58] she wins a promise from King Aegeus that because she can make him fertile, she may live under his protection in Athens.

The desire to avenge erotic betrayal is characteristic of women in Greek poetry, as we see from the chorus's sympathetic reaction to Medea and from Medea's own words (263–66; see also Jason at 909–10); so is Medea's choice of weapon, poison, and the deceptive rhetoric and gestures (tears, suppliancy) with which she manipulates her masculine enemies. Yet the side of Medea that plans and executes revenge, and especially the death of the children, is not represented in the language of the play as "feminine."[59] Above all, as Knox and Bongie in particular point out, the avenging Medea thinks and acts not like a classical woman but like an archaic and Sophoclean hero when he feels he has been wronged. Her first offstage words, her screams of suicidal rage, which threaten to endanger even those she loves, may be deliberately reminiscent of Sophocles' Ajax.[60] Her brilliance, craft, and drive for survival recall the Homeric Odysseus. Like Ajax or Achilles, she would deliberately sacrifice friends to defend her honor against a public slight from a peer. She has the stubborn individualism, intransigence, power, near-bestial savagery, and lack of pity of such beleaguered heroes. As hero, she wants to do good to her friends and bad to her enemies, quell injustice, win fame (810), and protect her reputation. She is so fearless that the sword would be her weapon of choice if circumstances permitted its use (379–85, 393). Poison, the feminine weapon, is her choice of necessity (ironically, she goes back to the sword to kill her helpless children). No woman in tragedy—none of all those who take revenge—models her self-image so explicitly on a masculine heroic and even military model (see esp. 1242–45).[61] Like a hero, she wishes to live up to her identity as the child of noble ancestors, she is the granddaughter of the sun: "Advance into danger. Now is your trial of courage. You see what you suffer. You must not be mocked

---

[58] See the scholiast at *Medea* 9 and 264.

[59] As was emphasized earlier, when Medea describes her plans she stresses the rational and heroic motivations for her revenge and virtually ignores the erotic ones.

[60] See Knox 1977: 96. Friedrich 1993: 223 argues that Medea does not represent a genuine example of heroic ethos because she flatters, lies, abases herself. Nevertheless, Medea does adopt an heroic ethos, even if her actions in some respects betray it.

[61] See Bongie 1977: 28 and 30–31 on Medea's masculinity, in contrast to Knox 1977, who sees Medea as heroic on the Sophoclean model regardless of sex. When they speak and act as Attic women could not or should not, many tragic heroines, and especially Sophoclean heroines, are characterized by the text as masculine. Medea's behavior is set apart from that of any other "masculine" tragic heroine above all by the language in which she describes her revenge. Even Clytemnestra, with her man-counseling (*Agamemnon* 11) mind, describes her killing of her husband in *Agamemnon* not with military metaphors but with language that perverts ritual and cycles of nature. Hecuba in Euripides' *Hecuba*, whose situation and revenge are very similar to Medea's, lacks her sense of heroic dignity at all costs. She says that she would accept slavery in exchange for the chance to obtain revenge (756–57).

by Jason's Sisyphean marriage, for you are descended from a noble father and the sun" (403–6).

What is shocking about Medea, as opposed, for example, to Clytemnestra in *Agamemnon*, where we are told from the first of her masculine aspects, is that Medea's heroic side emerges fully only as the play goes on, as she shrugs off the mask of subservience she has accepted as Jason's wife and finds the means to effect her revenge.[62] I have argued that the audience, like the chorus, is at first partly deceived by Medea's view of her plight as typically female. The first scene hints at Medea's outrage and capacity for violence, but those hints are obscured by her threats of suicide, her domestic confinement, her solidarity with the chorus, and her use of "feminine" wiles to manipulate Creon, Jason, and even Aegeus. Euripides' audience probably did not know that Medea would deliberately destroy her children or escape in the sun's chariot at the end.[63] It may even have feared for some time, as T. Buttrey argues,[64] that Medea was unwittingly destroying herself by leading her children into a death trap.

Medea plays for Creon, Aegeus, and finally Jason the part of the tragic damsel in distress in need of a masculine rescue, which she finally acquires in part from Aegeus.[65] But as the feminine mask gradually slips to reveal first an archaic hero and finally a near-goddess, the story of her revenge takes on a pattern typical of divine rather than human action.[66] Dionysus in Euripides' *Bacchae*, for example, punishes disbelievers who fail to revere him and to penetrate his disguise. Similarly, the once victimized and seemingly powerless Medea appears finally as a semidivine Fury whose nature and authority were not recognized by the mortals around her (except, to some degree, the nurse). While fully aware of Medea's intelligence, Creon (286), Jason (527–28, 555,

---

[62] Gellie 1988: esp. 16 laments the lack of psychological coherence in the portrait of Medea. "All these Medeas cannot fail to get in each others' way." This is arguable, but at least in this play the generation of contradictory aspects in the character seems consistent and deliberate. On the question of continuity in Greek, and especially Euripidean (Gould 1978: 51–52) characterization, see further the introduction to this book.

[63] Even if Neophron's version of the play, in which Medea chooses to kill the children herself, came first (Manuwald 1983 and Michelini 1989), the audience would not be certain whether Euripides' Medea would do so, or whether, as in other versions of the myth, the Corinthians killed them. See Page [1938] 1971: xxi–xxv, Buttrey 1958: 13–14, McDermott 1989: 25–42, and the appendix to this chapter.

[64] Buttrey 1958: 12. Ohlander 1989 expands considerably on his approach.

[65] Gredley 1987: 30–32 notes Medea's consistent control of her performance and her transformation of a position of ritualized inferiority—suppliancy—into one of dominance. Boedeker 1991: 106–9 stresses the way that she authors, rehearses, and directs her own story.

[66] This shift from a rescue to a revenge plot-pattern is implied in Buttrey's discussion of the structure of the play (1958: 10; see also Burnett 1973: 8). Burnett argues that the messenger speech describes the death of the princess in an explicit fashion characteristic of divine revenge plays (17). Many critics have noticed the similarities between the conclusion of *Bacchae* and *Medea*. On Medea as dea ex machina, see esp. Cunningham 1954: 152, Collinge 1962: 170–72, Knox 1977: 206–11, Worthington 1990, and Ohlander 1989: 189, who emphasizes Medea's human side in this final appearance.

568–73, 1338), and even the chorus (1291–92) see Medea as a woman, and therefore as motivated only by jealousy (whereas she herself mentions this motive only at 265–66, 1354, and 1368 and in each case more is at stake in her anger over her bed than sexual jealousy). For Jason, Medea is a temperamental barbarian concubine (and a typical woman) who must be cast aside for the advantages of a real Greek marriage. Jason mistakenly fails to treat Medea as a hero, to value their mutual oaths and her favors to himself. He cannot hear the heroic language and values she adopts for herself in their first encounter.[67] And so, like Pentheus, he pays for his misunderstanding.

But before the final revelation of her superhumanity, Medea has been shown to have a masculine and a feminine side, each exercising its capacity for reason and emotion. The two sides at first establish an uneasy complicity in the pursuit of revenge but finally split in tragic conflict during the famous monologue. By the conclusion of the monologue Medea's female self is once more a victim, this time both of her masculine self and of Jason, for at 1074 (see also 1364 and 1397–98) she blames her husband for the children's death (presumably because she cannot succeed in punishing him without killing the children). What is Euripides' point in turning the tragedy of jealousy that we expect in the first scene into a tragedy of gender? By this I mean, not that Medea's tragedy is *about* gender, but that it raises its tragic issues as a double conflict between male and female, both on stage in the external world and within Medea's self. And what is the significance of the structure of the play, in which the hero and finally the divinity in Medea emerge to dominate, if not entirely obscure, the victimized woman?[68]

Euripides' plays tend to leave us, as here, with more questions and (possible) revolutionary critiques than answers. The attitude of the chorus of ordinary women reminds us that for Euripides' audience a proper Greek wife had no fully autonomous sense of self, no muse, no public voice (421–30, 1085–89). As we have seen, legally she was under the permanent supervision of a guardian and could make no significant decisions. Any independent action on the part of a classical Athenian woman, or any pursuit of her own desires, was not acceptable in a wife unless it involved carrying out household duties such as weaving, cooking, or guarding and caring for household property and children (see also the *Odyssey*'s Penelope, who takes action only in these matters). Nor did a woman, living confined to the household and religious activities, have the

[67] See Bongie 1977: 42; see Gill 1996 on Jason's general failure to comprehend Medea and her positions.

[68] My previous discussion does not intend to question the reality of Medea's female and victimized self; she remains, despite her rhetoric, confined within female social limits until her final supernatural departure. Her use of the magical poison (see Knox 1977: 214) does not by itself characterize her as a witch. A similar poison, a typical female weapon, is used (unintentionally) by the feminine Deianeira of Sophocles. As Segal 1996: 28 puts it, her ethos may be masculine, but her crime is feminine.

knowledge or the educated discipline needed to make independent decisions (see, e.g., Sophocles' Deianeira in *Women of Trachis*). Tragic heroes like Medea frequently do not play by the rules governing the conduct of Attic women, yet these limits are, I think, implicitly present in the language and structure of all tragedies.[69] For every action a tragic woman takes in her own interest—every action outside of self-sacrifice for family or community—receives explicit criticism within the plays as unfeminine and has destructive consequences. Even Antigone is condemned for her unfeminine behavior and brings two other deaths in her wake.

Is Euripides' *Medea*, then, confirming the audience's worst fears of what will happen when a woman takes action?[70] Is it anticipating Aristotle in arguing that women are naturally *akuros*, without autonomous moral authority,[71] that because they cannot control their emotions with reason they cannot be permitted moral independence but must, as Jason thinks Medea should, obey the plans of their more reasonable husbands (see 565–75)? And all the more so because women are so clever at the rational planning of ways to achieve the goals dictated by their emotions (see esp. 407–9 and Creon's fear of Medea's intelligence)? These are in fact the very cultural clichés that Medea exploits in her second scene with Jason, where she pretends to accept and conform to his notions of what a woman is like and what she should be. In her speech at 869–905, Medea plays on women's supposed inferiority to men in making judgments (889–93) and emphasizes the wisdom of obeying those planning wisely for herself, the king and her husband, and the folly of her anger (873–78, 882–83, 885, 892–93). Later in the scene she hides the true reason for her tears at the sight of the children by remarking that women are given to tears (928).

Although Greek tragedy generally tends by displaying the devastating consequences of inverting cultural norms ultimately to affirm those norms, our earlier discussion of the monologue has made it clear that this interpretation of *Medea* cannot be true in any simple sense. For we must not forget that Euripides has presented in a negative light and even punished the ethical behavior of all the male characters in the play except Aegeus,[72] who sides with Medea and displays a heroic integrity comparable with the heroine's, and that the

[69] See esp. Loraux 1987, Harder 1993, and Seidensticker 1995.

[70] Rabinowitz 1993: 125–27, 149–50 takes this view (see also McDermott 1989: 50 and 64). She argues that the victimized Medea loses the audience's sympathy through her crimes and affirms its fears that women may escape the nets of male domination and become threats to male children. Female subjectivity is dangerous, especially if women are willing to harm themselves to gain revenge.

[71] Implied in Fortenbaugh's discussion at 1970: 238–39. See also Euripides fragment 362.34 N[2] on the *gunaikophrōn thumos* quoted earlier. As was remarked before, Jason repeatedly sees Medea's only motive for action as *erōs*. Medea flatteringly distracts Jason from his view of female nature by pretending to imitate him.

[72] See Schlesinger 1966: 45. Burnett argues that this atmosphere of moral corruption makes tragic Medea's otherwise monstrous and archaic revenge.

vengeful Medea deliberately imitates a heroic brand of masculinity. Because there is for the Greeks no model of autonomous and heroic femininity outside of self-sacrifice, Medea can only turn to a male model if she wishes to act authoritatively and with *timē* (honor). If she acts in a way that guarantees self-preservation and child preservation, she will in male public terms lose face and fail to make a dramatic display of her wrongs. Like all disfranchised rebels, she can tragically imagine no other self or self-defense to imitate than that of her oppressors. By this I mean, not that she sets out to imitate Jason or Creon, but that the heroic code itself oppresses women, both because it traditionally excludes and subordinates them and because it gives priority to public success and honor over survival and the private concerns of love and family. The debate between Hector and Andromache in *Iliad* 6, in which the views of the proper wife lose out to those of the warrior responsible to the welfare of his people, makes this clear in a more benign way. In this play we see that oppression in the inability of Jason to recognize Medea's heroic self and in Medea's own failure to accept the arguments of her maternal voice.[73] Furthermore, as G. B. Walsh and Pietro Pucci have shown, the Medea who contests Jason's injustice and pursuit of profit at the cost of emotional pain (598–99) ends up adopting all too similar goals for herself.[74] She chooses to accept emotional pain in order to achieve her revenge; a victim of injustice, she ends up like Jason, wronging her friends and rejecting suppliants (the chorus who pleads for the children at 853–55, and, by implication, the children, 863).[75] She wants to be understood and accepted for what she is (215–24; 292–305), but ends by doing everything to hide what she is from those around her. Thus, by pursuing her heroic code she ends by imitating even her despised immediate oppressors and harming herself.

For a moment in the monologue we may hope that her maternal side will successfully contest the masculine heroic logic, but everything in Medea and her circumstances has conspired against this frail possibility. For Medea has tried to suppress this voice too long. In addition, she has come to envision all

---

[73] Rehm 1989 independently offered a discussion along these lines. I differ from him largely in thinking that the female voice that opposes the heroic masculine logic in Medea is less articulated in the play and far more fragile. Ohlander 1989: 144 argues that Medea's desire to kill the children rather than allow the Corinthians to do so arises from her need to enlist her mother love in the cause of her revenge.

[74] See the very different arguments of Walsh 1979: 296–99 and Pucci 1980: esp. chs. 2 and 4, who emphasizes how the oppressed Medea adopts the position of a master. Strohm 1957: 3 shows how the positions of Jason and Medea have been precisely reversed by the exodus (for linguistic echoes of the earlier scene in the later one, see Burnett 1973: 22). The same is true for prologue and exodus. Jason begins by devaluing children for expedient reasons and ends as movingly paternal. Medea, in her movement toward masculinity, follows the reverse course.

[75] At 1250 Medea, just before killing the children, admits they were *philoi:* but it is too late to recognize the full irony of her position. Schein 1990 now elaborates on these points and Boedeker 1991 stresses the contemporary political resonance of Jason's perversion of oaths, supplication, and persuasion.

that is female as despicable,[76] a source of oppression that denies her need to be accepted for her own capacities and to achieve due recognition, a source of bad and never of good (407–9). For Medea, women are cowards except when they are wronged in bed (263–66); they are forced to depend on one person (247); they must buy a master for their bodies (232–34); any reputation they have must be to their disadvantage (215–24, 292–93). Maternity and *erōs*—emotional dependence on others—have tied her to Jason and led her to the predicament in which she is now trapped. In the monologue the maternal voice appears to her masculine self to present only the "soft arguments" of a cowardice to be expected from women (1052; see also 1242–46 and 776). Finally, Medea's repeated use of her femininity to manipulate and deceive has reduced her womanly side to a role so lacking in heroic integrity that she can only wish to slough it off.

Moreover, through the chorus, we have already seen how the female voice, silenced for centuries, lacks the confidence and authority necessary to make a reply to a long masculine tradition. The women of the chorus hoped to find this female voice in Medea, after her brilliant exposure of marriage and Jason's betrayal; but even they did not really expect a victimized woman to live up to their hopes (410–45). Later, aware after the monologue that they have lost their spokeswoman[77]—or, in fact, that they had never had one—the previously timid women struggle to give voice to the female muse in themselves and fail (1081–1115). Pitifully, their reasoning leads them to lose their grip on their one certainty, their commitment to maternity and the preservation of the lives of the children, as they wonder if it would not be better never to experience parenthood at all.[78] If the women of the chorus can be swayed momentarily to abandon the core of their self-interest as women, it is hardly surprising that the brilliant and semidivine princess Medea finds in her maternity no positive basis for action.[79]

Is Euripides, then, making in *Medea* a tragic point about social oppression and social change? Medea has been treated unjustly by men, and her eloquent indictment of women's lot is never denied.[80] By developing the case for

[76] On the general point, see Pucci 1980: 64. Jason, Creon, and even the chorus make other negative judgments of women. Galis 1992: esp. 77 sees Medea as betrayed by the very womanhood and reproductive capacity that she comes to hate.

[77] The third and fourth stasima reverse the chorus' earlier hopes and reveal its despair and horror at Medea.

[78] As Wolff 1982: 240 notes, by coming, like Medea, to overvalue self-sufficiency, the women deny the human need for reproduction. Reckford 1968: 346 sees in this chorus a divorce between reason and feeling.

[79] We do not know that the chorus comprises married women, but it consistently champions Medea's maternal interests as critical to her female identity and welfare.

[80] Even if, as Pucci 1980: 65–69 argues, Medea's argument contradicts itself, it presents a substantially accurate indictment of contemporary Attic reality. See Knox 1977: 219–21, Reckford 1968: 336–39, Paduano 1968: 259–71, and Barlow 1989 and 1995, who argues that Euripides' challenge to female stereotypes and the marriage system in the play survives the reemergence of popular misogyny at the conclusion.

Medea's oppression first, the play seems to urge us to understand Medea's later behavior as a reaction to this oppression. We saw in the monologue how Medea's female side predictably (especially given the gender relations obtaining in Greek culture) fell victim to her masculine side and Jason. Jason's failure to treat Medea as the fully human (rather than, in a traditional Greek sense, female) and even heroic being he married with a clasp of right hands and supplicated in times of trouble propels her to ever greater daring. His own significant—if not, as Medea sometimes claims, exclusive—responsibility for the tragic outcome seems confirmed both by the appearance of the sun's chariot and by the plot pattern that structures the final scenes. Reckford sees in the alienation and corruption of Medea the self-fulfilling power of prejudice.[81] Yet Euripides also seems to imply that the oppressed, by being trapped into imitating their oppressors, can in the end only tragically silence what should have been their own true (here maternal) voice, destroy themselves, and confirm an unjust status quo.

Or is Euripides, as Wolff suggests, also using Medea to bring home a point about masculine ethics?[82] Greek poets repeatedly demonstrated the tragic consequences of the brand of heroic individualism imitated by Medea and of the "do good to friends, bad to enemies" ethic. Here Medea, like Achilles (or Ajax), destroys (or threatens to destroy) in her heroic wrath those who are her friends. She talks herself into believing that her revenge will be inadequate without the death of the children; for when the chorus asks her how she could endure to kill her own offspring, she replies that her husband would above all be tortured (dēchtheiē, 817; see also 1370) by this. Yet unlike Achilles, who regains a fuller humanity in Iliad 24, Medea finally leaves female and even human limits (including human ethical limits) behind. The audience is literally distanced from her as she appears high above the stage, and for the first time it is invited to feel pity for Jason, who, wracked with paternal anguish, has lost all identity with the loss of his children. By choosing Medea, a barbarian woman, to display the contradictions inherent in this heroic ethic and behavior, Euripides has achieved a particularly devastating and grotesque demonstration of the problematic (above all because self-destructive) nature of this archaic heroism—and one he might have hesitated to make through a Greek or male protagonist.[83]

---

[81] Reckford 1968: 345. See also Reckford 346 n. 26 on the possible allusions in Medea's case to the plight of noncitizen wives in Athens after Pericles' citizenship law of 451/0. Knox 1977: 222 sees in the hostility expressed toward Medea as a sophē a reflection of Euripides' own reception by his contemporaries.

[82] Wolff 1982: 238–39. Michelini 1989: 132 thinks that the play offers a critique of the heroic code's sacrifice of social obligation.

[83] Burnett 1973 argued that Euripides stripped Medea's revenge of all the circumstances that mitigate other tragic revenges. Burnett 1998 now takes a more sympathetic view of the heroine's revenge; the crime is meant to produce not only horror and consternation, but pity for the seriously wronged heroine (194).

True, there is a certain integrity in Medea's single-minded pursuit of this archaic masculine ethic, especially when we are offered as an alternative the dubious sophistic or unprincipled masculine behavior of Creon and Jason. The play uses Medea's heroic ethic to expose the callous amoral pragmatism of the unheroic Jason[84] and Creon, and then turns on the ethic itself as it deteriorates into a ghastly version of her enemies' behavior. By implicitly taking as her heroic models both the avenging archaic warrior Achilles and the clever and crafty survivor Odysseus, and thus conflating two brands of heroism that epic views as partially contradictory, Medea shows herself a pathetically confused imitator of heroic masculinity.[85] By adhering blindly to her warrior code, she ironically comes to the peak of daring (394): the slaughter of her own children.[86] She achieves not the fame she sought but infamy. By going beyond the tragic, by not paying for her revenge with suicide or death (as in the case of Ajax, or Ino and Procne;[87] see Medea's own earlier courageous resolve to face death at 393), Medea further destroys the heroic integrity of her ethic. Unlike the Sophoclean hero who gains a certain authority not only by dying but by remaining tragically alienated from the world to the bitter end, the once mistreated and misunderstood Medea goes off to fit all too well into the contemporary world; indeed, she will very likely marry Aegeus and go on, after denying progeny to Jason, to produce the child Medus.[88] Medea's final transformation into an amoral deity, something beyond the human female or male, expresses not only the death and betrayal of her maternal self[89] but what she has become through her abuse of her masculine ethic. Unlike Sophocles in the *Ajax*, with its concluding recognition of the hero's epic glory despite his earlier brutality and dehumanization, Euripides seems finally to have little nostalgia for the epic past. Indeed, we might view the play as—at least in part—an implicit attack on the typical Sophoclean hero. But, above all, the poet comes close to labeling the "friends-enemies" ethic as destructive of humanity and human values and thus suitable only for gods.

[84] See von Fritz 1962a: 322–429 on how the play deprives Jason of his epic heroism.

[85] Deceptiveness is, of course, also thought to be a typically feminine vice, and Odysseus' heroism had become suspect by the fifth century.

[86] Bongie 1977: 32, 50, and 55 tends to view Medea's excessive pursuit of her code in terms that better suit the Sophoclean hero.

[87] See Mills 1980: 289–96, on the similarities and differences between Ino and Procne's story and Medea's, which includes a supernatural dimension. Newton 1985: 501–2 speculates that if, as seems likely, Euripides invented Ino's killing of her children, Medea's crime truly lacks precedent.

[88] In other versions (although this one was certainly known in Attic tragedy) Medus was the son of a barbarian king whom Medea married after she fled from Athens. For a discussion and ancient sources, see Graf 1997: 37 and Sfyoeras 1995: esp. 127 n. 9, who stresses the importance of Medea's future in Athens for the interpretation of the Aegeus scene and the play as a whole; he argues that Jason makes Medea into a symbolic (wicked) stepmother like Ino. Burnett 1998: 224 n. 30 is appropriately cautious about the status of Medea's myth in Athens at this period.

[89] See Schlesinger 1966: 51. In her 1976 Stanford dissertation, Suzanne Mills, noting the similarities established between Medea and her rival, the princess, intriguingly suggests that Medea moves toward divinity through the sacrifice of a double.

In his long career Euripides created adulterous and murderous women, as well as male characters, like Jason here (esp. 573–75) or Hippolytus (*Hippolytus* 616–68), who indulge in misogynistic outbursts. He also created courageous female sacrificial victims, female advocates of public ideals, defenders of the female sex like Melanippe, and a Helen who sat out the Trojan War guarding her virtue in Egypt. Aristophanes' accusation of misogyny in *Thesmophoriazusae* must be viewed in relation to that poet's own (mis)representations of women; besides, his Euripides is finally exonerated on the basis of his *Helen* and *Andromeda*.[90] Knox argues that *Medea* is neither feminist nor misogynist but a play about the wrongs done to and by women.[91] *Medea* exposes male suppression of women in marriage and the tragic results of a male refusal to recognize in women the capacities, feelings, and needs that they accept for themselves; and it shows the corrupting effects of this mistreatment on a woman of tremendous feeling and intelligence.[92] At the same time Medea's overly literal imitation of an anachronistic masculine code, her dehumanization, and her betrayal of her own sex could be said equally to confirm woman's ultimate incapacity for independence and civilized behavior. For if Euripides is using Medea to examine critically masculine heroism and masculine ethics, he cannot be arguing that women should be liberated to pursue these same goals, and there is a certain irony in the heroine's pursuit of a code that even Sophocles' *Ajax* displayed as politically if not emotionally outmoded.

Yet this play is equally about the wrongs done to and by men. By showing how Medea's concern for status and revenge at all costs can disintegrate into something uncomfortably close to the callous utilitarianism of Jason and destroy those whom her ideals were meant to protect, Euripides makes a devastating philosophical case against both the shallow modern ethics of Jason and Creon and the heroic ethics of the archaic past. Only Athens, with its harmonious blend of *erōs* and *sophia*, and Aegeus, who shows respect both for Medea's person and for her oaths, appear exempt from the general indictment; yet Athens itself is about to be visited by Medea. Medea seems to make at first an eloquent case for her own truth, integrity, and justice. Yet in the end her inability to trust her own maternal voice in the monologue destroys any hopes for a more enlightened form of human ethics, for the creation of an authoritative female identity and integrity that could contest masculine ethics, whether archaic or contemporary. By dividing Medea's self along sexual lines, Euripides creates, not a private psychological drama and/or an abstract struggle between reason and passion, but an ambiguous inquiry into the relation between human ethics and social structure.

[90] See Zeitlin 1981: 186–94.

[91] See Knox 1977: 211 and also Reckford 1968: 339–40.

[92] Gill 1996 offers a valuable expansion of this point. In his view, Medea's infanticide is an exemplary, reasoned response to Jason's refusal, especially in their first debate, to recognize their mutual responsibility to their relationship (marriage as an ethical partnership), her past favors to Jason, the legitimacy of her complaints, and her status as a fully human agent.

Appendix

The other two main arguments against accepting the present text of Medea's monologue are as follows.

1. The children are told to go off-stage at 1053 but are still there at 1069, awkwardly witnessing in person Medea's struggle over whether to kill them. We can justify the extant text only by assuming that the children leave the stage (1053) and return at Medea's call (1069),[93] or, as seems far less dramatically awkward, that they begin to leave the stage but are temporarily arrested in their departure by Medea's distraught behavior.[94] In any case, the children are probably too young to understand Medea's words fully. Her language is euphemistic about the murder except between 1053, after she has dispatched the children to the house, and 1063. She addresses the children again at 1069, so that they would have been moving away from her during the only explicit lines, and in production this fact could be made visible by having the actor turn away from the children at appropriate moments, or speak 1053 to himself, 1069 more emphatically to the children.[95] The visual contrast between the distraught mother and the innocent children makes a stage effect worth prolonging.

2. Medea at 1045 and 1058 speaks of taking the children with her to Athens, but later in the speech (1060–63) and before (see 791 and 1013–14) and after (1236–43) this speech she invokes a necessity that requires their death—if Medea does not kill the children herself, the Corinthians will (see also 1303–5, 781–82, 1380).[96] Apparently there is a serious inconsistency here; if Medea

[93] Dodds 1952: 14–15. He alters *dot'* in 1069 to *deut'*.

[94] This is the view of Page [1938] 1971: 148 on line 1053, supported by Voigtländer 1957: 230–31, Steidle 1968: 163, Mastronarde 1979: 110, Lloyd-Jones 1980: 57, Seidensticker 1990: 92–93, and with slight variations, Burnett 1998: 210. Stage directions in Greek drama generally appear in the texts and mutes generally obey instructions promptly (Bain 1981: 33). Yet in a comparable situation earlier in the play, the nurse twice directs the tutor to take the children inside (89, 100–105); the first time they do not go in. Kovacs' objection (1986: 345) to this example, that the nurse continues to address the pedagogue, thereby preventing prompt obedience, applies also to the monologue, if the children are arrested by Medea's continuing speech. For a discussion of other less likely explanations of the staging here (e.g., Grube's [1941] 1961 view that Medea imagines addressing the children from 1021–80), see Reeve 1972: 54–56.

[95] See Steidle 1968: 163–64.

[96] Most scholars view 1062–63 as interpolated from 1240–41, and this deletion receives support from a Berlin papyrus fragment that lacks these lines (Luppe 1995); Seeck 1968: 291, brackets 1060–63; Christmann 1962: 133–36 (see Reeve's objections, 1972: 59 n. 1) proposes a lacuna here. Lloyd-Jones 1980 advocates deleting 1059–63 (yet Kovacs 1986: 352 n. 17 rightly notes the problematic absence of an adversative in 1064 to show a mind change), and Kovacs deletes 1056–64. As Lesky 1983: 226 rightly objects, Seeck's deletion ignores the implications of 1059 and leaves the audience unprepared for 1236–41 (see also the chorus at 976–77 and Medea at 791 and 1013–14; Medea would not lament the necessity invoked here if it did not imply the killing of the children [Steidle 1968: 161]). Kovacs' proposal is ingenious, but he has no strong grounds for deleting 1056–58 (see Lloyd-Jones 54 on *ekei* and, more generally, Michelini 1989: 117–119 and Seidensticker 1990: 91–92); the parody in *Acharnians* of Medea (see *Acharnians* 450–52 and 480–89, and

can take the children to Athens, why are the Corinthians a threat? In my view, the only possible explanation short of deleting or emending the text is that of Schlesinger, who argues that what makes the killing of the children necessary is her revenge plan (see esp. 791–93, 817, 1059).[97] Medea has at this point abandoned her initial plans to attack Jason's person directly (374–75), and could not do so once her crime against the royal family has succeeded. Hence, without killing the children she cannot take fully effective revenge on her husband and will be made to look like a fool before her enemies (1049–50). If Schlesinger is right, the seeming inconsistencies of the passage represent a momentary hesitation over whether to take the children and abandon the full revenge plan or to pursue her revenge plan.[98] Once she has determined on the latter (as 1059 implies),[99] she must kill the children herself, rather than surrender them to the Corinthians. It makes no sense to eliminate the motif of the Corinthian threat from this speech, because it is repeated both before and after this passage,[100] and, although Medea seems confident that she herself can escape from Corinth, we have no idea until the end how she will do so. Hence

---

in addition *Medea* 1242–46) almost certainly refers to Euripides', not Neophron's, address by Medea to her *thumos*. In short, bracketing all or part of 1056–80 does not fully resolve the problems raised by those objecting to the lines.

[97] Schlesinger 1966: 30–32; Voigtländer 1957: 234–35 and Diller 1966: 362 make a similar argument. While the text never makes this point explicitly, the motif of the threatening insolence of enemies appears often in her deliberations (781–82, 1060–61, 1238–39, 1301–5), as does the desire to punish Jason fully; moreover, Medea seems to feel that both the tutor's news and the messenger's speech confirm the children's doom. Lloyd-Jones 1980: 55 argues against Schlesinger that a Medea who earlier made no apologies for her revenge need not offer to herself the excuse of necessity. In my view it is precisely because Medea is both determined on revenge and confronting the painful consequences of this decision that she needs at this crucial moment the reinforcement of additional arguments to make the revenge seem inevitable (the argument for necessity does not replace the argument for revenge).

[98] We have no reason to find implausible either alternative that Medea mentions concerning the children. As noted earlier, Medea never doubts her own ability to escape. Though she does not explain to the audience how she will make this departure, we cannot be sure that her plan to take the children with her is a lapse into wishful fantasy or delusion (Erbse 1981 and Ohlander 1989: 149–51), a powerful example of psychological realism. It may be significant, however, that she has not asked Aegeus for asylum for the children as well. The appearance of the chariot of the sun is reserved as a surprise for the audience and perhaps, since she feels so pressed for time (Steidle 1968: 161), for Medea herself. Previous mythological tradition had the children die in Corinth, and in one version the Corinthians killed them in revenge for Medea's deeds (see Page [1938]: 1971 xxi–xxv for a review of the mythic tradition here). The audience would thus have found convincing Medea's argument that if the children are to remain in Corinth, she must kill them to avoid their deaths at the hands of her enemies.

[99] The transition from 1058 to 1059 is disturbingly abrupt, and the argument implied by 1060–63 very condensed. Yet the invocation of deities of revenge in 1059 can serve as a succinct indication that Medea has shifted back to favoring her revenge plan (Voigtländer 1957: 234) and must now pursue its implications for the children. Page [1938] 1971: 149 offers a psychological defense of Medea's sudden vacillations here.

[100] See esp. Seidensticker 1990: 95.

the Corinthian threat seems plausible up to the surprising conclusion. More-over, it is repeated in conjunction with the need to steel herself to commit the revenge in the lines she utters just before exiting to kill the children (1236–50), whereas the possibility of taking the children to Athens is not mentioned once the plot is in motion. Finally, it should be noted that the ambiguities of the monologue in this respect have one decisive dramatic advantage: the killing of the children appears tragically determined by a combination of ex-ternal and internal pressures,[101] yet the way remains open for Medea's surpris-ing antitragic escape from Corinth in the chariot of the sun.[102]

[101] As many critics have seen (see esp. Diller 1966: 362, Voigtländer 1957: 225, Easterling 1977a: 188, Steidle 1968: 162, Lloyd-Jones 1980: 52 and 59, and Kovacs 1986: 344–45), there is no real possibility that Medea will choose to save the children. External necessity limits her op-tions and favors the revenge plan; the audience expects the children's death and does not know about the chariot of the sun; Medea has already invoked the gods' aid for her revenge plan (see 160, 764, 1013–14); above all, her powerful identity with her revenge plan makes the outcome inevitable. Yet to interpret the monologue simply as displaying the divided Medea's struggle to confront the costs of a predetermined revenge (see, e.g., Lloyd-Jones) is to play down the text's moments of genuine hesitation. A combination of predetermination and active choice is typical of tragedy, but Medea's unique situation—she makes a conscious choice with full knowledge of the bad consequences of her action—makes the monologue exceptionally striking.

[102] Ohlander 1989 stresses how the lack of full explanation for the shifts in the monologue pre-serves suspense, maintains audience identification with Medea, and leaves open the question of whether she herself will kill the children until the final moment. Michelini 1989: esp. 121, who thinks the speech is rhetorically effective regardless of seeming inconsistencies (self-address is in any case illogical and contradictory, 127), and Gibert 1995: 80–83, who argues that mind or mood shifts are often not fully explained in tragedy, also defend the dramatic effectiveness of the passage.

III.6

Tragic Mothers: Maternal Persuasion in Euripides

SOPHOCLES' *Antigone* pits the heroine, who justifies her action by reference to the unwritten laws and the gods below, against Creon, whose edict was based on what he conceived to be the interest of the *polis* in denying burial to traitors. This pointedly male-female conflict is resolved in favor of the traditional laws. The burial of Polyneices is, as it turns out, in the interest of the city-state, but Antigone offers no larger insights concerning the exercise of civic power, from which she is in any case excluded by her gender. In other words, because Antigone's defense of her action is one-sided and fails to confront directly the interest of the state, both in distinguishing between patriot and traitor and in quelling civil disobedience, Antigone remains partially excluded from the realm of public moral thinking.

Antigone is not the only female character in tragedy to challenge positions taken by men. Nor, as we shall see, is she the only woman to defend traditional laws on the tragic stage. By the standards of popular morality, however, a Greek woman should not normally, like Antigone, take autonomous action. Instead, the conventional female submits to male guidance, or persuades those men responsible for her to act on her behalf. Persuasion is thus a critical moral activity for women both on and off the tragic stage. In this chapter I want to examine the role of three older tragic mothers who attempt to persuade men to take action in a public context. In my first two examples, Aethra in Euripides' *Suppliants* and Jocasta in his *Phoenissae*, the plays appear to validate the stance taken by the women, although only Aethra succeeds in persuading her son Theseus to adopt her point of view. In the third and far more complicated case, Agamemnon recognizes the moral authority of positions taken by the barbarian queen Hecuba in Euripides' *Hecuba* but initially refuses to support her in any active fashion. Although Agamemon finally sides with Hecuba in the play's closing mock trial, her act of bloody revenge against the Thracian Polymestor and his sons compromises, at least in the eyes of many critics, the moral authority that she acquires in the play's earlier debates.[1] Although Hecuba's

I would like to thank audiences at Oberlin and SUNY Buffalo and Carolyn Dewald, Josh Ober, Diana Robin, and Richard Seaford for their comments on an earlier draft of this chapter.

[1] See esp. Matthaei 1918: 156, Abrahamson 1952, Conacher 1967: esp. 21, Luschnig 1976, King 1985, Reckford 1985: esp. 114 and 118, Nussbaum 1986, or Rabinowitz 1993: esp. 108–9 and 113. Michelini 1987: 140–41 stresses the corrupting effects of rhetoric on Hecuba. For Gellie 1980: 36 Hecuba is too evil to serve as an example of moral disintegration. Burnett 1998: 166–

case may appear very different from that of the two other Greek mothers, it is in fact used to raise comparable social and political issues.

All three of these mothers make speeches that are rhetorically sophisticated, well reasoned, and directed at larger public as well as private concerns. All, like Antigone, base their appeals on laws or customs, *nomoi* or *nomima*, that may be envisioned as of interest to the gods or rooted in nature, ancestral, and common to all Greeks, or even to all humanity. In contrast to Sophocles' *Antigone*, the laws cited in these plays are not specifically characterized as unwritten or even timeless—written law may in any case be considered anachronistic in the mythical world of tragedy—but they often fall into categories that are elsewhere described as unwritten.[2] Such laws typically relate on the individual level to the proper treatment of parents, strangers, and friends and, on the intrastate level, to the regulation of war: the rights of the dead or of suppliants and prisoners of war, piety toward the gods and their rituals, the keeping of oaths, and respect for the rules of hospitality and reciprocity. What is important to consider here, then, is what is at stake in having older mothers adopt this particular kind of ethical position in the complex dialectic of these plays and why Euripides makes a point of having these women attempt a decisive intervention in a public debate.

In both tragedy and in Attic culture the persuasive powers of women often meet with considerable ambivalence. The laws attributed to Solon, for example, aimed to control the influence of women not only in death ritual (see part I), but in private life. To quote Plutarch's *Solon*, Solon "was highly esteemed also for his law concerning wills. . . . He did not permit gift giving without restriction or restraint, but only gifts not given under the influence of sickness, drugs, imprisonment, necessity, or *the persuasion of a woman/wife*. He thought, very rightly and properly, that being persuaded into wrong was no better than being forced into it, and he placed in the same category both deceit and compulsion, pleasure and affliction, believing that both were alike able to pervert a man's reason" (*Solon* 21.2–3, trans. Perrin 1982, modified). Solon's views concerning the potentially dangerous influence of women on matters of inheritance was still very much alive in the fourth century, when the orator Isaeus asserts that when a women undermines a man's reason in such matters she insults the *polis* itself: "the woman who destroyed Euctemon's reason and laid hold of so much property is so insolent that . . . she shows her contempt not only for the members of Euctemon's family, but also for the whole city" (6.48, trans. Forster 1983; see also Demosthenes 46.14, Isaeus 2.19).

72, by contrast, considers the Trojan women as ethically instructive to the Greeks, who have been "desocialized" (166) by war in relation to the fundamental mores of reciprocity. For a history of the criticism on this issue, see Heath 1987: 63.

[2] On such unwritten (and closely related) laws, see Hirzel 1900, Ehrenberg 1954, de Romilly 1971, Ostwald 1973, and Cerri 1979. On written law, see Ostwald 1969.

Elpinice, the sister of the general and statesman Cimon, became the prototype of the aristocratic woman who inappropriately dared to offer her views on
public affairs to Attic men. Plutarch tells us that when Pericles returned to
Athens after subduing Samos, many of the women crowned him with garlands.
But the elderly Elpinice reportedly came up to him and said, "'This was a noble
action, Pericles, and you deserve all these garlands for it. You have thrown away
the lives of these brave citizens of ours, not in a war against the Persians or
Phoenicians, such as my brother Cimon fought, but in destroying a Greek city
which is one of our allies.' Pericles listened to her words unmoved, so it is said,
and only smiled and quoted to her Archilochus's verse, 'Why lavish perfumes
on a head that's grey?'" (Plutarch, *Pericles* 28, trans. Scott-Kilvert 1960) This
dismissal of Elpinice does not mean that women were not informed about and
even, when rhetorically convenient, entitled to opinions on both public and
private matters. Female relatives of the deceased are both present at and briefly
addressed in Pericles' famous funeral oration in Thucydides (2.45). In the
fourth century, orators can claim that jurymen will have to justify their decision on the infamous Neaera to wife, mother, or daughter ([Demosthenes]
59.110), or that wives will not permit their husbands to give evidence on family matters (Isaeus 12.5).

Despite common agreement in classical Athens on the silence and discretion that becomes women and a general insistence that women should defer to
their husbands rather than asserting their own views, lawcourt cases occasionally cite with respect the positive role a woman might undertake on behalf of
her male relatives in family councils. In Lysias 32, for example, a widow is reported to have spoken up on behalf of her children, who had been defrauded
of their inheritance by their guardian, Diogeiton. (The story may be apoc-
ryphal, but the speaker considered the anecdote appropriate.) After the relatives assembled "she asked him [Diogeiton] what sort of a man he was to think
it right to act in the way he had acted towards the boys. . . . If you have no feeling of embarrassment towards any man, you ought to have feared the gods."
After she proves her account of his financial mismanagement with records from
an account book, "all of those present were so affected by what this man had
done and by the things which she said to him, when we saw the boys and the
injuries inflicted upon them, and remembered the deceased and how unworthy a trustee he had left for his possessions, and when we reflected on how difficult a thing it is to find a man who could be trusted with what he ought to be
trusted, none of us who were there could utter a word, gentleman of the jury,
we could only weep as sadly as the victims of these doings and depart in silence"
(Lysias 32.12–18, trans. Lacey 1968: 160–61). Similarly, in Isaeus 8.21–22 the
speaker claims that he deferred to the wishes of his grandmother to conduct
his grandfather's funeral from the house of the deceased rather than from his
own house. Another speaker cites the case of a man who "came to my mother,
his own sister, for whom he had greater regard than for anyone else, and ex-

pressed a wish to adopt me and asked her permission, which was granted"
(Isaeus 7.14–15, trans. Murray 1988; see also Demosthenes 40.10). Clytemnestra in Euripides' *Iphigeneia in Aulis* insists on her entitlement to participate in
and help plan her daughter's wedding (718–36). Euripides' Andromache may
well be reflecting actual domestic practice when she asserts of the proper wifely
influence that "I gave / my lord's presence the tribute of hushed lips, and eyes
/ quietly downcast. I know when my will must have its way / over his, knew
also how to give way to him in turn" (*Trojan Women*, 654–56, trans. Lattimore
1959).

In tragedy, women regularly speak both persuasively and publicly and the
texts repeatedly cite the cultural ambivalence that we have observed about the
moral or practical influence of women. In Aeschylus' *Agamemnon*, for example, the chorus expresses doubts about female persuasion and credulity (485–
86);[3] rumors generated by women swiftly come to nothing (486–87). Yet the
action turns on the persuasive powers of women, both Clytemnestra, whose description of the beacon and of the fall of Troy awes the chorus into comparing
her words with those of a prudent man (351) and who persuades Agamemnon
to walk on tapestries that he well knows should be reserved for gods, and Cassandra, who fails to persuade the chorus of the truth to which the audience is
privy (see III.4). To give a few more examples from tragedy, Euripides' Medea
rivals Clytemnestra in her ability to use her persuasive powers to deceive and
avenge herself on Creon and Jason. The nurse in Euripides' *Hippolytus* relies
on her specious persuasive powers to put her mistress Phaedra in her hands, and
hence to destroy her. Euripides' female characters in particular adopt the full
range of rhetorical techniques that were normally the province of men and acquired as part of an education for public life from which women were excluded
(at *Hecuba* 815–19 the heroine regrets that she has not paid to receive a rhetorical education).

Such rhetoric by women did not go unnoticed by Aristophanes, who has Euripides criticized in his *Frogs* for teaching everyone to argue (1070). By contrast, in the opening scene of his *Ecclesiazusae*, the women who are plotting
to vote themselves into power in the assembly in disguise as men have to
be taught proper political rhetoric, and his articulate female protagonists,
Praxagora and Lysistrata, make a point of explaining how they acquired their
unusual rhetorical skills (by imitating men). Praxagora camped on the Pnyx as
a refugee with her husband (*Ecclesiazusae* 243–44); Lysistrata learned wisdom
from listening to her father and other elders (*Lysistrata* 1125–27). Since Lysistrata here quotes a line from Euripides' *Wise Melanippe* (fragment 483 N²),
Aristophanes may be implicitly mocking Euripides' articulate heroine, who was
criticized by Aristotle for displaying unfeminine knowledge, because she
claimed to have acquired otherwise masculine skills from her mother Hippe.

---

[3] See Denniston and Page 1957: ad loc.

Such monumental examples of the dangers of female persuasion can make us forget, however, that while stressing cultural norms about the discreet behavior proper to women, tragedy also offers examples of women like Aethra, Jocasta (in both Euripides and Sophocles), or Praxithea in the fragmentary *Erectheus*, who attempt to play a critical and positive mediating role in public affairs. Antigone, Aethra, Jocasta, and Hecuba are by no means the only tragic characters to defend positions on the basis of ancestral laws that derive their authority from the gods or nature or by being shared by all the Greeks. In Sophocles' *Ajax*, Odysseus cites the *nomoi* of the gods as one reason for burying Ajax (1343; see also 1129–31),[4] although he stresses above all the issue of self-interest (1365–67). He too wants to be buried, he argues; hence, upholding traditional burial customs is in his own and Agamemnon's self-interest. In Euripides' *Heracleidae*, both the rulers of Athens, the two sons of Theseus, and the chorus of old men at Marathon rely on such traditions in deciding to accept the suppliancy of the children of Heracles. In doing so, these men act in accordance with an Attic ideology spelled out not only in tragedy, but in the Attic funeral oration, where Athens is typically represented as a courageous defender of the laws common to all the Greeks; similarly, Pericles in his Thucydidean funeral oration indicates that democracy relies on and is best suited to preserve unwritten as well as written laws (2.37).

As noted earlier, women are, however, a marked category in tragedy, men unmarked. When women defend a specific variety of *nomoi* and the concerns of the gods to men who have other concerns, they not only cross social boundaries that contain them but draw attention to the fact that these men are not performing the full public role assigned to them. As marginal figures, women can implicitly marginalize or threaten to marginalize the positions they defend simply by their association with them. What kind of political statement is Euripides making in these plays, then, in pointedly assigning women (specifically mothers) to defend these ancestral laws to men? Overall, I shall argue that Euripides uses women to reflect a changing and increasingly marginalized status for these laws during the Peloponnesian War between Athens and Sparta.

At the opening of Euripides' *Suppliants* Adrastus and the mothers of the seven against Thebes are supplicating Aethra, mother of Theseus the king of Athens, in the temple of Demeter at Eleusis. They wish Athens to help them win burial for the dead champions. In her prologue, Aethra stresses the Theban violation of the gods' laws (*nomim' atizontes theōn*, 19), the strong necessities of suppliancy (*anangkas hikesious*, 39), and her pity (*oiktirousa*, 34) for the gray-haired mothers who have lost their children. She has sent for Theseus, who will determine what should be done with the suppliants. "For it is appro-

---

[4] He also cites the violation of *dikē* (1335) and *eusebeia* (1350). It is not just to dishonor or harm a brave man if dead (1332–45). His *aretē* outweighs enmity (1357). Ajax' wife and son are suppliants at the corpse of Ajax in this scene.

priate for women to act through men, if they are wise" (40–41). The mothers then reinforce their appeal to Aethra, reminding her of her living son, as they long to lament the ones they have lost (67–70). Theseus enters fearing for his mother (89–91). Aethra insists that the suppliants should present their own case (109).

At this point Theseus probably turns his attention from the women, who surround Aethra in the orchestra, to Adrastus and the sons of the warriors, probably located at the back of the orchestra. The staging thus underlines a contrast between male and female points of view, with the women positioned more prominently and closer to the audience.[5] Theseus questions Adrastus, discovering that he went into battle against the advice of the seer Amphiaraus, after surrendering to the desire of his young warriors (155–61). Adrastus supplicates Theseus. Athens, he says, has the power to stand up to Thebes and a reputation for pity (188–190). The chorus too urges compassion (193–94). But Theseus does not respond to this appeal.[6] The gods have provided for human beings all that they need, he says. Why, then, should humans arrogantly fail to be satisfied with these divine gifts? (201–15). Adrastus should not have wed his daughters to aliens, ignored divine omens, and surrendered to the youthful passion for war (219–37). It is best for cities to respect the wisdom of the middle classes (238–45). Theseus wishes no alliance with Adrastus, and bids the suppliants depart (246–49). Adrastus moves to leave; the mothers of the chorus make the typical suppliant appeal to kinship by reminding Theseus that, through his grandfather Pittheus, he shares their blood, and they plead once more with Theseus to pity them (263–85). Theseus, moved by the old women, turns to ask his mother why she weeps, holding her veil before her (286–87).

Aethra then asks to speak on behalf of Theseus and Athens. Theseus agrees, remarking that many wise things come even from women's mouths (294). Aethra hesitates; Theseus argues that it is shameful to conceal good advice from friends (296). Aethra begins a long and rhetorically sophisticated *rhēsis* (speech).[7] She will neither blame herself for speaking nor fear the taunt that women's good advice is worthless (297–300). Though otherwise sensible, Theseus should take care not to err in matters relating to the gods (301–3). She would have held her peace if it were not right to be bold on behalf of victims of injustice (*adikoumenois*, 304). The violent Thebans are confounding the laws of Greece (*nomima te pasēs sungcheontas Hellados*, 311). Preserving the laws (*nomous*, 313) is the bond that holds cities together (*to gar toi sunechon anthrōpōn poleis / tout' esth'*, 312–13).[8] Furthermore, Theseus will appear cowardly

---

[5] See Rehm 1988 and 1992: esp. 124, and Warren and Scully 1995: 6.

[6] Mastronarde 1986: 203–4 argues that his refusal of the suppliants is inadequate to the reality of fortune stressed in a tragic world. See Aethra at 331.

[7] Collard 1975: 2, 187 and 190.

[8] While the *nomima* of Greece are unwritten, the *nomoi* of 313, at least when this political cliché appears elsewhere (for examples, see Collard 1975: ad loc.), include written laws.

if he forgoes this opportunity to win glory for Athens (314–20). Will Theseus not help the dead and the wretched women (326–27)? Aethra trusts in the justice of Athens' cause and in divine retribution on the Thebans (328–31).

Theseus insists that his criticisms of Adrastus were just, but he sees the force of Aethra's warnings (334–39). His reputation has been built on punishing wrongdoers (339–41). If his mother, who fears more for him than anyone else, bids him act, how can he avoid the slurs of enemies if he fails to do so (343–45)? He will attempt to persuade the Thebans before resorting to force and consult the people (346–50). He later pointedly echoes Aethra's concerns with Panhellenic or divine laws (*nomos palaios daimonōn*, 563, *ton Panhellēnōn nomon*, 526, 671), instability (549–57), and fame and toil (*eukleia* and *ponos*, 573–77). He asks the suppliants to release his mother (359–61). At the close of the scene, Theseus leads Aethra off stage, never to return; he here remarks on the importance of children paying the debts owed to their parents (361–64).

As many critics have noted, this is an unusual suppliant scene. Characters in Euripides generally respect suppliants.[9] In contrast to Euripides' earlier play *Heracleidae*, where the sons of Theseus immediately and without hesitation (even though they are about to be attacked) accept the suppliancy of Iolaus and the children of Heracles, Theseus is prepared to ignore the Argive pleas for political reasons until his mother intervenes.[10] In *Heracleidae*, appeals to Athens' reputation for justice (104, 330), courage, kinship (205–12, 224, 240), gratitude (for Heracles' rescue of Theseus from the underworld, 213–19, 240–41), pity (129, 232), shame (223, 242, over suppliants being dragged from the altars),[11] and the moral duty to help suppliants, over which gods preside (107–8, *atheon hikesian / metheinai polei xenōn prostropan*; 258, 260, 264, 461–63), sway both the rulers and the chorus of old men of Marathon at once.[12] We do not know when Athens' championing of the seven against Thebes became a topos in the Greek funerary oration.[13] Aeschylus' *Eleusinioi* dealt with the same incident as Euripides' *Suppliants* at an earlier date, and may have helped to establish the topos.[14] In *Heracleidae*, which is generally thought to predate *Suppliants*, Athens' role as champion of suppliants and the laws of the gods is already well established. It is true, as others have argued, that Theseus' change

[9] Mercier 1990.

[10] See also Theseus' ready acceptance of the refugee Oedipus in Sophocles' *Oedipus at Colonus* (see 260–62 on Athens' treatment of strangers and suppliants).

[11] Demophon does offer to settle the issue in the courts, *Heracleidae* 250–52.

[12] To drag suppliants from an altar is characteristic of barbarians, not Greeks (*Heracleidae* 130–31). Also rejected is Copreus' argument that the Athenians will do better to side with the stronger rather than the weaker side (176–78). In addition, Demophon, at the chorus' urging, declines to strike a herald (271–73).

[13] On Athens' treatment of suppliants, see, e.g., Lysias 2.7–16; Plato, *Menexenus* 239b and 244d–e; Andocides 3.28; Isocrates, *Panegyricus* 52–65; [Demosthenes] 60.8; or Hyperides 6.5.

[14] We know little of the plot of this play. At Herodotus 9.27.3 the Athenians cite this deed to justify their place on one of the fighting wings against the Persians at Plataea.

of heart highlights his own and Athens' altruism and a democratic receptivity to persuasion,[15] and he certainly champions the cause of the dead with vigor in the remaining scenes of the play. Theseus does not, as in other suppliant plays, face an immediate military threat and thus has a genuine choice about how to treat the suppliants; yet he is initially reluctant to adopt a role for Athens that is very much part of her role in her funerary orations.

Characters in tragedy and even in Euripides rarely change their minds, and even more rarely respond to good advice.[16] Euripides here seems to be going out of his way to emphasize that Theseus was on the verge of making a critical error and that he adopts the cause of the dead because he has been persuaded to do so by a woman. In contrast to the elderly Adrastus, who unwisely bowed to the will of the young and ignored the signs of the gods, Theseus is persuaded by the wisdom of age (albeit the wisdom of a mother) and decides to respect the laws of the Greeks and their gods. Care and respect for parents is another canonical traditional law in Athens. Indeed, improper treatment of parents could disqualify a man for public office in Athens.[17]

Aethra's role certainly contrasts pointedly with that of the other women in the play. The mothers of the seven, as I argue in part I, are deprived of their traditional role in the burial of the seven once it has become a public, political issue. They are characterized as emotionally incompetent to control themselves before the maimed bodies of their sons. Evadne, wife of one of the dead champions, breaks loose of all male control and commits a spectacular suicide, and the play concludes with the mothers failing to dissuade the sons of the champions from wishing to avenge their fathers' deaths in another war against Thebes (see part I). Aethra not only observes proper female reticence but goes beyond her maternal pity for the suppliants to take a rational and principled stance that entails the interests of the city as a whole and echoes the rhetoric of the city-state. Her appeal to the concerns of the gods and the Panhellenic *nomima* that protect suppliants is combined with an interventionist stance— atypical for a mother, as Theseus points out—that it is in Athens' self-interest to take action on their behalf. In instilling military courage into her son, her actions are perhaps more typical in Greek tradition of the Spartan mother, who was famed for this role.

Aethra has come to the temple to perform religious rituals as part of the festival to Demeter at Eleusis, the Proerosia.[18] Even while besieged by the chorus, she persists in carrying out her religious duties, as she appeals to Demeter for the prosperity of the land and the royal family. Theseus becomes disturbed that she is weeping at Demeter's hearth (289–90), although Demeter is in her myths the mourning mother par excellence. Eleusis, as a Panhellenic site, and

[15] Collard 1984: 132.
[16] Knox 1966 and Gibert 1995.
[17] See Dover 1974: 298.
[18] On the setting at the Proerosia, see part I and Goff 1995a: 73–76.

the Proerosia, as a festival that invited participation from other Greek states, is an appropriate location for an appeal to Panhellenic laws.[19] In Euripides other female characters make persuasive speeches in religious contexts, and rules governing religious cults are often characterized as traditional and unwritten. Hence the setting and religious role may go some way to justifying Aethra's authoritative intervention here. In Euripides' *Helen*, the virgin priestess Theonoe justifies her willingness to facilitate the escape of Menelaus and the suppliant Helen against the interest of her brother on religious grounds (998–1029). Praxithea in Euripides' *Eurystheus* becomes the first priestess of Athena Polias at the conclusion of the play; she earlier shows herself worthy of this upcoming honor by freely offering her daughter's life for the city in a similarly patriotic speech that is quoted with approval by the orator Lycurgus.[20] In comedy, Aristophanes apparently makes a point of linking his persuasive heroine Lysistrata with the historical priestess of Athena Polias, Lysimache.[21] Among the rare recorded instances in which women asserted themselves publicly in Athens, two concerned priestesses reportedly spoke out under the aegis of religious roles. When the Spartan King Cleomenes tried to enter the Acropolis, the priestess of Athena told him that it was unlawful for a Dorian to enter (Herodotus 5.72). When Alcibiades was condemned in absentia in 415 for parodying the Eleusinian Mysteries, the priestess Theano refused to curse him publicly, as had been required of all priests and priestesses (Plutarch, *Alcibiades* 22.4). Nevertheless, Aethra is not necessary to the plot, as we know from *Heracleidae* and other suppliant dramas where male rulers resolve comparable issues without female intervention; hence, these are not fully satisfactory explanations for Aethra's assertive role in this scene, for the special link established between mothers and the traditional laws, and for Theseus' striking change of mind.

Before examining these larger questions, we must look at our other examples. In *Phoenissae*, Jocasta, like Aethra, delivers the prologue. Here she establishes her moral seriousness and her clear vision of the family history. The prologue is followed by a scene in which the young Antigone, chaperoned by her pedagogue, breathlessly observes the enemy from the palace roof (88–201). This scene reminds the audience of traditional limits on female behavior by stressing Antigone's virginity, the dangers of her appearing outside the house, and, in the final lines of the scene (196–201), the threat of female gossip. The chorus of Phoenician virgins enters and confounds any expectation that they will reflect this dangerous side of womanhood (202–60). On their way to a cultic role at Delphi, they are calm and sympathetic observers of Thebes' dangers

---

[19] Goff 1995a: 73.

[20] *Against Leocrates* 100; Euripides, *Erectheus*, fragment 50 Austin. On the importance of the ritual setting in explaining the role of Aethra, see Goff 1995a: 74–75, who also mentions Praxithea (77).

[21] See Lewis 1955 and Henderson 1987: xxxviii.

and its history. Polyneices then makes a nervous entrance (261). He has been summoned by Jocasta, who is attempting to mediate between the brothers and avert the war against Thebes. The ensuing dialogue stresses the family relations between mother and son. Jocasta, her hair shorn and dressed in mourning clothes, greets her son in an emotional aria, which stresses Oedipus' curse and the family disasters (301–54). Polyneices' cooler response in iambics laments the loss of his fatherland, the altars of Thebes' gods, Dirce's spring, his parents and sisters (357–78). Jocasta questions Polyneices about the misfortunes of life in exile (387–426). Eteocles, impatient to return to his martial duties, abruptly intervenes in this family dialogue (446). Jocasta attempts to slow the speech of her impatient sons and to create a familial intimacy by making them look into each other's eyes (454–64).

Polyneices, as plaintiff, speaks first. The conventional and aristocratic Polyneices characterizes the justice of his cause in a "simple tale of truth," which has no need of the sophistries used by the unjust (469–72). He argues that Eteocles has been unjust, since he reneged on his promise to share the sovereignty of Thebes with his brother. Polyneices will call off the battle if Eteocles will compromise. Otherwise he will attack the city. The chorus approves his sensible speech (*suneta*, 498). Eteocles argues in sophistic style that if the same thing were good and wise for all, men would not quarrel. But nothing is similar or equal for mortals except in name (499–502). Eteocles is a naked pursuer of power. Polyneices, he argues, should not attack his fatherland, and Eteocles would be a coward if he surrendered to force. Injustice (*adikein*) is most noble in the pursuit of kingship (*turannidos*), although one ought to be pious (*eusebein*) in relation to everything else (524–25). The chorus, in a second and unusually assertive judgment for a chorus, criticizes this speech for its adeptness in glossing over bad deeds and for its injustice (526–27).[22]

Jocasta now makes her highly rhetorical and ornate mediating speech (528–85). As an arbitrator, Jocasta fits Aristotle's prescriptions for the role, because she "looks to equity" (*to epieikes*—unwritten laws are part of what Aristotle has in mind here), whereas a juror looks to the law (*Rhetoric* 1374b20–21). This speech is far longer than any other speech by a third party to an *agōn* (formal debate)—indeed it is the longest of extant *agōn* speeches—and dominates the scene to an unusual extent.[23] Citing the wisdom of age, she criticizes Eteocles for his attachment to ambition (*philotimia*, 531–32). She argues for honoring equality (*isotēs*), which binds friends, cities, and allies (535–38). Equality (*to ison*) is by nature (*ephu*) lawful (*nomimon*) for humans (538). Inequality (the lesser and greater) breeds hatred (541–45). Jocasta then counters Eteocles' denial of a natural basis to morality, by making equality a cosmic principle. *Isotēs* provided weights and measures to men, the rotation of sun and moon, which

---

[22] Choruses rarely praise and blame pairs of speeches in an *agōn* so pointedly (Mastronarde 1994: ad loc.). This perhaps reinforces the sense that the scene is a trial as well as an arbitration.

[23] Lloyd 1992: 90 and Mastronarde 1994: 297.

serves humankind (541–45). By the principle of *isotēs*, Eteocles should share his inheritance (546–48). Royal power is an injustice that gives happiness; the honor that comes with it is empty (549–51). Power requires hard work and yields profit in name only (552–53). Mortals have no private possessions, but are overseers of what belongs to the gods (555–57). Wealth is transient (558). Eteocles should put the safety of Thebes before power and wealth (559–67). In attacking his own fatherland, Polyneices is, in Jocasta's view, very much to blame as well (568–85). Although on the surface Jocasta's arguments are designed to persuade the brothers to share power, for the audience the appeal to *isotēs* in the speech becomes as well an implicit defense of democracy, because ruling in turn and in yearly cycles is critical in democratic theory.[24]

Jocasta fails to persuade the brothers, who soon descend into a quarrel so hostile that they are eager to meet and kill each other in the upcoming battle. Later in the play Jocasta wrenches the maiden Antigone from seclusion and rushes to try to prevent the final duel of the brothers. She kills herself over the bodies of her dead sons with a sword, leaving Antigone to face her by now traditional dilemma over the burial of Polyneices and, finally, to join Oedipus in exile.[25] The selfishness of the brothers thus not only destroys their household but drags women from their place within the household into activities in the public realm.

As we saw from the court cases cited earlier, there is nothing surprising in a mother's attempt to mediate a family quarrel. Jocasta had already adopted this role in the earlier literary tradition; in a fragment of the archaic poet Stesichorus, she tries to resolve the brothers' quarrel at an earlier stage and appeals to the survival of the fatherland (P Lille 76abc). In Sophocles' *Oedipus*, she successfully intervenes in the quarrel between Creon and Oedipus. Despite the warning of the pedagogue to Antigone about the danger of female speech, no reservations about female advice occur in this scene. The arbitration scene in *Phoenissae* retains a discreet, domestic atmosphere because it is witnessed only by the chorus of maidens, and no other male citizens are present. Jocasta is clearly the wise participant in the *agōn* (arbitration), who is nevertheless powerless to persuade her ambitious sons to resolve their quarrel. The family setting for Jocasta's arbitration makes the brothers' claims appear more unnatural and the outcome implicitly reinforces Jocasta's claim for the binding force of *isotēs* at all levels of human society—families, cities, and allies (535–38). Because Polyneices makes an appeal to justice, which is marred by his own willingness to sacrifice his fatherland to his cause, and Eteocles espouses the cause of his own power, Jocasta here establishes herself not simply as mediating mother but as defender of the city and its concerns in a play in which all the male characters refuse to do so, except the boy Menoeceus and the blind

---

[24] See further Mastronarde 1994: ad loc.

[25] The text of this last scene is uncertain. See ibid.

prophet Tiresias, who plays a strictly advisory role. The brothers kill each other and refuse to compromise. Creon will not sacrifice his son for Thebes. Oedipus, who has survived in Thebes up to this point, fails to demonstrate the civic concern of his earlier Sophoclean counterpart. It is Jocasta and the chorus of foreign women who concentrate on the state of the city and see the patterns of its history emerging. In *Phoenissae*, then, those outside the political realm act heroically in the city's defense, citing areas where nature and human law purportedly intersect. The play seems to suggest that power is inherently corrupting, and hence those formally outside politics—women, the young, and the old—must speak the truth to those in authority.[26]

In *Hecuba*, the newly enslaved former queen of Troy Hecuba makes two appeals for assistance to her Greek masters. First, she tries to persuade Odysseus to intervene and prevent her daughter Polyxena's sacrifice at the tomb of Achilles; then she asks Agamemnon to exact justice from the barbarian Polymestor. In the first scene, she counters her powerlessness by evoking Odysseus' past debt to her. Odysseus had been her suppliant when he came disguised into the city of Troy. Hecuba spared him then, and now supplicates Odysseus for a return of the favor (239–47). If Odysseus rejects her appeal, he will be harming his friends to please the many (256–57). From the standpoint of justice (271, *tō(i) . . . dikaiō(i)*), she argues that human sacrifice is unfitting and that Achilles should have demanded Helen rather than the innocent Polyxena, who is everything to Hecuba (280–81). There are things over which the powerful should not have power; nor should they assume that prosperity will be lasting (282–83). The Greeks now kill those whom they formerly pitied and dragged from altars (288–90). For Greeks the law (*nomos*) is the same (*isos*) for slave and free (291–92).[27]

Hecuba fails to save Polyxena. Odysseus interprets her suppliant appeal narrowly. He is willing to save Hecuba's life but argues that matters of state must take precedence in Polyxena's case. Achilles died for Greece. A friend while he lived, he should not be treated differently in death. Honors for the dead are lasting, and men will not fight without them. Hecuba should endure her sufferings; Greek women and old men have after all suffered equally from the war (299–325).

In this scene, Hecuba bases her appeal on *charis* (reciprocity, 257, 276) and *to dikaion* (justice). Like Aethra (*Suppliants* 331), she reminds Odysseus of the

[26] See Foley 1985: esp. 144.

[27] Athenian law protected both free men and slaves in sanctuary, because their blood would pollute the altar (see Demosthenes 21.46–50 and Collard 1991: ad loc.). Otherwise, the law only protected slaves against their master's maltreatment. See MacDowell 1978: 80–81. Nevertheless, Athens prided itself in its humane treatment of slaves, and by Attic standards it was probably Agamemnon's duty, as Hecuba requests in a later scene, to see to the punishment of the murderer, Polymestor (Meridor 1983: 15).

tragic mutability of human life (282–85). She tries to blur the boundaries between male and female, slave and free, and friend and enemy by defining Odysseus as in her debt, and by evoking the legal protection from unjust death that even slaves deserve. Odysseus has been represented earlier in the play as an aspiring demagogue, who persuades a divided army to sacrifice Polyxena. Only Agamemnon, whose position is suspect in the eyes of the army due to his relation to his new concubine Cassandra, opposes the sacrifice (120–21). Despite Odysseus' questionable character, Hecuba cannot counter his defense of a public interest that here overrides private debts to herself and the injustice of the sacrifice, even though, in reality, too active a pursuit of such aims, when they conflicted with personal obligations, could—surprisingly, given the general civic ideology favoring the interest of the state—be frowned upon in Athens. Aeschines, for example, criticizes Demosthenes for personally torturing a suspected spy who had previously entertained him and causing an outcry in the assembly by saying that he rated the city's salt above the table of hospitality (*On the Embassy* 22, *Against Ctesiphon* 224–25).[28]

In her scene with Agamemnon, Hecuba, as a slave and a woman should, asks a man to take action on her behalf. She supplicates her master Agamemnon, asking him to be her avenger against the Thracian Polymestor. Polymestor has violated the relations between host and guest by killing Hecuba's son Polydorus and casting him into the sea unburied in order to get the gold that came with him from Troy. Hecuba says that although mortals may be slaves and powerless, the gods and the *nomos* that rules the gods are powerful (799–800). People believe in gods by virtue of *nomos* (800) and live distinguishing the just from the unjust (801).[29] If this *nomos* is corrupted, and those who kill guest friends and plunder what is sacred to the gods do not pay the penalty, there will be no equity among humans (802–5; I read with the manuscript *ison* at 805, not *sōn*, "safe").[30] Agamemnon must consider Polymestor's acts shameful, and pity Hecuba (806–8). At this point, Agamemnon apparently tries to withdraw physically from the suppliancy (812). Hecuba then makes a second desperate appeal based on personal *charis* (reciprocity). She has already heard that Agamemnon defended Polyxena before the army because of his relation to Cassandra (120–22). Hence she tries to use her daughter to establish a bond of *philia* with her master that would then make Polydorus a "relative" for whom the king should act (824–35).[31] In closing, Hecuba returns to her former point

[28] For a discussion, see Dover 1974: 302.

[29] See Collard 1991: ad loc. on the difficulties of interpreting this famous passage. On the concept of *nomos* here and elsewhere in the play, see Lanza 1963: 416–22 and Kirkwood 1947.

[30] See Collard 1991: ad loc.

[31] Hecuba's appeal for *charis* here has in the eyes of some critics made her into a mere pimp who prostitutes her daughter (Conacher 1967: 162, Buxton 1982: 176, Luschnig 1976: 232, Kirkwood 1947: 167, and Michelini 1991: 151–52). Gregory 1991: 106, however, following the scholiast who cites Tecmessa at *Ajax* 520–22 on the gratitude a man owes a woman for sexual favors, rejects this interpretation (see also Zeitlin 1991: 79 and Burnett 1998: 164 n. 87). Segal 1993b: 210 ar-

in a fashion that universalizes it. Agamemnon as a good (*esthlos*) man should serve justice and treat bad men badly *everywhere* (844–45).

Unlike Odysseus, Agamemnon does pity Hecuba and her suppliancy. (He echoes her language at 1249.) For the sake of the gods and justice, he wants Polymestor to pay for his unholy act. Yet Agamemnon does not wish to appear to the army to be acting for Cassandra's sake, because the army considers Polymestor an ally (*philios*, 858), and Hecuba's Trojan son Polydorus an enemy (*echthros*, 859). He concludes that he will help if he can avoid the army's calumny (860–63).

Hecuba frees Agamemnon from his dilemma by asking for Agamemnon's complicity, while she and her women undertake the revenge themselves (868–75). In the final mock trial of Polymestor, after the Trojan women have blinded Polymestor and killed his two sons, Hecuba takes care to release Agamemnon from his obligations by showing that Polymestor was not a true ally to the Greeks (1200–1232).[32] Hence Agamemnon will appear bad if he tolerates Polymestor's unholy and unjust behavior (1232–35). This gives Agamemnon the opening he wants; because Polymestor acted for gold and not for the Greeks, Agamemnon could not escape censure unless he condemned Polymestor for killing guests, an action that is *aischron* (shameful) to Greeks (1248–49).

In these scenes with Agamemnon and Odysseus, Hecuba attempts to win justice for herself and her family. The competing claims put forth are hard to evaluate. Odysseus, characterized as a demagogue, ignores Hecuba's valid appeals for personal justice by citing what he views as the higher claims of the public interest (a typical democratic argument). In Hecuba's view, this subservience to the particular claims of the many is slavish (256–57). Similarly, it is the slave Hecuba who ironically liberates (869) Agamemnon, slave to the mob (*ochlos*, 868). Agamemnon gives her a trial—or formal arbitration—unique in revenge tragedy outside the *Oresteia* and finally pronounces her revenge just, but here he acts not on principle but only because the winds do not yet permit his departure.[33] Hecuba may appear narrow and aristocratic in arguing for personal claims against the interests of the military group, yet she defends her position with principles that are, she claims, universal to a stable social and religious order and to political equality.[34] Moreover, she gradually

---

gues that Hecuba turns to this argument because her more traditional arguments were not effective.

[32] See Adkins 1966: 204.

[33] In the view of Segal 1993b: 206, Agamemnon here reduces justice to convenience.

[34] At 866–67 Hecuba argues that no one is free but is the slave of wealth (*chrēmatōn*), fortune (*tuchēs*), or written laws (*nomōn graphai*), which restrict a person from following his or her own bent (*kata gnōmēn tropois*). For Hecuba's aristocratic arguments, see Kovacs 1987: esp. 80–83 and 98–99. See my subsequent assessment of the argument by Hirzel 1900 and Cerri 1979 that aristocrats had a particular interest in the traditional and unwritten *nomoi*.

expresses greater self-consciousness about skillful persuasion and includes in her last speech arguments reflecting the political self-interest of the Greeks in support of traditional laws.

In the eyes of the Greeks, Hecuba is the quintessential suffering mother and female victim of war. Yet the play also draws specific attention to Hecuba's final and shocking violation of the limits of womanhood.[35] Agamemon, surprised that Hecuba intends to exact her own revenge, assumes that women are unable to take effective action to achieve justice (885). Hecuba deceptively plays the woman to Polymestor, claiming that she is ashamed to look him in the eyes (968–75). Finally, when Agamemnon decides in favor of Hecuba in the play's closing trial, Polymestor is outraged to have been defeated by a slave and a woman (1252–53). Thus both men raise questions about the possibility and legitimacy of female action.[36]

In all three of these scenes, then, our central older mothers appeal to male characters to act justly and appropriately by urging the claims of ancestral *nomoi* that are universally recognized by all Greeks or all humanity, supported by the gods, or based on nature. All three see respect for these *nomoi* as critical to the orderly functioning of cities and to the maintenance of civic equality. Aethra and Hecuba base their appeal on traditional and divinely supported laws concerning the burial of the dead, suppliants, and (in Hecuba's case) reciprocity between human beings. Jocasta's attempt to root justice in natural equality counters the sophistic position taken by her son, who believes that human laws are relative and derive from convention. In these plays, Euripides has gone out of his way to make the defenders of these particular *nomoi* female. Because they are older women, sexuality plays no role in motivating their pleas; they speak as mothers, more concerned for their children and (marital) family interests than for themselves. And although these female characters have personal and emotional reasons (typical of women in the Greek mind) for taking the position that they do and their role as suffering mothers gives them a certain authority, their entirely rational arguments extend more fully than Antigone's beyond the interests of the family to encompass the order of society as a whole. In *Antigone,* Ismene makes clear that a passive citizenship is required of virgins like herself (61–68, 78–79), but Aethra and Jocasta actively advocate the public interest; Hecuba, despite her anger at personal injustice, claims that her position has public implications and is permitted a public defense of her revenge. Yet in all three cases practical political considerations (expediency) override or threaten to override their pleas.

Let us now turn to examining more closely why Euripides may have chosen

[35] On women undertaking revenge, see Burnett 1998: 142–44.

[36] On the negative stereotypes of women at play here (above all in the myths of the homicidal Danaids and the Lemnian women, 886–87), see Rabinowitz 1993: esp. 113–21 and Zeitlin 1991. Once men abdicate authority, the effect on women is Dionysiac (Zeitlin 1991: 56–57 and Schlesier 1989).

these women to champion these particular causes. On the most general level, women's social position potentially aligns them with unwritten or traditional laws. First, they are excluded from making or executing written law or decrees, but actively follow and even administer (to some degree) both written and un-written laws in religious cults. The possible links between female persuasive dis-course and women's role in cult were mentioned earlier in relation to Aethra. Second, although (as was discussed in part I) the state usurped many of the ear-lier female roles in death ritual—public lamentations and even funerary dis-course—it never fully excluded women from public funerals. Hence women re-main logically more concerned with burial traditions than with some other political issues. Aethra invokes Panhellenic laws about burial; Hecuba insists on the universality of the laws concerning hospitality to which she appeals. By dissolving the boundaries between Greek and barbarian with her claims to rec-iprocity with Odysseus and Agamemnon, she in a sense demonstrates her point. Aristophanes also makes women the source of Panhellenic unity and salvation in *Lysistrata*, and of traditionalism and communism in *Ecclesiazusae*. Because women tend to be viewed in Greek literature as an undifferentiated group (a separate "tribe of women" or *genos gunaikōn*)[37] and do not determine the pol-icy of particular states, perhaps they were more readily imagined as able to ig-nore the boundaries between states and conflicting interests among political groups. Tragedy, for example, includes barbarian female choruses in plays set in Greek cities, but not barbarian male choruses (see e.g., *Choephoroi*, *Phoenissae*, *Bacchae*). As survivors of war who will be forced to adapt to the ways of other cities, the Trojan women in the chorus of *Hecuba*, for example, imaginatively share the sufferings of a Spartan woman (650–56) or join the women of the Greek cities to which they will come as slaves in ritual (455–74).

More important, with children, old men, and prisoners of war like Eurys-theus in Euripides' *Heracleidae*,[38] women are particularly vulnerable to chance and to abuse, and most dependent on traditions designed to protect the weak (e.g., oaths, supplications, rules of hospitality). In tragedy, women are more likely to have recourse to supplication than men, since both in principle and in reality they could not defend their own interests directly. Although Home-ric epic does not characterize male supplication as shameful, men in tragedy find it humiliating to have recourse to suppliancy, as does the aged Adrastus in the *Suppliants* (164–67). Menelaus in Euripides' *Helen* views it as beneath his masculine dignity, and leaves the role of suppliant to his wife (830). In both the literary and historical tradition, women may also intervene on behalf of suppliants. Arete in the *Odyssey* apparently plays a critical role in Odysseus'

[37] See Loraux 1978.

[38] *Heracleidae* 1010. Eurystheus, an Athenian prisoner of war, argues that since he was not killed when he wanted to be, he should not by the *Hellēnōn nomoi* be killed now (because it would be a source of pollution). See further Wilkins 1993: ad loc. On the relation between suppliancy and the powerless, see Michelini 1987: 176.

acceptance as suppliant among the Phaeacians,[39] and one historical instance
suggests that, at least in the archaic period, Attic women could in fact play an
active role in supplications of the kind adopted by Aethra. During the sixth-
century feud between the aristocrats Megacles and Cylon, Cylon and his fellow conspirators had taken refuge in the temple of Athena. Cylon persuaded
them to abandon the sanctuary and stand trial. In Plutarch's version of the
story, on their way down the Acropolis, the thread that they had fastened to
the image of the goddess broke at the shrine of the Erinyes. Megacles and his
fellow archons seized and killed most of the conspirators, on the grounds that
the goddess had refused to protect them. But those who supplicated the wives
of the archons were spared (Plutarch, *Solon* 12).

Finally, women's social roles orient them toward some of the concerns involved in traditional laws. As Lin Foxhall has pointed out,[40] Greek women's
lives are temporally defined in different ways than men's. Unless they died in
childbirth, their lives were more likely than that of their husbands to link three
generations, because they married young to older men. In public rituals, in reproducing children in marriage, and in caring for family graves their activities
were directed toward assuring the future and maintaining bonds with the past,
whereas men were actively responsible in the assembly, in the courts, and in
war for responding to the issues of the moment and to the interests of the state.
Yet we have also seen that male discourse, especially in the funeral oration, at
least ideally defended the traditions and unwritten laws of the Greek world.

Champions of the unwritten, traditional, and divine laws appear throughout Sophocles' plays, and are indifferently male or female.[41] Odysseus in *Ajax*
(1130, 1343) and Antigone, later supported by Tiresias, defend the rights of
the dead to burial. Electra, in deciding to avenge her improperly buried father,
is characterized by the chorus as winning, through her piety to Zeus, the best
prizes given by the mightiest laws that ever came to birth (*ha de megist' eblaste
nomima*, 1095–96). In *Oedipus at Colonus* Theseus presumably relies on such
traditions in accepting the polluted Oedipus into Athens; Oedipus himself invokes as the power behind his just curse primeval justice sitting enthroned with
Zeus by right of ancient laws (1382). The chorus of old men in *Oedipus Rex*,
reacting to Oedipus and Jocasta's dismissal of Apollo's oracles, wishes to live
by the eternal divine laws of Olympus (863–71). As in the case of Antigone,
these laws, which oppose tyranny, are eternal, inviolable, and without a known

---

[39] Pitt-Rivers 1977.

[40] Foxhall 1994.

[41] In Aeschylus, the examples are too limited to identify any trend in the reference to traditional laws. The chorus of women in *Suppliants* refers to the three *thesmioi dikas* (708–9), which
involve giving justice to strangers, honoring the gods with sacrifices, and revering parents. The
Erinyes are also champions of the traditional *nomoi*—reverencing gods, parents, and strangers and
upholding justice (*Eumenides* 269–72, 538–49).

origin. The action of Sophocles' plays tends to vindicate the superior status of such laws and stresses their links with divinity.

In the historical arena, denial of burial or exhumation of the dead, often accompanied by exile of the progeny of the guilty party, could apparently serve like ostracism as a weapon in the arsenal of the Attic *polis* against aristocrats who overstepped their bounds (the Alcmaeonids, Themistocles), including traitors to the state.[42] At the same time, when Giovanni Cerri interprets the conflict over funerary practice and the unwritten laws in Sophocles as a reflection of class warfare between aristocrats and the democratic majority, he oversimplifies the case.[43] The unwritten laws, when deployed publicly within the city-state, could serve as a convenient weapon for those who felt excluded from or in conflict with the democratic majority, precisely because these laws were not codified but categorized as older than and superior to written law, and hence theoretically impervious to political modification. Unwritten and religious law had important links with the aristocracy;[44] in some cases aristocratic *genē* (clans), like the Eumolpidae who presided over the Eleusinian Mysteries, interpreted a body of esoteric unwritten laws concerning cult and perhaps other religious matters for the city.[45] Yet unwritten laws are not, at least by the age of Pericles, imagined as the property of the aristocracy, but as functioning in a complementary fashion to written law in the democracy. For Pericles, in the funeral oration attributed to him by Thucydides, democracy relies not only on (presumably written) laws that protect the interests of those treated unjustly, but on unwritten laws, supported by a general popular consensus, that induce fear of wrongdoing in the population (2.37). In *Antigone* it is the general populace that is said by Haemon to side secretly with the heroine (692–700, 733), whereas the chorus, comprising longtime supporters of the royal family, does not directly oppose Creon until after Tiresias' prophecy (1091–

[42] See Cerri 1979: ch. 1 and 43–44 and Herman 1987: 161: "in the Greek world of cities, then, the notions 'treason' and 'patriotism' had overtones of class conflict."

[43] Cerri 1979, in contrast to Erhenberg 1954, de Romilly 1971, and Ostwald 1973 (although Cerri does not take account of the work of these last two scholars), interprets the province of the unwritten laws narrowly. He argues that Antigone's citation of the unwritten laws is a technical reference to a body of oral law linked with the aristocratic *genē* and applied to members of their group, rather than a supreme human law inscribed in the conscience and religious sensibility (13, 38–42, 81; Cerri sees the same dynamics at work in Sophocles' *Ajax*). Virtually all of our evidence on unwritten law comes from the fourth century, and, as Ostwald 1973 has shown, there is no coherent concept of "unwritten law" before this time. Pericles' funeral oration does not have to represent a new trend, as Cerri argues (67–72), but an appropriation of unwritten law by the democracy to serve its own interests that could easily have begun as early as Sophocles' plays (see the examples from Aeschylus in note 41) and appears in many fourth-century passages as well. If Sophocles' election as general the year after *Antigone* related to the play (Cerri 59–60 invokes this story in support of his thesis), Pericles was elected this same year (see Ronnet 1980: 349).

[44] See Hirzel 1900: 43–47.

[45] See pseudo-Lysias *Against Andocides* 6.10 and Andocides, *On the Mysteries* 115–16.

1107, although see its possible reserve at 219–20).[46] This popular support makes clear that Antigone's advocacy of the unwritten laws is not simply aristocratic propaganda but of interest to the whole population; this is not surprising, given that the Athenian championship of the dead after the war of the seven against Thebes, was, according to Herodotus, an element in Athenian propaganda and democratic imperialism since the Persian Wars (9.27.3).[47] These Panhellenic traditions, which supposedly protected the interests of the gods and the vanquished in war, but in reality were often deployed in the interests of democratic imperialism, are in Euripides, above all in the plays involving suppliancy or concerned with war and the aftermath of war, of direct interest to the city and protective of civic order and equality as they are not in Sophocles.[48] Where traditional laws are invoked to serve the interests of an aristocratic group against the supposed interests of the majority, as in the case of *Hecuba*, the heroine argues for the universal relevance of her claims, and their importance for the preservation of equality.

Yet in Euripides as opposed to Sophocles, the status of traditional, divine, or natural laws (they are never explictly characterized as unwritten) is far more fragile, and, unless this trend is simply an accident of the plays transmitted to us, the appeals based on them become increasingly futile, and more explicitly open to sophistic challenge. It may be significant that Euripides' *Heracleidae*, which as noted earlier gives the claims of suppliants immediate priority, is probably earlier than the three plays central to our consideration, and early in the Peloponnesian War as well.[49] To take our three plays in their probable chronological order, it seems likely that *Suppliants* was immediately preceded by the

[46] The body of unwritten law interpreted by priestly clans like the Eumolpidae seems in the examples given to relate specifically to cult practices—for example, to defining a limited range of matters of impiety. There is no indication that such laws involved proscription of burial, or that they dealt with issues specific to the state, like the punishment of traitors. Unwritten laws could be invoked in conjunction with written law, as in Cerri's major supporting example (pseudo-Lysias, *Against Andocides* 6.10), even if from 403 on written law took precedence over unwritten traditions. There is nothing esoteric about the laws invoked by Antigone—she expects the chorus to know and support them—or the similar though not specifically unwritten laws invoked by the chorus of women (representing the city) in *Electra*. In *Antigone*, Tiresias broadens the burial issue to all of the war dead, and Creon recognizes the general validity of these traditions concerning the dead at the end of the play.

[47] On the connection between Panhellenic law and imperialism, see Perlman 1976, Cerri 1979: esp. 86, and Hall 1989: 181–90.

[48] Cerri 1979: 71–72 notes that Euripides' *Suppliants* 433–37 makes a point of treating written law as the defender of equality, of the weak against the powerful, whereas Sophocles has his characters turn to unwritten or traditional laws to resist tyranny. (Cerri takes his cue from Hirzel 1900: 69–71 who links Sophocles with unwritten law, Euripides with written.) Yet Theseus also invokes Panhellenic law (unwritten, but the province of the whole state, not the absolute monarch) in this play (as Cerri notes, 84–86). Hence, Cerri's most important observation is that these plays of Euripides are apparently less concerned with the rights of individual nobles than those of Sophocles.

[49] Theseus' offer of a refuge to the polluted Heracles in *Heracles* should perhaps also be considered in this general category of plays.

battle of Delium in 424, which was followed by a Boeotian refusal to permit the Athenians to bury their dead.[50] If so, Theseus' initial reluctance to respect the pleas of the suppliants at Eleusis is all the more striking. In the closely contemporary *Hecuba*, perhaps performed shortly after *Suppliants*, traditional *nomoi* would without Hecuba's intervention have been sacrificed to the public interest in a postwar context. *Phoenissae* was produced in circa 409, shortly after the oligarchic revolution of 411 in which the disrespect of the oligarchs for traditional *nomoi* and their perversion of public power for private ends were notorious. In this play men reject state interest and the principle of equality in favor of private gain, and Jocasta, unlike Aethra and Hecuba, does not explicitly attribute divine authority to the law of equality she finds in nature. Pentheus in the *Bacchae* of 406–5 is punished for his outright rejection of divine traditions (331, 890–92, 895–96), but here the initiative is divine rather than mortal.[51] In Euripides, champions of such laws are increasingly female, not only in our three plays, but in other late plays like *Erectheus* (fragment 50.45 Austin, *progonōn palaia thesmi'*) and *Helen* (traditional burial rites, 1270, 1277) as well; hence, these laws come to depend dramatically on those who can only speak but cannot act to defend them. Historical pressures may thus be partly responsible for the increasing vulnerability attributed to these particular *nomoi* in Euripides, and we see a parallel, but critically different, transition in the status of traditional *nomoi* in the historian Thucydides' analysis of the Peloponnesian War (to be discussed shortly).[52]

Yet the implications of implicitly genderizing ethical positions in these particular plays may be even more far reaching than it appears on the surface. Let me begin with a more recent historical example. Joan Tronto has examined the way that the eighteenth century, especially in England, engendered an ethical division between reason and sentiment or feeling. She argues that a new morality based on abstract and formal universal premises relegated moral sentiments to the household and to the women who presided over it. This new impartial morality, based on reason, displaced a more contextual morality, which depended on intimacy between members of a moral community, and valued educating citizens about virtue and a sense of the ends of human and political life.[53] Historical changes, both economic and political, were critical to this transition. The spheres of domesticity and production gradually separated, and economic bonds acquired a new status. The politics of empire required a change in the way citizens interacted and dealt with different peoples and ways of life. In the service of a large, diverse, and market-oriented world, virtue became dislodged from social practices and linked with self-interest. The role of

---

[50] See Thucydides 4.98–99. On the date of the play, see Collard 1975: 1: 8–14.

[51] See also *Cyclops* 299–300 on the rights of suppliants.

[52] These tensions are important throughout the fifth century B.C.E in Greece but seem to be exacerbated as the century wears on.

[53] Tronto 1993: ch. 2.

the virtuous citizen declined. A virtue thus dislodged from social and political practices had to be sustained on the one hand by reason and on the other hand by sentiment. The household became the symbolic bulwark against corruption and self-interest in the public world. In Tronto's view, marginalizing sentiment by linking it with the private sphere, women, and the disempowered, and defining it as "natural," had far reaching implications for public policy and political ethics. (It also served to contain women within the boundaries of the household and the private world.) A sense of connection, of attachment to others and community, of sympathy for those other than members of one's own group, became relatively devalued in favor of formal bonds among the formally equal.

Tronto's analysis, which is based above all on her interpretation of the Scottish enlightenment, may well offer an oversimplified picture of eighteenth-century England. In any case, the situation in a preindustrial society like Athens was obviously different; but because of the Athenian Empire and the rise of democracy, some similar issues are at stake. The attempt to privilege the interest of the state and, in practice, the interest of the democratic majority led to the development of a public ethics not known in Homer. Within the *polis*, the democracy aimed to ensure political equality and favored the interest of the majority. The interests of the state took precedence over those of the individual when these two came into conflict and the role of the virtuous citizen is said by Thucydides and others to have declined in favor of those who made a profession of claiming to serve the interests of the *dēmos*. The empire and Athens' ever growing contacts with distant peoples created increasing pressures to conceptualize ethics beyond the boundaries of the city-state. In Euripides, this can even take the form of arguing that differences of status and nationality may be irrelevant to ethical decisions. "I reckon the good man *philos*—however far away in the world he lives, and even if I have not set eyes on him" (fragment 902 N²).[54] In matters concerning international relations, the assembly and the army gradually privileged in their deliberations the advantage of Athens over considerations of justice and appeals to emotion or altruism. This becomes particularly clear in Thucydides' Mytilenean debate, where Diodotus challenges Cleon's claim that justice and the national interest are compatible in this instance (3.47.5). Diodotus argues that justice would demand the severe punishment of Mytilene on which the assembly had earlier determined, but Athens' interest demands a lesser punishment. Both Cleon and Diodotus rule out emotional appeals to pity and decency (*epieikeia*) (3.40.2–4, 3.48.1). Cleon had argued that the vengeance that follows on the very heels of an outrage exacts a punishment that most nearly matches the of-

[54] Trans. Dover 1974. There is some question as to whether this fragment belongs to Euripides. See also Euripides' *Phaethon* fragment 163 Diggle, Euripides fragment 1047 N², or Menander fragment 475, "No one is alien to me if he is good." Such cosmopolitan statements are rare, however. See Dover 1974: 283 and Daitz 1971: 223.

fense (3.38.1; see also 3.40.7), whereas Diodotus rules out the influence of haste and passion (3.42.1).

In many respects, Greeks in the early stages of the Peloponnesian War assumed that the legal and ethical practices of their cities should extend at least to some degree to interstate and international "law."[55] Athens' defense of its empire partly turned on its claim to defending its subject states, who would have been otherwise helpless to preserve their lives and traditions; allies were required in some cases to adjudicate quarrels in Attic courts. Similarly, the Spartan ephor Sthenelaidas argues in Thucydides 1.86 that Sparta must go to war to defend its allies and redress a violation of international justice. Yet in relation to those categorized first as enemies, then as neutrals, then those even within cities, practice soon deviated from this aim. Thucydidean debates frequently show that arguments based on power and self-interest overcame pleas for moderation, justice, pity, decency or equity (*epieikeia*), traditional laws, or the rights of suppliants and the dead. In Thucydides' book 1 the Athenians claim to be motivated by honor, fear, and advantage but add that they are fairer than power obliges them to be (1.76.2–3). Pericles, however, soon argues that the Athenian Empire requires injustice (2.63.2). The later Melian debate (5.84–111) takes the position that justice is only possible among equals. The result was a system of justice and public ethics that operated in increasingly different ways on different levels. Ideally, Aristotle's *Rhetoric* 1.3.5.1358b21–26 and the *Rhetorica ad Alexandrum* 1.1421b24–25 make clear that *to dikaion* and *to nomimon* should be included with *to sumpheron* as the aim of deliberative oratory. In fact, justice operated in one way in the lawcourts and among citizens, friends, and allies, and in another in the assembly and among unallied cities. Diodotus, for example, underlines this divergence by pointedly reminding his audience in the Mytilenean debate that they are not engaged in deliberations over a lawsuit (where pity or equity would presumably apply [3.44.4]).[56] The reverse was equally a threat, as *stasis* (revolution) created "a seepage between the morality required by war and the domestic morality of cities."[57]

The traditional *nomoi*, which ideally served as a foundation for justice in relations among individuals and cities, yet whose role was clearly formalized in

---

[55] I here adopt the argument of Sheets 1994 that there was a genuine and operative conception of international law in Greece at this period. He argues (62–63) that "international law *in substance* is" not "any less determinate or stable than municipal law. It does mean that *in application* international law is much more obviously subject to political pressures than municipal law appears to be." On the informal rules governing intra-Greek warfare, see Ober 1994 with earlier bibliography. Problems with observing international law existed at all times in the fifth century but were exacerbated in the last quarter of the century.

[56] Cleon makes a point of contrasting insiders and outsiders here, by stressing that Athenians have no fear and intrigue in their relations in daily life. This makes them vulnerable to pity (3.37.2).

[57] See Lintott 1993: esp. 27 (with the critique of Winton).

none, become a locus of contradictions in the system as a whole. Pericles' funeral oration insists that privileging the interests of the state did not lead to disrespect for the unwritten laws; indeed the state relies on them (Thucydides 2.37). Nevertheless, events such as the Corcyrean stasis or the Athenian plague demonstrated their vulnerability. In international relations, reliance on unwritten law and arbitration was even more critical and less enforceable.[58] Josiah Ober views the informal rules of war, for example, as the product of hoplite ethos and practice from circa 700–450 B.C.E.; the Athenian democracy was no longer interested in maintaining these rules and was largely responsible for their gradual breakdown.[59] The discourse of the funeral oration, which championed the traditional *nomoi*, both within and in the relations among states, and the discourse of empire and assembly that often violated them came into increasing contradiction.

Suppliancy is a case in point for these emerging contradictions. In suppliant tragedies, the ruler often wishes to respond to the appeals of the suppliants, but when this requires force, he must also consider the sacrifices that will be required of his countrymen. In the imaginary world of drama and the funeral oration, city-states decide consistently in favor of the suppliants. By contrast, at Plataea, the Plataeans who surrendered to the Lacedaemonians appeal to the laws protecting suppliant captives who have voluntarily surrendered (*ho de nomos tois Hellēsi mē kteinein toutous*, 3.58.3; *ta koinon tōn Hellenōn nomima*, 3.59.1).[60] They expected justice (3.52.2, 3.53.1–2) but discover that the Lacedaemonians had not planned to have them offer a plea in their own defense. Given leave to speak nevertheless, the Plataeans try to establish their good character and their past service to the Lacedaemonians on the basis of exploits in the Persian Wars. They remind the Lacedaemonians that they are parties familiar to each other (3.53.4) and invoke the common gods of the Hellenes, past oaths, the uncertainty of fortune, pity (*oiktō(i) sophroni*), and restraint (3.58.1, 3.59.1).

These pleas might stand up well in an Attic court of justice or in tragedy, which gives a central role to pity and the vagaries of fortune. But in the political arena, the Plataean pleas are undermined by the Thebans, who argue that none of the Plataean claims in fact apply and pity should only be bestowed on those suffering something *aprepes* (unsuitable, 3.67.4).[61] The Thebans clearly fear that pity, justice, and suppliancy may persuade the Lacedaemonians to spare the Plataeans, thus indicating that these pleas still have some potential

[58] See Sheets 1994: esp. 55.

[59] Ober 1994.

[60] They also refer to a *kata ton pasi nomon kathestōta* permitting the use of force in self-defense (3.56.2).

[61] Cleon similarly argues that pity and *epieikeia* are only just and appropriate toward those who can respond in kind (3.40.3).

force in interstate relations.[62] Yet expediency wins. The Plataeans are put to death because they cannot answer in the affirmative the Lacedaemonians' single question (relating to advantage)—whether they had done the Lacedaemonians and their allies anything good in the present war (3.52.3–4, 3.63.3). By the time of Thucydides' Melian debate,[63] the Athenians rule out of order pleas to justice, the gods, decency or equity, and the instability of human life; the laws of power are described in language that once belonged to the timeless, traditional, and authorless *nomoi*: "We neither enacted this *nomos* nor when it was enacted were the first to use it, but found it in existence and expect to leave it in existence for all time" (5.105, trans. Smith [1921] 1966).

In terms of justice among individuals, the Athenian democracy attempted to preserve intimacy and feeling among members of its community, by relying at all periods on private arbitration as a mode of resolving disputes among citizens. Athenian arbitrators were chosen by the parties to the dispute;[64] they had an intimate knowledge of the people and situations involved in the case, and, despite their attempt to be impartial, a personal sympathy toward them. As Aristotle points out, juries look to the law, whereas arbitrators are more able to put into practice *to epieikes* (*Rhetoric* 1.13.1374b19). Even in the lawcourts, where the larger juries prevented intimate knowledge of the litigants, character witnesses, citation of past behavior and civic benefactions, and even open pleas for pity and suppliancy were as important as the facts of the case. If the jury looked to the law and the interest of the city, it did not lose sight of the citizen. Arbitrations were not necessarily enforced or respected, aristocrats complained that juries did not offer them impartial justice in the courts, and comedy satirized the corruption of jurors and their love of power. Yet in fact it appears that recourse to illegal forms of self-help justice (the system required or permitted self-help in some cases) appears to have been rare in Athens.[65] By and large, Aristotle's plea for a contextual morality, which relies on virtue as a disposition inculcated by education and a stress on the critical role of a full knowledge of context in reaching the proper ethical decision, develops logically in a society that had not entirely outgrown its ability to adapt an archaic morality largely based on relations among (powerful) individuals to the new context of the democratic courts.

[62] See further Connor 1984: 93.

[63] In his discussion of the Corcyrean stasis later in 3.82–84, Thucydides shows that respect for suppliancy had further deteriorated. Some men were persuaded to leave a temple and were killed; those who refused to do so committed suicide.

[64] The date at which legislation was passed making an arbitrator's judgment legally binding is uncertain, but there were legally binding arbitrations before 404 B.C.E. (MacDowell 1978: 204). On the development and procedures of arbitration at Athens, see Humphreys 1983b.

[65] See Cohen 1995, Herman 1993, 1994, and 1995, and Griffith 1995. Self-help was permitted in, e.g., the case of adulterers caught in the act (see Lysias 1).

Although both Euripides' tragedy and Thucydides attempt, perhaps ten-
dentiously, to show how the pressures of war and politics erode the force of the
traditional *nomoi* both within and among cities, the process works in different
ways in the two genres. Thucydides confines himself to the public sphere and
public policy and to a secular interpretation of events. Tragic plots dissolve to
shocking effect the boundaries between public and private and divine and
human worlds, and between different modes of justice, and in so doing they
show the potential coextensivity of these worlds as well as the growing gaps between them.[66] Tragedy insists on bringing into questions of civic or international justice both pity and a detailed knowledge of the circumstances and the
characters and motives of individuals.[67] Charles Segal remarks in passing that
in *Hecuba* the standards of public policy in the assembly confront the standards
of private justice in the lawcourts.[68] The play painfully demonstrates the rift
between different ethical modes operating in two different spheres. We have
already noted the way that Hecuba's appeals to reciprocity with Odysseus and
Agamemnon counter her status as slave, foreigner, and enemy, or how Aethra,
as Theseus' mother, wins legitimacy for female advice in a public context.
Hecuba's claims to Agamemnon are all based on her status as an individual,
and as such they are perfectly legitimate: *philia* and *charis*, suppliancy, the responsibility of a family member to seek legal restitution or revenge for close kin
unjustly murdered, the appeal of slave to master for justice.[69] Yet she can only
receive what is on the private level injustice, because her pleas conflict with
the interest of the army, which defines Polymestor as a friend, even though he
is both a barbarian and the violator of *nomoi* on which Greek civilization
rested. As mentioned earlier, the conflict here between priorities of state and
family are colored in the case of Hecuba by her aristocratic rhetoric. Lurking
behind these debates, and especially behind Hecuba's appeal to personal bonds
established between herself and Odysseus and Agamemnon, are very probably
the conflicts posed to the Athenian democracy by the ritualized friendships between Athenian aristocrats and those in the upper or ruling classes of other
cities, which respected neither cultural nor ethnic boundaries.[70] Although
these friendships occasionally proved advantageous to Athens, they in fact

---

[66] Thucydides' characterization of the Plataeans, who invoke traditional claims that no longer
have weight in the context in which they find themselves, does something similar, however.

[67] Adkins 1966: 209 argues that *Hecuba* displays a new interest in motives.

[68] Segal 1993b: 211, developing Matthaei 1918, who argues that the justice of the community
here does injustice to the individual (vii). For Matthaei, tragedy defends both the individual life
and the values of the community, showing that the community may be too impersonal, the individual too limited and instinctive (148–50).

[69] On the obligation of the families of murdered kin to see that the murderer meets justice, see
Meridor 1978: 29.

[70] See Herman 1987: esp. ch. 5.

rarely coincided with the interests of the democracy: "structurally and inherently, they were opposed to them."[71]

At the same time the play challenges the relegation of Hecuba's apparently private concerns to the private sphere and the world of helpless women, slaves, or fallen aristocrats. For Hecuba wants to argue that violating traditional *nomoi* will, regardless of the particular current interest of the army, destroy civilized life and the possibility of equality (and thus, by implication, democracy itself). Hecuba's painful turn to self-help justice and a violent revenge when her plea for justice fails demonstrates the implications of these very claims.[72] The Melians make a similar point about the violation of traditional *nomoi* (Thucydides 5.90) when they argue that it is useful if a party in danger has something to which to appeal even if its arguments are not rigorously compelling.[73] The balance of power may someday reverse. And indeed, both the Sicilian expedition and, in *Hecuba*, the prophecy of Agamemnon's own future murder by Clytemnestra, which will demand an act of vendetta justice comparable with Hecuba's, show that this reversal can lurk, both in play and reality, in the not-so-distant future.

[71] Herman 1987: 142. Pearson 1962: 144, on the other hand, argues that *Hecuba* is concerned with the kind of "misapplied *charis*" ("the disaster that comes when favours are wrongly asked and given and returned") particularly common in democracies. On aristocratic ethics in *Hecuba*, see most recently, Stanton 1995.

[72] Gregory 1991: 108 argues that the play reverses the plot of the *Oresteia*; vendetta returns when the appeal to institutional justice fails. Despite Hecuba's abuse of *xenia* and the killing of Polymestor's innocent children (see Hogan 1972a: 254, Thalmann 1993: 149 n. 61), I have deliberately refrained from further judgment of Hecuba's revenge. It is very difficult to gauge the affect of a revenge tragedy on a highly competitive culture, even if competition and revenge were largely pursued by legal means (see esp. Adkins 1960: 55, Meridor 1978, Heath 1987: 65, Kovacs 1987: esp. 99, Gregory 1991: 94 and 110–12, Mossman 1995, Cohen 1995, and Burnett 1998). The final shift of wind after the trial may hint at divine support of Hecuba (Kovacs 1987: 105). Even Hecuba's final metamorphosis into a dog remains an ambiguous sign (see Gellie 1980: 40, Meridor 1978: 34, Collard 1991: 197, Burnett 1994: esp. 160–62 and 1998: 172–76, and Zeitlin 1991). Zeitlin 1991: 82–83 may be correct that the critical obsession with judging Hecuba is misguided; she is in any case the only "standard bearer for an objective moral order" in the play; Burnett 1998: 159 and 166–72 sees Hecuba and the Trojan women as the locus of civilized values. In the view of several critics, the godless and amoral Greeks and their ambivalent leaders play a critical role in necessitating the final tragedy (Kovacs 1987: 111); the Thracians are stereotypically negative barbarians, equivocal and untrustworthy (Hall 1989: 109 and Meridor 1978: 32). For Segal 1993b: 210 the play is a critique of a "world that has lost touch with basic moral values and with a language that could articulate them." For Nussbaum 1986 "deep human agreements (or practices) concerning value are the ultimate authority for moral norms" (400); the play shows that the annihilation of convention can destroy a stable character (417).

[73] On other similarities between *Hecuba* and the Melian dialogue, see Gregory 1991: 113; she interprets the play as a reflection on Athenian imperialism and the relations between the powerful and the powerless (85). Hogan 1972 stresses the similarities between the issues in *Hecuba* and the episode with the Plataeans in Thucydides 3 discussed earlier.

Phoenissae similarly blurs the boundaries between modes of resolving disputes among kin normally resolved by arbitration or the lawcourts and issues of public policy. Within families, inheritance was shared equally by all sons. Jocasta extends this (democratic) policy to the state and naturalizes it. Similarly, *Suppliants* links Theseus' pity for and piety toward a parent, a virtue generally practiced in the private sphere, with his public acceptance of the suppliants (here we can contrast Creon in *Antigone*). As with *Hecuba*, the intermingling of personal and public spheres creates a critical interaction between diverging and sometimes contradictory ethical standards that have in the course of the late fifth century become characteristic of each sphere, and demonstrates the dangers of a leakage of wartime or imperial values into civic and domestic life (see esp. Thucydides 3.82–84 on the Corcyrean revolution). Eteocles' argument that injustice is most noble in pursuit of power, although one ought to be pious in relation to everything else (*Phoenissae* 524–25), for example, echoes the kind of arguments made in Thucycides for Athenian imperialism.

Although in reality men as well as women were victims of a breakdown of traditional law in the later years of the war, Euripides' tragedy apparently aims to highlight the effects of a political ethics based on self-interest or advantage by putting a defense of tradition into the mouths of the categorically weak and innocent women, and by making its violators men concerned with issues of power and expediency.[74] Although the funeral oration claims a place for traditional *nomoi* in the world of war and the assembly, in situations where women defend traditional *nomoi* in conflict with men, they can bring to the unwritten laws things otherwise linked with themselves in Greek literature and thought: nature, pity, religion, or the private world. Yet in contrast to Tronto's claim about the eighteenth century, the positions adopted by these tragic mothers are by no means linked only with the private world or with sentiment rather than reason. Instead, as often in tragedy, these Euripidean women occupy a mediating position between public and private worlds. As mothers and citizens, they have children and freedom to lose in the face of war, and thus their lives are more clearly and self-consciously tied than those of some of the tragic virgins to the fortunes of the state. Age and maternal suffering have given them a broader, if limited wisdom. Although recognizing the risks that defending the suppliants may entail, Aethra's plea to Theseus heroically denies her interest as a mother and Praxithea in *Erectheus* gives an entirely public definition to motherhood, claiming that she bore children to protect the state and the altars of the gods (50.14–15 Austin), and hence she must sacrifice children of both sexes for these ends. These mothers emphasize the role of civic concerns and general principles far more than the tragic virgins Antigone and Electra,

[74] Comedy does this quite openly. Women in Aristophanes advocate peace, Panhellenism, or communism against war-obsessed or selfish men. In *Acharnians*, Dikaiopolis is willing to share his private peace only with a new bride who wants her husband to stay at home—because women are not to blame for war (1059–62).

whose horizons are more limited, although they never lose sight of the emotional and familial implications of their positions.[75]

The speech of women has no formal status or authority in the *polis*. We saw this reflected in the inability of Jocasta in the arbitration scene of *Phoenissae* to make her judgment binding on her sons. Hecuba does defend her cause publicly and successfully but will lose her ability to speak (if not to sign in her role as beacon) once changed into a dog.[76] After Aethra's departure, women's speech is ignored or problematized in the later scenes of *Suppliants* (see part I). Similarly the traditional, ancestral *nomoi* make claims, especially on the international level, that cannot be reliably enforced. We have seen that the link with women gives to these traditional laws a secondary and fragile status in relation to the hegemonic democratic discourse of the army and assembly (*Hecuba*), the politics of interstate relations (*Suppliants*), or the politics of power (*Phoenissae*). The traditional *nomoi*, with their reputed origins in the divine, in nature, or in traditions common to all Greeks offer a weak refuge from relativity or the sophists. Like the women who defend them in these Euripidean plays, they rely above all on persuasion. In these plays the ethical views of those in power continue to have more weight in practice, yet are inadequate to the demands of both an ideal morality and to the tragic instability of human fortunes. Euripides' tragic mothers are there to demonstrate this point.

[75] The psychological dimension of this dramatic representation of mothers remains beyond the scope of this book.

[76] On the silencing of Hecuba, see Rabinowitz 1993: 109. Yet as Burnett 1994 and 1998: 172–76 shows, her transformation into a dog may well be less important than her role as beacon for sailors at the opening of the Bosporus.

Part IV

ANODOS DRAMAS: EURIPIDES'
ALCESTIS AND *HELEN*

> The finding of an object is in fact
> the refinding of it.
> (*Freud,* Three Essays on the Theory of Sexuality)

Homer's *Odyssey* bestows on Penelope *kleos*, the immortal fame conferred by epic poetry, for her chastity and her brilliance in devising the stratagem of the web (2.125 and 24.196–97, *kleos . . . aretēs*). At the same time the poem pointedly contrasts the heroine's creative fidelity to her husband with the adultery and treachery of Clytemnestra and (more discreetly) Helen. Attic tragedy, apparently preferring to dramatize the Clytemnestras over the Penelopes,[1] rarely pronounces women worthy of an eternal reputation for *aretē* (virtue or excellence) that even in epic is largely reserved for men. Euripidean drama awards *kleos* to its sacrificial virgins, like Iphigeneia at Aulis, who die to preserve family, state, or nation, although even here the ironic context in which such sacrifices often occur partially undercuts the heroic gesture. Considerably rarer in drama is the adult woman who, like Penelope, acts to secure her husband's survival and wins a glorious reputation in her private capacity as wife. Alcestis and Helen are in fact our only extant examples—and in Helen's case what she achieves is above all (or, perhaps, at best) an escape from *duskleia* (ill repute).[2]

Although Odysseus compares Penelope to a king who has won *kleos* for his good rule (19.108), Penelope insists that her *kleos* would be greater and fairer if Odysseus were present (18.255). The *Odyssey* is similarly careful throughout to insist that Penelope's reputation for excellence, like the mind of the ideal wife (6.181–84), complements that of her husband rather than undercutting or surpassing it. (For detailed discussion of Penelope as wife and moral agent, see III.1). Euripides, on the other hand, presents a virtuous Alcestis and Helen whose reputation for excellence threatens to overshadow or to compromise permanently that of their respective spouses. Although it comes as no surprise that tragedy should rework an epic story pattern to emphasize sexual tensions that remain largely implicit in Homer[3] and to devalue for its democratic audi-

This chapter is a revised version of Foley 1992. Earlier versions of the original article benefited from the comments of audiences at the December 1987 American Philological Association meeting in New York, at University of Pennsylvania, and at UCLA. I wish to thank the following for their detailed comments and suggestions: Erwin Cook, Duncan Foley, Richard Seaford, Daniel Selden, Christian Wolff, and the anonymous referee for *Innovations of Antiquity*. The following relevant discussions were published after Foley 1992: Austin 1994, Holmberg 1995, Juffras 1993, Luschnig 1995, Meltzer 1994, O'Higgins 1993, Pucci 1997, Rabinowitz 1993, Segal 1993a and b, Rehm 1994, and Wohl 1998.

[1] See Aristophanes' *Thesmophoriazusae* 545–48 on this failing of Euripides.

[2] See *Helen* 135 (*aischron . . . kleos*) and 1506 (*duskleian*); *Alcestis* 623 and 938. Alcestis' deed will make the reputation (in her case, *eukleia*) of all women fairer; she thus reverses (as Penelope could not) the infamy Clytemnestra bestowed on her sex at *Odyssey* 24.199–202. For the reputation won by sacrificial virgins, see Euripides' *Iphigeneia at Aulis* 1383, 1504 (also 1440) and *Heracleidae* 534. Medea, by contrast, pursues a masculine-style victory over her enemies (*Medea* 810).

[3] The relation between Helen and Menelaus in *Odyssey* 4 or between Helen and the Trojans

ence the *kleos* won by a traditional archaic hero,[4] the dynamics of Euripides' play with male and female reputation need closer examination.[5] It is curious to find tragedy publicly celebrating the courage and ingenuity of married women before a society that did not include the possibility of a public reputation for virtue in its definition of the ideal wife (dead wives could be celebrated in funeral epitaphs). Pericles, in speaking of feminine *aretē* in his funeral oration, for example, paradoxically asserts that the greatest *kleos* will belong to the widow who is least talked of among the men, whether for good or for bad (Thucydides 2.45). Although both plays draw on a range of mythical story patterns and activities associated both in literature and reality with women and, in particular, women's significant role in Greek rituals and cults, they do not aim primarily to promote iconoclasm concerning Attic society's evaluation of women and their capacities. Instead, as in the other plays studied in this book, they modify traditional sex roles to explore symbolically a broad set of contemporary political, religious, and social issues. Both plays confront simultaneously contradictions and problems in the marital system and with masculine identity, including male public roles in war or in host-guest relations.

Defining *Anodos* Drama

In this chapter I shall borrow the term "*anodos* drama" from Jean-Pierre Guépin to describe those Euripidean plays—*Alcestis, Helen,* and *Iphigeneia among the Taurians* are the three extant examples—that are plotted against the mythical story pattern most familiar both to ourselves and, I think, to the Athenian audience, in the story of the rape and descent (*kathodos*) of the goddess Kore/Persephone and her subsequent ascent (*anodos*) to the upper world.[6] In the well-known version of the Kore myth represented in the Homeric *Hymn to Demeter*, the virgin Kore/Persephone is abducted by Hades, the god of the underworld. The goddess of grain, Demeter, wins her daughter's return to the

---

in the *Iliad* is uneasy but not openly hostile; Clytemnestra's adultery alone is singled out for direct criticism. Even in the *Odyssey* Penelope's fidelity stands out in implicit contrast to other contemporary poetic traditions in which she was unfaithful. Odysseus takes his time about testing the virtue of his wife before he reveals his identity, and the poem occasionally allows its audience to wonder about Penelope's behavior (e.g., when, shortly after Odysseus' arrival in disguise as a beggar, she displays herself to the suitors to acquire gifts; see further III.1). For the phenomenon in tragedy generally, see, with further bibliography, Foley 1981.

[4] Recent criticism of tragedy, and above all the work of Jean-Pierre Vernant, has emphasized the ambivalent relation between tragedy, the public literature of a democratic *polis*, and epic, which celebrates the glory of the individual aristocratic warrior. See esp. Vernant 1981: 6–27 and 1970: 273–95.

[5] Meltzer 1994 has expanded on my 1992 discussion of *kleos* in Helen.

[6] Guépin 1968: esp. 120–33 and 137–42 and Lattimore 1964: 53. Further refinements on the pattern are my own.

world above by withdrawing fertility from the earth and thus threatening humankind with extinction. Because she ate a pomegranate seed in the world below, Persephone must live one-third of her existence with her husband; but in compensation for her stay among the dead, she receives new honors in her role as queen of the underworld. As a result of her experience, Demeter establishes on earth the Eleusinian Mysteries, which promise to initiates a better lot after death. The story of Persephone also became paradigmatic in Greek art, literature, and in some cults relating to marriage: for the mortal bride, marriage is a symbolic death transitional to a new role in another household.[7]

In these three plays of Euripides a heroine who has been abducted into a world of literal or symbolic death is rescued and brings with her return to civilization a mitigation of past suffering and destruction. As in the divine story of the two goddesses, the fortunate denouement of these tragedies brings with it a modified perspective on the relation among gods, men, and the world of death. As in the case of Kore, the plays also promise each female protagonist an immortal reputation through the establishment of a cult in her honor. Yet Euripides' *Helen* and *Alcestis* make the striking gesture of adapting what was in the divine version of the *anodos* story pattern a case of violent abduction, loss of virginity, and entry into maturity to the experience of a *married* (yet, as we shall see, simultaneously young and virginal) woman who is forcibly removed from her private domestic world, but finally achieves a reunion or symbolic *remarriage* with her spouse.[8]

In order to comprehend better the way that these plays manipulate gender relations to examine a series of larger social and philosophical issues, especially questions relating to mortality and reputation, this essay begins by looking at the *anodos* story pattern and its function in *Alcestis* and *Helen*, placing special emphasis on the way that allusions to marriage and funerary ritual and to cult enrich the authority of this mythic pattern in its human context. It then examines the way that Admetus and Menelaus come to share with their wives the story pattern's symbolic experience of death and loss of previous identity followed by a return to a renewed marriage and reputation. Returning to the issue of male and female reputation with which it began, it places particular emphasis on the way in which the wife secures a full recognition in cult that she cannot attain as mortal wife without compromising the reputation of her spouse. As in the case of Penelope, these wives make active and celebrated choices in defense of marriage and family, even, as in Helen's case, in the ab-

---

[7] See Foley 1994: esp. 81–82 for further discussion and bibliography.

[8] On her return to earth and Olympus, Kore becomes once more the virgin daughter of her mother. The heroines of these plays symbolically repeat the goddess' yearly transition from "virgin" to married woman. The *Odyssey* seems to reflect aspects of this same underlying story pattern. Like Helen and Alcestis, Penelope's youthful beauty still dazzles the suitors; after a symbolic remarriage to Odysseus, she went on in some versions to attain immortality through her marriage to Telegonus on Circe's island.

sence of her spouse. Admetus temporarily adopts the mourning role more often played by women, whereas Helen uses lamentation to rescue both herself and Menelaus (see part I). Hence both tragedies bring into play all of the topics that are central to this book—women's roles in death ritual, contradictions in the marital system, and female moral agents engaging in active, and, in this case, virtuous, ethical choices—and permit us to examine them operating in conjunction with each other.

Traditional Story Patterns in *Helen* and *Alcestis*

As many critics have pointed out, *Helen* intertwines the Kore myth with the *Odyssey*'s rewooing, recognition, and symbolic remarriage of its own long-separated spouses.[9] As in the *Odyssey*, a shipwrecked husband, disguised in rags, reencounters after a long separation his faithful, eternally lamenting wife who is besieged by an unwelcome suitor (or suitors) and beset with confusing prophecies concerning his imminent arrival; both stories include a delayed recognition between the spouses and an escape and symbolic remarriage set in motion by the ruse of the woman, but completed by the heroic violence of her spouse.[10] Like Persephone, Helen was abducted while gathering flowers (244–49, roses for Athena of the Brazen House). Although her image (*eidōlon*) brings war and destruction to Troy, Helen remains in innocent obscurity in an Egypt colored with underworld associations;[11] at the opening of the play she has taken refuge at the tomb of the former king of Egypt, Proteus. Egypt's current king Theoclymenus (whose name evokes Hades' epithets Clymenus and Periclymenus)[12] dwells in a rich (and, Menelaus hopes, hospitable) palace not un-

[9] Critics who have put particular stress on aspects of this universally accepted point are Golann 1943: 31–46; Pippin, 1960: 156; Wolff 1973: 63–64; Segal 1971: 569–73, 578, 582, 598, and 600; Hartigan 1981: 23–24 and 29; Eisner 1980: 31–37; and Seidensticker 1982: 160–61. Euripides has perhaps chosen to exploit the fact that the plots of the *Odyssey* and the Homeric *Hymn to Demeter* are built on the same traditional story patterns (Lord 1967).

[10] For other similarities, see Steiger 1908 (whose interpretation of these parallels is contested by Segal 1971 and Eisner 1980). Menelaus encounters Helen among a group of young women who have just been washing, just as Odysseus encounters Nausicaa drying her washing with her maidens. The returns of both heroes, who have each descended into some kind of Hades, are enabled by the advocacy of goddesses arguing in a divine assembly. Both heroes bathe and change their clothes before the symbolic remarriage to their wives; each recites or is asked to recite a catalog of his wanderings to his spouse. Segal and Eisner do not, however, fully confront the dramatic point made by many of these Odyssean allusions, to say nothing of the play's appropriation of the *Odyssey* as a whole. For example, why does Euripides have Helen insist that, like Penelope and Odysseus, she and Menelaus can recognize each other through certain tokens known only to the two of them (290–91), and then fail to use this device in the actual recognition scene?

[11] On this much discussed point, see esp. Bacon 1961: 137–38, Guépin 1968: 128–33, Pippin 1960: 156, Wolff 1973: 64, Iesi 1965, and Robinson 1979. Helen and Persephone are also linked in myth through an actual or attempted rape by Theseus and Perithous.

[12] See Guépin 1968: 131, Wolff 1973: 64 n. 11, and Robinson 1979: 166.

like Pluto's (69) and threatens to kill all Greeks who enter his realm. Helen is represented as a young, almost virginal[13] woman resisting threats to her chastity by Theoclymenus and even, for a comic moment, by the as yet unrecognized Menelaus.[14] The chorus compares her cries of lament to those of a nymph pursued by Pan (184–90); in her suffering Helen calls on Persephone (174–78), as Menelaus later calls on Hades (969–71). A choral ode, which details the Mother goddess' sorrow, anger, and final reconciliation with the Olympians over the rape of her daughter (1301–68), marks the moment at which Helen initiates her plan to escape from Egypt and return to her daughter Hermione at Sparta, a return permitted by the Egyptian priestess Theonoe's decision to side with Hera in her quarrel on Olympus.[15]

Extensive textual allusions to epic and to the Kore myth play no comparable role in *Alcestis*.[16] U. von Wilamowitz and other Victorian critics, who saw a divine origin for the human story in Thessalian chthonic cults of Hades and Persephone, emphasized in particular the name and characteristics of Admetus, who shares with Hades a name (Hades' epithet is *adamastos*, *Iliad* 9.158), the possession of wide realms and many cattle, and a boundless hospitality.[17] More tellingly, Alcestis' disappearance, like Persephone's, makes life in the upper world barren, whereas her return brings life and a new toleration of death. For Admetus, a life won through the sacrifice of a woman, an irreplaceable woman, is hardly worth living. In a non-Euripidean version of the myth it is thus quite appropriately Kore herself who returns Alcestis to the upper world in admiration for her courage (Apollodorus, *Bibliotheca* 1.9.15).

---

[13] She is addressed as *pai* (1356) and *neani* (1288). The scene of her abduction has specifically virginal associations, as does her return to join choruses of maidens in Sparta (1465–77) to be discussed later. In the opening scenes of the play she leads a chorus of young women in a fashion that prefigures this later role.

[14] The scene with Menelaus may be deliberately reminiscent of the scene, well known in poetry and the fine arts, of Menelaus' recovery of Helen hiding at an altar after the sack of Troy. According to the lyric poet Ibycus, Helen fled to Aphrodite's temple and conversed with Menelaus from there; he then dropped his sword from love (Scholiast on Euripides' *Andromache*, 627–31; the scene also appeared in the *Little Iliad* of Lesches). For a discussion of artistic representations of this scene, see Clément 1958.

[15] Despite controversy, scholarly opinion now generally accepts the view that the ode does refer to the Demeter-Kore myth, but assimilates elements from the cults of Cybele and Dionysus. See esp. the mistaken views of Golann 1943 and the convincing arguments of Kannicht 1969: 2: 328–33, Wolff 1973, and Robinson 1979.

[16] Garner 1988 argues that Euripides associates Alcestis' heroic death with that of the male epic heroes Hector and Patroclus through brief textual allusions to the *Iliad*. I would note, however, that the play's final allusion to the games celebrated for Patroclus (*Alcestis* 1026–34 and *Iliad* 23.257–70) makes Alcestis no longer the hero but a prize for heroes (for further implications of this point, see my subsequent argument). Bassi 1989: 25–26 notes that like male heroes Alcestis boasts of her achievement, expresses disdain for enemies (Admetus' parents), and asks for rewards worthy of her deeds. O'Higgins 1993: 91 remarks that as with Achilles, Alcestis' irreplaceability can only be recognized in her absence.

[17] See Wilamowitz-Moellendorf 1886: 67–77 and 1906: 68–69 and Séchan 1927: esp. 9–10. For further theories and references, see Lesky 1925: 5–9.

We can agree with Albin Lesky, in his effective critique of the interpretation of Wilamowitz and others,[18] that the Alcestis story does not correspond literally to the divine story of Hades and Persephone; but then neither does the plot of *Helen*, where the links between Helen's story and the Kore myth are explicit in the language of the text. Lesky's own widely accepted views on the origins of the Alcestis myth, however, throw out the baby with the bathwater. The similarities in the plots of *Helen*, *Alcestis*, *Iphigeneia among the Taurians*, and the Kore myth may well derive from a mythic story pattern that appears with important variations in Old Comedy and satyr plays (whose rescue plot has also been recently argued to derive from the mysteries by Richard Seaford),[19] or in the closely associated myths of Orpheus and Heracles (e.g., Heracles' rescue of Theseus from the underworld). In *Alcestis*, Heracles does repeat his familiar role as a boundary crosser who successfully challenges death, and the Orpheus paradigm is explicitly mentioned only to be rejected (unless, as some have thought, there was a version of the Orpheus myth in which the poet successfully rescued his wife).[20] Yet origins are only part of the issue here, and to an audience familiar with the Eleusinian mysteries and related cults like the Thesmophoria, this particular kind of plot would naturally take on affinities with the divine story pattern. In particular, both the Kore myth and these plays revolve around the successful rescue of a female protagonist from a literal or metaphorical death that brings with it a renewal of life and good fortune as well as a new divine status for its heroine. Tragic plots frequently conflate several traditional story patterns, and in my view Euripides' version of the Alcestis myth incorporates the obscure folktale elements identified by Lesky—the sacrifice of the bride and the struggle with death—to serve a more familiar and far more authoritative mythical pattern.[21] For it is precisely the link with a story

[18] Lesky 1925: esp. 7–8. Admetus is not consistently associated with Hades, because he loses his wife to death; Alcestis is rescued by Heracles, not Demeter. In one story the barrenness produced by the wife's disappearance is literal, in the other case metaphorical or psychological, and so on.

[19] Seaford 1984b: 41–42. The plots of Old Comedy and satyr plays frequently involved the rescue and return of a figure (or figures) from bondage to a monster or even from the underworld itself; Euripides appropriated the story pattern for tragicomic plays with a female protagonist. On the plots of satyr plays, see the summary by Seaford, esp. 33–38; on the affinities between *Helen*, *Iphigeneia among the Taurians*, *Alcestis*, and satyr drama, see Sutton 1972 and 1973.

[20] At 357–60 Admetus regrets that he lacks the tongue of Orpheus, by which he might secure the return of his wife (see also 966–69); in contrast to Apollodorus' version of the Alcestis story, as well as in the Orpheus myth and in the case of Heracles' rescue of Theseus, Euripides makes no mention of Persephone's permission in this play. Heracles' rescue is achieved by force, not persuasion or poetry. For a discussion of different versions of the Orpheus myth, see Graf 1987.

[21] Lesky 1925, who relies almost exclusively on non-Greek examples of these folktale patterns, would make *Alcestis* an anomalous tragedy, whereas the interpretation of Wilamowitz-Moellendorf and others assimilates the play to a familiar dramatic plot pattern. My objection to Lesky was in part anticipated by Séchan 1927: 10.

pattern familiar through its epic and dramatic variations that authorizes and makes inevitable from the beginning the untragic outcome of *Alcestis*, the "fairy tale" ending that has so disturbed some critics of the play.

My point is, then, that affinities between *Alcestis* and *Helen* and the divine *anodos* story pattern bring to each play not a scenario to imitate in any literal fashion but a set of implications and expectations that color the action and enrich its significance.[22] From a thematic perspective, for example, the *anodos* story pattern naturally takes on associations with a resistance to or modification of traditional views on mortality and reputation, though this challenge can take various forms. *Alcestis* establishes a profound link with its mythic story pattern through developing and partially resolving a tension between its miraculous plot and the normal inevitability of death,[23] whereas *Helen* exploits the Kore myth in part to serve its Odyssean attack on traditional views about heroic reputation. In the Kore myth, Demeter, unable to immortalize the baby Demophon, fails to transgress the boundaries between gods and mortals, life and death; the return of Persephone similarly promises initiates not an escape from death (though Demeter makes the resurrection of her daughter a permanent feature in the cycle of the seasons) but a better experience after death. The Mysteries thus mitigate the fear of death and make the struggle to attain an immortal reputation at least marginally less important; their benefits are both individual and communal and are dispensed without regard to sex, social status, or military prowess. In contrast to Asclepius' attempt to make a practice of resurrecting the dead (*Alcestis* 3–6, 969–72), the return of Helen and Alcestis, like that of Persephone, sets no dangerous precedents. Death remains traditionally undesirable (without the mitigation offered by the Mysteries), and reputation remains a compelling concern. Yet the experience of death, loss of reputation, and separation—inherent also in the transition experienced by every bride in marriage—modifies each husband's priorities and promises each couple "a better life than before" (*Alcestis* 1157–58).

[22] The plot of the *Iphigeneia among the Taurians* is virtually identical to that of *Helen* and is colored by many of the same affinities with the *anodos* story pattern (for the parallels between the two plots, see esp. Sutton 1972). The heroine has been transported to a land associated with Hades and its king, and her rescue (effected, as in the case of Helen, largely by devising a fictive ritual and through divine assistance) brings salvation to herself and to her brother, who can now return to rule his leaderless country. Orestes barely escapes being sacrificed in the same fashion as his sister was at an earlier date. Thus, as with Menelaus and Admetus, he echoes a female experience; is rescued by a woman; and cannot escape the past and return from the world of "death" without a specific woman/wife (here his sister/the statue of Artemis). The play similarly concludes with the establishment of a new cult—for Artemis and Iphigeneia. Iphigeneia begins and ends the play as a virgin; however, her sacrifice is represented in both Aeschylus' *Agamemnon* and Euripides' *Iphigeneia at Aulis* with marital imagery.

[23] These seemingly contradictory views of mortality in *Alcestis* have disturbed many critics. For useful recent discussions of the theme of mortality in *Alcestis*, see Nielsen 1976, Bradley 1980, and above all Gregory 1979 (revised in Gregory 1991: 19–50).

Marriage and Death

As *anodos* dramas, both *Helen* and *Alcestis* also appropriately capitalize on the similarities between marriage and funerary rites. Persephone's rape/marriage is an entry into the realm of death, and the associations between marriage and death were so powerful in Greek myth, literature, and cult that at their death both real and tragic virgins were often called brides of Hades.[24] The conclusion of the *Odyssey* plays on the association between marriage and death rites by staging a wedding ceremony to conceal both the actual death of the suitors and Penelope's symbolic remarriage to Odysseus.[25] In *Alcestis*, as Richard Buxton has argued in the greatest detail,[26] Heracles returns Alcestis to Admetus with gestures that pointedly evoke the Greek wedding rite. Admetus is made to grasp the hand of the unknown young woman with the possessive marriage gesture of *cheir epi karpō(i)*, right hand on wrist (1115); then Heracles initiates the *anakaluptēria* by unveiling Alcestis to the gaze of her husband (1121).[27]

What has not been noticed is the way that the play has visually prepared for Alcestis' symbolic remarriage with Admetus from her first appearance. We know from the language of the last scene that the veiled[28] Alcestis appears to Admetus as a beautiful and desirable young woman with an uncanny physical resemblance to his dead wife. The stranger is youthful in her *esthēti* and *kosmō(i)* (clothing and ornament, 1050), the very words used earlier by the maidservant to describe the costume Alcestis dons in preparation for her death (161, *esthēta kosmon t'*); the word *kosmos* can have both festive and funereal (see also 149, 613, 618) associations. Her form and figure are like that of Alcestis (1061–63); seeing her Admetus thinks he sees his wife (1066–67). For the last scene to work for the audience, Alcestis must wear a costume that looks suitable for a bride. Yet she must also wear the funeral dress in which she departed. Here Euripides apparently makes dramatic capital of a potential ambi-

---

[24] For an extensive recent discussion with earlier bibliography, see Seaford 1987.

[25] See now the further elaboration of Seaford 1994: 53–65. On the conflation of funeral and wedding ritual in tragedy generally, see Rehm 1994.

[26] Buxton 1987a notes the reference in the concluding scene to two aspects of the marriage rite, the *anakaluptēria* and the *cheir epi karpō(i)*. See also my own brief earlier discussion of *cheir epi karpō(i)* in Foley 1982b: 170 and Halleran 1988.

[27] Luschnig 1995: 78 argues that if Alcestis unveiled herself, as the bride can in vase paintings, the gesture would suggest her positive response to Admetus in a scene where she is otherwise silenced.

[28] See the scholiast on 1050 and Dicaearchus' hypothesis to the play. Dicaearchus emphasizes the covering (with the veil or *esthēs*) and, in manuscript LP, the uncovering of Alcestis. At the same time, the veil does not obscure the resemblance of the woman to Alcestis in form and costume. I disagree with those scholars who think that Alcestis is not veiled (see most recently Masarrachia 1992). Any respectable woman in such a context should have been veiled. But even if she is not, Admetus' recognition of this woman as his wife symbolically repeats the first glance of the couple central to the wedding ceremony.

guity between funeral and wedding attire. Although we know little about funerary dress at any period in Greece, corpses, like brides, were more often
dressed in white than black. Both might wear wreathes and fine jewelry as well
as a special *peplos*. Virgins and newly married young women could be buried in
bridal attire;[29] Evadne in Euripides' *Suppliants* dresses in wedding attire to prepare for her suicide over her husband's pyre (1054–55).[30]

Before she appears on stage, we are told that Alcestis, whose youth is repeatedly emphasized in the play despite her matronly status (see 55, 288–89,
471–72, 1050–51), has performed her own preliminaries to her funeral rite
(which are also the preliminaries to a marriage rite) by bathing, anointing, and
dressing herself, and by making dedications to the gods. Alcestis says farewell
to her home and makes a last prayer to Hestia (162–69), goddess of the hearth;
she later recalls her own wedding and laments her future absence at the wedding of her daughter (248–49, 317; see also 165–66). The Greek bride may
leave behind the Hestia cult of her father's house, a cult with which she was
intimately associated, for probable incorporation into the Hestia cult of her
husband's household.[31] Alcestis, in her vision of her coming death and of
Charon, calls attention to the journey she is about to begin as corpse (252–72,
esp. 263); the bride undertakes a similar journey into the control of an unknown male (e.g., *Iphigeneia at Aulis* 668–71).[32] Reinforcing the association
between her marriage and her death, Alcestis, immediately before her vision
of Charon, invokes the halls and bridal chambers of her original home in Iol-
cus (248–49).

In preparation for the *anakaluptēria* and *cheir epi karpō(i)* of the final scene,
the chorus and Admetus emphasize what it means not to be able to look into
the face of his wife again (876–77) or to touch her hand (917; note also the
emphasis on seeing and touching in the final scene). Admetus hovers at the
threshold to his house and recalls the joys of his former wedding, where
the crossing of the threshold is an important symbolic moment;[33] he laments
that his wedding song has turned to a *goos* (funeral lament, 922), that his bed
is empty and he now wears black clothes instead of white (923). In short—as
would be comprehensible to an audience who anticipates Alcestis' return from
the moment of her death—Alcestis' preparations for her funeral rite both ver-

[29] See Peek 1955: 1: 1238, Alexiou 1974: 5 and 206 n. 11, Seaford 1987: 107, and Garland
1985: 25. On burial dress generally, see Garland: ch. 3, esp. 24–26.

[30] See Seaford 1987: 121 and Collard 1975: 2:358.

[31] Pomeroy 1997: 70–71 questions this view. On the *katachusmata*, or rites of incorporation, and
the role of the virgin daughter in the cult of Hestia, see Vernant 1969: esp. 136, 142, and 149–52.

[32] Music and torches also accompanied both bride and corpse; the staging of Alcestis' funerary
procession might have included both elements. For general parallels between marriage and funeral
ritual, see, with further references, Redfield 1982: 188–91.

[33] See Buxton 1987a: 18 on the symbolic role of the doorway and Roberts 1978: 182 on the
ambiguity in visual representation between the wedding doorway and the portal to Hades. Similarly, the gesture of *cheir epi karpō(i)* is also used for rapes and for Hermes escorting corpses to the
world below. See Jenkyns 1983: 140–41.

bally and visually anticipate with a gradually emerging comic irony the symbolic remarriage completed in the final scene. Heracles plays the pivotal role
in converting funeral to marriage. Although Alcestis has been incorporated
into her husband's household and has become according to him a dearer relation than his own parents, Admetus soon finds himself forced to describe her
to Heracles as *othneios* (532–33; see also 646, 810–11, and *thuraios*, 778, 805,
814), a foreigner like the bride she is soon to become once more. Heracles' inappropriately festive male banquet (*thoinaō*, 542, 549) at the house of the bereaved Admetus leads directly, as in a wedding, into his inauguration, as *kurios*
(guardian) to the bride, of the *anakaluptēria*.

The curious conflation between marriage and funeral rite that we also find
in the concluding scene of *Helen* is made especially vivid by the contrasting
costumes of the spouses in each play. In the final scene of *Alcestis*, Admetus
wears black and Alcestis is dressed suitably for both corpse and bride (she has
been for most of the play quite literally in a state between death and life). In
Helen, the lamenting Helen wears shorn hair and black robes while the freshly
bathed and newly attired Menelaus appears the groom to be. The couple's marriage has earlier been twice recalled (638–43, 722–25); now, under cover of
the fictive funeral rite for Menelaus and of false preparations for a marriage to
Theoclymenus, Menelaus will abduct his bride (911, *apolazusthai*, and 1374,
anerpasen')[34] and renew the couple's married life in Sparta. Yet Helen's dress
may well have the same ambiguity as Alcestis'; her funeral rite for Menelaus
may evoke aspects of the Spartan marriage rite. Here the bride was also married by *harpagē* (abduction); a young woman in her full bloom, she cut her hair
(also a funerary gesture), disguised herself, and lay in the dark awaiting a groom
dressed, like Menelaus, in normal clothing (Plutarch, *Lycurgus* 15.3–5).[35] The
final exit of Helen and Menelaus thus repeats their original nuptial departure.[36] Here both plays exploit the symbolic similarities, noted by anthropologists cross-culturally, between marriages and funerals as rites of transition. For
just as death is a passage to a new state, marriage is for the woman a symbolic
death transitional to a new life in another household.[37]

Symbolic Death and Rebirth

In both *Helen* and *Alcestis* the male protagonists follow the lead of their wives
in experiencing the *anodos* story pattern: each undergoes a symbolic or living
death before reemerging into a new life, identity, and prosperity.[38] Early in the

---

[34] See the similar vocabulary used for the abduction of Helen by Hermes (247) and Paris (50).
The departure is an abduction because of Theoclymenus' opposition.

[35] See Wolff 1973: 67 n. 17.

[36] Pippin 1960: 155.

[37] See van Gennep [1909] 1960. On the issue in Greek literature and culture, see esp., Foley
1982b, Jenkyns 1983: esp. 142, and Alexiou and Dronke 1971.

[38] Downing 1990: 7 notes that Teucer has similar experiences to those of Helen and Menelaus.

play Alcestis enters the realm of death; before the play opens the misunderstood Helen has suffered many years of obscurity in the deathlike world of Egypt and her initial exchange with the chorus draws pointedly on the language and tradition of lamentation (164–251). Arriving in Egypt, the shipwrecked Menelaus falls unwittingly into the power of a figure symbolically associated with Hades who threatens him with destruction. Similarly, Admetus wins through Alcestis' sacrifice not an escape from death but a life worse than death (863–71, 939–40, 960–61)—an existence to be marked by no marriage, festivity, or social intercourse, but by endless mourning and the cold embraces of a statue of his former wife.

Admetus and Menelaus both temporarily suffer in their symbolic encounter with a world of death a partial loss of their previous heroic and/or masculine identity and reputation. In this respect their experience echoes that of Odysseus, who entered the underworld and then suffered for a time obscurity and enforced passivity on the island of Calypso.[39] Menelaus loses his former identity as king and successful warrior at Troy. At his entrance he is worsted and humiliated by a slave porteress, who refuses to see through his rags to his essential nobility and has no interest in his Trojan reputation. In Egypt all Greeks are the same, and king Theoclymenus will sacrifice, rather than entertain, any Greek that he discovers. Not only is Menelaus' former reputation compromised by the discovery that the ten-year venture at Troy was fought for a phantom, but he finds himself in a world in which the war and his role in it has lost its former significance. His attempts to invoke his former glory or to escape his predicament by relying on his Trojan prowess repeatedly prove (until the final battle with the Egyptians on shipboard) not only fruitless but at some points almost ludicrous.[40] He (again like Odysseus) is forced instead to rely on supplication (1083–86)—a mode of behavior he explicitly views as apt for women and not for men (825–31)—as well as the plans, persuasive speeches, and favors of women. Helen initiates the escape plan; it is her speech, not Menelaus' forceful blustering, that decisively persuades Theonoe to side with the couple.[41] This plan entails imagining that Menelaus has died unheroically; like Helen, he is temporarily the victim of a false reputation.

[39] Helen has also lost her true identity, only in her case she wishes to replace the public lie with the hidden and private truth. The dead Alcestis is in a different situation. Like all the dead, she has undergone a change of state; but in the world above she has acquired an immortal reputation for her courage. On these aspects of the *Odyssey*, see Foley 1978.

[40] Menelaus is Odysseus' unintelligent double here (Arnott 1990: 14). Menelaus' first appearance on stage has the dramatic effect of a second beginning with its own prologue, because the chorus has unexpectedly left the stage with Helen (Arnott, 12–13). The comic tone of this entrance almost puts the hero into a different and less serious generic milieu from which he must be rescued by his wife.

[41] The only argument Menelaus puts forward that proves persuasive to Theonoe was already introduced by Helen; his plans for escape are also shown to be useless. Holmberg 1995 expands on this point; because Helen's plans work, she can control her story in a fashion that her epic predecessors, Helen and Penelope, could not.

Similarly Admetus, earning through Alcestis' sacrifice the reputation of cowardice, will be cut off from the hospitality that won him fame and divine favor. He will be comfortable neither outside nor inside of his house (941–61), a house degenerating into domestic disorder due to the absence of its mistress (944–50).[42] For although Alcestis died to preserve her household and the future of her children, Admetus now comes to recognize (940, *arti manthanō*), as Alcestis' son and the servants confirm, that the identity and security of the household now rests less on himself than on Alcestis (see 414–15, 879–80). Just as Menelaus is returned to a fortunate existence in Greece largely through the help of Theonoe and Helen, Admetus is rescued from misery and a lost reputation by Heracles and his wife's return.

In these plays, then, husband and wife both come to experience the "death"/change of identity initially suffered by the wife and then share in a rescue/return to marriage and a new existence characteristic of the *anodos* story pattern. Nevertheless, whereas the *anodos* story pattern, like marriage itself, entails a radical and permanent change in the status and reputation of the woman who experiences it, Menelaus and Admetus, in ways to be discussed shortly, eventually regain their former reputations for military glory and hospitality and return to live out lives that precisely reflect the cultural status quo.

Spousal Reputation

Helen and *Alcestis* do more than enact the education of their male protagonists through their experience of loss of identity/death and return, however. For Euripides seems in these plays to be experimenting, along the lines of the Kore myth and the *Odyssey*, with allowing a wife to win a *kleos* of her own. Although the Athenian wife was ideally confined to chastity and silence in the interior of her household (her role in ritual represents the important exception), unusual circumstances force Alcestis and Helen to seek or to protect a public reputation as an ideal wife. The plays deliberately exploit this implicit tension between fiction and reality, for in each case the reputation sought and/or achieved by the virtuous wife creates—contrary to the wife's intent—embarrassment for the husband and, in the case of *Alcestis*, the threat of a permanent imbalance in the traditional relationship between the sexes.[43]

---

[42] G. Smith 1983: 129–45, esp. 136–40, stresses that Admetus comes to recognize that a living Alcestis is more valuable than a wife who will die for him.

[43] By engaging in what is initially a female experience, both in the plot of the plays and in the *anodos* story pattern and cults associated with it, Menelaus and Admetus enter into a context in which a temporary modification of traditional gender roles and relations can quite naturally take place. Hippolytus in Euripides' *Hippolytus* and Pentheus in Euripides' *Bacchae* similarly undergo an experience that is socially and ritually female, but here the consequences are disastrous and permanent. On *Hippolytus*, see Zeitlin 1985b. Temporary sex role reversals were a common feature of Greek initiation rituals generally, although in the case of marriage (as in Sparta) the role reversals usually involved women taking on attributes of men.

Alcestis' selfless sacrifice ironically puts Admetus' reputation in jeopardy, as the hero himself realizes in the aftermath of his humiliating argument with his father Pheres (704–5; 939–40, 952–61).[44] In contrast to Admetus, Alcestis has in her remarkable onstage, highly public death scene displayed far more courage and acceptance of mortality than her spouse;[45] Pheres sees Admetus as bested (*essēmenos*) in courage by his heroic wife (696–98). Having made her own feminine version of the epic choice for death with fame over an inglorious life without (323–25), Alcestis will be *eukleēs* (famous, 938) and her husband can boast that he took the best of wives (323–24), whereas Admetus faces a *lupron . . . bioton* (painful life, 940) of permanent and excessive mourning (a role more suitable for a woman because a mourner is isolated from normal and public existence).[46] Alcestis will thus usurp the male role of protecting the reputation of the house while Admetus will feel alienated from every social role normal for men. When Admetus insists that the *othneios* Alcestis has become for him a replacement for father and mother (646–47), he reminds his audience that he has become an Andromache to Alcestis' Hector at *Iliad* 6.429–30. Intending to assuage Admetus' grief, the chorus announces Alcestis' future celebration in song and her coming worship as a heroine. She has already gained the status, the chorus claims, of a *makaira daimōn* (blessed spirit, 1003; she will also be addressed as *potnia*, divine mistress, 1004); her tomb will not be treated as belonging to a dead person, but viewed as divine (995–99). She will also be perpetually celebrated in song both at the Carneian festival in Sparta and in Athens (445–54). The important Carneian festival for Apollo was said to involve a "copy of the soldierly way of life" and included musical contests, choral dances for youth and maidens, and foot races;[47] hence Alcestis takes a prominent place with her husband in the sphere of Apollo and becomes part of a context linked with heroic male prowess and youthful initiation.[48] With this announcement, then, the chorus unwittingly increases Admetus' humiliation.

[44] Both Lloyd 1985: esp. 121 and Dyson 1988: 15 stress the richness of the life Alcestis has given up, in contrast to Euripides' other sacrificial victims.

[45] The other notable onstage death (but see also the fragmentary *Niobe* of Sophocles) is that of Sophocles' *Ajax*. As Chalkia 1983 stresses, Alcestis' heroic public death, unusual for a woman, and her occupation of space outside the house contrast with Admetus' equally anomalous move toward future confinement within the household. On Admetus' behaviour in this scene, see Bradley 1980: 115–16 and Smith 1960: 130–31. As Smith remarks (131) what Admetus finds notable in Alcestis' death is his own suffering.

[46] The chorus implies repeatedly that Admetus' mourning may be excessive (416–19, 891–94, 903–11, 931–33). Funeral lamentation was above all a female role and province; in this play, however, Alcestis only weeps in private. Rivier 1973: 135 notes that Admetus gets his mourning formulas slightly wrong in Alcestis' death scene by ignoring its uniqueness. His exaggerated vows of fidelity are not required by his wife (see further Michelini 1987: 329). For additional discussion of mourning in *Alcestis*, see now Segal 1993b: 51–72. He stresses that tragedy permits men to act out fear, grief, and anxiety about the body and loss of emotional control in ways not normally permitted to them (71).

[47] Burkert 1985: 234–36.

[48] Although virtually nothing is known about the actual cult of Alcestis (see Wide [1893] 1973:

Alcestis seems finally to resolve the tensions created by this paradoxical contrast between the humiliating living death of Admetus and the eternal *kleos* of Alcestis, partly by gradually undermining the value of Alcestis' heroic sacrifice to Admetus,[49] and partly by returning Alcestis to relative anonymity as Admetus' wife—for his lifetime—in the concluding scene. For Admetus, unable despite his promises to Alcestis to abandon the male role of dispenser of hospitality that won him fame,[50] regains his former life and reputation with the return of a silent Alcestis, an Alcestis defined by Heracles as a prize (*nikētēria*, 1028, and *kerdos*, 1033, as she was when Admetus first won her from her father) and a servant (*prospolein*, 1024) who, like a proper Athenian wife, silently disappears into the interior over which she formerly presided with such perfection. Admetus' symbolic gesture of *cheir epi karpō(i)* puts his wife once more under the domination of the husband. The *anakaluptēria* allowed the bride and groom to look at each other's faces for the first time;[51] but the moment may also have permitted their first exchange of speech. The wedding gifts presented at the *anakaluptēria* were called both *optēria, theōrētra*, and *athrēmata*, gifts of the look, and *prosphthengktēria*, gifts of addressing one another.[52] Pherecydes (fragment 7 [B] 2 Diels-Kranz) gives an etiology for the *anakaluptēria* that in-

---

356), we have no definite evidence that Euripides invented it. For this reason, and because Greek literature elsewhere makes Alcestis the paradigm of wifely virtue and courage, the promise of a cult to Alcestis after her death will not be permanently undermined by her temporary return to life at the end of Euripides' play. Nevertheless, in contrast to *Helen*, the conclusion of *Alcestis* deemphasizes the future cult status of its heroine, and male concerns over hospitality take the center stage. Yet Segal 1993b: 47 argues that "the true monument to Alcestis' glory is not the epitaph on the tomb but the play that denies that there is a tomb." The honor of the tomb is replaced by the "enacted commemoration of the play."

[49] On this point, see esp. G. Smith 1983: 134–35, Gregory 1979: 265, Beye 1959: esp. 115, 119, 121, and 124, and Erbse 1972; Masarrachia 1993 sees this failure as an attack on epic heroism and sacrifice. For Wohl 1998: 137 Alcestis' preservation of the *oikos* and patrilineal succession and her redemption of marriage is the root of Admetus' problem.

[50] By admitting Heracles into his house, Admetus renegs on his promise to put an end to revelry in his house (343–44), although he does not participate in it himself; by accepting the unknown woman in a context so suggestive of marriage, he is well on his way to breaking his vow not to remarry (see the influential article of von Fritz 1962). O'Higgins 1993: 83 thinks that Admetus' ban on music indirectly challenges the future *kleos* of Alcestis in song. Halleran 1988: 129 remarks on the double irony of accepting a woman into the house who is in fact his wife. Some critics (especially those who delete lines 1119–20—but see the recent critique of this position by Halleran 1988: 123–34) argue that Admetus does not violate this second promise, however. In their view Admetus does not actually take in a second wife in bowing to the demands of friendship; he could not marry a woman entrusted to him by Heracles (see esp. Lloyd 1985: 127–29 and Dyson 1988: 22). Furthermore, his reception of Heracles ultimately leads to the rescue of Alcestis.

[51] Halleran 1988: 124 notes that a double *antilabē* at 390–91 and 1119–20 twice accompanies the theme of looking in the play (390 and 1121), and links Alcestis' death scene with her return.

[52] See Pollux' *Onomasticon* 3.36 on *prosphthengktēria*. For a brief discussion of these aspects of the *anakaluptēria*, see Armstrong and Ratchford 1985: 9.

cludes a greeting by the god Zas to his divine bride Chthonie, followed by a response from the bride. After the unveiling, Admetus asks Heracles if he can address his wife; encouraged by Heracles, he tells Alcestis of his unexpected joy at seeing her face (literally, *omma* or eye) and form (1131–34). Yet the play does not allow its heroine to complete the exchange of words with her husband apparently permitted by the normal ritual; for it is not *themis* (lawful) for Admetus to hear the words of Alcestis for three days (1144–46).[53]

At the end of *Alcestis*, the heroine is silenced (on stage if not for life) and passively rescued by and for a man;[54] at least for her lifetime her story is in some sense not only experienced but finally appropriated by her husband. The initial choral promise to Alcestis of eternal fame and a cult for her courageous sacrifice was an established part of her mythical tradition, but this promise is far from an audience's mind in the concluding scene. The later *Helen* allows its heroine a far more active role in educating and rescuing her husband that surpasses even that permitted to her literary model Penelope; for it is Helen who, in order to regain her reputation as innocent and faithful wife, insists on recognition from Menelaus, initiates the deception that ensures their departure, persuades the priestess Theonoe to protect them, and tricks the Egyptian king Theoclymenus. Menelaus defeats the Egyptians as Helen—unlike Penelope, an active witness to the bloodshed—cheers her husband on. Furthermore, it is Helen whose reputation, as we shall see in more detail shortly, receives at the close of the play both a divine defense and a lavish recognition from Theoclymenus.

As Jean-Pierre Vernant in particular has pointed out, the Greek wife is threatening precisely because she must be both sexual and chaste.[55] Paradoxically, he argues, without experiencing sexuality, she cannot produce children; but once she has experienced it, she no longer has reliably the perfect chastity also required of the wife. *Helen* confronts this ambivalent nature of the wife in the person of the most notorious of all wives, Helen. It begins by splitting the chaste (virginal) and the adulterous (sexual) wife into the actual Helen and deceptive *eidōlon*. But the recognition of the real Helen by Menelaus does not

---

[53] On the possible ritual motives for Alcestis' silence here, see Betts 1965, Trammell 1968, Parker 1983: 61 n. 2, and Buxton 1987a: 22. The parallel examples come from situations in which the corpse has been inhumed, however, whereas in *Alcestis* the corpse was apparently burned on a pyre (608, 740). In the deviant *anakaluptēria* of Alcestis, Admetus also resists looking at Alcestis as he reaches for her hand (1117–18).

[54] Feminist readings of this silence tend to be pessimistic. See esp. Bassi 1989: 28, O'Higgins 1993, esp. 78, Rabinowitz 1993: esp. 72 and 93, and Wohl 1998. For a modern audience these aspects of the play are certainly highly problematic; Wohl 1998: 157 seems correct that the play could not tolerate the inclusion of Alcestis' voice (which might expose Admetus and reveal secrets of death) in the final scene. Yet in the original context this conclusion had, I think, different connotations.

[55] Vernant 1969. See also Rabinowitz 1993: esp. 67–69, 98–99 on Alcestis' supposed threatening sexuality in the play.

at once restore, as she hopes, Helen's true *kleos*. Troy cannot be dismissed so quickly as a cruel trick of the gods, for it was an event experienced by mortals as a terrible and destructive reality. Helen seems content for the world to view her as the faithful wife who never went to Troy, a woman who had no story beyond that of virtuous wife; she is even willing to mar her famous beauty or sacrifice her life to escape her Trojan reputation.[56] The chorus of women, affirming Helen's own regrets about the public and private disasters her beauty has caused, underlines the play's reevaluation of the Trojan experience with its own meditations on the futility of war (see esp. 1107–64).

The disappearance of the *eidōlon* prevents Menelaus from exercising his announced preference for his Trojan *ponoi* (labors) over the apparently innocent Helen (593). Nevertheless, the innocent Helen poses a problem for Menelaus, who continues to resist returning to Sparta simply as the man who fought a needless war for an illusion. Dressed finally in noble clothing rather than rags, he must reestablish his former reputation by reenacting his Trojan victory, this time for an innocent Helen. Helen once more (but here deceptively) promises her favors to a barbarian, in this case to Theoclymenus rather than to Paris, and cheers Menelaus on to a dubious victory against unarmed barbarians.[57] Her brilliant fictional rite again turns her into a commodity to be exchanged among men by abduction, and in fashioning her escape she reproduces, despite her innocence, the seductiveness and destructiveness of her rejected alter ego.

Helen's attempt to achieve survival and a happy private life after "death" in Egypt through persuasion, intelligence, and ritual is associated in the play with its Odyssean critique of the Iliadic tradition and with the *anodos* story pattern. Helen wins her return to Sparta through the performance of a fictive *ritual* she has invented: a false funeral that is actually an escape from death and a symbolic remarriage with Menelaus (as in the Kore myth, between a "raped" wife and a "dead" lord). Relying on the beneficence of the gods and Theonoe as well as their own ingenuity, Helen and Menelaus supplicate and persuade the priestess both to maintain the silence that will allow their escape and to side with the goddess Hera, who favors Helen's return. Pippin argues that Theonoe plays the role of "a demythologized Demeter, offering, in her religion of justice and

---

[56] Helen repeatedly laments the effects of her beauty, to the point that she would prefer metamorphosis into a beast (the price paid for beauty and rape in many Greek myths) to survival in her present situation (375–85; see also 260–66). For Helen to abandon her beauty, as she does when she cuts off her hair and furrows her face with nail marks to mourn Menelaus, is virtually equivalent, in the eyes of the world, to abandoning her identity. Wolff 1973: 71 notes that Helen's appearance in mourning immediately follows the ode in which Helen is accused of neglecting the cult of Demeter and trusting too much in her beauty (1353–68). Notice Theoclymenus' amusing concern that Helen not carry her disfigurement too far (1285–87, 1419). On her willingness to commit suicide, see 350–59, 835–42.

[57] On the possible ironies and ambiguities in this scene, where the new Helen assimilates the Trojan Helen, see esp. Wolff 1973: 72 and 81–82, Segal 1971: 606–7, and Papi 1987: 35–37 and 40.

the immortal *gnōmē*, the philosophical counterpart of the Eleusinian promise, but adding the threat of punishment";[58] others have linked Theonoe with the virgin goddess Athena.[59] As we shall see in more detail shortly, the play seems to link the innocent Helen with Penelope, Kore, and future honors for Helen in ritual. Echoing the pattern of the Kore myth, Helen's sojourn in Egypt begins with her abduction by Hermes into a symbolic death as she plucks flowers in virginal fashion for Athena and ends with her restored family life and her rejoining of Spartan maidens in cults that will, again in a parallel fashion to the Kore myth,[60] play a role in the transition to marriage and fertility of young Spartan women.

Yet Helen's attempt to return to Sparta and to transform her epic reputation by nonviolent and religious means stands in tension at the end of the play with a return to an emphasis on a public display of masculine virtue that we find also in Odysseus' violent slaughter of the suitors and Admetus' (seemingly treacherous) adherence to hospitality. The *Iliad* can offer to its hearers no mitigation of mortality but the *kleos* won above all by public success (especially a glorious death) that is celebrated in song. The *Odyssey* reevaluates the Iliadic stance by celebrating intelligence and survival, a survival won as much by deception and eloquence as by military prowess; Odysseus returns to Ithaca not as the hero of Troy, but as a teller of tales who has won from the Phaeacians a return and a treasure through his civilized behavior and his gift with language. In the manner of Odysseus, the Menelaus of *Helen* survives by participating in Helen's fiction of his own death and playing the no-man and beggar. Yet in *Helen*, we are also told that the gods offered success to Helen and Menelaus because of their good birth, while pitilessly sacrificing the nameless masses to relieve the earth's overpopulation and to bring fame to Greece (36–41, 1678–79).[61] The concluding scenes of the play seem to represent a return to the *Odyssey*'s ultimate unwillingness to abandon, despite its critical response to the Iliadic tradition, the *kleos* achieved by good birth, military prowess, and song.[62]

Euripides' play thus reiterates a challenge to epic reputation present in both the *Odyssey* and, as mentioned earlier, in the Mysteries of Demeter and Kore; it exposes the contradictions present in the *Odyssey*'s critique of Iliadic values by demonstrating with self-conscious irony the impossibility of escaping fully

---

[58] Pippin 1960: 159.

[59] At Plato, *Cratylus* 407b, Athena is etymologized as *theonoa*. See Kannicht 1969: 2: ad loc., Sansone 1985, Burnett 1971: 89, and Austin 1994: 173–74.

[60] For interpretations of the Homeric *Hymn to Demeter* that stress the goddesses' resistance to and final acceptance of marriage, see Arthur 1977, Rudhardt 1978, and Foley 1994: 104–12. There are close links throughout the play between Helen's association with Kore and with Penelope.

[61] See further Juffras 1993. Aristocracy also rescues Admetus (Wohl 1998: 172).

[62] The treatment of *kleos* in *Helen* is more complex than this discussion implies. For example, the concern for reputation motivates Menelaus to survive and Theonoe to spare the couple. For a positive interpretation of Theonoe's concern for *kleos*, see Wolff 1973: 81–83 and for a negative interpretation, see Sansone 1985: 17–36.

from the authority of these traditional views and the myths, like those about Helen and the Trojan War, that rely on them. And the ultimate irony is that the innocent Helen can escape "death" in Egypt and her literary past only by playing simultaneously the parts of Kore/Penelope and the image that destroyed Troy.[63]

The living Helen cannot, by repeating the original Trojan scenario with a crucial difference, fully undo the damage accomplished by epic poetry, her *eidōlon*, and the Trojan war. For this, we require a divine intervention promising to Helen a role in Spartan cult that will confirm in perpetuity her reputation for chastity. The chorus of captured young Greek women lay the groundwork for the final appearance of Helen's brothers, the Dioscuroi, by praying to these gods for help in securing Helen's return and in restoring her tarnished reputation (1495–1511). In addition, the women invoke a Helen who presided in Spartan cult as a heroine over the initiation of young women on the verge of matrimony.[64] They imagine Helen rejoining maidens in their cults at Sparta (1465–78), as if she herself were once more the Helen she had been when Hermes abducted her as she was picking flowers for Athena of the Bronze Temple (242–45; though Helen was married, this is an activity typical for virgins): "may she [Helen] in fact encounter the maiden Leucippides by the river's swell or before the temple of Pallas, rejoining at last their dances or the revels for Hyacinthos, a night-long festival" (*ē pou koras an potamou / par' oidma Leukippidas ē pro naou Pallados an laboi / chronō(i) xunelthousa chorois / ē kōmois Huakinthou / nuchion es euphrosunan*, 1465–70). The cults of Hyacinthus and of the Leucippides[65] in which Helen will participate also marked stages in the initiation of Spartan girls, and their myths, like that of Helen in this play, resemble the story of Demeter and Kore. (We might contrast here Alcestis' future cult role in a far more masculine context, although choruses of young girls also danced at the Carneia festival.) Young girls rode into Hyacinthus' festival on special wagons and performed in choral dances; as is well known, Spartan girls were prepared for marriage and motherhood by such choral dancing (as well as athletics).[66] The story of this young man accidently killed by Apollo, god of adolescents at Sparta, and then reborn to a new life with his sister, the

---

[63] Pippin 1960: 154 shows how Helen's escape plan imitates the original divine deception. Segal 1971: 584 points out that the language used to describe Helen's own departure recalls the *eidōlon* (see 605–6 and 1516).

[64] For Helen's initiatory role in Spartan cult, see especially the sources and discussion presented in Wide [1893] 1973: esp. 343 and the detailed discussion in Calame 1977: 1: esp. 333–55, 443, and 447. Theocritus 18 gives the *aition* for a Spartan tree cult of Helen, in which Helen was celebrated by adolescent girls (see Calame 1: 338 and Gow [1950] 1965: 2: 358).

[65] The Leucippides are here represented as maidens, reflecting their role after death in cult and not their living status as wives of the Dioscuroi. Similarly, the living Helen is represented as joining in festivities in which she participated after death as a cult figure.

[66] These wagons or *kannathra* were also used in a festival in honor of Helen (Hesychius). See Calame 1977: 1: 340 n. 329 and Clader 1976: esp. 68.

virgin Polyboea, is similar in its pattern of death and rebirth to that of Kore, who was in fact represented with Demeter among the other figures on his tomb.[67] The Leucippides, together with the Dioscuroi and Helen, were associated with a slightly later stage in the transition to adulthood of young Spartan women and men; as in the case of Helen and Kore their stories began with a rape, in this instance by the divine twins who were to become their husbands.[68] Finally, Helen will return to a reunion with her daughter Hermione (like that of Demeter and Persephone), who can now be married (1476–78).[69]

Aristophanes' Lysistrata (1308–15) confirms an Athenian familiarity with the Helen of these Spartan cults; there she is the pure (hagna) and beautiful child of Leda, leading girls who dance like colts, their hair flowing like Bacchants. Indeed, as Claude Calame argues, Helen incarnates the choral leader of Spartan young women at the height of an adolescent beauty that was Helen's special province;[70] the images of Bacchants and colts used both in Aristophanes and in Helen are drawn directly from a poetic tradition devoted to celebrating female initiation.[71] In the cults dedicated to initiating marriageable Spartan girls, Helen eternally preserves a liminal position between the sphere of the virgins Artemis and Athena and that of the goddesses of sexuality and marriage, Aphrodite and Hera.[72] The Spartan cult thus permits to Helen an

---

[67] Pausanias, Description of Greece 3.19.4. Leading women in the festival were chosen for their sōphrosunē, semnotēs, and aretē (IG V 1, 586–87). For sources and discussion on the cult of Hyacinthus, see Wide [1983] 1973: 285–93, Kannicht 1969: 2: 383–85, and Calame 1977: 1: esp. 309–17.

[68] On the cults and myths of the Leucippides, see esp. Wide [1893] 1973: 326–32, Kannicht 1969: 2. 381–83, and Calame 1977: 1: 323–30. Some artistic representations of the Leucippides show their willing consent to abduction by their future hubands (Calame, 329–30); this representation reflects the positive role they played in Spartan initiation. Spartan marriage itself, as mentioned earlier, was viewed as a form of harpagē.

[69] Helen is linked with both Demeter and Persephone in this play; similarly in cult she facilitates the transition from daughter to married mother.

[70] On Helen as leader of choral dances, who is superior because her initiation is virtually complete, see esp. Calame 1977: 1: 92, 127, 136, 345–46, and 397–98; the ship that will take Helen to Sparta is a chorage tōn kallichorōn delphinōn (Helen 1454–64). Spartan girls participated in beauty contests, and Alcman's partheneia, choral songs that celebrate the transition of young women into adulthood, emphasize the beauty of the girls. Helen, as a deity of beauty with marriage as its end (Calame, 349), was reported to have made ugly girls miraculously beautiful (Herodotus 6. 61; Pausanias, Description of Greece 3.7.7).

[71] Kōmoi (1469) have Bacchic connotations; Helen is earlier compared to a colt (dromaia pōlos; young women ran races on the Dromos at Sparta) and a Bacchant (543–44) when she faces an imagined threat to her chastity from the unrecognized Menelaus; Hermione is called a moschos (1476), another typical image for young women about to be domesticated by matrimony. On the complex relation between Dionysus and the transition to marriage and adulthood, see Calame 1977: 1: 330 and Seaford 1988. Guépin 1968: 126, points out that due to cultic syncretism, Demeter's search for her daughter in the Helen ode is resituated in a Bacchic context.

[72] Calame 1977: 1: esp. 340–41, 443, and 447 argues that in their education to become mothers, young Spartan women participated in gymnastics and in dance and song, first in the rites of Artemis, Athena, and Hyacinthus (at a festival of Apollo), then in the cults of Athena, Helen,

eternal celebration of her seductive beauty in a context of chastity and virginity that bears no relation (historically or in myth)[73] to the role of her image in the Trojan venture. Although Helen earlier in the play feared that if she returned to Sparta she would inevitably receive a rejection appropriate to the *eidōlon* that dominated her literary tradition (287–89), the very existence of this Spartan cult, predating Euripides' own play, guarantees an alternative context in which Helen can escape *duskleia*. As elsewhere in Euripidean tragedy, the destructive repetitions of tragedy are dissolved through ritual, a form of action that is also repetitive, but serves to facilitate a constructive and collective social transition.[74]

In their final speech from the machine the Dioscuroi announce that Helen will be worshipped after death as a *theos* (god) and receive libations at a *theoxenia* with her brothers (*theos keklēsē(i) kai Dioskorōn meta / spondōn methexeis xenia t' anthrōpōn para / hexeis*, 1667–69).[75] We are not sure of the precise role of Helen in this rite—indeed, Euripides may have invented it, because Helen is otherwise not known to have been worshipped with her brothers. *Orestes* 1683–90 indicates that Helen and the Dioscuroi acted as guardians of sailors at sea.[76] Vase paintings and reliefs depict the Dioscuroi rushing through the air to reach a table and couches on which amphorae, sometimes entwined with snakes, are set out for the gods.[77] Elsewhere the Dioscuroi at least were expected to assist their table companions in confronting other dangers, including interventions in battle. As they once saved the virgin Helen from the rape of Theseus, the Dioscuroi, here apparently responding directly to the chorus' call to be saviors of Helen and to exonerate her from ill fame (*duskleian . . . barbarōn lecheōn*, 1495–1511), now escort their sister safely to Sparta and establish the

---

and the Leucippides, arriving finally in the domain of Dionysus, Aphrodite, and Hera. Thus, in celebrating both Helen's virginal achievements and her recent marriage to Menelaus, Theocritus 18 reflects Helen's role in presiding over the transition from virginity to the sphere of Aphrodite. In the Mountain Mother Ode the story moves from the rape of the daughter resisted by Artemis and Athena to the dissolution of the mother's grief by Aphrodite (*Helen* 1301–68).

[73] It is generally agreed that Helen was a pre-Greek fertility goddess (see especially her frequent rapes) who eventually became an epic heroine; on Helen as an early Greek goddess, see above all Nilsson 1967: 1: 475–76 and 1932: 73–76 and 170–71. Helen's worship by young women at Sparta would thus derive from her role as a goddess originally very similar to Kore.

[74] On this function of ritual in Euripidean tragedy, see esp. Foley 1985.

[75] On the cults of the Dioscuroi and their sister, see the discussion and additional references in Wide [1893] 1973: 304–25, Chapoutier 1935, Burkert 1985: 212–13, Kannicht 1969: 2: 433, Clader 1976: 69–82, and Calame 1977: 1: esp. 347. There seem to have been two traditions about the Dioscuroi; in one they were local Spartan heroes buried at Therapne; in another more Panhellenic tradition they were gods.

[76] The Dioscuroi may not have been guardians of sailors in Spartan cult, but from the Athenian perspective this was probably their most familiar role.

[77] See Burkert 1985: 213 and for the early Spartan monuments, with further discussion of the cult, Pipili 1987: 54–58.

truth of her extraordinary Egyptian story.[78] Helen's cult role as guardian may be reflected in the Dioscuroi's promise that the island to be named for Helen (1670–75), will guard (1673, *phrouron*) the coast of Attica from incursion.[79]

Curiously, the Dioscuroi do not mention the Spartan cult that Menelaus and Helen shared—as gods—in the Menelaion at Therapne, a cult that in archaic times at least included the Dioscuroi as well (Alcman, PMG fragment 7; and Pindar, *Pythian* 11.61–64). Menelaus is instead promised a place after death in the Isles of the Blest (1676–77); in the *Odyssey* Menelaus is accorded a similar destiny simply as a result of his marriage to Zeus' daughter Helen, not for his own achievements (Menelaus will go to the Elysian Field and the limits of the earth [*Odyssey* 4.561–69]). By including a reference to this well-known (see Isocrates, *Helen* 63) cult at Therapne, in which Helen is celebrated as wife as well as virgin and sister,[80] Euripides could have promised to Helen the paradoxical chastity and mature fertility that cannot be fully possessed by a mortal woman.[81] The omission, then, seems pointed. Instead, Helen goes on to a divine destiny that, like the cult promised to Alcestis, transcends her role as wife, breaks the links that bind her reputation to that of her spouse, and returns to her an immortality uncompromised by her husband's own desire for historical significance through his Trojan reputation.

The final scenes promise to Helen a cult cycle that repeats in another form

[78] *Helen* insists on the connection between the dei ex machina and the rest of the text; thus it offers a particularly good clue as to the possible function of these much-disputed appearances in Euripides' plays.

[79] Dunn 1996: 136–42 sees no meaningful connection between the plot of the play, the world of the audience, and these concluding etiologies. This seems very unlikely—why would Euripides create an entirely pointless conclusion? Dunn is misled by ignoring the connections between the predictions of the earlier choral stasimon at 1465–78 (also etiological) with the words of the Dioscuroi.

[80] For the cult of the divinized Menelaus and Helen at Therapne, see esp. Wide [1893] 1973: 340–46 and Calame 1977: 1: esp. 337, 341 n. 331, and 346–48. In Egypt, Menelaus and Helen were also worshipped as divine in cults founded during the early Arcadian and Laconian colonization (Wide 344 and Clader 1976: 69). The interpretation here depends partly on how well known Spartan cults were to Euripides and his audience, and how inseparable the cults of Helen and the Dioscuroi and Helen and Menelaus were at the end of the fifth century B.C.E. In archaic Sparta they appear to have been closely linked, in postclassical periods quite separate; our limited knowledge precludes an answer to either point; indeed, we cannot be sure whether Euripides has invented these cults, in whole or in part.

[81] Perhaps, like the Spartan Hera, the cultic Helen could even symbolically renew her virginity, as Helen renews her purity in Euripides' play (cf. Pausanias, *Description of Greece* 2.2.3, on Helen's *loutron*, or ritual bath). Even in epic, Helen may either be compared with the virgin Artemis (*Odyssey* 4.121–22) or equated with her patron deity Aphrodite. Theocritus 18 links the Helen who presides over Spartan virgins with the married wife of Menelaus; this may well have been true of the Leucippides as well. Kore herself is married in the world below, the virgin daughter of Demeter in the world above. So perhaps the worship of Helen at Sparta always assumed the connection between all her cults and she was in that context, as in Euripides' play, always simultaneously chaste and married.

the events of Euripides' play. In the play Helen as *korē* is sexually threatened and departs the world of symbolic death in Egypt and a chorus of young women for remarriage and a role (after her death a cultic role) among other choruses of young women in Spartan cult. As savior of her husband, the shipwrecked sailor, she will also assume a divine role as a guardian of sailors in the cult that she shares with her brothers. In both epic and drama the wife who loses her virginity in marriage can, like Penelope and Euripides' Helen, regain its symbolic equivalent by reconfirming her chastity against contrary traditions. The success of the Dioscuroi's defense of Helen is reflected in the closing lines of the play. The previously angry Theoclymenus now congratulates the Dioscuroi for Helen's *eugenestatē gnōmē* (extemely noble judgment or intelligence, 1686–87), a quality she now shares with the wise and virtuous virgin Theonoe. As their sister she has proved both *aristē* and *sōphronestatē* (outstanding and very self-controlled or chaste, 1684). Theonoe's childhood name, Eido, and her role as "object of her mother's delight" or "her mother's image" (*to mētros agalaisma*, 11), link her with the *eidōlon* that replaced Helen at Troy.[82] Her adult name Theonoe, which means "knowing the divine," detaches the root *eid-* from its links with image and foregrounds those with knowledge and judgment.[83] After Helen persuades Theonoe to side with her by invoking *kleos* as an ideal to be pursued and not polluted by violence, falsehood, or injustice, she herself is promised a cult role as a model to virgins. The Egyptian priestess and innocent, virginal Helen begin to become doubles to each other in the realm of wisdom rather than appearance.[84] In the play's concluding dialogue about Helen there is again no mention of Menelaus. Perhaps the play suggests that only in the fairy tale world of Egypt can Helen regain a fame that remains partially compromised in a Greek "reality."

Symbolic Remarriage

As married women, Alcestis and Helen, who have already experienced as young brides the symbolic death and rebirth of marriage, in these plays make the *anodos* story for a second time their own. The sacrifice of life each is willing to make for her marriage is enriched, especially in contrast to Euripides' sacrificial virgins, by her maturity and her knowledge of motherhood and sexuality. Alcestis may in earlier myth have made the choice to sacrifice herself on her wedding night (Apollodorus, *Bibliotheca* 1.9.15); in Euripides her heroic

[82] See Kannicht 1969: 2: 20 and 76, Downing 1990: 4 and 14, and Meltzer 1994: 249.

[83] Theonoe is asked by the chorus to offer a judgment to please all (996–97), a plea that links her judgment, in the view of Downing 1990: 14, with Euripides' own plot.

[84] Yet Papi 1987: 32–33 stresses Helen's shift from arguing that gods hate the violent and unjust treatment of possessions to promoting violence; in the end, what becomes important is not the justice of Helen and Menelaus' reunion, but "their reintegration into their lost status" (40).

sacrifice is deepened by the shared life of the couple between the time of the promise and the appointed day of Alcestis' death. Alcestis' decision is an entirely free one. She could, as she explains, have married a Thessalian of her choice and occupied the wealthy royal house (285–86). Despite fully enjoying the delights of youth, she did not find life to be worth living without Admetus and with orphaned children (287–89). Concerned for these children, she asks only that Admetus refuse remarriage for their sake, not because she resists personal replacement. Alcestis' reasoning does not extend much beyond the domestic environment, but it is exercised with admirable self-control and mature knowledge of the situation and of the proper status of the *oikos*. In this play, as in the *Odyssey*, the text presents male and female as moral equals subject to the demands of different social roles. Indeed, it is Admetus, not Alcestis, who makes public displays of grief and dependence, while the heroine confines hers to the privacy of her bedroom, but is otherwise remarkably composed (173–74).

Helen similarly promises to die for or with Menelaus, even if in the end she only temporarily mars her beauty. The play, however, gives her numerous opportunities to display her freely chosen marital devotion and the full battery of female tools for effecting her goals. Before Menelaus' entrance she has employed suppliancy to avoid remarriage. Later she takes the lead in supplicating and persuading Theonoe and one-ups even Penelope by her clever planning of their escape—including the deceptive use of lamentation (see part I). Indeed, her argument to Theonoe demonstrates her active assimilation to a patriarchal marital system. Theonoe (in accordance with her social role as virgin) should imitate her virtuous *father's* past commitment to preserving Helen's marriage, win *kleos* for so doing (941), and preserve her brother from further unjust behavior; justice entails returning property (including herself) to those who own it (900–916); Helen's return will restore her reputation for wifely *sōphrosunē* (*epi to sōphron*, 932) and permit the marriage of the couple's only child (926–35). Helen's arguments concerning property in this speech are deliberately universalizing and timeless, in the manner of the mothers in III.6; she regrets but does not question the plans of the gods for herself. Menelaus' speech, which immediately follows Helen's, displays a masculine unwillingness to supplicate or weep, an evocation of Theonoe's father's ghost and of Hades, and threats of violence to Theoclymenus or of joint suicide for himself and Helen (947–95). Overall, he attempts to shame Theonoe into saving himself and Helen. This aggressive speech characterizes him as a man of action but lacks the positive and idealizing moral arguments made by Helen. The virtuous Theonoe responds more directly to the high tone of the former speech (998–1029).

By sharing in their wives' experience of the *anodos* story pattern, Admetus and Menelaus are each given a similar opportunity to acquire a new perspective on reputation and mortal existence and to regain in place of an image (the *eidōlon* and the statue that Admetus promises to make of Alcestis) a wife now recognized fully for her virtue. Admetus, echoing his wife's original choice, learns to tolerate death rather than pursue a life without his former reputation and the presence of Alcestis. Menelaus accepts the innocent Helen as his bride, despite his reluctance to abandon the Trojan reputation that depended on the reality of the *eidōlon*, and temporarily allows his wife's plans to take precedence over his penchant for military force. Each acquires a more nuanced sense of the complexities of existence and, especially in the case of Menelaus, of the relation between reality and illusion.[85] In a strictly private sense, the plays promise each couple a marriage with a mutual recognition of worth that Greek literature had not celebrated since the reunion of Odysseus and Penelope. Yet from a public perspective, the conclusion of both plays remains compromised by the need to rescue for the husband a reputation for virtue challenged or nearly preempted by the wife. Here, as often in Euripides, the poet turns to cult and the gods to endow his female protagonists with a *kleos* that history and mortal marriage cannot fully offer them.

The plays' celebration of marital romance, as in the *Odyssey*, takes place not in the context of marriage for the first time, in which a mature love between spouses was precluded by the arranged marriages of Greek custom, but in the context of *remarriage*. In the Kore myth, the emotional bond between Demeter and the unmarried Persephone largely excluded the father Zeus and the husband Hades; in *Helen*, *Alcestis*, and the *Odyssey*, the experience of sexuality, children, and painful separation results in the substitution of marital for filial love. Yet despite this affirmation of marriage, the mother-daughter bond so powerfully celebrated in the Kore myth continues to play an important secondary role in both plays, and it should be emphasized that this feature is so unusual in extant tragedy that it may be a special feature of *anodos* dramas.[86] At her death Alcestis insists on securing the future of her daughter (see 309–19; her son will be more effectively protected against a stepmother by his father), and regrets that she will not be there to help initiate her into marriage and childbirth. Above all, it is in making Admetus promise not to remarry for the sake of the children (and especially the daughter) that Alcestis unwittingly undercuts the value of her sacrifice to her husband. In *Helen*, atoning for the death of her mother Leda and remedying the plight of her unmarried daughter

---

[85] For thoughtful discussions of what Menelaus experiences and learns in *Helen*, see esp. Pippin 1960: 153 and Segal 1971: esp. 575–79 and 594–97. Segal emphasizes Menelaus' new recognition of ambiguity, both in relation to the issues of appearance and reality in the play, and in relation to language itself.

[86] Tragedy tends more often to stress the father-daughter bond; the mother-daughter bond is as in the Homeric *Hymn to Demeter* potentially hostile to or exclusive of husband or father. In extant tragedy, the mother-daughter relation can be hostile, as in the case of Electra and Clytemnestra. Where it is not, as in the case of *Iphigeneia at Aulis* (where the Demeter-Kore relation almost certainly looms behind the violent separation of Clytemnestra and Iphigeneia by her father's plans for his daughter's marriage/sacrifice) or the *Phoenissae*, the father-daughter relation ultimately takes precedence.

Hermione are central motives for the heroine's actions,[87] and the play concludes by returning her to that daughter and to a cult role in which she will be worshipped by young women. The cults promised to each heroine apparently leave the earthly marriage to the husband behind in favor of reassimilating her story with that of the Kore myth pattern, in which Persephone's confinement to the underworld and marriage to Hades is mitigated by her acquisition of her own honors in cult (Homeric *Hymn to Demeter* 360–69). In this respect, it may be important that Alcestis and Helen are ultimately rescued not by their husbands but by Heracles and the Dioscuroi, all three of whom were known to have been initiated into the mysteries at Eleusis. Helen's continuing link with her brothers also affirms her tie—at least after death—to her natal family.

Moral Equality

In the aristocratic society of epic, men and women have separate but complementary roles; the husband presides over war, agriculture, and relations with strangers, whereas the wife weaves, supervises and guards the internal sphere of the household, and nurtures children. In the presence of her husband she participates in the public life of the court; in his absence, remaining in her own quarters, she devotes herself to chastity and to preserving her husband's interests. Endowed with the same moral capacities and intelligence as a man, Homer's Penelope can win an immortal reputation of her own for her devoted pursuit of her prescribed role (see III.1). In classical Athens, the sexual division of labor within the household was virtually identical. Yet no living respectable wife was meant to have a public reputation of her own, and, with the important exception of her extensive participation in religious ritual, she played little or no role in the social and political life of the city. The social contexts in which archaic epic and tragedy were apparently composed (our knowledge of the actual role of women is tenuous in either period) may go some way toward explaining the differences between the *Odyssey*'s treatment of Penelope and Odysseus and the reworking of the similar plot in Euripides' *Helen*.

On the one hand, Athenian democracy favored collective celebrations of the citizens' heroic contributions to their city over the celebration of the glory won by individuals;[88] in their celebration of the Kore myth the Mysteries re-

---

[87] See Helen at 134–36, 200–202, 280, 282–83, 686–90, and 933–35 and the chorus at 219. For the emphasis on Helen's relation to Leda in the play, see Hartigan 1981.

[88] For tensions between public and private life in classical Athens, see esp. Humphreys 1983a: esp. 132, Finley 1981: 77–94, and Loraux 1986. For the same issues in tragedy and the City Dionysia, see Vernant 1970 and 1981 and Goldhill 1987. Individuals could be singled out for commendation at the City Dionysia because of special contributions to the city (Demosthenes, *De Corona* 120), and athletes and others could be awarded dining privileges at the Prytaneion. Funeral orations, however, celebrated the war dead collectively (yet *stēlai* also listed the names of the war dead; see Goldhill 1987: 66), and each citizen was meant to put the welfare of the *polis* above his own.

inforced this civic ethic by offering an alternative path for every individual to confront death. Tragedy repeatedly acknowledges the seductive power of heroic *kleos*, yet reveals its destructive consequences when not exercised for the benefit of and shared with a whole society; *Helen* was presented just after the disaster of the Sicilian expedition, when an Odyssean reevaluation of military ambition may have seemed particularly relevant. That each play finds a final resolution through ritual again resonates with the Athenian context, in which cult—including women's cults that centered on the reenactment of the Kore myth—was acknowledged to be a sphere in which women could act constructively for the good of family and society.[89]

Helen thus becomes a part of a late-fifth- and early-fourth-century reevaluation of domestic life and of public and private priorities represented in Xenophon's later treatise on household management, the *Oeconomicus*, in vase paintings that celebrate domestic themes,[90] or in romantic tragedies like Euripides' *Andromeda*, where the young couple in love defend their marriage against a resisting father. Yet, if Athenian society did not include the possibility of a public reputation for virtue in its definition of the ideal wife, it is hardly surprising that tragedy could not cast off its ambivalence toward the achievements of Helen and Alcestis even as it claims to celebrate them. In part, Euripides' plays use the example of Helen and Alcestis to point up contradictions and problems in the masculine ethics of Admetus and Menelaus concerning the reputation acquired by hospitality and war: the difficulties of balancing public and private priorities and the destructive consequences that result from pursuing these goals without regard for context. We have seen, for example, how Menelaus repeatedly wishes to use force and directness and to protect his Trojan reputation where anonymity, nonviolent strategies, and an innocent Helen are more persuasive and effective for winning him a fortunate return home. Similarly, Admetus does not wish to face the contradiction that arises between keeping his promises to the dead Alcestis and the, in his view, even more compelling obligation to entertain a Heracles who is ignorant of his host's loss.[91] Heracles' final ruse with the veiled Alcestis forces Admetus painfully to reconfront this contradiction between these private and public priorities in a new form. On the other hand, the plays move toward affirming another set of values by restoring significance to a specifically feminine *kleos* acquired (as in the *Odyssey*) by devotion to survival and to private rather than public life.

As in the case of the Hollywood comedies of remarriage studied by Stanley Cavell in *Pursuits of Happiness*, Euripides seems in these plays, but above all

[89] Compare similar resolutions by and for the female protagonists of the *Oresteia* (the cult given to the Erinyes at Athens) or *Iphigeneia among the Taurians*. See more generally, Foley 1981. Most of the (fertility) cults exclusive to women in Athens, and above all the Thesmophoria, celebrated the Demeter-Persephone myth.

[90] See esp. Sutton 1981 and Osborne 1997.

[91] Both Heracles and the chorus criticize Admetus for this, while admiring his hospitality at the same time (see 551–52, 561–62, 808–16, 1017–18 and 597–605, 858–60).

in *Helen,* to have uncovered in this plot pattern the possibility of using remarriage and ritual to offer indirect comments and questions about social values and institutions and about the future of a society in transition. As Cavell
puts it:

> Our films may be understood as parables of a phase of the development of con-
> sciousness at which the struggle for the reciprocity or equality of consciousness be-
> tween a woman and a man, a study of the conditions under which this fight for recog-
> nition (as Hegel put it) or demand for acknowledgement (as I have put it) is a struggle
> for mutual freedom, especially of the views each holds of the other. This gives the
> films of our genre a Utopian cast. They harbor a vision which they know cannot be
> fully domesticated, inhabited, in the world we know. They are romances. Showing
> us our fantasies, they express the inner agenda of a nation that conceives Utopian
> longings and commitments for itself. . . . The conversation of what I call the genre
> of remarriage is, judging from the films I take to define it, of a sort that leads to ac-
> knowledgement; to the reconciliation of a genuine forgiveness; a reconciliation so
> profound as to require the metamorphosis of death and revival, the achievement of
> a new perspective on existence.[92]

Like Cavell's films or Shakespeare's late romances, (e.g., *The Winter's Tale,*)
these two plays by Euripides allow women to present their own case and to defend their own goals in dialogue with their spouses, to appropriate glory and to
display competence in some respects superior to that of their men. We are invited to consider what the experience of marriage can mean to women, and
how their husbands can learn from encountering a comparable experience.
The plays challenge what appears to have been the standard attitude in Attic
society (see further III.1) by assuming that women can be rational, self-
controlled, courageous, and capable of constructive and voluntary decisions
and actions.[93] Yet both dramas then reassert the norm by demonstrating the
disastrous social consequences for men of any challenge to the traditional balance of roles between the sexes. They cannot rest content with the utopian vision of gender relations that closes Cavell's films, or even to some extent the
Odyssey, which unambivalently permits Penelope permanent *kleos* as wife and
stresses a demonstrated like-mindedness (*homophrosunē*) between spouses that
neither tragic couple attains to the same degree.

In part II, we saw that attractive and loyal tragic concubines could appropriate the virtues of epic or ideal wives to express a wifely ideal free of the en-
cumbrances of the Attic marital system such as dowry, threats of divided loy-

---

[92] Cavell 1981: 17–19. See Foley 1978 for a similar claim about the marriage of Penelope and
Odysseus in the *Odyssey.*

[93] In contrast to *Medea* or *Agamemnon, Helen* and *Iphigeneia among the Taurians* in particular
tolerate women for their capacity to contrive a way out of difficulties that require strategy rather
than physical strength (*Helen* 830, 1049 and *Iphigeneia among the Taurians* 1032; see also *Iphigeneia
among the Taurians* 1054–64).

alty, and uncertain possession of the wife. In *Alcestis* and *Helen*, the wife retains the attractiveness and virginal charms of a young bride or freely chosen
concubine, but (like Penelope) actively proves her full assimilation to her marital family.[94] Indeed, the returning Alcestis, as a fictional concubine and prize
of Heracles given to Admetus with strong hints of wedding ritual, literally embodies the fantasized combination of concubine and spouse otherwise absent
from tragedy. Helen, too, becomes both bride and prize abducted from Egypt
by her once more heroic husband. Each wife voluntarily becomes the full and
genuinely virtuous possession of her spouse; indeed, both would have preferred
from the start the domestic obscurity and the traditional wifely role that they
finally obtain. Helen's brothers intervene only to preserve her marriage to
Menelaus, and her future ties to her natal family will come into play only after
death. In *Alcestis*, the "foreign" wife replaces Admetus' parents as friend/rela-
tive to her husband. Admetus' parents were *philoi* in name, not deed, whereas
Alcestis' sacrificed what was dearest to her for his life (340–41). He will now
give all that he owes to his parents—nurture in old age and burial—to the
(ironically dead) Alcestis (662–68).[95] Both Menelaus and Admetus turn in-
ward to evaluate their marriages and private lives on terms more generally expected of women.[96]

   The marital ideal offered in these plays proves difficult to maintain in reality, due to the demands of traditional sex roles. Admetus' feminizing excursion
into lamentation and permanent mourning and his extreme attempts to live
up to Alcestis' sacrifice by isolating himself from both his kin and the public
world prove as impossible to maintain as a publicly heroic Alcestis.[97] Like her
epic predecessor Penelope, Helen deploys deception—a standard negative
characteristic of women in Attic thought—in the service of marriage and
household. Yet because the straightforward use of military force proves initially
useless in Egypt, because trickery is practiced on a barbarian who has not lived
up to the virtues of his father, and because the pure Theonoe bows to Helen's
argument and agrees to support her ruse with silence, female deception gains
a positive valence that transcends its customary ambivalence.[98] Its suspect
links with lamentation (see part I) and sexuality remain, but the play at least

---

[94] After death Helen reestablishes a primary relation with her natal family.

[95] See Thury 1988: 203–4 on the use of legal language here.

[96] Saïd 1997 argues that the play enforces a reevaluation of traditional gender roles. At the conclusion, the male role remains concerned with affairs outside the *oikos* (especially, in this case, hospitality), but it must be balanced by the irreplaceable and critical role of the wife within.

[97] Rabinowitz 1993: 99 remarks that "textual praise of a woman who actively seeks her own
passivity is one way to achieve feminine complicity with patriarchy." (See similarly Wohl 1998:
175.) This underestimates, however, the sacrifices that Attic society regularly demanded of men
as well as women.

[98] Downing 1990 argues that *apatē* (deception) is revalued in *Helen* through its connection to
fiction.

introduces the possibility for wisdom and virtuous action on the part of those helpless to defend their autonomy with force and power.

The final silence of Alcestis and the recommodification of Helen are, quite reasonably, difficult for a modern audience to tolerate. Yet *Alcestis* and *Helen* treat the dangers of a shift in sex roles in a considerably more subtle and tolerant fashion than is the case, for example, in Euripides' *Hippolytus* or *Bacchae*, where the blurring of gender boundaries has permanent and tragic consequences. For the sexuality and mature experience of Helen and Alcestis only marginally compromise their dramatic representation. In part the happy denouement of these tragicomic plays is permitted because Helen and Alcestis cross gender boundaries in the service of their marriage and their husbands, rather than simply pursuing their own independent desires; in part it results, as in other romances, because suffering and recognition, and in *Helen* time and geographical distance, have permitted the transformation of tragic confusion into high-comic fantasy.[99] Perhaps most important of all, the *anodos* story pattern itself provides authority for the plays' tentative experiment with granting to its married female protagonists an immortality of their own. In this respect, both plays once more affirm that tragic play with gender is permitted in a sphere carefully circumscribed and authorized by the structures of myth and ritual, but ultimately subject at its conclusion to the constrictions of social and political reality.

---

[99] Aristotle characterized as tragedies plays with both a fortunate and an unfortunate outcome. Later critics have viewed *Helen* and *Alcestis* as partially satyric (*Alcestis* was presented as a fourth-place play in the slot of a satyr drama) or, perhaps anachronistically, as tragicomedies or romances. Genre definition was apparently fluid and loosely defined throughout the fifth century, and the topic is too complex to address here. (See esp. Seidensticker 1982, who comments on the "comic" and ironic aspects of Helen's symbolic remarriage [159–60, 192–95]). The fortunate denouement and the comic tone of some scenes are not sufficient to explain fully the particular role played by these two heroines, however, since Euripidean tragedies with an unfortunate outcome can celebrate the behaviour of adult women, like Jocasta in *Phoenissae*, Megara in *Heracles*, or Praxithea in *Erectheus*, in their role as mothers (see III.6).

Conclusion _____

U NQUESTIONABLY, ancient Greece left a legacy to later Western culture that reinforced symbolic links between female, "nature," domestic/private, emotion/the irrational, and passivity and male, culture, public, rational/the self-controlled, and activity.[1] Greek conceptions of the self and of models of human achievement were also structured in our remaining documents from a male point of view, with women, barbarians, slaves, and children serving to define less fully human alternatives. The characters of Greek tragedy can openly articulate such clichés about gender, and tragic action can directly or indirectly reinforce them, in part through conformity to cultural ideals and in part through its representation of rebellious, transgressive, and/or androgynous women like Medea or Clytemnestra. Performed at a festival for Dionysus, a god specifically linked in his myths with the kind of authorized festal inversion characteristic of such rituals cross-culturally, tragedy can invert and destabilize norms in a fashion that questions the cultural status quo and reveals the social world to be socially and historically constructed rather than natural and inevitable. Yet such temporary inversions and queries can also serve in the end to reinforce cultural ideologies, and we should not be fooled into thinking that the prominent, articulate, active, or resistant women of tragedy represent a genuine impulse for social change.

At the same time, tragedy offers a dialogue in which women, slaves, barbarians, and even divinities are represented in a complex and powerful public performance. As noted in the introduction, both Plato in the *Republic* and Aristophanes in *Frogs* articulate their fears about domesticating the results of these performances, whether they involve the dangers of men enacting roles unworthy of and dangerous to their identity as citizens (Plato) or of keeping in their place those who need the guidance of Greek male authority. Indeed, Aristophanes' Euripides boasts to the outrage of his Aeschylus that he democratized tragedy by making wives, maidens, old women, and slaves not only speak but argue in a subtle fashion and examine and question everything (*Frogs* 948–79). Moreover, because tragedy often views public issues through the lens of the family and its conflicts, it inevitably not only collapses but blurs boundaries between public and private worlds. Rhetoric or philosophy explores important social and ethical questions in a context that keeps public goals and issues, both general and specific, at the forefront, largely excludes the uncertain relations between divine and mortal worlds, and rarely views the domestic world as wor-

---

[1] I treat all these terms as subject to different definitions and/or constructions in different cultural contexts.

thy of serious exploration. Tragedy typically does the reverse. In the tragic debate, the concerns of those generally silenced in the public arena, such as
women or children, are not excluded; hence, for example, we experience
vividly in such instances as the sacrifice of Iphigeneia the repercussions of public policy on her family. In such cases, the tragic household can find itself in
tension with public goals, but it can also serve as a microcosm of the larger
world that brings both central and marginalized issues to the forefront.

As I argued in my study of tragic lamentation, civic life in Athens outside
tragedy attempted to control the public expression of grief and the confrontation with death. Legislation targeting both women, whose cultural function
was to perform grief and an engagement with death far more vividly, physically,
and emotionally than men, and probably wealthy aristocrats, whose private funerary display was curtailed, allowed the *polis* to put death ritual into the civic
realm in the form of the public funeral. The public funeral appropriated the
display of the aristocratic funeral to heroize the city's military casualties and to
suppress the elements of traditional female lament that stressed the cost of
death and heroic values to family and loved ones. Tragedy, however, allowed
citizen men to play this predominantly female role and often put female lamentation into a central, resistant, and even creative role. The fact that during the
Peloponnesian War, and especially in its later years, tragedy apparently became
less permissive in this respect seems to indicate an increasing uncertainty about
giving free rein even to fictional public expressions of grief in a difficult historical period. This shift also coincides with a return in actual practice to more
funerary display on the part of private families that was once again restricted
in the fourth century. Unease about female lamentation is never absent from
the tragic stage at any period, yet its powerful voice, the pleasures of the grief
it generated from epic on, and the emotional authority that it gave to revenge
or justice apparently continued to play a sufficiently important theatrical function to keep it in a prominent role even in the final years of the fifth century.

Both Plato and Aristotle expressed an interest in controlling marital life and
practices far more than the contemporary Attic democracy, which apparently
attempted to control private life through gossip as well as relatively limited legislation. This philosophical response to keeping women, wealth, and private
interests under control confronts a set of genuine tensions in the Attic marital system concerning the role of heiresses, dowry, women's informal powers in
the household, and the reproduction of the household more generally. Tragedy
turns to an implicit comparison between the epic marital system, which apparently incorporated a wife fully into her marital household, did not endow
her with a dowry, and permitted the reproduction of the household through
concubines as well as wives with a classical Attic system in which a wife is
"lent" to her marital family to produce children but retains a relation to her
natal family that can be activated if the natal family lacks heirs; in which a wife
can be said to "buy" a husband with a dowry and "enslave" him with a large

one; and in which reproducing a household is hampered by laws controlling citizenship, inheritance, and adultery, and disenfranchising the offspring of concubines. This system curtailed the ability of aristocrats to play politics and especially international politics through marriage alliances while supposedly reinforcing the survival of individual citizen households. It also, judging from frequent complaints in Euripides and New Comedy, provoked a tragic attraction to myths featuring conflicts between natal and marital families, childlessness, and aggressive and adulterous wives. Tragedy looks back to epic in favoring spouses, whether aristocratic wives or epic-style concubines, who resemble Homeric ideals like Penelope or Andromache. A tragic wife modeled on Penelope like Euripides' Egyptian Helen can even, as she begins to spin a plot that rescues her husband from disaster, stand in for the plot-making playwright and, with divine help, invent solutions to seemingly insoluble mythical dilemmas (the virgin sister Iphigeneia performs among the Taurians a similar rescue of her brother, Orestes). Moreover, both the implicit contrast or comparison between epic and classical Athenian marriage and family structures and the open critiques of or resistance to marriage by female characters like Clytemnestra or Medea keep in view the historically constructed nature of democratic households and permit tragedy to question them.

Greek culture did not view women as ethical adults, partly due to the limitations imposed by their social role, which confined them to the household and the religious realm, and partly due to their putatively unstable bodies and emotions. Tragedy, however, can treat some female characters as autonomous moral adults. It offers approval to female characters who, without abandoning their female character, voluntarily choose to sacrifice themselves for city or nation like Euripides' Iphigeneia at Aulis, or to favor the interests of the *polis* over the family, like Euripides' older mothers Aethra, Praxithea, or Jocasta; the voluntary rather than merely culturally prescribed nature of such female choices is what gives them striking dramatic authority. It also celebrates wives who, like Euripides' Alcestis or Egyptian Helen, play the role of the epic Penelope, and make choices that, even in the absence of their husbands, heroically serve the interest of their marital family.

Tragedy also treats the domestic as well as the public world as an important moral realm. Some female characters take ethical positions that bring what seem to be specifically female concerns and approaches into play in both domestic and public debates. Age, status, and kin position can weigh even more specifically for them than for their male counterparts. These characters do not hesitate to act or advocate acting on a combination of principled and emotional grounds rarely adopted in the same form by male characters, although their stances are pointedly limited by their status as unmarried daughters, wives, and mothers. At the same time, women, by being even more confined to their social roles and more dependent on others, can serve to embody in a particularly self-conscious form the tragic image of the human, whose actions and decisions are often nullified by a series of uncontrollable contingencies, including ignorance and misfortune. Awareness of the corrosive effects of cultural prejudice can weigh particularly heavily with female characters (i.e., Phaedra or Medea), as can a sense of tragic self-division. No male character faces an extended internal debate between two compromised alternatives in the fashion of the heroic and androgynous Medea, or ruminates at length on the difficulties of controlling or confronting erotic desire like conventional wives Phaedra and Deianeira. Indeed, as all three of these characters demonstrate, the lack of a confident, knowledgeable, and autonomous female self capable of representing positive alternatives to the heroines in such self-debates both affirms the danger of allowing women to make choices independent of men and, because men have put them in the impossible positions in which they find themselves, reveals the dangers of not educating them to do so.

Most important, tragedy implicitly asks whether public and private morality can operate on the same terms. It seems to recognize that ethical decisions made in smaller-scale contexts like the household may not require the same ethical mode as those in the public realm, but also that public realm cannot always be as insulated through abstraction from specific contexts and private concerns as might first appear. Sophocles' Creon in *Antigone* attempts to conduct public morality by deploying generalities without full attention to context, and by suppressing emotional and kinship considerations in favor of what he defines as the rational interest of the *polis*. His Antigone, though limited in her perspective by her youth and social role, attempts to establish the importance of familial and emotional concerns and care for others, in alliance with principle, in a public context. At the same time, Greeks did not necessarily advocate any simple separation between reason and educated, controlled emotion or between public and private concerns even in ethical decision making by men, and characters like Creon are (as we can see from his debate with Haimon) not meant to represent a masculine ideal in practice.

The series of tragic debates in which Clytemnestra defends her killing of Agamemnon to the chorus of old men in Aeschylus' *Agamemnon* and to her daughter Electra in Sophocles' and Euripides' *Electras* make clear that her choice looks very different from a public and private perspective. The elders in *Agamemnon*, who are nevertheless confused by Clytemnestra's subversive arguments, cannot conceive a wife's killing of her heroic husband/the king as justice. Their concerns are principled and public in orientation. For the Electras the familial repercussions are central. Such a mother can no longer share the same domestic space with her legitimate children without destroying their lives and characters. Living with injustice and the memory of injustice corrodes morality and even eventually begins to make telling right from wrong impossible. Yet taking action against such a mother is, for example, far more complex and vivid for Sophocles' Electra than it is for his Orestes, who can view his revenge in abstract terms because he has not lived with his mother, and more compromised for Euripides' Electra, who is trapped in a web of jealousy, resentment, and social and economic deprivation and deliberately exploits her mother's maternity in order to destroy her. Such plays can permit the male characters to shoulder the weight of public and private duties and to maintain self-control without silencing legitimate, if messy, concerns that are shared with and articulated through women.

Tragic women can also be used to argue out other sorts of private-public conflicts for men as well. Transition from the face-to-face aristocratic culture of archaic Greece to a larger-scale democratic city-state left a legacy of tensions for masculine (and perhaps above all for aristocratic) identity. Male reputation remained important, but lasting fame belonged first and foremost to collective service to the city-state. Male honor required revenge, but revenge in Athens needed to be pursued in the lawcourts, where the citizen could become the victim of slander, superior rhetoric, and even false testimony. The traditional ethic of doing good to friends and bad to enemies remained equally vital, but acting on this principle could also be problematic in the democratic civic context. Tragedy often (if not exclusively) allowed women and barbarians like Medea or Hecuba to explore the full negative or ambivalent consequences of pursuing such traditional honor-related goals. Women's pursuit of *kleos* consistently endangers male interests and threatens to masculinize the women themselves; by implication the male pursuit of individual *kleos* can also endanger the city to which he is supposed to subordinate his interests. Finally, the Athenian Empire and the Peloponnesian War made it clear that ethical standards that could be maintained within a *polis* became virtually impossible to implement outside it. Although many tragic characters uphold the traditional or unwritten laws against the interests of political expediency, this role seems to fall increasingly to the older women of Euripides' later plays and in an increasingly international context.

This book has deliberately confined itself to what I have characterized as an anthropological approach to tragic representation that locates gender issues in a specific dramatic and cultural context but has paid relatively little attention to a range of other psychological or aesthetic issues. My purpose in taking this approach was at least in part to capture the strangeness and difference of Greek representations of cultural, historical, and ethical issues from our own. At the same time, I do not want to lose sight of why tragic conceptions of women can illuminate the study of a broader range of concerns both within tragedy itself and for the twenty-first century. From my perspective Greek tragedy is fascinating precisely because, despite all the familiar clichés about gender relations that it expresses and even reaffirms, it allows us by its self-consciousness, its festal inversions and perversions of the norm, and its open obsession with imagining a range of public questions through the lens of gender and family to explore sex roles, cultural institutions, and morality in a fashion that remains of interest to us today. Philosophers and especially feminist philosophers who are interested in alternative moralities might be one audience for further discussion of these issues, for tragedy offers us an examination of ethical issues colored by a contextual and narrative appreciation rarely provided by philosophy. Anthropologists and historians who want to see a traditional culture self-consciously responding to itself in an unusually sophisticated fashion might be another. Theater scholars curious about what is at stake intellectually in composing drama for a tradition where men both write and play the other might compose a third audience. Above all, Greek tragedy remains compelling for the modern reader because it both consistently queries and struggles to push beyond the clichés voiced by its characters and complicates, in ways that we can only begin to isolate, any predictable relation to its contemporary environment.

Bibliography

Abrahamson, E. 1952. "Euripides' Tragedy of Hecuba." *Transactions and Proceedings of the American Philological Association* 83: 120–29.

Abu-Lughod, L. 1986. *Veiled Sentiments: Honor and Poetry in a Bedoin Society*. Berkeley.

Achtenberg, D. 1996. "Aristotelian Resources for Feminist Thinking." In J. K. Ward, ed., *Feminism and Ancient Philosophy*, 95–117. New York and London.

Addelson, K. P. 1987. "Moral Passages." In E. F. Kittay and D. T. Meyers, eds., *Women and Moral Theory*, 87–110. Totowa, N.J.

Adkins, A.W.H. 1960. *Merit and Responsibility: A Study in Greek Values*. Oxford. Reprint, Chicago, 1975.

————. "Basic Greek Values in Euripides' *Hecuba* and *Hercules Furens*." *Classical Quarterly* 60, n.s., 16: 193–216.

Ahlberg, G. 1971. *Prothesis and Ekphora in Greek Geometric Art*. Göteberg.

Aldrich, K. M. 1961. *The Andromache of Euripides*. University of Nebraska Studies 25. Lincoln, Neb.

Alexanderson, B. 1966. "On Sophocles' *Electra*." *Classica et Medievalia* 27: 79–98.

Alexiou, M. 1974. *The Ritual Lament in Greek Tradition*. Cambridge.

Alexiou, M., and P. Dronke. 1971. "The Lament of Jephta's Daughter: Themes, Tradition, Originality." *Studi Medievali* (Spoleto) 12.2: 819–63.

Allen, D. S. 2000. *The World of Prometheus: The Politics of Punishing in Democratic Athens*. Princeton.

Amory, A. 1963. "The Reunion of Odysseus and Penelope." In C. H. Taylor Jr., ed., *Essays on the "Odyssey,"* 100–121. Bloomington, Ind.

Armstrong, D., and E. A. Ratchford. 1985. "Iphigenia's Veil: Aeschylus, *Agamemnon* 228–48." *Bulletin of the Institute of Classical Studies* 32: 1–12.

Arnott, W. G. 1990. "Euripides' New Fangled *Helen*." *Antichthon* 24: 1–18.

Arthur, M. 1977. "Politics and Pomegranates. An Interpretation of the Homeric *Hymn to Demeter*." *Arethusa* 19: 7–48.

Austin, C. 1968. *Nova fragmenta Euripidea in papyris reperta*. Berlin.

Austin, N. 1994. *Helen of Troy and Her Shameless Phantom*. Ithaca, N.Y., and London.

Bacon, H. 1961. *Barbarians in Greek Tragedy*. New Haven, Conn.

————. 1964. "The Shield of Eteocles." *Arion* 3: 27–38.

Bain, D. 1981. *Masters, Servants and Orders in Greek Tragedy: Some Aspects of Dramatic Technique and Convention*. Manchester.

Balme, D. M. 1991. *Aristotle: History of Animals*. 3 vols. Loeb Classical Library. Cambridge, Mass.

Bamberger, J. 1975. "The Myth of Matriarchy: Why Men Rule in Primitive Society." In M. Rosaldo and L. Lamphere, eds., *Woman, Culture, and Society*, 263–80. Stanford, Calif.

Barlow, S. 1989. "Stereotype and Reversal in Euripides' *Medea*." *Greece and Rome* 36.2: 158–71.

————. 1995. "Euripides' *Medea*: A Subversive Play." In A. Griffiths, ed., *Stage Directions: Essays in Honor of E. W. Handley*, 36–45. London.

Bassi, K. 1989. "The Actor as Actress in Euripides' *Alcestis.*" *Themes in Drama* 11: 19–30.

———. 1998. *Acting Like Men: Gender, Drama, and Nostalgia in Ancient Greece.* Ann Arbor, Mich.

Benardete, S. 1967, 1968. "Two Notes on Aeschylus *Septem.*" *Wiener Studien* 80: 22–30 (Part I); 81: 5–17 (Part II).

———. 1975. "A Reading of Sophocles' *Antigone.*" *Interpretation: A Journal of Political Philosophy* 4.3: 148–96; 5.1: 1–55; 5.2: 148–84.

Benedetto, V. di. 1984. "La casa, il demone e la struttura dell'*Orestea.*" *Rivista di Filologia e di Istruzione Classica* 112: 11–25.

Benhabib, S. 1987. "The Generalized and the Concrete Other: The Kohlberg-Gilligan Controversy and Moral Theory." In E. F. Kittay and D. T. Meyers, eds., *Women and Moral Theory*, 154–77. Totowa, N.J.

Bennett, L. J., and W. B. Tyrrell. 1990. "Sophocles' *Antigone* and Funeral Oratory." *American Journal of Philology* 111: 441–56.

Bergk, T. 1884. *Griechische Literaturgeschichte.* Vol. 3. Leipzig.

Bergson, L. 1993. "Herakles, Deianeira und Iole." *Rheinisches Museum* 136.2: 102–15.

Betensky, A. 1978. "Aeschylus' *Oresteia:* The Power of Clytemnestra." *Ramus* 7: 11–25.

Betts, G. G. 1965. "The Silence of Alcestis." *Mnemosyne*, 4th ser., 18: 181–82.

Beye, C. 1959. "Alcestis and Her Critics." *Greek, Roman and Byzantine Studies* 2: 111–27.

Black-Michaud, J. 1975. *Cohesive Force: Feud in the Mediterranean and the Middle East.* Oxford.

Blok, J. 1987. "Sexual Assymetry. A Historiographical Essay." In J. Blok and P. Mason, eds., *Sexual Assymetry: Studies in Ancient Society*, 1–58. Amsterdam.

Blum, L. A. 1988. "Gilligan and Kohlberg: Implications for Moral Theory." *Ethics* 98: 472–91.

Blundell, M. W. 1989. *Helping Friends and Harming Enemies: A Study in Sophocles and Greek Ethics.* Cambridge.

Blundell, S. 1995. *Women in Ancient Greece.* Cambridge, Mass.

Boedeker, D. 1991. "Euripides' *Medea* and the Vanity of *LOGOI.*" *Classical Philology* 86: 95–112.

———. 1997. "Becoming Medea: Assimilation in Euripides." In J. J. Clauss and S. I. Johnston, eds., *Medea: Essays on Medea in Myth, Literature, and Philosophy*, 127–48. Princeton.

Boeghold, A. L. 1994. "Perikles' Citizenship Law of 451/0 B.C." In A. L. Boeghold and A. C. Scafuro, eds., *Athenian Identity and Civic Ideology*, 57–66. Baltimore and London.

Boehm, C. 1984. *Blood Revenge: The Anthropology of Feuding in Montenegro and Other Tribal Societies.* Lawrence, Kan.

Bollack, J. 1999. *La mort d'Antigone.* Lille.

Bollack J., and P. Judet de la Combe. 1981–82. *L'Agamemnon d'Eschyle.* 3 vols. Lille.

Bongie, E. B. 1977. "Heroic Elements in the *Medea* of Euripides." *Transactions and Proceedings of the American Philological Association* 107: 27–56.

Bonnafé A. 1989. "Clytemnestra et ses batailles: Eris et Peitho." In E. Roland, M.-T. le

Dinahet, and M. Yon, eds., *Architecture et poésie dans le monde grec. Hommages à Georges Roux,* 149–57. Lyons and Paris.

Boserup, E. 1970. *Women's Role in Economic Development.* London.

Boulter, P. N. 1966. "*Sophia* and *Sophrosyne* in *Andromache.*" *Phoenix* 20: 51–58.

Bowra, C. M. 1944. *Sophoclean Tragedy.* Oxford.

Bradley, E. M. 1980. "Admetus and the Triumph of Failure in Euripides' *Alcestis.*" *Ramus* 9: 112–27.

Bremmer, J. N. 1997, "Why Did Medea Kill Her Brother Apsyrtus?" In J. M. Clauss and S. I. Johnston, eds., *Medea: Essays on Medea in Myth, Literature, and Art,* 83–100. Princeton.

Broughton, J. M. 1983. "Women's Rationality and Men's Virtues: A Critique of Gender Dualism in Gilligan's Theory of Moral Development." *Social Research* 50.3: 597–642.

Brown, A. L. 1976. "The End of the *Seven against Thebes.*" *Classical Quarterly* 70, n.s., 26: 206–16.

———. 1977. "Eteocles and the Chorus in the *Seven against Thebes.*" *Phoenix* 31: 300–318.

———. 1987. *Sophocles: Antigone.* Warminster.

Brown, P. G. McC. 1990. "Plots and Prostitutes in Greek New Comedy." *Papers of the Leeds International Latin Seminar* 6: 241–66.

———. 1993. "Love and Marriage in New Comedy." *Classical Quarterly* 43: 189–205.

Burian, P. 1985. "*Logos* and *Pathos.* The Politics of the *Suppliant Women.*" In P. Burian, ed., *Directions in Euripidean Criticism,* 129–55, 212–21. Durham, N.C.

Burkert, W. 1979. *Structure and History in Greek Mythology and Ritual.* Sather Classical Lectures, vol. 47. Berkeley.

———. 1985. *Greek Religion.* Cambridge, Mass.

———. 1990. "Ein Datum für Euripides' Electra: Dionysia 420 v. Chr." *Museum Helveticum* 67: 65–69.

Burnett, A. P. 1971. *Catastrophe Survived: Euripides' Plays of Mixed Reversal.* Oxford.

———. 1973. *Medea* and the Tragedy of Revenge." *Classical Philology* 68: 1–24.

———. 1994. "Hekabe the Dog." *Arethusa* 27: 151–64.

———. 1998. *Revenge in Attic and Later Tragedy.* Berkeley, Los Angeles, and London.

Buttrey, T. V. 1958. "Accident and Design in Euripides' *Medea.*" *American Journal of Philology* 79: 1–17.

Buxton, R.G.A. 1982. *Persuasion in Greek Tragedy: A Study of Peitho.* Cambridge.

———. 1987a. "Euripides' *Alkestis:* Five Aspects of an Interpretation." In *Papers Given at a Colloquium in Honor of R. P. Winnington Ingram,* 18–27. London. Originally published in *Dodone (Philologia)* 14 (1985): 75–90.

———. 1987b. "Le voile et le silence dans l'*Alceste* d'Euripide." *Cahiers du Groupe Interdisciplinaire du Théâtre Antique* 3: 167–78.

Calame, C. 1977. *Les choeurs de jeunes filles en Grèce archaïque.* Vol. 1. Rome.

Calder, W. 1968. "Sophocles' Political Tragedy, *Antigone.*" *Greek, Roman and Byzantine Studies* 9: 389–407.

Caldwell, R. 1973. "The Misogyny of Eteocles." *Arethusa* 6: 197–231.

Cameron, H. D. 1970. "The Power of Words in *Seven against Thebes.*" *Transactions and Proceedings of the American Philological Association* 101: 95–118.

Cannon, A. 1989. "The Historical Dimension in Mortuary Expression of Status and Sentiment." *Current Anthropology* 30.4: 437–51.

Caraveli, A. 1986. "The Bitter Wounding: The Lament as Social Protest in Rural Greece." In J. Dubisch, ed., *Gender and Power in Rural Greece*, 169–94. Princeton.

Carey, C. 1995. "Rape and Adultery in Athenian Law." *Classical Quarterly* 45.2: 407–417.

Cavell, S. 1981. *Pursuits of Happiness: The Hollywood Comedy of Remarriage.* Cambridge, Mass.

Cerri, G. 1979. *Legislazione orale e tragedia greca. Studi sull' Antigone di Sofocle e sulle Supplici di Euripide.* Naples.

———. 1987. "Le message dionysiaque dans l'*Hélène* d'Euripide." *Cahiers du Groupe Interdisciplinaire du Théâtre Antique* 3: 197–216.

Chalkia, I. 1983. "L'*oikos* et l'espace de la mort dans l'*Alceste* d'Euripide." *Epistemonike Epeterida tes Philosophikes Scholes tou Aristoteleiou Panepistemiou Thessalonikes* 21: 55–82. Reprinted in *Lieux et espace dans la tragédie grec*, 226–48. Thessaloniki, 1986.

Chamberlain, C. 1984. "The Meaning of *Prohairesis* in Aristotle's *Ethics*." *Transactions and Proceedings of the American Philological Association* 114: 147–57.

Chapoutier, F. 1935. *Les Dioscures au services d'une déese.* Paris.

Chodorow, N. 1978. *The Reproduction of Mothering, Psychoanalysis and the Sociology of Gender.* Berkeley and Los Angeles.

Christmann, E. 1962. "Bemerkungen zum Text der Medea des Euripides." Dissertation, Heidelberg.

Clader, L. 1976. *Helen: The Evolution from Divine to Heroic in Greek Epic Tradition.* Leiden.

Clairmont, C. 1970. *Gravestone and Epigram.* Mainz.

Clément, P. 1958. "The Recovery of Helen." *Hesperia* 27: 47–73.

Cohen, D. 1990. "The Social Context of Adultery at Athens." In P. Cartledge, P. Millet, and S. Todd, eds., *Nomos: Essays in Athenian Law, Politics, and Society*, 147–65. Cambridge.

——— 1991. *Law, Sexuality, and Society: The Enforcement of Morals in Classical Athens.* Cambridge.

———. 1995. *Law, Violence and Community in Classical Athens.* Cambridge.

Cohn-Haft, L. 1995. "Divorce in Classical Athens." *Journal of Hellenic Studies* 115: 1–14.

Cole, S. G. 1981. "Could Greek Women Read and Write?" In H. P. Foley, ed., *Reflections of Women in Antiquity*, 219–46. New York and London.

Collard, C. 1972. "The Funeral Oration in Euripides' *Supplices*." *Bulletin of the Institute of Classical Studies* 19: 39–53.

———. 1975. *Euripides Supplices.* 2 vols. Groningen.

———. 1991. *Euripides Hecuba.* Warminster.

Collard, C., M. J. Cropp, and K. H. Lee. 1995. *Euripides: Selected Fragmentary Plays* Vol. 1. Warminster.

Collinge, N. E. 1962. "Medea *ex Machina*." *Classical Philology* 57: 151–60.

Conacher, D. J. 1956. "Religious Attitudes in Euripides' *Suppliants*." *Transactions and Proceedings of the American Philological Association* 87: 8–26.

———. 1967. *Euripidean Drama: Myth, Theme, and Structure.* Toronto.

———. 1974. "Interaction between Chorus and Characters in the *Oresteia*." *American Journal of Philology* 95: 323–43.

————. 1987. *Aeschylus' Oresteia: A Literary Commentary*. Toronto.

————. 1988. *Euripides Alcestis*. Warminster.

Connor, W. R. 1984. *Thucydides*. Princeton.

Cox, C. A. 1988. "Sisters, Daughters, and the Deme of Marriage." *Journal of Hellenic Studies* 108: 185–88.

————. 1998. *Household Interests: Property, Marriage Strategies, and Family Dynamics in Ancient Athens*. Princeton.

Cozzi, D. E. 1910. "La vendetta del sangue nelle Montagne dell' Alta Albania." *Anthropos* 5: 654–87.

Craik, E. M. 1984. "Marriage in Ancient Greece." In E. M. Craik, ed., *Marriage and Property*, 6–29. Aberdeen.

Cropp, M. J. 1988. *Euripides Electra*. Warminster.

————. 1997. "Antigone's Final Speech (Sophocles, *Antigone* 891–928)." *Greece and Rome* 44.2: 137–60.

Cunningham, M. P. 1954. "Medea *apo mechanes*." *Classical Philology* 49: 151–60.

Daitz, S. 1971. "Concepts of Freedom and Slavery in Euripides' *Hecuba*." *Hermes* 99: 217–26.

Dale, A. M. 1967. *Euripides Helen*. Oxford.

Dalfen, J. 1977. "Gesetz ist nicht Gesetz und fromm ist nicht fromm: Die Sprache der Personen in der sophokleischen Antigone." *Wiener Studien* 11: 5–26.

Danforth, L. M. 1982. *The Death Rituals of Rural Greece*. Princeton.

Daube, B. 1939. *Zu Rechtsprobleme in Aischylos' Agamemnon*. Dissertation, Basel.

Davidson, J. F. 1988. "Homer and Sophocles' *Electra*." *Bulletin of the Institute of Classical Studies* 35: 45–72.

Davies, J. K. 1977–78. "Athenian Citizenship: The Descent Group and the Alternatives." *Classical Journal* 73: 105–21.

Dawe, R. D. 1967. "The End of the *Seven against Thebes*." *Classical Quarterly* 61, n.s., 17: 16–28.

————. 1978. "The End of the *Seven against Thebes* Yet Again." In R. D. Dawe, J. Diggle, and P. E. Easterling, eds., *Dionysiaca*, 87–103. Cambridge.

Dawson, C. M. 1970. *The Seven against Thebes by Aeschylus*. Englewood Cliffs, N.J.

Dean-Jones, L. 1994. *Women's Bodies in Classical Greek Science*. Oxford.

Deliyanni, H. 1985. "Blood Vengeance Attitudes in Mani and Corsica." University of Exeter. Unpublished manuscript.

Denniston, J. D. [1939] 1977. *Euripides Electra*. Oxford.

————. 1975. *The Greek Particles*. 2nd ed. Oxford.

Denniston, J. D., and D. L. Page. 1957. *Aeschylus Agamemnon*. Oxford.

de Romilly, J. 1971. *La loi dans la pensée grecque*. Paris.

de Ste Croix, G.E.M. 1981. *The Class Struggle in the Ancient World*. London and Ithaca, N.Y.

de Wet, B. X. 1977. "The *Electra* of Sophocles—A Study in Social Values." *Acta Classica* 20: 23–36.

des Bouvrie, S. 1990. *Women in Greek Tragedy: An Anthropological Approach*. Oslo.

Dewald, C. J. 1981. "Women and Culture in Herodotus' *Histories*." In H. P. Foley, ed., *Reflections of Women in Antiquity*, 91–126. New York and London.

Diels, H., and W. Kranz, eds. 1951. *Die Fragmente der Vorsokratiker*. Vol. 1. 6th ed. Berlin. Reprint, Dublin, 1966.

Diggle, J. 1981. *Euripides Fabulae*. Vol 2. Oxford.

———. 1984. *Euripides Fabulae*. Vol. 2. Oxford.

———. 1994. *Euripides Fabulae*. Vol. 3. Oxford.

Dihle, A. 1977. *Euripides' Medea.*" Sitzungsberichte der Heidelberger Akademie der Wissenschaften. Heidelberg.

Diller, H. 1966. "*THUMOS DE KREISSON TON EMON BOULEUMATON.*" *Hermes* 94: 267–75. Reprinted in *Kleine Schriften*, 359–69. Munich, 1971.

Dillon, J. 1997. "Medea among the Philosophers." In J. J. Clauss and S. I. Johnston, eds., *Medea: Essays on Medea in Myth, Literature, and Philosophy*, 211–18. Princeton.

Dirlmeier, F. 1960. "Vom Monolog der Dichtung zum 'inneren' Logos bei Platon und Aristoteles." *Gymnasium* 67: 26–41.

Dodds, E. R. 1952. "Three Notes on *Medeia*." *Humanitas* 4: 13–18.

———. 1990. "Morals and Politics in the *Oresteia*." *Proceedings of the Cambridge Philological Society* 186: 19–31.

Doherty, L. E. 1991. "The Internal and Implied Audiences of *Odyssey* 11." *Arethusa* 24.2: 145–76.

———. 1992. "Gender and Internal Audiences in the *Odyssey*." *American Journal of Philology* 113: 161–77.

———. 1995. "Sirens, Muses and Female Narrators in the *Odyssey*." In B. Cohen, ed., *The Distaff Side: Representing the Female in Homer's Odyssey*, 81–92. Oxford.

Dover, K. J. 1973. "Some Neglected Aspects of Agamemnon's Dilemma." *Journal of Hellenic Studies* 93: 58–69. Reprinted in *Greek and the Greeks, Collected Papers*, 1: 135–50. Oxford, 1988.

———. 1974. *Greek Popular Morality in the Time of Plato and Aristotle*. Berkeley and Los Angeles.

Downing, E. 1990. "*Apate, Agon*, and Literary Self-Reflexivity in Euripides' *Helen*." In M. Griffith and D. Mastronarde, eds., *Cabinet of the Muses: Essays on Classical and Comparative Literature in Honor of Thomas G. Rosenmeyer*, 1–16. Atlanta.

Doyle, R. E. 1984. *Ate: Its Use and Meaning*. New York.

Dunn, F. M. 1996. *Tragedy's End: Closure and Innovation in Euripidean Drama*. New York and Oxford.

Durham, E. (1909) 1987. *High Albania*. Boston.

Dyson, M. 1987. "Euripides Medea 1056–80." *Greek, Roman and Byzantine Studies* 28: 23–34.

———. 1988. "Alcestis' Children and the Character of Admetus." *Journal of Hellenic Studies* 108: 13–23.

Easterling, P. E. 1973. "Presentation of Character in Aeschylus." *Greece and Rome* 20: 3–19.

———. 1977a. "The Infanticide in Euripides' *Medea*." *Yale Classical Studies* 25: 177–91.

———. 1977b. "Character in Sophocles." *Greece and Rome* 24: 121–29.

———. 1984. "The Tragic Homer." *Bulletin of the Institute of Classical Studies* 31: 1–8.

———. 1985. "Anachronism in Greek Tragedy." *Journal of Hellenic Studies* 105: 1–10.

———. 1988. "Women in Tragic Space." *Bulletin of the Institute of Classical Studies* 34: 15–26.

———. 1990. "Constructing Character in Greek Tragedy." In C. Pelling, ed., *Characterization and Individuality in Greek Literature*, 82–99. Oxford.

————. 1994. "Euripides Outside Athens: A Speculative Note." *Illinois Classical Studies* 19: 73–80.

Edwards, M. W. 1977. "Agamemnon's Decision: Freedom and Folly in Aeschylus." *California Studies in Classical Antiquity* 10: 17–38.

Ehrenberg, V. 1954. *Sophocles and Pericles*. Oxford.

Eisner, R. 1980. "Echoes of the *Odyssey* in Euripides' *Helen*." *Maia* 32: 31–37.

Elliott, A. 1969. *Euripides Medea*. Oxford.

Emlyn-Jones, C. 1984. "The Reunion of Penelope and Odysseus." *Greece and Rome* 31: 1–18.

Erbse, H. 1972. "Euripides' Alcestis." *Philologus* 116: 32–52.

————. 1978. "Zu Elektra des Sophokles." *Hermes* 106: 284–300.

————. 1981. "Medea's Abschied von Ihren Kindern (Zu Eur. Med. 1078–80)." *Archaiognosia* 2: 67–82.

Erdmann, W. 1934. *Die Ehe im alten Griechenland*. Munich.

Falkner, T. M. 1989. "The Wrath of Alcmene: Gender, Authority and Old Age in Euripides' *Children of Heracles*." In T. M. Falkner and J. de Luce, eds., *Old Age in Greek and Latin Literature*, 114–31. Albany, N.Y.

Fantham, E. 1986. "Andromache's Child in Euripides and Seneca." In M. J. Cropp, E. Fantham, and S. E. Scully, eds., *Greek Tragedy and Its Legacy: Essays Presented to D. J. Conacher*, 267–80. Calgary.

Fantham, E., H. P. Foley, N. B. Kampen, S. B. Pomeroy, and H. A. Shapiro. 1994. *Women in the Classical World: Image and Text*. Oxford.

Faraone, C. 1994. "Deianira's Mistake and the Demise of Heracles: Erotic Magic in Sophocles' *Trachiniae*." *Helios* 21: 115–35.

Felson-Rubin, N. 1988. "Penelope's Perspective: Character from Plot." In J. M. Bremer, I. F. De Jong, and J. Kalff, eds., *Beyond Oral Poetry: Recent Trends in Homeric Interpretation*, 61–83. Amsterdam.

————. 1994. *Regarding Penelope: From Character to Poetics*. Princeton.

Finley, J. H. 1955. *Pindar and Aeschylus*. Cambridge, Mass.

Finley, M. I. 1955. "Marriage, Sale and Gift in the Homeric World." *Revue internationale des droits de l'antiquité*," ser. 3, 2: 167–94.

————. 1978. *The World of Odysseus*. Rev. ed. Harmondsworth.

————. 1981. *Economy and Society in Ancient Greece*. London.

Fisher, N.R.E. 1981. Review of D. M. Schaps, *The Economic Rights of Women in Ancient Greece*. *Classical Review* 31: 72–74.

————. 1992. *Hybris: A Study in the Values of Honour and Shame in Ancient Greece*. Warminster.

Fitton, J. W. 1961. "The *Suppliant Women* and the *Heracleidae* of Euripides." *Hermes* 89: 430–61.

Flintoff, E. 1980. "The Ending of the *Seven against Thebes*." *Mnemosyne* 33: 244–71.

Flory, S. 1978. "Medea's Right Hand: Promises and Revenge." *Transactions and Proceedings of the American Philological Association* 108: 69–74.

Foley, H. P. 1975. "Sex and State in Ancient Greece." *Diacritics* 5.4: 31–36.

————. 1978. "'Reverse Similes' and Sex Roles in the *Odyssey*." *Arethusa* 11: 7–26.

————. 1981. "The Conception of Women in Athenian Drama." In H. P. Foley, ed., *Reflections of Women in Antiquity*, 127–68. New York and London.

———. 1982a. "The 'Female Intruder' Reconsidered: Women in Aristophanes' *Lysistrata* and *Ecclesiazusae.*" *Classical Philology* 77.1: 1–20.

———. 1982b. "Marriage and Sacrifice in Euripides' *Iphigeneia in Aulis.*" *Arethusa* 15: 159–80.

———. 1985. *Ritual Irony: Poetry and Sacrifice in Euripides.* Ithaca, N.Y.

———. 1988. "Women in Greece." In M. Grant and R. Kitzinger, eds., *Civilization of the Ancient Mediterranean,* 1301–17. New York.

———. 1989. "Medea's Divided Self." *Classical Antiquity* 8.1: 61–85.

———. 1992. "*Anodos* Dramas: Euripides' *Alcestis* and *Helen.*" In R. Hexter and D. Selden, eds., *Innovations of Antiquity,* 133–60. New York and London.

———. 1993. "The Politics of Tragic Lamentation." In A. H. Sommerstein, S. Halliwell, J. Henderson, and B. Zimmermann, eds., *Tragedy, Comedy and the Polis,* 101–43. Bari.

———. 1994. *The Homeric Hymn to Demeter.* Princeton.

———. 1995a. "Tragedy and Democratic Ideology: The Case of Sophocles' *Antigone.*" In B. Goff, ed., *History, Tragedy and Theory,* 131–50. Austin, Tex.

———. 1995b. "Penelope as Moral Agent." In B. Cohen, ed., *The Distaff Side: Representing the Female in Homer's Odyssey.* 93–115. Oxford.

———. 1995c. Review of N. S. Rabinowitz, *Anxiety Veiled: Euripides and the Traffic in Women. Classical Philology* 90: 82–86.

———. 1996. "Antigone as Moral Agent." In M. S. Silk, ed., *Tragedy and the Tragic: Greek Theatre and Beyond,* 49–73. Oxford.

———. 2000. "The Comic Body in Greek Art and Drama." In B. Cohen, ed., *Not the Classical Ideal: Athens and the Construction of the Other in Greek Art,* 275–311. Leiden.

Forster, E. S. [1927] 1983. *Isaeus.* Loeb Classical Library. Cambridge, Mass.

Fortenbaugh, W. W. 1970. "On the Antecedents of Aristotle's Bi-Partite Psychology." *Greek, Roman and Byzantine Studies* 11: 233–50.

Foxhall, L. 1989. "Household, Gender and Property in Classical Athens." *Classical Quarterly* 39. 22–44.

———. 1994. "Pandora Unbound. A Feminist Critique of Foucault's *History of Sexuality.*" In A. Cornwall and N. Lindisfarne, eds., *Dislocating Masculinity: Comparative Ethnographies,* 133–46. New York and London.

Fraenkel, E. 1962. *Aeschylus Agamemnon.* 3 vols. Oxford.

———. 1975. *Early Greek Poetry and Philosophy.* Trans. M. Hadas and J. Willis. Oxford.

Fredricksmeyer, H. C. 1997. "Penelope *Polutropos:* The Crux at *Odyssey* 23.218–24. *American Journal of Philology* 118: 487–97.

Freeman, K. 1971. *Ancilla to the Pre-Socratic Philosophers.* Oxford.

Freese, J. H. [1926] 1967. *Aristotle: The Art of Rhetoric.* Cambridge, Mass.

Freud, S. [1908] 1909. "Family Romances." In J. Strachey, ed., in collaboration with A. Freud and assisted by A. Strachey and A. Tyson, *The Standard Edition of the Complete Psychological Works of Sigmund Freud,* 9:235–41. London, 1953–74.

Friedrich, R. 1993. "Medea *apolis:* On Euripides' Dramatization of the Crisis of the Polis." In A. H. Sommerstein, S. Halliwell, J. Henderson, and B. Zimmermann, eds., *Tragedy, Comedy and the Polis,* 219–39. Bari.

Friedrich, W. H. 1967. "Schuld, Reue und Sühne der Klytaimestra." In *Vorbild und Neugestaltung. Sechs Kapitel zur Geschichte der Tragödie,* 140–57. Göttingen.

Gagarin, M. 1976. *Aeschylean Drama.* Berkeley and Los Angeles.

Gailey, C. W. 1987a. *Kinship to Kingship: Gender Hierachy and State Formation in the Tongan Islands.* Austin, Tex.

———. 1987b. "Evolutionary Perspective on Gender Hierarchy." In B. Hess and M. Ferree, eds., *Analyzing Gender.* Beverly Hills, Calif.

Galis, L. 1992. "Medea's Metamorphosis." *Eranos* 90: 65–81.

Gamble, R. B. 1970. "Euripides' *Suppliant Women:* Decision and Ambivalence. *Hermes* 98: 385–404.

Gantz, T. 1982. "Inherited Guilt in Aeschylus." *Classical Journal* 78: 1–23.

———. 1983. "The Chorus of Aischylos' *Agamemnon.*" *Harvard Studies in Classical Philology* 87: 65–86.

———. 1993. *Early Greek Myth: A Guide to Literary and Artistic Sources.* Baltimore and London.

Gardiner, C. P. 1987. *The Sophoclean Chorus: A Study of Character and Function.* Iowa City.

Garland, R. 1985. *The Greek Way of Death.* Ithaca, N.Y., and London.

———. 1989. "The Well Ordered Corpse: An Investigation into the Motives behind Greek Funerary Legislation." *Bulletin of the Institute of Classical Studies* 36: 1–15.

Garner, R. 1988. "Death and Victory in Euripides' *Alcestis.*" *Classical Antiquity* 7: 58–71.

Garton, C. 1957. "Characterization in Greek Tragedy." *Journal of Hellenic Studies* 77: 247–54.

Garvie, A. F. 1986. *Aeschylus Choephoroi.* Oxford.

Garzya, A. 1951. "Interpretazione dell 'Andromaca' di Euripide." *Dioniso* 14: 109–38.

Gaskin, R. 1990. "Do Homeric Heroes Make Real Decisions?" *Classical Quarterly* 40: 1–15.

Gasti, H. 1993. "Sophocles' *Trachiniae:* A Social or Externalized Aspect of Deianeira's Morality." *Antike und Abendland* 39: 20–28.

Gellie, G. H. 1972. *Sophocles: A Reading.* Melbourne.

———. 1980. "Hecuba and Tragedy." *Antichthon* 14: 30–44.

———. 1988. "The Character of Medea." *Bulletin of the Institute of Classical Studies* 35: 15–22.

Gernet, L. 1921. "Sur l'épiclerat," *Revue des Études grecques* 34: 337–79.

———. 1937. "Notes de lexicologie juridique." In *Mélanges E. Boisacq,* 391–98. Annuaire de l'Institut de Philologie et d'Histoire Orientales et Slaves de l'Université libre de Bruxelles. Brussels.

Gibert, J. 1995. *Change of Mind in Greek Tragedy.* Hypomnemata 108. Göttingen.

Giddens, A. 1979. *Central Problems in Social Theory.* Berkeley and Los Angeles.

Gill, C. 1983. "Did Chrysippus Understand Medea?" *Phronesis* 28: 136–49.

———. 1984. "The *Ethos/Pathos* Distinction in Rhetorical and Literary Criticism." *Classical Quarterly* 34.1: 149–66.

———. 1986. "The Question of Character and Personality in Greek Tragedy." *Poetics Today* 7: 251–73.

———. 1987. "Two Monologues of Self-Division: Euripides' *Medea* 1021–80 and Seneca, *Medea* 893–977." In M. Whitby, P. Hardie, and M. Whitby, eds., *Homo Viator: Classical Essays for John Bramble,* 25–37. Bristol.

———. 1990a. "The Articulation of Self in Euripides' *Hippolytus.*" In A. Powell, ed., *Euripides, Women and Sexuality,* 76–107. London.

———. 1990b. "The Character-Personality Distinction." In C. Pelling, ed., *Characterization and Individuality in Greek Literature*, 1–31. Oxford.

———. 1996. *Personality in Greek Epic, Tragedy, and Philosophy: The Self in Dialogue*. Oxford.

Gilligan, C. 1982. *In a Different Voice*. Cambridge, Mass.

———. 1983. "Do the Social Sciences Have an Adequate Theory of Moral Development?" In N. Haan, R. N. Bellah, P. Rabinow, and W. M. Sullivan, eds., *Social Science as Moral Inquiry*, 33–51. New York.

Gilligan, C., J. V. Ward, and J. M. Taylor. 1988. *Mapping the Moral Domain*. Cambridge, Mass.

Goff, B. 1995a. "Aithra at Eleusis." *Helios* 22.1: 65–78.

———, ed. 1995b. *History, Tragedy, Theory: Dialogues on Athenian Drama*. Austin, Tex.

Goheen, R. F. 1951. *The Imagery of Sophocles' Antigone: A Study in Poetic Language*. Princeton.

———. 1955. "Aspects of Dramatic Symbolism: Three Studies in the *Oresteia*." *American Journal of Philology* 76: 126–32.

Golann, C. P. 1943. "The Third Stasimon of Euripides' *Helena*." *Transactions and Proceedings of the American Philological Association* 76: 31–46.

Golden, M. 1990. *Children and Childhood in Classical Athens*. Baltimore and London.

Golder, H. 1983. "The Mute Andromache." *Transactions and Proceedings of the American Philological Association* 113: 123–33.

Goldhill, S. 1984a. *Language, Sexuality, Narrative: The Oresteia*. Cambridge.

———. 1984b. "Two Notes on *telos* and Related Words in the *Oresteia*." *Journal of Hellenic Studies* 114: 169–76.

———. 1986. *Reading Greek Tragedy*. Cambridge.

———. 1987. "The Great Dionysia and Civic Ideology." *Journal of Hellenic Studies* 107: 58–76.

———. 1990. "Character and Action, Representation and Reading: Greek Tragedy and Its Critics." In C. Pelling, ed., *Characterization and Individuality in Greek Literature*, 100–127. Oxford.

———. 1994. "Representing Democracy: Women at the Great Dionysia." In R. Osborne and S. Hornblower, eds., *Ritual, Finance, Politics: Athenian Democratic Accounts Presented to David Lewis*, 347–69. Oxford.

Goldhill, S., and R. Osborne. 1999. *Performance Culture and Athenian Democracy*. Cambridge.

Gomme, A. W. 1925. "The Position of Women in Classical Athens." *Classical Philology* 20: 1–25.

Gomme, A. W., and F. H. Sandbach. 1973. *Menander: A Commentary*. Oxford.

Goody, J. R. 1976. *Production and Reproduction: A Comparative Study of the Domestic Domain*. Cambridge.

Goody, J. R., and S. Tambiah. 1973. *Bridewealth and Dowry*. Cambridge.

Gould, J. 1978. "Dramatic Character and Human Intelligibility." *Proceedings of the Cambridge Philological Society* 24: 43–63.

———. 1980. "Law, Custom, and Myth: Aspects of the Social Position of Women in Classical Athens." *Journal of Hellenic Studies* 100: 38–59.

Gow, A.S.F. [1950] 1965. *Theocritus*. 2 vols. Cambridge.

Graf, F. 1987. "Orpheus: A Poet among Men." In Jan Bremmer, ed., *Interpretations of Greek Mythology*, 80–106. London and Sydney.

———. 1997. "Medea, the Enchantress from Afar: Remarks on a Well-Known Myth." In J. J. Clauss and S. I. Johnston, eds., *Medea: Essays on Medea in Myth, Literature, and Philosophy*, 21–43. Princeton.

Gredley, B. 1987. "The Place and Time of Victory: Euripides' *Medea*." *Bulletin of the Institute of Classical Studies* 34: 27–39.

Gregory, J. 1979. "Euripides' *Alcestis*." *Hermes* 107: 259–70.

———. 1991. *Euripides and the Instruction of the Athenians*. Ann Arbor, Mich.

Griffin, J. 1998. "The Social Function of Greek Tragedy." *Classical Quarterly* 48.1: 39–61.

Griffith, M. 1995. "Brilliant Dynasts: Power and Politics in the *Oresteia*." *Classical Antiquity* 14: 62–129.

———. 1998. "The King and the Eye: The Rule of the Father in Greek Tragedy." *Proceedings of the Cambridge Philological Society* 44: 20–84.

———. 1999. *Sophocles Antigone*. Cambridge.

Groeneboom, P. 1944. *Aeschylus' Agamemnon*. Groningen. Reprint, Amsterdam, 1966.

Grube, G.M.A. [1941] 1961. *The Drama of Euripides*. London.

Guépin, J.-P. 1968. *The Tragic Paradox: Myth and Ritual in Greek Tragedy*. Amsterdam.

Gundert, H. 1960. "Die Stichomythie zwischen Agamemnon und Klytaimestra." In F. von Eckstein, ed., *Theoria, Festschrift für W. H. Schuchardt*, 69–78 Baden-Baden. Reprinted in H. Hommed, ed., *Wege zu Aischylos*, vol. 2: 219–31. Darmstadt, 1974.

Hall, E. 1989. *Inventing the Barbarian: Greek Self-Definition through Tragedy*. Oxford.

———. 1993. "Asia Unmanned: Images of Victory in Classical Athens." In J. Rich and G. Shipley, eds., *War and Society in the Greek World*, 107–33. London.

———. 1996. *Aeschylus Persians*. Warminster.

———. 1997. "The Sociology of Athenian Tragedy." In P. E. Easterling, ed., *The Cambridge Companion to Greek Tragedy*, 93–126. Cambridge.

———. 1999. "Actor's Song in Tragedy." In S. Goldhill and R. Osborne, eds., *Performance Culture and Athenian Democracy*, 96–124. Cambridge.

Halleran, M. 1988. "Text and Ceremony at the Close of Euripides' *Alkestis*." *Eranos* 86: 123–29.

Halliwell, S. 1986. *Aristotle's Poetics*. London.

———. 1997. "Tragedy and Athenian Rhetoric." In C. Pelling, ed., *Greek Tragedy and the Historian*, 121–42. Oxford.

Hamilton, E., and H. Cairns. 1961. *Plato: The Collected Dialogues*. Princeton.

Hammond, N.G.L. 1965. "Personal Freedom and Its Limitations in the *Oresteia*." *Journal of Hellenic Studies* 85: 47–55.

Hanson, A. 1990. "The Medical Writer's Woman." In D. Halperin, J. J. Winkler, and F. I. Zeitlin, eds., *Before Sexuality: The Construction of Erotic Experience in the Ancient Greek World*, 309–37. Princeton.

Harder, M. A. 1995. "'Right' and 'Wrong' in the *Electras*." *Hermathena* 159: 15–31.

Harder, R. 1993. *Die Frauenrollen bei Euripides*. Stuttgart.

Harrison, A.R.W. 1968. *The Law of Athens*. Vol. 1, *The Family and Property*. Oxford.

Harsh, P. W. 1950. "Penelope and Odysseus in *Odyssey* XIX." *American Journal of Philology* 71: 1–21.

Hartigan, K. V. 1981. "Myth and the *Helen*." *Eranos* 79: 23–31.

Heath, M. 1987. "*Jure principem locum tenet.* Euripides' *Hecuba*." *Bulletin of the Institute of Classical Studies* 34: 40–68.

Hecht, A., and H. Bacon. 1973. *Seven against Thebes*. Oxford.

Henderson, J. 1987. *Aristophanes' Lysistrata*. Oxford.

———. 1991. "Women and the Athenian Dramatic Festivals." *Transactions and Proceedings of the American Philological Association* 121: 133–47.

Henry, M. M. 1985. *Menander's Courtesans and the Greek Tradition*. Frankfurt am Main, Bern, and New York.

Herman, G. 1987. *Ritualized Friendship and the Greek City*. Cambridge.

———. 1993. "Tribal and Civic Codes of Behaviour in Lysias I." *Classical Quarterly* 43: 406–19.

———. 1994. "How Violent Was Athenian Society?" In R. Osborne and S. Hornblower, eds., *Ritual, Finance, Politics: Athenian Democratic Accounts Presented to David Lewis*, 99–117. Oxford.

———. 1995. "Honour, Revenge, and the State in Fourth-Century Athens." In W. Eder, ed., *Die athenische Demokratie im 4. Jahrhundert v. Chr. Vollendung oder Verfall einer Verfassungsform?*, 43–66. Stuttgart.

Hester, D. A. 1971. "Sophocles the Unphilosophical: A Study in the *Antigone*." *Mnemosyne* 24: 11–59.

———. 1980. "Law and Piety in *Antigone*. A Reply to J. Dalfen 'Gesetz ist nicht Gesetz.'" *Wiener Studien* 14: 5–11.

Hirzel, R. 1900. *Agraphos Nomos*. Leipzig.

Hogan, J. C. 1972a. "Thucydides 3.52–68 and Euripides' *Hecuba*." *Phoenix* 26: 241–57.

———. 1972b. "The Protagonists of the *Antigone*." *Arethusa* 5: 93–100.

Holmberg, I. E. 1995. "Euripides' *Helen*: The Most Noble and the Most Chaste." *American Journal of Philology* 116.1: 19–42.

Holst-Warhaft, G. 1992. *Dangerous Voices: Women's Lament and Greek Literature*. New York and London.

Holt, P. 1995. "Metaitios, with Special Reference to Sophokles, *Trach*. 1234." *Rheinisches Museum* 138.1: 33–40.

Hommel, H. 1974. "Schicksal und Verantwortung: Aischylos' Agamemnon 1562." In H. Hommel, ed., *Wege zu Aischylos II*, 232–63. Darmstadt.

Horsley, G.H.R. 1980. "Apollo in Sophokles' *Elektra*." *Antichthon* 14: 18–29.

Houston, B. 1988. "Gilligan and the Politics of a Distinctive Women's Morality." In L. Code, S. Mullett, and C. Overall, eds., *Feminist Perspectives. Philosophical Essays on Methods and Morals*, 168–89. Toronto.

Humphreys, S. C. 1978. *Anthropology and the Greeks*. London.

———. 1983a. *The Family, Women and Death: Comparative Studies*. London and Boston.

———. 1983b. "The Evolution of Legal Process in Ancient Attica." In E. Gabba, ed., *Tria Corda. Scritti in onore di Arnaldo Momigliano*, 229–56. Como.

———. 1986. "Kinship Patterns in Athenian Courts." *Greek, Roman and Byzantine Studies* 27.1: 57–91.

———. 1995. "Women's Stories." In E. D. Reeder, ed., *Pandora: Women in Classical Greece*, 102–110. Princeton.

Hunter, V. 1994. *Policing Athens: Social Control in Attic Lawsuits, 420–320 B.C.* Princeton.

Hutchinson, G. O. 1985. *Aeschylus. Septem contra Thebas.* Oxford.

Ierulli, M. 1993. "A Community of Women?: The Protagonist and the Chorus in Sophocles' *Electra*." *Métis* 8.1–2: 217–29.

Iesi, F. 1965. "L'Egitto infero nell' *Elena* di Euripide." *Aegyptus* 45: 56–69.

Jachmann, G. 1936. *Binneninterpolation.* Vol. 2. Nachr. Götting. Ges. der Wissenschaften, 185–215.

Jameson, M. 1997. "Women and Democracy in Fourth-century Athens." In P. Brulé and J. Oulhen, eds., *Esclavage, guerre, économie en Grèce ancienne: Hommages à Yvon Garlan*, 95–107. Rennes.

Jebb, R. [1924] 1962. *Sophocles, the Plays and Fragments.* Part VI: *The Electra*. Amsterdam.

Jenkyns, I. 1983. "Is There Life after Marriage? A Study of the Abduction Motif in Vase Paintings of the Athenian Wedding Ceremony." *Bulletin of the Institute of Classical Studies* 30: 137–45.

Jens, W. 1967. "Antigone-Interpretationen." In H. Diller, ed., *Sophokles*, 295–310. Darmstadt.

Johansen, H. Friis. 1964. "Die Elektra des Sophokles: Versuch einer neuen Deutung." *Classica et Medievalia* 25: 8–32.

Johnson, P. J. 1997. "Woman's Third Face: A Psycho-Sexual Reconsideration of Sophocles' *Antigone*." *Arethusa* 30.3: 369–98.

Johnston, S. I. 1999. *Restless Dead: Encounters between the Living and the Dead in Ancient Greece.* Princeton.

Jones, J. 1962. *On Aristotle and Greek Tragedy.* London.

Jouan, F. 1997. "Les rites funéraires dans les *Suppliantes* d'Euripides." *Kernos* 10: 215–32.

Judet de la Combe, P. 1989–90. "La force argumentative du dérisoire: *Ag*. 931–43." *Sacris Erudiri* 31: 209–37.

Juffras, D. M. 1991. "Sophocles' *Electra* 973–85 and Tyrannicide." *Transactions and Proceedings of the American Philological Association* 121: 99–108.

———. 1993. "Helen and Other Victims in Euripides' *Helen*." *Hermes* 121: 45–57.

Just, R. 1975. "The Conception of Women in Classical Athens." *Journal of the Anthropological Society of Oxford* 6.3: 153–70.

———. 1989. *Women in Athenian Law and Life.* New York and London.

Kamerbeek, J. C. 1974. *Electra.* Leiden.

Kannicht, R. 1969. *Euripides Helena.* 2 vols. Heidelberg.

Katz, M. A. 1991. *Penelope's Renown: Meaning and Indeterminacy in the Odyssey.* Princeton.

———. 1992. "Patriarchy, Ideology, and the *Epikleros*." *Studi italiani di filologia classica*, 3d ser, 10, fasc. 1–2: 692–708.

———. 1994a. "Homecoming and Hospitality: Recognition and the Construction of Identity in the *Odyssey*." In S. Oberhelman, V. Kelly, and R. J. Golsan, eds., *Epic and Epoch: Essays on the Interpretation and History of a Genre*, 49–75. Lubbock, Tex.

———. 1994b. "The Character of Tragedy: Women and the Greek Imagination." *Arethusa* 27.1: 81–103.

Kells, J. H. 1973. *Sophocles Electra*. Cambridge.

Kessel, R. 1973. "Kritische und Exegetische Kleinigkeiten IV." *Rheinisches Museum* 116: 97–112.

King, H. 1983. "Bound to Bleed: Artemis and Greek Women." In A. Cameron and A. Kuhrt, eds., *Images of Women in Antiquity*, 109–27. Detroit.

———. 1998. *Hippocrates' Women: Reading the Female Body in Ancient Greece*. New York and London.

King, K. C. 1985. "The Politics of Imitation: Euripides' *Hekabe* and the Homeric Achilles." *Arethusa* 18: 47–66.

Kirkwood, G. 1942. "Two Structural Features of Sophocles' *Electra*." *Transactions and Proceedings of the American Philological Association* 73: 85–95.

———. 1947. "Hecuba and Nomos." *Transactions and Proceedings of the American Philological Association* 78: 61–68.

———. 1958. *A Study of Sophoclean Drama*. Ithaca, N.Y.

———. 1965. "Homer and Sophocles' *Ajax*." In M. J. Anderson, ed., *Classical Drama and Its Influence*, 53–70. New York and London.

Kitto, H.D.F. 1969. *Greek Tragedy*. London.

Kitzinger, R. 1976. "Stylistic Methods of Characterization in Sophocles' *Antigone*." Ph.D. dissertation, Stanford University.

———. 1991. "Why Mourning Becomes Elektra." *Classical Antiquity* 10.2: 298–327.

Knox, B.M.W. 1964. *The Heroic Temper: Studies in Sophoclean Tragedy*. Berkeley and Los Angeles.

———. 1966. "Second Thoughts in Greek Tragedy." *Greek, Roman and Byzantine Studies* 7: 213–32.

———. 1977. "The *Medea* of Euripides." *Yale Classical Studies* 25: 193–225. Reprinted in *Word and Action: Essays on Ancient Theater*, 292–322. Baltimore and London, 1979, 1986.

Kohlberg, L. 1981. *The Philosophy of Moral Development: Moral Stages and the Ideology of Justice*. San Francisco.

———. 1984. *The Psychology of Moral Development*. San Francisco.

Konishi, H. 1989a. "Agamemnon's Reasons for Yielding." *American Journal of Philology* 110: 220–22.

———. 1989b. *The Plot of Aeschylus' Oresteia: A Literary Commentary*. Amsterdam.

Konstan, D. 1996. "Greek Friendship." *American Journal of Philology* 117.1: 71–94.

Kovacs, P. D. 1980. *The Andromache of Euripides: An Interpretation*. American Classical Studies 6. Chico, Calif.

———. 1986. "On Medea's Great Monologue." *Classical Quarterly* 36: 343–52.

———. 1987. *The Heroic Muse: Studies in the Hippolytus and Hecuba of Euripides*. Baltimore.

Kranz, W. 1919. "Zwei Lieder des Agamemnon." *Hermes* 54: 301–20. Reprinted in *Studien zur antiken Literatur und ihrem Fortwirken. Kleine Schriften*, 264–78. Heidelberg, 1967.

———. 1933. *Stasimon*. Berlin.

Kurke, L. 1991. *The Traffic in Praise: Pindar and the Poetics of Social Economy*. Ithaca, N.Y.

———. 1992. The Politics of *habrosyne* in Archaic Greece." *Classical Antiquity* 23.1: 91–120.

Kyriakou, P. 1997. "All in the Family: Present and Past in Euripides' *Andromache*." *Mnemosyne* 50.1: 7–26.

Lacey, W. K. 1966. "Homeric HEDNA and Penelope's KYRIOS." *Journal of Hellenic Studies* 86: 55–68.

———. 1968. *The Family in Classical Greece*. Ithaca, N.Y.

Lane, W. J., and A. M. Lane. 1986. "The Politics of *Antigone*." In P. J. Euben, ed., *Greek Tragedy and Political Theory*, 162–82. Berkeley and Los Angeles.

Lanza, D. 1963. "*Nomos* e *ison* in Euripide." *Rivista di Filologia* 91: 416–39.

Lattimore, R. 1959. *The Trojan Women*. In D. Grene and R. Lattimore, eds., *The Complete Greek Tragedies: Euripides*. Vol. 3. Chicago.

———. 1964. *Story Patterns in Greek Tragedy*. Ann Arbor, Mich.

Lavagnini, B. 1947. "Echi del rito eleusino in Euripide." *American Journal of Philology* 68: 82–86.

Lawrence, S. E. 1978. "The Dramatic Epistemology of Sophocles' *Trachiniae*." *Phoenix* 32: 288–304.

Leach, E. R. 1982. *Social Anthropology*. London.

Lebeck, A. 1971. *The Oresteia: A Study in Language and Structure*. Cambridge.

Leduc, C. 1992. "Marriage in Ancient Greece." In P. Schmitt Pantel, ed., *A History of Women in the West*. Vol. 1, *From Ancient Goddesses to Christian Saints*, 233–95. Cambridge, Mass.

Lee, K. H. 1975. "Euripides' *Andromache*: Observations on Form and Meaning." *Antichthon* 9: 4–16.

Leinieks, V. 1962. *The Plays of Sophocles*. Amsterdam.

Lesky, A. 1925. *Alkestis. Der Mythos und das Drama*. Sitzungsbericht der Akademie der Österreichischen Akademie der Wissenschaft in Wien, Phil.-Hist. Klasse, vol. 203, no. 2. Vienna.

———. 1966. "Decision and Responsibility in the Tragedy of Aeschylus." *Journal of Hellenic Studies* 86: 78–85.

———. 1983. *Greek Tragic Poetry*. Trans. M. Dillon. New Haven, Conn.

Letters, F.J.H. 1953. *The Life and Work of Sophocles*. London and New York.

Levine, R. A. 1982. "*Gusii funerals*." *Ethos* 10.1: 26–65.

Levy, C. S. 1963. "Antigone's Motives: A Suggested Interpretation." *Transactions and Proceedings of the American Philological Association* 94: 137–44.

Lewis, D. M. 1955. "Notes on Attic Inscriptions II: Who Was Lysistrata?" *Annual of the British School at Athens* 50: 1–12.

Linforth, I. M. 1961. "Antigone and Creon." *University of California Publications in Classical Philology* 15.5: 183–260.

———. 1963. "Electra's Day and the Tragedy of Sophocles." *University of California Publications in Classical Philology* 19.2: 89–126.

Lintott, A. W. 1993. "Civil Strife and Human Nature in Thucydides." In J. H. Molyneux, ed., *Literary Responses to Civil Discord*, 25–35. Nottingham.

Lloyd, M. A. 1985. "Euripides' *Alcestis*." *Greece and Rome* 32: 119–31.

———. 1992. *The Agon in Euripides*. Oxford.

———. 1994. *Euripides' Andromache*. Warminster.

Lloyd-Jones, H. 1959. "The End of the *Seven against Thebes*." *Classical Quarterly* 53, n.s. 9: 80–115.

———. 1980. "Euripides' *Medea* 1056–80." *Würzburger Jahrbücher für die Altertums-*

wissenschaft, n.s., 6a: 51–59. Reprinted in *Greek Epic, Lyric, and Tragedy: The Academic Papers of Sir Hugh Lloyd-Jones*, 440–51. Oxford.

———. [1979] 1993. *Aeschylus: The Oresteia*. Berkeley and Los Angeles. Originally published 1990. Englewood Cliffs, N.J., 1979.

Lloyd-Jones, H. 1994. *Sophocles*. Vols. 1–3. Loeb Classical Library. Cambridge, Mass.

Long, A. A. 1968. *Language and Thought in Sophocles*. London.

———. 1986. "Pro and Contra Fratricide. Aeschylus' *Septem* 653–719." In J. H. Betts, J. T. Hooker, and J. R. Green, eds., *Studies in Honor of T.B.L. Webster*, 179–89. Bristol.

Loraux, N. 1978. "Sur la race des femmes et quelques-unes de ses tribus." *Arethusa* 11.1–2: 43–88.

———. 1986. *The Invention of Athens*. Trans. Alan Sheridan. Cambridge, Mass., and London.

———. 1987. *Tragic Ways of Killing a Woman*. Trans. A. Forster. Cambridge, Mass.

———. 1990. *Les mères en deuil*. Paris.

———. 1993. *The Children of Athena: Athenian Ideas about Citizenship and the Division between the Sexes*. Trans. C. Levine. Princeton.

———. 1995a. *The Experiences of Tiresias: The Feminine and the Greek Man*. Princeton.

———. 1995b. "Therefore, Socrates Is Immortal." In *The Experiences of Tiresias: The Feminine and the Greek Man*, 145–66. Princeton.

Lord, M. L. 1967. "Withdrawal and Return: An Epic Story Pattern in the Homeric *Hymn to Demeter*." *Classical Journal* 62: 24–48.

Lupas, L., and Z. Petre. 1981. *Commentaire aux Sept contre Thebes d'Eschyle*. Bucarest and Paris.

Luppe, W. 1995. "Ein neuer früher Medeia-Papyrus P. Berol. 21257." *Archiv für Papyrusforschung und verwandte Gebiete* 41: 34–39.

Luschnig, C.A.E. 1976. "Euripides' *Hekabe*: The Time Is Out of Joint." *Classical Journal* 71: 227–41.

———. 1995. *The Gorgon's Severed Head: Studies of Alcestis, Electra, and Phoenissae*. Leiden.

Lutz, C. A. 1988. *Unnatural Emotions: Everyday Sentiments on a Micronesian Atoll and Their Challenge to Western Theory*. Chicago and London.

MacDowell, D. M. 1963. *Athenian Homocide Law in the Age of the Orators*. Manchester.

———. 1978. *The Law in Classical Athens*. Ithaca, N.Y., and London.

———. 1989. "The *Oikos* in Athenian Law." *Classical Quarterly* 39: 10–21.

MacKay, L. A. 1962. "Antigone, Coriolanus and Hegel." *Transactions and Proceedings of the American Philological Association* 93: 166–74.

MacKinnon, J. K. 1971. "Heracles' Intention in His Second Request to Hyllus." *Classical Quarterly* 65, n.s., 21: 33–41.

Macleod, C. 1983. *Collected Essays*. Oxford.

Maddalena, A. 1963. "La Medea di Euripide." *Rivista di Filologia* 93.3: 129–52.

Manuwald, B. 1983. "Der Mord an den Kindern: Bemerkungen zu den Medea-Tragödien des Euripides und des Neophron." *Wiener Studien*, n.s., 17: 27–61.

Masaracchia, E. 1992. "Il velo di Alcesti." *Quaderni Urbinati di Cultura Classica* 42: 29–35.

———. 1993. "La 'estraneità' di Alcesti." *Quaderni Urbinati di Cultura Classica* 45: 57–82.

Mastronarde, D. J. 1979. *Contact and Discontinuity: Some Conventions of Speech and Action on the Greek Tragic Stage*. Berkeley and Los Angeles.

———. 1986. "The Optimistic Rationalist in Euripides: Theseus, Jocasta, Teiresias." In M. J. Cropp, E. Fantham, and S. E. Scully, eds., *Greek Tragedy and Its Legacy: Essays Presented to D. J. Conacher*, 201–11. Calgary, Alberta.

———. 1994. *Euripides Phoenissae*. Cambridge.

Matthaei, L. 1918. *Studies in Greek Tragedy*. Cambridge.

McClure, L. 1997a. "Clytemnestra's Binding Spell (*Ag.* 958–74)." *Classical Journal* 92: 123–40.

———. 1997b. "*Logos Gunaikos*: Speech, Gender, and Spectatorship in the *Oresteia*." *Helios* 24.2: 112–35.

———. 1999. *Spoken Like a Woman: Speech and Gender in Athenian Drama*. Princeton.

McDermott, E. 1989. *Euripides' Medea: The Incarnation of Disorder*. University Park, Pa.

McDevitt, A. S. 1983. "Shame, Honour and the Hero in Sophocles' *Electra*." *Antichthon* 17: 1–12.

McIntyre, A. 1985. *After Virtue: A Study in Moral Theory*. 2nd ed. London.

McKeon, R., ed. 1941. *The Basic Works of Aristotle*. New York.

McManus, B. F. 1990. "Multicentering: The Case of the Athenian Bride." *Helios* 17: 225–35.

Méautis, G. 1936. *Eschyle et la trilogie*. Paris.

Meiggs, R., and D. Lewis, eds. 1969. *A Selection of Greek Historical Inscriptions*. Oxford.

Mellon, P. 1974. "The Ending of the *Seven against Thebes* and Its Relation to Sophocles' *Antigone* and Euripides' *Phoenissae*." Ph.D. dissertation, Stanford University.

Meltzer, G. 1994. "Where *Is* the Glory of Troy? *Kleos* in Euripides' *Helen*." *Classical Antiquity* 31.2: 234–55.

Mercier, C. E. 1990. "Suppliant Ritual in Euripidean Tragedy." Ph.D. dissertation, Columbia University.

———. 1993. "Hekabe's Extended Supplication (*Hek.* 752–888)." *Transactions and Proceedings of the American Philological Association* 123: 149–60.

Meridor, R. 1978. "Hecuba's Revenge: Some Observations on Euripides' *Hecuba*." *American Journal of Philology* 99: 28–35.

———. 1983. "The Function of Polymestor's Crime in the *Hecuba* of Euripides." *Eranos* 8: 13–20.

———. 1987. "Aesch. *Ag.* 944–57: Why Does Agamemnon Give In?" *Classical Philology* 82: 38–43.

Michelini, A. N. 1979. "Character and Character Change in Aeschylus: Clytaimestra and the Furies." *Ramus* 8: 153–64.

———. 1987. *Euripides and the Tragic Paradox*. Madison, Wis.

———. 1989. "Neophron and Euripides' *Medea* 1056–80." *Transactions and Proceedings of the American Philological Association* 119: 115–35.

———. 1991. "The Maze of the Logos: Euripides, *Suppliants*." *Ramus* 20.1: 16–36.

Mills, S. 1976. "Euripides' *Medea*: A Study in Dramatic Mythopoeia." Ph.D. dissertation, Stanford, University.

———. 1980. "The Sorrows of Medea." *Classical Philology* 75: 289–96.

Minadeo, R. W. 1967. "Plot, Theme, and Meaning in Sophocles' *Electra*." *Classica et Medievalia* 28: 114–42.

Mirto, M. S. 1984. "Il lutto e la cultura delle madri: le *Supplici* di Euripide." *Quaderni Urbinati di Cultura Classica* 18: 55–88.

Mitchell-Boyask, R. 1993. "Sacrifice and Revenge in Euripides' Hecuba." *Ramus* 22.2: 116–34.

Modrzejewski, J. M. 1981. "La structure juridique du mariage grec." In E. Bresciani, G. Geraci, S. Perigotti, and G. Susini, eds., *Scritti in onore di Orsolina Montevecchi*, 231–68. Bologna.

Monsacré, H. 1984. *Les larmes d'Achille. Le heros, la femme et la souffrance dans la poésie d'Homère*. Paris.

Moody-Adams, M. M. 1991. "Gender and the Complexity of Moral Voices." In C. Card, ed., *Feminist Ethics*, 195–212. Lawrence, Kan.

Moreau, A. 1985. *Eschyle. La violence et le chaos*. Paris.

Morris, I. 1986. "The Use and Abuse of Homer." *Classical Antiquity* 5: 81–138.

———. 1987. *Burial and Ancient Society*. Cambridge.

———. 1989. "Attitudes towards Death in Archaic Greece." *Classical Antiquity* 8.2: 296–320.

———. 1994. "Everyman's Grave." In A. L. Boeghold and A. C. Scafuro., eds., *Athenian Identity and Civic Ideology*, 67–101. Baltimore and London.

Mossé, C. 1981. "La femme dans la société homérique." *Klio* 63: 149–57.

Mossman, J. 1995. *Wild Justice: A Study of Euripides' Hecuba*. Oxford.

Most, G. 1994. "Sophocles, Electra 1086–87." In A. Bierl and P. von Moellendorf, eds., *Orchestra: Drama, Mythos, Bühne*, 129–38. Stuttgart and Leipzig.

Mukta, P. 1999. "The Civilizing Mission—The Regulation and Control of Mourning in Western India." *Feminist Review* 63: 25–47.

Müller, G. 1951. "Interpolationen in der *Medea* des Euripides." *Studi Italiani di Filolologia Classica*, n.s., 25: 65–82.

Murnaghan, S. 1986a. "Penelope's *Agnoia*: Knowledge, Power and Gender in the *Odyssey*." *Helios* 13.2: 103–16.

———. 1986b. "Antigone 904–920 and the Institution of Marriage." *American Journal of Philology* 107: 192–207.

———. 1987. *Disguise and Recognition in the Odyssey*. Princeton.

———. 1994. "Reading Penelope." In S. Oberhelman, V. Kelly, and R. J. Golsan, eds., *Epic and Epoch: Essays on the Interpretation and History of a Genre*, 76–96. Lubbock, Tex.

Murnaghan, S. 1995. "The Plan of Athena." In B. Cohen, ed., *The Distaff Side: Representing the Female in Homer's Odyssey*, 61–80. Oxford.

Murray, A. T. [1935] 1988. *Demosthenes*. Vol. 6. Loeb Classical Library. Cambridge, Mass.

Murray, G. [1902] 1963. *Euripidis Fabulae*. Vol. 1. Oxford.

Musurillo, H. 1967. *The Light and the Darkness*. Leiden.

Naerebout, F. G. 1987. "Male-Female Relationships in the Homeric Epics." In J. Blok and P. Mason, eds., *Sexual Symmetry: Studies in Ancient Society*, 109–27. Amsterdam.

Nagy, G. 1990. *Pindar's Homer: The Lyric Possession of an Epic Past*. Baltimore and London.

Nails, D. 1983. "Social Scientific Sexism: Gilligan's Mismeasure of Man." *Social Research* 50.3: 643–64.

Neuberg, M. 1990. "How Like a Woman: Antigone's 'Inconsistency.'" *Classical Quarterly* 40.1: 54–76.

———. 1991. "Clytemnestra and the Alastor: Aesch. *Ag.* 1497ff." *Quaderni Urbinati di Cultura Classica* 38: 37–68.

Neustadt, E. 1929. "Wort und Geschehen in Aischylos' Agamemnon." *Hermes* 64: 243–265.

Newiger, H.-J. 1969. "Hofmannsthals Elektra und die griechische Tragödie." *Arkadia* 4: 138–63.

Newton, R. M. 1985. "Ino in Euripides' *Medea.*" *American Journal of Philology* 106: 496–502.

———. 1989. "Medea's Passionate Poison." *Syllecta Classica* 1: 13–20.

Nielsen, R. M. 1976. "*Alcestis*: A Paradox in Dying." *Ramus* 5: 92–109.

Nilsson, M. 1932. *The Mycenean Origin of Greek Mythology.* Berkeley.

———. 1967. *Geschichte der griechischen Religion.* Vol. 1. Munich.

North, H. 1966. *Sophrosyne: Self-Knowledge and Self-Restraint in Greek Literature.* Ithaca, N.Y.

Norwood, G. 1948. *Greek Tragedy.* 4th ed. London.

Nussbaum, M. 1986. *The Fragility of Goodness.* Cambridge.

Oakley, J. H., and R. H. Sinos. 1993. *The Wedding in Classical Athens.* Madison, Wisc.

Ober, J. 1989. *Mass and Elite in Democratic Athens: Rhetoric, Ideology and the Power of the People.* Princeton.

———. 1993. "The *Polis* as a Society: Aristotle, John Rawls and the Athenian Social Contract." In M. H. Hansen, ed., *The Ancient Greek City-State,* 129–60. Copenhagen.

———. 1994. "Classical Greek Times." In M. Howard, G. J. Andreopoulos, and M. R. Shulman, eds., *The Laws of War: Constraints on Warfare in the Western World.* New Haven, Conn. 12–26, 227–30. Reprinted as "The Rules of War in Classical Greece." In *The Athenian Revolution: Essays on Ancient Greek Democracy and Political Theory,* 53–71. Princeton, 1996.

O'Connor-Visser, E.A.M.E. 1987. *Aspects of Human Sacrifice in the Tragedies of Euripides.* Amsterdam.

O'Daly, G.J.P. 1985. "Clytemnestra and the Elders: Dramatic Technique in Aeschylus' *Agamemnon* 1372–1576." *Museum Helveticum* 42: 1–19.

Ogden, D. 1996. *Greek Bastardy in the Classical and Hellenistic Periods.* Oxford.

O'Higgins, D. 1993. "Above Rubies: Admetus' Perfect Wife." *Arethusa* 26.1: 77–98.

Ohlander, S. 1989. *Dramatic Suspense in Euripides' and Seneca's Medea.* American University Studies, ser. 17. Classical Languages and Literature 6. New York, Bern, Frankfurt am Main, and Paris.

Okin, S. 1979. *Women in Western Political Thought.* Princeton.

Ormand, K.W.B. 1996. "Silent by Convention? Sophocles' Tekmessa." *American Journal of Philology* 117.1: 37–64.

———. 1999. *Exchange and the Maiden: Marriage in Sophoclean Tragedy.* Austin, Tex.

Ortner, S. 1996. *Making Gender: The Politics and Erotics of Culture.* Boston.

Ortner, S., and H. Whitehead. 1981. *Sexual Meanings: The Cultural Construction of Gender and Sexuality.* Cambridge.

Orwin, C. 1980. "Feminine Justice. The End of the *Seven against Thebes.*" *Classical Philology* 75: 187–96.

Osborne, R. 1985. *Demos: The Discovery of Classical Attica.* Cambridge.

———. 1993. "Women and Sacrifice in Classical Greece." *Classical Quarterly* 43.2: 392–405.

————. 1997. "Law, the Democratic Citizen and the Representation of Women in Classical Athens." *Past and Present* 115: 5–33.

Ostwald, M. 1969. *Nomos and the Beginnings of Athenian Democracy*. Oxford.

————. 1973. "Was There a Concept *agraphos nomos* in Classical Greece?" *Phronesis*, suppl. 1: 70–104.

Oudemans, C. W., and A.P.M.H. Lardinois. 1987. *Tragic Ambiguity: Anthropology, Philosophy and Sophocles' Antigone*. Leiden.

Owen, A. S. 1936. "The Date of Sophocles' *Electra*." In C. Bailey, E. A. Barber, C. M. Bowra, J. D. Denniston, and D. L. Page, eds., *Greek Poetry and Life: Essays Presented to Gilbert Murray on His Seventieth Birthday*," 145–57. Oxford.

Padel, R. 1990. "Making Space Speak." In J. J. Winkler and F. I. Zeitlin, eds., *Nothing to Do with Dionysus? Athenian Drama and Its Social Context*, 336–65. Princeton.

————. 1992. *In and Out of the Mind: Greek Images of the Tragic Self*. Princeton.

————. 1995. *Whom the Gods Destroy: Elements of Greek and Tragic Madness*. Princeton.

Paduano, G. 1968. *La formazione del mondo ideologico e poetico di Euripide*. Pisa.

Page, D. [1938] 1971. *Medea*. Oxford.

————. 1962. *Greek Literary Papyri*. Cambridge, Mass.

Papi, D. G. 1987. "Victors and Sufferers in Euripides' *Helen*." *American Journal of Philology* 108: 27–40.

Parker, R. 1983. *Miasma: Pollution and Purification in Early Greek Religion*. Oxford.

Patterson, C. B. 1981. *Pericles' Citizenship Law of 451–50 B. C.* Salem, N.H.

————. 1986. "Hai Attikai: The Other Athenians." *Helios* 13: 49–67.

————. 1990. "Those Athenian Bastards." *Classical Antiquity* 9: 40–73.

————. 1991. "Marriage and the Married Woman in Athenian Law." In S. B. Pomeroy, ed., *Women's History and Ancient History*, 48–72. Chapel Hill and London.

————. 1998. *The Family in Greek History*. Cambridge, Mass.

Pearson, A. C. 1930. "Aeschylus' *Agamenon* 1525ff." *Classical Review* 44: 55.

Pearson, L. 1962. *Popular Ethics in Ancient Greece*. Stanford, Calif.

Pearson, M. P. 1983. "Mortuary Practices, Society, and Ideology: An Ethnoarchaeological Study." In I. Hodder, ed., *Symbolic and Structural Archaeology*, 99–113. Cambridge.

Pedrick, V. 1988. "The Hospitality of Noble Women in the *Odyssey*." *Helios* 15.2: 85–102.

Peek, W. 1955. *Griechische Vers-Inschriften*. Vol 1. Berlin.

Pelling, C., ed. 1990. *Characterization and Individuality in Greek Literature*. Oxford.

————. 1997. *Greek Tragedy and the Historian*. Oxford.

————. 2000. *Literary Texts and the Greek Historian*. London and New York.

Peradotto J. 1969. "The Omen of the Eagles and the *ethos* of Agamemnon." *Phoenix* 23: 237–63.

Perlman, S. 1976. "Panhellenism, the Polis and Imperialism." *Historia* 25: 1–30.

Perrin, B. [1914] 1982. *Plutarch's Lives*. Vol. 1. Loeb Classical Library. Cambridge, Mass.

Philippo, S. 1995. "Family Ties: Significant Patronymics in Euripides' *Andromache*." *Classical Quarterly* 45: 355–71.

Pintacuda, M. 1978. *La musica nella tragedia greca*. Maggio.

Pipili, M. 1987. *Laconian Iconography of the Sixth Century B.C.* Oxford University Committee for Archaeology, Monograph no. 12. Oxford. 54–58.

Pippin, A. N. 1960. "Euripides' *Helen*: A Comedy of Ideas." *Classical Philology* 55: 151–63.

Pitt-Rivers, J. 1977. "The Law of Hospitality" and "Women and Sanctuary in the Mediterranean." In *The Fate of Schechem or The Politics of Sex: Essays in the Anthropology of the Mediterranean*, 94–112 and 113–25. Cambridge.

Podlecki, A. J. 1965. *The Political Background of Aeschylean Tragedy*. Ann Arbor, Mich.

———, ed. 1989. *Aeschylus Eumenides*. Warminster.

———. 1990. "Could Women Attend the Theater in Ancient Athens? A Collection of Testimonia." *Ancient World* 21: 27–43.

Pomeroy, S. B. 1975. *Goddesses, Whores, Wives, and Slaves: Women in Classical Antiquity*. New York.

———. 1984. *Women in Hellenistic Europe from Alexander to Cleopatra*. New York.

———. 1997. *Families in Classical and Hellenistic Greece*. Oxford.

Porter, D. 1987. *Only Connect: Three Studies in Greek Tragedy*. Lanham, Md.

Porter, E. J. 1991. *Women and Moral Identity*. North Sydney, Australia.

Prott, J. de, and L. Ziehen. 1896–1906. *Leges Graecorum Sacrae*. Leipzig.

Pucci, P. 1980. *The Violence of Pity in Euripides' Medea*. Ithaca, N.Y.

———. 1994. "Peitho nell'*Orestea* di Eschilo." *Museum Criticum* 29: 75–138.

———. 1997. "The *Helen* and Euripides' 'Comic Art.'" *Colby Quarterly* 33.1: 42–75.

Pulleyn, S. 1997. "Erotic Undertones in the Language of Clytemnestra." *Classical Quarterly* 42.2: 565–67.

Rabinowitz, N. S. 1981. "From Force to Persuasion: Aeschylus' *Oresteia* as Cosmogonic Myth." *Ramus* 10: 159–91.

———. 1993. *Anxiety Veiled: Euripides and the Traffic in Women*. Ithaca, N.Y., and London.

Reckford, K. 1968. "Medea's First Exit." *Transactions and Proceedings of the American Philological Association* 99: 329–59.

———. 1985. "Concepts of Demoralization in the *Hecuba*." In P. Burian, ed., *Directions in Euripidean Criticism*, 112–28. Durham, N.C.

Redfield, J. 1982. "Notes on the Greek Wedding." *Arethusa* 15: 188–91.

Reeve, M. D. 1972. "Euripides' *Medea* 1021–80." *Classical Quarterly*, 65, n.s., 22: 51–61.

Rehm, R. 1988. "The Staging of Suppliant Plays." *Greek, Roman and Byzantine Studies* 29: 263–307.

———. 1989. "Medea and the Logos of the Heroic." *Eranos* 87: 97–115.

———. 1992. *Greek Tragic Theatre*. London.

———. 1994. *Marriage to Death: The Conflation of Wedding and Funeral Rituals in Greek Tragedy*. Princeton.

Rehrenboeck, G. 1988. "Pherekrates Persai fr. 193K und die Datierung der sophokleischen Elektra." *Wiener Studien* 101: 47–57.

Reiner, E. 1938. *Die rituelle totenklage der Griechen*. Stuttgart-Berlin.

Reinhardt, K. 1979. *Sophokles*. Trans. H. Harvey and D. Harvey. Oxford.

Rickert, G. A. 1987. "*Akrasia* and Euripides' *Medea*." *Harvard Studies in Classical Philology* 91: 91–117.

Rivier, A. 1973. "En marge d'*Alceste* et de quelques interprétations récentes, II." *Museum Helveticum* 30: 130–43.

Roberts, S. R. 1978. *The Attic Pyxis*. Chicago.

Robinson, D. B. 1979. "Helen and Persephone, Sparta and Demeter." In G. Bowersock, W. Burkert, and M. Putnam, eds., *Arktouros: Hellenic Studies Presented to Bernard M. W. Knox on the Occasion of his 65th birthday,* 162–72. Berlin and New York.

Rohdich, H. 1968. *Die Euripideische Tragödie.* Heidelberg.

———. 1980. *Antigone, Beitrag zu einer Theorie des Sophokleischen Helden.* Heidelberg.

Roisman, H. M. 1987. "Penelope's Indignation." *Transactions and Proceedings of the American Philological Association* 117: 59–68.

Roisman, J. 1996. "Creon's Roles and Personality in Sophocles' *Antigone.*" *Helios* 23.1: 21–42.

Ronnet, G. 1980. Review of G. Cerri, *Legislazione orale e tragedia greca. Revue de Philologie* 54: 348–49.

Rosaldo, M. Z. 1980. *Knowledge and Passion: Ilongot Notions of Self and Social Life.* Cambridge.

Rosaldo, M. Z., and L. Lamphere. 1974. *Woman, Culture, and Society.* Stanford, Calif.

Rosaldo, R. 1980. *Ilongot Headhunting, 1883–1974: A Study in Society and History.* Stanford, Calif.

Rose, H. J. 1956. "Aeschylus the Psychologist." *Symbolae Osloenses* 32: 1–21.

Rosenmeyer, T. G. 1961. *The Masks of Tragedy.* Berkeley and Los Angeles.

———. 1982. *The Art of Aeschylus.* Berkeley and Los Angeles.

Roy, J. 1999. "*Polis* and *Oikos* in Classical Athens." *Greece and Rome* 46: 1–17.

Rudhardt, J. 1978. "À propos de l'hymne homérique à Demeter." *Museum Helveticum* 35: 7–31.

Russo, J. A. 1968. "Homer against His Tradition." *Arion* 7.2: 275–95.

———. 1982. "Interview and Aftermath: Dream, Fantasy, and Intuition in *Odyssey* 19 and 20." *American Journal of Philology* 103: 4–18.

Ryzman, M. 1991. "Deianeira's Moral Behaviour in the Context of the Natural Laws in Sophocles' *Trachiniae.*" *Hermes* 119: 385–98.

Saïd, S. 1981. "La tragédie de la vengeance." In R. Verdier, ed., *La vengeance dans la pensée occidentale,* 4: 47–90. Paris.

———, 1997. "Alceste ou la tragédie de l'*oikos*." In *Euripide Alceste: Du texte à la scène,* 55–71. Toulouse.

———. 1998. "Tragedy and Politics." In D. Boedeker and K. A. Raaflaub, eds., *Democracy, Empire, and the Arts in Fifth-Century Athens,* 275–96. Cambridge, Mass. and London.

Sandbach, F. H. 1977. "Sophocles' *Electra* 77–95." *Proceedings of the Cambridge Philological Society* 23: 71–73.

Sansone, D. 1985. "Theonoe and Theoclymenus." *Symbolae Osloenses* 60: 17–36.

Scafuro, A. 1990. "Discourses of Sexual Violation in Mythic Accounts and Dramatic Versions of 'The Girl's Tragedy.'" *Differences* 2.1: 126–59.

———. 1997. *The Forensic Stage: Settling Disputes in Graeco-Roman New Comedy.* Cambridge.

Schaps, D. D. 1977. "The Woman Least Mentioned: Etiquette and Women's Names." *Classical Quarterly* 71, n.s., 27: 323–31.

Schaps, D. M. 1975. "Women in Greek Inheritance Law." *Classical Quarterly* 69, n.s., 25: 53–57.

———. 1979. *The Economic Rights of Women in Ancient Greece.* Edinburgh.

———. 1982. "The Women of Greece in Wartime." *Classical Philology* 77: 193–213.

Schein, S. L. 1982. "*Electra*. A Sophoclean Problem Play." *Antike und Abendland* 28: 69–80.

———. 1990. "*Philia* in Euripides' Medea." In M. Griffith and D. J. Mastronarde, eds., *Cabinet of the Muses: Essays on Classical and Comparative Literature in Honor of Thomas G. Rosenmeyer*, 57–73. Berkeley and Los Angeles.

Schlesier, R. 1989. "Die Bakchen des Hades: Dionysische Aspekte von Euripides' Hekabe." *Métis* 3: 111–35.

Schlesinger, E. 1966. "Zu Euripides' Medea." *Hermes* 94: 26–53.

Schmiel, R. 1972. "The Recognition Duo in Euripides' *Helena*." *Hermes* 100: 274–94.

Schütrumpf, E. 1970. *Die Bedeutung des Wortes Ethos in der Poetik des Aristoteles*. Zetemata 49. Munich.

Scott-Kilvert, I. 1960. *Plutarch, Rise and Fall of Athens*. Harmondsworth, Middlesex.

Seaford, R.A.S. 1984a. "The Last Bath of Agamemnon." *Classical Quarterly* 34: 247–54.

———. 1984b. *Euripides Cyclops*. Oxford.

———. 1985. "The Destruction of Limits in Sophokles' *Elektra*." *Classical Quarterly* 35.2: 315–23.

———. 1986. "Wedding Ritual and Textual Criticism in Sophocles' *Women of Trachis*." *Hermes* 114: 50–59.

———. 1987. "The Tragic Wedding." *Journal of Hellenic Studies* 107: 106–30.

———. 1988. "The Eleventh Ode of Bacchylides: Hera, Artemis, and the Absence of Dionysus." *Journal of Hellenic Studies* 108: 118–36.

———. 1989. "Funerary Legislation and the *Iliad*." Paper presented at American Philological Association, Boston.

———. 1990a. "The Structural Problems of Marriage in Euripides." In A. Powell, ed., *Euripides, Women and Sexuality*, 151–76. London.

———. 1990b. "The Imprisonment of Women in Greek Tragedy." *Journal of Hellenic Studies* 110: 76–90.

———. 1994. *Reciprocity and Ritual: Homer and Tragedy in the Developing City-State*. Oxford.

———. 2000. "The Social Function of Attic Tragedy: A Response to Jasper Griffin." *Classical Quarterly* 50.1: 30–44.

Seale, D. 1982. *Vision and Stagecraft in Sophocles*. Chicago.

Sealey, R. 1984. "On Lawful Concubinage in Athens." *Classical Antiquity* 3: 111–33.

———. 1990. *Women and Law in Classical Greece*. Chapel Hill, N.C., and London.

Séchan, L. 1927. *Le Dévouement d'Alceste*. Paris.

Seeck, G. A. 1968. "Euripides' *Medea* 1059–68: A Problem of Interpretation." *Greek, Roman and Byzantine Studies* 9: 291–307.

Segal, C. P. 1966. "The *Electra* of Sophocles." *Transactions and Proceedings of the American Philological Association* 97: 473–545.

———. 1971. "The Two Worlds of Euripides' *Helen*." *Transactions and Proceedings of the American Philological Association* 102: 553–614.

———. 1975. "Mariage et sacrifice dans les *Trachiniennes* de Sophocle." *L'antiquité classique* 44: 30–53.

———. 1981. *Tragedy and Civilization: An Interpretation of Sophocles*. Cambridge, Mass.

———. 1992. "Time, Oracles, and Marriage in the *Trachiniae*." *Lexis* 9–10: 63–92.

———. 1993a. "Euripides' *Alcestis*: How to Die a Normal Death in Greek Tragedy." In

S. W. Goodwin and E. Bronfen, eds., *Death and Representation*, 213–41. Baltimore and London.

———. 1993b. *Euripides and the Poetics of Sorrow: Art, Gender, and Commemoration in Alcestis, Hippolytus, and Hecuba*. Durham, N.C. and London.

———. 1994a. "Bride or Concubine? Iole and Heracles' Motives in *Trachiniae*." *Illinois Classical Studies* 19: 59–64.

———. 1994b. "Female Mourning and Dionysiac Lament in Euripides' *Bacchae*." In A. Bierl and P. von Moellendorff, eds., *Orchestra: Drama, Mythos, Buhne*, 13–18. Stuttgart and Leipzig.

———. 1996. "Euripides' *Medea*: Vengeance, Reversal, and Closure." *Pallas* 45: 15–54.

Seidensticker, B. 1982. *Palintonos Harmonia. Studien zu komischen Elementen in der griechischen Tragödie*. Göttingen.

———. 1990. "Euripides' *Medea* 1056–80: An Interpolation?" In M. Griffith and D. J. Mastronarde, eds., *Cabinet of the Muses*, 89–102. Berkeley and Los Angeles.

———. 1995. "Women on the Tragic Stage." In B. Goff, ed., *History, Tragedy, Theory: Dialogues on Athenian Drama*, 151–73. Austin, Tex.

Seremetakis, C. N. 1991. *The Last Word: Women, Death, and Divination in the Inner Mani*. Chicago.

Sevieri, R. 1991. "Linguaggio consapevole e coscienza individuale di Clitennestra nell'*Agamemnone* di Eschilo." *Dioniso* 61: 13–31.

Sfyroeras, P. 1995. "The Ironies of Salvation: The Aigeus Scene in Euripides' *Medea*." *Classical Journal* 90.2: 125–42.

Shapiro, H. A. 1989. "The Iconography of Mourning in Athenian Art." *AJA* 95: 629–56.

Sharples, R. W. 1983. "'But why has my spirit spoken me thus?': Homeric Decision-Making." *Greece and Rome* 30: 1–7.

Shaw, M. H. 1975. "The Female Intruder in Fifth-Century Drama." *Classical Philology* 70: 255–66.

———. 1982. "The Ethos of Theseus in the *Suppliant Women*." *Hermes* 110: 3–19.

Sheets, G. A. 1994. "Conceptualizing International Law in Thucydides." *American Journal of Philology* 115: 51–73.

Sheppard, J. T. 1918. "The Tragedy of *Electra*, According to Sophocles." *Classical Quarterly* 12: 80–88.

———. 1927a. "*Electra*: A Defence of Sophocles." *Classical Review* 41: 2–9.

———. 1927b. "*Electra* Again." *Classical Review* 21: 163–65.

Siegel, H. 1980. "Self-Delusion and the Volte-Face of Iphigenia in Euripides' *Iphigenia at Aulis*." *Hermes* 108: 300–321.

Silberbauer, G. 1995. "Ethics in Small Scale Societies." In P. Singer, ed., *A Companion to Ethics*, 14–28. Oxford.

Silk, M., ed. 1996. *Tragedy and the Tragic: Greek Theatre and Beyond*. Oxford.

Simpson, M. 1977. "Why Does Agamemnon Yield?" *La Parola del Passato* 26: 94–101.

Slater, P. 1968. *The Glory of Hera: Greek Mythology and the Greek Family*. Boston.

Smith, C. F. [1921] 1966. *Thucydides* III. Loeb Classical Library. Cambridge, Mass.

Smith, G. 1983. "The *Alcestis* of Euripides. An Interpretation." *Rivista di Filologia e di Istruzione Classica* 111: 129–45.

Smith, N. D. 1983. "Plato and Aristotle on the Nature of Women." *Journal of the History of Philosophy* 21.4: 467–78.

Smith, W. D. 1960. "The Ironic Structure in *Alcestis*." *Phoenix* 14: 127–45.

————. 1966. "Expressive Form in Euripides' *Suppliants*." *Harvard Studies in Classical Philology* 71: 151–70.

Snell, B. 1948. "Des früeste Zeugnis über Sokrates." *Philologus* 97: 125–34.

————. 1960. *The Discovery of the Mind*. New York and Evanston, Ill.

————. 1964. *Scenes from Greek Drama*. Berkeley and Los Angeles.

Snodgrass, A. M. 1974. "An Historical Homeric Society?" *Journal of Hellenic Studies* 94: 114–25.

Sokolowski, F. 1955. *Lois sacrées de l'Asie Mineure*. Paris.

————. 1969. *Lois sacrées des cités grecques*. Paris.

Solmsen, F., ed. 1970. *Hesiodi Theogonia Opera et Dies Scutum. Fragmenta Selecta*, ed. R. Merkelbach and M. L. West. Oxford.

Sommerstein, A. H. 1988. "The End of Euripides' *Andromache*." *Classical Quarterly* 38: 243–46.

————. 1989. *Aeschylus Eumenides*. Cambridge.

Sorum, C. E. 1978. "Monsters and the Family." *Greek, Roman and Byzantine Studies* 19: 59–73.

————. 1982. "The Family in Sophocles' *Antigone* and *Electra*." *Classical World* 75.4: 201–11.

Sourvinou-Inwood, C. 1983. "A Trauma in Flux: Death in the Eighth Century and After." In R. Häag, ed., *The Greek Renaissance of the Eighth Century BC: Tradition and Innovation*, 33–48. Stockholm.

————. 1989a. "Assumptions and the Creation of Meaning: Reading Sophocles' *Antigone*." *Journal of Hellenic Studies* 109: 134–48.

————. 1989b. "The Fourth Stasimon of Sophocles' *Antigone*." *Bulletin of the Institute of Classical Studies* 36: 141–65.

————. 1990. "Sophocles' *Antigone* as a 'Bad Woman.'" In F. Dieteren and E. Kloek, eds., *Writing Women into History*, 11–38. Historisch Seminarium van de Universiteit van Amsterdam. Amsterdam.

————. 1991. "Sophocles *Antigone* 904–20: A Reading." *Annali dell'Instituto Universitario Orientale di Napoli* 9–10 (1987–88): 19–35.

Sparshott, F. 1985. "Aristotle on Women." *Philosophical Inquiry* 7.3–4: 177–200.

Stanton, G. R. 1987. "The End of Medea's Monologue, *Medea* 1078–80." *Rheinisches Museum* 130.2: 97–106.

————. 1995. "Aristocratic Obligation in Euripides' *Hekabe*." *Mnemosyne* 48: 11–33.

Stears, K. 1998. "Death Becomes Her: Gender and Athenian Death Ritual." In S. Blundell and M. Williamson, eds., *The Sacred and the Feminine in Ancient Greece*, 113–27. New York and London.

Steidle, W. 1966. "Zur Hekabe des Euripides." *Wiener Studien* 79: 133–42.

————. 1968. *Studien zum antiken Drama unter besonderer Berücksichtigung des Bühnenspiels*. Studia et Testimonia Antiqua 4. Munich.

Steiger, H. 1908. "Wie Enstand die Helena des Euripides." *Philologus* 67: 202–37.

Steiner, G. 1986. *Antigones*. Oxford.

Stevens, P. T. 1971. *Euripides Andromache*. Oxford.

————. 1978. "Sophocles' *Electra*, Doom or Triumph?" *Greece and Rome* 25: 111–20.

Stewart, A. 1995. "Rape?" In E. D. Reeder, ed., *Pandora*, 74–90. Princeton.

Storey, I. C. 1989. "Domestic Disharmony in Euripides' *Andromache*." *Greece and Rome* 36: 16–27. Reprinted in I. McAuslan and P. Walcot, eds., *Greek Tragedy*, 180–92. Greece and Rome Studies 2. Oxford, 1993.

Strauss, B. S. 1993. *Fathers and Sons in Athens: Ideology and Society in the Era of the Pelo-ponnesian War*. Princeton.

Strohm, H. 1957. *Euripides*. Zetemata 15. Munich.

Sutton, D. F. 1972. "Satyric Qualities in Euripides' *Iphigeneia in Tauris* and *Helen*." *Rivista di Studi Classici* 20: 321–30.

———. 1973. "Satyric Elements in *Alcestis*." *Rivista di Studi Classici* 21: 384–91.

Sutton, R. F. 1981. "The Interaction between Men and Women Portrayed on Attic Red-Figure Pottery." Ph.D. dissertation, University of North Carolina.

Swart, G. 1984. "Dramatic Function of the 'Agon' Scene in the *Electra* of Sophocles." *Acta Classica* 27: 23–29.

Synodinou, K. 1987. "Tecmessa in the *Ajax* of Sophocles. Amid Slavery, a Moment of Liberation." *Antike und Abendland* 33: 99–107.

Taplin, O. 1977. *The Stagecraft of Aeschylus: The Dramatic Use of Exits and Entrances in Greek Tragedy*. Oxford.

Tetzlaff, I. 1965. *Einlandung nach Sardinien*. Munich.

Thalmann, W. G. 1977. *Dramatic Art in Aeschylus' Seven against Thebes*. New Haven, Conn.

———. 1985. "Speech and Silence in the *Oresteia* 2." *Phoenix* 39: 221–36.

———. 1993. "Euripides and Aeschylus. The *Hekabe*." *Classical Antiquity* 12.1: 126–59.

Thomson, G. [and W. Headlam]. 1966. *The Oresteia of Aeschylus*. 2nd ed. 2 vols. Amsterdam.

Thompson, W. E. 1967. "The Marriage of First Cousins in Athenian Society." *Phoenix* 21: 273–82.

Thornton, A. 1970. *People and Themes in Homer's Odyssey*. London and Dunedin.

Thury, E. M. 1985. "Euripides' *Electra*: An Analysis through Character Development." *Rheinisches Museum* 128: 5–22.

———. 1988. "Euripides *Alcestis* and the Athenian Generation Gap." *Arethusa* 21.2: 197–214.

Todd, S. C. 1993. *The Shape of Athenian Law*. Oxford.

Tormey, J. F. 1976. "Exploitation, Oppression and Self-Sacrifice." In C. C. Gould and W. M. Wortofsky, eds., *Women and Philosophy: Towards a Theory of Liberation*. New York.

Torrance, R. M. 1965. "Sophocles: Some Bearings." *Harvard Studies in Classical Philology* 69: 269–327.

Trammel, E. P. 1968. "The Mute Alcestis." In J. R. Wilson, ed., *Twentieth Century Interpretations of Euripides' Alcestis*, 85–91. Englewood Cliffs, N.J.

Trapp, M. 1996. "Tragedy and the Fragility of Moral Reasoning: Response to Foley." In M. Silk, ed., *Tragedy and the Tragic: Greek Theater and Beyond*, 74–84. Oxford.

Tronto, J. C. 1993. *Moral Boundaries: A Political Argument for an Ethic of Care*. New York and London.

Tucker, T. G. 1908. *The Seven against Thebes of Aeschylus*. Cambridge.

Turner, J. A. 1983. "*Hiereiai*: Acquisitions of Feminine Priesthoods in Ancient Greece." Ph.D. dissertation, University of California at Santa Barbara.

Tyrrell, W. B., and L. J. Bennett. 1998. *Recapturing Sophocles' Antigone*. Lanham, Md.

van Erp Taalman Kip, A. M. 1996. "The Truth in Tragedy: When Are We Entitled to Doubt a Character's Words." *American Journal of Philology* 117.4: 517–36.

van Gennep, A. 1960. *The Rites of Passage*. Trans. M. B. Vizedom and G. L. Caffee. London. Originally published as *Les rites de passage*. Paris, 1909.

van Wees, H. 1999. "A Brief History of Tears." In L. Foxhall and J. Salmon, eds., *When Men Were Men*, 10–53. New York and London.

Vermeule, E. 1979. *Aspects of Death in Early Greek Art and Poetry*. Berkeley, Los Angeles, and London.

Vernant, J.-P. 1969. "Hestia-Hermes: The Religious Expression of Space and Movement among the Greeks." Trans. H. Piat. *Information sur les Sciences Sociales-International Social Sciences Information*. 8.4: 131–68.

———. 1970. "Greek Tragedy: Problems in Interpretation." In R. Macksey and E. Donato, eds., *The Structuralist Controversy*, 273–95. Baltimore.

———. 1980a. "Marriage." In *Myth and Society in Ancient Greece*, 45–70. Trans. J. Lloyd. Sussex, N.J.

———. 1980b. *Myth and Society in Ancient Greece*. Trans. J. Lloyd. Sussex, N.J.

———. 1981. "Tensions and Ambiguities in Greek Tragedy." In J.-P. Vernant and P. Vidal-Naquet, *Tragedy and Myth in Ancient Greece*, 6–27. Trans. J. Lloyd. Sussex, N.J.

Vernant, J.-P., and P. Vidal-Naquet 1981. *Tragedy and Myth in Ancient Greece*. Trans. J. Lloyd. Sussex, N.J. Originally published Paris, 1972.

Versnel, H. S. 1987. "Wife and Helpmate: Women of Ancient Athens in Anthropological Perspective." In J. Blok and Peter Mason, eds., *Sexual Assymetry: Studies in Ancient Society*, 59–86. Amsterdam.

Vickers, B. 1973. *Towards Greek Tragedy*. London.

Vidal-Naquet, P. 1972. "Chasse et sacrifice dans *l'Orestie*." In J. P. Vernant and P. Vidal-Naquet, eds., *Mythe et tragédie en Grèce ancienne I*, 135–158. Paris. Translated as "Hunting and Sacrifice in Aeschylus' *Oresteia*." In *Tragedy and Myth in Ancient Greece*, 150–74. Atlantic Highlands, N.J., 1988.

———. 1981a. "The Black Hunter and the Origin of the Athenian *ephebeia*." In R. L. Gordon, ed., *Myth, Religion and Society*, 147–62. Cambridge. Originally published as "Le chasseur noir et l'origine de l'ephébie athénienne." *Annales: Economies, sociétés, civilisations* 23 (1968): 947–64.

———. 1981b. "Slavery and the Rule of Women in Tradition, Myth and Utopia." In R. L. Gordon, ed., *Myth, Religion and Society: Structuralist Essays by M. Detienne, L. Gernet, J.-P. Vernant, and P. Vidal-Naquet*, 187–200. Cambridge.

———. 1986. *The Black Hunter: Forms of Thought and Forms of Society in the Greek World*. Baltimore and London. Originally published Paris, 1981.

———. 1988. "The Shields of the Heroes." In J.-P. Vernant and P. Vidal-Naquet, eds., *Myth and Tragedy in Ancient Greece*, 273–300. New York.

Visser, M. 1986. "Medea: Daughter, Sister, Wife, and Mother—Natal Family versus Conjugal Family in Greek and Roman Myths about Women." In M. Cropp, E. Fantham, and S. E. Scully, eds., *Greek Tragedy and Its Legacy: Essays Presented to D. J. Conacher*, 149–66. Calgary.

Vlavianos, B. 1924. *Blutrache*. Jena.

Voigt, C. 1933. *Überlegung und Entscheidung*. Berlin.

Voigtländer, H.-D. 1957. "Spätere Überarbeitungen im grosser Medeamonolog?" *Philologus* 10: 217–37.

von Fritz, K. 1962a. *Antike und moderne Tragödie*. Berlin.

————. 1962b. "Euripides' Alkestis und ihre modernen Nachahmer und Kritiker." In *Antike und Moderne Tragödie*, 356–21. Berlin.

Waldock, A.J.A. [1951] 1966. *Sophocles the Dramatist*. Cambridge.

Wallace, R. W. [1985] 1989. *The Areopagos Council, to 307 B.C.* Baltimore and London.

Walsh, G. B. 1979. "Public and Private in Three Plays of Euripides." *Classical Philology* 74: 294–309.

Walsh, J. J. 1973. *Aristotle on Moral Weakness*. New York.

Ward, J. K., ed. 1996. *Feminism and Ancient Philosophy*. New York and London.

Warren, R., and S. Scully. 1995. *Euripides, Suppliant Women*. New York and Oxford.

Webster, T.B.L. 1967. *The Tragedies of Euripides*. London.

————. 1969. *An Introduction to Sophocles*. London.

Weinstock, H. 1937. *Sophokles*. Berlin.

West, M. L. 1990. *Studies in Aeschylus*. Stuttgart.

————. 1991. *Aeschyli Agamemnon*. Teubner. Stuttgart.

Whitehorne, J.E.G. 1986. "The Dead as Spectacle in Euripides' *Bacchae* and *Supplices*." *Hermes* 114: 59–72.

Whitman, C. H. 1951. *Sophocles: A Study of Heroic Humanism*. Cambridge, Mass.

Wide, S. [1893] Darmstadt 1973. *Lakonische Kulte*. Leipzig.

Wiersma, S. 1984. "Women in Sophocles." *Mnemosyne* 37: 25–55.

Wilamowitz, T. von. 1969. *Die dramatische Technik des Sophokles*. Zurich.

Wilamowitz-Moellendorf, U. von. 1886. *Isyllos von Epidauros. Philologische Untersuchungen* 9. Berlin.

————. 1906. *Griechische Tragödie* 3. Berlin.

Wiles, D. 1989. "Marriage and Prostitution in Classical New Comedy." *Themes in Drama* 11: 31–48.

Wilkins, J. 1990. "The State and the Individual: Euripides' Plays of Voluntary Self-Sacrifice." In A. Powell, ed., *Euripides, Women and Sexuality*," 177–94. London.

————. 1993. *Euripides Heracleidae*. Oxford.

Williams, B. 1993. *Shame and Necessity*. Berkeley, Los Angeles, and Oxford.

Williams, P. 1997. "Woman's Third Face: A Psycho/Social Reconsideration of Sophocles' *Antigone*." *Arethusa* 30.3: 369–98.

Williamson, M. 1985. "A Woman's Place in Euripides' *Medea*." *Joint Association of Classical Teachers Review* 3: 16–20. Revised in Anton Powell, ed., *Euripides, Women and Sexuality*, 16–27. London and New York, 1990.

Wilson, J. R., ed. 1968. *Twentieth Century Interpretations of Euripides' Alcestis*. Englewood Cliffs, N.J.

Wilson, S. 1988. *Feuding, Conflict, and Banditry in Nineteenth-Century Corsica*. Cambridge.

Winkler, J. J. 1990a. "Penelope's Cunning and Homer's." In *The Constraints of Desire*, 129–61. New York.

————. 1990b. *The Constraints of Desire*. New York and London.

Winnington-Ingram, R. P. 1980. *Sophocles: An Interpretation*. Cambridge.

————. 1983. *Studies in Aeschylus*. Cambridge.

Wohl, V. J. 1993. "Standing by the *Stathmos*: The Creation of Sexual Ideology in the *Odyssey*." *Arethusa* 26.1: 19–50.

———. 1998. *Intimate Commerce: Exchange, Gender, and Subjectivity in Greek Tragedy.* Austin, Tex.

Wolf, E. 1910. *Sentenz und Reflexion bei Sophokles.* Leipzig.

Wolff, C. 1973. "On Euripides' *Helen.*" *Harvard Studies in Classical Philology* 77: 61–84.

———. 1979. "A Note on Lions and Sophocles' *Philoctetes* 1436." In G. W. Bowersock, W. Burkert, and M.C.J. Putnam, eds., *Arktouros: Hellenic Studies Presented to B.M.W. Knox on the Occasion of His 65th Birthday,* 144–50. Berlin.

———. 1982. "Euripides." In T. J. Luce, ed., *Ancient Writers: Greece and Rome,* 1:233–65. New York.

Wolff, H. J. 1944. "Marriage Law and Family Organization in Ancient Athens." *Traditio* 2: 44–95.

Woodard, T. M. 1964, 1965. "*Electra* by Sophocles: The Dialectical Design." *Harvard Studies in Classical Philology* 68: 163–205 and 70: 195–233.

Worthington, I. 1990. "The Ending of Euripides' *Medea.*" *Hermes* 118: 502–5.

Young, M., and P. Wilmott. [1957] 1986. *Family and Kinship in East London.* London.

Zeitlin, F. I. 1965. "The Motif of Corrupted Sacrifice in Aeschylus' *Oresteia.*" *Transactions and Proceedings of the American Philological Association* 96: 463–508.

———. 1978. "The Dynamics of Misogyny in the *Oresteia.*" *Arethusa* 11: 149–84. Revised in *Playing the Other: Gender and Society in Classical Greek Civilization,* 87–119. Chicago, 1996.

———. 1981. "Travesties of Gender and Genre in Aristophanes' *Thesmophoriazasae.*" In H. Foley, ed., *Reflections of Women in Antiquity,* 186–217. New York and London. Revised in *Playing the Other: Gender and Society in Classical Greek Civilization,* 375–416. Chicago, 1996.

———. 1982. *Under the Sign of the Shield: Semiotics and Aeschylus' Seven against Thebes.* Rome.

———. 1985a. "Playing the Other: Theater, Theatricality, and the Feminine in Greek Drama." *Representations* 11: 63–94. Revised in *Playing the Other: Gender and Society in Classical Greek Civilization,* 341–74. Chicago, 1996.

———. 1985b. "The Power of Aphrodite: Eros and the Boundaries of the Self in the *Hippolytus.*" In P. Burian, ed., *Directions in Euripidean Criticism,* 52–111. Durham, N.C. Revised in *Playing the Other: Gender and Society in Classical Greek Civilization,* 219–84. Chicago, 1996.

———. 1986. "Thebes: Theater of Self and Society in Athenian Drama." In P. Euben, ed., *Greek Tragedy and Political Theory,* 101–41. Berkeley and Los Angeles.

Zeitlin, F. I. 1990. "Patterns of Gender in Aeschylean Drama: The *Seven against Thebes* and the Danaid Trilogy." In M. Griffith and D. Mastronarde, eds., *Cabinet of the Muses: Essays on Classical and Comparative Literature in Honor of Thomas G. Rosenmeyer,* 103–15. Atlanta.

———. 1991. "Euripides' *Hekabe* and the Somatics of Dionysiac Drama." *Ramus* 20: 53–94. Revised in *Playing the Other: Gender and Society in Classical Greek Civilization,* 172–218. Chicago, 1996.

———. 1995. "Figuring Fidelity in Homer's *Odyssey.*" In B. Cohen, ed., *The Distaff Side: Representing the Female in Homer's Odyssey,* 117–54. Oxford. Revised in *Playing the Other: Gender and Society in Classical Greek Civilization,* 19–52. Chicago, 1996.

————. 1996. *Playing the Other: Gender and Society in Classical Greek Civilization.*
   Chicago.
Zellner, H. M. 1996–97. "Antigone and the Wife of Intaphrenes." *Classical World* 90.5:
   315–18.
Zuntz, G. 1963. *The Political Plays of Euripides.* Manchester.
Zwierlein, O. 1978. "Die Tragik in den Medea-Dramen." *Literaturwissenschaftliches
   Jahrbuch* 19: 27–63.

General Index

abduction (*harpagē*), 312, 318, 320, 321n.68. *See also* Kore/Persephone; myth

Achilles, 222; compared with Antigone, 196; compared with Medea, 249, 255, 260, 266, 267; decision in *Iliad* book 9, 140nn.74, 76, 78, 244; in *Hecuba*, 283; in *Iphigeneia at Aulis*, 124; mourning behavior in *Iliad*, 42 n.74, 44; promised to Iphigeneia, 226, 236. *See also* Agamemnon; Homer

Achtenberg, D., 120–21

Adkins, A., 128–29n.52

Admetus: compared with Alcestis, 315–16, 330; compared with Hades, 307; compared with Menelaus, 305, 325–26, 328 330; educated by his wife, 304, 312–14 and n.43, 325–26 and n.85; feminized, 315, 330. *See also* Alcestis; Euripides

Adonis, 48

adoption, 274–75

Adrastus: eulogy in *Suppliants*, 37–38; as suppliant in *Supplices*, 276–78, 279

adultery, 65, 70–71, 84–85 and nn.135, 137, 304n.3; in *Agamemnon*, 213–15, 216 and n.59; in *Choephoroi*, 230 and n.101, 231 and n.105, 233; Dracon on, 88; in Euripides' *Electra*, 238; in Sophocles' *Electra*, 149. *See also* marriage

Aegeus: Medea's protector, 260, 261, 263, 267, 268, 270n.98

Aegisthus, 160 and n.75, 166–67 and n.100, 202, 213, 223n.81, 241n.133, 228–29 and n.95; as *alastōr*, 220–21 and n.74, 228; Clytemnestra on, 213–14 and n.50, 221, 228, 231, 233; defense of, 206 and n.14, 220 and n.72; Electra (Euripides') on, 237; language of, 206–7 and n.17; as Thyestes' child, 220; murder of, 222n.77; as woman, 224. *See also* Aeschylus; Clytemnestra

Aeschines: against Demosthenes, 189, 284

Aeschylus: *Agamemnon*, 30, 41n.72, 46, 85n.137, 87n.147, 88, 92–94, 202–3, 208–25, 226–29, 260n.61, 275, 309n.22; —, tapestry scene, 209–11 and nn. 32, 39, 220n.70, 275; *Athamas*, 85; *Choephoroi*, 26, 27, 29n.30, 33–36, 202, 204, 225, 229–30;

—, compared with Homer, 158–59; —, compared with Sophocles' *Electra*, 146 and n.5, 148, 150n.23, 154–58 and n.65, 160, 166, 169; —, parodied by Euripides, 158n.65, 333; — response to *Agamemnon*, 230–31; *Danaids*, 83 and n.128; *Eleusinioi*, 37, 45n.86, 278 and n.14; *Eumenides*, 34, 53n.121, 86, 157, 222–23, 224, 232, 233; *Mysioi*, 86n.141; *Oresteia*, 51, 53n.121, 202–4 and nn.4–5, 207–8, 234, 285; — compared with Euripides' *Electra*, 238–39, 240n.132, 242 (*see also individual titles*); *Persians*, 29, 46, 143; *Prometheus Bound*, 28, 54n.124, 86n.141, 122; revival of, 52n.116; *Seven against Thebes*, 37–38, 45–54, 122; — compared with *Suppliants*, 53, 54; *Suppliants*, 28, 53 and n.121, 54, 122. *See also Index Locorum*

Aethra, 121, 236, 272, 276–78, 279; assertiveness in *Supplices*, 279–80, 286

Agamemnon: burial of, 217, 226–27, 230n.103; as debased hero, 217, 221, 224–25, 226 and n.91, 227–28, 232, 288; in *Hecuba*, 272, 283n.27, 284–86; in *Odyssey*, 127, 134, 141–42; as sacrificial victim, 210. *See also* Aeschylus; Clytemnestra

agency, 16–17 and n.60

agōn (debate), 44–45, 151–52, 161, 169, 214n.43, 252n.39, 273; Antigone vs. Creon, 172–73, 174–76; Clytemnestra vs. Electra, 160n.74, 201n.1, 238, 240n.131, 241; Diodotus vs. Cleon (Thucydides), 292–93, 293 and n.56; Jocasta mediates Eteocles vs. Polyneices 281–82; Euripides as teacher of (Aristophanes), 275; Hector vs. Andromache, 50, 90, 142, 259, 264, 268n.92; Melian, 293; —, parallels with *Hecuba*, 297 and n.73. *See also* choice; ethics

agriculture: effects of advance in, 61, 63, 79n.115

aidōs (shame), 118, 150, 207–8, 233; in *Choephoroi*, 230 and n.101, 233–34; shame culture, 248; —, internalization of other in, 118. *See also aitia*

36; as counter—cultural, 82, 204, 208–9, 212, 215–16, 226–28, 232–33; death of, 166, 241 and n.134; defense of, 207, 211–34 (apologia), 234–42; defied by Electra (Sophocles), 150, 151–52, 153, 160n.74, 169; in Euripides' Electra, 234–42; as monster, 221, 230, 231and n.109, 233; on moral imbalance, 232–33; in Odyssey, 141–42, 303–4n.3; pleads with Orestes (Sophocles), 158; refeminizing of, 228–29 and n.95, 233–34; tragic portrayals compared, 201 and n.1. See also Aeschylus; Sophocles; woman/wife

Cohen, D.: on adultery, 70n.58; on Oresteia, 170

Cohn-Haft, L., 100n.204

comedy, 48, 298n.74; New Comedy, 59 and n.3; scholiast on, 103n.223. See also Aristophanes; New Comedy; Old Comedy

Conacher, D. J., 103n.203, 206n.17, 216n.60, 219nn.66, 67

concubine(s) (pallakē / pallakai), 60–61; in Athens, 89–90; in Homer, 104; to produce heirs, 62, 76 and nn.91, 92; in tragedy, 87–105, 233; wicked, 94n.177; as wife, 95–98, 126, 236, 329–30. See also hetaira(ai); marriage; woman/wife

Corsica: blood revenge in, 162; lament in, 162n.79, 163

Cox, C. A., on epiklēros, 68–69n.49; on Attic marriage, 72–73 and nn. 71, 72, 74, 77

cremation, 38

Creon: in Antigone, 31–33 and n.38, 121, 172–200 passim, 336; abuse of Antigone, 180; allegiance to polis, 183–84, 196–97; defense of (modern), 185–86n.43; ethical stance of, 183–87; failure in Antigone, 184–88 and nn.47, 48, 222n.78; use of maxims, 185. See also Antigone; Eteocles; Haemon; Ismene; Polyneices; Sophocles

Cropp, M. J., 176n.12, 178n.20

Cylon: dispute with Megacles, 288

daimōn: as avenging spirit, 216–17 and n.60, 218, 219n. 69, 221 and n.75, 205, 222, 223, 224, 227, 229; Aegisthus as, 228; Alcestis as blessed spirit, 315; Helen as, 228. See also aitia; alastōr; gods

Darius, 178

Daube, B., 214n.49, 215, 218n. 64, 220n.73

Davies, J. K., 59

death: countering fear of, 309; and marriage,

309–12; and rebirth (symbolic), 312–14; tragic, on—stage, 315 and n.45. See also death rituals; rebirth; rite of passage

death ritual: of Agamemnon, 217, 226–27, 230n.103; in Antigone, 33, 172–200; of Antigone, 155n.54; in Choephoroi, 34n.43; denial of, 32, 288; details of, 39–40 and n.64; eulogy at itaphios logos) (Adrastus) 37–38, 40, 44, 276, 278, 294; for hero, 217, 276, 288, 298; gender roles in, 233; in Homer, 40; political use of, 27n.27; as men's work, 179–80; public, 25, 39 and n.63; 167–68; — vs. private, 40, 334; as rite of passage, 312; in Seven against Thebes, 49, 51, 52; simulated, 47–48; sixth-through fourth-century Athens, 22–25, 196n. 83; Solon's legislation on, 22–23 and nn.5, 6, 7, 11; in Suppliants, 36–39. See also death; lamentation; mourning; rite of passage; rituals

debate. See agōn

deception (dolos): in Greek tragedy, 158 and n.66, 159nn.69, 70, 206–7, 226, 229n.98, 230, 267n.85. See also apatē

defense (i.e., legalistic exoneration): of Aegisthus, 206–7 and n.14; of Clytemnestra, 207, 211–34 (apologia); of Creon, 185–86n.43; of Orestes, 204–5

Deianeira, 116, 262n.68; vs. Iole, 95–97. See also Heracles; Sophocles

Deliyanni, H., 162n.79

Demeter: Homeric Hymn to, 305n.8, 319n.60, 326n.86; inversion of myth, 43n.78; myth as prototype for anodos drama, 304–6; in Suppliants, 41 and n.69, 279–80. See also Kore (Persephone); myth; Proerosia

Demetrius of Phaleron, 27

democracy: and isotēs (Jocasta), 281–82; Pericles on, 276, 289; evolution of ethics within, 292–93, 295; private life within, 78; in tragedy, 82–83; women in, 78. See also aristocracy; equality; polis

Demosthenes, 189, 197, 209; criticized by Aeschines, 189, 284

de Ste. Croix, G.E.M., 64n.20

des Bouvrie, S., 12

desire, 137 and n.72. See also erōs

deus (dea) ex machina, 239–40, 261n.66, 266, 267, 270n.98, 323n.78

De Wet, B. X., 147n.9, 161n.78

Dicaearchus, 310n.28

Didot Papyrus, 84n.134

Thucydides, 39, 293; on Corcyrean revolution, 298; on international law in wartime, 292–95, 297–98. *See also* Herodotus; history; Pericles

thumos (physical source of decisions): and *bouleumata,* 249–54; defined, 252–53 and n.42; in Euripides, 245–46, 249–57; —, compared with Homer, 253–56 *passim;* as "masculine" aspect, 245, 246; *oxuthumos,* 252n.38; Plato on, 256; *prothumos,* 246; as self, 253; *thoumoumenēn,* 252n.38. *See also* emotion

Thyestes: as father of Aegisthus, 206, 216, 218, 220, 221, 228, 231. *See also* Aegisthus; Aeschylus; Agamemnon; Clytemnestra; Electra; Orestes

Tiresias, 175, 184, 185n.41, 186, 187, 195, (appendix.) 197, 282–83. *See also* prophecy

Todd, S., 73

tragedy, ancient Greek: "antitragedy," 271; borders on comic, 331 and n.99; characterization in, 109–12; democratization of (Aristophanes), 333; as dialogue between past and present, 3, 55, 98, 99, 168–71, 235, 241, 290–91, 328, 334–35, 337–38; departure from epic codes, 92, 335; as dissent, 14, 54; etiology in, 51; extreme situations in, 196; as "feminist" genre, 335; and history, 16, 17–18, 296–97, 328; as initiation (Zeitlin), 10; inversions in, 4, 5, 331, 333; as lamentation, 14; marriage in, 80–87; and philosophy, 116–20, 333–34, 337–38; as public mourning, 25 and n.17; slave nurses in, 122. *See also* comedy; history; *individual names and titles,* New Comedy; Old Comedy; philosophy; theater

trial by jury, 24 and n.12, 27, 33, 157, 248, 337. *See also* vendetta

Tronto, J., 291–92, 298

Troy: fall of, 208, 210, 318. *See also* Homer

Tyndareus, 235–36

van Wees, H.: on mourning practices, 26

vendetta: in Aeschylus compared with Sophocles, 158; in ancient Athens, 154 and n.50; consequences of, 248–49; ethics of, 151–52, 202n.3, 206; and funeral rituals, 23–24 and nn.11, 14, 34–35, 36, 38; fear of, 41; Hecuba's, 285–86, 297 and n.72; Lysias on, 154; male role in, 157, 158–59, and n. 68; Medea's, 109, 243, 244–46, 248, 258 and

n.54, 260n.59, 261, 262, 263, 264 and nn.73, 75, 266 and n.81, 267, 268n.92, 269–71 and nn.97–98 and 101–2; modern-day, 161–63, 179, 205n.9; in *Odyssey,* 153–54, 159n.68; in *Oresteia,* 202–4, 226, 297; replaced by trial, 27, 33, 154, 157, 170; revenge as goal, 33–35, 151, 153; and tragedy, 27, 115, 146–47, 150 and n.21, 153, 158 and n.65, 167; woman as instigator of, 154, 160, 161–64, 233, 241. *See also* lamentation; trial by jury

Vernant, J.-P., 62n.9, 63n.17; on Athenian marriage, 65; on the role of wife, 317–18; on Homeric marriage, 64; on tending the hearth, 214n.50; on tragedy, 304n.4

Vickers, B., 208n.23, 211n.36, 212n.43, 216n.60, 218n.64, 229n.95

Vidal-Naquet, P., 45n.88, 158n.66, 226n.89

virgins, 123–25, 199–200 and n.97, 303; Antigone (Sophocles), 172–200, Electra (Sophocles), 145–71; Helen as model to, 324; tragic, compared with tragic mothers, 298–99. *See also individual names;* woman/wife

virtue (*aretē*): as mean, 120; in Homer, 127–28, post-Kantian "virtue ethics," 117–20; as "quiet," (Adkins), 118n.24, 128n.52; in women, 91, 92–93, 97, 98–99, 103, 104, 109–13, 115, 151, 303, 304, 331. See also *aretē*

Visser, M., 258n.54

Voigtländer, H.-D., 244n.3, 245n.8, 251n.34

von Fritz, K., 267n.84

Waldock, A.J.A., 181n.30

Walsh, G. B., 264

West, M. L., 224, 225 and nn. 85, 86, 226n.91

Whitman, C., 168n.106, 177n.15, 198n.92

Wilamowitz-Moellendorf, U. v., 307, 308 and n.21

Williams, B.: on Homeric decision making, 140–41n.79; on shame culture ethics, 118, 222

Wilson, S., 162n.79

Winnington-Ingram, R. P., 46n.92, 169, 178n.20, 220n.74, 232

wives: in ancient Athens, 314; Clytemnestra, 201–42; compared with virgins, 324; as concubines, 329–30; overshadowing spouses, 303, 324, 326, 329; Medea, 243–71; winning *kleos* (Euripides), 314–24. *See also* concubine; marriage; woman/wife

Index Locorum

(*Note*: boldfaced line numbers are those quoted verbatim (in their entirety) in text; where a selection is quoted verbatim once and occurs otherwise more than once, the page number instead will appear in boldface.)

Ecology of desert organisms

Gideon Louw and Mary Seely

Longman
London and New York

Longman Group Limited
Longman House
Burnt Mill, Harlow, Essex, UK

*Published in the United States of America
by Longman Inc., New York*

© Longman Group Limited 1982

First published 1982

Library of Congress Cataloging in Publication Data

Louw, Gideon, 1930–
    Ecology of desert organisms.

    Bibliography: p.
    Includes index.
    1. Desert ecology. I. Seely, Mary, 1939–
II. Title.
QH541.5.D4L68   574.5'2652 81–6027
ISBN 0–582–44393–8   AACR2

British Library Cataloguing in Publication Data

Louw, Gideon
    Ecology of desert organisms.
    1. Desert biology
    2. Ecology
    I. Title   II. Seely, Mary
    574.5'2   QH88

ISBN 0-582-44393-8

Printed in Great Britain by
William Clowes (Beccles) Ltd
Beccles and London

Contents

Preface

Although many impressive volumes have been published on desert biology, very few have attempted to synthesize the main principles involved at a reasonable length. This is essentially what we have tried to do, namely to concentrate on the main principles involved in desert ecology and to use a limited number of examples from the literature and our own experience to explain these principles. In doing so we have necessarily been obliged to treat many aspects rather superficially. The physiological ecologists may complain that we have not discussed their field in sufficient depth, while the traditional ecologists could fairly claim that too much space has been allocated to physiology and autecology. We have, however, tried to strike a reasonable balance but wish to apologise to many of our colleagues for omitting so many of their excellent papers.

This volume is aimed at various levels, but particularly at the undergraduate who wishes to broaden his ecological knowledge and at the same time absorb some important principles in ecology and ecophysiology, which are applicable to all kinds of biomes. It is not directed at the specialist in desert biology who nevertheless may enjoy those sections outside his immediate field of interest.

We wish to thank our many friends and colleagues around the world who have so kindly shared their knowledge and experience, and thank them for their hospitality in their respective deserts. In this respect we are particularly grateful to Amiram Shkolnik and Heinrich Mendelssohn of Israel, Neil Hadley of Arizona, Dr López Ocaña and Professor P. Aguilar of Peru. The financial support provided by the CSIR, the Transvaal Museum and the University of Cape Town, made our travels and research over the past ten years possible. We also thank Sandra Hardman, Jennifer Day, Sue Nicolson and Leonora Fox who assisted with the preparation of the manuscript. We are especially grateful to Claire Louw and Eckart Pfeifer who assisted in innumerable ways.

Anthony Bannister and John Visser supplied the colour transparencies used in the plates.

Chapter 1

Introduction

What is a desert?

If we were philosophers we could spend a great deal of time arguing about an exact definition of a desert. Fortunately ecology is a younger science and allows itself more latitude in the use of such arbitrary terms. Nevertheless, as there is considerable confusion and little agreement about the usage of the term desert, it is important to define it for the purposes of this volume.

To the layman a desert is merely a hot, dry area of the earth's surface where the vegetation is usually stunted, often bizarre in form and either absent or patchily distributed. This concept could serve us quite well, but an examination of some of the contradictions is also justified. Firstly, how dry or how hot must an area be before it is described as a desert? Should we include the polar regions which could qualify on the grounds of aridity alone; in fact should heat be a criterion at all? Furthermore, in some areas which enjoy reasonably high rainfall the rate of evaporation is so rapid that the effect of rain is greatly reduced. Alternatively, rainfall in certain areas, although quite high when measured as an annual mean, can be so erratic as to produce desert-like conditions for prolonged periods.

Several attempts have been made in the past to combine the variables of temperature, rainfall and evaporation to produce a suitable definition of a desert area. In view of the contradictions described previously, however, these suggestions have not gained general acceptance. For this reason modern authors have tended to use rainfall as the sole criterion. For example, McGinnies (1968) based the following classification of arid regions on the rainfall criteria employed in the well-known maps of the world's deserts compiled by Meigs (1953):

E – Extremely arid (less than 60–100 mm mean annual precipitation)
A – Arid (from 60–100 mm to 150–250 mm)
S – Semi-arid (from 150–250 mm to 250–500 mm)

Obviously this classification leaves a great deal to be desired, but it is a reasonably practical one as it can be associated, in a broad sense, with vegetation types and agricultural practices. Moreover, Noy-Meir (1973) has argued that in view of the pre-eminent role of water in controlling productivity in desert ecosystems, this classification is the most pragmatic. He assigns three main attributes to arid ecosystems: (1) precipitation is so low that water is the predominant controlling factor for most biological processes; (2) precipitation is highly variable throughout the year and occurs as infrequent and discrete events; and (3) variation in precipitation has a large unpredictable component.

Let us then accept Noy-Meir's definition of a desert ecosystem: a 'water-controlled ecosystem with infrequent, discrete and largely unpredictable

1

water inputs', for the purposes of this discussion. The polar deserts will not be described and the discussion will centre mainly on deserts falling within the A and E classification of Meigs.

Where are the deserts?

In Fig. 1.1 both the major and minor deserts of the world have been illustrated. A study of their distribution shows that they lie predominantly within the tropics of Cancer and Capricorn, or close to these latitudes. They are either situated on the west coasts of large continents adjacent to cold ocean currents, or in the interior of large continents. This distribution has led to several generalisations on the climatic patterns which allow the development of desert areas.

McGinnies (1968) has selected three general causes which can act either individually or in combination to produce an arid environment. Firstly, if the area is separated from a source of oceanic moisture by either large distances or a topographical barrier such as a massive mountain range (rain-shadow), then arid conditions usually develop. Secondly, aridity is frequently caused by the persistence of dry stable air masses that resist convective currents. Thirdly, aridity can result from the lack of storm systems which would create unstable environments and provide the lifting necessary for precipitation. The second factor, the persistence of high-pressure belts, is particularly important in sub-tropical deserts and is caused by the peculiar flow pattern of air within pressure cells near the equator (Fig. 1.2). Trade winds blow in the direction of the equator in both hemispheres, gathering moisture which rises and cools adiabatically in the equatorial region. The cooling of this air mass results in condensation and, as a consequence, the high-level winds which move in the opposite direction to the trade winds are relatively dry. This means that when stable high-pressure regions develop over the sub-tropics, this relatively dry air mass descends towards the surface of the earth. In doing so it becomes compressed and heated and the relative humidity is markedly reduced. Cloudsley-Thompson (1977) has used these causal factors to provide a broad classification of the more important deserts of the world:

Sub-tropical deserts
These are largely the result of persistent high pressure cells and lie within the latitudes 30 °S and 30 °N.

Cool, coastal deserts
The primary cause of aridity in deserts of this nature is again the dry air conditions produced by descending, high-pressure air masses. These conditions are intensified by the proximity of cold ocean currents, although the latter frequently also bring relief from high temperatures and low humidities in the form of either cool, moist oceanic winds or condensing advective fog. Examples are the Namib, Atacama and Baja California deserts which are adjacent to the Benguela, Humboldt and California currents respectively.

Rain-shadow deserts
When the flow of moist oceanic winds is interrupted by a topographical barrier such as a mountain range, the air mass is deflected upwards and cools adiabatically. Relative humidity rises rapidly and so-called orographic precipitation occurs on the windward slopes of the mountain range. Consequently when the air mass reaches the

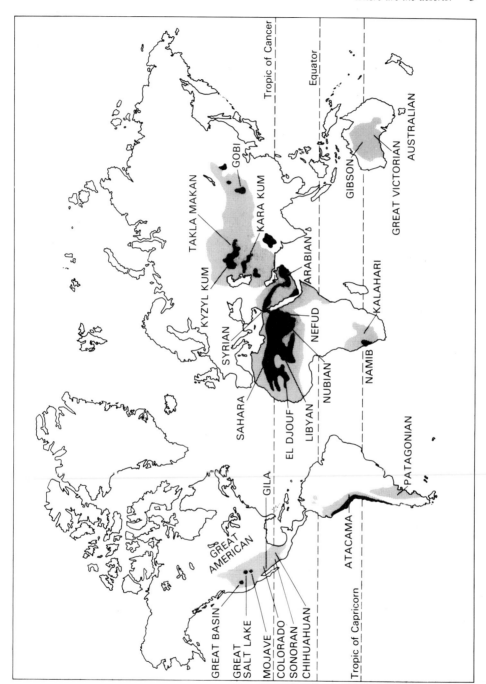

Fig. 1.1 The major deserts of the world. (Adapted from Cloudsley-Thompson 1977.)

leeward side of the mountain, it has lost much of its moisture and this is aggravated by compressional heating as the air mass descends on the leeward side. Deserts falling in

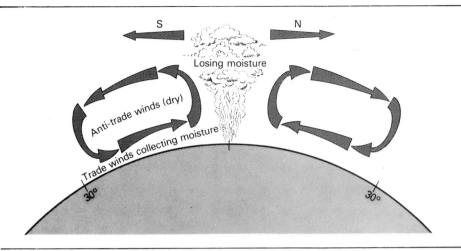

Fig. 1.2   Air-circulation patterns within cells near the equator show how moisture is lost from the trade winds at the equator. (After Arnon 1972.)

this category are the Mojave, the deserts of Patagonia, the deserts of the Great Basin of North America and part of the Great Australian Desert.

Interior continental deserts
These owe their aridity to their distance from sources of marine moisture, their position between major wind belts and the associated storm systems. These, in turn, are all related to the large continental land masses surrounding these areas. Typical examples are large areas within the Australian, North American and Great Palaearctic deserts.

Why study deserts?

Man seldom requires an excuse to satisfy his insatiable curiosity, but in these days of increasing restrictions on research funding a few remarks in defence of desert research may be appropriate.

Interest in deserts is certainly not new. Aristotle has commented on the problems of desert survival in plants and animals. For millennia nomadic tribes have survived in desert areas by relying on their expert knowledge of the applied ecology of a particular desert region. In fact, deserts do not differ basically from other terrestrial ecosystems inhabited by man, but the limited resources and harsh climate impose a certain discipline and respect for nature. Also, the limited resources have never been able to support dense populations and, although life may be difficult, it also has a tranquil and mystical quality. It is not surprising therefore to learn that several of the major religions of the world have emerged from arid and semi-arid regions.

The interest of modern industrial man in desert areas has largely been centred on the exploitation of minerals and fossil fuel. Geology was therefore one of the first disciplines to be involved seriously in desert research. The earlier biological research was mostly of an exploratory nature with the emphasis on systematics. During the past three decades, however, research has expanded rapidly on a broad front to

include physiological, ecological and behavioural aspects of biology. Applied aspects of biology including agricultural and fisheries research have grown equally rapidly.

Why this fascination with desert research? No doubt the exploding populations of the world and increasing pressures on arid lands have contributed significantly. Nevertheless, other important considerations have also been involved. For example, if we accept that the most important unifying theme in basic biological research is the study of evolution, then few ecosystems in the world offer as rich a variety of unique adaptations as does the desert. In many instances the intense heat and extreme aridity create conditions which are so hostile to the normal requirements of living protoplasm, that bizarre and fascinating adaptations evolve in response to these influences. Furthermore, many deserts are still in remote areas, undisturbed by man, and consequently provide the biologist with some of the few remaining natural ecosystems for study. Finally, the paucity of vegetative cover makes deserts ideal situations for studying animal behaviour, and the relative simplicity of the ecological interactions within desert ecosystems greatly facilitates ecological analyses and the construction of predictive models.

Chapter 2

The desert environment and principles of adaptation

Before embarking upon a detailed discussion of the adaptations of organisms to the desert environment, it is first necessary to examine the most important abiotic and biotic factors impinging upon these organisms and the major principles involved in their adaptive responses.

Radiation, heat and temperature

Most of the desert situations we shall be discussing are characterised by intense solar radiation, high air temperatures and extremely high soil surface temperatures. For example, Cloudsley-Thompson (1977) lists the following maximum shade temperatures for various desert areas:

El Azizia, Libya	58 °C	(136 °F)
San Luis Potosi, Mexico	58 °C	(136 °F)
Death Valley, California	56.5 °C	(134 °F)

These temperatures admittedly represent unusually high single records but mean maximum temperatures during summer can also remain at remarkably high levels in certain areas such as the Sonoran Desert, where mean summer maxima of 40 °C have been recorded. Moreover, in summer in the Sonoran Desert minimum temperatures at night frequently remain above 37 °C. All these temperatures, however, were recorded under standard meteorological conditions inside a shaded screen and are only of limited value in evaluating the actual micro-climate to which desert organisms are exposed. To illustrate this principle, Fig. 2.1 shows how high sand surface temperatures can rise (84 °C) when air temperatures are only moderately high (40 °C) in a desert area such as Wadi Halfa in the Sudan. More dramatic differences are, however, found at high altitudes, as for example in the Andes, where body temperatures of *Liolaemus* lizards have been recorded 30 °C above an ambient air temperature of 5 °C. This remarkable difference is the result of intense radiation and behavioural thermoregulation by the lizards and emphasises the importance of first gaining a working knowledge of the more important physical principles associated with terms such as radiation, heat and temperature.

Solar radiation

Solar radiation is a form of electromagnetic energy and is transmitted, depending upon the conceptual viewpoint employed, as waves or quanta of energy at a velocity of 3×10^8 m s^{-1}. The relationship between velocity (c), frequency of oscillation (ν) and wavelength (λ) is often expressed as:

$$c = \lambda \nu$$

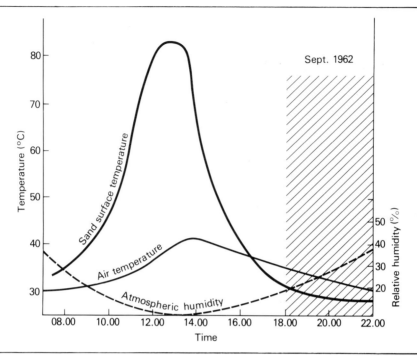

Fig. 2.1 Example of extreme sand surface temperature measured at Wadi Halfa in the Sudan in relation to atmospheric temperature and humidity. (Cloudsley-Thompson and Chadwick 1964.)

where $\lambda = $ m and $\nu = s^{-1}$. However, because the energy transmitted in a particular wave band is relative to the frequency of oscillation rather than the wavelengths, spectral distribution is frequently expressed as $1/\lambda = \nu$ and stated as wave number in units of cm^{-1}. The relationship between wavelength, wave number and visibility is illustrated in Fig. 2.2. In practice the biologist is interested in measuring direct solar radiation, diffuse radiation, reflected radiation and re-radiation in terms of energy per unit surface area, per unit of time. The units employed are either joules $m^{-2} min^{-1}$ or watts m^{-2} (1 W $= 1$ joule s^{-1}). Obviously the intensity of solar radiation at one point in time will depend upon the altitude of the sun (elevation

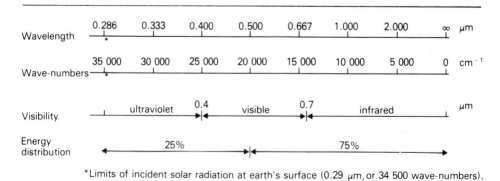

*Limits of incident solar radiation at earth's surface (0.29 μm, or 34 500 wave-numbers).

Fig. 2.2 Relationship between wavelength, wave-numbers, visibility and energy distribution.

above the horizon), the declination of the sun and to what extent dust, water vapour and cloud obscure the sun's rays. For this reason radiation intensity at the earth's surface is often integrated over long periods and expressed as radiation intensity per month, season or even year. A commonly used meteorological term employed for this purpose is langleys (ly) per min. (1 ly min^{-1} = 69.75 mW cm^{-2}). For example the Tucson area in the Sonoran Desert receives about 190 kly yr^{-1} with a winter average of approximately 300 ly day^{-1} and a maximum during May before the start of the monsoon season of close to 800 ly day^{-1}. In contrast, in Britain the radiant energy impinging upon plant cover is in the region of 25 kly yr^{-1}. In temperate climates as much as 95–99 per cent of this incident energy is lost from the plants in the form of sensible heat loss and evaporation, while only 1–5 per cent is actually used for photosynthesis.

The radiant environment, to which a desert animal or plant is typically exposed, is illustrated in Fig. 2.3. This illustration shows that the organism is exposed to direct

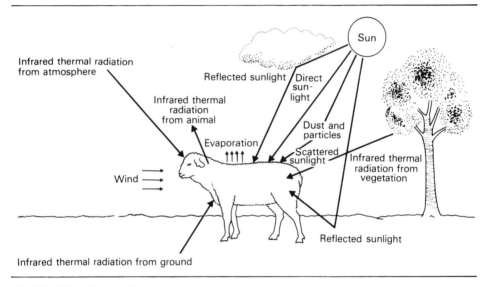

Fig. 2.3   The radiant environment

solar radiation, diffuse radiation from clouds and the atmosphere, and a considerable amount of short-wave radiation which is reflected from the soil's surface and other objects in close proximity to the organism. In addition, direct solar radiation is partially absorbed by the soil surface, the surface of the organism and other objects. It is then reradiated as long-wave radiation which may or may not impinge upon the organism. If we should now add the metabolic heat of the animal as well as heat losses by radiation, conduction, convection and evapo-transpiration to the diagram, it is clear that the thermal relationships of free-living organisms are very complex indeed. We can, however, draw some important conclusions from the energy flux diagram in Fig. 2.3 without considering these complexities in detail. Firstly, it immediately becomes apparent that desert organisms, because of the low water vapour content of the air and the lack of cloud cover, are often exposed to severe loads of direct solar radiation. This component is naturally intensified in deserts which are situated in the lower latitudes. Secondly, the most obvious way in which to reduce solar loads would be to escape, in the case of animals, to a favourable micro-environment by shading,

burrowing or sand-diving. In the case of plants or large animals without access to shade, this is not possible. These organisms can, however, reduce the solar load very significantly through reduction of the surface area exposed to radiation by orientation of the leaves or, in the case of animals, orientation of the long axis of the body relative to the sun's rays. Finally, the nature of the outer covering of both plants and animals can influence the reflectance, absorbance and transmittance of solar radiation. A thick dense pelage will, for example, reduce the penetration of solar energy while a glossy, light-coloured pelage will reflect more energy than a dull, dark-coloured hair coat. These aspects will be discussed later (Ch. 4) in considerable detail.

Heat and temperature

Heat, like solar radiation, is a form of energy and is a function of the total kinetic energy of the molecules contained within a substance. It follows then that all substances which possess kinetic energy will contain heat and that energy will be transferred in the form of heat from a substance with greater kinetic energy to another with less kinetic energy. Temperature, on the other hand, is a measurement of the mean kinetic energy possessed by the molecules of a substance, and at absolute zero (-273 °C or 0 Kelvin) kinetic energy is nil.

The ways in which heat is transferred from one system to another are very relevant to this text and a brief discussion of these mechanisms is justified. The subject has been reviewed by various authors recently and the reader who wishes to gain a deeper understanding is referred to an excellent treatment by Monteith (1973) in his book *Principles of Environmental Physics*. We shall use the principles and equations outlined by Mitchell (1977) in view of their clarity.

Energy flux through any organism must obey the first law of thermodynamics, namely that energy may be transformed from one form to another but is neither created nor destroyed. This concept is embodied in the well-known equation to describe energy flux through an animal:

$$M + W + K + R + C + E - S \qquad [1]$$

where M = metabolic rate, W = energy expenditure on physical work, K = energy exchange with the environment by conduction, R = by radiation, C = by convection, E = by evaporation. S represents the amount of heat stored and when the organism is in thermal equilibrium it will be equal to 0.

Metabolic heat production (M)

In animals (M) is influenced by a complex of factors including: body size (surface area), ambient temperature, reproductive status, nutrition, wind speed, incident radiation, the nature of the integument and most importantly by their thermal response to ambient temperature. Endotherms (mostly mammals and birds) will increase their metabolic heat production in response to cold while ectotherms, which rely on an external source of heat for maintaining body temperature, do not. Although physical work (W) represents a loss of energy to the organism, it is one of the swiftest ways in which to increase the heat load of an animal. We have seen this demonstrated many times by monitoring the body temperatures of desert gazelles (springbok) by means of radio-telemetry. The animals will graze calmly under conditions of high ambient temperature and intense solar radiation while maintaining a constant body temperature of 39–40 °C. If they are disturbed by a predator, however, a short sprint of 300–400 m will result in an immediate rise in

body temperature of 2–3 °C. The rate of loss of this heat load will again depend on body size (surface area), nature of integument and the influence of ambient conditions on heat loss by conduction, convection, radiation and evaporation.

Radiant heat transfer (R)

Together with conduction and convection, radiant heat transfer (R) is categorised as sensible heat transfer between an animal and its environment. Mitchell (1977) has pointed out that no accurate calculations are possible as yet of radiant heat transfer in environments in which solar radiation is present, because of the presence of wavelengths less than 2 μm. He has, however, proposed the following equation for estimating the rate of long wave (> 2 μm) radiant heat transfer between the environment and the animal, which is derived from the Stefan–Boltzmann law:

$$R = h_r (A_r/A_b)(\bar{T}_r - \bar{T}_s) \tag{2}$$

where T_r is the mean temperature of the surrounding solid surfaces, T_s is the mean surface temperature of the animal, A_b is the total surface area of the animal, A_r is the total surface area exposed to radiant heat exchange and h_r is the linear heat transfer coefficient. Important inferences to be drawn from this equation are that radiant heat transfer between desert organisms and their environment will be strongly influenced by the intensity of the radiation, the surface area exposed to direct radiation and the nature and colour of the integument.

Conduction (K)

As a mechanism of heat transfer, conduction (K) involves the movement of heat from regions of high kinetic energy to adjacent regions of low kinetic energy without mass motion of the medium through which the energy is transferred. This mechanism is particularly important for animals that adpress the ventral surface of their bodies to the surface of the substrate, such as lizards or snakes (thigmothermic thermoregulation). In the case of a large ungulate standing on hooves with a relatively small surface area it becomes insignificant. In spite of the importance of this mechanism in certain ecological situations, the physicists have not yet provided us with a suitable equation to quantify the process. Nevertheless, it is clear that the surface areas involved will play an important role, as will the temperature gradient between the surfaces and the nature of the integument.

Convection (C)

Convection (C) involves the transfer of heat through a fluid medium by mass transport in currents. Mitchell (1977) has proposed the following equation to estimate the rate of convective heat transfer between the surrounding air and an animal:

$$C = h_c (\bar{T}_a - \bar{T}_s) \tag{3}$$

where T_a is the air temperature and h_c the convective heat transfer coefficient. The latter coefficient, in turn, depends upon wind speed and air density and, when considering free convection, on surface and air temperature as well. Convective heat transfer in air is therefore strongly influenced by wind speed and the temperature gradient between the organism and the environment. So much so that in certain specialised conditions heat loss can be predicted as a function of the square root of the wind speed. Another important component influencing convective heat transfer is the surface area of the organism. Obviously a large desert ungulate with a relatively small surface area will lose heat relatively more slowly by convection than a smaller

animal with its proportionally greater surface area. Because convective heat transfer is so frequently thought of as a mechanism of heat loss, it should, however, be emphasised that if the temperature of the air is greater than that of the surface of the body, it will represent a heat gain to the body. Consequently high wind speeds with ambient temperatures in excess of 40 °C can cause serious thermal problems for both animals and man in the desert. Finally, convective heat transfer in water, because of its much higher specific heat, takes place at a rate which is several orders of magnitude greater than that in air. For example, the convective heat transfer coefficient for a nude man at low wind speeds is approximately 4 $W\,m^{-2}C$, while at rest in water it is 230 $W\,m^{-2}C$ (Mitchell 1977).

Evaporative heat exchange (E)
The only avenue open to desert organisms for losing heat when ambient temperatures exceed surface and core temperatures is evaporative heat exchange (E). The following equation has been suggested by Mitchell (1977) for estimating the rate of evaporative heat exchange:

$$E = wh_e(A_e/A_b)(\phi P_{wa} - P_{ws}) \qquad [4]$$

where P_{ws} is the saturated vapour pressure at the mean temperature of the surface of the animal, P_{wa} is the saturated vapour pressure at the temperature of the air, ϕ is the fractional humidity, A_e is the surface area available for heat transfer and wh_e the evaporative heat transfer coefficient; w is the wetted area and is equal to 1 when the surface is completely wet. Because of the difficulties of measuring the factor h_e this equation is seldom used. More direct methods such as measuring the weight loss of the subject or collecting water vapour from an air stream passing over the subject and then multiplying the change by the latent heat of evaporation are more commonly employed. Nevertheless, the equation allows us once again to conclude how important surface area and water vapour pressure gradients are in determining rate of heat loss. Also, wind speed has an important influence on the evaporative heat transfer coefficient h_e and consequently on evaporative heat loss as well.

Heat loss by evaporation in plants occurs as a result of transpiration but is not nearly as biologically significant as sweating and panting in animals. Even when active sweating and panting are absent in animals, some insensible heat loss occurs slowly as a result of continuous transepidermal water loss. This has been demonstrated by Hattingh (1972) who found that cooling rates ranged from 10 $W\,m^{-2}$ (snake) to 150 $W\,m^{-2}$ (bat) via this mechanism.

Examination of equations [1], [2], [3] and [4] for energy flux and the various pathways of heat transfer allows us to draw certain general conclusions which will be applied later during detailed discussions of the adaptive responses of various desert organisms. For example, the size of the organism plays a key role in determining the rate of energy exchange between the organism and the environment, and in consequence will also affect the type of adaptive response exhibited by the organism. This relationship is largely a result of the well-known allometric association between size and surface area. As the size of the organism increases there is a proportional decrease in relative surface area which can be described by the equation: surface area = body weight$^{2/3}$ (Fig. 2.4). In all of the preceding equations the importance of surface area in determining rate of heat transfer has been emphasised, and it follows therefore that size of the organism is a very important consideration when evaluating the interacting effects of wind speed and temperature gradients upon the thermal ecology of desert organisms. Body size will also affect thermal inertia directly as large

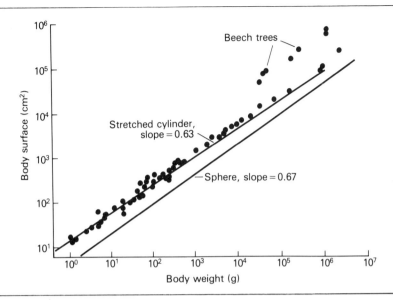

Fig. 2.4 Relationship between body weight and body surface in vertebrates and beech trees. (Adapted from Hemmingsen 1960 and McMahon 1973.)

organisms will gain heat more slowly than smaller ones, while the metabolic rate of larger animals is relatively much lower than in small animals. This relationship between body size and metabolic rate is depicted in Fig. 2.5 and has long been a subject of study and speculation, but as yet no really satisfactory explanation for the phenomenon has been provided. For our purposes, however, the implications of this phenomenon in the thermal ecology and nutrition of desert animals should be clear and require no elaboration at this stage. It should be equally clear that the colour and other physical characteristics of the cuticle in plants and the integument and pelage in animals are of major importance in determining heat exchange with their environment.

Wind

The preceding equations have highlighted the importance of wind speed in certain heat transfer mechanisms such as convection and evaporative water loss and for this reason a consideration of wind in the desert environment is relevant. Unfortunately no generalisations can be made in respect to wind speed and frequency of strong winds for the desert environment in view of the marked differences between deserts. High frequencies of moderately strong winds are a feature of narrow coastal deserts such as the Atacama and Namib deserts. These are usually cool winds with a high moisture content which blow off the surface of the cold ocean in response to intense insolation on land. Because of their low temperature animals will respond behaviourally to exploit the convective cooling effect of these winds. We have frequently observed how the large desert antelope (*Oryx gazella*) will climb to the crest of the dunes in the Namib Desert during the hottest time of the day to maximise this effect. Also the normally nocturnal Namib dune tenebrionid beetle (*Lepidochora discoidalis*) will respond facultatively to wind by emerging from the sand during the late afternoon as the wind reduces the sand surface temperature and

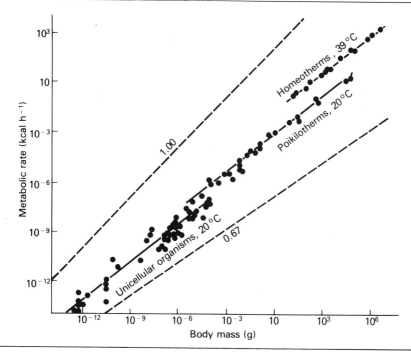

Fig. 2.5 Relationship between metabolic rate and body mass for various classes of organisms. (From Hemmingsen 1960.)

redistributes the grass detritus, which provides the beetles with food. Ground-nesting birds such as the ostrich and sandgrouse will orientate the long axis of the body towards this wind, raise themselves above their eggs and allow the eggs to become cooled convectively.

In continental deserts such as the Sonoran Desert the frequency of strong winds is less regular than in coastal deserts. Nevertheless, wind remains an important abiotic factor in the ecology of these deserts, frequently producing spectacular dust- or sand-storms (Fig. 2.6) with a pronounced abrasive and desiccating action, particularly on delicate ephemeral plants. Perennial desert plants are not spared, however, and there is no doubt that wind has a profound effect on the distribution of desert plants and animals. The sand-blasting action of wind in the desert also has an important effect on the production and redistribution of plant litter or detritus, which characteristically accumulates in certain deserts because of the low decomposition rates. The effect on animals is perhaps less severe because of their ability to escape to a favourable micro-climate but large animals, exposed to high temperature winds, will gain heat remarkably swiftly and, as a result, will lose large amounts of water by evaporative cooling. When evaluating the effect of wind on desert animals and plants it is important to consider the boundary effect at the surface and the gradient of wind speeds in relation to height above the surface as illustrated in Fig. 2.7. Examination of this principle shows that an 80 mg tenebrionid beetle or 2 g lizard moving across the surface of a desert dune is exposed to minimal wind effects, even though the wind may be strong enough to change the shape of the crest of the dune.

A cultural criterion which could possibly be used to evaluate the importance of

Fig. 2.6 Dust- and sand-storms are a typical feature of certain desert climates. This sand-storm in the Namib Desert was followed by one of the heaviest rainfall events to be measured in 40 years.

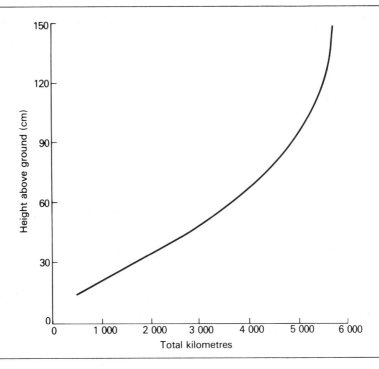

Fig. 2.7 Wind gradient above the surface of the ground shows how wind speed increases exponentially with increase in height above the ground. (From Whitman and Wolters 1967.)

desert winds is the usage of idiomatic names for winds by the local inhabitants. Examples are the Khamsin of the Middle East and North Africa, the Simoon of Iran and Pakistan and the Berg or Ooswind of the Namib Desert. When no special idiomatic term has been coined in the local language, as for example in the Sonoran Desert, wind effects are usually less frequent or less obvious.

Water

Water, as described in the introduction, is the most important single limiting factor in the productivity of desert ecosystems. It is the universal biological solvent, provides turgor to cells and when evaporated has a high cooling potential ($2\,400\,J\,g^{-1}$). Less obvious functions are the effect upon transport of soil nutrients and upon microbial decomposition of litter or detritus to allow recycling of nutrients. We have therefore used rainfall as our sole criterion for defining a desert and for classifying desert areas as extremely arid, arid and semi-arid. The rainfall ranges assigned to these categories (Ch. 1) are purposely wide because of the highly erratic nature of desert rainfall. This is exemplified by the rainfall pattern in the Central Namib Desert where a mean annual precipitation of 14 mm was measured for seven consecutive years to be followed abruptly by an annual precipitation of 118 mm. Because of the low density of plant cover in deserts run-off is swift, flash-floods occur and the high intensity of solar radiation results in rapid evaporation of rain-water. In fact, we have frequently seen how rain can evaporate just before or as it reaches the surface of the soil. All these factors contribute to reducing the effectiveness of rainfall in deserts and bring about a patchy distribution of areas with high soil moisture subsequent to a rainfall event. Areas which retain considerable moisture are eroded washes, the sand at the base of dunes and beneath dry river beds as well as the periphery around rocky outcrops or inselbergs. This distribution pattern is nearly always mirrored by the distribution of the vegetation and in specialised geological and topographical situations oases can form.

Water transport, like heat transfer, is controlled by well-described physical laws and like heat transfer is strongly influenced by differences in water content (concentration gradient) and the surface areas involved in water exchange. When water moves from an area of high water content to one of low content the phenomenon is known as passive diffusion. When this process occurs through a membrane which is selectively permeable to water it is familiarly called osmosis. It is beyond the scope of this text to discuss the intricacies of membrane physics which control water transport but certain important principles are relevant. One of these is the relationship between temperature and the vapour pressure of the air. In Fig. 2.8 the relationships between ambient temperature, humidity ratio and saturation temperature have been illustrated. A cursory examination of these data shows that as the temperature of air rises, its capacity to hold water vapour increases markedly and vice versa. In practice this means that desert plants and animals which are frequently exposed to high ambient temperatures and insolation are also exposed to air with a low water vapour pressure, and this marked water vapour deficit will have a profound desiccating effect, in the absence of specialised adaptive responses which evolve to overcome this problem. In contrast many deserts, because of the low water vapour content of the air, re-radiate the accumulated heat of the day as long-wave radiation very rapidly at night. Ambient temperatures fall swiftly and the relative humidity increases rapidly until the dew-point is reached. This means that both animals and plants can benefit from this dramatic reversal in humidity conditions for several hours. This phenomenon is a prominent feature of

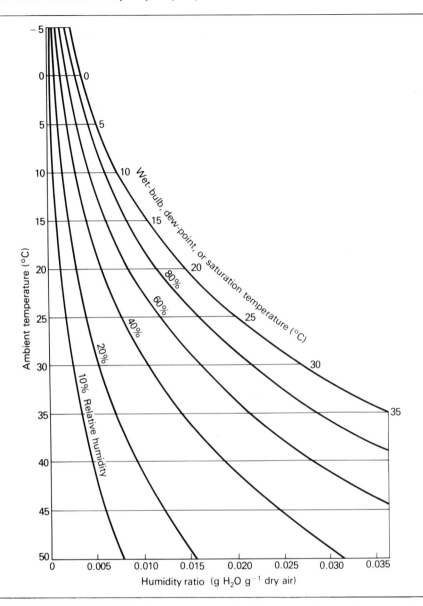

Fig. 2.8 The relationship between ambient temperature, humidity ratio and saturation temperature. (From Chambers 1970.)

the climate of the Namib Desert where we have frequently measured 100 per cent relative humidity with either dew or fog at 08.00 hr in the morning to be followed 4 hours later at 12.00 hr by a relative humidity of less than 35 per cent.

Water balance in plants
In plants water can be absorbed over the entire surface area, although the major portion of the water supply to higher plants is usually absorbed through the roots. In

lichens, however, which in certain deserts comprise the most important component of the plant biomass, water vapour can be absorbed from humid, unsaturated air. Moreover, even dead plant material can adsorb water vapour hygroscopically from unsaturated air and the important implications of this phenomenon to desert animals will be discussed in detail in Chapter 5.

Water uptake by plant roots from the soil is a complex physical process but the rate of uptake can be described in general terms by the equation of Gardner, cited by Larcher (1975):

$$W_{abs} = A \frac{\Psi_{soil} - \Psi_{root}}{\Sigma_r}$$ [5]

where W_{abs} = rate of absorption, A = surface area available for absorption, Ψ_{soil} − Ψ_{root} = the difference in water potential between the soil and the roots and r = the resistances to water transport in the soil and between the soil and the plant. Once again, therefore, the importance of surface area and gradient differences are involved, but in the case of water absorption by roots the physical properties of the soil provide additional complicating factors. For example certain soils will store more water than others. The storage capacity of a soil is usually defined as the weight of water which a soil will retain under a force of 1 000 times gravity and this is known as the *moisture equivalent*. More familiar is the term *field capacity* which is the water content of a saturated soil *in situ* after natural gravitational forces have removed the excess water by percolation. The degree to which water will be retained in a soil depends upon capillary forces present in the soil and the adsorption of water to colloids. When these two forces are added together the force is known as the *matrix potential*. In practice this means that the sands of desert dunes will have a low field capacity and matrix potential while certain desert soils containing a high percentage of colloids for adsorption of water will exhibit high matrix potential. The latter situation is common in alluvial soils on the banks of certain dry river beds. Eventually, however, under dry conditions plants will exhaust the available soil moisture. At first this may be a temporary phenomenon and the plants will wilt during the day and recover at night when the relative humidity rises in response to declining ambient temperature. When they are no longer able to recover, the condition is known as the *permanent wilting point* and the soil is said to have reached the permanent wilting percentage, because the water content at this stage is usually determined gravimetrically as a percentage of the oven-dried weight of the soil. The permanent wilting percentage (PWP) will naturally differ among plant species and Larcher (1975) gives permanent wilting percentages (expressed in soil–water potentials) of −7 to −8 bar for herbs, while in plants growing in moderately arid environments the PWP can reach −30 bar. Larcher (1975) has also described a simple but useful and practical criterion for measuring the available water that a soil can store in the following equation:

$$W_{av} = W_{FC} - W_{PWP}$$ [6]

where W_{av} = the readily available water, W_{FC} = the water content at field capacity and W_{PWP} = the permanent wilting percentage.

Loss of water from plants is collectively known as transpiration and includes water loss via the stomata as well as through the cuticle. As would be expected, transpiration rates are greatly influenced by temperature, radiation, vapour pressure gradients, surface area and wind speed. Naturally all these variables interact with one another in determining the rate of transpiration and the adaptive responses of the

plants to specific climatic conditions. These interactions and responses will be discussed in more detail in Chapter 5 and only the more important principles involved require attention at this stage. For example, the most important ways in which plants can respond adaptively to the desert environment are by escape (ephemerality), reducing the surface area of leaves, the development of elaborate root systems, efficient stomatal closure, water storage in specialised tissues, orientation of leaves and the reduction of transpiration by evolving a specialised cuticle morphology. The effectiveness of these types of adaptations is reflected in the large differences which have been found in the transpiration rates of plants in widely divergent climatic conditions. Transpiration rates in evergreen Ericaceae with closed stomata amount to 45 mg $H_2O\,dm_2^{-2}\,hr^{-1}$, while in certain herbaceous plants it can exceed 2 000 mg $H_2O\,dm_2^{-2}\,hr^{-1}$. Also, the survival time of leaves excised from various plants can vary from 1 000 hr in the case of the succulent *Opuntia camanchica* to only 0.5 hr in a soft-leaved plant such as *Pulmonaria officinalis* (Larcher 1975).

Water balance in animals
In animals water balance, as we have seen, is governed by the same physical laws as in plants. The overall water balance of a large mammal is depicted in Fig. 2.9. Sources of water gain to the animal are provided by free drinking water, water in the food and the water resulting from the oxidation of nutrients such as protein, carbohydrates and fats. Because fats contain a larger number of hydrogen atoms per unit weight,

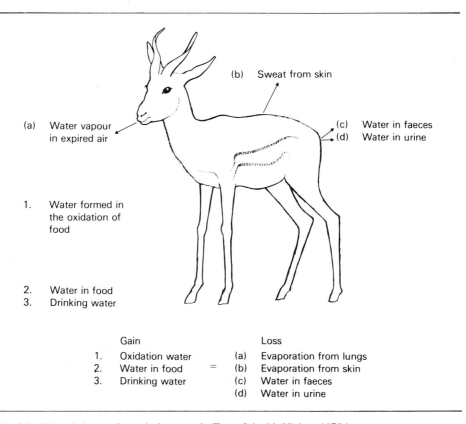

	Gain		Loss
1.	Oxidation water	(a)	Evaporation from lungs
2.	Water in food =	(b)	Evaporation from skin
3.	Drinking water	(c)	Water in faeces
		(d)	Water in urine

Fig. 2.9   Water balance of a typical mammal. (From Schmidt-Nielsen 1970.)

more metabolic water is produced during the oxidation of fat than in the case of the other major nutrients (*ca*. 1.1 g of H_2O per g fat oxidised). The amount of water in the food will vary markedly from 70–80 per cent in the case of lush green pasture to 8 per cent in air-dry grass seeds in a desert environment. Water losses from the animal occur via the respiratory tract, in the faeces, in the urine, by active sweating and slowly by continuous transepidermal water loss.

The major factors influencing the rate of water loss are radiation, ambient temperature, surface area (body size), the nature of the integument, wind speed, vapour pressure deficit and heat loads resulting from locomotion. These factors have already been discussed in some detail under heat transfer and do not require further

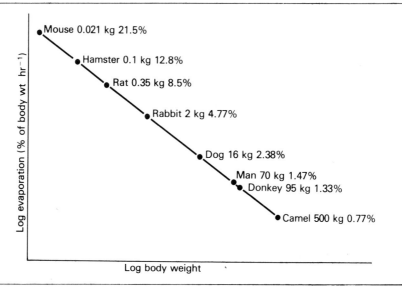

Fig. 2.10 The theoretical relationship between the amount of water, expressed as a percentage of body weight, required to maintain a constant body temperature at 40 °C. (From Folk 1974.)

elaboration here. It is, however, important to realise how these factors interact with one another. For example, a small desert gazelle standing in a strong cool wind will lose heat by convection rapidly because of its relatively large surface area and the high wind speed. If it is obliged to sprint away from a predator the heat load resulting from locomotion will be more rapidly dissipated than in the case of a large antelope with a relatively smaller surface area. The net result is a saving in evaporative water loss. Conversely, if a strong hot wind is blowing the small gazelle will gain heat more rapidly by convective heat transfer than a large antelope. The high wind speed and large water vapour deficit would enhance water loss if the animal were to sweat actively. This important interaction between body size or surface area and evaporative cooling raises an additional principle. From Fig. 2.10 it is apparent that, because of the increase in relative surface area which occurs with decreasing body size, the evaporative water loss required to maintain a constant body temperature, expressed as a percentage of body weight, under hot desert conditions, will be far greater in the case of small mammals (21.5% per hour) than in large mammals (0.8% per hour). There must therefore theoretically be a minimum critical body size, below which it is physiologically impossible to employ evaporative cooling to maintain a

constant body temperature in the desert environment (Fig. 2.10). No exact figure can be selected for this theoretical minimal size because small diurnal mammals will ameliorate the desiccating effects of the desert environment by retreating temporarily to a favourable micro-environment between foraging excursions. Nevertheless, mammals below 16 kg will clearly fall within the critical range. Finally, the employment of active sweating as opposed to thermal panting as a means of evaporative cooling also requires comment. There is a reasonably good correlation between the employment of sweating and body size. Small mammals, because of the principle illustrated in Fig. 2.10, do not sweat. Some large mammals sweat profusely under certain conditions, for example the rhinoceros, while others like the oryx engage in thermal panting in response to heat loads and sweat facultatively, depending on their degree of hydration. The use of active sweating seems also to be closely related to locomotory patterns. Mammals capable of long-distance sustained running, such as man and the equids, favour sweating over thermal panting, the canids being an obvious exception (Taylor 1977). Non-mammalian species do not sweat but evaporative cooling is nevertheless of critical importance in many other animals, particularly in birds, in which both thermal panting and gular fluttering are well developed.

Adaptive responses to minimise water loss in animals include escape to favourable micro-environments, the storage of heat (adaptive heterothermy), efficient reabsorption of water from faecal material in the rectum, production of a highly concentrated urine, a low metabolic rate, specialised integuments and pelages, particularly the highly impermeable cuticles of arthropods. Certain animals also have the ability to store significant amounts of water and others are able to tolerate marked dehydration of their tissues, while others increase their water intake by selecting plants with a high water content or restricting foraging times to the early hours of the morning, when even dead plant material contains appreciable amounts of moisture.

Nutrition

The nutrition of desert plants has not received a great deal of attention. This is probably due to the critical importance of water in the life and productivity of these plants and the priority which this aspect has enjoyed among plant physiologists. Hadley and Szarek (1980), in reviewing nutrient cycling in desert ecosystems, conclude that nitrogen is a key limiting nutrient in North American deserts. Charley and Cowling (1968) have suggested that phosphorus is limiting in arid regions of Australia, while Seely and Louw (1980) report that the Namib Desert dune sand is deficient in all three macro-nutrients – nitrogen, phosphorus and potassium. Decomposition rates in deserts are also notoriously slow and this means that the characteristic swift and ephemeral growth of many desert plants will exhaust nutrients rapidly from the soil and that these nutrients will be recycled very slowly. In this respect Noy-Meir (1974) has also observed that the nutrient supply in arid regions is mostly confined to the upper 5 cm of the soil and that soil strata below this level are frequently impoverished. In addition to nutrient deficiencies, some desert plants are faced with the problem of an excessive concentration of salts in the soil, particularly sodium chloride and gypsum. The reader should not, however, be left with the impression that all desert soils are impoverished. Water remains the key limiting factor and this is demonstrated by the frequently spectacular yields obtained from crops grown under irrigation in the desert, especially from alluvial soils on the margins of dry river beds. Nevertheless, because of the nature of rock weathering in

deserts, the frequent accumulation of excessive salts, the instability of dune substrates and the slow rate and amount of decomposition, low fertility of soils must be considered an important limiting factor in the primary productivity of desert ecosystems.

In the case of desert animals, a superficial examination of the desert environment with its low primary productivity and patchy distribution of plants, immediately suggests that energy would be in short supply. This may be so when considering the nutrition of large herbivores but recent work by Seely and Louw (1980) suggests that energy in absolute terms may not be deficient, especially in the case of small primary consumers. The patchy dispersion of this energy may, however, result in a localised deficiency of energy. In contrast, in many arid and semi-arid ecosystems a severe protein deficiency can occur for prolonged periods. This is also true for certain micro-nutrients such as vitamins which are essential for maintenance and particularly reproduction in animals. In this respect, the advantages of ruminant digestion should be considered. The rumen provides ideal conditions for fermentation of fibrous plant material. The micro-organisms responsible for the degradation of this material are also capable of synthesising water-soluble vitamins, as well as amino acids from recycled urea. Ruminants would then appear to be the ideal type of animal to exploit arid and semi-arid areas, were it not for the fact that they are usually fairly large animals and as such have a high requirement for energy, in absolute terms, and cannot easily retreat to micro-environments.

There is no doubt therefore that periodic nutritional stress is an important factor in the overall unpredictability of the desert environment, particularly in the case of protein and certain vitamins, while energy in certain situations may also be limiting. The more important adaptive responses of animals to nutritional stress include the storage of energy in the form of fat, migration, the reduction of metabolic rate through aestivation or diapause, sun-basking and selection for small body size. These factors will be discussed in detail in Chapters 4 and 5, but brief consideration of some of the principles involved in selection for body size is pertinent here. A large animal will, as we have seen, have a relatively lower resting metabolic rate than a small animal. Its energy requirements will therefore be proportionally less and because of the large amount of elastic energy stored in the muscles, the cost of locomotion will be reduced (Fig. 2.11) and migration will be facilitated. In contrast, a small animal has a much lower energy requirement in absolute terms, it can retreat easily to a favourable micro-environment to aestivate and can reproduce more swiftly when favourable conditions develop in the desert. The advantages of being small usually outweigh the advantages of being large, and this is reflected in the fact that most permanent residents in deserts are small animals while large herbivores and carnivores are usually periodic visitors.

The preceding discussion of principles allows us to conclude that the desert ecologist, especially a physiological ecologist, should give careful consideration to micro-climate, body size, surface areas, temperature and water vapour pressure gradients, the physical nature of the epidermis, wind speed, the storage of energy and water and the interdependence of all these factors. He should also be aware of the similarity in the adaptive responses of both plants and animals to the hostility of the desert environment. Finally, the zoologist will be impressed by the fact that the desert is an ideal environment for the small ectotherm. There is an abundance of radiant energy for behavioural thermoregulation during the day and a warm substrate at night for thigmothermic thermoregulation. Moreover, in terms of nutritional stress the small ectotherm can retreat well below the surface and reduce

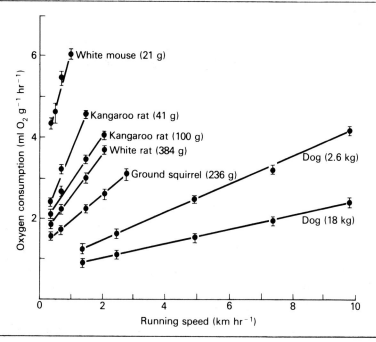

Fig. 2.11   The cost of locomotion and the effect of running speed decreases in relation to increasing body size. (From Taylor *et al.* 1970.)

body temperature, metabolic rate and water requirements, emerging periodically to exploit the irregular pulses of water and nutrition, so characteristic of the desert environment.

Chapter 3

Escape from the desert environment

We could perhaps begin this chapter with the bold generalisation that most plants and animals survive in the desert because they do not live in the desert. This is of course not entirely true but it does serve to emphasise how important the exploitation of favourable micro-climates is within the desert ecosystem. We could also use an all-encompassing term such as avoidance to describe this phenomenon but we have chosen to distinguish between escape, a long-term phenomenon, and retreat, a short-term behavioural response. Volumes could be filled with examples of how desert organisms avoid the harshness of the desert climate, as it is the most commonly employed of all adaptive responses. The major concepts and principles involved are, however, relatively simple and treatment of the subject will therefore be relatively brief.

Escape

Ephemerality and micro-climate exploitation in plants

One of the earlier experiments performed in plant physiology showed that the seeds of common cereal grains were able to withstand exposure to surprisingly high temperatures (100 °C) and low levels of relative humidity. The metabolic rate of seeds is also so low that for all practical purposes they can be considered ametabolic. It is not surprising therefore that so many desert plants have evolved ephemerality, whereby most of their lives are spent in an arrested embryonic stage which is extremely resistant to high temperatures and desiccation. With the advent of favourable conditions, usually a threshold amount of rain, these seeds germinate rapidly and a very efficient and rapid rate of photosynthesis allows them to reach maturity and set seed swiftly. The majority of ephemeral plants are annuals because perennial ephemerals are required to maintain a greater proportion of dormant tissue in the form of corms, roots or bulbs during prolonged dry periods. Survival potential of ephemeral annuals is therefore theoretically greater in very arid deserts. This is reflected in the preponderance of annuals (96% of plant cover) in the most arid areas of the North American deserts such as Death Valley, where the coefficient of variation in rainfall is 50 per cent. Where the variability in annual rainfall is lower (20%), the percentage of annuals drops dramatically to only 1 per cent of the total plant cover (Schaffer and Gadgil 1975). This distribution pattern of annual versus perennial ephemerals probably holds good for most arid and semi-arid regions of the world but in certain specialised situations it is not applicable. For example, a transect from east to west across the narrow Namib Desert has shown that rainfall decreases rapidly from the escarpment in the east to reach minimal levels on the coast in the

west. Variability increases markedly in the same direction. Perennial ephemerals predominate in the eastern portion of the desert as expected, but are gradually replaced by ephemeral annual grasses in a westerly direction. In the coastal region, however, where extremely arid conditions and high variability of rainfall prevail, the annuals are replaced again by perennials. This is probably owing to the fairly frequent occurrence of fog in the west which can sustain the growth of widely dispersed perennials.

Because ephemeral plants complete their life cycles under favourable conditions, they seldom exhibit any specialised morphological adaptations to the desert climate and often possess mesophytic leaves. Many of them, however, employ the so-called C_4 photosynthetic pathway, apparently to sustain very rapid photosynthesis and therefore growth. The significance of this metabolic pathway will be discussed in more detail in Chapter 5. In any event, whatever the ecological and physiological implications are, desert ephemerals provide us, from an aesthetic viewpoint, with one of the most spectacular examples of natural beauty. This is heightened by the contrasting barrenness which precedes their dramatic growth and is perhaps best exemplified by the flora of Namaqualand in southern Africa.

In addition to ephemerality, some desert plants avoid desiccation by growing in favourable micro-climates. Rock fissures, the stable moist sand at the base of dunes, the banks of certain washes or wadis and the shade beneath trees in dry river beds can all provide suitable conditions for plant growth in specialised situations. One of the more striking examples of this phenomenon is provided by the western slopes of the isolated hills or inselbergs on the gravel plains of the Namib and the *lomas* in the Peruvian Desert, which act as fog collectors and support a different flora from that of the eastern slopes and the plains below. Nevertheless, most of these plants show at least some form of adaptive reponse to minimise desiccation.

Seed dispersal of both ephemeral and perennial plants in the desert raises some interesting questions, reviewed in considerable detail by Cloudsley-Thompson (1965). Most of the plants fall into two broad categories; those which have evolved elaborate mechanisms to enhance dispersion (e.g. *Aristida* sp.) and those which produce seeds morphologically adapted to minimise dispersion. The former category is not entirely peculiar to deserts while the latter would enhance the survival of the seedling by limiting its dispersion to the habitat, which has already proved to be favourable for the growth and reproduction of the parent plant. One mechanism for limiting seed dispersion is known as *hygrochasy* which occurs in the 'Rose of Jericho', *Anastatica hierochuntica*. Apparently hygrochastic plants are limited to arid environments. In these plants dissemination does not follow ripening of the plant but is delayed until the next rainy season. In certain species, the seed coat becomes mucilaginous in contact with water as the rain washes it from the seed capsule. These so-called *myxospermic* seeds act as an additional restriction on dispersion.

Diapause and temporary pond inhabitants

The term *diapause* was originally restricted in its usage to describe the resting stage during blastokinesis. Today, however, it is used to describe any situation in which the development of an organism is arrested. If we accept the latter interpretation, then there are literally thousands of examples among invertebrates in which diapause occurs and they are certainly not limited to deserts. The desert environment, however, with its irregular pulses of food and water, will naturally favour the evolution of invertebrate animals with protracted diapause. During diapause metabolic demands are minimal and, if it occurs in a moist micro-climate, water loss

is also minimised. Favourable conditions will provide the environmental cue to trigger rapid development of the organism to maturity and, following reproduction, an organism can again enter diapause at a developmental stage which is most suitable for its particular life form. There are many examples to draw from but our discussion will be limited to one of the more dramatic, the temporary pond inhabitants.

Anyone who has experienced the transition from a dry to a wet period in a desert can hardly have failed to be impressed by the explosion of life which occurs in a temporary pond. Natural depressions on desert plains which vary in size from several metres to several kilometres, known *inter alia* as *playas* in the south-western United States and *panne* in the Kalahari Desert, remain in a dry and apparently lifeless condition for years on end. When these depressions are periodically flooded with rain, algae, bacteria and protozoans appear in great numbers within a matter of hours. Within 1 to 2 days a variety of small crustaceans appear and grow to maturity very rapidly. Their large numbers and active feeding habits give the pond the appearance of teeming life (Fig. 3.1). These crustaceans are the predominant

Fig. 3.1 Temporary ponds in desert areas frequently support a teeming mass of phyllopod crustaceans after being dry and lifeless for many years.

metazoan animals in most desert ponds and usually include anostracans (fairy shrimps), conchostracans (clam shrimps) and notostracans (tadpole shrimps), collectively known as phyllopods. Intense insolation in the desert environment causes rapid evaporation of the pond water, high water temperatures and consequently a low O_2 tension in the water. In these highly unstable conditions the animals must develop swiftly and reproduce before conditions become intolerable for life. Naturally, ephemeral life in temporary ponds is not restricted to the desert environment but in the desert the period of dormancy is longer and far more

unpredictable. The wet phase is usually shorter and the physical conditions during this phase are highly unstable. One would therefore expect that the temporary pond inhabitants in deserts would show greater tolerance to fluctuating salinity, O_2 tension and water temperature. One would also expect that these organisms would exhibit adaptations which allow for longer periods of dormancy as well as well-controlled responses to environmental cues which initiate reactivation during the wet phase. This has been shown to be the case in specific species and is perhaps best exemplified by the well-known brine shrimp (*Artemia salina*). Nevertheless, some temporary pond inhabitants in mesic areas show equally high tolerance of the unstable conditions described.

In spite of the interesting biological problems posed by life in temporary desert ponds, research in this direction has been surprisingly limited and of a rather fragmentary nature. The field has been reviewed by Cole (1968) and Belk and Cole (1975). As expected, most research has been directed towards studying the adaptations exhibited by these animals during the dormant or diapause phase, the environmental cues which synchronise reactivation from the dry to the wet phase, and those which allow the free-living forms to cope with highly unstable aquatic conditions. We shall restrict our discussion to diapause.

In their review Belk and Cole (1975) distinguished between obligatory diapause, which occurs every generation and is endogenously controlled, and facultative diapause, which is cued by an environmental factor that predicts a future change to unfavourable conditions. They point out that obligatory diapause is well suited to an environment in which cyclic change is regular and predictable, while facultative diapause is eminently suitable for the highly unpredictable environment of the temporary desert pond. They cite several examples of facultative diapause among phyllopods in desert ponds but, in our opinion, the distinction is perhaps too sharply defined and the life histories of these animals are more probably controlled by the interaction between an endogenous rhythm and exogenous cues.

The most common stage in which diapause in phyllopods occurs is the egg. In the egg stage the organism is virtually ametabolic and, even though the nutrient reserves are limited, it is able to survive for many years in this form. A further prerequisite for survival which would be expected to develop, is some form of waterproofing to prevent desiccation of the eggs. This, however, does not seem to be the case. For example, the thick spongy tertiary shell of phyllopod eggs is not watertight but is thought to be a protective structure against abrasion and sunlight. Also, the ephippium of cladoceran eggs is not impermeable to water and Belk and Cole (1975) conclude that the shells of these crustraceans only play a secondary role in protecting them against desiccation. It would seem therefore that the embryos possess inherent tolerance to desiccation, which still has to be explained. In fact Clegg (1964) has shown that desiccation of *Artemia* eggs is a prerequisite for normal development in the life history of this species. Also, Carlisle (1968) has found that the eggs of the tadpole shrimp (*Triops granarius*) survived 16 hr of exposure to 98 °C and that death only occurred after the last small amount of water had been driven off above the boiling-point of water. Exact data on tolerance limits for the various species are, however, still very limited.

Not all temporary inhabitants of desert ponds undergo diapause as eggs. Rzóska (1961) reports that the cyclopoid copepod (*Metacyclops minutus*) survives extremely hot conditions in the Sudan in the resting copepodid stage for 9 months. Edward (1968) has shown that chironomid larvae, surrounded by capsules, can survive 56–60 °C for up to 2 hr per day in desiccated rock pools in Australia. What determines the stage of development in which diapause occurs? Probably a complex

of factors but an obvious influence would be body size. Animals which are small in the adult form would be unable to store sufficient nutrient reserves as adults to sustain life for prolonged periods, even though metabolic rate was greatly reduced. In the embryonic egg stage, before complex tissues have developed, metabolic demands would, however, be far lower and less specific. On the other hand a large adult would be able to store sufficient reserves, and with the advent of favourable conditions would be able to reproduce immediately, a distinct advantage in an ephemeral situation. The question is, nevertheless, far from resolved and the whole field of temporary pond ecology is a fertile one for further investigation.

Aestivation

Aestivation, like hibernation, describes a condition of prolonged dormancy or torpor in vertebrate animals during which metabolic rate and body temperature are significantly reduced. Aestivation is, however, usually used to describe this condition in a hot arid environment, whereas hibernation is typically associated with a more profound dormancy in response to prolonged cold stress. The adaptive value of both conditions is obvious, particularly to endothermic animals which expend approximately four times as much energy as ectothermic animals on maintenance. The physiological control of hibernation has been exceedingly well researched but is not pertinent to this discussion. Suffice it to say that a complex of interactions is involved between environmental cues and the response of various organ systems.

Bartholomew (1977), in a recent review on body temperature and energy metabolism, explains how hibernation can occur in ground squirrels of the genus *Citellus*, inhabiting the cold northern latitudes of North America, while representatives of the same 'genus' aestivate in hot, arid regions. Congeneric species in warm temperate regions neither aestivate nor hibernate. A sharp distinction between hibernation and aestivation should therefore not be drawn. Moreover, there appears to be no phylogenetic pattern associated with this ability. Aestivation in endotherms is probably most common in rodents but has also been recorded in one species of marsupial (*Cercaertus nanus*). The poorwill (*Phalacnoptilus nuttallii*) is probably the best-known example of hibernation in birds. Leopold (1962) describes how Edmund Jaeger first observed this phenomenon. He discovered a dormant poorwill in a rocky crypt in southern California and ringed it. The same bird returned to the identical location for three consecutive years where it was observed to hibernate for weeks at a time. Not only does the poorwill exhibit long periods of dormancy under dry conditions, when food is usually scarce, but its basal metabolic rate under summer conditions is still less than half that of most other birds. Reference to equation [1] in Chapter 2 will show that this confers a significant advantage to the bird in maintaining thermal equilibrium under conditions of intense radiation, because of the reduction in metabolic heat production (Bartholomew 1977).

In ectothermic vertebrates aestivation is a somewhat different concept and again involves us in the confusing terminology used in this field. For example, because aestivation in endotherms is accompanied by a marked reduction in body temperature from the normally high level, special physiological adjustments are required to induce this phenomenon. In contrast, ectotherms normally exhibit a marked diurnal variation in body temperature and the physiological adjustments required to induce aestivation in these animals, although still complex, are of a different type. For this reason various authors prefer to use the terms *brumation* for reptilian aestivation and *retraherence* for amphibians. Brumation in reptiles has been described for several species. The animals usually seek out a cool, moist

micro-habitat and their metabolic rate is markedly reduced as they slowly use up their nutrient reserves. In the case of tortoises their survival under these conditions is greatly enhanced by the storage of large amounts of hypo-osmotic urine in the bladder. Amphibian retraherence has, however, enjoyed more attention and will be used as an example.

Amphibians, because of their almost universal dependence upon water for reproduction, are restricted in arid regions to specialised habitats, which periodically provide sufficient water for this purpose. They cannot therefore be considered true desert animals. Nevertheless, through specialised physiological and behavioural adaptations, they are able to survive long periods of drought and epitomise the concept of escape from the desert environment. Reproductive patterns in desert amphibians have been reviewed by Low (1976) and a general account of their adaptations to desert scrub has been provided by Blair (1976).

Amphibians which undergo retraherence exhibit similar patterns of adaptive responses. Normally they have the ability to burrow to remarkable depths beneath the surface to seek out a fairly moist micro-habitat. *Scaphiopus* or the spadefoot toads of the Sonoran Desert are probably the best-known examples of this type. They can reach depths of 91 cm where they remain for as long as 9 months (Ruibal *et al.* 1969) and a horny projection on the hind foot facilitates burrowing in this species (Fig. 3.2). While in a state of retraherence the metabolic rate of adult amphibians is

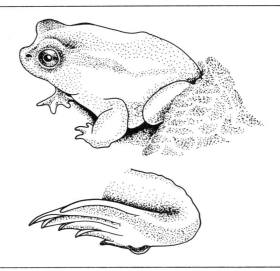

Fig. 3.2 The spadefoot toad of the Sonoran Desert can escape to depths as great as 90 cm below the surface during unfavourable climatic conditions. Digging is facilitated by the presence of a horny projection on the foot.

markedly reduced and they are largely dependent on fat reserves, located in special fat bodies within the abdominal cavity. The marked reduction in metabolism is also accompanied by several adaptations to reduce water loss. Some amphibians become surrounded by a mud cocoon while others produce a cocoon of dry dead skin which is relatively impervious to rapid water loss. Alternatively, or concomitantly, the animals accumulate urea within their tissues, which raises the osmoconcentration of the body fluids above that of the matrix potential of the surrounding soil. The result

of this change is a net flow of water from the soil to the animal's tissues. This requires the catabolism of protein and the development of a high tolerance, particularly of the muscles, to hypertonic urea solutions as well. Retention of urea in response to osmotic stress is, however, not confined to desert species but occurs also in the highly aquatic *Xenopus laevis* and the marine frog (*Rana cancrivora*). Finally, survival will be greatly enhanced by storage of water and the tolerance of marked dehydration of the tissues. The former is fairly common in desert-adapted species in the form of dilute urine which is stored in a diverticulum of the digestive tract, commonly referred to as a bladder. High tolerance to dehydration is essential since a 40–50 per cent loss of body weight frequently occurs. It also involves a marked change in the electrolyte composition and osmotic concentration of the body fluids. All the above changes have been quantified in several species and are perhaps best exemplified in the African bullfrog (*Pyxicephalus adspersus*) (Loveridge and Withers 1981).

Seasonal migration

The most obvious form of escape from the desert is emigration. It is, however, restricted to those animals in which locomotion is not too costly, usually large mammals or animals capable of flight. There are many accounts of seasonal migration to and from the desert environment, but they are nearly all of an anecdotal nature. In fact, very little quantitative data, using marked mammals and birds, are available. For example, we have been repeatedly impressed by the immigration of very large flocks of sandgrouse (*Pterocles namaqua*) into the Namib Desert, when soil-surface temperatures fall to sufficiently low levels during winter to allow these ground-nesting birds to reproduce. The phenomenon has, however, not been quantified. Many similar examples could be cited, particularly in the case of birds which range over enormous distances in arid areas to exploit localised food resources, including temporary ponds and lakes, and then move on as the ephemeral resources become depleted. Perhaps the best-documented example of seasonal migration to and from the desert environment is provided by the Phainopepla (*Phainopepla nitens*), a small 24 g bird which belongs to the fly catcher family. This species has been well studied by Walsberg (1977). He provides data that show that this species winters in the deserts of the south-western United States and, with the advent of hot summer conditions, moves to the more mesic environments surrounding the desert areas (Fig. 3.3). In California these birds winter in the Colorado Desert where they breed in March and April, and then leave this area in late April to enter the coastal oak and riparian woodlands where breeding occurs once again from late May through July. Interestingly, the main food item for Phainopeplas in the desert during winter is the berry of the desert mistletoe. In its summer range aerial insects are abundant and the fruits of *Rhamnus crocea* are utilised. The change in habitat is accompanied also by significant changes in this species' behaviour and general life style, presumably to allow the unusual employment of a double breeding season in two very different habitats.

Seasonal migration in large mammals has been well documented in the case of the wildebeest (Pennycuick 1975). Although the wildebeest is not strictly a desert animal and requires access to a regular water supply, parts of its habitat range become seasonally very arid. In East Africa it responds to this seasonal effect by migrating, employing a wide circular pattern which allows it to follow seasonal changes in the rainfall pattern. Large-scale migration of springbok, an arid-adapted gazelle in southern Africa, has been the subject of much speculation over many years. Reports of thousands of these animals in mass migrations or *treks* are

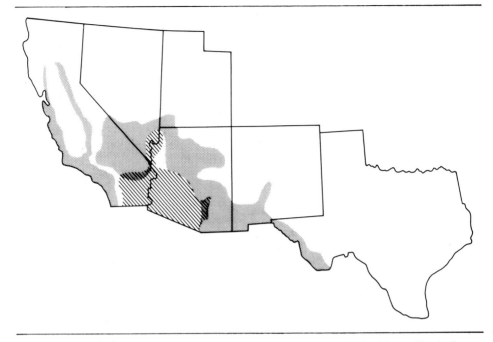

Fig. 3.3 Seasonal migration of *Phainopepla nitens* in the south-western United States. Hatched areas represent the winter range and stippled areas the summer range. (From Walsberg 1977.)

commonplace in the literature of early explorers. Although there can be little doubt that these very mobile antelope, like most ungulates of the savanna and arid steppe, can move across large distances to exploit localised effects of rain, the reports remain largely anecdotal. More localised movement of large desert mammals, which cannot be strictly classed as true migration, has, however, been the subject of considerable study. For example, Hamilton *et al.* (1977) have reported on the movement of oryx (*Oryx gazella*) to and from the large Namib dune sea. When rain falls in the dune sea it triggers the growth of ephemeral grasses, particularly in the inter-dune valleys and at the base of the dunes. The oryx then move into the dune sea and graze upon these grasses in surprisingly large numbers. As conditions in the dunes become progressively drier, the animals migrate to the dry Kuiseb River bed which, with its riparian vegetation, provides shelter, food in the form of *Acacia* pods and water. The animals excavate the sand in the dry river bed to maintain the water-holes but compete for food with several other species, including chacma baboons, in this narrow linear oasis which transects the entire desert from east to west.

Retreat

The term retreat, in the context of this discussion, is applied to the short-term escape behaviour of desert animals. It usually assumes the pattern of a daily rhythm and can occur with or without a period of circadian torpor. Examples are legion, but only a few have been chosen for illustrative purposes.

The escape behaviour of tenebrionid beetles in the Namib Desert has been well studied by Hamilton (1975). Figure 3.4 shows how two species of tenebrionids

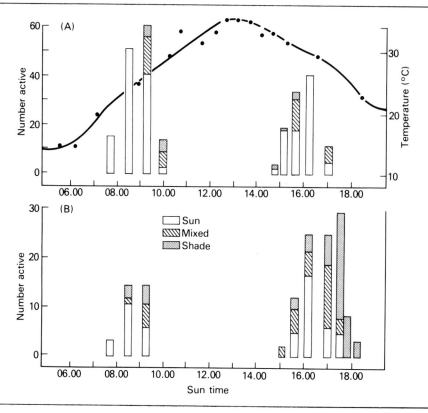

Fig. 3.4 Activity patterns of (A) a white desert tenebrionid *Onymacris langi* and (B) a black species *Physosterna globosa* in an area of overlap. (From Hamilton 1975.)

respond to high soil-surface temperatures by employing a bimodal activity rhythm which allows them to escape the fiercest heat of the midday hours. The interesting interaction between the colour of the beetles and their activity rhythm will be discussed in Chapter 4. Many other species of Tenebrionidae employ a similar bimodal diurnal activity rhythm for the same purposes, while others, notably the nocturnal *Lepidochora* species, avoid the excessive heat of the day entirely. One member of the latter species, *L. discoidalis*, will, however, emerge during late afternoon by responding facultatively to wind in the Namib dunes. The wind cools the surface of the dune sand sufficiently for these normally nocturnal beetles to emerge from beneath the sand and forage upon the wind-blown grass detritus. Of interest also is the fact that the nocturnal activity of these beetles is basically controlled by an endogenous rhythm, which will persist for several days under conditions of constant light and ambient temperature. This endogenous rhythm is, nevertheless, not only modified in the field by a facultative response to wind, but as the beetles are gregarious, the larger the population is, the more sharply synchronised the activity rhythm becomes (Louw and Hamilton 1972). This phenomenon is known as social facilitation.

The above examples of nocturnal and diurnal activity rhythms raise challenging evolutionary and ecological questions. Why, for example, are all the Namib tenebrionids not nocturnal? Perhaps by being diurnal a particular species can

maintain a higher body temperature for longer periods and thus capitalise on a more rapid metabolism and reproductive rate. It could, however, be argued that a nocturnal species, employing a set of specially adapted iso-enzymes, could maintain the level of metabolism at an equally high rate. Obviously the correct answer will have to consider a complex set of influences including predation intensity, food availability and other variables; this information is not yet available.

The escape behaviour of Namib dune lizards provides another example of contrasting behaviour patterns. The diurnal, sand-diving lizard, *Aporosaura anchietae*, lives in the soft wind-blown sand of the slipfaces near the crests of the dunes. Under normal summer conditions these slipfaces receive intense solar radiation in the forenoon and, as a result, the temperature of the surface of the sand rises very rapidly and remains for only a short period within the preferred range (*ca*. 30–40 °C). This means that this species suffers from what ecologists idiomatically call a 'time crunch'. It has very little time on the surface for foraging and social behaviour before temperatures become excessively high. In order to extend the time spent on the surface as long as possible, it engages in what could perhaps be described as a thermoregulatory dance. At surface temperatures of approximately 30 °C it emerges from beneath the sand and adpresses the ventral surface of the body to the warm substrate. In this position the whole body is dished convexly with all four limbs and the tail held in the air while the body temperature rises rapidly to the preferred level. The animal then moves swiftly across the surface of the slipface while foraging for food and engaging in various forms of social behaviour. As the surface temperatures approach 40 °C, the gait of the lizard changes to a stilt-like walk and the body is held as high as possible above the hot substrate. Periodically the animal interrupts this behaviour and raises diagonally opposite limbs into the air while using the heavily cornified tail for support. This is presumably to assist in convective or radiant cooling of the extremities and gives the same impression as a barefoot child dancing on a hot pavement. Eventually, however, when surface temperatures move into the 40–45 °C range the animal escapes to a cooler environment beneath the sand with a flick of its tail. It remains beneath the sand until the surface temperatures fall to within an acceptable range once again in the afternoon (*ca*. 40–30 °C). This characteristic, bimodal, surface activity is illustrated in Fig. 3.5 and, although it is basically controlled by an endogenous diurnal rhythm, it is entrained by environmental cues and can be facultatively modified by environmental conditions. For example, the activity patterns in Fig. 3.5 show that the lizards will remain below the surface all day when strong desiccating winds are blowing, whereas when cool conditions prevail, they frequently remain above the surface all day with no sign of a bimodal pattern of activity. In contrast to *Aporosaura*, *Palmatogecko rangei* is strictly nocturnal. Its integument is almost transparent and its feet are provided with broad and extensive webbing, which allow it to dig deep burrows beneath the compacted sand on the slopes of the dunes (Fig. 3.6). It remains secluded in this comparatively cool and moist environment for the entire day.

Desert birds, because of their efficient mode of locomotion, are able to retreat easily from unfavourable desert conditions. There are many examples of bird species which shelter in nests, rock overhangs, trees and dense shrubs to avoid the hottest hours of the day. A unique example of this type of behaviour is provided by the social weaver (*Philetairus socius*), which invades the semi-arid steppe on the periphery of the Namib Desert and is common in the Kalahari. This species builds an enormous communal nest in the branches of *Acacia* trees and its range is therefore limited by the presence of these trees. In the absence of these trees it will attempt to use unlikely artificial structures such as telephone poles (Fig. 3.7). The significance of this

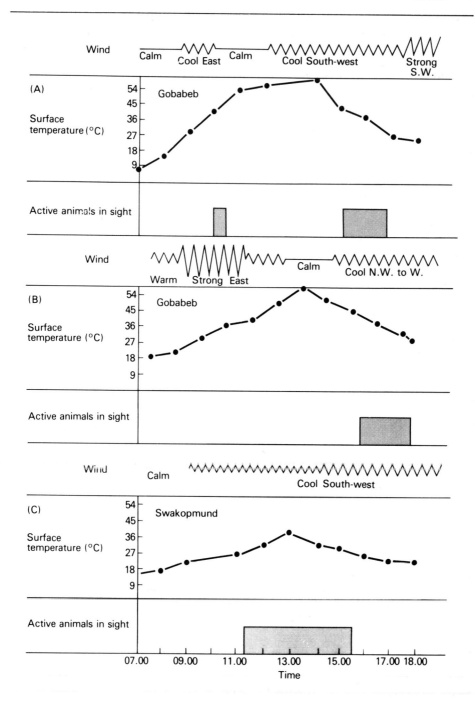

Fig. 3.5 Activity patterns of the Namib sand-diving dune lizard are normally of a bimodal nature, but can become unimodal when cool conditions prevail or the animals can remain below the surface for most of the day when hot desiccating winds are blowing. (From Louw and Holm 1972.)

Fig. 3.6   The strictly nocturnal Namib dune gecko *Palmatogecko rangei* spends the entire day in a cool moist burrow beneath the sand. The wide webbing on the feet facilitates the digging of this burrow.

Fig. 3.7   The social weaver, *Philetairus socius*, constructs enormous communal nests which insulate the community against the excessive heat and cold of the desert environment.

unusual nest in the thermal biology of this species has been examined by Bartholomew *et al.* (1976) who found that the insulation provided by the nest dampened the effect of the widely fluctuating diurnal range in ambient temperature, which is so characteristic of the desert environment. The birds are therefore protected from both the extreme cold at night and excessive heat during the day. Social weavers, like ourselves, do not, however, live in a perfect world and the nest also provides a suitable retreat for a large species of cobra which preys heavily upon these birds.

One of the first examples of retreat in desert animals to be studied thoroughly was the kangaroo rat (Fig. 3.8). Schmidt-Nielsen (1964) has described the behaviour of

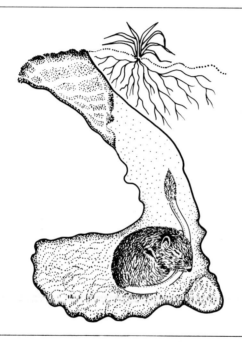

Fig. 3.8   The burrow of the kangaroo rat provides shelter from predators, radiation as well as desiccation. When the entrance is sealed water vapour in expired gases contributes to keeping the relative humidity above a critical level.

this animal in detail in relation to its water balance. When the animal retreats to its burrow during the day it seals the entrance with soil and, as a result, the relative humidity of the air in the burrow remains reasonably high throughout the day (> 30%). The water vapour expired in the respiratory air contributes significantly to maintaining this level of relative humidity and, as we shall discover in Chapter 5, is a crucial factor in allowing the animal to balance its finely adjusted water budget. Pocket mice (*Perognathus californicus*) exhibit a similar behavioural pattern to the kangaroo rat but, probably because of their extremely small size, also enter a state of torpor while sheltered in their burrows. The torpor can be of a circadian nature or for a fairly prolonged period. Another striking example of retreat in small desert animals is provided by the antelope ground squirrel (*Citellus leucurus*). This small diurnal mammal allows its body temperature to rise to unusually high levels of *ca*. 42 °C

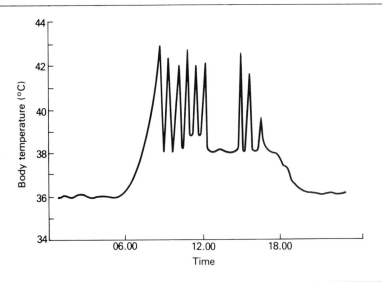

Fig. 3.9   Fluctuation in body termperature of the antelope ground squirrel as it periodically retreats to the cool burrow after foraging forays on the hot surface. (From Hudson 1962.)

Fig. 3.10   The largest desert mammal in the Namib dune system, *Oryx gazella*, excavates sand in the dry Kuiseb River bed to construct semi-permanent water-holes.

while foraging on the surface. When the body temperature reaches these peak levels it retreats to its cool underground burrow, flattens its body against the cool substrate and loses heat by both conduction to the substrate and radiation to the ambient air. Thus they avoid the necessity of wasting valuable water on evaporative cooling (Fig. 3.9).

Chapter 4

Tolerance of the desert environment: I
Morphological adaptations

Although small animals survive in the desert largely through avoidance of extreme conditions, some of them also show important adaptations which allow them to tolerate these extremes. Nevertheless, tolerance is of greater importance to plants and large animals that are unable to escape from the exigencies of the desert environment. Tolerance usually involves both physiological and morphological adaptation but these characteristics are frequently so dependent upon one another that it is unrealistic from a biological viewpoint to differentiate between them. For the sake of convenience, however, we shall discuss morphological and physiological attributes separately. Also, because the adaptations exhibited by plants and animals are surprisingly similar (Hadley 1972), the sequence in which plants and animals will be treated has been chosen to highlight these similarities. Finally, a brief reference to terminology may be justified here. The adaptive responses discussed in this chapter are now commonly described as strategies in the modern eco-physiological literature. A strategy, however, implies that a rational choice has been made by the organism and is therefore the antithesis of the evolutionary concept of chance and necessity. The term is philosophically misleading and will consequently be avoided.

Plant morphology

The principal characteristics of desert plants have been reviewed by McCleary (1968), Hadley (1972) and Solbrig and Orians (1977). Solbrig and Orians have tabulated (Table 4.1) these main characteristics and from their summary it is clear that deep root development, and the development of either small specialised leaves or a large succulent body without leaves constitute the major forms of morphological adaptation in arid-adapted plants. The orientation of leaves is also an important consideration as it will determine the surface area exposed to light for photosynthesis as well as the heat load from solar radiation. For example, Treshaw (1970) has shown that vertically orientated pads and stems of cacti absorb less solar energy and remain cooler than those orientated at right angles to the sun's rays (Fig. 4.1). It has also been shown that east–west facing pads of the desert prickly pear (*Opuntia engelmannii*), gained heat more swiftly than those orientated in a north–south direction. The latter pads exhibited a bimodal temperature profile with two peaks, while the former exhibited a unimodal profile with a single peak (Gibbs and Patten 1970). Because of the patchy distribution and low biomass of plants in the desert, there is also very little inter-plant obstruction and consequently leaf orientation, to maximise sunlight absorption for photosynthesis, is not usually an important consideration.

Hadley (1972) has pointed out the importance of surface projections and irregularly shaped surfaces in reducing incident radiation and, therefore, the heat

Table 4.1 *Major features of desert plants. (From Solbrig and Orians 1977.)*

	Drought evaders	Phreatophytes	Evergreen shrubs	Succulents
Life span	Mostly ephemerals; some perennials	Perennials	Perennials	Perennials
Principal phenotypic characteristic	No obvious specialisation	Long deep roots	Small and specialised leaves, or no leaves	Succulent body, usually without leaves
Photosynthetic characteristics	High photosynthetic rate during periods of water availability (many C_4 plants)	No obvious photosynthetic specialisation	Relatively low photosynthesis but can photosynthesise under water stress (mostly C_3 plants)	Very low photosynthetic rates but can photosynthesise under almost all conditions (CAM photosynthesis)
Water economy	No specialisation to conserve water	Tap underground sources of water	Specialised to withstand water stresses; high resistance to water loss	Store water

loads on desert plants. This adaptation is particularly prominent in certain desert cacti, such as the teddy bear cholla (*Opuntia bigelovii*), in which the temperature of the tissues underlying the spines can be as much as 11 °C cooler than if the spines were absent (Fig. 4.2). The spines not only absorb and reflect incident radiation but also create a boundary layer of air between the surface of the plant and the spines, which retards heat transfer to the surface of the plant. This, however, also means that heat loss will be slower from these plants at night than from those with a less dense

Fig. 4.1 The orientation of cactus pads can reduce the profile area exposed to incoming solar radiation, thereby reducing the heat load on the plant significantly.

Fig. 4.2 Spines of *Opuntia* species reduce heat loads by increasing reflectance and creating a boundary layer of air between the spines and the surface of the plant.

spiny covering. Spines are also involved in the protection of the plant against herbivory and in dispersion of the species, thus illustrating a common phenomenon in biology, that of the multi-purpose value of a single adaptation. Not all cacti have spines to protect them from excessive radiation, and the totem pole cactus (*Cereus schottii*) is an excellent example of a highly irregular surface which scatters incident radiation and reduces heat loading of the plant. The stem is fluted with alternating convex and concave surfaces, giving the appearance of a carved totem pole (Fig. 4.3). Probably the most unusual life form exhibited by a desert succulent is, however, found in the *Lithops* genus (Fig. 4.5). In these southern African species virtually the entire plant grows beneath the soil surface with only the peculiar leaf tips appearing above the surface. These tips are rounded and flattened on the dorsal surface in such a way as to give them the appearance of a small pebble. The cryptic coloration further enhances the effect and the leaf tips are almost indistinguishable from the surrounding pebbles, while the major portion of the plant remains protected from intense solar radiation beneath the surface. Even more impressive is a species of cactus which is entirely subterranean apart from the flower. A layer of quartz and other pebbles allows sufficient light to penetrate to the upper surface of the plant for photosynthesis (Wiesser *et al.* 1975).

In addition to leaf orientation and the architecture of the plant's surface, the nature of the plant cuticle plays a very important rôle in determining the rate of water loss. Hadley (1972) was the first to draw attention in this regard to the striking similarities between insect integument and plant epicuticle (Fig. 4.6). Water loss from plants by transpiration through the cuticle amounts to only about 10 per cent of

Fig. 4.3 In *Cereus schottii* the alternating concave and convex surfaces are thought to scatter and reflect a significant amount of incoming solar radiation.

Fig. 4.4 The old man cactus (*Cephalocereus senilis*) has dense, light-coloured spines which are ideal for protection against intense solar radiation.

the total water loss. Water loss occurs mostly as a result of transpiration through open stomata. Cuticular transpiration is largely controlled by the thickness of the epicuticular wax layer and the lipid deposits (cutin) in the cuticle layer. In the case of most desert-adapted plants, including both succulents and shrubs, the wax coating in the epicuticular layer and the thickness of the cuticle layer are particularly well developed. So much so that the wax layers on the tall stems of the Candelilla, *Euphorbia antisymphilitica*, are commercially exploited in northern Mexico. It is clear then that xerophytic plants, endowed with a well-developed epicuticular and cuticular layer, need only close their stomata during the hottest hours of the day in order to reduce total water loss very significantly.

Arthropod cuticle

Arthropod cuticle has been the subject of intensive research by both biologists and biophysicists. Detailed discussion of the various hypotheses which have been proposed to explain the movement of water through the cuticle and the remarkable

waterproofing properties of this structure are not warranted in an ecological review. The serious student is referred to an excellent recent treatment of the subject by Edney (1977).

Examination of Fig. 4.6 reveals the remarkable similarities between insect and plant cuticle in respect of general structure and the importance of lipid-like deposits in providing waterproofing properties. There can also be no doubt that the impermeability of arthropod cuticle to water contributes greatly to the success of this phylum in the desert, particularly when the high surface area to volume ratio of these small animals is considered. The importance of lipid material in waterproofing arthropod cuticle has been amply demonstrated by treating the cuticle with organic solvents. This results in a marked increase in water permeability, as does abrasion of the cuticle or heating of the animal beyond a critical 'transition temperature', at which presumably the integrity of the lipid layer is affected. Recent experiments have also shown that the chemical composition of epicuticular lipids is associated with the degree of water impermeability exhibited by a particular species. This field has been reviewed by Hadley (1979) and he has provided convincing experimental evidence to support the conclusion that hydrocarbons, the most abundant epicuticular lipid, are also the most important contributors to the water barrier. From Hadley's studies it would also appear that the amount of hydrocarbon, the degree of saturation and the length of the carbon chains all affect the efficacy of the water barrier. For example, the beetle species (*Eleodes armata*) produces greater quantities of hydrocarbons and a greater percentage of long-chain components in summer than in winter (Hadley 1977).

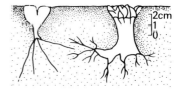

Fig. 4.5 *Lithops* species are very cryptic succulents, resembling stones, and are protected by the surrounding soil from excessive radiation. Two different species are depicted in the diagram. (After Walter 1939.)

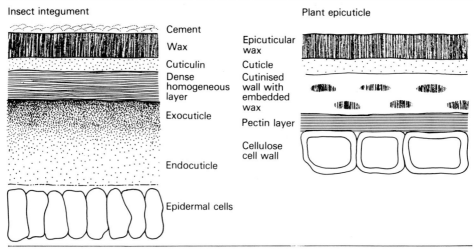

Fig. 4.6 Diagrammatic sections showing the similarities in structure of insect integument and plant epicuticle. (After Hadley 1972.)

Comparisons of rates of water loss from various arthropods are difficult to make because much of the experimental work has been carried out under a variety of environmental conditions. Nevertheless, certain comparisons are valid and Edney (1977, p. 58) has assembled a considerable amount of comparative data in this respect. These data show that the permeability of adult arthropods can vary from 270 μg cm^{-2} hr^{-1} mm Hg^{-1} in the case of a hygric myriapod (*Lithobius* sp.) to as low as 0.8 μg cm^{-2} hr^{-1} mm Hg^{-1} in the xeric scorpion (*Androctonus australis*). Hadley (1972) has gone even further and assembled comparative data for evaporative water loss from a variety of plants, arthropods and vertebrates (Table 4.2). Again these data should be interpreted with caution but the superiority of arthropods, particularly of desert scorpions, in reducing evaporative water loss is quite remarkable. Water loss from plants approaches that of desert birds and mammals but it should be remembered that plants, particularly deep-rooted plants, can replenish water losses from the soil under certain conditions, whereas in many instances desert arthropods must rely almost entirely on metabolic water. The extremely high evaporative water loss recorded for man, although admittedly at a high ambient temperature (35 °C), should also be noted for comparative purposes.

Vertebrate integument and pelage

Amphibians, as we have seen, are not true desert animals and survive by escaping to favourable micro-environments. The integument of most adult amphibians is highly permeable to water which precludes their survival in a true xeric environment. Recent studies by Loveridge (1970), however, on a species of African tree frog, *Chiromantis*, have shown that the evaporative water loss from these animals at certain times of the year is as low as that from desert reptiles (Fig. 4.7). This attribute allows them to survive in the hot African savanna without access to water, and the explanation for the low permeability of *Chiromantis* integument is based on the presence of a dense layer of chromatophores in the dorsal skin. Similar results have

been reported for the South American genus *Phyllomedusa* by Shoemaker and Nagy (1977), but in these species low permeability is attributed to a lipid film secreted on to the skin surface (Mclanahan *et al.* 1978). The use of skin cocoons in aestivating frogs has already been discussed (Ch. 3) and although the above examples are of great biological interest the general conclusion can be drawn that the high permeability of amphibian integument, which is related to their mode of water uptake and respiration, is the most important single morphological factor limiting the survival of this class of vertebrate in the desert.

Water loss through reptilian integument has been the subject of considerable study and the results obtained show that the permeability, particularly that of desert-adapted species, is very low. In the case of the desert lizard *Sauromalus obesus* values as low as 0.05 mg cm^{-2} hr^{-1} were obtained by Bentley and Schmidt-Nielsen (1966), which is only slightly higher than the results obtained in a desert scorpion (Table 4.2). No satisfactory explanation has as yet been advanced for the low

Table 4.2 *Comparison of rates of evaporative water loss from desert organisms. (See Hadley 1972 for original references.)*

Species	Water loss $(mg\ cm^{-2}\ h^{-1})$	Remarks
Plants:		
Echinocereus fenderli (hedgehog)	0.57	30 °C
Aeonium haworthii	3.14	T_a = 31–32 °C; light
Ananas cosmosus (pineapple)	0.75	T_a = 31–32 °C; light
Agave americana (century plant)	1.64	T_a = 31–32 °C; light
Agave americana	1.46	light
Agave americana	3.00	dark
Glossyprium barbadense (cotton)	3.0	
Opuntia polyacantha (prickly pear)	6.7	47% RH; 26 °C
Opuntia polyacantha (prickly pear)	1.9	90% RH; 26 °C
Opuntia engelmannii (prickly pear)	1.59	30 °C; 5–15% RH; light
Zygophyllum coccineum	0.7	mean mon. values (July)
Zilla spinosa	4.8	both surfaces
Arthropods:		
Eleodes armata (beetle)	0.20	30 °C; 0% RH
Hadrurus arizonensis (scorpion)	0.02	30 °C; 0% RH
Buthotus minax (scorpion)	0.03	33 °C; dry air
Locusta migratoria (locust)	0.70	30 °C; 0% RH
Amphibian:		
Cyclorana alboguttatus (frog)	4.90	25 °C; sat. atmos.
Reptiles:		
Gehydra variegata (gecko)	0.22	30 °C; dry air
Uta stansburiana (lizard)	0.10	30 °C
Sauromalus obesus (lizard)	0.05	23 °C
Pituophis catenifer (snake)	0.23	25 °C; 26–31% RH
Birds:		
Excalfactoria chinensis (quail)	1.50	25 °C; adults
Amphispiza belli (sparrow)	1.48	30 °C
Phalaenophlus nuttallii (poorwill)	0.86	35 °C
Mammals:		
Peromyscus eremicus (cactus mouse)	0.66	30 °C
Oryx beisa (African oryx)	3.24	22 °C
Man	22.32	70 kg; nude, sitting in sun; 35 °C

permeability of the integument of desert reptiles, although very recent work by Roberts (unpublished) suggests that lipids may be involved, as they are in the insect integument.

In spite of the fact that birds do not sweat, a considerable amount of transepidermal water loss occurs in this group. There are also marked differences between species in this respect, as illustrated by the much higher rate of water loss in the quail (1.50 mg cm^{-2} hr^{-1}) when compared with the more xeric-adapted poorwill (0.86 mg cm^{-2} hr^{-1}) (Bernstein 1971 and Lasiewski 1969). Detailed studies on the reasons for these differences have not yet been undertaken. Permeability of mammalian skin to water loss is obviously high in mammals that sweat actively and surprisingly low in small desert rodents which do not sweat. In the latter respect Macmillen (1965) reports of water loss as low as 0.66 mg cm^{-2} hr^{-1} in the case of the cactus mouse *Peromyscus eremicus* at 30 °C.

The plumage of birds and the pelage of mammals are obviously of great importance in the thermal biology and water balance of these groups. Colour of these structures will be dealt with later in this chapter and only a few examples are required to highlight their important role in the ecology of desert animals.

The plumage of birds acts as a protection or thermal shield against excessive insolation in the desert. Nevertheless, a very dense plumage of fine feathers, such as is found in the snowy owl, would also retard loss by radiation and convection. The optimal solution for desert birds would seem to be a compromise between the two

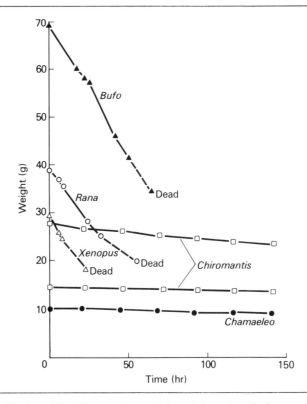

Fig. 4.7 The arid-adapted frog *Chiromantis*, apart from being uricotelic, has remarkable resistance to desiccation which approaches that of a reptile. (After Loveridge 1970.)

demands, for protection against incoming radiation and for facilitation of heat loss via convection and radiation. This compromise is perhaps best illustrated by the plumage of the ostrich, *Struthio camelus*. The feathers of the ostrich are long but very sparsely distributed over the dorsal surface of the bird, and when the bird is exposed to high ambient temperatures, it erects the feathers on its back, thus increasing the thickness of the barrier between incident solar radiation and the skin. The sparse distribution of the feathers, however, allows considerable lateral air movement over the skin surface while they are in the erect position. This results in significant heat loss by convection if given sufficient wind and an ambient air temperature below that of body temperature (Fig. 4.8). Smaller desert birds do not exhibit the same degree of adaptation in this respect as they, unlike the large flightless ostrich, are able to escape to a favourable micro-environment. Nevertheless, similar patterns of response have been observed in other birds, for example in the ground-nesting sandgrouse, *Pterocles namaqua*. This bird lays its eggs on the hot surface of the soil and incubation is largely a process of shielding the eggs from solar radiation to keep them below a critical maximum temperature. To reduce the effect of the high intensity of radiation while covering the eggs, this bird orientates the long axis of its body towards the sun and erects the mantle feathers over the back. The air space below these erected mantle feathers then acts as a barrier to incoming radiation (see Fig. 6.2). It should, however, be emphasised that survival in the desert environment is not exclusively determined by the ability to reduce heat loading and to facilitate heat loss. The nights are frequently very cold and the plumage must also provide protection against heat loss at certain times. The ostrich has solved these conflicting demands of the environment by erecting its sparse plumage during the hottest part of the day and depressing the interlocking feathers close to the body at night, thereby trapping a layer of insulating air between the skin and the feathers which reduces heat loss very effectively (Fig. 4.8).

Exactly the same conflicting demands are made on the pelages of desert mammals. A naked skin would be ideal for loss of heat by radiation, convection or conduction, but would offer no thermal shielding against solar radiation during the day, nor would it provide any insulation at night. The ideal compromise would appear to be a short glossy coat, as is found in certain African antelope and in indigenous African cattle, such as the Afrikaner breed. The advantages of this type of hair coat in extensive cattle ranching in hot areas, as opposed to the long woolly coat of certain British cattle breeds, has been convincingly demonstrated by Bonsma and Pretorius (1943) who have pioneered this field of research. Schmidt-Nielsen (1964) has also drawn attention to the importance of the pelage of desert camels in providing a compromise between thermal shielding and the facilitation of heat loss. An additional demand placed on the pelage of certain mammals is that of effective sweating. Sweating takes place at the skin surface and if the skin is covered by an insulated layer of air beneath a thick woolly pelage, the efficacy of sweating can be markedly reduced. For this reason mammals which depend heavily on sweating as a means of evaporative cooling usually have a short hair coat (equids) or none at all (man). In contrast, if sweating is less important in the thermoregulation of a mammal, as in sheep, the thick fleece provides an ideal thermal shield against intense solar radiation. In fact, the outer surface of the fleece of Merino sheep can reach a temperature as high as 85 °C in still air when exposed to a solar radiation load of 930 W m^{-2}, while the skin temperature remains at only 42 °C (Macfarlane 1964). The net result of this phenomenon is a loss of heat from the surface of the fleece to the ambient air, although the animal will still have to employ a measure of evaporative cooling by means of thermal panting. The thermal shielding effect of the Merino's

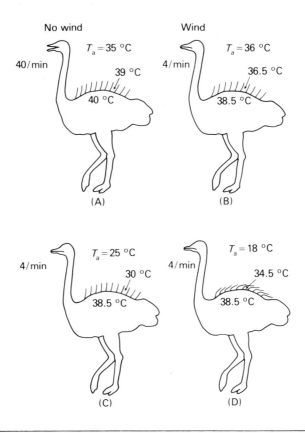

Fig. 4.8   Thermoregulation in the ostrich involves thermal panting and feather erection under conditions of no wind and high ambient temperature (A). In windy conditions, feather erection alone is frequently sufficient to allow body cooling (B, C), while at low ambient temperatures at night the feathers are flattened to provide an insulating layer of air (D).

fleece undoubtedly contributes importantly to its success in hot, semi-arid regions of Australia. This type of adaptation has, however, not been produced by natural selection in similarly sized wild mammals, such as desert antelope. In the latter animals, selection pressure has favoured the evolution of a short sleek pelage. It is tempting to speculate that the facilitation of heat loss, particularly when sprinting away from predators, is more important to these animals than is either thermal shielding or insulation against the cold. The pelage of mammals is therefore an excellent example of an optimal compromise, which can occur through natural selection.

Animal colour

Animal coloration has been the subject of much study and speculation for years. A recent book, which not only summarises much of this speculation but also suggests several new concepts, has been written by Hamilton (1973) and is commended to the

interested student. In essence, colour in animals serves the function of mimicry, camouflage (crypsis), communication between animals or modification of the effect of thermal radiation upon the animal. Cryptic coloration is particularly well developed in many desert animals (see colour illustrations). This can probably be attributed to the sparsely distributed vegetation and consequent lack of cover for the animals. Certain diurnal lizards, snakes, grasshoppers and the precocious chicks of some ground-nesting birds are remarkably well camouflaged and match the substrate, be it rock, sand or scattered pebbles, almost perfectly. In contrast, certain diurnal desert beetles are pitch-black and stand out clearly against the sandy substrate of the dunes. We shall attempt to explain this anomaly, but first a few brief remarks on some of the complex physical phenomena involved, are required. Colour, as perceived by the human eye, is a form of electromagnetic energy and comprises that portion of the spectrum between 400 nm and 700 nm, usually referred to as visible light. It is therefore important, when appraising the cryptic coloration of animals, to realise that the visual sensors of animals, other than humans, may be sensitive to energy outside this range. For example, certain insects and some birds appear to have this sensitivity, and the fact that white polar bears appear to be black when photographed in the ultraviolet region of the spectrum, cautions against an anthropomorphic interpretation of the ecological rôle of colour (Lavigne and Øritsland 1974). Also, animal colours perceived by the human eye are sometimes not the result of pigment synthesis and deposition in the animal's integument, but are produced by peculiar optical properties of the surface covering. These so-called structural colours are dramatically exhibited by certain humming-birds in which a slight turn of the body can cause the colour of the head and neck to change immediately from brilliant scarlet or iridescent green to a dull grey.

One of the main concerns of the desert biologist in animal coloration, however, centres on the interrelationship between colour and the thermal biology of the animal. The relationship at first would appear to be a simple one in the belief that light-coloured animals would reflect more heat and dark animals would absorb more heat, but the situation in free-ranging wild animals is far more complex. For example, colour is not the only factor determining the rate of absorption or reflectance of radiation, but the physical nature of the plumage or pelage will also affect the optical properties of these structures. In this respect we could compare cotton wool with glass wool. Both appear to be white but their optical properties differ markedly and as a result their thermal properties as well. Gloss on the coats and plumages of certain mammals and birds may therefore be important in reflecting radiation but this has not been well studied. It has also been suggested that the white pelage of polar bears behaves like a series of optical fibres allowing the penetration of short-wave radiation to the skin surface, thereby contributing to the heat gain of the animal. It is therefore most important to measure the penetrance of thermal energy to the skin surface when evaluating the rôle of colour in the eco-physiology of desert mammals and birds. This is because much of the radiation may be trapped near the outer surface and not penetrate to the skin surface. A case in point is provided by black ravens in which the temperature just below the outer feathers can rise as high as 84 °C (Marder 1973). Examination of the thermal environment of a large desert mammal, as depicted in Fig. 2.3, will also reveal additional complexities which have to be considered when evaluating the rôle of colour. These include the relationship between wavelength and reflectance as well as the important rôle of wind speed. These complexities have received considerable attention from biophysicists, notably Cena and Monteith (1975a & b), Hutchinson *et al.* (1976) and Porter and Gates (1969). In spite of the impressive physical theory employed by these investigators it

remains an open question as to the extent that their results, obtained from excised skin and restrained animals, can be applied to free-ranging animals. The following examples have been selected to illustrate certain important concepts as well as to highlight many of the unresolved questions pertaining to the rôle of colour.

We have already examined the bimodal activity patterns of black and white Namib Desert beetles (Ch. 3). Hamilton (1975) has extended these studies in an attempt to explain the apparent paradox of the occurrence of so many species of black beetles in the hot sand dunes of the Namib. In brief, his explanation rests on the hypothesis that it is to the advantage of many animals to maintain their body temperatures at the maximum preferred level of *ca.* 38 °C for as long as possible. In doing so, the animals are also able to maintain various essential life processes such as feeding, digestion, metabolism and reproduction at peak levels, and these advantages may be of critical survival value. This so-called hypothesis of 'maxithermy' would then explain the advantages of being black, as black beetles would theoretically heat up more rapidly than pale-coloured ones and consequently enjoy some of the above advantages. This concept has been criticised on various grounds, including the argument that the use of iso-enzymes would be equally effective in maintaining high metabolic rates at lower body temperatures. Also, Hamilton has pointed out that wind speeds in excess of 4 m s^{-1} reduce the superior absorptive properties of black beetles to negligible levels. Nevertheless, the fact that so many animals, both ectothermic and endothermic, maintain a body temperature within the range of 38–40 °C, is sufficient reason to give serious consideration to the imaginative hypothesis of maxithermy. Alternative explanations for the black coloration of desert beetles are based on the waterproofing properties of melanin and the strengthening properties that this material confers on the cuticle. The latter property would be a distinct advantage in the abrasive environment of sand dunes (Hamilton 1975). Porter (1967) has also suggested that black coloration would protect the internal organs of animals against harmful effects of ultraviolet radiation.

A species of tenebrionid in the Sonoran Desert, *Cryptoglossa verrucosa*, exhibits a remarkable colour change, when exposed to different levels of relative humidity. The light-blue colour phase, which develops at low humidity and is produced by wax filaments from the tips of minute tubercles, contrasts sharply with the jet-black appearance at high humidity (Fig. 4.9). The mesh of wax filaments reduces transcuticular water loss at low humidities and may reduce heat loading by increasing reflectance (Hadley 1979).

Unlike desert tenebrionids, certain desert snails such as *Sphincterochila boissieri* in the Negev Desert have chalky white shells which reflect as much as 90 per cent of visible light and 95 per cent of the near infrared radiation (Schmidt-Nielsen *et al.* 1972). This property is undoubtedly of critical importance in reducing the temperature of a snail's tissues when it aestivates for as long as a year on the hot desert substrate. The desert chameleon, *Chamaeleo namaquensis*, also depends on a very light coloration to reflect the intense radiation while walking across the hot soil surface in arid regions of southern Africa. In the early morning and late evening it changes to an almost uniform black colour and gains heat rapidly, presumably to maintain body temperature at the preferred level for as long as possible (Burrage 1973). Birds and mammals are, however, not able to change colour and the thermal significance of plumage and pelage colour has received considerable attention in these two groups. Riemerschmid and Elder (1945) undertook one of the first studies on reflectance of excised cattle hides of various colours and showed the superiority of lighter colours in this regard. Bonsma and Pretorius (1943) confirmed Riemerschmid's findings in live animals and urged cattle breeders in sub-tropical

Fig. 4.9 The desert tenebrionid *Cryptoglossa verrucosa* changes from a jet-black colour to light blue when the relative humidity decreases. The colour phases are created by wax filaments and this meshwork of filaments reduces transcuticular water loss. (Hadley 1979.)

regions to select for glossy light-red coats. The rôle of colour in the mammalian pelage is, however, not quite so clear-cut when considering the total heat balance of the animal and its ecology. For example, Hutchinson and Brown (1969) have shown that penetrance of heat through the pelage is the most critical consideration, and that absorption and penetrance are not necessarily related. Moreover, above a certain critical wind speed of 4 m s^{-1}, which frequently occurs under natural conditions, differences in absorptivity of various colours disappear. Similar findings have been reported by Walsberg *et al.* (1978), who found that, although black plumage in pigeons acquired a much greater heat load at low wind speeds than white plumage, the penetration of radiation into white plumage was greater and the radiative heating of white plumage was less affected by convective cooling. The heat loads of black and white plumage tend therefore to converge as wind speed increases and, at wind speeds greater than 3 m s^{-1}, black plumage actually acquires lower radiative heat loads than does white plumage. These authors then go so far as to suggest that black could be thermally advantageous to desert species and white coloration of advantage to polar animals.

From the preceding discussion it should be apparent that it is no easy task to evaluate the true ecological significance of animal coloration under natural free-ranging conditions. Nevertheless, the abundant solar radiation in the desert would suggest that certain mammals and birds could use this source of energy to assist in the maintenance of normal body temperatures, under cold conditions, and show some colour adaptation to facilitate this process. This appears to be the case in

the black vulture and roadrunner in the south-western United States. Both these species become hypothermic at night and employ sun-basking to raise body temperature in the morning, thus saving a considerable amount of energy. The roadrunner exhibits a specialised basking posture to facilitate heat gain. The cervical plumage is erected in such a way that the black skin of the interscapular apterium and the black plumage of the dorsal spinal tract are exposed to direct radiation. Ohmart and Lasiewski (1971) have estimated that the energy savings of sunning roadrunners amount to 551 calories per hour. Similarly Finch *et al.* (1980) have demonstrated that black Bedouin goats absorb heat 1.8 times more rapidly at the skin surface than do white goats. The ecological significance of the preference among Bedouins for black goats in the desert is therefore puzzling, but the findings of Shkolnik *et al.* (1977) that black Bedouin goats have a metabolic rate 25 per cent lower than that of white goats, when standing in the winter sun, provide an explanation. During winter when food is scarce this metabolic advantage may be critical in the survival of black goats and may have resulted in their preferential selection by the Bedouins. Although all these results are of great interest, the final appraisal of the importance of colour under ecologically realistic conditions will require analysis of the activity and energy budgets of free-ranging animals throughout an entire annual cycle of seasons. For example, it would be of great interest to know for how many hours in the year the air temperature and wind speed in the Negev is sufficiently low while the sun is shining, to allow black goats to benefit over white ones. This advantage would have to be balanced against the increased water requirements of black goats during the summer for evaporative cooling. The advantages may be marginal in the final analysis but, nevertheless, sufficient to tip the scales in favour of being black.

Water storage

Both plants and animals employ water storage as a mechanism of defence against prolonged droughts in the desert. Even the most casual observer of desert vegetation must have been impressed by the water-storing capacity of the giant cacti such as the saguaro. These plants have surprisingly shallow root systems, but are able to store literally tons of water after a brief rainy season and they shrink and swell in relation to their degree of hydration. Other prominent succulents in deserts and semi-arid regions are the prickly pears *Opuntia*, and the Mesembryanthemaceae. The hydrature of succulents has been reviewed by Walter and Stadelman (1974) and they emphasise that, in spite of the large water loss which these plants incur during prolonged droughts, there is little change in the relative water content. They cite *Opuntia phaeacantha-toumeyi* as an example in which the percentage of water decreased from only 84.8 to 72.7 per cent in spite of a 60 per cent loss in original weight during 189 days of drought. During dry periods the fragile and superficial lateral roots of many succulents die off, but immediately the surface layer of soil is moistened the roots start to develop rapidly, within 8 hr in the case of *O. puberula*. This is one of the reasons why these plants are able to survive in shallow soils on stony hillsides, although they do best in arid areas which receive two rainy seasons per year. Under these conditions, which prevail in the Sonoran Desert and parts of the Karoo, they are able to replenish their depleted reserves of water twice annually. Not all succulents store water above ground, however, and several so-called root-succulents such as *Pachypodium succulentum* have received the attention of plant physiologists. This species is found in the semi-arid Kalahari and grows in fairly deep dry sand. In one specimen the tuber was found to contain 950 per cent of its dry weight in the form of water (Walter 1964).

Although water storage in animals is not as dramatic as in plants, it is nevertheless of key importance to some desert species. A few examples will suffice to illustrate this. We have already seen the importance of the storage of hypo-osmotic urine in the bladders of certain frogs. A similar mechanism is employed by certain desert tortoises. Henderson and Loveridge (1980) have examined the role of hypo-osmotic urine in the water economy of *Chersina angulata*. They established that when these animals were exposed to starvation and desiccation, there was a progressive reduction in urine volume and concluded that 'bladder urine' was potentially an important source of water for this species.

A more unusual example of water storage is found in the 'bladder' of the sand-diving Namib lizard *Aporosaura anchietae* (Robinson 1980). This small lizard emerges from beneath the sand soon after cold advective fog has condensed on the sand dunes and drinks as much as 12 per cent of its body weight in the form of fog droplets. This water is stored in a voluminous diverticulum of the lower intestine (bladder) and is extremely dilute (25 mOsm kg^{-1}), thereby providing the animal with a water source upon which it can draw for many weeks. The intake of water in this animal is equivalent to a 75 kg man drinking 7.5 litres of water in 3 minutes. It is a remarkable feat, as the lizards are obliged to emerge from beneath the sand at temperatures which are much lower than their normally preferred range of 30–40 °C. After drinking fog they have a plump appearance as the lateral skin-folds stretch to accommodate the enlarged bladder and reflection of the ventral skin and muscles reveals a large volume of clear water surrounded by a transparent delicate membrane. Water storage in reptiles is, however, not restricted to specialised storage structures. The tissues, including the blood, can also act as water-storing spaces.

Ruminant mammals are also capable of water storage and this phenomenon has been well studied in the small black Bedouin goat (Choshniak and Shkolnik 1978). These goats are able to lose as much as 30 per cent of their initial body weight when deprived of water and can replace this loss within 2 minutes when given access to drinking water. Much of this large volume of ingested water is apparently stored in the rumen which protects the tissues from osmotic shock, while the water is slowly absorbed into the tissues. As we shall see later, this ability is of great importance in allowing the Bedouins to exploit desert pastures far from permanent watering points in the Negev.

Shape and size

In Chapter 2 some of the important eco-physiological implications of body size in animals were examined. Larger animals have a relatively smaller surface area and lower metabolic rate. For this reason the thermal biology of large animals is different from that of smaller animals, and the cost of locomotion is much lower and less affected by increasing speed. Body size as measured by weight is, however, not the sole criterion as shape also has an important influence on metabolic rate. For example, Brown and Lasiewski (1972) have shown that the weasel, a long thin animal with a relatively large surface area, exhibits a metabolic rate 50–100 per cent greater than normally shaped mammals of the same weight when subjected to cold stress. This high cost of living is apparently offset by the advantages of being able to squeeze into small rodent burrows to capture prey. In addition there is a marked difference in size between the sexes. This allows the females to enter smaller burrows to capture prey which is denied to the males, better able to overpower larger prey in wider burrows. In this way intersexual competition for food is reduced.

Body size and shape are therefore most important considerations in evaluating the

adaptation of desert animals, in spite of the fact that the inverse correlation between body size and relative, or mass-specific, metabolic rate is still not fully understood. Let us examine a large desert mammal such as the oryx as an example. This species, because of its large size, has a high thermal inertia and will be able to store a large amount of heat in its body tissues during the day without resorting to the evaporation of precious water for cooling purposes. Its large size also means that the cost of locomotion will be relatively low, thereby allowing the animal to traverse long distances at low energetic cost in search of food. Its energy requirements for maintaining essential life processes will be relatively low, in view of its low metabolic rate. The relatively small surface area of these large animals will also reduce the relative size of the profile area exposed to solar radiation. There are, however, three important disadvantages to being large, which, incidentally, may have also contributed to the extinction of the dinosaurs. Firstly, the absolute requirements of maintenance energy are high; secondly, the relatively small surface area reduces the rate of heat loss by convection and radiation; and finally, large animals cannot escape to favourable micro-environments. The reduced potential for heat loss, which is a consequence of the smaller relative surface area, is particularly important during locomotion when ungulates store large amounts of heat. It is not surprising therefore that the large ungulates of the hot and semi-arid African savanna, including the oryx, have either very short coats, or none at all. This phenomenon has been examined by plotting the length of the pelage against body size in African savanna ungulates (Fig. 4.10). This semi-log plot shows that the pelage in the smaller antelope such as the grysbok and klipspringer is relatively long, but with increasing body size there is a marked exponential decrease in hair length until the hair coat completely disappears in the largest ungulates, the rhinoceros and elephant. We have interpreted these data as being an adaptation in the case of the larger animals for facilitating heat loss, particularly during locomotion. The opposite argument could also be advanced: because of the high surface area of the smaller animals, they require protection against heat loss at night, hence the longer pelage. Both arguments are probably valid but the marked difference in pelage length between a large desert ungulate such as an oryx and a large temperate ungulate such as a moose gives considerable support to the former hypothesis. The size and shape of extremities in desert animals also appear to have been adapted to facilitate heat loss (Allen's rule). The large ears of the jack rabbit (Fig. 4.11) are an excellent example of this, but less pronounced examples are also common and equally important. Arid-adapted ungulates tend to have a flatter conformation and larger ears and dewlaps than similarly sized temperate species.

If we consider all the above implications of body size in animals, we could conclude that most animals in the desert must be either small enough to escape from the desert environment or large enough to enjoy the benefits discussed previously. This generalisation is probably true with certain notable exceptions, such as the desert gazelles and the Bedouin goat, which exhibit specialised physiological adaptations. The thermal implications of animal size and geometry are generally also applicable to plant size. Energy flux and evaporative water loss are naturally again related to surface area and smaller plants will have a greater surface area to volume ratio than larger ones. For this reason, giant cacti such as barrel cactus and saguaro will heat up more slowly than fine-leaved desert shrubs, largely because of their greater thermal inertia, but also because of the relatively small profile area exposed to radiation. Eventually, however, the giant cacti reach temperatures 10–15 °C above ambient while the finer-leaved shrubs such as the creosote bush maintain leaf temperatures close to that of the ambient air. The reason for this large difference is to

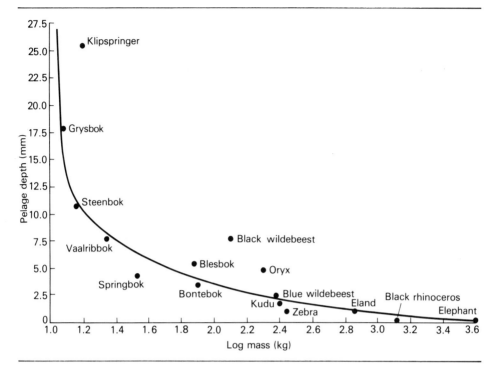

Fig. 4.10 As body size increases in the African ungulates, which inhabit the hot and frequently dry savannas, there is an exponential decrease in the thickness of the pelage. See text for discussion of the thermal implications. (Hofmeyr and Louw 1980.)

be found in the greater relative surface area of the fine-leaved shrubs which are able to dissipate heat more rapidly by convection (Hadley 1972). In fact, this is probably the major reason why so many non-succulent perennials in the desert are fine-leaved and not, as was first thought, as an adaptation to reduce water loss. The finer leaves with their greater surface area would in fact enhance water loss. Gates *et al.* (1968) have calculated that convection is the major pathway of heat loss in leaves which are less than 1 cm² in size, in spite of a significant contribution by evaporative cooling from transpiration. Leaf shape can also be modified in desert plants to provide a mutual shading effect and reduce penetration of radiation into the plant, as in the Namib dune plant *Trianthema hereroensis* (Seely *et al.* 1977).

The ratio of roots to shoots would at first appear to be an important form of adaptation in desert plants. This is certainly true for many arid-adapted species. As many as 80 species of plants in the south-western United States have been classified as phreatophytes, that is plants in which the roots extend as much as 20 m to the water-table, with maximum lateral growth in the capillary fringe just above the water-table. Probably the most dramatic example of this type of plant is the desert mesquite *Prosopis* in which a taproot of 53 m in length has been recorded in one specimen. In contrast, desert ephemerals have very shallow root systems. Even the giant cacti such as the saguaro have relatively shallow root systems with well-developed lateral roots, often extending more than 20 m in a horizontal plane (McCleary 1968). It is not possible, therefore, to generalise about root/shoot ratios in desert plants as different taxa have evolved separate solutions to the same problem of an erratic supply of water.

Fig. 4.11   The enormous ears of the jack rabbit assist this animal in off-loading excessive body heat.

Ectopic storage of fat

Certain lipids, as we have seen, play an important rôle in the waterproofing of various animals and plants. The triglycerides or fats are equally important in providing an energy store for animals. They are particularly well suited to serve this function, being light and containing a large number of hydrogen atoms for potential electron transfer. In fact, fat contains approximately 2.25 times as much potential energy as other tissues of the body. One would also expect that, in the unpredictable desert environment, fat storage in animals would be especially important to allow survival during prolonged periods of drought and shortages of food energy. This, however, remains an assumption and it has not been shown that desert animals are more dependent on fat storage than are temperate animals.

In addition to being energy-rich, fats are also good insulators and this property is of great importance to certain polar animals that deposit large amounts of adipose tissue subcutaneously. In the case of desert vertebrates, this could be a distinct embarrassment as subcutaneous fat would retard heat loss by radiation and convection. In heliothermic animals such as reptiles, which depend heavily on sun-basking to raise their body temperature, it would also retard the flow of heat from the skin to the viscera. These animals have therefore evolved special fat bodies which lie in the abdominal cavity and do not interfere with energy flux into the animal. Large desert-adapted mammals show a similar form of adaptation. The large antelope do not have particularly large fat stores and fat is mostly deposited around the viscera, particularly the kidneys. The camel deposits most of its fat in its hump as do zebu cattle to some extent, while arid-adapted sheep use their large tails as fat stores (Fig. 4.12).

Fig. 4.12 The ectopic storage of fat is a characteristic of many arid-adapted mammals. (A) Humped zebu cattle, (B) camel, (C) fat-tailed sheep.

Chapter 5

Tolerance of the desert environment: II
Physiological and behavioural adaptations

The study of physiological adaptation in desert organisms was one of the first aspects of desert biology to receive serious attention. As early as 1923 Buxton published his fascinating account of animal life in deserts. More recently, Schmidt-Nielsen has pioneered this field and, included among his many publications, is a standard work, *Desert Animals* (1964). He must certainly be considered the pace-setter in this field and his influence has spread throughout the world, leading to the publication of many significant papers. The following account can unfortunately only touch on several selected topics.

Tolerance of tissue to high temperatures

In Chapter 3 we discussed the impressive tolerance of some seeds and phyllopod eggs during diapause to very high temperatures. Certain free-living organisms such as mosquito larvae and algae exhibit an equally impressive tolerance but they must be considered exceptional, as most organisms cannot tolerate temperatures much in excess of 42 °C. The standard explanation given for this phenomenon is that tissue enzymes become denatured at these high temperatures and, as a result, important metabolic pathways cease to function normally. In practice, however, the situation is not quite so simple, as enzymes vary significantly in terms of the optimum temperature at which they function, as well as the critical 'lethal' temperature at which they become denatured. Enzymes are proteins, consisting of chains of amino acids joined together by peptide bonds. These chains form branches which are often folded in a complex manner. Slight changes in the spatial configuration and bonding of these proteins can alter their critical 'lethal' temperature as well as their optimum temperature, without necessarily changing their metabolic function. In other words an organism may produce a spectrum of enzymes, all with similar function, but in view of slight differences in their configuration they may have different temperature optima. These are known as iso-enzymes or isozymes, and the adaptive advantages they confer on an organism are important. For example ectothermic animals, such as arthropods and reptiles, that rely on an external heat source to raise their body temperature, usually exhibit a progressive increase in metabolic rate with increasing ambient temperature. The metabolic rate frequently doubles with each increase of 10 °C in ambient temperature (Q_{10} effect), similar to the increase in reaction rate of a mixture of chemicals in a test tube. Under certain ecological conditions, however, this may be a distinct embarrassment to the organism. This is particularly true for certain desert animals which have evolved to make sparing use of fat stores, accumulated during a brief rainy season. In these cases reliance on suitable isozymes at high temperatures could prevent the dramatic increase in metabolic rate and thus ensure the husbanding of valuable tissue nutrients, particularly fat. This

56

phenomenon is known in some circles as metabolic or temperature compensation and is particularly common in inter-tidal marine invertebrates (Hochachka and Somero 1973). More recently it has been discovered in desert scorpions (Riddle 1979). Another important rôle played by isozymes in desert organisms is found in the evolution of specific enzymes which are able to tolerate unusually high temperatures.

Many studies have been conducted on the thermal tolerance of both plants and animals but they frequently suffer from the lack of standardised exposure times and standard pre-conditioning procedures. Nevertheless, marked differences in tolerance have been recorded under reasonably standard conditions. For example, Levitt (1972) has listed a wide range of maximum tolerances for plants, ranging from 44 °C for *Trichomanes erosum* in a rain forest habitat to 55 °C for a desert grass *Aristida pungens*. The reasons for these differences in tolerance are complex and not yet fully explained. They include an increase in the rate of replacement of damaged protein, an increased concentration of 'anti-denaturing' substances, particularly sugar, and an altered configuration of proteins (enzymes) which provides the protein with thermostable bonds. In other words, tolerance largely centres on the conformational flexibility of the cellular proteins (Alexandrov *et al.* 1970). The biochemical details are beyond the scope of this text.

Thermal tolerances of animals show perhaps even greater variation than those of plants. Prosser and Brown (1961) list a range of upper lethal body temperatures in animals, varying from 25 °C in certain aquatic invertebrates to as high as 46.8 °C for the house wren. With few exceptions, terrestrial vertebrates exhibit an upper lethal limit of 42–43 °C. One exception is the desert iguana, *Dipsosaurus dorsalis*, which tolerates body temperatures as high as 47 °C. Again, as in plants, this adaptation is closely associated with enzyme configuration and temperature optima. This is substantiated by *in vitro* studies on the effects of temperature on the activity of ATPase enzymes from skeletal muscle of lizards with different temperature preferenda. Figure 5.1 shows a graded difference in temperature optima of these ATPases which corresponds very well with the preferred body temperatures of the respective lizard species.

For many years the Death Valley pupfish, *Cyprinidon milleri*, was thought to possess high heat tolerance. This belief arose from the very high air temperatures which can occur in Death Valley, California (56 °C). Laboratory measurements have, however, shown that the critical thermal maximum for this species is only 43 °C. It is most adept at seeking out regions of low water temperature in shallow pools and shaded areas beneath the projecting salt crust surrounding the water. It does, however, possess remarkable resistance to high salinity (Naiman *et al.* 1973).

Tolerance of high temperatures in insects is also well developed. Mosquito larvae are notoriously tolerant and recently Heinrich (1979) has shown that honey-bees can tolerate thoracic temperatures of 47 °C when forced to fly for extended periods. Under these conditions the bee extrudes a droplet of fluid from its mouthparts, resulting in evaporative cooling of the head. African dung beetles which occur in semi-desert areas are obliged to increase their body temperatures dramatically prior to take-off, to provide sufficient power for flight. This phenomenon of pre-flight thermogenesis is made possible by a very high metabolic rate of the thoracic flight muscles. These tissues are in fact considered to be the most metabolically active cells found in any living system and, judging by the highest thoracic temperatures measured (45 °C), the enzymes must also possess considerable temperature tolerance (Heinrich and Bartholomew 1979). Also of interest is that male dung beetles exhibiting the highest body temperatures appear to gain ascendency over cooler beetles in the competition for both dung and females! The upper lethal

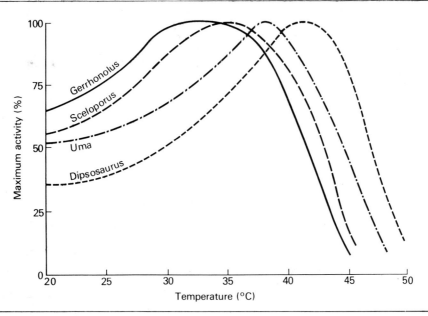

Fig. 5.1   The effect of temperature on the percentage of maximum activity of skeletal muscle ATPases, extracted from lizards with distinctly different temperature preferenda. The activity peaks correspond with the ranking of temperature preferenda. (Licht 1964.)

temperature limit of insects is, as expected, generally related to the type of habitat. Dramatic examples of chironomid larvae breeding in hot springs at 49–51 °C have been recorded and the larva of the cheese fly, *Piophila casei*, can resist 52 °C for 1 hr. Also, desert insects appear to have higher thermal tolerances than those from mesic climates. This is reflected in the melting-point of the cuticular waxes. For example, the melting-point of the epicuticular wax in bumble-bees from a mesic climate lies between 35–45 °C, while that of *Icerya purchasi* is 78 °C and the wax of *Coccus cacti* is 99–101 °C. Generally speaking, however, desert insects tend to avoid thermal stress by behavioural means and temperature tolerance should not usually be considered of critical importance.

Most desert mammals maintain body temperatures within the 'normal' range of 37–42 °C, and tissue tolerance to excessively high temperatures has only been reported in the oryx and Grant's gazelle. Taylor (1969) found that, when oryx were dehydrated and exposed to ambient temperatures of 45 °C in an artificially heated room, they survived body temperatures above 45 °C for 8 hr. Similar results have, however, not yet been recorded in free-ranging oryx under natural conditions.

Tolerance to dehydration

Plants, as we have seen, usually avoid dehydration whenever possible either by ephemerality, or through the development of an adaptive morphology which protects the plant from desiccation. Certain species are, however, truly tolerant to desiccation and among these the lichens must be considered the most specialised. They can survive periods of dryness lasting for years and their metabolism can be reactivated merely by increasing the water vapour content of the air. Condensation

a

b

Plate 1 The term 'desert' is used to describe a wide variety of ecosystems ranging from: *(a)* the relatively lush vegetation of the Sonoran Desert in Arizona to *(b)* the extreme aridity of the Namib Desert. See Ch. 1 for detailed discussion.

a

b

Plates 2 and 3 Because of the paucity of plant cover in deserts many animals have evolved remarkable cryptic coloration: (2*a*) The sidewinding adder of the Namib, *Britis peringveyi,* half-submerged on the surface of a sand dune. (2*b*) The same animal, with only the eyes visible, lying in wait for its prey. (3*a*) The stone cricket *Crypsicerus cubicus* matches the stony substrate of the gravel plains almost perfectly, while the solpugid *Metasolpuga picta* (3*b*) matches the sandy substrate of the inter-dune valleys.

of water on the organism is not required. In fact, in certain lichens the rhythm of metabolic activity is synchronised with diurnal fluctuations in the water vapour content of the unsaturated ambient air. According to Larcher (1975) very few tolerant species of flowering plants exist. Most of these are found in the arid regions of South Africa and belong to the families Scrophylariaceae, Velloziceae, Myrothamnaceae, Cyperaceae and Poaceae. In spite of our fairly good understanding of the morphological and physiological factors which protect plants from desiccation, no really acceptable explanation of the mechanisms involved in true tolerance to desiccation has as yet been advanced.

Tolerance to desiccation in vertebrate animals is perhaps best exemplified by desert amphibians which can tolerate losses of 40–50 per cent of body water (see Ch. 3). Certain desert lizards, however, are not only capable of storing large amounts of water in both their tissues and specialised storage organs, but are also able to tolerate a considerable degree of dehydration. The sand-diving Namib lizard (*Aporosaura anchietae*) tolerates fairly wide fluctuations in the osmoconcentration of its plasma from the hydrated to the dehydrated state (312–420 mOsm kg^{-1}). Khalil and Abdel-Messeih (1959) have suggested that *Varanus griseus* can store an amount of water in its tissues equal to 15 per cent of its body weight. When deprived of water there is a minimal loss of water from the most active tissues, namely the heart and central nervous system, but this species is well able to tolerate water loss from the remaining tissues. Dantzler and Schmidt-Nielsen (1966) have shown that the tortoise (*Gopherus agassizii*) can also tolerate significant dehydration and large increases in the ionic concentration of its plasma. Small desert mammals, such as rodents, avoid desiccation by behavioural means as far as possible. Under normal conditions metabolic water production will balance evaporative water losses in well-adapted species. In an emergency, however, or under artificial laboratory conditions, these animals can survive a remarkable degree of dehydration amounting to 20–30 per cent of their body weight (Macmillen and Christopher 1975).

Probably the most spectacular example of desiccation tolerance in large mammals is found in the desert camel, *Camelus dromedarius*. Schmidt-Nielsen (1964) studied the tolerance of camels to dehydration in the Sahara and, together with his colleagues Macfarlane and Morris, found that these animals easily tolerated a loss of 30 per cent of their total *body water* over a period of 9 days. In most large mammals a 12–14 per cent weight loss represents the critical limit. Of equal interest was the finding that 50 per cent of this loss was from water contained in the gut, 30 per cent from the intracellular water space and only 20 per cent from the extracellular water space. In practice this means that camels lose relatively small amounts of water from their plasma and are thus able to maintain a normal blood circulation during dehydration. In contrast, in most other large mammals that have been studied, there is a disproportional loss of water from the plasma. This reduces circulatory efficiency to such an extent that the circulation is no longer able to transport metabolic heat to the skin surface and an explosive increase in body temperature occurs, that can be fatal. The physiological mechanisms that are peculiar to the camel in this respect have not yet been elucidated fully and it is a subject that should be well worth pursuing with more modern critical methods.

The camel is also able to maintain an almost normal rate of food intake during long periods of dehydration, whereas in most large mammals food is refused soon after withdrawal of water. Recovery from dehydration is equally spectacular and Schmidt-Nielsen has recorded that after a 20 per cent loss in body weight, camels would drink enough to restore their original weight in less than 10 minutes. In fact one female drank 66.5 litres of water (33.1% of body weight) in one session. The

largest quantity recorded was 186 litres in the case of a castrated male, which first drank 94 litres and 92 litres some hours later.

Since Schmidt-Nielsen's studies on the camel, Shkolnik *et al.* (1975) have recorded equally interesting results for the black Bedouin goat. He and his co-workers in Israel have found that these animals can lose as much as 30 per cent of their initial body weight and replenish this loss within 2 minutes when given free access to drinking water. We have already seen that the black colour of these animals confers a metabolic advantage on them during winter, as they are able to absorb more heat than white goats. The black colour is, however, a disadvantage in summer and the animals must compensate by evaporating more water. To sustain this increased water loss without daily access to drinking water is indeed remarkable, and this adaptation is largely mediated by the capacious rumen, or fore-stomach, which these animals possess. The large rumen allows rapid drinking of large volumes of water when the animals visit isolated drinking points at intervals of 2–3 days. At the same time the rumen acts as an osmotic barrier, preventing osmotic shock to the tissues following rapid rehydration. Like camels, the goats continue to feed during a period of dehydration and this capability together with their unusual water metabolism, makes them ideal pastoral animals for desert nomads (Chosniak and Shkolnik 1978).

Cold tolerance

Because unusually high temperatures are such a major feature of most desert climates, the majority of eco-physiological studies have been directed towards studying adaptations to heat. The low relative humidity of the desert atmosphere, however, favours rapid loss of heat from the surface at night and cold stress, although a neglected field of research, is a significant factor in the lives of many desert animals.

Most ectothermic animals merely escape excessive cold by burrowing beneath the surface but in some instances, for example the Namib dune tenebrionid beetle, *Lepidochora discoidalis*, and many species of spiders and scorpions, they have adapted to the cold nocturnal niche and are seldom, if ever, active during the day. In these animals the body temperature will be the same as the ambient air and we must assume that their suite of isozymes is adapted in such a way as to compensate for activity at low temperatures.

In the case of endothermic animals such as mammals, entirely different considerations pertain. Under cold conditions these animals must either enter a state of torpor and allow their body temperatures to decline or they must expend a great deal of energy, either by shivering or through non-shivering thermogenesis, to maintain a constant body temperature. The insulation of a desert mammal, as determined by both the thickness and physical quality of its pelage, is, as we have seen, usually a compromise between thermal shielding and the facilitation of heat loss via radiation and convective cooling. As such, it seldom offers really effective protection from the cold and desert mammals are therefore frequently required to expend considerable amounts of energy on cold nights to maintain body temperature. In this respect, Haim and Borut (1976) have found interesting differences in the ability of different populations of the golden spiny mouse, *Acomys russatus*, to withstand cold. This species occurs only in extreme desert regions and specimens from a population inhabiting the Sinai mountains, where snow occurs frequently, were able to maintain their body temperatures with ease when exposed to cold (6 °C) for 6 hr. They achieved this by apparently employing non-shivering thermogenesis exclusively. In contrast, specimens from a population inhabiting the warm Ein Gedi area were unable to maintain body temperature when exposed to the

same treatment. Offspring of these two populations, raised at the same ambient temperature (28 °C) showed responses similar to their parents, suggesting that the characteristic is genetically controlled. It was, however, possible to increase the cold resistance of the Ein Gedi mice with large doses of thyroid hormone. This hormone may therefore be intimately involved in cold adaptation.

Large desert mammals (> 4 kg) do not exhibit non-shivering thermogenesis and, as their pelage is better adapted for facilitating heat loss than for heat retention, they are obliged to shiver and expend energy whenever ambient temperatures fall below the lower critical temperature of their thermal neutral zone. This situation, together with low primary production of herbage in deserts which does not usually allow the deposition of large fat reserves, means that these animals are frequently walking an energetic tight-rope. Severe cold after prolonged drought can therefore lead to extensive mortality in desert antelope, particularly when they are prevented from migrating to more favourable areas. The effect of cold can, however, be considerably ameliorated by behavioural means such as huddling, insulation of 'thermal windows' in the pelage by lying down and particularly by sheltering from cold winds.

Adaptive heterothermy

Adaptive heterothermy refers to an endothermic animal's ability to allow its body temperature to fluctuate in response to some form of environmental stress. For example, in the case of very small birds and mammals, such as humming-birds and certain species of bats, the energetic cost of maintaining a uniformly high body temperature for 24 hr is enormous. This is because of the high ratio of surface area to volume in these animals and their extremely high metabolic rate (see Ch. 2). Moreover, their small volumes exacerbate this disadvantage because storage of energy is also limited. Consequently, these animals exhibit a circadian torpor and allow their body temperature to fall during their periods of rest, thereby saving very significant amounts of energy. It would also be of advantage to large desert mammals to employ some measure of adaptive heterothermy, as this would allow them to store considerable amounts of heat without resorting to the evaporation of precious water. In contrast a large mammal, such as man, that maintains a body temperature within very narrow limits is at a serious disadvantage. During the desert day he loses large amounts of water through profuse sweating and at night, unless warmly clothed, he will expend considerable energy to maintain a constant body temperature.

We have already seen that the ground squirrel, while foraging on the surface of the desert, allows its body temperature to spike at temperatures as high as 42–43 °C. This is, however, a very transient phenomenon, as the animal immediately retreats to its burrow after reaching these temperatures, to off-load heat by conduction against the cool wall of the underground burrow. To find a better example of adaptive heterothermy we must again turn to that remarkable beast of burden, the camel. This animal, which has served man for millennia throughout North Africa, the Middle East and Asia, not only possesses unusual tolerance to dehydration, but minimises evaporative water loss by employing a marked degree of adaptive heterothermy. Schmidt-Nielsen *et al.* (1957) were the first to describe this phenomenon and clearly showed (Fig. 5.2) that, when the camel is dehydrated under desert conditions, its body temperature will fluctuate by as much as 6.2 °C during 1 day (34.5 °C at 08.00 hr and 40.7 °C at 19.00 hr). The data in Fig. 5.2 also show that, while the average degree of fluctuation over a period of 4 days in a dehydrated animal lay between 35 °C and 40.5 °C, when the animals were watered daily the range in

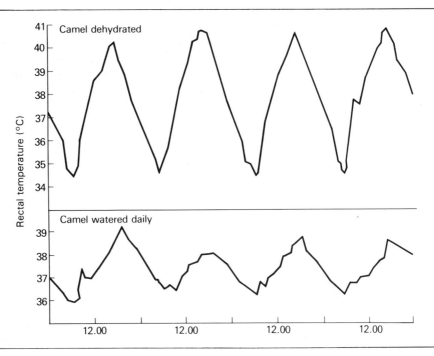

Fig. 5.2   The dehydrated camel shows a much more marked degree of adaptive heterothermy than when it is watered daily. (Schmidt-Nielsen *et al.* 1957.)

fluctuation was markedly reduced to a range of about 36–39 °C. The advantages to the animal are obvious. By allowing its body temperature to drift slowly down at night to a temperature as low as 34.5 °C, the heat-storing capacity of the tissues is greatly increased. Also, these animals are very large and consequently possess a high thermal inertia. Therefore by allowing its body temperatures to rise from 34.5 °C to 40.5 °C during the day, a 500 kg camel would be storing approximately 2 500 kcal. This heat is then lost by radiation and convection during the cool night and the necessity to evaporate water is minimised. The camels that were watered daily employed evaporative cooling to maintain their temperatures within the narrower range of 36–39 °C. This suggests that a control system involving osmoreceptors or volume receptors must be integrated in some unexplained way with the thermoregulatory control systems of these animals.

Camels are therefore what the French would describe as *animaux formidables*. Not only is their adaptive physiology remarkable but their endurance over long distances under the harshest conditions has become legendary. Alan Moorehead, in his book *Coopers Creek*, has vividly described the vital rôle played by camels in supporting Burke and Wills' heroic crossing of the Australian continent during the last century. Australians had little experience of these animals and when the camels sweated, they interpreted it as a 'sweat of fear', in response to the hostile landscape the animals were crossing. The treatment consisted of bathing of the animals in hot springs and even the occasional tot of rum. The camels survived it all and were even able to negotiate the swampy tropical areas in the Northern Territories, although with difficulty. Finally they provided food for their masters when the latter were faced with starvation.

An even more dramatic example of adaptive heterothermy is provided by two large antelope, the eland and the oryx, which survive well in arid and semi-arid areas of Africa. Richard Taylor has investigated the adaptive physiology of these animals, together with his colleague Charles Lyman of Harvard University, and has written a fascinating, semi-popular account of their results (Taylor 1969). When exposed to day temperatures of 40 °C and night temperatures of 22 °C, the eland allowed its body temperature to fluctuate through more than seven degrees (33.9 °C to 41.2 °C) and the oryx more than six degrees (35.7 °C to 42.1 °C). During these experiments the animals were fully hydrated but, when the oryx was dehydrated and exposed to a temperature of 45 °C, it did not sweat and its body temperature exceeded 45 °C for 8 hr. The advantages to these animals are again obvious, because of the significant amount of water saved and also because of the reversal of the heat gradient which now flows from the animal to the environment. Nevertheless, it is a remarkable achievement for a mammal to survive body temperatures of 45 °C for such long periods, as a temperature of 42 °C is usually lethal for most mammals. Taylor ascribes the survival of these animals to the cooling effect the carotid rete has on the brain. The carotid rete is a small network of blood vessels situated beneath the brain in certain mammals (Fig. 5.3). Just before the carotid artery enters the brain case, it breaks up into a fine network of vessels which is surrounded by cool venous blood returning from the nasal sinuses. This venous blood is cooled because, although the dehydrated oryx has ceased to sweat at these high ambient temperatures, it continues to pant. Consequently, the venous blood returning from the nasal sinuses is several degrees cooler than the hot arterial blood from the heart, which flows through the carotid artery. When the hot carotid blood reaches the carotid rete, it is

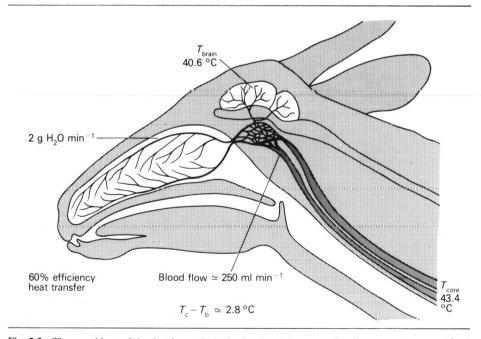

T_{brain}
40.6 °C

2 g H_2O min^{-1}

60% efficiency
heat transfer

Blood flow ≃ 250 ml min^{-1}

$T_c - T_b \simeq 2.8$ °C

T_{core}
43.4
°C

Fig. 5.3   The carotid rete, lying just beneath the brain of certain mammals, allows counter-current heat exchange between hot arterial blood from the heart and cool venous blood from nasal sinuses. The hypothetical figures demonstrate how a temperature difference of 2.8 °C can be maintained between the brain and the core of the body. (Modified from Taylor 1969.)

flowing in the opposite direction to the venous blood and an ideal opportunity therefore exists for counter-current heat exchange. In this respect, Taylor has measured differences between carotid blood temperature and brain temperatures as great as 2.9 °C in running gazelles. It would seem feasible therefore that the hyperthermic, panting oryx would be able to reduce its carotid blood temperature from 45 °C to approximately 42 °C before this enters the brain. In this way, the presumably delicate tissues of the brain would be protected from excessively high temperatures. Taylor (1972) reports that sustained high body temperatures of 45 °C also occur in the small desert gazelle, *Gazella granti*, and he proposes that this is the reason for this species' superior adaptation to the desert environment, when compared with the very similar *G. thomsonii*.

The above phenomenon is sometimes referred to as adaptive hyperthermia but, as the lower limit of the fluctuating body temperature in these animals is equally important in determining the total amount of heat stored, we prefer the term adaptive heterothermy. Besides, it should be remembered that Taylor measured these extremely high body temperatures in an artificially heated room in which the animals were not able to thermoregulate behaviourally, and equivalent temperatures have not as yet been measured in free-ranging oryx under natural conditions. Adaptive heterothermy is, nevertheless, an important physiological adaptation for large desert mammals, and the carotid rete appears to fulfil an important supportive function in this respect. If this is so, one would expect that the surface area of the nasal sinuses would be enlarged in arid-adapted mammals to provide maximum cooling of the venous blood returning from this area to the rete. We found this to be the case when comparing arid-adapted sheep breeds (Afrikaner) with mesic breeds (Romney Marsh), and also when comparing *Bos indicus* cattle (Afrikaner) with a *B. taurus* breed (Friesland). It is possible therefore that the proud Roman nose of Afrikaner cattle may have adaptive value, as might also be the case with the grotesquely developed nasal region of the Saiga antelope, *Saiga tatarica*. The latter usually inhabits treeless plains, including cold arid areas of Mongolia. More research on the adaptive value of the carotid rete is, however, still required because its distribution is not limited to arid-adapted mammals. Its major function would appear to be the cooling of the brain in sprinting predators and prey animals (mammals) when their body temperatures rise dramatically during vigorous exercise (Baker 1979). Nevertheless a dual function or at least a more critical function for this heat exchanger may exist in certain desert-adapted mammals.

Behavioural thermoregulation and the concept of the 'thermal niche'

In Chapter 3, when escape behaviour was discussed, we provided several examples of behavioural thermoregulation. These included the sand-diving lizard, *Aporosaura*, and certain tenebrionid beetles. These examples, together with the ostrich and certain antelope, will serve well to develop the theme further.

The ostrich, *Struthio camelus*, is not only the largest living bird but can survive successfully in some of the most arid regions of Africa. This ability is in large measure due to minimising water loss by behavioural thermoregulation. When faced with a high intensity of solar radiation and ambient temperature, the birds orientate towards the sun and move their wings downwards and away from the thorax. This manoeuvre both shades and exposes the thorax which, because of its naked surface, now functions as a large 'thermal window' by facilitating radiant and convective heat loss (Fig. 5.4). In addition, the sparsely distributed dorsal feathers are erected, as described previously (see Fig. 4.8), and the slightest breeze can now provide a

Fig. 5.4 Ostriches in typical desert habitat increase convective and radiant cooling by orientation, feather erection and wing drooping.

movement of air over a large area of skin surface of the bird. In this way the animal maximises convective cooling and, as long as the temperature of the air remains below body temperature (about 40 °C), the birds will not be required to employ evaporative cooling. Under these conditions the respiration rate remains slow and deep (4 resp. min^{-1}) but on still, hot days the birds are forced to resort to rapid, shallow thermal panting (about 40 resp. min^{-1}). Nevertheless, the conservation of water on hot ($\sim$40 °C) days with reasonable wind speed is critical in the overall water balance of this species and its survival in the desert. At night, however, when the desert air cools rapidly, the birds are faced with the opposite problem of conserving heat. This they solve by folding their wings close to the thorax, interlocking the dorsal feathers and tucking their naked legs beneath them as they huddle close to the ground. In this position the plumage traps an insulating layer of air around the skin and the temperature of the air space between the skin and the feathers rises to a uniformly high level (see Fig. 4.8). The heart rate drops during the night to a minimum level of 23 beats min^{-1} indicating a low metabolic rate, thus obviating unnecessary use of energy to maintain body temperature. This thermoregulatory behaviour is supported by efficient renal function, thereby ensuring superior adaptation to an arid environment.

Even the casual visitor to the massive Namib dune sea is impressed by the relatively large variety of tenebrionid beetles in this area, as well as by the variety of temporal niches which the various species occupy. Some are strictly nocturnal, others facultatively crepuscular while some are strictly diurnal. The spatial separation of these beetle species is also remarkable. For example, if you were to walk from the crest of one dune to another by crossing the wide, flat inter-dune valley or street, you would notice that certain species never leave the dune slopes while others are confined to the dune streets. A suitable comparison is provided by a large pitch-black species, *Onymacris plana*, which is confined to the dune slope, whereas a much smaller beetle, *Stenocara phalangium*, with a much lighter coloration and longer legs, inhabits the flat dune street exclusively. Henwood (1975) examined both the micro-climate surrounding these two species and their thermoregulatory behaviour, in order to construct a mathematical thermoregulation model for both species, which

he then tested in the field. His observations showed that a very steep temperature gradient existed above the ground, with temperatures falling rapidly by about 10 °C between 0–5 cm above the ground and even significantly between 0–1 cm. This steep gradient is exploited behaviourally by the long-legged *S. phalangium*, which incidentally has the longest legs, relative to body size, of any insect in the world. On cool mornings these beetles bend their legs, moving the abdomen as close as possible to the substrate while orientating the long axis of the body perpendicularly to the sun's rays. As the substrate temperature rises, the beetles extend their long legs, move the abdomen away from the substrate and engage in a stilt-like walk. When substrate temperatures become intolerably high the insects clamber on to small stones which cover the dune street. They then occupy the highest point on the small stone in a stilted position, with the white posterior pointed towards the sun. In this position they remain inactive during the hottest midday hours but will defend their 'thermal' refuge vigorously against intruding conspecifics. In contrast, the larger *O. plana* with a smaller relative surface area and much darker coloration has greater thermal flexibility on the soft dune-slope habitat. However, when Henwood used his mathematical model to test the theoretical response of *O. plana* in the micro-habitat occupied by *S. phalangium*, he found that its body temperature would exceed 55 °C when placed on a 5 cm high stone. He concluded that *O. plana* was 'thermally excluded' from the dune street habitat. This concept of the 'thermal niche' is in our opinion a very useful one in evaluating community ecology and resource partitioning in the desert, and deserves far more attention than it has enjoyed in the past.

Orientation of the long axis of the body in relation to incident solar radiation is a fairly common form of thermoregulatory behaviour and is not confined to desert animals. Nevertheless, it is particularly important to certain desert species as it can reduce the heat load significantly. This reduction in heat load eventually represents a critical reduction in evaporative water loss, thereby allowing the animal to survive on minimal water intake. In this regard Hofmeyr *et al.* (1980) have examined the behaviour of the springbok, *Antidorcas marsupialis*, a gazelle which can survive without free drinking water in arid regions of southern Africa. These animals, while grazing, will orientate either the head or the rump towards the sun under conditions of intense solar radiation. This behaviour will naturally reduce the profile area exposed to direct radiation, but in the case of the springbok, there is an added advantage, in that both the rump and the head are white in colour and consequently have superior reflectance. The data represented in Fig. 5.5 show how the percentage of springbok orientating towards the sun depended on the intensity of radiation, which obligingly fluctuated during this particular day owing to intermittent cloud cover. How efficient is this behaviour in reducing radiation loads? To answer this we have drawn the profile areas of an arid-adapted sheep, orientated both horizontally and perpendicularly towards the sun's rays, at various elevations of the sun (Fig. 5.6). When these profile areas are multiplied by the radiation intensity, it can be seen (Fig. 5.6) that orientation towards the sun can effectively reduce direct solar loads by approximately 50 per cent (Hofmeyr 1980).

One of the more photogenic mechanisms of thermoregulatory behaviour to be seen in desert animals is provided by the African ground squirrel *Xerus inauris*. On hot windless days these animals flare and raise their tails above their backs, using them as portable sunshades as they forage for food on the surface. In Fig. 5.7 it is clear, from the shadows cast by the animals, that they also orientate their bodies away from the sun to obtain maximum shading effect from the tail.

Many more examples could be cited but one further example of a slightly different nature should suffice. We have previously seen that muscular activity, particularly

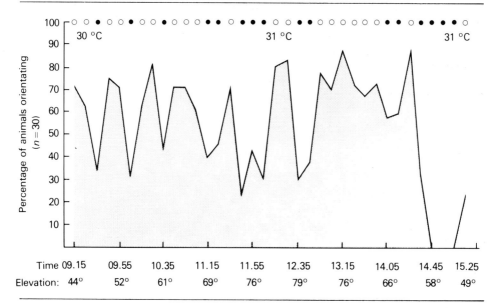

Fig. 5.5 The percentage of springbok orientating the long axis of the body towards the sun. In doing so the profile area exposed to direct radiation is significantly reduced. When the sun is obscured by intermittent cloud, indicated by closed circles, orientation becomes random. (Hofmeyr and Louw 1980.)

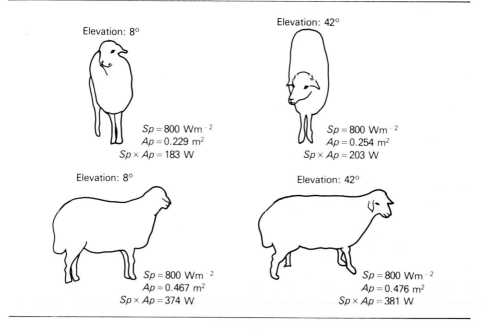

Fig. 5.6 Demonstrating the extent to which profile areas (Ap), exposed to direct radiation (Sp), can be reduced by orientation of the long axis of the body in an arid-adapted sheep. At sun elevations of both 8° and 42° the heat load ($Sp \times Ap$) is almost halved. (Hofmeyr 1980.)

Fig. 5.7 Thermoregulatory behaviour in *Xerus inauris.* The animals employ the flared tail for shading and simultaneously orientate their bodies in the opposite direction from the incoming insolation. Note the position of the shadows cast by the animals. (Marsh *et al.* 1978.)

rapid locomotion, can cause a swift rise in body temperature. For this reason many arid-adapted animals restrict activity to an absolute minimum during the hottest part of the day. Stan Tomkowitz, a graduate student at Arizona State University, has recently confirmed this while studying burros in the Sonoran Desert. He also found that the stallions restricted activity more carefully than the mares and, as a result, maintained their body temperatures at a slightly lower level than the females during the day. He has called this difference in temperature the 'thermal reserve' and advances the hypothesis that the stallions must maintain a thermal reserve to allow for intermittent aggression, for example when competing for females.

Osmoregulation in arthropods

Water balance in desert arthropods has been the subject of a great deal of research. In this respect, as we have seen, the cuticle plays a key rôle in providing an almost impermeable barrier to water, thereby reducing evaporative water loss to a minimum and ensuring a slow rate of water turnover. Also of great importance in minimising water loss from desert insects is the ability of these animals to reabsorb water very efficiently from the contents of the hindgut. This subject has attracted the attention of biochemists, physicists and physiologists, and complex physical models have been

proposed to explain the process. A detailed discussion of the phenomenon is beyond the scope of this text and the interested reader is referred to a recent review by Edney (1977). In brief, however, the Malphigian tubules, which lie in the haemocoel of insects and are bathed in haemolymph, are of central importance in the process. These tubules are joined to the junction between the midgut and the hindgut and have the ability to transport ions actively from the haemolymph into the lumina of the tubules. This results in water following the secreted ions passively and this iso-osmotic fluid is then conveyed along the tubules to the hindgut. In the hindgut the fluid is exposed to active transport through the action of specialised rectal pads. Once again water passively follows the actively transported ions. The end result is that the final products of excretion, faecal matter and uric acid, can be voided in an extremely dry state with a minimum loss of water. Alternatively, if the insect is overloaded with water, reabsorption in the rectum is reduced and excessive water is excreted (Fig. 5.8). The process of tubular secretion is under the control of specific hormones. As

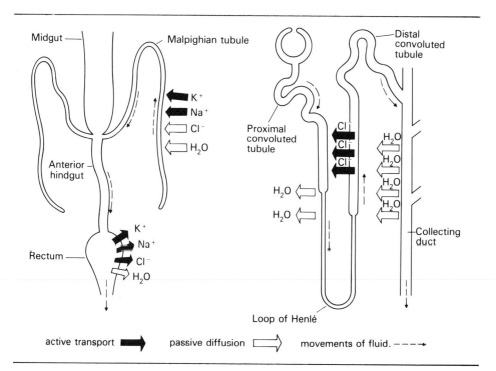

Fig. 5.8 Although the structures employed in urinary excretion in insects and mammals are different, the biophysical principles involved are very similar. See text for explanation of functioning of Malpighian tubules in insects (left) and mammalian nephron (right).

the end-product of nitrogen metabolism is uric acid in insects, the above process is greatly facilitated because uric acid is very insoluble in water and can therefore be excreted in an almost dry crystalline state. Guanine, which is the end-product of protein catabolism in desert scorpions and spiders and is equally insoluble, confers similar advantages on these animals. In insects with cryptonephric tubules, excretion is somewhat different because of the position of the tubules but the same principles apply.

From the foregoing it should be clear that desert insects, because of the impermeable nature of their cuticle and their highly efficient reabsorption of water in the hindgut, can survive almost exclusively on the water produced from oxidation of tissue nutrients. This so-called metabolic water therefore plays an important part in the osmoregulation of insects and deserves more attention. In Chapter 2 we mentioned that fats, because of the relatively larger number of hydrogen atoms present, can potentially produce more water when oxidised than proteins and carbohydrates. If fats and carbohydrates are fully catabolised to CO_2 and H_2O, 1 g of these substrates will yield 1.07 g and 0.56 g of H_2O respectively, while 1 g of protein, when catabolised to urea, will yield only 0.40 g of water. It would appear then as if metabolism of fat would be most advantageous to desert insects during periods of dehydration or starvation. A shift to fat metabolism has been confirmed in the locust under these conditions. The advantages involved are, however, not quite so clear-cut. For example, Loveridge and Bursell (1975) have pointed out that when metabolism is measured in terms of energy produced as ATP, and not as amounts of oxygen consumed, the oxidation of carbohydrates will yield 0.133 g H_2O kcal^{-1} while only 0.112 g H_2O is produced when the same amount of energy is produced by fat. Switching to fat metabolism therefore has disadvantages in terms of the bio-energetics involved. Nevertheless, fat still yields the most water per unit weight of substrate oxidised and, for this reason and others, is the most suitable nutrient to store in the tissues of both small and large animals.

In spite of the large volume of papers published on the water relations of desert

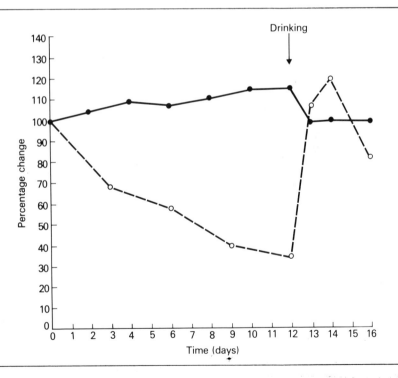

Fig. 5.9 Changes in the haemolymph of the desert beetle, *Onymacris plana*, during dehydration and rehydration. Changes in haemolymph volume (o ----- o) and osmolarity (●——●) shown as percentages of original values. Drinking (day 12) marked by arrow. (Nicolson 1980.)

arthropods, relatively few investigators have examined the actual osmoregulation of the body fluids in these animals. In a recent study Nicolson (1980) has followed the changes in haemolymph volume and osmoconcentration in a Namib dune tenebrionid during a period of dehydration and rehydration. During dehydration the animals were continuously exposed to a low relative humidity (10–15%) which they are unlikely to encounter continuously even under severe desert conditions. In spite of this, they were able to maintain the osmoconcentration of their haemolymph at an almost constant level throughout the dehydration period, even though the blood volume was markedly reduced (Fig. 5.9). The concentration of the major cations (Na^+ and K^+) in the haemolymph remained relatively constant during this period and it is clear that these desert beetles are remarkably good osmoregulators. The actual physiological mechanisms involved are, however, more difficult to explain but it is thought that absorption of ions by the fat body during dehydration may be involved.

Another interesting study on haemolymph osmoregulation in desert arthropods has been described by Riddle *et al.* (1976). They also found that tenebrionid beetles regulated the osmolarity of their haemolymph, while scorpions tolerated increasing osmolarity when both groups were subjected to desiccation. In the case of desert millipedes the males tended to tolerate increasing osmolarity during desiccation, whereas the females exhibited finer control over osmolarity. This distinction, however, tended to disappear when the period of dehydration was extended from 20–40 days. We can conclude then that the osmoregulatory capacity and the physiological mechanisms involved in minimising water loss during excretion are as complex in desert arthropods as in certain vertebrates. These mechanisms obviously also play an essential supportive rôle to the 'waterproofed' cuticle in ensuring these animals' survival in the desert environment.

Renal and extra-renal osmoregulation in desert vertebrates

Even a superficial examination of the heat and water balance equations in Chapter 2 will reveal the importance to desert vertebrates of minimising water loss via the digestive, renal and respiratory routes. Nearly all desert vertebrates are able to reabsorb water very efficiently from the terminal portion of the digestive tract and the faecal pellets, produced from this process, consist of only 40 per cent water in certain well-adapted species. In temperate animals the percentage of water in the faeces is often as high as 80 per cent. In this section we shall direct our attention mostly to water conservation mechanisms brought about by the renal system and specialised salt glands. Frequent use will be made of the units milliosmoles (mOsm) and a brief explanation of this terminology may be justified. A one molar solution of a non-dissociating compound such as glucose is said to have an osmoconcentration or, more correctly, osmolarity of one osmole 1 Osm 1^{-1}) and will consist of 180 g glucose made up to 1 litre of solution. Because the concentrations of most body fluids of vertebrates are far weaker than 1 Osm1^{-1} preference is usually given to the unit milliosmole (1 Osm = 1 000 mOsm).

Important considerations when evaluating renal function in vertebrates are the evolutionary patterns of nephron development and obligatory nitrogen excretion, exhibited by modern vertebrates. Amphibians, with few exceptions, excrete nitrogen in the form of urea as do mammals. Reptiles and birds on the other hand, excrete uric acid and this is of great advantage during the embryonic development of these animals within their enclosed or 'cleidoic' eggs. If the embryos of reptiles and birds were to excrete urea, this highly soluble compound would cause severe osmotic disturbances within the embryonic tissues, as there is no means of eliminating it from

the enclosed egg. The marked difference in solubility of urea and uric acid has further important implications insofar as the almost insoluble uric acid can be excreted as a crystalline paste, with minimum water loss by so-called uricotelic animals, while urea excretion by ureotelic animals, because of the high solubility of urea, requires a certain minimum amount of water as a vehicle for excretion. This is well illustrated in the ostrich, a uricotelic animal. When these birds are given free access to water, they void a large volume of watery light-coloured urine. When water is withheld from them the volume of urine is markedly reduced, water virtually disappears from the urine and the uric acid is voided in the form of a sticky white paste (Fig. 5.10). The

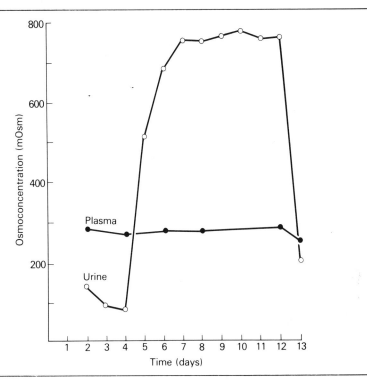

Fig. 5.10 Homoiostatic control of the osmoconcentration of the plasma of the ostrich during dehydration, largely through adjusted kidney function. The period of dehydration extended from day 4 to day 12. (Louw *et al.* 1969.)

major vehicle employed for expulsion of the uric acid under the latter conditions is mucus, which is secreted by special goblet cells lining the ureters. Uricotelism therefore has definite advantages in balancing water budgets in the desert and it is no surprise that it is employed by insects and reptiles, two of the most successful groups in the desert. The frog species best adapted to semi-arid conditions, *Chiromantis xerampelina*, is also uricotelic (Loveridge 1970) and, also noteworthy, when proteins are catabolised to uric acid they yield more metabolic water than when broken down to urea.

A second important evolutionary development among certain vertebrates which must be considered is the evolution of the nephron or, more specifically, the loop of Henlé in the kidney. This tubular structure, in the form of a hairpin loop, is essential

for the production of urine which is hyperosmotic to the blood of the animal in question (Fig. 5.8). In these vertebrates the blood filtrate enters the tubule via the glomerulus as a result of a process known as ultrafiltration. At first the tubular fluid has the same osmolarity as the plasma but, as it passes down the descending limb, ions move into the tubule from the surrounding tissue and as the fluid passes around the hairpin bend it attains its maximum osmolarity. The reason for the movement of ions from the surrounding tissue into the descending limb is to be found in the function of the ascending limb. As the filtrate passes up the ascending limb, ions are actively transported out of this structure into the surrounding tissues but, as this portion of the tubule is impermeable to water, water does not follow passively. The net result is that peritubular tissue surrounding the hairpin loop attains a very high osmolarity and, when the filtrate finally passes down the collecting ducts, it is exposed to this strong gradient and water is removed rapidly from the filtrate. The rate of reabsorption of water during this final passage down the collecting ducts is controlled by a hormone, anti-diuretic hormone (ADH), synthesised in the brain and stored prior to release in the posterior pituitary. Consequently, only those vertebrates which possess the loop of Henlé are able to produce a concentrated urine (hyperosmotic to plasma) and this structure is absent in all vertebrates apart from birds and mammals. Very recent studies also suggest that blood levels of ADH are higher in desert mammals than in temperate species.

The efficiency with which the loop of Henlé functions in producing a concentrated urine differs markedly among mammals. It is also thought that the longer the loop is, the more efficient it is. As the major portion of the loop lies within the medulla of the kidney, this has given rise to the concept that the relative medullary thickness of any mammalian kidney could serve as an index of its concentrating ability. The data contained in Table 5.1 appear to support this hypothesis and show that arid-adapted animals exhibit a greater relative medullary thickness and produce a far more concentrated urine than temperate animals of a similar size. Also of interest is that smaller mammals, particularly small desert rodents, have a concentrating ability far superior to that of larger mammals. There are probably several reasons for this. Firstly, larger mammals have greater thermal inertia and are better able to tolerate heat loads than smaller ones and, secondly, the efficient locomotion of the larger

Table 5.1 *Relative medullary thickness* * *and maximum urine/plasma osmotic ratios in selected mammals.* (*See Marsh* et al. *for original references.*)

Mammal	Relative medullary thickness	Maximum urine/plasma osmotic ratio
Beaver (*Aplodontia rufa*)	1.3	2.7
Man (*Homo sapiens*)	3.0	4.2
Cat (*Felis domesticus*)	4.8	–
Bontebok (*Damaliscus dorcas dorcas*)	4.9	5.4
Springbok (*Antidorcas marsupialis*)	5.5	8.3
White rat (*Rattus rattus*)	5.9	8.9
Jerboa (*Jaculus jaculus*)	9.3	–
Gerbil (*Gerbillus gerbillus*)	10.5	14.0
Ground squirrel (*Xerus inauris*)	12.4	14.9[†]
Desert mouse (*Psammomys obesus*)	12.9	17.0

* Calculated as $\dfrac{\text{medulla thickness (mm)} \cdot 10}{\text{kidney size}}$

[†] Theoretical maximum

mammals allows them to seek out plants with a higher moisture content and travel to remote and isolated water-holes. The loop of Henlé is therefore of critical importance in the survival of small desert mammals which are forced to survive on the food resources in their immediate vicinity. Several challenging physiological problems in respect of the functioning of this structure are, however, still to be explained. For example, if length is a critical factor in the production of a highly concentrated urine, why do the longer loops (in absolute terms) in the larger mammals, not function more efficiently than the loops in the small mammals which are only relatively longer? Also, how do delicate proteins survive their passage in the bloodstream through the peritubular tissues which can reach osmolarities as high as 7 000 mOsm l^{-1} in certain rodent species? Most proteins become denatured at much lower osmolarities.

An examination of the many results obtained from studying water balance in small desert mammals suggests that the critical urine concentrating ability, which these mammals must have in order to survive on an air-dry diet without drinking water, is approximately equal to 4 000 mOsm l^{-1}. The highest urine concentration measured to date is 9 400 mOsm l^{-1} for Australian hopping mice. Also, Schmidt-Nielsen's data (1964) on the complete water balance of *Dipodomys*, the kangaroo rat, clearly show the importance of efficient renal function in the overall water balance of this animal (Table 5.2). This independence of drinking water is therefore a prerequisite for

Table 5.2 *Overall water balance of a kangaroo rat during the consumption of 100 g of barley over a period of about 4 weeks. (Schmidt-Nielsen 1964.)*

Water gains	ml	Water losses	ml
Oxidation water	54.0	Urine	13.5
Absorbed water	6.0	Faeces	2.6
		Evaporation	43.9
Total water gain	60.0	Total water loss	60.0

desert rodents but, as Macmillen and Lee (1967) have pointed out, only certain desert species are able to survive indefinitely on air-dry seed without drinking water. In this respect, Withers *et al.* (1980) have demonstrated that a remarkably large proportion of Namib Desert rodents have this ability, which is not surprising in view of the extreme aridity of this region. In the same study water turnover rates (WTR) in these rodents were measured under field conditions by injecting the animals with radioactive water (H^{3}OH) and retrapping them at intervals to obtain blood samples. The results confirmed that the rate of water turnover in these animals was remarkably low, even under harsh field conditions. In the case of *Petromyscus collinus* WTR was as low as 0.8 ml day^{-1} but, interestingly enough, rose to 1.4 ml day^{-1} after heavy advective fog had occurred in the habitat.

Birds, like mammals, possess a loop of Henlé but are not capable of producing nearly as concentrated a urine as the latter. Nevertheless, the ability to produce a hyperosmotic urine is still of importance to desert birds. This is reflected in the marked changes which occur in urine osmolarity of an ostrich, exposed to dehydration, while the osmolarity of the plasma remains perfectly constant (Fig. 5.10). Of greater importance to certain birds, however, is the possession of a nasal salt gland which is capable of excreting a solution with an osmolarity as high as 1 800 mOsm l^{-1}, thereby allowing the bird to excrete excess ions with minimal water loss. The nasal salt gland functions as a support system to the efficient reabsorbing ability

of the cloaca and terminal portion of the digestive tract in certain avian species. When the fairly dilute urine reaches these structures, where it is temporarily stored, ions are actively transported from this fluid and water follows passively. The end result is that the obligatory excretion of nitrogen in the form of uric acid takes place with a minimum of water loss; but the animal is still faced with the problem of excreting the reabsorbed ions that have now entered its blood stream. It is at this point that the nasal salt gland fulfils its supportive function by excreting these excess ions in the form of a hyperosmotic solution. Marine birds that are excluded from a source of fresh water rely heavily on salt gland function to balance their water budgets, and certain desert birds also employ this mechanism. It is, however, interesting how different species of desert birds have solved this problem in different ways. The Rueppell's bustard *Eupodotis vigorsii rueppellii* and the sandgrouse *Pterocles namaqua* are both ground-nesting species in the Namib desert and produce precocious chicks which must, immediately after hatching, fend largely for themselves. The bustard chicks employ efficient salt glands to minimise water loss, while the sandgrouse chicks rely on the male parent to ferry water to them, often from distant water-holes. The males wade into the shallows of the water-hole and thoroughly wet their breast feathers. These feathers can absorb as much as 20–40 ml of water (Cade and Maclean 1976), which is more efficient than a nylon sponge. After the return of the male, the chicks drink copiously from the breast feathers and we have measured as much as 3 ml of water in the crop of a sandgrouse chick. This amounts to almost 30 per cent of the total body weight of the chick which is in itself remarkable (Dixon and Louw 1978). How the parent is able to return and find its cryptically coloured chicks, isolated on a vast monotonous desert plain, is even more astounding.

Nasal salt glands are also of great importance to desert lizards which, it will be remembered, do not possess the loop of Henlé and are therefore not able to produce hyperosmotic urine. Cloacal reabsorption of water is important to this group, as in birds, and they have the advantage of being uricotelic as well. Because nearly all desert reptiles are exclusively carnivorous, their diet contains between 60–70 per cent water which is a distinct advantage over seed-eating birds and mammals. In unusual cases, such as the sand-diving Namib lizard *Aporosaura anchietae*, which feeds facultatively on dry seeds, a special organ (bladder) has developed for storage of relatively large amounts of water.

Specialised respiration and transpiration

The process of respiration in terrestrial plants and animals ultimately involves the exchange of gases at a gas–liquid interface. Because the gases involved are usually unsaturated with water vapour, particularly in the desert environment, respiration is potentially a major avenue of water loss to the organism. For this reason both desert plants and animals have evolved specialised morphological and physiological adaptations to minimise water loss via this route.

The importance in reducing water loss of a thick, lipid-containing cutin layer on the surface of desert plants has already been emphasised. The stomata, however, still represent a potential avenue of water loss when open. To reduce this avenue of loss the stomata of desert plants are frequently depressed below the surface of a leaf and, as a result of their position at the bottom of this cavity, the resistance to the outward diffusion of water vapour is increased (Fig. 5.11). This is due to an increased depth of the boundary layer, which acts as a barrier between the steep water vapour gradient that exists between the air in the sub-stomatal cavity and the free air above the

boundary layer. To enhance the efficiency of these specialised stomata, certain xerophytes keep their stomata closed during the day and open them only at night, when the relative humidity of the air rises in response to declining temperatures. The process of photosynthesis, however, requires both light and carbon dioxide and these plants solve these conflicting demands as follows. At night, when the stomata are open, CO_2 is absorbed and combined with phosphoenolpyruvate to produce malate. These organic acids accumulate in the cells during the night and with the advent of sunlight they are broken down to release CO_2, which is then incorporated into carbohydrates by the enzymes of the Calvin cycle. This metabolic pattern is known as crassulacean acid metabolism or CAM and is especially common in succulent plants, including members of the families Cactaceae, Crassulaceae and Bromeliaceae (Solbrig and Orians 1977). Although the above adaptations are effective in protecting xerophytes from arid conditions, Solbrig and Orians have pointed out that xerophytic leaves, which are capable of photosynthesising under high negative water potentials, are energetically more costly to grow than mesophytic leaves. They base this assumption on the fact that the small cells, thick cell walls, high osmotic pressure, thick cuticles and specialised stomata found in xerophytic leaves require more material per unit volume than mesophytic leaves. It is also possible that maintenance costs in the xerophytic leaves are higher.

If we now turn to respiratory adaptations in desert arthropods, we are again struck by the similarities in the adaptations exhibited by desert plants and insects. Hadley (1972) has compared both the physical structure and the function of plant stomata with those of the insect spiracle (Fig. 5.11). That the structure of these openings is remarkably similar is not unexpected, as the same physical factors, such as water vapour gradients and the barrier rôle of the boundary layer, are involved in the functioning of both stomata and spiracles. For this reason xeric arthropods have small spiracles which are frequently hidden or sunken and, in some instances, are surrounded by a basketwork of outgrowths to reduce loss of water vapour. Probably the most specialised adaptation in this respect, however, is to be found in tenebrionid beetles in which the abdominal spiracles open into the subelytral space, a humid cavity, and are not directly linked with the dry atmosphere (Ahearn 1970).

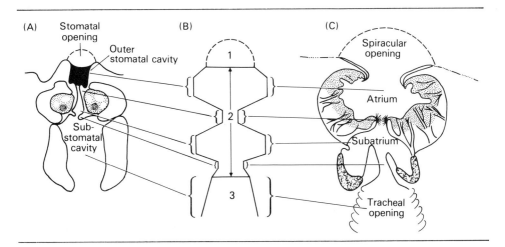

Fig. 5.11   Similarities in the structure of a plant stoma (A) and insect spiracle (C) and a comparison of the diffusion resistances in these structures with those in an aperture with varying diameters (B). (Hadley 1972.)

Respiratory water losses from these animals are therefore minimal and are, in fact, significantly lower than cuticular transpiration at temperatures from 25 °C to 42.5 °C and at 0 per cent rh.

Mammals also display respiratory adaptations to reduce water loss and one of the more interesting is to be found in desert rodents. The air breathed in by these animals in the desert is well below saturation point and, consequently, when this air moves across the moist mucous membranes, lining the nasal sinuses, it takes up moisture and is warmed to body temperature. This results in cooling of the surfaces of the nasal sinuses because of the latent heat of evaporation. On expiration the warm saturated air from the lungs is cooled as it returns through the nasal sinuses. When the temperature of saturated air is reduced, condensation of water occurs and this water is therefore not lost to the surrounding dry atmospheric air. Behavioural adaptations such as nocturnality and the use of humid burrows during the day would naturally minimise water loss via this route as well.

Large desert mammals also appear to be able to reduce respiratory water losses. Recently Shkolnik *et al.* (1980a) have reported that the camel expires unsaturated air at night under desert conditions. Whether this is solely due to recondensation in the nasal sinuses during expiration or some other physiological mechanism is still to be explained. Nevertheless, it is an intriguing and significant discovery, and we have recently shown that the desert ostrich expires unsaturated air under certain environmental conditions (Withers, Louw and Siegfried 1981). Perhaps a more subtle respiratory adaptation is to be found in the oryx. At night, as ambient temperatures decline below their thermal neutral zone, these animals are eventually obliged to increase their metabolic rate, and therefore their oxygen consumption as well, to maintain body temperature. This has two important implications, namely that the increased metabolism will produce more metabolic water and secondly that the ventilation of the respiratory system must be increased to provide the increased requirement for oxygen. The oryx apparently solves the latter problem by breathing more deeply, instead of more rapidly, to satisfy the increased demands for oxygen. In this way the dead space in the respiratory tract (sinuses, trachea, bronchi, etc.) is exposed less frequently to the dehydrating effect of the inspired air, while the alveoli, which are involved in the actual gas exchange, still receive sufficient oxygen (Taylor 1969). Whether large surface-dwelling mammals benefit from metabolic water, however, remains a moot point. Whenever a nutrient substrate in the tissues is fully catabolised to yield metabolic water, it requires a specific amount of oxygen from the surrounding atmospheric air. The process therefore involves ventilation of the respiratory tract with a concomitant water loss. The critical factor is of course the relative humidity of the inspired air. During the typical desert day with high temperatures and very low air humidity no advantage would accrue to the animal, but at night, if the humidity rose sufficiently (>70%), the animal might benefit from the production of metabolic water.

Imbibition of fog, dew and water vapour

Condensed water droplets, in the form of dew or condensed fog, represent an important source of water to desert organisms. What may appear to us as a tiny droplet of almost useless water is of course frequently large enough for a small arthropod to drown in. As the importance of this water source for desert organisms has long been realised (Buxton 1923), we have collected condensed fog in the Namib for chemical analysis. The osmolarity of these samples was surprisingly low

(25 mOsm l^{-1}) and it is therefore an ideal source to replenish tissue water in both plants and animals.

The fact that plants are able to absorb water through their leaves is well known and both nutrient solutions and systemic insecticides are often administered via this route. It is possible, however, that the thick lipid-containing cutin layer on the surface of desert plants may act as a barrier to the absorption of water in this way. We have tested this hypothesis in the Namib by spraying a fine aerosol of tritiated water on to the leaves of a desert succulent, *Trianthema hereroensis*, to simulate a condensing fog. The radioactive water was rapidly absorbed by the leaves and this result, together with the fact that this plant is confined to the fog belt of the Namib, leads us to believe that condensed fog is a major source of water for this particular species. This may not be true for all desert plants, particularly those with a highly modified cutin layer for minimising water loss from the plant to the atmosphere. A case in point is the coarse perennial grass, *Stipagrostis sabulicola*, which has spiky, tightly rolled leaves unsuitable for water collection and absorption. It grows on the slopes of high, shifting sand dunes and possesses an extensively developed lateral root system, which lies just beneath the surface of the sand and can extend for as much as 20 m from the main plant (Fig. 5.12). We wished to know if these superficial roots were able to absorb water from the top centimetre of sand, which reaches field capacity for several hours during a condensing fog, although the sand below this zone remains perfectly dry. The condensed fog is rapidly evaporated when the fog clears. To test this idea we sprayed tritiated water on the surface of the sand surrounding the plant, using a predetermined volume to bring the top centimetre to field capacity. Not only did we find that the tritiated water was rapidly absorbed but we also established that even after 7 weeks almost one-third of the radioactive water was still present in the form of photosynthates. This suggests that these plants make efficient use of condensed fog-water and that the turnover rate of the water is low.

In contrast to the Namib dune grass discussed above, the epiphyte *Tillandsia recurvata* utilises fog-water in the Peruvian Desert without a root system (Fig. 5.12). The advective fog which rolls in over the Peruvian Desert is a high fog and usually only condenses on the highest dunes and hills which interrupt the desert plain. As a result, one frequently sees two sharply demarcated zones on a high hill. The lower slopes appear to be completely barren of any life, while rows of *Tillandsia* plants occupy the crests. The absence of roots is an advantage to these plants, as they are not subjected to toxic levels of either salinity or gypsum, which often occur in the substrate. Belonging to the pineapple family, *T. recurvata* has long fluted leaves with an orientation ideal for fog-water collection and, in addition, the surface of the leaves has been modified for trapping condensed fog droplets (Fig. 5.13). In certain areas of the Peruvian Desert these plants have been rearranged on the surface of hills on either side of the Pan-American Highway to produce impressive political 'phyto-grafitti'. The artists, however, are not biologists and when plants are moved below the critical fog zone they die. This frequently has disastrous consequences for the original syntax! The flowering plants of the Namib do not appear to have evolved quite such specialised adaptations for fog collection. The closest ecological equivalent to *Tillandsia* in the Namib is probably the sausage-shaped lichen, *Omphalodium convoluta*, which occurs near to the coast. As a result of wind action, these plants collect in shallow washes and when fog condenses on them the cylindrical shape changes almost immediately to a flat absorbing surface. Being completely free of the substrate, they survive on soils with high gypsum levels.

The most impressive effect of fog on plant life is, however, to be seen in the so-called *lomas* of the Peruvian Desert. We have studied such a site, some 20 km

Fig. 5.12 A comparison of the extensive lateral root system of (A) *Stipagrostis sabulicola* in the Namib dunes compared with (B) the fluted leaves of *Tillandsia recurvata* in the Peruvian Desert. Both structures are responsible for absorption of condensed fog-water.

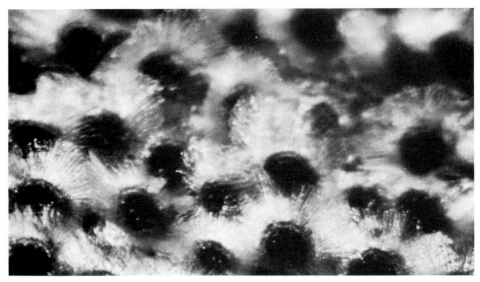

Fig. 5.13 Micrograph (×50) of the modified leaf surface of *Tillandsia recurvata*. The fine projections are thought to aid the plant in the absorption of condensed fog-water.

south-east of Lima and were struck by the contrast the *loma* provided with the lifelessness of the surrounding desert. This seaward-facing slope at an altitude of 300–800 m receives heavy fog condensation during the winter months, sufficient to cause the germination and growth of a variety of ephemerals, geophytes and shrubs. Lichens and mosses are, as expected, an important feature of the flora, and during the winter these hillsides are used for grazing domestic animals by local herdsmen. A particularly interesting plant to be found in this area is a species of amaryllis, *Stenomesson coccineum*. This plant produces luxuriant leaves during the winter months when fog precipitation is greatest. Water and photosynthates are then stored until the height of the dry summer when attractive flowers are produced on a long stem without any leaves. This could be an adaptation to reduce competition for pollinators. During our visit pollination of the plants was accomplished by a variety of humming-birds, their flashing colours an unexpected contrast with the starkness of the surrounding desert plain.

Although absorption of condensed fog and dew is of critical importance to many desert organisms, a more subtle adaptation is to be found in the absorption of water vapour from unsaturated air. This aspect has received less general attention but has been well studied in various species of lichens. Recent studies have demonstrated that the metabolic rhythm of these alga–fungus symbionts is synchronised with the water vapour content of the air and that they can withstand extreme desiccation and very high temperatures on the rock surfaces, which they frequently occupy (Lange *et al.* 1975). It is also significant that in certain desert situations lichens make up the largest percentage of the total biomass. Absorption of water vapour is, however, not restricted to living plants. We have measured the relative humidity of the air simultaneously with the water content of dead grass tissue in the Namib during one day (Fig. 5.14). The results showed that even this dead plant tissue had hygroscopic properties and that the water content of the grass followed the relative humidity of the air throughout the day, reaching a maximum of 27 per cent during the early hours of the morning. Animals that restrict their grazing periods to these hours, such as the

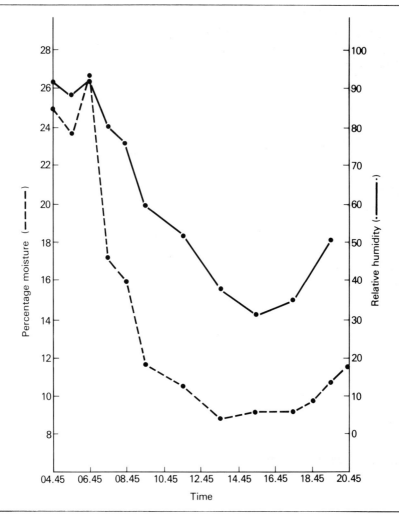

Fig. 5.14 The effect of the relative humidity of the air during one day upon the moisture content of a dry, perennial desert grass (*Stipagrostis uniplumis*) during dormancy. Animals that restrict their grazing to the early hours of the morning therefore favour their water balance.

oryx and the ostrich, could therefore increase their water intake very significantly. From our field observations this appears to be the case.

As expected, animals make equally good use of condensed fog or dew in the desert. An unusual example is provided by the Namib tenebrionid beetle, *Onymacris unguicularis*, which engages in fog-basking. These animals are ordinarily diurnal, emerging on to the warm sand surface of the dunes during the day while remaining buried in soft slipface sand during the night. When nocturnal fogs occur they will, however, emerge from the sand and climb slowly to the crest of the dune where fog condensation is greatest. Once near the crest they adopt a head-down stance and face into the fog-bearing wind (Fig. 5.15). The fog droplets condense on the dorsal surface of the elytra and trickle down to the mouthparts where they are imbibed. The average gain in water, expressed as a percentage of body weight after drinking, was

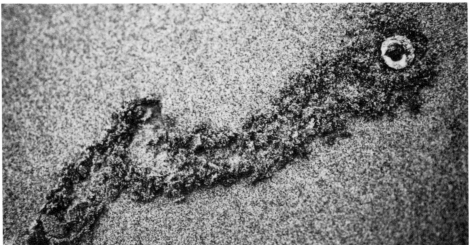

Fig. 5.15 *Onymacris unguicularis* in a typical fog-basking stance. Water collects on the dorsum and trickles down to the mouthparts where it is ingested. (Below) in contrast the sympatric *Lepidochora sp.* constructs fog-collecting trenches to capture fog-water and then extracts water from the moister sand on the ridges.

12 per cent, with a maximum of 34 per cent (Hamilton and Seely 1976). Even more unusual is the fog-trapping behaviour of the much smaller Namib dune beetle, *Lepidochora discoidalis*. These beetles are nocturnal and, when advective fog occurs, they construct narrow trenches on the surface of the sand, perpendicular to the fog wind. The ridges of these trenches collect more water than the surrounding sand and when the beetles return along the trench they flatten the trench, while extracting water from the sand (Fig. 5.15). This was established by determining the moisture content of the ridges before and after the beetles had returned along the trench. The

mean water uptake of the beetles during this process amounted to 13.88 per cent of their original body weight (Seely and Hamilton 1976). Although perhaps less spectacular, we have also observed that many other Namib dune species are active on cold foggy mornings and direct collection of fog-water from sand appears to be important to ants, spiders, lepismids and other tenebrionids. The actual physics or mechanics of moving water from the wet sand past the mouthparts of these arthropods must still be explained.

Again, as in plants, the uptake of water vapour from unsaturated air by animals has received less attention from biologists than the direct collection of condensed water. All adult tenebrionids studied to date do not seem to have the ability to absorb water vapour from unsaturated air. Their larvae, however, do have this ability and the process is dependent on relative humidity and not vapour pressure deficit. Also, the process appears to be mediated by the cuticle as it does not occur during ecdysis but begins again 2 days after ecdysis (Coutchié and Crowe 1979). Similarly, Edney (1966) has established that adult females of the desert cockroach, *Arenivaga*, which occurs in southern Californian deserts, are capable of absorbing water vapour from sub-saturated air.

Vertebrates also make use of condensed fog and dew both directly or indirectly through the plants they eat. We have frequently seen how jackals lick condensed fog or dew from the surfaces of rocks on the barren Skeleton Coast of Namibia. In this same area, when a group of shipwrecked passengers off the *Dunedin Star* became desperate for water during the Second World War, they licked condensed fog droplets off the wing surfaces of a crashed aircraft that had been sent to rescue them. A far more efficient animal in this respect is of course the Namib sand-diving lizard, *Aporosaura* (see Ch. 3). Even more remarkable is the ability of the Australian lizard, *Molloch horridus*, to absorb water into fine capillary-like channels or depressions in the skin. Water absorbed into these channels spreads over the skin and eventually some reaches the mouth. There it is absorbed by hygroscopic secretions of mucous glands at the edge of the lips. It then passes into the mouth and is swallowed.

Metabolic rate

The importance of nutrition and metabolic adjustments, such as torpor, aestivation and metabolic temperature compensation, has been emphasised previously (Ch. 3 and 4). More subtle adaptations may, however, be equally important. For example, examination of the heat balance equations in Chapter 2 shows that a reduced metabolic rate in desert endotherms would significantly reduce the total heat load on these animals, thereby contributing indirectly to water conservation. The diurnal reduction need not be large as a small critical adjustment could well be significant over a long period of, say, a complete desert summer. This would then seem to be the reason why certain arid-adapted mammals, such as zebu cattle and the North American ground squirrel, exhibit a lower metabolic rate and thyroid activity than expected (Hudson *et al*. 1972). Ectothermic animals naturally have the advantage of being able to seek out a cool micro-environment and, as the ambient temperature falls, so does their metabolic rate. Not only does this represent a reduction in water turnover rate but it also represents large savings in stored tissue nutrients. Just how large these savings can be is well illustrated by the xeric lizard, *Coleonyx variegatus*. During a 4-day feeding period these animals increased their body weight by 50 per cent, and the nutrient reserves stored in this manner were sufficient to last the lizard for 6–9 months (Bustard 1967). The pulmonate snail, *Sphincterochila boissieri*, which aestivates on the rocky surface of the Negev Desert, fully exposed to sun and

the desiccating desert air, also provides an excellent example of this phenomenon. Although its light-coloured shell ameliorates the effect of the intense radiation, the snail's low metabolic rate is of critical importance in ensuring its survival during long periods of dormancy. Schmidt-Nielsen *et al.* (1972) have calculated that, because of this low metabolic rate, the nutrient reserves in this animal are sufficient for several years' survival in the dormant state.

Conclusions

From the preceding discussion in Chapters 4 and 5, we can now draw several major conclusions in regard to the morphological and physiological adaptations exhibited by desert organisms.

1. Shape and size are important to both plants and animals. This is because size is inversely related to relative surface area, which in turn determines the rate of flux of both heat and water. Small size in animals also allows escape to a favourable micro-environment.
2. Orientation of leaves and the long axis of animal bodies reduces the profile area exposed to incident radiation and can be of critical importance.
3. Both the colour and physical nature of the integument in plants and animals are of great significance in determining heat gain from the environment and reducing water loss from the organism. The arthropod cuticle probably represents the most advanced development in this regard.
4. The ability to absorb and store small amounts of water from precipitated dew and fog allows certain species to survive in very arid areas indefinitely.
5. The use of a threshold amount of precipitation as an environmental cue for seasonal reproduction ensures survival of the progeny under the most favourable conditions.
6. Tolerance of both high temperatures and tissue dehydration is a feature of certain desert plants and animals.
7. Specialised respiratory patterns, such as crassulacean acid metabolism in plants and recondensation of respiratory water vapour in animals, confer obvious advantages in the desert environment.
8. The ability to excrete nitrogen and electrolytes in a highly concentrated form is of great importance in conserving water.
9. Reduction of metabolic rate during diapause, aestivation, torpor or merely through significant reductions in thyroid activity ensures slow usage of stored nutrients and low water turnover rates.
10. Ruminant-type digestion, which allows the transformation of cellulose to fatty acids and the synthesis of B vitamins and amino acids with the aid of symbiotic micro-organisms, has important advantages in certain desert situations.
11. There is, as first pointed out by Hadley (1972), a striking similarity in the adaptive responses of desert plants and animals. Moreover, their survival in the desert is often due to several favourable adaptations acting in concert, rather than a single adaptation.
12. Suitable behaviour by animals can ameliorate the exigencies of the desert environment very significantly.

Finally, one is again impressed by the fact that the desert environment, because of the high intensity of solar radiation and periodic pulses of food and water, is most suitable for the small ectotherm. It is no surprise therefore that the most abundant animals in the desert are arthropods and reptiles.

Chapter 6

Reproduction in the desert environment

In previous chapters we have described how flexibly plants can adapt their reproductive patterns to the desert environment. They can survive for years as seeds in this unpredictable environment and then, as a result of an ephemeral existence, they can escape long periods of unfavourable conditions. Similarly, geophytes and other perennial plants can store water and nutrients in underground storage organs during long periods of dormancy. The environmental cue for inducing germination in the ephemerals and new growth in the perennials is, naturally, sufficient rain. As expected, a threshold amount of rain is required to prevent a false start and desiccation after insufficient rain. The threshold amount required will be influenced by various climatic variables and differs between different desert environments. We have, for example, found that 20 mm of rain during late summer is required in the central Namib Desert for the germination of annual grasses and most perennial shrubs. The situation in certain other deserts is, however, more complex than a simple response to sufficient rain. In the Sonoran Desert most plants appear to respond to threshold amounts of rain which fall in the winter, thereby providing maximum growth and flowering during spring. During summer, when extremely high temperatures prevail, if the same amount of rain falls it is far less effective in eliciting growth and germination. Also, certain deep-rooted desert trees and large shrubs respond to a changing photoperiod or temperature gradient rather than to rain. Environmental cues for germination, growth and reproduction in desert plants can therefore consist of a complex sequence or association of climatic variables, including day-length and temperature as well as rainfall. Nevertheless, sufficient water remains the primary controlling factor in the periodicity of desert plants. The resistance of seeds to desiccation and their dispersion has been discussed in Chapter 3.

Animals, particularly vertebrate animals, do not possess the same potential flexibility as plants in coping with the irregular food and water supply of the desert. This is largely due to their inability to remain dormant for such extended periods. Their adaptations are therefore probably more complex and subtle and, for this reason, we shall concentrate on animal adaptations in this chapter.

Physiological principles

The periodicity of seasonal breeding in desert animals is controlled by a series of complex interactions between certain environmental cues and a sequence of delicately controlled physiological responses on the part of the animal. In this respect the central nervous system in vertebrates and the neurosecretory cells in arthropods fulfil an important integrating function. Let us examine a hypothetical desert mammal as an example to explain the sequence of physiological events involved.

Our mammal, the size of a ground squirrel, is too small to migrate over long distances to seek out new food resources and must by necessity survive on the resources within a fairly restricted home range. In view of the arid conditions prevailing in the area, these animals are obliged to survive on tubers and bulbs with a low protein content for most of the year. During spring, however, sporadic thunder-showers may occur in the area producing a flush of ephemeral new plant growth and an explosion of insect life which lasts for a period of 8–10 weeks. In order to exploit this short period of favourable nutrition, reproduction in this species has evolved into the following pattern.

During early spring the increasing photoperiod is sensed by both the male and female animals. This stimulus is conveyed via the central nervous system to the hypothalamus, which, because of its ability to secrete releasing hormones, plays an important integrating rôle in controlling subsequent physiological events. The photoperiod in this instance is known as the primary factor or cue. The reason why this species has evolved a dependence on this cue is that the sporadic rains, if they fall, always fall during the spring months and that the photoperiod is constant from year to year.

Once the hypothalamus has received the photoperiodic stimulus it will secrete luteinising hormone–releasing hormone (LH–RH) into the portal blood system, which links the hypothalamus to the anterior pituitary gland. This gland in turn will now produce just sufficient gonadotropic hormones (follicle-stimulating hormone and luteinising hormone) to stimulate the male and female gonads to recrudesce. This will involve a delicate interplay as well as feedback control between the hypothalamus, the pituitary and the sex hormones produced by the gonads. The details are beyond the scope of our discussion but the end result is that both the male and female reproductive tracts, which have been in a quiescent state for many months, are now slowly becoming functional again. The germinal epithelium of the male slowly recommences spermatogenesis and the interstitial cells start producing testosterone. The follicles in the ovaries of the female commence their growth and the increasing levels of oestrogenic hormones begin to stimulate growth and development of the uterus and mammary glands. Of equal importance are the effects of the male and female sex hormones on the behaviour of the two sexes. Sufficient testosterone will eventually manifest itself in suitable courtship behaviour and perhaps aggression in the male. Meanwhile increasing oestrogen levels in the blood of the female will eventually bring her into the so-called condition of oestrus, when the female is receptive to the male's advances and will allow copulation to take place. In our specific species of mammal it would, however, not be in their interest to proceed automatically from primary stimulation by the primary cue, in this case the photoperiod, to reproduction, because of the unpredictable nature of the rainfall. For this reason, in addition to their dependence on the photoperiod as a primary cue, they have also evolved a dependence on a secondary cue, namely the level of protein in their diet.

In other words the primary cue, the photoperiod, has brought the male and female animals into a state of what may be termed sub-threshold sexual activity. When sufficient rain falls and a sudden increase in dietary protein or some other nutrient occurs in fresh new vegetation, the absorbed nutrients in the circulation will provide the secondary cue for the hypothalamic-pituitary complex to initiate full sexual development, mating, gestation and lactation. This secondary cue may only be required by one of the sexes. For example, it may bring about courtship behaviour in the male and this behaviour, in turn, could be responsible for providing the secondary cue to the females. They would then attain full sexual activity and enter into a state of

oestrus. Alternatively, the females may be the sex that is sensitive to the secondary cue, producing suitable olfactory pheromones, which could stimulate final and full sexual activity in the males. In any event, whichever pattern is employed, the goal of synchronising reproduction with the most favourable environmental conditions has been achieved.

Once conception has taken place, foetal growth and development occurs rapidly in this particular species and again, through a delicate interplay of the hormones of the hypothalamus and pituitary, gestation is terminated after 4 weeks. A large number of altricial, or poorly developed, young are then born in well-protected underground nests. Suitable adjustments in the endocrine status of the females finally initiate lactation and the altricial young grow rapidly to become independent within 4–6 weeks. In this way the nutritional demands for foetal growth, particularly for protein, as well as the very high demand for protein and energy during lactation and the early growth of the young, are met during the most favourable season of the year.

In discussing our hypothetical mammal we have described only one particular pattern. There are many more variations on the same theme and their ecological significance will be discussed presently. For example the photoperiod, although the most reliable and consistent cue of all environmental factors, does not always serve as the primary cue. This is particularly true in the desert environment, where rainfall is erratically distributed and not related to the photoperiod. In some desert birds, for instance, the mere sight of rain is apparently sufficient to entrain the necessary endocrine changes required for reproduction. In other cases temperature or nutrition may act as primary cues while auditory stimuli, such as birdsong or vocalisations by amphibians and geckos, could provide secondary cues. Optical stimuli such as courtship behaviour, nest-building, the sight of secondary male sexual characters, as well as the chemical stimuli of pheromones, are equally important. Alternatively, the reproductive pattern of a particular animal may not require both primary and secondary cues. A single cue is frequently sufficient in animals with a very short sexual cycle. The reader should also not be left with the impression that the physiological knowledge of endocrine changes, accompanying seasonal breeding, is as superficial as our discussion has been. It is a most advanced science and involves the application of very refined techniques to unravel the complex interplay between the environment and the endocrine system of the animals being studied. An example of this complex interplay is provided in Fig. 6.1.

In the case of invertebrate animals there is a greater flexibility in reproductive patterns. This is largely because of their small size, which allows them to grow and reproduce rapidly, as well as their ability to enter long periods of diapause when their metabolic requirements are reduced to a minimum. Nevertheless, similar physiological principles still apply. When favourable environmental conditions occur, be they moisture, temperature, nutrition or length of day, the stimulus is sensed by the nervous system, and neurosecretory cells secrete the necessary humoral factors for either metamorphosis and/or reproduction. Moreover, as we shall discuss later, diapause in invertebrates can occur at various stages of their complex life cycle, which introduces even greater flexibility for synchronising reproduction with the erratic pulses of food and water, so typical of the desert environment.

Ecological and evolutionary considerations

It would be not only axiomatic but also trite to state that successful reproduction is

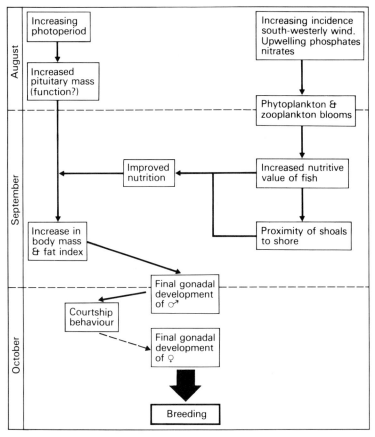

Fig. 6.1 Example of the complex interaction between environmental cues and seasonal breeding in a marine bird, the Cape cormorant, which breeds in large numbers on the coast of the Namib Desert. (Berry *et al.* 1979.)

essential for the survival of a *species*. Nevertheless, it is necessary to emphasise that both adults and offspring are involved, because so many recent discussions of this topic have tended to emphasise that seasonal breeding is synchronised for the sole purpose of ensuring survival of the offspring. While readily conceding that natural selection could rapidly remove the genotype of offspring, born outside the most favourable season of the year, from the gene pool, there are also other important factors to consider. For example, in mammals the various phases of reproduction which include courtship, mating, gestation, parturition and lactation could theoretically all be equally vulnerable to adverse environmental conditions. If a certain phase in the reproductive cycle is particularly vulnerable, we can expect that natural selection will ensure that it will take place at a time when conditions are optimal for its execution, while other less critical phases may of necessity occur during less favourable periods (Millar 1972). In addition, as Millar has indicated, various patterns of social behaviour may place constraints upon the reproductive rhythm employed by a particular species. In non-social animals parturition could theoretically be synchronised without any deleterious effects, whereas in a highly social species the synchronised arrival of a large number of offspring may disrupt the

social structure very severely. For the above reasons and others, such as predator evasion, an extremely wide variety of reproductive patterns has evolved in the animal kingdom. These include sexual and asexual reproduction, ovoparity, ovoviviparity, viviparity and marsupial reproduction. Also, the phylogenetic distribution of the various patterns makes it difficult to distinguish which are of monophyletic and which are of polyphyletic origin.

In addition to the seasonality of reproduction, there are also the quantitative aspects of reproduction to consider. Why do certain species produce thousands of offspring with a minimum of parental care, while others may produce a single offspring and invest heavily in parental care? Can we assume that animals are reproducing as rapidly as possible within the constraints of their biology and the environment, as suggested by Lack (1948), or are they breeding as slowly as they can as proposed by Baker (1938)? These questions have been the subject of lively debate among ecologists for many years and we can only briefly examine the most important factors involved.

If we assume that an organism is reproducing in a so-called ecological vacuum in which resources are unlimited, then the rate of population growth can be expressed as:

$$dN/dt = rN$$

where r = the biotic potential or innate biological capacity of that organism to increase.

The resources in all ecosystems are, however, limited and as these resources become progressively depleted, the ability to increase will decrease proportionally, as expressed by the Verhulst–Pearl equation:

$$\frac{dN}{dt} = rN \frac{(1-N)}{K}$$

where K = the carrying capacity of the habitat.

Under these circumstances, as pointed out by Callow (1978), the fitness of the population depends on the extent to which populations can share in the limited resources or, in terms of the above equation, maximise their own K. Callow is also of the opinion that in order to maximise K, parents must produce offspring that are competitively superior, which is likely to lead to an increase in body size of both parents and their young. Simultaneously, because reproduction represents a risk to the parents, there will probably also be a tendency to reduced reproductive effort.

The above considerations led to the concept of r-selected and K-selected species, proposed by MacArthur and Wilson (1967). Pianka (1970) has summarised the more important correlates of r- and K-selection (Table 6.1). From his summary it is evident that r-selection is associated with an unstable environment with unpredictable resources, catastrophic mortality, highly variable population size, rapid development, a short life span, small body size and high productivity. In contrast, K-selection is mostly correlated with the opposite conditions and characteristics. Although this concept is useful in analysing the evolution of reproductive patterns, relatively few species fit the extreme categories of r- and K-selection. We should rather visualise an r–K continuum, as suggested by Pianka (1970), and evaluate the position of a particular organism upon this continuum. If we now apply these concepts to the desert situation, with its unpredictable pulses of food and water, we could intuitively conclude that the desert environment would favour r-selection. This would seem to be the case as small arthropods make up the greatest proportion of endemic desert animals. The large vertebrates of the deserts

Table 6.1　*Certain correlates of* r- *and* K-*selection. (From Pianka 1970.)*

	r-*selection*	K-*selection*
Climate	Variable and/or unpredictable: uncertain	Fairly constant and/or predictable: more certain
Mortality	Often catastrophic, non-directed, density-independent	More directed, density-dependent
Population size	Variable in time, non-equilibrium; usually well below carrying capacity of environment; unsaturated communities or portions thereof; ecologic vacuums; recolonisation each year	Fairly constant in time, equilibrium; at or near carrying capacity of the environment; saturated communities; no recolonisation necessary
Intra- and interspecific competition	Variable, often lax	Usually keen
Relative abundance	Often does not fit MacArthur's broken stick model	Frequently fits the MacArthur model
Selection favours	1. Rapid development 2. High r_{max} 3. Early reproduction 4. Small body size 5. Semelparity: single reproduction	1. Slower development greater competitive ability 2. Lower resource thresholds 3. Delayed reproduction 4. Larger body size 5. Iteroparity: repeated reproductions
Length of life	Short, usually less than 1 year	Longer, usually more than 1 year
Leads to	Productivity	Efficiency

(*K*-selected) are often temporary visitors to the desert and their efficient locomotion allows them to migrate over long distances in search of new resources. As with most generalisations, however, there are many exceptions to this conclusion. For example, some desert tenebrionid beetles are surprisingly long-lived and reproduce comparatively slowly. Certain reptile species in the desert also tend more towards *K*-selection than *r*-selection. These exceptions possibly fit Murphy's (1968) concept of 'bet hedging'. When environmental conditions are unpredictable, as in the desert, the parent may have a better chance of surviving than the offspring, which could lead to reduced reproductive output per reproductive cycle but to more frequent breeding. This adaptation has been described as 'bet hedging'. Nevertheless, as we have previously emphasised, the desert environment favours the ectotherm with small body size for a variety of other physiological and ecological reasons. The relative abundance of *r*-selected species in the desert again fits fairly neatly into this pattern.

Finally, we must consider the important consequences of the cost of reproduction in the evolution of reproductive patterns. Animals with a short life span, that reproduce once and then die (semelparous), usually invest very heavily in reproductive effort when compared with iteroparous animals that are longer-lived and reproduce repeatedly. Iteroparity, as Callow (1978) has pointed out, provides an insurance against the mass loss of progeny at any one time and it is surprising that it has not evolved more frequently. Theoretically, then, the most successful reproductive pattern would be a long life span, high reproductive output and repeated breeding. The reason that this pattern has not evolved, apart from examples of certain endoparasites and domestic animals, is self-evident and lies in the high cost of reproduction and the fact that animals must use energy and nutrients for a host of activities other than reproduction. It is not surprising, therefore, that an inverse relationship has been established between reproductive output and repeated breeding within taxa (Callow 1978). We could, however, refine our examination of

a

b

a

b

Plate 4 Apart from water, the nature of the substrate is one of the most important abiotic factors influencing the structure and function of desert ecosystems. (*a*) A stony desert is contrasted with (*b*) the unstable, shifting sands of a dune system.

the cost of reproduction by posing the question of the relative cost of producing altricial and precocious young in birds and mammals. These considerations, together with the questions raised in the preceding discussion, can perhaps best be examined in their relationship to the desert environment by analysing specific examples.

Some examples

In Chapter 3 we discussed the remarkable changes which occur in temporary desert ponds after rain. These depressions, that have remained in an apparently lifeless condition for years on end, suddenly explode with life. Our discussion was, however, largely limited to a description of diapause in the phyllopods and their impressive resistance to high temperatures and desiccation. The environmental cues for hatching and the reproductive patterns of these animals must still be examined. As far as the cue for hatching is concerned no generalised statement can be made, because the cues appear to differ from species to species. Obviously rain is the primary cue, but in certain anostracans low O_2 tension triggers hatching, while in some conchostracans low O_2 tension and darkness will inhibit hatching. Therefore those eggs, buried deeply under silt or sand, will remain unhatched until disturbed by the next inundation of rain. In ostracods and cladocerans, which are generally much smaller with a very short generation time, hatching appears to be delayed until a few days after rain. When suitable conditions have persisted for a reasonable time, the probability increases that conditions will remain favourable sufficiently long for them to complete their life cycles. Temperature also seems to play an important rôle in regulating hatching. In fact Belk (1977) considers temperature to be the overriding environmental factor controlling hatching in Arizonan anostracans.

Growth rate in phyllopods is extremely rapid with a very short larval life. For example, Day (1980) has shown that the branchiopod *Triops namaquensis* can reach a carapace length of 9 mm within 6 days at 30 °C. The adults, as expected, are remarkably tolerant to changes in pH, temperature, O_2 tension and salinity. Parthenogenesis is known to occur in at least some species of all orders of branchiopods. Generally they exhibit parthenogenesis as long as conditions are favourable and the eggs, produced in this way, are often not able to withstand desiccation. Males are produced as the pond begins to dry and the eggs produced from sexual reproduction are resistant to desiccation and, therefore, suitable for the long diapause phase. The number of eggs produced by crustaceans in ephemeral waters is very large. Takahashi (1977) has estimated, for example, that a *Triops* female will produce several thousand eggs in her lifetime.

The phyllopods of ephemeral desert ponds are, therefore, an excellent example of *r*-selection with their short life span and high reproductive output in a very unstable environment. It appears also that they have escaped the major hazard of this reproductive pattern, namely mass mortality, because of the differential hatching of the eggs. The mechanism whereby some eggs delay hatching is unknown but it may be merely due to the random distribution of the eggs within a pond. For example, eggs are dropped by females at different levels in the pond and those settling near the edge will only become inundated during rains of similar or greater magnitude. Also some eggs will be buried more deeply than others where light and O_2 tension are reduced. These may not hatch until a subsequent rainy season, or until the bottom layer of the pond is mechanically disturbed, for example, by a large vertebrate drinking from the pond. It is even possible that eggs from different females may be genetically variable with regard to threshold cues for hatching, but this has not been tested (Day 1980). In any event, whatever the cause of delayed hatching, it acts as an

important insurance policy against the hazards of the *r*-selected reproductive pattern.

Desert insects, with their characteristically short life span and high reproductive output, also tend towards *r*-selection. The complex life cycles of holometabolous insects, however, allow these animals great flexibility in delaying certain phases of the cycle by entering diapause during unfavourable periods. In certain species, for example, individuals may remain as prepupae for as long as 13 years. This flexibility can often compensate for the disadvantages inherent in *r*-selection, but not all insects have evolved r_{max} reproduction. In the Namib Desert dunes, plant litter accumulates in large cushions on or near the surface of the sand. This detritus does not decompose rapidly and, as it is continuously being redistributed by the wind, it provides a stable source of energy to the tenebrionid beetles living there. Water is provided by periodic fog condensation and under these conditions many of these tenebrionids continue to reproduce almost continuously during prolonged dry periods at a moderate rate. They are also surprisingly long-lived (at least 3 years). Admittedly these are unusually stable conditions for a desert, but this example does serve to caution against the simplistic categorisation of all desert insects as being *r*-selected.

Desert scorpions, with their remarkably long and stable evolutionary history, have also not become adapted to *r*-selection, in spite of the unpredictable nature of the desert environment and their relatively small body size. Instead they grow fairly slowly, often reproduce seasonally, are ovoviviparous and invest in a modicum of parental care. Polis and Farley (1979) found that the desert scorpion, *Paruroctonus mesaensis*, matured at 19–24 months. Mating occurs during the summer in southern California (May through October) and gestation lasts 10–14 months. The first surface appearance of the newborn is synchronous and occurred in August for 5 consecutive years. They also found that, on average, 19.9 young/female survive to appear on the surface but that the population biomass of newborn was positively correlated with precipitation and vegetation cover. This is clearly not an *r*-selected reproductive pattern and, in view of the adults' superior survival potential, could perhaps best be classed as 'bet hedging'. The fact that cannibalism occurs in scorpions substantiates this view.

A comparison of the reproductive patterns employed by desert reptiles reveals a fairly wide spectrum upon the *r–K* continuum. Some lizards have a short life span with relatively high reproductive output, while others have become adapted to a slower reproductive rate and longer life span. Tinkle (1969) has also shown that shorter-lived lizards are at greater risk to accident and predation, presumably because more frequent courtship, copulation and oviposition makes them more conspicuous. Life span is, however, not the only factor influencing the reproductive patterns of desert lizards. Climate and the nature of the habitat are equally important. In deserts with sharply defined seasons of low and high temperature, reproduction tends to be seasonal. In areas such as the fog belt of the Namib dunes, with a fairly stable climate, reproduction in several lizard species is, however, aseasonal. Climate and habitat also appear to have a strong influence on the mode of reproduction. For example, the sidewinding adder, *Bitis peringueyi*, is exclusively restricted to a sand-dune habitat and it is no surprise to find that this species is ovoviviparous, in view of the unstable nature of the substrate. In this respect an interesting comparison can also be made between the desert chameleon *Chamaeleo namaquensis* and its mesic congener *C. pumilus pumilus*. The desert species is exposed to a wide range of temperatures and the habitat affords little in the way of a thermal refuge. In fact, Burrage (1973) has measured body temperatures ranging from just above zero to almost 40 °C in *C. namaquensis* within a single day, hardly

suitable conditions for embryonic development. In contrast, *C. p. pumilus* maintains body temperatures within a much narrower range in a well-vegetated mesic habitat. These environmental considerations therefore appear to be mainly responsible for viviparity in *C. p. pumilus* and oviparity in the desert species *C. namaquensis*. The latter species lays its eggs some 13 cm below the desert substrate where temperature and moisture conditions are remarkably stable.

Reproductive patterns in desert reptiles are therefore very variable and cannot be simply related to *r*- and *K*-selection criteria. Rather the animal's whole ecology should be considered. This approach has been used by Congdon *et al.* (1978) in evaluating parental investment and the comparative reproductive energetics in bisexual and unisexual lizards. Their conclusions (summarised in Table 6.2) suggest

Table 6.2 *Flow diagram comparing the correlates of unisexual and sexual reproduction in cnemidophorine lizards. (Adapted from Congdon* et al. *1978.)*

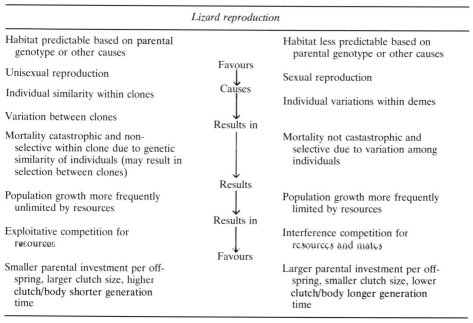

Lizard reproduction	
Habitat predictable based on parental genotype or other causes	Habitat less predictable based on parental genotype or other causes
	Favours
Unisexual reproduction	Sexual reproduction
	Causes
Individual similarity within clones	
	Individual variations within demes
Variation between clones	
	Results in
Mortality catastrophic and non-selective within clone due to genetic similarity of individuals (may result in selection between clones)	Mortality not castastrophic and selective due to variation among individuals
	Results
Population growth more frequently unlimited by resources	Population growth more frequently limited by resources
	Results in
Exploitative competition for resources	Interference competition for resources and mates
	Favours
Smaller parental investment per offspring, larger clutch size, higher clutch/body shorter generation time	Larger parental investment per offspring, smaller clutch size, lower clutch/body longer generation time

that in an unpredictable environment sexual reproduction is favoured. This is associated with larger parental investment per offspring, smaller clutch size and longer generation time. In a more predictable environment unisexual reproduction is favoured with the opposite correlates.

Reproduction in birds is generally controlled by the changing photoperiod but, because of the unseasonal nature of rainfall in deserts, it has become popular to assume that desert birds employ rainfall rather than the photoperiod as a primary cue or *Zeitgeber* for synchronising reproduction. Nevertheless, as Serventy (1971) has indicated, this viewpoint has largely arisen from observations obtained from the arid areas of Australia. Many studies in central and north-western Australia have shown how reproduction is associated with the irregular rainfall pattern, so typical of these areas. In some cases local thundershowers permit breeding in very circumscribed areas, measuring only 7 × 2 km, while the birds in surrounding areas remain inactive. The rapidity with which these desert birds respond to rain is also most impressive.

Immelman (1963) cites the example of the blackfaced woodswallow, *Artamus cinereus*, which started courtship behaviour within minutes after rain began to fall. The first copulation occurred 2 hr later and the birds began to build nests the next day. Although this example and many others may lead one to accept the hypothesis that desert birds have 'broken free' from photoperiodic synchronisation, it is still necessary to examine the previous endocrine history of these birds. For example, it is possible that other cues, such as photoperiod or temperature, may have acted as primary cues while rainfall merely fulfils the function of a secondary cue. None of the field studies was carried out in sufficient detail to confirm this. Also, Serventy (1971) has emphasised that, although many examples of rainfall-induced breeding have been recorded in arid regions of Australia, this is certainly not the case in all the deserts of the world. Maclean (1974), however, is of the opinion that most birds of the arid zones in Ecuador, southern Africa, Eritrea, Somalia and elsewhere in North African deserts rely on rainfall and its effects for initiating and maintaining breeding activity. Rainfall not only provides an adequate food supply but also material for nest-building and the necessary cover and framework for nesting sites. Nevertheless, Maclean (1974) also gives examples of important exceptions to the above rule where breeding is seasonal. He makes the interesting point that in extremely arid areas (< 50 mm), where rainfall is very erratic, rainfall cannot be used advantageously as a *Zeitgeber*. An example of the latter is the bustard or koshaan, *Eupodotis vigorsii rueppelli*, in the Namib Desert. It would seem then that simplistic analyses of the breeding biology of desert birds are not realistic and, again, consideration of the total ecology of the organisms in question is more appropriate.

Examples of the rather complex interaction between environmental factors and the organism in shaping the breeding biology of desert birds are to be found in the reproduction of three species of ground-nesting birds, inhabiting the Namib Desert. They also differ markedly in body size and feeding behaviour. The ostrich, *Struthio camelus*, weighing approximately 90 kg, breeds in response to summer rains by laying its large eggs in a simple depression on the soil surface. The rain causes the fresh growth of ephemeral and perennial grasses, which form the major portion of the diet of the ostriches and their precocious chicks. The parents protect the eggs from the intense insolation and high surface temperatures by incubating them and simultaneously engaging in vigorous thermoregulation. Incubation during the day is, therefore, in effect designed to keep the eggs cool and the large size of the birds, and consequently their greater thermal inertia, facilitates this procedure. In contrast, the sandgrouse, *Pterocles namaqua*, which also lays its eggs in the simplest of scrapes on the soil surface, weighs only 180 g but as a result of its low thermal inertia, cannot nest successfully when soil surface temperatures are too high (Figs. 6.2 and 6.3). Sandgrouse therefore favour the cooler winter months for breeding and are able to do so because their food supply, small, very cryptic seeds scattered on the surface of the desert plain, is not immediately dependent on rain. On the other hand, Gray's lark *Ammomanes grayi*, never drinks water, weighs only 20 g and is dependent on sufficient insect life for its altricial young. Like the ostrich and the sandgrouse, it is a ground-nesting bird but, because of its very low thermal inertia, is obliged to expend considerable energy in building an elaborate nest. This is usually excavated on the southern (shade) side of a grass tuft or beneath an overhanging rock and is well insulated with grass to reduce conductance of heat from the soil surface to the eggs. These precautions, together with the bird's efficient thermoregulation, allow it to keep nest temperatures at ground level within reasonable limits. This is possible even when the birds nest after summer rains when soil surface temperatures are very high (Fig. 6.4). These examples illustrate how complex interactions between diet, body

Fig. 6.2 (A) The ground-nesting sandgrouse shades its eggs during the hottest hours of the day and reduces the radiation load by erecting the mantle feathers. (B) By facing into the wind and raising itself above the nest, convective cooling of the shaded eggs is facilitated. (Dixon *et al.* 1978.)

size, *Zeitgeber* and nesting behaviour can be, as well as the desirability of assessing an animal's total ecology when analysing its breeding biology.

The above comparison also raises the question of the relative advantages, if any, of producing precocious as opposed to altricial chicks. Ricklefs (1974) has reviewed the energetic cost of reproduction in birds in great detail and concludes that natural selection will usually favour precocity, because independent feeding by the chicks usually increases the number of chicks that can be raised. Precocity, however, is primarily determined by the kind of food resources available, such as vegetation, seeds or insect larvae that demand relatively little strength or skill to capture and ingest. This analysis fits the feeding behaviour of the precocious ostrich and sandgrouse chicks, which feed on vegetation and seeds. In contrast, Gray's lark feeds on insects, which require considerable skill to capture, and it therefore raises altrical young.

Small desert mammals, particularly rodents, tend towards *r*-selection. Their gestation and lactation periods are short and, therefore, they do not require a long

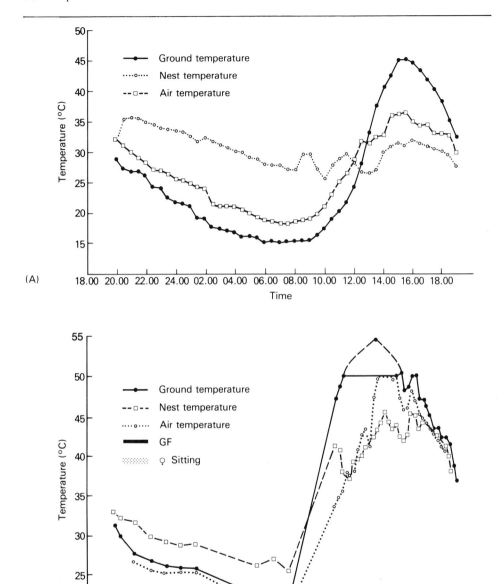

Fig. 6.3 (A) When soil surface temperatures remain below 50 °C, the shading of eggs and thermoregulatory behaviour of the sandgrouse is sufficient to prevent overheating of the eggs. (B) When soil surface temperatures exceed 50 °C the embryos do not survive. For this reason these desert birds breed mostly in the cooler winter months. (GF = gular fluttering.)

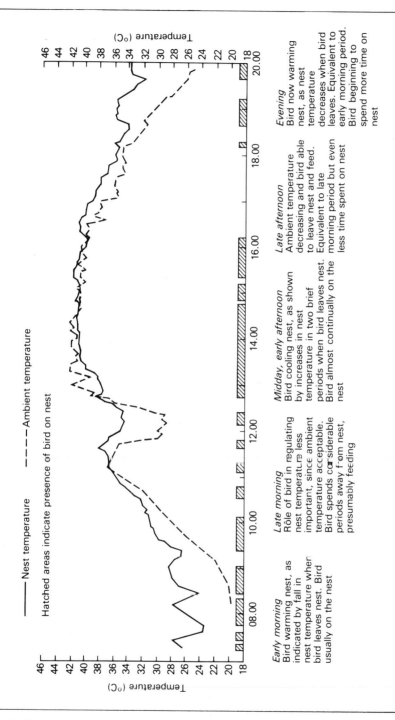

Fig. 6.4   Unlike the sandgrouse and ostrich, Gray's lark (20 g), because of its very low thermal inertia, must insulate its nest from high soil-surface temperatures. This precaution, together with its efficient thermoregulation, prevents overheating of the eggs.

period between the sensing of the primary and secondary cues for breeding. Rainfall, with its attendant increase in both the quantity and quality of vegetation, is usually the trigger for increased breeding and populations frequently increase explosively after good rains. In this respect the quality of the vegetation should be stressed and the conclusion that specific compounds, perhaps proteins, in the fresh new growth are involved in triggering reproduction is gaining wider acceptance. Again there are important exceptions and in deserts where very cold winters prevail, temperature can act as an additional constraint upon breeding. A most unusual exception is provided by the naked mole rat, *Heterocephalus glaber*, which occurs in the arid regions of Kenya, Ethiopia and Somalia. Jennifer Jarvis (1978) has established that a definite caste system exists in these colonial animals: the first discovery of a truly eusocial mammal. In these colonies reproduction is limited to a single female which is larger than the other females and is presumably the most genetically fit. Reproduction in other females and in most of the males is suppressed and these animals assume the rôle of the worker caste, enlarging the burrow and foraging for scarce food resources. The reproductively active members are therefore spared the costly process of foraging and can, as a result, channel most of their energy into reproduction. Jarvis has suggested that this unusual reproductive pattern has evolved in response to the limited food supplies which consist of scattered underground tubers. Reproduction appears to be aseasonal which is not surprising, in view of the constant darkness and uniform temperatures which prevail in the burrow system, and because the food resource, unlike surface vegetation, is slow to respond to rainfall.

The large desert mammals are obviously K-selected. Their long gestation periods prevent them from evolving a dependence on rainfall as an environmental cue for seasonal breeding. By the time parturition occurs the beneficial effects of erratic rainfall may well have disappeared. For this reason many of the large mammals, which breed seasonally, appear to rely on the photoperiod as a primary cue. Their ability to migrate efficiently over long distances can also compensate for unfavourable local conditions at the time of parturition. Not all large mammals are seasonal breeders, however, and there are several interesting examples of the influence of social structure on the breeding patterns of these animals. Blue wildebeest, which inhabit the semi-arid savannas of Africa, congregate in very large herds with a loose social structure. Parturition in this species is surprisingly well synchronised (3–4 weeks), so much so that the normal predators of wildebeest, lion and hyena, are unable to capture too many of the vulnerable calves. In this way a significant number of offspring always survives. In contrast, Burchell's zebra, *Equus burchelli*, which shares the same habitat with the blue wildebeest and is preyed upon by the same predators, produces young throughout the year in Kenya. The marked difference between these two species is most likely due to the much tighter social structure which exists in the fairly small family groups of zebra. If the zebra were all to calve simultaneously, the co-operation which exists for alerting and protecting the cohesive family group from predation may break down. Similarly, synchronised seasonal breeding in a social species such as the chacma baboon would severely disrupt their highly structured social organisation. In the latter case, the disadvantages of producing young during unfavourable conditions are largely compensated for by migration and particularly by very flexible feeding behaviour. In this respect Hamilton *et al.* (1978) have shown that, when chacma baboons and oryx compete for food supplies in a dry river bed of the Namib Desert, the baboons are able to process toxic and unpalatable foods, thereby rendering them palatable and broadening their resource base.

Further examples of the effect of social structure on breeding patterns are provided by the Kalahari lion and the wild Cape hunting dog. These animals rely on close co-operation when hunting in cohesive prides or packs. In the case of the hunting dogs, after returning from a distant hunt, food is frequently regurgitated by several members of the pack to feed the pups of a single breeding female. Not surprisingly, neither of these species has evolved synchronous seasonal breeding.

The question of the adaptive value and relative energetic cost of precocious and altricial breeding was raised when discussing birds. Similar questions could be raised in respect of mammals. Why, for example, do some mammals produce a large number of altricial young while others produce a few, very precocious young after longer gestation periods? The answers to these questions are not yet clear and involve a complex of interacting factors. For example, the energetic cost of providing nutrition to the young via the placenta *in utero* is probably somewhat less than via lactation, which requires additional synthesis of nutrients. This difference is, however, not likely to be critical. More important are considerations such as the availability of a suitable substrate in the natural habitat, for constructing well-protected nesting sites for altricial young and the amount, nature and distance of the food resource. Evasion of predators and social structure are again important considerations, as is body size, because the large K-selected vertebrates must produce precocious young that can escape from predators almost immediately after birth. In small r-selected mammals, however, unlike birds, selection will favour the production of altricial young because a larger number of individuals can be produced per litter. We could perhaps then tentatively conclude that in view of the high surface temperatures and low humidity in the desert, small mammals are in any event obliged to excavate elaborate burrow systems to provide a favourable micro-environment. These burrows simultaneously provide a suitable environment for constructing well-protected nests for raising altricial young, and r-selection criteria would then naturally favour altricial reproduction.

Probably the most unusual breeding pattern found in arid areas is that exhibited by marsupials. In the kangaroo, copulation and fertilisation occur shortly after parturition. After the embryonic joey has completed its hazardous journey to the pouch and become attached to the mammary gland, further development of the new blastocyst is arrested. The blastocyst remains in this quiescent state until the joey is no longer attached to the mammary gland, whereupon it immediately begins to develop and, after a short time, parturition of a second 'embryonic' joey occurs. This pattern has great adaptive value in arid environments with an unpredictable food supply. For example, if the joey were to perish due to unfavourable environmental conditions, immediate development of the next generation can begin without the necessity of a protracted oestrous cycle, the finding of a suitable mate and elaborate courtship ritual.

It would seem then that body size, the social structure, predation and food supply are the major determinants in the evolution of the breeding patterns of mammals. The field has been reviewed by Sadlier (1969) and Millar (1972).

Chapter 7

Structure of some typical desert communities

In Chapter 1 we used the amount of precipitation within an area as a criterion to define a desert. Although this is suitable for defining deserts as a whole, when one wishes to compare typical communities found in the various deserts, other criteria must also be considered. Two of the most important additional factors are the distribution of the precipitation through the year and the substrate upon which it falls.

Rainfall in deserts may occur (1) mainly in summer, (2) mainly in winter, (3) at two distinct times during the year, (4) throughout the year or, (5) only very occasionally, at any time, as episodic rain in the extreme desert areas (Fig. 7.1). Moreover, as amount of rainfall decreases, its regularity and predictability decrease also. Most contiguous desertic areas are large enough to experience different periods of rainfall in different parts of a single desert. For example in the northern Sahara, what little rain occurs, falls in winter. In the central Sahara rainfall is aseasonal and almost absent, while in the southern Sahara rain only occurs in the summer months.

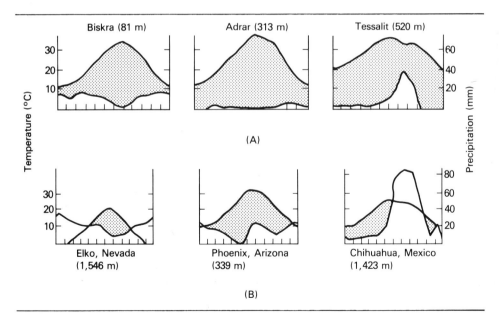

Fig. 7.1 Simplified climate diagrams from (A) the northern central and southern Sahara, and (B) the Great Basin, Sonoran and Chihuahuan deserts of North America. (After Walter 1971.) Divisions on the abscissa indicate the months from January to December. The stippled areas indicate periods of water stress.

100

In contrast, the southern hemisphere deserts, e.g. the Australian deserts, the Atacama and Peruvian deserts of South America and the Namib of southern Africa, experience more summer rainfall in their northern reaches and more winter rainfall towards the south. In North America, winter rainfall occurs in the northerly located Great Basin and in the westernmost Mojave Desert. Two rainfall periods occur in the centrally located Sonoran Desert and summer rainfall predominates towards the east in the more tropical Chihuahuan Desert. These different rainfall regimes normally result in different types of dominant vegetation.

Although not a hard-and-fast rule, arid and semi-arid regions which experience summer rainfall tend to support a plant community in which grasses are an important component. Grasslands are of special significance in some deserts, for example the Namib, where they provide most of the wind-borne plant detritus upon which many invertebrate species depend. Summer grasslands also figure prominently in the southern Sahara, the semi-arid Mitchell grass plains of Australia (Walter 1971) and the northern Namib. In Australia Mott (1972) notes that annuals which are summer germinating are largely grasses, while after winter rains dicotyledons predominate. In contrast, succulents often dominate where there are two short rainy seasons each year. Examples are the Karoo of southern Africa and the Sonoran Desert, both of which are situated in a transition zone between summer and winter rainfall.

Seasonality of the water source in deserts also has a variable effect when the source of water is fog. In the South American coastal deserts of Peru and Chile precipitating fog occurs mainly in winter. On the slopes of the foothills a dense vegetation develops for the winter months of each year at elevations between 300 and 800 m where fog-water precipitation is greatest. In this vegetation woody plants as well as geophytes are present among the dominant herbaceous species. However, fog in the Namib Desert on the coast of south-western Africa is more evenly distributed throughout the year. Here fog-water is important for at least two perennial plant species, growing in the dunes, and for a number of succulents growing on low, rocky hill slopes where fog-water is concentrated by run-off.

This varying response to different rainfall regimes is partly, if not entirely, based upon the manner in which nutrients and water are stored to allow survival during prolonged dry periods (Noy-Meir 1973). Succulents persist through dry periods by accumulating a large internal water reserve. This water reserve will, however, not last indefinitely and relatively regular replenishment is required. It is for this reason that succulents flourish where rainfall occurs in two distinct seasons of the year or where fog is a regular phenomenon. In contrast, the nutrient reserve of annuals lies in the seeds. This store of energy and nutrients may often persist for decades until sufficient rainfall causes germination.

Grass occurs more frequently with summer rainfall. In the Namib Desert, where we have gained most of our desert experience, grass grows in response to smaller amounts of rainfall (< 10 mm) than do dicotyledons (~ 30 mm), although both respond to the late summer rains. The grasses are all C_4 species which are able to grow rapidly in all periods and latitudes, with high radiation inputs. This gives them a competitive advantage over the mainly C_3 dicotyledonous species. In winter the situation is reversed because the reduction in evaporation would result in greater availability of water for germination and growth. The reduced radiation could also place C_4 plants at a disadvantage.

Substrate is the second factor with a marked effect on the type of plant community found in deserts. This is because of a strong influence of substrate on water regimes. Substrate may even be responsible for the development of a desert in areas where rainfall appears to be sufficient to support a more luxuriant community. Examples of

these edaphic deserts are to be found in the 'thirst land' of the Kalahari of southern Africa where a deep sand layer prevents the accumulation of surface water, and in parts of the interior of Australia on the Nullarbor Plain, where lack of surface water is the result of effective drainage by an extensive karstland plateau (Walter 1971).

The effects of substrate on differential water-holding capacities of sand, rocky hills and the various desert soils are readily observed in any desert area. The more sandy soils, often found in dry watercourses as well as dunes, store more water and often support more vegetation than surrounding gravel or stony plains. A good example of the effect of sand is to be found in the sandy loess soils of the Negev. Loess is an aeolian soil common in Asia and the Middle East. When loess subsoil is protected against excessive evaporation by a superficial layer of sand, it can be very productive (Zohary 1973). Near rocky hills or outcrops the presence of bare rock surfaces effectively increases the water catchment surface and smaller amounts of rainfall may support a greater than expected vegetation cover. It is the gravel plains of low relief, with limited water storage and concentrating capacities, that often support the lowest standing biomass in a desert.

Experience has shown us that when most people think of deserts it is a vision of sand dunes or succulents. Although the sand dunes of Libya towering over 300 m high and the giant saguaro cactus of the Sonoran Desert are indeed spectacular, they represent only a small fraction of the possible desert landscapes. As a detailed classification of deserts would require endless discussion, we have selected only a few examples to illustrate the range of communities rather than attempt to cover all the deserts of the world. Something of the variety of deserts can be seen in Figures 7.2–7.5.

The Namib Desert

Situated on the south-western coast of southern Africa, the Namib lies in the zone

Fig. 7.2 Maktesh Ramon in the Negev Desert, Israel.

influenced by the dry, subsiding air masses of the sub-tropical anticyclones (McGinnies 1979). In the central Namib, the most arid portion of the southern Africa warm arid zone (Leistner 1979), desert sand dunes up to 300 m high (Fig. 7.3), gravel plains, rocky hills and dry watercourses, situated in close proximity,

Fig. 7.3   Unvegetated dune crests.

experience similar amounts of rainfall and fog-water precipitation. They therefore provide us with a series of good examples of the different interactions between substrate and rainfall. The effect of the substrate in this area is very clear-cut; different species of plants are limited to the dunes, to the gravel plains, low hills or watercourses. Overlap of species occurs only where there is an overlap of substrate material, for example on accumulations of wind-blown sand on the hills. The effects of varying rainfall or fog-water precipitation are·less abrupt but become obvious across the narrow width of the central Namib.

The gradual increase in elevation, only 1 000 m in 100 km, clarifies relationships between precipitation and plant community, which would be obscured in an area of greater relief. Near the coast in the western Namib, rain is infrequent (annual average precipitation is less than 5 mm at Pelican Point, Walvis Bay) and fog is the main water source. In the dunes two perennial fog-using plant species occur but only infrequently. The largest diversity of perennial vegetation occurs on the low, rocky inselbergs where fog-water run-off supports a succulent vegetation. Watercourses are devoid of vegetation except following rain. On the gravel plains lichens, dwarf shrubs (e.g. *Arthraerua lubnitzia* and *Zygophyllum stapffii*) and *Welwitschia mirabilis* constitute the only perennial growth (Fig. 7.4). The distribution of *A. lubnitzia* provides an interesting example of 'diffuse' vegetation (Monod 1954), suggesting that despite the minimal rainfall, this area is not an extreme desert. The only possible explanation must lie in the use of fog-water as a moisture source to alleviate the extreme aridity. A sparse grassland (*Stipagrostis* spp.) develops after

Fig. 7.4   Dwarf shrubs in the coastal fog zone on the Namib Desert plains.

approximately 20 mm of rain has fallen over a short time span, an irregular event occurring less than once a decade.

Forty to eighty kilometres inland the average rainfall increases (15 mm at 56 km inland) and fog is still frequent. Here the dunes support up to ten plant species and the standing biomass is greater. This vegetation occurs mainly on the dune slopes as a result of the water-storing characteristics of dune sand and the instability of the dune crests. The dry watercourses of the plains support several perennial shrubs (*Zygophyllum stapffii* and *Salsola* sp.) and the occasional stunted tree (e.g. *Acacia reficiens* and *Euclea pseudebenus*). They thus provide an example of 'contracted' vegetation formation, which is to be expected in an extreme desert area (Monod 1954). In the rocky areas rainfall run-off supports a few small trees, perennial shrubs and woody succulents. The plains are generally bare except following rain, when a grassland composed of mainly *Stipagrostis* spp. develops.

The advent of rain in this marginal area causes dramatic fluctuations of standing biomass in all habitats. For example, on the dune slopes an increase of 56-fold was measured following one rainfall event (Seely and Louw 1980). Variations from year to year as large as this are not to be found in higher rainfall areas.

One hundred kilometres east of the coast on the 100 mm rainfall isohyet, fog occurs very infrequently. Here, because of the increased storage of rain-water, the dunes support a much denser cover of grasses (mainly *Stipagrostis* spp., *Eragrostis spinosa*, *Asthenatherum glaucum*) and barren dune crests are reduced in area. Several dicotyledonous species grow in numbers. In the dry watercourses of the plains, where water is stored, trees (*Acacia erioloba*, *A. reficiens*, *Boscia albitrunca*, *B. foetida*, *Maerua schinzi*, *Moringa ovalifolium*) and perennial shrubs are common. The rocky hills also support a number of tree, shrub and large succulent species (*Aloe dichotoma*, *A. namibensis*, *Euphorbia virosa*, *Commiphora* spp.). The plains support a grassland (predominantly *Stipagrostis* spp.), which is dependent on the late

summer rains. Dicotyledonous species are somewhat more common here than on the plains further west where rainfall is less. In the vicinity of the 100 mm isohyet, the perennial vegetation continues to exhibit a 'contracted' growth pattern. It is only further inland, where the rainfall averages more than 150–200 mm a year, that perennial vegetation exhibits a 'diffuse' growth pattern.

Crossing this rain/fog gradient, perpendicular to the coast, are large ephemeral rivers with headwaters located outside the desert. An almost yearly surface flow results in a permanent supply of underground water and subsequent independence of the local rainfall. Hence the riverine vegetation is similar from east to west throughout their desert reaches. These watercourses also represent a series of linear oases important for animal movement (Fig. 7.5).

Fig. 7.5 Occasional floods carry water from higher rainfall regions into the desert. Sossusvlei, Namib Desert.

The effects of climatic factors, other than precipitation, on the community structure of deserts have as yet not received sufficient attention to draw any definite conclusions. Nevertheless, maximum and minimum temperatures, annual temperature variations and the effect of prevailing winds on plant growth and animal activity have important influences on shaping community structure.

South American coastal deserts

The coastal deserts of South America, the Atacama and Peruvian deserts, should be very similar to the Namib by virtue of their parallel geographic situations on the west coast of a southern hemisphere continent. They are both affected by dry, subsiding air masses, with cold currents present offshore (Lyndolph 1957). Indeed, the causes of aridity and the overall climate are similar, but there are several distinct differences, which significantly affect the ecology of these two deserts.

In the Peruvian and Atacama deserts the fog, known as the *garua* or *camanchaca*, is seasonal, thus affecting the vegetation only in the winter months (Ellenberg 1958). This fog vegetation, the *loma* vegetation, does not have the many succulent species that are present in the fog-influenced vegetation of the Namib. The *loma* vegetation is well developed with relatively discrete upper and lower boundaries because of the steepness of the hills where the fog is intercepted. These two factors, the seasonality of the fog and the steep relief of the South American deserts, have resulted in an ecological pattern very different from that observed in the Namib (Fig. 7.6). However, at an isolated locality, Paposo, on the coast of northern Chile, Rundel (1976) described a situation where the hills rise steeply within 1 km from the coast. Here, because of the proximity to the coast, moist, foggy conditions are experienced daily in winter but also intermittently in summer, thus supporting a flourishing succulent vegetation.

Sand dunes are of localised distribution on the South American west coast and, in contrast to the Namib, are not known to support an endemic vegetation restricted only to this substrate. The proximity of the Andes ensures an annual flow of water along the numerous watercourses dissecting the narrow coastal desert plain. Also, because of the narrowness of the coastal plain, the extensive grasslands, which border the Namib dunes in some years, are absent in the Atacama and Peruvian deserts. This, in turn, has resulted in less plant litter accumulating in these dunes than

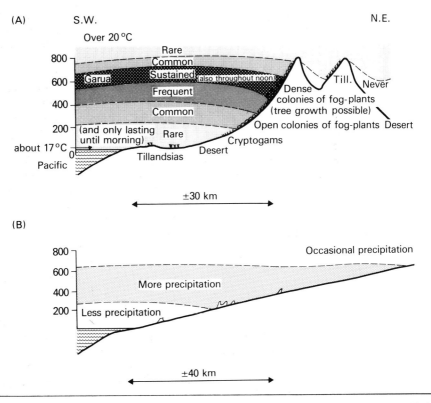

Fig. 7.6   Diagram of the distribution of fog relative to the land-forms (A) in Peru, and (B) the Namib. (A) is modified from Ellenberg (1958).

in the Namib dunes. It is perhaps for this reason that far simpler animal communities exist in the Peruvian dunes than in the Namib.

Of particular interest is the bromeliad, *Tillandsia* spp. which occurs commonly in the Peruvian Desert and is the only true vascular fog plant known (Walter 1976). Nevertheless, non-vascular fog plants, the lichens, are important in both coastal desert systems (Rundel 1978). The most barren desert landscape we have ever seen is to be found on the sand-covered salt deposits overlying hills of coastal Peru.

The Sahara

The largest desert in the world, the Sahara stretches from the Atlantic coast of North Africa eastward to the Red Sea. From there desertic conditions extend to India and northwards to the Gobi Desert of China. The Sahara extends from the Mediterranean in the north over 2 000 km south to grade into the savanna of the Sahel. The Sahara, similar to the Australian deserts, is influenced by the dry, subsiding air masses of sub-tropical anticyclones. The Mediterranean climate of the north gives way to predominantly irregular and scanty rainfall in the southern Sahara and then to the more regular summer rainfall of the Sahelian zone. From west to east across its 5 000–6 000 km expanse, the climate is uniform with the exception of the localized foggy area on the Atlantic coast (McGinnies 1979; Walter 1971). Gravel plains occupy about 68 per cent of the surface area and rocky mountains and stony desert pavement less than 10 per cent.

Although sand dunes occupy only 22 per cent of the surface area of the Sahara they represent some of the largest sand accumulations on earth, attaining heights of over 300 m. The dunes have been formed by differing wind regimes into a variety of shapes (Fig. 7.7). The final form is a result of a combination of factors including the amount of sand, vegetation, wind and physical barriers on the desert surface (McKee 1979). For example, barchan dunes form where sand is sparse and the wind blows from a single dominant direction. Barchans do not, however, comprise major portions of sand-dune seas. The formation of linear dunes is more complex and the processes less clearly understood, although they are one of the major dune types.

In the arid areas of the Sahara where average annual rainfall varies between 100–400 mm, annual productivity of above-ground phytomass varies from 200 kg ha^{-1} to 1 200 kg ha^{-1} (le Houérou 1979). Where the annual average rainfall is approximately 50–100 mm, the vegetation on the gravel plains is distributed in a 'diffuse' pattern. At approximately 20–50 mm average rainfall, the vegetation is in a 'contracted' pattern and restricted to depressions and dunes. At less than 20 mm average annual rainfall, perennial vegetation is restricted to major watercourses that have their catchment areas in adjacent areas outside the desert (Fig. 7.8). This variation of vegetation type with rainfall parallels, but on a much larger scale, the detailed example of the Namib Desert, if the effects of fog are excluded. Nevertheless, for its size, the Sahara is floristically impoverished and lichens and succulents are common only on the fog-rich Atlantic coast.

Animals in the Sahara have been greatly affected by the advent of man with his attendant domestic herds and agriculture. Many large animals have disappeared or become quite rare within the last several hundred years and consequently rodents, reptiles, birds and insects are the more common groups to be found. Today the productivity of the natural ecosystem is estimated to be 25 per cent of that possible under appropriate management (le Houérou 1979).

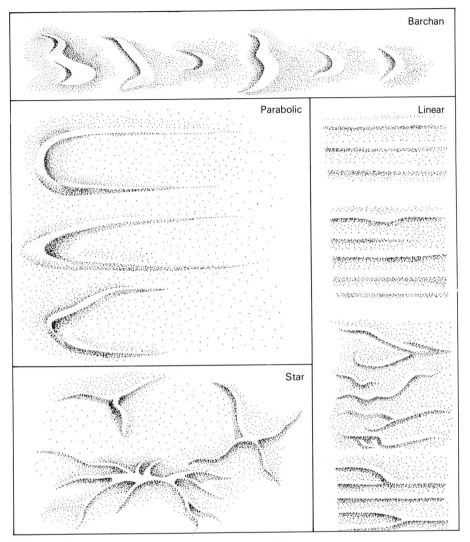

Fig. 7.7   Some major, typical dune patterns. (After McKee 1971.)

Central Asia

Deserts comprise more than half the area of Central Asia (Fig. 7.9). They extend from the Red and Caspian seas to the Yellow River and possess many romantic sounding names: Kara-Kum, Kyzyl-Kum, Taklamakan, Alashan, Ordos and Kzungaria. Throughout the entire area the climate is arid and drainage is internal. There are large sand deserts, pebble sand and gravelly gypsiferous surfaces and massive rocky deserts. Characteristic are the large and deep intermontane depressions of Tarim, Tsaidam and southern Alashan rimmed by high, folded mountain ranges (Petrov 1976).

The deserts of Central Asia lie in the temperate zone. The eastern parts come under the influence of the East China monsoon and, therefore, have a distinct maximum summer precipitation. Towards the west, summer precipitation becomes

Fig. 7.8 Water stored in the sand of dry watercourses supports a limited number of trees in the Mouydir Mountains of the Sahara. (Kind permission: M. J. Selby.)

less significant and in the far west moist Atlantic air provides some rain throughout the year. Annual precipitation ranges from 10 mm in the most arid areas of Kashgaria, Tsaidam and Beishan, to 250 mm in the east. Consequently, the vegetation is very sparse, especially in the western and central regions. Shrubs and annual herbs predominate although large trees grow in isolated watercourses.

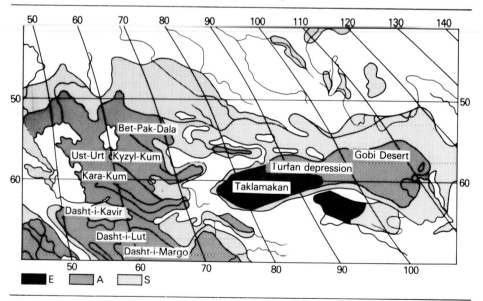

Fig. 7.9 Deserts of Central Asia. (After Petrov 1976.) (E = extremely arid, A = arid, S = semi-arid).

Much of the sand covering the extensive deserts of Central Asia originates from the natural process of deflation of bedrock. But especially toward the east, man, who has inhabited this arid area for thousands of years, has had a deleterious effect and overgrazing has resulted in the development of vast areas of moving sand (Petrov 1976).

Australian deserts

Because the Australian deserts receive more rainfall than large parts of the desert areas already described (> 100 mm annual average), they cannot be directly compared with the Namib, South American deserts or the Sahara (Fig. 7.10).

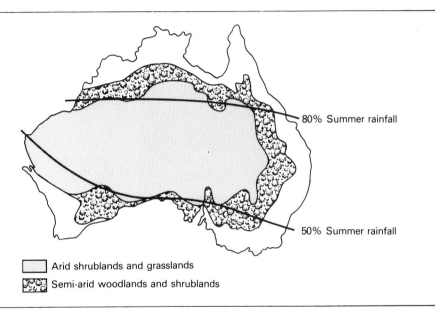

Fig. 7.10   Distribution of vegetation communities and rainfall in Australia. (After Williams 1979.)

Because of the irregularity of this rainfall and the lack of surface water, they are, however, edaphic deserts and uninhabitable in places. Australian deserts are positioned between major wind belts and their associated storm systems and are influenced by the dry, subsiding air masses of the sub-tropical anticyclones (McGinnies 1979). In addition, the nitrogen and phosphorus content of the soils of Australia are thought to be substantially lower than in arid-zone soils elsewhere (Charley 1972), and, as a result, the occasional good rains may produce less biomass than expected.

The Simpson Desert is considered to be the most extreme desert in Australia, where the irregular rainfall has been estimated to vary between 100 and 250 mm per year. Here the dunes consist of parallel sandy ridges about 8–30 m high, 250–500 m apart and 250 km long (Walter 1971). Only the crests of the dunes are mobile, the lower dune slopes and interdune areas support a sclerophyllous grassland of predominantly *Triodia* and *Zygochloa* species, with associated perennials and annuals which grow only after rains. On stony soils the Chenopodiaceae dominate (Walter

1971). As in our example of the Namib Desert, soil factors such as water storage capacity and sand mobility influence species distribution.

North American deserts

The North American deserts should be more readily comparable with the Australian deserts as only about 5 per cent of the land is extremely arid, 40 per cent is arid and 55 per cent is semi-arid (MacMahon 1979). Nevertheless, despite the similarity in average annual rainfall, the deserts of North America have a greater pattern of relief. The southern regions of the North American deserts lie in an area of subsiding, sub-tropical dry air, but the northern deserts are the result of rain-shadow effects.

The deserts of North America consist of four adjacent areas with different rainfall regimes and vegetation patterns. Furthest north lies the Great Basin Desert with its winter precipitation of which more than 60 per cent occurs as snow. Further south, from west to east, the Mojave Desert experiences winter rainfall, the Sonoran Desert biseasonal winter and summer rainfall and the Chihuahuan Desert summer rainfall only.

The Great Basin Desert contains few shrub species and consequently has a very monotonous appearance. Most abundant within this cold desert, although not restricted thereto, are the big sagebrush, *Artemisia tridentata*, and shadscale, *Atriplex confertifolia*. The Sonoran Desert is typified by numerous forms of cacti which are most diverse and well developed here (Fig. 7.11). Sub-trees and shrubs are also dominant plant types. The Mojave is intermediate between the Great Basin and Sonoran deserts with the addition of a very rich annual flora. In the Chihuahuan Desert shrubs and grasslands are well developed.

Of particular interest are the ephemerals which have been derived from different

Fig. 7.11   Cactus and other succulents are a feature of the Sonoran Desert of North America.

geographic origins. Their dynamics are greatly affected by temperature and the timing and amount of rain, which triggers germination. In contrast to the ephemerals in Old World deserts, summer rainfall species will not respond to winter rainfall nor will winter species germinate with summer rains.

In our brief description of five desertic areas we have illustrated the main characteristics of each desert (Table 7.1). No two deserts have identical climates or

Table 7.1 *Some major characteristics of six of the world's desert areas. (The numbers in the three right-hand columns refer to the importance of the characteristic in each desert: 0 = absent, 1 = present, 2 = important, 3 = very important.)*

| | Location | Rainfall | | Fog | Sand dunes | Succulents |
		seasonality	minimum (mm)			
Namib	coastal	summer to winter	10	3	3	2
Peru	coastal	summer to winter	10	3	1	1
Sahara	continental	summer to winter	10	1	3	1
Central Asia	continental	summer to winter	10	0	3	0
Australia	continental	summer to winter	100	0	2	0
North America	continental	summer to winter	100	1	1	3

substrates. Sand dunes, which are thought to typify deserts, figure prominently in only three of the six areas described. Succulents, the 'most typical of desert plants', are commonly found in only two of these deserts. On closer inspection, sand dunes and succulents can be found somewhere in almost every desert area but certainly do not typify deserts in general.

We have not yet mentioned animals in this discussion of the structure of various desert areas. The same major factors, substrate and seasonality of precipitation, which affect vegetation also influence the distribution and abundance of animals. Larger, more mobile mammals and birds, however, are less restricted to one area and often range over several desert substrate types and across different rainfall regimes. The oryx (*Oryx gazella*) and the large bird, Ludwig's bustard (*Neotis ludwigii*) of the Namib Desert are good examples. When conditions are favourable in the sand dunes, they occupy this substrate in great numbers. When conditions deteriorate there, they escape by moving to other desert areas or even leave the desert entirely.

Arthropods, reptiles and small mammals are usually the most numerous species in the desert environment and the substrate strongly influences their methods of retreat or escape from unfavourable conditions. For example, those species dependent on sand swimming are restricted to sandy areas, while those dependent on burrow construction or stones, under which they hide, occupy more stable substrates.

Seasonality of precipitation also affects the smaller desert animals through its effect on the vegetation as a source of food and shelter. However, in some of the extremely arid areas with more uniform annual conditions, for example in the southern hemisphere coastal deserts, plant detritus may provide a continuous source of energy. In such a situation the effect of seasonality of precipitation is less marked and reproduction and growth is aseasonal for many species.

Although the desert areas of the world are varied, we can make a few

generalisations regarding their characteristics. Most deserts lie between latitudes 15° and 30° where they are influenced by the dry, subsiding air masses of the sub-tropical anticyclones. This aridity may be greatly enhanced if the desert is located either in the interior of a large, continental land mass or on the west coast of a continent where a cold current runs parallel to the shore. The desert substrates are also variable depending on the parent rock, nevertheless certain formations such as sand dunes, desert pavement and wind erosion surfaces are more common in deserts than elsewhere. Weathering processes are directly influenced by the paucity of rainfall and vegetation cover.

Precipitation is the dominant climatic factor in deserts because of its scarcity and infrequent, unpredictable nature. Seasonality of precipitation influences the character of the plant community which, in turn, affects the desert fauna. As a result of the controlling rôles played by substrate and precipitation, autecological relationships between a desert organism and the environment are, in many cases, more important than interactions between organisms. Because of this strong element of environmental control, the structure of habitats in divergent deserts is often similar. Nevertheless, the available habitats in the different deserts have been partitioned in different ways. For this reason, examples of convergent evolution are numerous in deserts and will be discussed in Chapter 9.

Chapter 8

Functional aspects of desert communities

In earlier chapters we used the amount of rainfall to define a desert and the seasonality of rainfall to characterise communities further in selected deserts. The reason for using rainfall as the basic criterion is that it exerts a primary controlling effect on production in desert environments. In fact Noy-Meir (1973) has gone so far as to suggest that use of a 'water flow model' alone is sufficient to describe life processes in a desert ecosystem, since energy flow cannot take place in the absence of water. In arid areas water, rather than the amount of solar and/or heat energy available to the plants, is the main limiting factor. Water cannot be recycled in deserts and is exhaustable. Hence productivity is dependent upon rainfall. Productivity, in turn, characterises the community.

The very dramatic effect of rainfall on production was recently measured in the Namib Desert (Fig. 8.1). The standing biomass of both plants and animals was determined in the dune ecosystem during a period of average rainfall (14 mm) and after an exceptional rainfall event (118 mm). The potential energy in plant, detritus and animal biomass increased nine-, seven- and six-fold respectively. While such dramatic variations are only to be found in the extreme desert environment, they are indicative of the central rôle of water in desert ecosystems.

Production

Primary production

Energy transformations throughout an ecosystem are, as expected, subject to the laws of thermodynamics. The first law of thermodynamics states that matter and energy may be transformed from one form to another but are neither created nor destroyed. The first law does not, however, predict how complete the conversions between forms of matter and energy will be. Each time energy is converted from one form into another, some is given off as heat. This we can summarise as:

(matter + energy) form 1 → (matter + energy) form 2 + heat.

The second law of thermodynamics states that energy of any kind tends to change spontaneously into a more random or less organised form (increase in entropy). This means that there must be a source of energy to maintain a live plant or animal. The energy required for all biological processes first enters the ecosystem as solar energy. Plants being autotrophs use this solar energy and transform it into chemical energy by photosynthesis. This process of transforming solar energy into chemical energy can be stated as:

$6H_2O + 6CO_2 + \text{solar energy} \rightarrow C_6H_{12}O_6 + 6O_2$

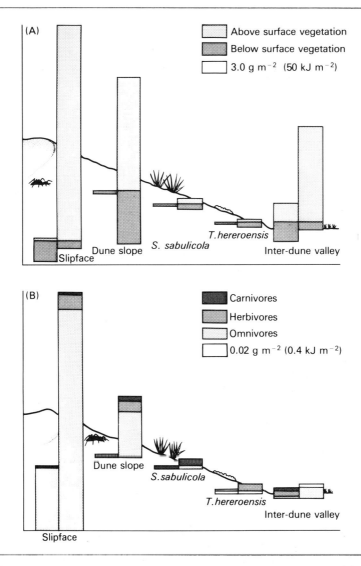

Fig. 8.1 The change of standing biomass of (A) plants and (B) animals from a dry period (left-hand side of each column) to a wet period (right-hand side of each column) was measured in the Namib dune system. (From Seely and Louw 1980.)

At the same time plants must also respire:

$$C_6H_{12}O_6 + 6O_2 \rightarrow 6CO_2 + 6H_2O + heat$$

Thus we have two measures of primary production:
gross production (energy fixed in photosynthesis)
− respiration (energy used for maintenance)
= net production (energy available for growth and reproduction)
which is illustrated in Fig. 8.2.

It is the net primary production which is then available for consumption by

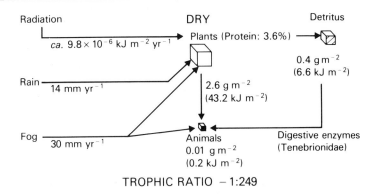

Fig. 8.2 A very small proportion of the available solar energy is incorporated into plants. Much of the net primary production is lost immediately to detritus and to respiration. Values represent standing crop in the Namib dune desert during one period of measurement. (From Seely and Louw 1980.)

animals, the heterotrophs in the community. Other organisms, particularly bacteria, have evolved alternative methods of energy assimilation but will not be discussed here.

All green plants use the Calvin cycle for the reduction of CO_2 and the consequent build-up of organic molecules such as carbohydrates. In most plants (called 'C₃' plants) the CO_2 enters the Calvin cycle directly, but in some the CO_2 is fixed in the form of organic acids prior to entering the Calvin cycle. Those plants in which this fixing occurs in the dark are called CAM (Crassulacean Acid Metabolism) plants, and those in which CO_2 is fixed in the light are called 'C₄' plants. Since the discovery of these two processes, various studies have considered their adaptive significance and competitive advantages. CAM plants have succulent tissues and are most common in hot, open arid areas with relatively low night temperatures (Ting *et al.* 1972). They are, however, thought to be at a competitive disadvantage because of their lower rates of carbon reduction (Mooney 1972). In contrast, C₄ grasses are common in tropical or sub-tropical areas with summer rainfall (Vogel *et al.* 1978), where their initial rapid growth rates apparently give them a competitive advantage.

In annuals of the Mojave and Sonoran deserts, Mulroy and Rundel (1977) have shown that winter annuals use the C_3 pathway, whereas the C_4 pathway is more common in summer annuals.

Individual CAM and C_4 plants are common in deserts although C_3 species may be more numerous, as Syvertsen *et al.* (1976) found in three Chihuahuan Desert plant communities. CAM plants in this area contributed 10 per cent of the species but 48 per cent of the total biomass in an alluvial plain community, while one C_4 grass species accounted for 90 per cent of the biomass in the bed of an ephemeral desert lake. In the central Namib dune ecosystem, C_4 grasses comprised 41 per cent of the species (Vogel and Seely 1977) but 99 per cent of the biomass. Some CAM plants, however, have the ability to alternate between CAM and C_3 metabolism. For example, the proportion of fixation by the two pathways in *Welwitschia mirabilis* is determined by temperature and water stress (Schulze *et al.* 1976). Szarek (1979) also points out that in all four North American deserts the dominant plants are C_3-type woody shrub species, which were found to be photosynthetically as efficient as the C_4 plants studied. It would appear then that the C_4 and CAM carbon-fixation pathways constitute effective but far from obligatory adaptations to desert environments. The advantages of CAM in reducing water loss during transpiration have been discussed in Chapter 5.

Many of the studies of net primary production in deserts, and elsewhere, have been made with the objective of correlating production with rainfall. Water as an essential factor for primary production will be considered in a later section describing limiting factors. Nevertheless, we will discuss the various relationships between water and production in this section in view of their intimate involvement with one another.

In deserts the efficiency of water use is important. Noy-Meir (1973) gives an estimated range of 0.5 to 2 mg production for every gram of water, while Webb *et al.* (1978) calculated an efficiency of 0.3 mg g^{-1} water for hot desert perennials, increasing to 0.38 mg g^{-1} water when annuals were included. In an extensive summary Szarek (1979) gives mean values of 0.42 mg g^{-1} annual efficiency (range 0.15 to 0.82 mg g^{-1}) and 0.73 mg g^{-1} growing season efficiency (range 0.26 to 1.60 mg g^{-1}) for sites from all four North American deserts. Rutherford (1980) concludes that 0.5 mg g^{-1} ($5 \text{ kg ha}^{-1} \text{mm}^{-1}$) is a good estimate up to an annual rainfall of about 600 mm, but points out that efficiencies of herbaceous plant production are greatly reduced in the presence of trees or shrubs (minimum values about 0.1 mg g^{-1}).

Also of interest in desert environments is the minimum annual precipitation necessary for any production to occur. Noy-Meir (1973) gives the zero production intercept as ranging from 25–75 mm yr^{-1}. For hot deserts of North America it has been calculated that 38 mm of annual precipitation is needed to sustain production of perennials, and 15 mm for annuals. For shortgrass, prairie-cold desert, the minimum calculated value is 170 mm yr^{-1} (Webb *et al.* 1978). Seely (1978b), using limited extrapolation from experimental points derived from a very arid area, gives a value of 20.6 mm yr^{-1}. Recent experimental work indicates that this value is lower than 10 mm for *Stipagrostis gonatostachys*, an endemic annual C_4 grass of the Namib dunes. It is to be expected that evolution of an arid endemic would lead to more effective use of a very limited resource.

Not only the amount but the allocation of the net photosynthetic production is of importance to the consumers of plants. For example, trunks and branches of trees consist mostly of cellulose and lignin, which are extremely indigestible and contain no nitrogen. Leaves contain more nitrogen-containing compounds and, if not also

endowed with tannins or other unpalatable compounds, are more suitable for consumption by animals. Seeds and fruits often contain the highest food value and are highly desirable as food. The ratio of net productivity to biomass (P/B) indicates availability of energy to herbivores. An average mean ratio of 0.27 (range 0.11 to 0.46) was measured at four North American sites where woody desert shrubs predominate (Szarek 1979). Grasslands have one of the highest mean ratios for natural habitats (0.33), indicating that relatively little energy is stored in supportive tissues including roots. Here too the highest average portion of net production is found in fruits and flowers (22%). In desert winter annuals, both monocotyledons and dicotyledons, Bell *et al.* (1979) found that maximum investment in reproductive structures varied between species from 16 to 50 per cent of total biomass. The variation was independent of habitat or soil moisture. Usually, smaller proportions are found in shrubland and forest habitats. Pitelka (1977) investigated the energy allocation patterns of three species of lupine, an annual, a perennial herb and a shrub. In the annual, 61 per cent of the energy ends up in reproductive tissues, 29 per cent in seeds alone. In the perennial herb similar values were 18 per cent and 5 per cent, whereas in the shrub at least 20 per cent of its energy goes into reproductive tissue and 6 per cent into seeds. Although grasses and/or annuals are not the only type of vegetation in deserts they nevertheless often figure prominently. Because much of the net primary production in annuals and grasses is readily available for consumption by herbivores, the energy flow in these areas closely reflects environmental conditions, particularly rainfall.

Secondary production

Until now we have discussed the rôle of plants as primary producers, with only brief reference to their use by consumers. Perhaps this is justified as 99.9 per cent of life on earth is tied up in green plants (Krebs 1972). Nevertheless, we will now redress the balance and discuss secondary production.

Plants (autotrophs) are eaten by animals (heterotrophs) which may be eaten by other animals. A simple system of this sort may be termed a food chain. But feeding relationships are seldom so simple and the complex feeding relations can better be illustrated by the use of food webs (Fig. 8.3). Although there are seldom more than five links in the food chains making up any one food web, complexity is introduced by the number of individuals and their numerous interactions with one another within the web. To simplify the model, the organisms may be grouped into primary producers, primary consumers, secondary consumers and tertiary consumers. Organisms may be represented on several levels if their food habits are complex. These groups of animals may be represented in a pyramid of numbers, a pyramid of biomass or an energy pyramid (Fig. 8.4). The first two configurations portray standing crop, that is number or biomass present at any one time, while an energy pyramid is based on the energy used over a longer, specified time period, such as 1 year. Each of the levels on a pyramid is known as a trophic level, representing producers, herbivores, carnivores and top carnivores.

Net production of consumers at any one level represents the energy available to the animals feeding upon them and is analogous to net plant production. Because information on production at the higher trophic levels is limited, we will only consider consumption of each level by the ensuing level. Whereas plants utilise captured solar energy efficiently for production, animals are far less efficient. This is a result of the amount of energy which animals must expend on maintenance, including activity; thus ectotherms are more efficient producers of biomass than are

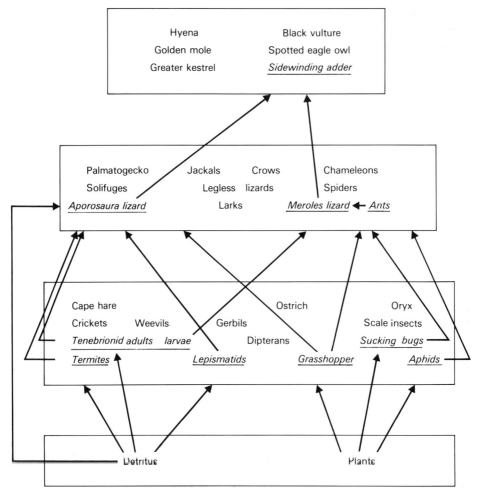

Fig. 8.3 A generalised food web for the Namib Desert. Because of the extensive overlap in feeding activities of the fauna only one major food web ending in *Bitis peringueyi* has been indicated. (From Seely and Louw 1980.)

endotherms because less energy is required to maintain a high body temperature. The number or biomass of animals on any trophic level is much lower than on the preceding level (Table 8.1) but the greatest difference in biomass between trophic levels is found between plants and the herbivores which consume them. This is simply because animal food is easier to digest than plant food. The relationships between exploitation, assimilation and production have been succinctly summarised by Ricklefs (1973) (Fig. 8.5). His summary on patterns of energy flow shows that: (1) assimilation efficiency depends largely on the quality of the food; (2) production efficiency depends largely on activity of the organism, which is highest for endotherms; and (3) exploitation efficiency is highest (10–100%) for predators (including seed and seedling eaters) and low (1–10%) for browsers. The reader is referred to Ricklefs for a more thorough discussion of these concepts.

An important consideration, ignored until now, is the amount of energy which

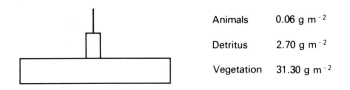

Fig. 8.4   A pyramid of standing crop of plant and animal biomass in a desert. (From Seely and Louw 1980.)

Table 8.1   *The production of a trophic level is always lower than that of the level immediately preceding it. (From Ricklefs 1973.)*

Trophic level	Harvestable production ($kcal\ m^{-2}\ yr^{-1}$)
Primary producer	704
Primary consumer	70
Secondary consumer	13

passes through the detritus food chain. Normally more than 90 per cent of net primary production is consumed by detritus feeders rather than herbivores (Fig. 8.6). The activities of detritus feeders are, however, poorly understood, although it is well known that bacteria and similar organisms are largely dependent on environmental moisture for normal activity.

Heal and MacLean (1975) have quantified the relative importance in a community of the saprovore food chain, or consumption of dead organic matter, in relation to the herbivore food chain, or consumption of living plant tissue. Consumption of net annual primary production in a grassland ecosystem is

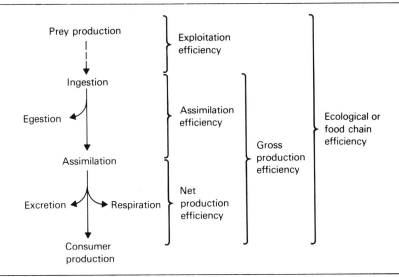

Fig. 8.5   Terminology used to describe the efficiencies that determine the flow of energy through a link in the food chain. (From Ricklefs 1973.)

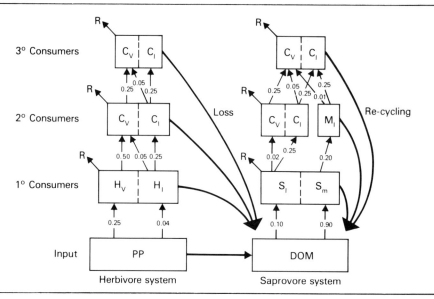

Fig. 8.6 A generalised trophic structure for terrestrial ecosystems emphasising the importance of the saprovore consuming dead organic matter (DOM) over the herbivore system consuming primary production (PP). H = herbivore, S = saprovore, M = microbe, C = carnivore, V = vertebrate, I = invertebrate, R = respiration. The numbers between levels refer to efficiencies of transfer to the next higher level. (From Heal and MacLean 1975.)

calculated to pass through the two chains in very different proportions (Table 8.2). Major variations in the pattern of heterotrophic production in different ecosystems are not obvious, with the exception of production by vertebrate herbivores in grasslands and non-grassland areas, however, heterotrophic productivity probably follows primary productivity.

What is the productivity of plants and animals in a desert ecosystem in the light of the foregoing discussion? Although low, values for a desert are not the lowest measured (Table 8.3). In the arid zone, Noy-Meir (1973) concludes that average annual net above-ground primary production varies between 100 and 400 g m^{-2} for arid and between 250 and 1 000 g m^{-2} for semi-arid communities. Le Houérou (1979) gives more specific values related to precipitation for the Sahara (Table 8.4), while Seely (1978b) measured a linear increase in production related to rainfall, from 0.75 to 49.92 g m^{-2} for 18 to 98 mm rainfall. That precipitation can be used to predict net primary production, in the face of all the other possible factors affecting plant growth, again stresses the importance of water in arid environments.

Table 8.2 *Percentage of net primary production passing through the herbivore and saprovore food chains. (From Heal and MacLean 1975.)*

	Herbivores (%)	Saprovores (%)
Ingestion	15.2	84.8
Egestion	42.9	57.1
Respiration	13.5	86.5
Production	1.6	98.4

Table 8.3   *Net primary production and standing crop of the main types of vegetation. (From Krebs 1972, after Rodin and Basilevich 1968 and Whittaker 1970.)*

Vegetation	Net primary production (dry g m^{-2} yr^{-1})	Standing crop (g m^{-2})	Green parts of total biomass (%)
Arctic tundras	100	500	15
Dwarf-shrub tundras	250	2 800	11
Fir forests			
North taiga	450	10 000	8
Middle taiga	700	26 000	6
South taiga	850	33 000	6
Beech forests	1 300	37 000	1
Oak forests	900	40 000	1
Steppes			
Temperate	1 120	2 500	18
Dry	420	1 000	15
Deserts			
Dwarf, semi-shrub	122	430	3
Sub-tropical	250	600	3
Sub-tropical forests	2 450	41 000	3
Dry savannas	730	2 680	11
Savannas	1 200	6 660	12
Tropical rain forests	3 250	50 000	8
Sphagnum bogs with forest	340	3 700	41
Mangroves	930	12 730	6
Open ocean	125	3	–
Continental shelf	350	10	–
Agricultural land	650	1 000	–

Table 8.4   *Primary production in the Sahara in semi-arid and arid areas. (From le Houérou 1979.)*

	Average annual rainfall (mm)	Production (kg ha^{-1})
	300–400	800–1 000
Semi-arid	200–300	400–500
	100–200	200–400
	50–100	100–200 (extreme 0–600)
Arid	20–50	~ 500 (10 yr^{-1})
	0–20	~ 0

Consumption of primary production, as well as of organisms at higher trophic levels, may well be controlled by availability of water, in the food as well as free drinking water, and by the water balance of the consumer (Noy-Meir 1973). Thus we would expect the amount of primary production consumed in deserts to be even less than in environments where water is freely available, and that this consumption would be restricted to brief periods after rainfall.

Few values of standing biomass of animals are given for arid environments. In the Namib, Seely and Louw (1980) obtained values ranging from 100 to 500 g ha^{-1} for all trophic levels in a dune ecosystem. In the Sonoran Desert, Nutting *et al.* (1974) give production values for a species in each of two genera of alate termites, of 44.27 g ha^{-1} and 3.28 g ha^{-1}. Crawford (1976) estimated the dry weight production during the active season of the millipede *Orthoporus ornatus* to be 850 g ha^{-1} in the Chihuahuan Desert.

Hadley (1980) provides some information on scorpions and spiders for warm North American deserts and gives values ranging from 5 to 10 individuals m^{-2} for scorpions (but 1.15 individuals m^{-2} for one dominant species on sand dunes) and 2.5 spiders m^{-2}. It is concluded that energy flow in desert invertebrates may be minimal when compared with invertebrates from other ecosystems occupying the same trophic levels. The small amount of data available for desert vertebrates has been summarised by Johnson and Schreiber (1979). For the 12 endothermic species listed, only about 2 per cent of biomass consumed resulted in production.

Limiting factors

A limiting factor is usually defined as a resource, required by plants or animals, that is scarce relative to the requirement for it. On occasion an excess of some resource may also play an inhibiting rôle. On a global scale, solar radiation, temperature and moisture are the most common limiting factors for primary production in the terrestrial ecosystem, whereas nutrients may be locally scarce.

As emphasised earlier and best described by Noy-Meir (1973, 1974, 1979/80), water is the most important limiting factor in a desert. The intake of solar energy and therefore the rate of primary production is mainly controlled by water, while the transfer of energy to higher trophic levels is also coupled with water flow. The effective use of rain may, in some instances, be influenced by edaphic factors, in which case the direct relationship between rainfall and primary production may be obscured.

Secondary production is also controlled by the amount of water available in the environment. For some animals the amount of water consumed with the food, plant or animal, supplies all their water requirements. However, free water is often necessary if the food being consumed is too dry. For example, in the Kuiseb Canyon of the Namib, oryx, *Oryx gazella*, were unable to make use of an abundant supply of *Acacia albida* pods when drinking water was not available (Hamilton *et al.* 1977). This may be a response to the low water content of the pods (5–13%) when compared with that of their usual food supply, or possibly to the high level of nitrogen found in the pods. In contrast, water availability appears to have no effect on feeding dispersion of the red kangaroo, *Megaleia rufa*, a desert herbivore of central Australia (Low 1979). Nevertheless, the amount of moisture present in the environment directly affects activity of detritus-consuming species. Because of the importance of saprovores in all ecosystems, the importance of water as a limiting factor cannot be overemphasised.

Beatley (1976) describes an interesting example of the water requirements of several rodent species in the Mojave and Great Basin deserts of North America. In the drier areas the water from winter annual plants is necessary for reproduction by the rodents, while in the moister areas reproduction can carry on in the absence of winter annuals, all the necessary moisture coming from the environment. Hence we must consider not only the limiting effect of water on growth but also on reproduction. For example, growth of perennial plants may continue for a time using water stored underground or within the plant or water condensing from fog or dew. These plants may even flower and set seed for many years. But rain is almost always necessary to induce germination of annual and perennial species. For some birds, insects, snails and possibly other animals, rain may be interpreted as a signal to begin reproduction (Immelmann 1963; Yom-Tov 1971). Consequently water as a limiting factor operates at two levels. It may affect the production of both plants and animals that are able to grow for long periods using some source of stored water, and it is also

necessary to induce reproduction. The spectacular show of annual flowers which occurs in the Mojave Desert and Namaqualand during some years is a good example of this latter effect.

Energy

Because of the great importance of water as a limiting factor in deserts, energy has received relatively little attention. The quality of available food, in particular the protein content, and not energy *per se*, is probably limiting in mesic (White 1978) as well as desert environments (Seely and Louw 1980). In a detailed study of three tropical grasslands in the Serengeti region of Tanzania, the consumption of net primary production by large ungulates, small mammals and grasshoppers was examined by Sinclair (1975). During a short period of 1 to 4 months each year the green component of primary producers, with a crude protein content of < 4 per cent, was the limiting resource. Thus net primary production cannot simply be equated with food as many plant species may be nutritious for only a short period of time. In concluding, Sinclair suggests that all trophic levels may be limited by their resources rather than by predators or parasites. White (1978) has proposed the same hypothesis.

In order to examine the relationship between available energy and production, the abundance of prey for two desert lizards was measured (Dunham 1978). Positive correlations were established between precipitation, estimates of food availability and individual growth rates of the iguanid lizard *Sceloporus merriami*. Similar correlations were found by Ballinger (1977) between the same two factors and reproduction in the lizard, *Urosaurus ornatus*. In some situations, however, surplus energy may be present but either not usable or unavailable. For example, it may be too widely dispersed, or hidden from predators with particular feeding habits, or be of too low a quality or too dry to consume in the absence of additional water.

Nutrients

The importance of nutrients in an arid environment may, after water, be critical (Ch. 2). Noy-Meir (1974) mentions four reasons why this may be so: (1) the rapid pulse of growth, particularly of annuals, after rain may tie up most of the available nutrients; (2) some desert soils are intrinsically low in nutrients; (3) as a result of low decomposition and leaching rates due to lack of moisture, nutrients are mainly concentrated at the surface layer; and (4) litter, and hence decomposition of the litter, is often localised in deserts because of the sparse vegetation cover and the action of winds. Most of the definitive work in this respect has been done on aquatic systems and agricultural land and, despite extensive research, the effects of nutrients are not well understood. For example, addition of nutrients often increases primary production but the addition of twice as much does not double the yield. Secondary limitations in the form of genetic capabilities and other unknown interactions are probably involved. One example of a possible interaction, namely sequential limitation of nutrients, may be drawn from work carried out on the water of the Sargasso Sea (Menzel and Ryther 1961). Their results suggested that iron was primarily limiting but that nitrogen and phosphorus were also limiting when iron was present in adequate amounts.

The nutrients limiting growth in desert environments are primarily nitrogen and phosphorus, although the list of less important limiting elements is also long. The idea that nutrients may be limiting in a desert environment developed from the

observation, made first in Australia, that plant and animal production declined in the second of two consecutive years of high rainfall (West and Skujins 1978). Phosphorus levels are often limiting there (Charley and Cowling 1968) while nitrogen is more frequently limiting in North American deserts. As a result of the work of the US/IBP Desert Biome Programme, the rôle of nitrogen in North American deserts is becoming clearer and a model of the nitrogen cycle has been constructed for the warm Mojave Desert (Wallace *et al.* 1978) (Fig. 8.7). Although

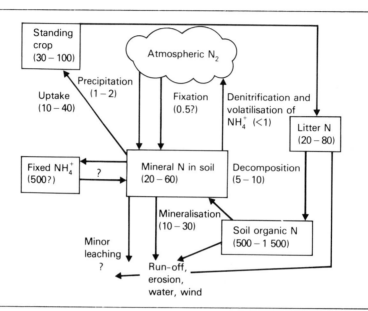

Fig. 8.7   The nitrogen cycle in the Mojave Desert has been worked out on a preliminary basis. (From Wallace *et al.* 1978.)

the nitrogen is concentrated in fertile islands around shrub clumps, with little in the spaces between, it appears to be sufficient over a wide range of precipitation.

    The importance of the limiting rôle of nitrogen, as opposed to energy, in food for very young animals has been pointed out by White (1978). Mispagel (1978), studying the acridid grasshopper, *Bootettix punctatus*, on the creosote bush (*Larrea tridentata*) suggests that nutrient availability, as a function of available soil moisture, may be a factor influencing the survivorship of early instar nymphs and the population as a whole.

Other factors

Radiation, temperature and wind may also limit production by being present in amounts too high or too low for optimal growth by plants and animals. Even in deserts radiation may be limiting (Noy-Meir 1973). This may occur when stomatal behaviour restricts photosynthesis to periods of low evaporation, such as early morning, when radiation levels would also be low. Perhaps the most graphic example of light as a limiting factor in desert environments is provided by the window algae growing on translucent quartz stones (Vogel 1955) (Fig. 8.8). Moisture is provided by dew condensing on the stones and is the primary limiting factor in the area of algal

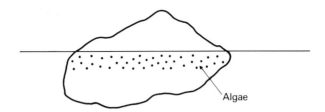

Fig. 8.8   Light is a secondary limiting factor for growth of algae living on quartz stones below the soil surface. (From Vogel 1955.)

growth. Light, however, can only penetrate the stone to a shallow depth, and limits growth of the algae to areas near the soil surface, despite the fact that moisture is available at greater depths. The soil itself plays a secondary limiting rôle by its controlling effect on the availability of water in some habitats. Stability of the substrate, particularly in a dune environment, also plays a limiting rôle in plant growth and animal activity.

Although water is the primary limiting factor for plants in an extremely arid desert, edaphic factors, nutrient availability and perhaps genetic capability can modify the effect of water. In the inter-dune valley habitat of the Namib, germination and growth will occur when the equivalent of 10 mm of rain has been applied to the bare sand surface. The equivalent of 20 mm causes more growth but the application of 30 mm results in growth not significantly more than that found at 20 mm. Nutritional restrictions or edaphic factors may thus prevent this rapidly growing, specialised grass, *Stipagrostis gonatostachys*, from taking advantage of increased amounts of rainfall. In contrast on the nearby gravel plains, a minimum of 20 mm precipitation causes germination, and production of the congeneric *S. ciliata* continues to increase linearly with rainfall to at least 90 mm.

In the dune habitat, differences in compaction of the sand grains lead to differences in water-holding capacity (Fig. 8.9) and germination does not usually occur on the uncompacted, unstable dune crests. However, should germination occur in or near this area, mobile sands will soon uproot or smother the young plant. Therefore, we may summarise the main factors limiting plant production in an extreme desert as primarily water, secondarily modified by edaphic factors, such as water-holding capacity and stability of the soil, thirdly nutrient availability and finally the genetic capabilities of the plants involved.

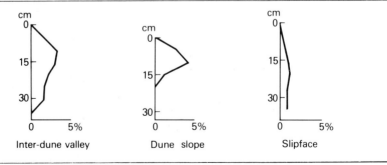

Fig. 8.9   Water-holding capacity of sand varies as substrate stability varies across a dune. Measurements of water content (w/w) were taken 1 week after a 20 mm rainfall.

Consumers in a desert are also water-limited. For primary consumers, water and nutrients are often closely related since the nitrogen content of plants tends to decrease as the plant dries. Values for protein content ranging from 21.1 per cent in a wet period to 3.6 per cent in a dry period were measured for plants in the Namib dune ecosystem. However, for secondary consumers, energy may be the main limiting factor as water and nutrients are usually adequately supplied by the prey animals. But in extreme deserts, environmental factors may be limiting for some of the more widely ranging predators. For example, the tenebrionid beetles, preyed on by Ludwig's bustard, *Neotis ludwigii*, are available in the dune system throughout the year although the bustard is only present in the cooler winter months. However, the departure of the bustards from the dunes may in fact depend on water availability rather than on temperature *per se*.

Decomposition: rates of energy and nutrient cycling

Decomposition is the term given to the process of breaking down the results of primary and secondary production into their inorganic components. A variety of detritus feeders, from vultures to microbes, consume non-living material. In a recent review Crawford (1979) has categorised most soil-dwelling desert detritivores as having either short lives and relatively rapid responses to changing conditions, or long lives with few close links to environmental change; some have life histories of intermediate length which are often complicated by eusociality. Nematodes and social insects, the ants and termites, are thought to have the greatest and most direct influence on the flow of nutrients and energy in warm deserts. Other detritivores may indirectly control rates of mineralisation, processing of excrement and carrion and accumulation of organic debris and may also interact with microbial–fungal decomposers.

As more than 90 per cent of primary production enters the detritus chain immediately, its importance to ecosystem production is clear. That part of the detritus which is cold-water soluble may be rapidly leached out if water is available. For example, 7 per cent of grass leaf-litter in a semi-arid grassland disappeared after 7 months in the absence of microbial activity (Vossbrink *et al*. 1979). Large detritus eaters break down available detritus material to yield further water-soluble products and smaller particles suitable, eventually, for bacteria and fungi. This process is often viewed essentially as yielding inorganic compounds to be used again by plants. It should, however, be remembered that each step is actually providing energy for the consumer organism involved.

The flow of nutrients is directly linked to the flow of water and energy. However nutrients, unlike energy and water, are retained and recycled through the system for long periods whereas water and energy are lost and must be replenished from external sources. The high efficiency of phosphorus cycling compared with energy flowing through an ecosystem is diagrammatically illustrated in Fig. 8.10.

The rate of nutrient and energy cycling is dependent on water as well as on temperature, on the density of the consumers and on the composition of the material being decomposed. Recently Meentemeyer (1978) has shown that in predicting litter decay rates in habitats ranging from sub-polar to warm temperate, evapotranspiration is several orders of magnitude more important than the quality, that is the lignin content of the litter. In phytoplankton communities the assimilated energy is dissipated in 9–18 days while 25 years may be required in a tropical rain forest. Weigert *et al*. (1967) used radioactive phosphorus to demonstrate the differing rates of uptake by various trophic groups in an old field community (Fig. 8.11).

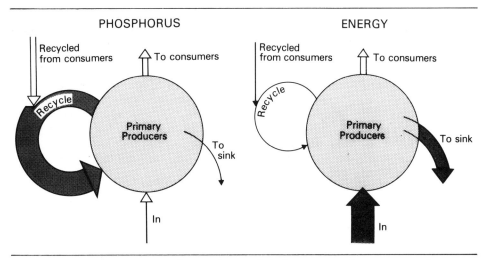

Fig. 8.10 Phosphorus and other nutrients tend to recycle in the ecosystem whereas energy and water pass through rapidly. (From Rigler 1975.)

In a desert environment the rate of decomposition is almost entirely determined by the availability of water. Whereas primary production enters the ecosystem as a pulse following sufficient rainfall, detritus may accumulate and be available in the presence of a source of moisture when photosynthesis is not taking place. Organic detritus thus constitutes a reserve of energy and nutrients which may be critical. These reserves are particularly important in deserts where moisture limits decomposition.

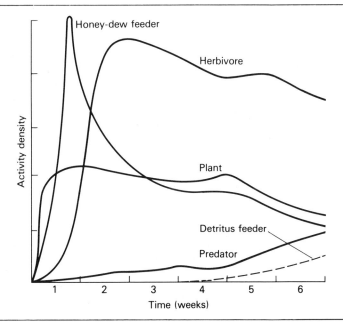

Fig. 8.11 Labelled phosphorus accumulates in the various trophic components of an old field community at varying rates. (Weigert *et al.* 1967.)

Densities of decomposers are usually lower in deserts than in more favourable environments. Nevertheless, they are probably as important for the cycling of nutrients in deserts as elsewhere. But, the lack of moisture may be a particularly significant limitation for microbial and fungal decomposers, leaving arthropods as 'macro-decomposers' to break down much of the litter (Noy-Meir 1974). An example from the Namib Desert illustrates the rôle of 'macro-decomposers' in an extremely arid ecosystem. Here wind-blown plant and other material accumulates at slipfaces on the dunes and is the sole energy source for several invertebrates, including tenebrionid beetles and silverfish, which occupy this habitat. Microbial forms are not numerous (le Roux 1970), probably as a direct result of the lack of environmental moisture. The tenebrionid beetles are the main detritus consumers and, because they are able to consume and store external moisture in the form of fog, they are able to feed on the detritus throughout the year. Consequently in this dune environment it is water, in the form of condensing fog, that controls the rate of energy flow through the 'macro-decomposers'.

Population dynamics and evolution of predator–prey relationships

A population has been defined as 'a group of organisms of the same species occupying a particular space at a particular time' (Krebs 1972). Populations have basic characteristics which may be statistically described. Of primary importance is size or density of a population, which may be affected by natality, mortality, migration and immigration. In addition, secondary characteristics such as age distribution, genetic composition and dispersion may also be used to describe a population further. Information concerning these parameters can lend insight into many aspects of the ecology and evolution of a population (for example, Tinkle 1967; Vinegar 1975).

What controls populations and regulates the changes in the numbers of individuals? Four general theories have arisen. Krebs (1972) summarises: (1) density-dependent factors, mainly natural enemies, determine average abundance and prevent increased numbers in many populations; (2) weather factors affect population size and may act predominantly as a density-independent control; (3) population changes are influenced by a combination of biotic and physical factors, both density-dependent and density-independent, which vary in space and time; and (4) abundance may change as the quality of individuals changes, i.e. through self-regulation. Density-independent processes are more important in fluctuating than in stable environments and may therefore be expected to be more important in deserts.

Quantitative demographic techniques are used to measure population changes. Perhaps the most important relationship to arise is termed the Verhulst–Pearl logistic equation describing the sigmoidal population growth curve for species with overlapping generations (Ch. 6).

Although extensive laboratory experiments indicate that the logistic curve adequately describes laboratory population growth for organisms with simple life cycles, it has never been demonstrated that the population of any organism with a complex life history follows the logistic curve. In natural populations, growth may or may not fit the logistic model, but a stable final density is almost never attained. Other models, such as time-lag and stochastic models, have been tried with mixed success.

Two aspects of population change are of particular interest in ecology: steadiness and resilience (Leigh 1975). Steadiness describes the year-to-year fluctuations which

occur under normal circumstances, while resilience measures a resistance to major disturbance or real catastrophe. Hence it is necessary to measure amplitude and frequency of the fluctuations of the population in question. Moreover, we must investigate the causes of these fluctuations. Limiting factors, particularly moisture, have already been discussed. Another factor which may be important in controlling populations is predation. But, based upon the earlier hypotheses describing environmental control of desert organisms, it is unlikely that predation will be an important factor in very arid environments. Examples have, nevertheless, been derived from less arid deserts and will be discussed here.

Predation occurs when an organism, a predator, adversely affects another organism, its prey, by killing and consuming it. Seeds and seedlings may also be considered prey; mature plants, however, are not often totally destroyed. A generalised model has been described by the Lotka–Volterra equations (Krebs 1972); their equation for prey population

$$\frac{dN}{dt} = (r_1 - K_1 P)N$$

where K_1 = a constant indicating ability of prey to escape predation, and their equation for predator population is

$$\frac{dP}{dt} = (-r_2 - K_2 N)P$$

where K_2 is a measure of the predator's skill in catching prey. Using these equations, populations of predator and prey are shown to oscillate in a systematic, cyclic manner.

Elton and Nicholson (1942) presented an excellent example of these classical oscillations in predator–prey interactions. The Canada lynx, *Lynx canadensis*, which eats snowshoe hares, *Lepus americanus*, has shown such cycles with peaks every 9 to 10 years for over 200 years. However, Keith (1963) has found that snowshoe hares also fluctuate in a 10-year cycle when lynx are absent. Thus, although lynx may be dependent on snowshoe hares, the hares are controlled by some factor in addition to predation by the lynx.

Stable oscillations of predator–prey interactions have been demonstrated but only under complex laboratory conditions. Moreover Pimental *et al.* (1963) have also demonstrated evolutionary changes under laboratory conditions, resulting in a reduction of the interaction between predator and prey. Under field conditions, however, where both predator and prey are influenced by many other environmental factors, simple oscillations of predator–prey interactions have not been demonstrated.

Do predators influence the abundance of prey at all under natural conditions? Several examples, where either predators have been reduced or new predators have been introduced into a system, seem to indicate that prey abundance is sometimes, but not always, influenced by predation. For example, within 20 years of the introduction of the sea lamprey into the Great Lakes of North America, the catches of lake trout decreased to almost nothing (Baldwin 1964). In contrast, predator control in the annual grasslands of California had no effect on the overall vole population (Pearson 1966). Why the differing results?

Predators may respond to an increased abundance of prey in two ways (Krebs 1972). There may be a numerical response, resulting in an increase in predator density, or there may be a functional response, in which individual predators change their rate of consumption of prey. Holling (1959) has given a very clear

demonstration of these two responses for three small mammals, *Sorex*, *Blarina* and *Peromyscus*, that prey on the cocoons of European pine sawfly, *Neodiprion sertifes*, in Ontario. As the density of cocoons increased so the number of *Sorex* increased to over 24 per acre, although the number of cocoons taken per animal per day remained at the same level. In contrast, *Blarina* density never increased above 6 per acre but each of these small mammals consumed up to 320 cocoons per day. The numerical and functional responses of *Peromyscus* were intermediate between those of the other two species. However, as the density of cocoons increased beyond a certain level the small mammals had a diminishing effect on the population increase of the prey (Fig. 8.12). Hence, the cyclic predator–prey interactions did not develop.

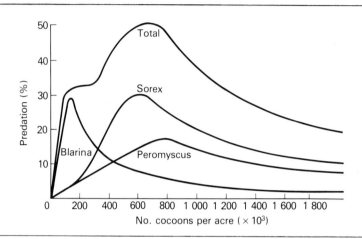

Fig. 8.12 The effect of predation by rodents on the European pine sawfly cocoons decreases as the cocoon density increases beyond a certain limit. (From Holling 1959.)

The population aspects of predator–prey relationships in deserts have rarely been studied. The saguaro, *Carnegiea gigantea*, is one of the massive columnar cacti growing in the Sonoran Desert. Individuals may live for 175 years or more and in many areas do not appear to be reproducing themselves. Shade and moisture are limiting factors during the first decade of a young saguaro's life, but predation by grazers such as rodents, rabbits, insects and cattle appears to be the controlling factor (Niering *et al.* 1963; Turner *et al.* 1969). However, this example of predator control of the saguaro populations must still await experimental confirmation.

Plant populations may be influenced by predation upon their seed reserves in deserts. Chew and Chew (1970) found that 87 per cent of seed production was consumed by small mammals in one desert shrub community. Soholt (1973) estimated that in one particular year kangaroo rats, *Dipodomys merriami*, in one North American desert locality, consumed enough of the available annual *Erodium* seeds to reduce the density of the plant by more than 30 per cent the following year. The Rose of Jericho, *Anastatica hierochuntica*, is an annual restricted to the driest parts of the Negev Desert. Friedman and Stein (1980) attribute this to effective predation on the seeds by rodents in the moister areas where perennials support rodent life. Similarly, predation on resistant and dormant forms of ephemeral animals may influence the prey populations (Noy-Meir 1979/80). The gerbils, *Gerbillus dasyurus*, consumed 42 per cent of the population of the snail, *Trochoidea*

seetzeni, in some localities in the Negev and dormice, *Eliomys melanurus*, an unmeasured but even greater number (Yom-Tov 1970). These rodents also have a very significant effect on populations of southern slopes of a wadi but not on the northern slopes.

More recently the behavioural aspects of predator–prey relationships have been receiving attention, particularly in the deserts of North America. Horned lizards, *Phrynosoma cornutum*, are the main predators of several species of ant, including *Pogonomyrmex desertorum* and *P. rugosus*, in the Chihuahuan Desert of southern New Mexico (Whitford and Bryant 1979). The lizards take only a few ants at one place, mainly those ants not found in association with nest discs or foraging columns. As a result of the lizard's behaviour, that of the prey is not disturbed, ensuring in the long term an adequate level of prey availability. The results of experimental simulation of predation indicate that the activity of *P. desertorum* ceased for up to 5 days when foragers were removed at a rate of five to ten per day, representing approximately 25 per cent of the forager population. The second prey species, *P. rugosus*, did not respond to a 25 per cent loss of foragers but ceased activity at 50 per cent loss and entered into frenzied activity at 75 per cent loss. The populations of lizards are probably food-limited and not limited by predation themselves, hence the pattern of utilization of ants which has evolved.

In the more arid desert areas of the world it is thought that predator–prey relationships are probably not well developed. The water content of the prey and the length of time moist prey is available, rather than prey density, are probably limiting to predators. As a result of the importance of environmental control, populations do not have sufficient time for biotic interactions to evolve. The occurrence of rain results in a flood of prey animals which are usually more *r*-selected than their potential predators so that lack of environmental stability reduces the possibility for evolution of numerous predator–prey relationships. Predation upon seeds undoubtedly exists but, as most desert animals have variable diets, seeds are only one of the types of food consumed. As a result, populations of plants may often be affected but are only occasionally eliminated from an area.

Preliminary observations in the extreme desert of the Namib dunes indicate that gerbils do not feed on seeds exclusively but require some succulent material to maintain water balance (Louw 1972). The sand-diving lizard, *Aporosaura anchietae*, consumes seeds when insects are less available (Robinson and Cunningham 1978). In contrast, when they are readily available seeds are preferred to plant detritus by several species of tenebrionid beetles.

Mammalian and avian predators in the extremely arid dune Namib are predominantly of two types. The golden mole, *Eremitalpa granti namibensis*, lives permanently in the dunes where it consumes beetle larvae and small reptiles and is not believed to have any controlling effect upon its prey. Instead, its own populations are probably food-limited despite its presence in owl pellets in some peripheral dune areas. One species of lark, *Certhilauda albescens erythrochlamys*, also lives permanently in the dunes, consuming all available soft-bodied insects. Again evidence suggests that this predominantly insectivorous dune lark is food-limited.

Non-resident predators enter the dune system only on its periphery or when potential prey populations are exceptionally dense. For example the jackal, *Canis mesomelas*, and the rock kestrel, *Falco tinnunculus*, may prey upon the adult forms of diurnal tenebrionid beetles where the dunes border on a dry watercourse or other suitable habitat. Other avian predators such as Ludwig's bustard, *Neotis ludwigii*, are resident in the dune environment for months at a time but only when tenebrionid population densities are high. When rain has not fallen for some years, the bustard is totally absent from the dunes, sometimes for decades at a time. Hence predator–prey

interactions in a very arid environment are mainly opportunistic in nature rather than being well developed interspecific relationships.

Competition and the niche concept

In addition to predation, we must consider other biotic interactions. Competitive interactions occur when two or more populations have an adverse effect on each other. This usually happens when two or more individuals require a common resource that is actually or potentially limiting. The resultant competition may take either of two forms. The first, interference competition, occurs when an individual defends a territory which includes a rich source of food, nesting sites, etc. Time, matter or energy expended during interference competition may affect the competitors adversely. In the second type of competition, termed exploitation, there is unlimited access to a resource, often food, leading to 'scramble competition' to obtain and utilise this resource. All competitors are adversely affected by reduction of the amount of the resource available.

Endotherms in a stable environment are more likely to compete through interference. Species that compete through exploitation, for example many insects, are more often controlled by physical factors. Therefore in more arid deserts we may predict that any competition which does occur would be predominantly through exploitation. Reports of field experiments which clearly differentiate between alternative types of interaction, including competition, are few. Although competition has been under discussion for a long time, remarkably few testable hypotheses have emerged (Miller 1967). Some have even questioned the validity of the concept, but for the sake of further discussion we will accept the importance of competition in structuring biological communities.

The 'principle' of competitive exclusion may be stated as follows: two species with identical ecological requirements cannot live together in the same place at the same time. Although this statement cannot be disproved, and is therefore of questionable value, it has served to emphasise that some degree of ecological differentiation may be necessary for coexistence in a saturated environment (Pianka 1974). This 'principle' was derived from several early laboratory experiments where the results were always conclusive and one of the two species was always eliminated. To demonstrate competition, Gause (1934) used cultures of related species of *Paramecium* feeding on a single type of food. Later Park (1962) and his colleagues, in a series of papers, used flour beetles, *Tribolium castaneum* and *T. confusum* to study competition. Although one species of flour beetle was always eliminated, that species varied depending on conditions of temperature and humidity used for the experiment. In each of the above cases elimination was based on competition for a limiting resource, while resources which are abundant, compared to their requirement by organisms, do not provide grounds for competition. The theoretical basis of competition, somewhat oversimplified, was established by Lotka (1925) and Volterra (1926). Their equations and the relationships derived may be found in any standard ecology text (for example, Pianka 1974; Ricklefs 1973).

Competition is much more difficult to demonstrate in natural communities than in the laboratory as most of the evidence has been lost in time. However, there is evidence, much of it circumstantial, to suggest that competition has occurred or is occurring in natural populations. Pianka (1974) categorizes four types of evidence: (1) studies on the ecological requirements of closely related species living in the same area; (2) character displacement; (3) studies on 'incomplete' floras and faunas and associated changes in niches, or 'niche shifts'; and (4) taxonomic composition of communities.

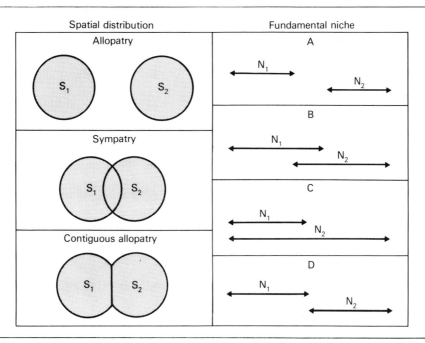

Fig. 8.13 Possible distribution patterns of two species and their related niche relationships. (After Miller 1967.)

Miller (1967) has graphically portrayed the relationships that may exist in the spatial distributions and fundamental niches of two populations (Fig. 8.13). Both sympatric and contiguous allopatric distributions may indicate competition. But it is also possible that they can be explained by ecological differences such as time of activity, food resources or use of space not arising through competition.

The concept of the niche is a necessary part of any discussion of competition. Nevertheless, it is a concept with widely varying definitions which range from very broad, to very specific such as 'food niche' or 'thermal niche'. We will not enter into this controversial discussion but instead accept the terminology of Pianka (1974) who defines the ecological niche as 'the sum total of the adaptations of an organismic unit', or as 'all of the various ways in which a given organismic unit conforms to its environment'. Hutchinson (1957) first proposed the n-dimensional hypervolume as a definition of an organism's niche. A model using only three environmental gradients with fitness as a fourth dimension illustrates this idea (Fig. 8.14). The optimal conditions under which an organism can live and replace itself have been called the fundamental niche. In this idealised niche the physical environment is optimal and the organism experiences no interactions such as competition. However, this ideal situation seldom if ever exists and instead the organism lives in its realised niche. Realised niches of relatively K-selected species may be strongly influenced by their biotic environments, while the physical environment may have more control on the realised niches of relatively r-selected species, a point to remember in view of our bias towards deserts.

Experimental evidence for niche overlap and competition may be obtained from manipulation of natural populations. Connell (1961a & b) was able to demonstrate competition for space between two species of inter-tidal barnacles, *Balanus*

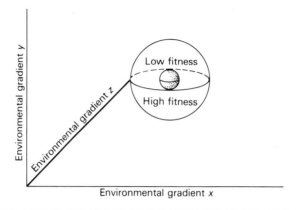

Fig. 8.14 A niche may be defined as the location of optimal fitness along many environmental gradients. (From Pianka 1974.)

balanoides and *Chthamalus stellatus*, by excluding a predatory snail and removing barnacles from selected areas. *Chthamalus stellatus* occupied a higher vertical position because of its ability to withstand greater desiccation than *B. balanoides*, even though *B. balanoides* out-competed *C. stellatus* lower down the shore. Many other examples are available of segregation by habitat as the end result of competition, particularly for well-studied groups such as birds.

Character displacement refers to a frequently observed phenomenon wherein two widely distributed species are more similar where only one of the two species occurs than where they both occur sympatrically. Character displacement may be of a morphological, behavioural or physiological nature, but food-gathering or 'trophic apparatuses' such as beaks or mouthparts are very frequently involved (Pianka 1974).

Of particular interest to us with respect to deserts is that competitive exclusion need not apply if external factors rarefy populations so that resources are not heavily exploited, or if environmental control results in unpredictable oscillations which prevent attainment of a state of equilibrium (Miller 1967). Noy-Meir (1979/80) points out that competition among desert ephemerals is more closely related to evaporative losses, than it is with other ephemerals.

Perennials, however, may have evolved a competitive chemical advantage over some annuals apparently by preventing germination (Friedman *et al.* 1977). In the northern Negev where two common shrubs dominate the landscape, *Artemisia herba-alba* releases an allelopathic substance which inhibits germination of several annual species while *Zygophyllum dumosum* does not. Halophytes which accumulate salt from or excrete it into the soil may also inhibit non-halophytes (Charley 1959, and Litov 1957).

Fortunately, there have been several recent studies of competition in desert environments, some of an experimental nature, and a few selected examples can be included. Yeaton and Cody (1976) and Yeaton *et al.* (1977) used nearest-neighbour analyses in two North American desert communities to demonstrate intraspecific and interspecific competition between dominant shrub species. In the first study, on *Yucca schidigera*, *Opuntia acanthocarpa* and *O. ramosissima*, competition occurred between all species-pairs. In the second study, incorporating five species, *Larrea tridentata* competes with three: *Franseria deltoidea*, *O. fulgida* and *Fouquieria*

splendens, whereas there is no evidence of *Carnegiea gigantea* competing with any of the other species. The authors have suggested that vertical root separation reduces interspecific competition.

Using a clear and simple experimental procedure, Fonteyn and Mahall (1978) have demonstrated competition for moisture between *Larrea tridentata* and *Ambrosia dumosa* in the Mojave Desert of California. Leaving one experimental plant in the centre of 100 m² circular plots, they removed either all *Larrea*, all *Ambrosia* or all individuals of both plant species. When the water potential of the experimental, centrally located plant was measured, it was found to be lower in the control plots from which no plants had been removed than in some of the experimental plots (Table 8.5). Although these data demonstrate interspecific

Table 8.5 *Water potentials of plants under different removal treatments. (From Fonteyn and Mahall 1978.)*

	Larrea		Ambrosia	
Treatment	Water potential (bar)	Treatment	Water potential (bar)
(a) Control	−39.0 ± 1.3	(a) Control	−44.2 ± 3.2
(b) Total removal	−33.7 ± 1.6	(b) Total removal	−30.5 ± 3.4
(c) *Larrea* removal	−39.3 ± 2.3	(c) *Ambrosia* removal	−44.6 ± 3.9
(d) *Ambrosia* removal	−34.6 ± 2.7	(d) *Larrea* removal	−36.5 ± 2.8

competition for soil moisture when water availability is low, the authors point out that the actual mechanism responsible for, and the basis of, the negative interspecific interactions cannot be explained.

Brown *et al.* (1979a) also conducted an experiment removing one taxon of competitor from a community containing seed-eating desert rodents and ants. Where rodents were excluded, the number of ant colonies increased 71 per cent relative to the unmanipulated control plots. In the absence of ants the number of rodents increased 20 per cent and their biomass 29 per cent with respect to the control plots. In plots where both ants and rodents were excluded there were more seeds and annual plants than on plots where either or both groups were present. They conclude that competition among distantly related organisms for a limiting resource, in this case seeds and annuals, plays a major rôle in the organisation of ecological communities.

Price (1978), using field experiments with four species of North American desert rodents, demonstrated the apparent importance of competition in the establishment of resource usage and abundance patterns. The four species differed in their use of a potentially limiting resource, foraging micro-habitat. When competitors were added to or removed from the experimental enclosures, each species shifted its use of foraging micro-habitats as expected. In addition, each species was most dense when its preferred micro-habitat was abundant and an increase in density of a species was recorded when its preferred habitat was increased. It is concluded that competition maintains the interspecific differences in foraging micro-habitat and consequently that the availability of appropriate micro-habitats determines abundance of the species on a local scale.

However, when we return to Noy-Meir's (1979/80) autecological hypothesis, the overall importance of competition in a desert environment comes into question.

Closer inspection of the examples available reveals that they are all from what might be termed semi-arid deserts, not the very arid areas in which Noy-Meir predicted his hypothesis would best apply. Nevertheless, even in these semi-arid areas of the North American deserts, competition occurs only when resources are abundant. Moreover, it is not the only force shaping the realised niches of the species studied.

The small pocket-mouse, *Perognathus amplus*, one of the seed-eating rodent species competing with ants in the Sonoran Desert, was shown to use hypothermic torpor to conserve energy during periods of food shortage, especially when these periods were coupled with low environmental temperatures (Reichman and Brown 1979). Granivorous ants may also employ dormancy to survive periods of climatic stress or resource scarcity (Brown *et al.* 1979b), although ectothermy and seed storage may reduce the necessity for dormancy during short-term environmental fluctuations.

In fact, there are several methods available to desert organisms for escaping from competition, some of them similar to the methods described in Chapter 3 for escaping from the desert environment. For example diapause, aestivation and seasonal migration may all be considered to reduce competition for resources with lowered availability during certain periods. Nevertheless, these may also be considered examples of environmental regulation as predicted for deserts where exploitation competition is more common. However, competition may not be a factor even during optimal growing conditions for those animals able to escape the desert environment during long, dry unsuitable periods. Some pond animals and other short-lived ephemeral organisms may totally avoid competition during their brief growing periods. They are instead entirely influenced by environmental conditions while food and other potentially limiting factors may be present in superabundant amounts.

Alternation between competition and environmental control has been observed in the central Namib Desert. There, during dry periods, four species of *Onymacris*, diurnal tenebrionid beetles, occupy four distinct locations in sandy habitats. *Onymacris rugatipennis* occupies the sandy, dry river bed and flood plain bordering the dune ecosystem, *O. plana* the dune bases and slopes near vegetation, *O. laeviceps* the dune slipfaces and isolated clumps of sparse vegetation and *O. unguicularis* the slipface only. At the location where observations were made, *O. unguicularis* is at the inland, eastern limit of its range. In 1976, over 100 mm of rain fell after more than a decade with a mean annual record value of 14 mm. The habitat occupied by *O. rugatipennis* expanded several kilometres into the dune ecosystem, but contracted again after completion of annual grass growth. The range of *O. plana* expanded to include the slipfaces while the other two species continued to occupy the same portion of the dune environment as during the dry period. In at least one area *O. unguicularis* disappeared from the slipfaces within 4 years, the eastern limit of its range retreating at least 10 km westward. This suggests that *O. plana*, occupying the slipfaces following the high rainfall, may have out-competed *O. unguicularis*. However, it is not known if this competition exists between the larval or adult stages of these two congeneric species. Following this same rainfall event the niches occupied by several other species were also observed to expand (and lead to competition?) during this temporary period of increased production.

In deserts, therefore, we would expect predominantly exploitation competition, although environmental control may reduce populations for long periods during which resources are no longer limiting. Here too, niche breadth is likely to be greater in general owing to the smaller plant biomass and variability of the environment (Goodall 1979).

Opportunism: generalists v. specialists

In deserts, where environmental conditions are variable and unpredictable and productivity is low, opportunism and flexibility are characteristics of many elements of the biota. Opportunistic behaviour allows plants and animals to take advantage of good conditions whenever these occur. However, in the following discussion of generalists and specialists we will sometimes be discussing contrasting physiological, as well as behavioural, adaptations. For example, camels exhibit physiological specialisations to allow them to live in the desert but are generalists with respect to feeding habits. Similarly, a Namib dune tenebrionid beetle, *Onymacris unguicularis*, employs very specialised fog-water drinking behaviour but has generalised feeding preferences. Nevertheless, both behaviour patterns of the beetle allow opportunistic utilisation of the environment.

We have repeatedly mentioned the temporal and spatial variability of rainfall in deserts and its effect on patchiness of primary producers. We must, however, again consider these important aspects of the desert environment. Patchiness affects different organisms in different ways. Highly mobile species are able to cover many suitable patches of food, substrate or other resources and use the environment in a 'fine-grained' manner. In extreme deserts such opportunistic generalists tend to be the larger or longer-lived species. They may rely predominantly upon one type of food or other resource, but when more attractive alternatives are available they will immediately take advantage of these varied resources. Specialists, in contrast, are often shorter-lived species occurring after adequate rainfall. They are usually less mobile than the generalists and use the dune environment in a more 'coarse-grained' manner.

Specialists are generally more common where productivity is higher. For example increases in precipitation, productivity and species diversity are paralleled by enhanced morphological, behavioural and ecological specialisation in harvester ants in the North American deserts (Brown *et al.* 1979b). *Veromessor pergandei*, a generalist inhabiting the least productive areas, shows size-polymorphism in workers and uses a diversity of seed-sizes efficiently. *Veromessor pergandei* is replaced, in habitats of greater productivity, by several species with workers of more uniform body size, each of which specialises in a narrow range of seed densities. That specialists in extreme deserts are usually found only during periods of increased productivity following rainfall is, therefore, not unexpected.

In very arid environments animals tend to be opportunistic, generalist feeders. There are very few true carnivores in a desert which will not consume alternative food sources when necessary. In the Namib the jackal, *Canis mesomelas*, consumes more vegetable matter in the more arid regions where meat is scarce. Where rainfall is higher, and in special situations such as on the coast where scavenging is more rewarding, meat forms a larger part of the diet (Stuart 1976). Larger, grazing herbivores feed only on plant material but are selectively opportunistic. They may consume one type of food when it is available but switch to other resources when necessary. Many smaller animals such as gerbils, beetles and some lizards will feed upon seeds, plants or insects, although they may prefer one category of food to another. Even pollinators in arid environments are often generalists and many desert plants are wind- or self-pollinated (Kislev 1972). Resources other than food may also be used in an opportunistic way. Gerbils in the Namib dunes usually burrow near vegetation where the sand is somewhat stabilised. However, in the absence of vegetation, the gerbils may locate their burrow entrances at patches of sand solidified by oryx urine (Seely 1976).

The great number of generalists may be a result of the importance of abiotic rather

than biotic factors in the desert environment. That is, interspecific competition and predation are not so important that specialisation need evolve. However, even in extreme desert areas many opportunistic specialists may be found. These specialisations are usually not the result of biotic interactions but are, instead, adaptations to the abiotic environment.

In contrast to the long-lived generalists of the Namib dunes, represented by the tenebrionid beetles (*Onymacris* spp.), a closely related species in the same tribe, *Eustolopus octoseriatus*, specialises in feeding on annual green grasses. Adults are only found on the surface for a few months following adequate rainfall, which may occur once or twice a decade. Amongst weevils of the genus *Leptostethus* we find the same dichotomy. The longer-lived species are generalists using all available plant species on the Namib dunes. However, one very short-lived blue species is found on the surface in an adult form for a very brief period after rain. As it feeds on a perennially green grass, *Stipagrostis sabulicola*, food quality rather than availability, or some other unidentified factor, may be the ultimate regulator. Moreover, the blue *Leptostethus* will emerge if rain occurs out of season in winter whereas *Eustolopus* only emerges following the somewhat more predictable late summer rains. Therefore even in extreme deserts opportunistic behaviour may be employed by animal specialists as well as generalists. Once again most of the specialisations are adaptations to the abiotic environment rather than to biotic interactions.

Opportunitistic specialists and generalists may also be found among desert plants. Annual plants often employ 'cautious opportunism', particularly with reference to seed germination (Koller 1972). Because of the variability of rainfall in deserts, full response to a simple signal may lead to a decrease in reproductive potential (Noy-Meir 1973). Seed longevity and seed heterogeneity, which allow delayed or differential germination, are common in desert plants. Particularly in North America many annuals have complex mechanisms regulating germination, and seeds only respond to precise combinations of environmental factors or sequences of events.

Growth response of the plant may also be opportunistic. Some plant species may have specialised roots which respond to soil heterogeneity, with exploring roots which locate any soil moisture. Others may be specialists in salt tolerance and occupy saline soils. Still others may be opportunistic generalists growing either as annuals or perennials depending upon the water-holding capacity of the soil in which germination occurs. In conclusion, we find a high degree of opportunism in both generalists and specialists, evolved as a response to the desert's basic characteristic, an unpredictable environment.

Chapter 9

Evolutionary ecology of deserts

Throughout the previous chapter we have examined the balance between biotic and abiotic components of the desert ecosystem. Although the abiotic influence is dominant, biotic interactions are not entirely absent. We will now examine the results of this delicate balance upon the organisms which occupy the arid environments of the world.

Diversity, stability and succession

Diversity

Tropical forests support many species of plants and animals, while only comparatively few occur in the arctic tundra. This tendency for a decrease in number of species from the tropics polewards has long been recognised by biologists, but the reason is still a topic for lively debate. The number of species present, or species density, however, provides only part of the picture. Also to be considered are the number of individuals of each species, and their biomass or their energy consumption as a measure of the relative importance of each component species. These two measures, species density and relative importance, have been combined into the concept of species diversity. Species diversity increases with increasing species density and with increasing equality of importance of the species considered. For example, a community with two species could be made up in two extreme ways:

	Species A	Species B
Community 1	50	50
Community 2	99	1

Community 1 would be considered more diverse. Several indices of diversity, Fischer's $\propto$ index, The Shannon–Wiener function (H') and Simpson's index (D) may all be used to summarise the information on diversity (Krebs 1972). However, the Shannon–Wiener index of diversity

$$H' = - \Sigma p_i \log p_i$$

when P_i is the proportion of the community belonging to the ith species (Pielou 1975), is probably the index most widely used by ecologists.

An increase in species diversity in any one area may occur as a result of increased partitioning of the niches occupied. Thus diversity may be generated along any of the three major niche dimensions: spatial, temporal and trophic (Pianka 1974). The spatial component of diversity may occur both horizontally and vertically. Ground-dwelling animals may partition habitats horizontally, some using open space

140

between vegetation and others using space near or in specific vegetation types such as grass, shrubs or trees. Vertical partitioning is employed by birds that occupy different vertical strata such as grass, shrubs and the lower and higher parts of the canopy of trees. Temporal separation, both daily and seasonal can also allow coexistence of more species and add to species diversity. Trophic differences may also lead to increased diversity. These may consist of subtle variations in the main differences between herbivores, omnivores and carnivores. Size and type of prey and overall composition of the diet may vary between consumers at various trophic levels.

The mechanisms determining diversity may be classified, depending on whether they act mainly through the physical environment alone (primary), the physical and biotic environments (secondary), or through the biotic environment alone (tertiary). Why are there greater species diversities in one community than in another? Attempts to explain this phenomenon have been numerous and we will present only a summary of one of several hypothetical mechanisms which have been proposed (Table 9.1). The reader is referred to any of the modern ecology texts for a more detailed discussion.

The several studies directed towards elucidating the mechanisms of species diversity have demonstrated correlations with habitat isolation (e.g. MacArthur and Wilson 1967), climatic stability (e.g. Sanders 1968), or predation (e.g. Paine 1966). Recently Connell (1978) has attributed the high diversity in tropical rain forests and coral reefs to the maintenance of a non-equilibrium state. This is the result of the severe disturbances which occur, preventing the establishment of a low-diversity equilibrium community. Recently studies concerning species diversity have been carried out in desert environments and we will discuss several of these examples.

Lizard communities were studied in three desert ecosystems varying widely in the total number of lizard species present (Pianka 1973, 1975). In North America 14 areas in the Great Basin, Mojave and Sonoran deserts support from 4 to 11 sympatric species of lizard. Ten study areas in the Kalahari of southern Africa support from 11 to 18 species of lizard and 8 study areas in the Great Victoria Desert of Australia support from 18 to 40 species. Lizard niches differ in the three niche dimensions of place, time and food. The trophic niches used by North American lizards vary greatly

Table 9.1 *Postulated factors contributing to species diversity. (From Pianka 1974.)*

Level	Hypothesis or theory	Mode of action
Primary	1. Evolutionary time	Degree of unsaturation with species
Primary	2. Ecological time	Degree of unsaturation with species
Primary	3. Climatic stability	Mean niche breadth
Primary	4. Climatic predictability	Mean niche breadth
Primary or secondary	5. Spatial heterogeneity	Range of available resources
Secondary	6. Productivity	Especially mean niche breadth, but also range of available resources
Secondary	7. Stability of primary production	Mean niche breadth and range of available resources
Tertiary	8. Competition	Mean niche breadth
Primary, secondary, or tertiary	9. Rarefaction	Degree of allowable niche overlap and level of competition
Tertiary	10. Predation	Degree of allowable niche overlap and level of competition

in contrast to Kalahari lizards, where differences in temporal and spatial niches are greater. All three dimensions separate niches in the Australian communities and overlap is greatly reduced. Pianka concludes that the difference in species diversity of the lizard communities is a result of the differences in the variety of resources used and of the reduced niche overlap as shown in the most diverse Australian communities. He found no obvious differences in the breadths of niches occupied.

In a study of the desert rodents of North America, Brown (1975) sampled sand dunes in the Mojave and Great Basin deserts, and sandy flatlands and rocky hillsides in the Sonoran Desert. The number of species that exist in any one habitat is dependent on historical as well as on ecological factors, so he restricted his analyses to interconnected deserts to ensure that there had been equivalent access to the habitats. Several conclusions could be drawn regarding species diversity. The close correlation between the number of common species and the predictable amount of rainfall (mean precipitation minus one standard deviation), indicates that species diversity within habitats depends largely on the abundance and predictability of the food resources in both sand dunes and sandy flats. The pattern of species diversity observed on a geographic scale differed from that observed within habitats. The largest number of common species was found where high species diversity was observed within habitats but also in the southern Mojave where low productivity supports low species diversity within habitats. The high species diversity with high productivity is a result of coexistence of several species in each kind of habitat but little habitat specificity and turnover of species between habitats. In contrast, areas of low productivity support only one or a few species in each habitat, but these species tend to have highly restricted habitat distributions and therefore a high turnover of species between habitats. Brown also found low species diversity in isolated deserts, which are essentially similar to islands. Unlike Pianka's (1975) findings for desert lizards, Brown has shown that the mean values for overlap of all pairs of species increase with species diversity.

In a more recent study in a small area of the Mojave Desert, Hafner (1977) found that the diversity of rodents was highly correlated with plant diversity. Neither rainfall nor habitat heterogeneity, proposed as controlling factors by Brown (1975) and Rosenzweig and Winakur (1969) respectively, appeared to affect rodent diversity directly. However, density in rodent communities responded indirectly and perennial shrub communities responded directly to amounts of rainfall. The different results obtained can be partially explained by differences in experimental design and particularly by extent and variation of experimental areas. Hafner (1977) concludes by emphasising the variations to be found within what are loosely termed 'desert habitats'. When responses to environmental parameters are discussed, perhaps the only generality which uniformly applies in all 'desert' areas is that rainfall will be an important factor in the system.

This generalisation agrees with the results of Davidson (1977) who found that the species diversity of seed-eating ants and rodents correlated with mean annual precipitation, an index of productivity, on a longitudinal gradient of increasing rainfall across the Mojave and Sonoran deserts (Fig. 9.1). She suggests that these parallels indicate that limits to specialisation and overlap may be specified by parameters such as resource abundance and predictability that affect unrelated taxa in a similar manner.

Similar results for plant species diversity and mean annual precipitation were recorded on a rainfall gradient from west to east across the Namib Desert dunes. Although not quantified, an increase in richness of plant species has been observed on the gravel plain substrate across this same rainfall gradient (Robinson 1977). We

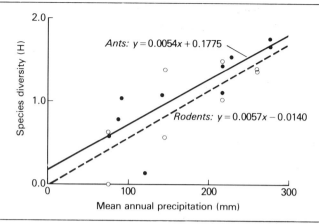

Fig. 9.1 Species diversity of seed-eating ants (●) and rodents (○) increases as precipitation increases in the North American deserts. (From Davidson 1977.)

may thus conclude that rainfall has a direct influence on species diversity, especially in the more extreme arid environments.

In extremely arid areas the large temporal and spatial variation of rainfall causes patchiness in the pattern of primary production, which also tends to increase species diversity. Patchy use of the desert by burrowing species may also contribute to species diversity through alteration of the substrate. For example, the burrowing activity of gerbils and ground squirrels creates suitable habitats for plant species otherwise excluded from undisturbed ground (Fig. 9.2). In less arid areas where the primary environmental parameters do not influence biological relationships so directly, varied secondary or tertiary factors other than rainfall may be more important in influencing species diversity of various taxa.

Fig. 9.2 Burrowing activities of rodents create suitable habitats for a variety of plants otherwise excluded from the central Namib plain. (Kind permission: W. Giess.)

Stability

Stability of an ecosystem is a somewhat elusive concept which is thought to depend on the diversity of the components. Odum (1975) has proposed an alternative explanation, that low diversity may result in stability when there is a high-quality energy flow and/or large nutrient input into a system, but that high diversity may be optimum in ecosystems limited by quality of energy input and/or dependent on internal nutrient cycling. Pielou (1975) has sought to clarify the concept of stability by differentiating between environmental and community stability. She proposes the following relationship:

environmental stability → community stability ⇄ high diversity, in which community stability may result in high diversity but where diversity does not create stability and may in fact have the opposite effect. Two aspects of the environment, predictability and productivity, may affect stability and hence diversity, although predictability is thought to be more important. With these ideas in mind we shall consider stability in a desert ecosystem.

Noy-Meir (1973) has listed four factors contributing to 'stability' in deserts when consideration is taken of the 'pulse and reserve' production pattern found in deserts (from Westoby 1972, and Bridges *et al.* 1972): (1) The flexible transition between an inactive (resistant) and active (susceptible) state is highly adaptive in an intermittently favourable environment; (2) the prevalence of this pattern among desert organisms explains the long-term stability of the system despite its extreme short-term variability; (3) this stability will only be endangered by mechanisms causing over-exploitation of the reserves or consistent prevention of back-flow to reserves; and (4) organisms at higher trophic levels must adapt either by adopting a pulse-reserve pattern, by using reserves of other organisms, or by flexible feeding habits.

Productivity in deserts, as we have discussed previously, is generally low and comes in pulses. Predictability is also low as a result of the large variances of the period and amplitude of environmental fluctuations. With rainfall, the primary limiting factor in deserts, the variability increases as the total declines. Hence we could expect deserts to be variable, particularly in the short term. But in the long term, deserts must be considered stable environments resulting in relatively stable communities, in that populations persist regardless of the degree of fluctuation. Stability of such an ecosystem varies around a steady state, which itself must also vary, depending on the amount and periodicity of the rainfall. Based upon data recently collected in the Namib Desert, the relative stability of the standing crop of vegetation in three dune habitats may be hypothetically portrayed (Fig. 9.3). Plants of the inter-dune valley respond to small amounts of precipitation (>10 mm) with the result that annuals appear every few years. As they dry out and disintegrate, wind eventually deposits the detritus on the slipface. Sufficient rain to cause germination of perennials on the dune slopes (± 50 mm) occurs less frequently. These plants break down more slowly but also eventually contribute to the detritus stores of the slipface. With the use of fog-water, tenebrionids and other macro-decomposers slowly break down the accumulated detritus, providing for long-term stability in a widely fluctuating, extremely arid environment.

Succession

Vegetation seldom occurs in discrete entities with sharp boundaries between communities. Instead there is usually a gradual change of species composition

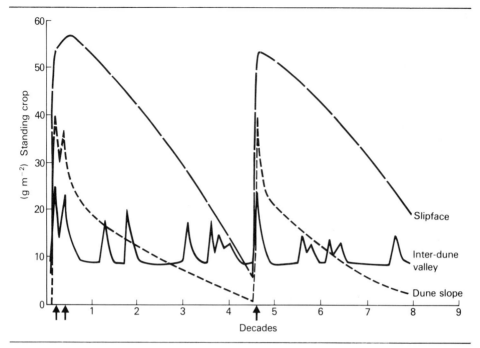

Fig. 9.3 The standing crop of detritus and vegetation in three Namib dune habitats varies independently with rainfall. Hypothetical curves are based on long-term precipitation records and measurements of standing crop preceding and following rain. (Arrows ↑ indicate high rainfall events.)

through both space and time. The change of community composition through space is usually in response to some environmental gradient such as elevation, moisture, temperature, soil factors, nutrients, etc. In an arid environment changes in species over an environmental gradient, particularly that of moisture, are often very clear-cut (we can refer to the example of the Namib in Ch. 7), while changes through time are not.

The change of vegetation through time may either be unidirectional, and is then called succession, or it may be cyclic. Succession occurs when a colonising species modifies the environment leading to occupation by other new species; this may include a change of pH, nutrients, moisture, organic matter, etc. In fact, most of these factors are also those which change through space, with the obvious exception of elevation. Succession continues until new species no longer alter the environment. But in deserts there is usually little or no modification of the environment by the vegetation. Thus in arid areas the invading species are usually the climax species, and succession in the classical sense does not occur. Ricklefs (1973) has tabulated the general characteristics of plants during early and late stages of succession (Table 9.2). The characteristics of the early stages could just as well be applied to annuals of arid environments. Any environmental modification which occurs may lead to germination of one species in the shade of another and then the continued growth of both species, rather than a change of species. Intimate growth patterns brought about as a result of micro-environmental changes by one species have been observed between, for example, *Welwitschia mirabilis* and *Colophospermum mopane* on the border of the Namib Desert.

Table 9.2   *Characteristics of plants during succession. Desert annuals show the characteristics of early successional stages. (From Ricklefs 1973.)*

Characteristic	Early	Late
Seeds	Many	Few
Seed size	Small	Large
Dispersal	Wind, stuck to animals	Gravity, eaten by animals
Seed viability	Long, latent in soil	Short
Root/shoot ratio	Low	High
Growth rate	Rapid	Slow
Mature size	Small	Large
Shade tolerance	Low	High

However, Kassas (1966) uses the term 'succession' to describe changes induced not by the vegetation itself but by seasonal and accidental changes. The example given earlier of the impact of burrowing animals on plant species composition may also then be considered to represent succession. Zemach (1974) describes the effects of rodents bringing up saline soil from deeper layers and causing replacement of non-halophytic winter annuals by halophytic annuals. Drastic succession or irreversible degradation of desert environment may result from over-use due to bad farming or recreational practices.

There is one example, however, wherein plants do modify the desert environment. Shrubs or other medium-sized plants can reduce wind speeds sufficiently to cause an accumulation of sand and organic detritus around the base of the plant. The micro-environment thus formed is often more favourable than the surrounding environment for germination and growth of other plants. Such mound-formation is an important component in the cyclic relationship between *Larrea tridentata* and *Opuntia leptocaulis* in the northern Chihuahuan Desert (Yeaton 1978) (Fig. 9.4). Nevertheless, this process of mound initiation and establishment may also lead to one of the few examples of autogenic succession in deserts (Danin 1978). A similar process, due to transport by water rather than by wind, may explain the vegetation bands or arcs which have been noted in some deserts (White 1969).

In conclusion, most observable change of vegetation in a desert environment is spatial and a response to some environmental gradient. Change through time is usually cyclic in nature. On a longer time scale, change is probably largely a response to climatic modification of the environment by plants themselves. True autogenic succession is not commonly a natural phenomenon in arid environments.

Parallel evolution, convergent evolution and coevolution

Thus far, we have emphasised the importance of abiotic factors, particularly water, in controlling life in deserts. In the desert environment interspecific interactions are limited in comparison to the overwhelming effect of climate. Moreover, because of the sparse vegetation, the environments in all deserts are dominated by geomorphological features rather than plant communities and are therefore relatively similar. As a result of the importance of abiotic factors and the limitations imposed on possible ways that living organisms can adapt to this relatively harsh environment, the number and variety of life forms should be limited. It is for these reasons that we find many examples of convergence between species in comparable deserts throughout the world. When examples of similar adaptations are found in distant areas, the species involved are known as 'ecological equivalents'. These may

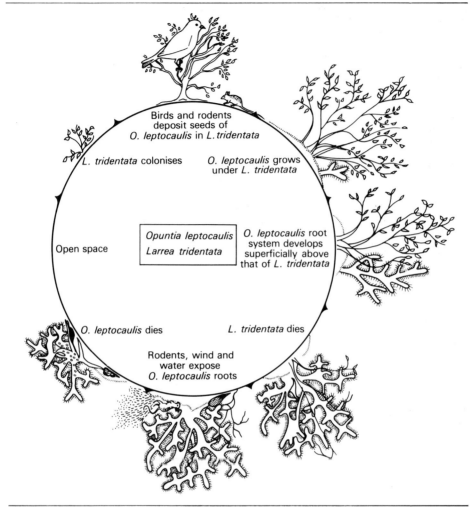

Fig. 9.4 Postulated cyclical replacement of *Larrea tridentata* and *Opuntia leptocaulis* in the northern Chihuahuan Desert. (From Yeaton 1978.)

have evolved from the same phylogenetic lineage through parallel evolution or from different origins by way of convergent evolution.

Similarities between communities experiencing similar environments have long been recognised by biologists. As stated by Whittaker (1975), 'adaptive convergence at the level of the community is one of the major generalisations about the geography of life'. Examples of convergence are most conspicious in tropical rain forests, where many plant species are all competing for one limiting resource, light. Mammals, too, show striking convergence in form, function and behaviour in tropical forests (Bourlière 1973) (Fig. 9.5). However, evolutionary convergence is also marked in environments, such as deserts, controlled mainly by abiotic elements. For example, we have been able to make generalisations about the adaptations of desert plants and animals because many of the same adaptations have been evolved by organisms from different phylogenetic origins in distant deserts (Fig. 9.6). The reasons for this are

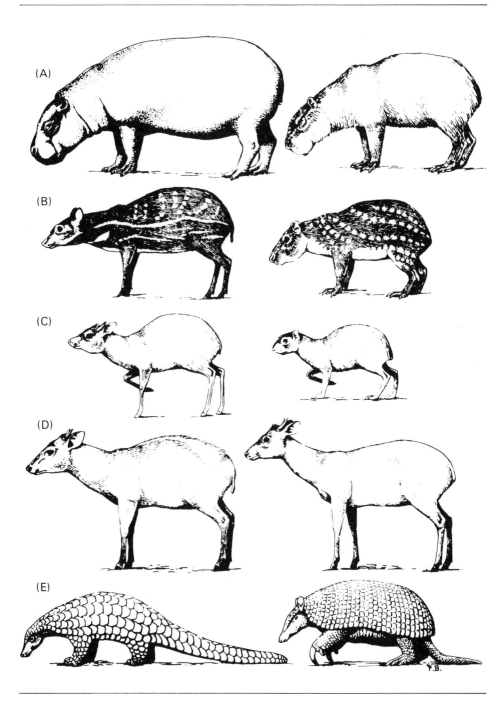

Fig. 9.5 African (left) and neo-tropical (right) rain-forest mammals show remarkable morphological convergence. From left to right: (A) pigmy hippopotamus and capybara; (B) African chevrotain and paca; (C) royal antelope and agouti; (D) yellowback duiker and brocket deer; (E) terrestrial pangolin and giant armadillo. Each pair of animals is drawn to the same scale (From Bourlière 1973.)

succinctly stated by Mayr (1963): 'If there is only one efficient solution for a certain functional demand, very different gene complexes will come up with the same solution, no matter how different the pathway by which it is achieved.' This emphasises that 'convergence is the adaptive response of species and not of communities as a whole. Two principles concerning convergent evolution have emerged from extensive study of this phenomenon (Whittaker 1975): (1) solutions to problems are not usually found by use of a single adaptation but by a combination of several; (2) species may therefore show some convergence but varied patterns of adaptation as a whole.

Many striking examples are known and often cited in discussions of convergent evolution. For example, flightless birds such as emu, ostrich and rhea, occupy similar niches on three different continents. Phenotypically the American cacti closely resemble the euphorbias of southern Africa (Fig. 9.7 (A), (B)). Jerboas of North African deserts and kangaroo rats of American deserts have different ancestors but are similar in form. All of these examples of convergence represent adaptations of several characters under similar environmental pressures. However, as pointed out by Pianka (1974), roughly similar ecological systems need not always support conspicuous ecological equivalents. There are a limited number of ways in which the niche space in a community may be exploited. How each individual species occupies the available space is determined in part by what other species in the community are doing. But in deserts, where abiotic factors are more important than interspecific interactions, the available niche space is limited, as is the array of possible adaptive responses. In a recent paper dealing with geographical trends in numbers of species, Schall and Pianka (1978) have pointed out that species densities of different groups of organisms, in this case insectivorous birds and lizards, may depend on different environmental factors. Lizards appear to be more restricted by abiotic factors and occupy a restricted range of habitats when compared to birds. Nevertheless, four times as many lizards coexist in the Australian desert as in North America. Australian lizards occupy the ecological niches of some North American mammals, snakes and perhaps arthropods as well. Hence we cannot expect one-to-one convergence between species of these two desert areas where different groups of organisms occupy, in different ways, the complex of available ecological niches.

Karr and James (1975) have suggested that if environments impose constraints on the adaptations of organisms, then sets of coexisting species should have predictable morphological and ecological properties. This was found to be the case for forest birds from three continents. Of particular interest were the findings that convergence occurred more commonly between ecologically similar species of different phylogenetic origin; divergence commonly occurred between ecologically different species of the same phylogenetic origin; and in many cases there was wider morphological spacing between congeners than between non-congeners. The convergences and divergences found crossing generic and familial lines suggest that ecological, behavioural and morphological characteristics represent closely knit adaptive complexes. Competitive displacement is thought to be a particularly important determinant of community structure.

Mares (1978) points out the value of deserts in studies on convergent evolution and that convergence is particularly evident in groups such as small mammals which are not extensively pre-adapted for a desert existence. From a study of almost all desert rodent genera from all deserts of the world, he concludes that only a limited number of broad niches have evolved in each desert. Moreover, although the organisms are only distantly related, the niches occupied are basically similar in each region. Similar functional niches in some deserts may be accompanied by reversed

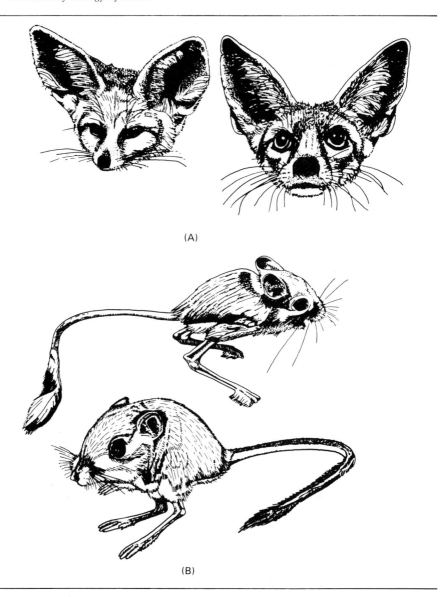

(A)

(B)

trophic and locomotory components, as for example in the Iranian Daskt-e-Kavir and the Sonoran Desert of North America. He found that fossorial root- and tuber-eating gophers and bipedal granivorous kangaroo rats inhabit the Sonoran Desert while, in contrast, extensively burrowing granivores and bipedal root- and tuber-eaters frequent the Daskt-e-Kavir. Thus the evolutionary history of an area, including the presence of ecological equivalents from non-mammalian assemblages, influences the overall composition and ecological adaptations of individual species in that community.

Brown *et al.* (1979b) studied a more varied community of desert granivores, mainly rodents and ants but also including birds. They also suggest that a combination of unique historical events, environmental factors and interspecific

Fig. 9.6 Many examples of convergent evolution may be found in deserts of the world. (A) Sahara fennec fox and American kit fox, (B) Saharan jerboa and American kangaroo rat, (C) Namib sidewinding adder and North American sidewinder rattler.

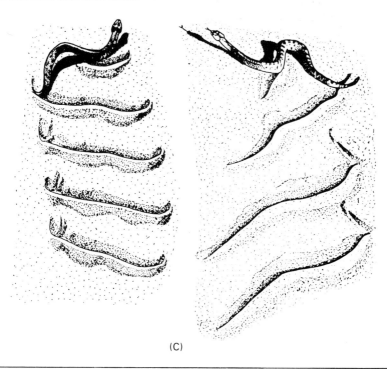

(C)

competition, within and between closely related taxa, have produced observed patterns of community organisation. In Australia and South America desert rodent faunas are impoverished for historical reasons. In the extensive deserts of other continents, specialised seed-eating rodents have evolved independently from distantly related, unspecialised ancestors. Examples of convergent evolution resulting in similar morphology, physiology and behaviour are particularly to be found in the genera *Dipodomys, Dipus, Gerbillurus, Gerbillus, Jaculus* and *Notomys*.

In Asian, African and North American deserts, seed-eating ants, rodents and birds are abundant and diverse (Brown *et al.* 1979b). However in Australia, the rodent fauna is impoverished and there are about three times as many species of harvester ant and six times as many granivorous bird species as in North America. In contrast in South America, where there is also an absence of seed-eating rodents in the desert communities, seed-eating ants and birds are not more abundant or diverse than in North America. The South American situation may be the result of a historical situation in which seed-eating rodents recently became extinct and this niche has been left unoccupied. In Australia, on the other hand, the high diversity of seed-eating birds and ants may be the result of these groups having evolved to exploit resources utilised by rodents in other deserts. Hence convergence of entire communities may occur as differing groups fill similar ecological rôles.

Convergent evolution was one of the focal points of the US/IBP Desert Programme and an initial summary has appeared (Orians and Solbrig 1977). This presents the results of extensive studies carried out in the hot deserts of North and

(A)

(B)

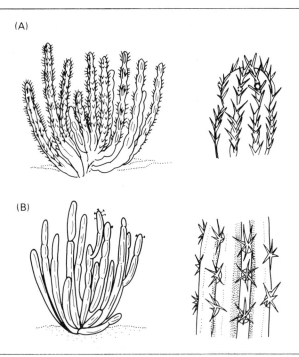

Fig. 9.7   (A) Namib euphorbia, and (B) North American cactus.

South America at selected sites where the physical environments are similar. In their summary, the authors conclude that those characteristics of organisms which are more influenced by abiotic factors will show a greater degree of convergence than will those in which biological interactions with competitors or predators are important. For example, results indicate that striking convergences are shown in individual morphological and physiological traits of plants. A number of closely matched species-pairs were found; however, many of these are congeneric and therefore represent parallel rather than convergent evolution. At the community level similarities were also found in patterns of distribution of total plant biomass, life form and spacing and density of shrubs. In contrast, those features of the plants related to interactions with animals were less similar.

Similar conclusions were derived from studies of selected animal taxa. Those groups most influenced by the abiotic environment showed the highest degree of convergence in both individual adaptive traits and equivalent species-pairs. For example, anurans showed a high degree of convergence while mammals did not. However, this latter, somewhat unexpected, result is thought to be due to historical rather than to ecological factors.

Another interesting pattern to emerge from these studies is that one is more likely to find convergent species-pairs in taxa with few species than in taxa with many species. When few species are present, they presumably have only a few ways of existing in the environment. This restriction is probably generated by strong influences from abiotic as well as biotic factors, and these pressures should also result in covergence of characteristics. In contrast, when many sympatric species in a taxon occur in an environment, biotic rather than abiotic factors are more likely to

influence the resultant pattern and therefore less convergence is to be expected.

In general we may say that the physical environment, rather than biotic interactions, is the main force resulting in convergence between species and communities of distant deserts. Many of the examples provided have come from deserts where rainfall averages at least 100 mm annually. Considering the importance of abiotic factors, we could predict that more examples of convergent characters may be found in the more extreme, very arid deserts, the same environment in which Noy-Meir (1978) suggests that the autecological hypothesis may be more valid.

Examples of very arid environments with approximately similar physical environments are found in the sand dunes of the Namib and Peruvian deserts. The dunes of the Namib occupy a larger area and the fauna has been exposed for a longer time to arid conditions (Seely 1978a). Nevertheless, because of the presence in both of fog, an important moisture source in the absence of rain, we may expect to find examples of convergence in these two deserts.

Wind, acting upon the sand, shapes the dunes of all deserts into similar configurations. Near the crests of the dunes, slipfaces often develop on the leeward slope. Here any organic detritus in the form of wind-blown plant or animal material accumulates. The slipfaces of the Namib support a fauna which uses wind-blown detritus as its major energy source. Tenebrionid beetles are the most conspicuous component of this fauna, which also includes silverfish, lizards and gerbils. Resident predators include trapdoor spiders, which prey upon adult beetles, as well as on other invertebrates and even small reptiles, and the golden mole which also preys upon beetle larvae and small reptiles.

A similar fauna, also dependent on detritus as its energy source, occurs on the slipfaces in the Peruvian dunes. Several coleopteran species, both tenebrionids and ptinids, comprise the detritivorous fauna. Predators on the adult Coleoptera include a scorpion species and perhaps ant lion larvae.

The slipface fauna of the Peruvian dunes appears to be somewhat impoverished when compared to the equivalent Namib fauna, but in the face of a combination of historical and geographical factors this observation is not unexpected. Hence, although an exact series of ecological equivalents are not to be found in the two desert slipface communities, comparable species of both primary and secondary consumers occupy similar trophic niches in both areas.

Coevolution

Coevolution refers to the simultaneous evolution of two or more taxa with close ecological interactions and, most frequently, to interdependent evolutionary interactions between plants and animals (Pianka 1974). These interactions are usually mutually advantageous or at least minimise the disadvantages that one or both associates may be exposed to. Because of the importance of abiotic interactions in a desert, few examples of coevolution have been discovered, nevertheless several instances have been observed in the North American deserts.

An interesting example, which demonstrates the evolution of interdependence between plants and animals, is provided by the moth, *Pronuba yuccaseila*, and the yucca plants of the deserts of the south-western United States. The yucca plants themselves are of unusual interest in that the attractive white flowers are produced on an incredibly tall spike, which must be energetically most expensive to grow. Presumably the plants make this heavy investment to facilitate successful pollination by the *Pronuba* moth. The female moth collects pollen from the anthers of one flower

and then moves to a different flower, climbs on to the pistil where it inserts the ovipositor in order to lay several eggs. After oviposition the moth moves up the pistil and deposits the pollen ball on the stigma. Apparently the moth does not feed on either pollen or nectar and much speculation has arisen as to whether the pollination is accidental or purposeful. In any event the larvae benefit from feeding on the developing seed pod, thus demonstrating the coevolution of interdependence between the two species. This intriguing phenomenon was first reported by Charles Riley during the last century and has been beautifully described by Krutch (1966) in his delightful book *The Voice of the Desert*.

Time is one of the factors which promotes coevolution (Ricklefs 1973), but geological time would not necessarily be a limiting factor in deserts. The low productivity and unpredictable occurrence of rainfall would, however, serve to limit the number of interactions between species during any one lifetime and so limit possibilities of coevolution in deserts.

Compromise and optimisation

During the evolutionary history of both plants and animals conflicting demands are often involved in the selection pressures acting upon living organisms. For example, it may hypothetically be to an animal's advantage to develop a square shape in order to exploit its food resources adequately, while a round shape may be ideal for escaping from predators. Depending on the genetic variation present in the population and the relative intensity of these two selection pressures, the animals could either become square or round. In both cases they are obliged to accept or 'trade off' the disadvantages of one shape to exploit the advantages of the opposite shape. Alternatively a compromise could develop if the animals become hexagonal! In the latter case we may be tempted to speak of an optimal compromise, although life is seldom optimal and we live in an imperfect world. Moreover, because of both the time factor involved in evolution, and the fluctuating environment, there will always be a time-lag between ideal and realised phenotypic characteristics. In any event, there are many examples of apparent evolutionary compromises brought about by natural selection, and a brief description of some of these is warranted.

On the coast of the Namib Desert literally millions of cormorants nest and raise their chicks without access to any fresh water. These birds are uniformly black in colour and even on relatively cool summer days (25 °C) they absorb excessive solar radiation. As a result they are obliged to evaporate a large amount of water by thermal panting to maintain a constant body temperature while shading either their eggs or chicks. As the birds have no access to fresh water, this water loss causes considerable stress and we were puzzled as to the reason why they should have evolved a black coloration. The answer is to be found in the demands made on these animals when foraging beneath the cold waters of the Atlantic Ocean. Unlike those of most marine birds, the cormorants' feathers do not repel water and consequently cold water at 12 °C comes into direct contact with the skin which is at 40 °C. The wettable feathers represent an additional evolutionary compromise but reduce the buoyancy of the birds, thus lowering the energetic cost of underwater swimming while they hunt their prey. The steep thermal gradient between skin and water, however, results in a rapid loss of heat and the birds do not remain in the sea for long periods. Instead, they return to the desert shoreline where they extend their wings and orientate the maximum surface area toward the incident insolation. Under these conditions the animals' black coloration is most advantageous in that they absorb heat rapidly and body temperatures are maintained without wasting energy. Black

colour in these birds therefore appears to represent an evolutionary compromise which on balance must favour the survival of the species.

In Chapter 4 we pointed out that the pelage of desert ungulates represented a compromise between thermal shielding and the facilitation of heat loss. In fact, selection pressure in ungulates of the semi-arid African savanna appears to have favoured heat loss. There is an exponential decline in the depth of the pelage with increasing body size and a concomitant decrease in relative surface area for losing heat. Facilitation of heat loss is particularly important when the ungulates are forced to sprint when escaping from predators. In contrast, certain artificially selected sheep breeds with a relatively long fleece can thrive in hot, semi-arid areas. The outer surface of the fleece reaches temperatures as high as 85 °C and the heat gradient is reversed from the fleece to the environment. The fleece therefore acts as an efficient thermal shield during the day and, equally important, as insulation during cold nights. The sheep are, however, protected by man from predators and, if forced to run even comparatively short distances under hot conditions, they would collapse from heat stress. The antelope, on the other hand, with their short sleek pelage, are able to lose heat fairly easily by radiation and convection after sprinting away from predators. This compromise in antelope is, however, achieved at considerable cost because during cold nights they lose heat rapidly and squander energy in maintaining their body temperatures by shivering. It is no surprise then that desert antelope, unlike sheep, seldom accumulate excessive fat; after long periods of nutritional stress, prolonged exposure to cold can be fatal. The compromise nevertheless appears to have been dictated by the strongest selection pressure, namely the need to lose heat when escaping from predation under hot arid conditions.

Compromises are not restricted to the effects of natural selection but also occur in systems of artificial selection. An excellent desert example of this is provided by the black Bedouin goat discussed in Chapter 4. The black colour increases absorption of solar radiation and, on cold but sunny winter days in the desert, the demand for energy to maintain body temperature is significantly reduced (25%). Again, however, this compromise is not without its disadvantages as the black goats are obliged to evaporate more water to maintain body temperature during the summer than white goats, because of the greater absorptivity of the black pelage. Presumably over centuries of goat herding the Bedouins have evaluated the relative survival value of the two coat colours and opted for the 'black' compromise.

Many examples of apparent evolutionary compromises could be cited and they often provide material for entertaining, if somewhat speculative, debate. These examples are also not limited to the morphological characteristics of animals but include physiological and behavioural traits. Perhaps one of the most reliably studied aspects in this respect is the analysis of optimised foraging behaviour in animals, which has been well quantified in certain species. The above examples should, however, serve to introduce the subject and the reader is referred to any standard text on ecology for further information.

Chapter 10

Man and the desert

The desert environment affects different people in different ways. To many it is a grotesque and frightening environment and to become lost in the waterless wastes of a hot desert is to understand the real meaning of despair. To the Tuareg, crossing the seemingly endless sandy plains of the Sahara together with a salt caravan, the environment is commonplace; he knows no other and takes pride in his prowess as a caravaner, hunter and warrior. His knowledge of the applied ecology of the desert is astounding and one is also impressed by the dignity and elaborate courtesy of desert people. In contrast, many European immigrants to deserts have romanticised the unusual beauty of the desert environment. Antoine de Saint-Exupéry and Joseph Wood Krutch, the Thoreau of the Desert, are just two of many writers who have successfully captured the special mystique of the desert. The desert biologist finds his niche somewhere in between, enjoying the remarkable beauty of the natural laboratory he is exploiting while keeping an analytical and quantitative eye on the processes he is studying. We could fill volumes on man's historical association with the desert environment, but space permits only a discussion of certain physiological considerations, together with some of the more important applied problems.

Physiological considerations

The same physical principles governing heat exchange in animals and plants naturally pertain to a discussion of human thermoregulation in the desert environment. These principles, together with the relevant equations, have been outlined in Chapter 2. Man, however, differs from other animals in two important respects. He is a naked endotherm and, because of his ability to modify his micro-environment, is probably the most adaptable organism on this planet. Special consideration of the physiological principles related to desert survival in man is therefore warranted.

When ambient temperatures rise above the thermal neutral zone of man the expected physiological and behavioural responses are evoked. Conductance of heat from the body is increased by vasodilation of the superficial blood vessels to allow increased flow of blood and therefore of heat to the surface of the body. Man, unlike many large mammals, does not pant in response to heat; otherwise it would be most awkward to play the flute in a symphony concert on a warm night. Instead, man sweats profusely and can produce over 1 litre of sweat per hour under hot conditions. This ability places man in a class of his own, as no animal studied to date can sweat nearly as efficiently and this is probably the reason for man's unusual stamina in long-distance running. Perhaps this unusual capacity for sweating can be traced back to our evolutionary origin in a warm African climate and our long history as hunter-gatherers when stamina for the long chase was essential.

In view of the great importance of the evaporative cooling effect of sweating, it is particularly important to appreciate that the efficacy of sweating is dependent on the water vapour pressure in the air surrounding the body. In tropical climates this is frequently high and associated with high ambient temperature. Consequently such climates cause physical and psychological distress to unadapted immigrants and even to natives of these regions. The desert climate, on the other hand, is characterised by low water vapour pressures in the atmospheric air and as a result efficacy of sweating is far higher. The desert climate is therefore far more acceptable to the European immigrant than are the tropics in terms of thermoregulatory stress.

Although the physiological adjustments mentioned above, sweating and vasodilation, are of critical importance, one should not overlook behavioural responses which are as important to an endotherm such as man as they are to an ectothermic reptile. Reduction in the amount of clothing, seeking out shade or a cool breeze and the adoption of a spread-eagled posture to increase the surface area for heat loss are all of significance. Their importance is overshadowed, however, by the effect of decreasing the amount of physical activity, because physical activity increases the metabolic rate and therefore the heat production of an individual very swiftly.

The question of critical temperatures now arises. As ambient temperature, wind speed, water vapour pressure and radiation intensity are all involved it is not possible to suggest a simple temperature range. All these factors cannot be integrated in strict physical terms but they have to be considered together when determining the critical conditions for human activity. Many attempts have been made to integrate these factors and probably the most widely used index is the Wet-Bulb Globe Thermometer Index (WBGT) which is calculated as follows:

WBGT = 0.2 globe temperature + 0.1 dry-bulb temperature + 0.7 wet-bulb temperature.

Globe temperatures are measured inside a copper sphere, 150 mm in diameter, which has been painted with matt black paint. Both radiation intensity and wind speed will affect this temperature and become integrated in the equation. The water vapour pressure in turn will affect the difference between the wet and dry bulb temperatures. Using WBGT as a criterion, the United States Army has recommended that physical training for recruits should be abandoned at 31.5 °C (WBGT), while well-trained military personnel are allowed to continue training to 33.0 °C (WBGT).

The different criteria applied to recruits and well-trained soldiers introduces the interesting phenomenon of acclimation to heat. It is a subject that has been well researched because of the importance of having acclimated troops who can be transported rapidly through different climatic zones in times of war. It is also of importance in industries such as mining where personnel are exposed to unusually high temperatures. In this context Professor C. Wyndham at the Human Sciences Laboratory in Johannesburg has been most successful in reducing the mortality rate due to thermal stress in the Witwatersrand gold mines by acclimating miners before they are exposed to the steep geothermal gradient thousands of metres below ground. These studies and many others have shown that acclimation to heat consists essentially of an increased ability to sweat. In one particular study it was shown that exposure to 40 °C dry bulb and 32 °C wet bulb with a wind speed of 0.4 m s^{-1} for 4 hours daily, increased the sweating rate of the experimental subjects very dramatically over a period of 30 days (Fig. 10.1). In this experiment it should be noted that exposure was not continuous for the 30-day period but for four periods of

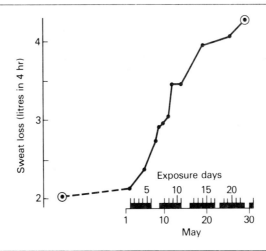

Fig. 10.1 The increase in mean sweating rate of 16 individuals exposed to hot room conditions for 4 periods of 5 consecutive days each. The first measurements (●) were made 4 weeks prior be the main experiment. (From Edholm 1978.)

5 consecutive days. Under these conditions the sweat loss over the 4-hour period increased from approximately 2 litres in the pre-acclimation period to over 4 litres after acclimation. It should also be noted that these sweating rates are by no means maximal and that a sweating rate of as much as $4\,l\,h^{-1}$ has been measured in a well-acclimated individual.

Acclimation to heat occurs merely by exposure to high ambient temperatures without any physical effort being required from the subjects. Acclimation will, however, be more rapid if physical work is included in the acclimation programme. In fact, if temperature chambers are not available for acclimating subjects in a temperate environment, vigorous physical exercise alone can provide a large measure of acclimation. This is because of the marked increase in heat production which accompanies vigorous exercise and the high sweating rate required to cool the body under these conditions. For this reason long-distance athletes and similarly trained sportsmen are usually well acclimated to hot environments even if they have trained in temperate countries.

Edholm (1978) has summarised the main conclusions which can be drawn from research on acclimation to heat. These are: (1) that all people, irrespective of age, sex and ethnic origin, respond similarly to heat exposure which eventually leads to a state of heat acclimation; (2) that continuous exposure to heat is not required as even daily exposure of as little as 2 hours will be sufficient, even if the remainder of the day is spent in a cool environment; (3) that short daily exposures to heat can allow men living in a cool temperate country to achieve an even higher degree of acclimation than people living permanently in a hot country; (4) although men and women both exhibit the above acclimation responses, it is generally accepted that sweating rates in women remain at a much lower level than in men, ~ 50 per cent (this finding has been advanced as the reason for the higher potential work output of men in hot desert conditions); and (5) with advancing age the acclimation response is reduced. Recently it has also been suggested that vitamin C supplementation facilitates heat acclimation.

In view of the central rôle played by sweating in acclimation and eventually in maintaining normal body temperatures under hot conditions, we should give some attention to the replacement of this large loss of body fluids. In earlier chapters we have seen that desert beetles, lizards and the camel, when they get the opportunity to drink, replace the loss of body water rapidly and exactly. In man, however, homoiostatic control over water replacement does not seem to be as refined as in these animals. Many people under hot conditions tend to allow considerable dehydration to occur before drinking enough to replace lost tissue fluids.

In this respect the Israeli Army conducted an interesting experiment on soldiers undertaking a vigorous route-march through the desert under hot conditions. The soldiers were divided into four groups and each group was assigned to drink as much of one of the following four fluids as they wished: water, water flavoured with fruit extract, milk and finally beer. Surprisingly, the group given plain water did not maintain a positive water balance throughout the route-march, as humans, for some unknown reason, perhaps palatability, are unable to drink sufficiently large quantities of plain water in a short enough time to replace losses through sweat under these conditions. Eventually they do, but it takes some time and usually occurs several hours after strenuous physical activity has ceased. The group given milk developed diarrhoea, which naturally would exacerbate their condition by adding to the dehydration process. Somewhat surprisingly, the group on beer were able to maintain their water balance but were hardly in a condition to engage in any military operation. The highest intakes of fluid were obtained with the flavoured water and this group maintained their water balance far more efficiently.

Any discussion of fluid replacement in the desert must include reference to the contentious issue of salt (NaCl) replacement or supplementation. For many years it was believed that the high sweating rates which developed under desert conditions were accompanied by severe depletion of the sodium chloride reserves of the body, leading to muscular cramps and other disabilities. For this reason salt tablets were issued, and still are in some instances, to military personnel and athletes who have to perform under hot conditions. More recent, refined measurements of electrolyte loss in sweat have, however, shown that, as the process of acclimation proceeds, the concentration of electrolytes in the sweat diminishes and well-acclimated individuals produce a very dilute sweat. Moreover, even in unacclimated individuals the loss of electrolytes is relatively small, seldom exceeding 60 mmol chloride per litre. This loss would be comfortably compensated for by the normal dietary intake of salt and many experts in this field today maintain that salt supplementation would be more harmful than beneficial. In the face of this expert opinion many lay-people, including marathon athletes, strongly maintain that salt supplementation is essential for preventing or treating muscular cramps. The weight of evidence, however, is clearly against salt supplementation, which can cause osmotic disturbances and renal complications. Under extraordinary conditions such as alcohol abuse in hot desert conditions by unacclimated individuals, the diuretic action of alcohol plus electrolyte loss in sweat could cause muscular cramps and justify the supplementation of salt (9 g per litre of H_2O) for a short period.

We move from acclimation physiology and fluid replacement to illnesses caused by thermal stress. Edholm (1978) has distinguished between *syncope* and *heatstroke* in this respect. Syncope is the more usual form of heat stress and is accompanied by a swift rise in body temperature and loss of consciousness (fainting), which is probably caused by vascular collapse and pooling of blood in the skin and muscles. Edholm (1978) also points out that in acclimated individuals the blood volume increases and peripheral pooling of blood is less probable. Treatment of syncope consists of

sponging the body with cool water and placing the patient in the shade and, if at all possible, a cool breeze to facilitate evaporation. Recovery is usually swift. Placing the patient in an ice bath is not recommended as this will cause shivering and peripheral vaso-constriction, thereby retarding heat loss to the environment (Strydom 1980).

Heatstroke is a far more serious condition than syncope. It is characterised by a swift rise in body temperature and is frequently associated with the cessation of sweating, known as anhidrosis. The elevated body temperature aggravates the condition by increasing metabolic rate and therefore heat production. At a body temperature of 39–40 °C most individuals will collapse from heat stress. Once the body temperature reaches 43 °C recovery is very unlikely as certain proteins may precipitate and enzyme functions become impaired at this temperature. In contrast, it would appear that the desert-adapted oryx is able to tolerate a body temperature of 45 °C for several hours without undue distress (see Ch. 5). The oryx, however, possesses a carotid rete for cooling the brain, while the sensitivity of the human brain to high temperatures is well known to anyone who has suffered from the delirium associated with a high fever.

In conclusion then, the physiological responses of man to heat are fairly typical of many large endotherms, with the important difference that man regulates his temperature within very narrow limits and relies heavily on copious sweating for this purpose. Acclimation is largely an adaptation for increased sweating rate, the sweat becoming progressively more dilute as acclimation proceeds. Acclimation is induced by increasing the body temperature either by exposure to high temperatures or by strenuous physical exercise or both. These treatments will naturally increase sweating rates and after repeated application will produce acclimation. If sweating ceases (anhidrosis) body temperatures rise explosively under hot conditions and this can lead to an irreversible heatstroke. The cause of anhidrosis is not yet clear but factors which may contribute to this condition are sweat-gland fatigue from too long an exposure to high ambient temperatures, insufficient water intake, and sunburn. In the latter case it is thought that the hyperaemia and swollen skin may block the sweat ducts. Heat cramps can be caused by a variety of factors including an inadequate blood supply, over-exertion, hyperventilation, a lack of any one of the electrolytes, and dehydration. Supplementation of the diet with salt is not recommended.

Clothing, diet and housing

If one reviews the physical principles governing heat exchange in animals, outlined in Chapter 2, it is clear that the naked skin of man is an ideal surface for losing heat by evaporative water loss. It is equally clear that it would be absurd to expose naked skin to the intense radiation encountered in desert environments. Apart from the destructive effects of the ultraviolet rays on the skin, the lack of thermal shielding would lead to high heat gains. The question then arises: what is the ideal form of clothing for the desert environment?

Surprisingly little research has been carried out in this field, but the physics of heat transfer would suggest that a highly reflective surface would be superior to a dull black surface and that loose-fitting clothes, which allow free circulation of air across the skin surface to facilitate evaporative water loss, would also be advantageous. The garment should cover most of the body surface including the neck and head and its insulative properties should be a good compromise between restricting heat gain from the environment (thermal shielding) and not being too thick to prevent heat loss from the body to the environment. With these considerations in mind we would probably design a garment which is very similar to the robes worn by typical desert

nomads such as the Bedouins. There is, however, one exception, and that is that the Bedouins' robes are black and not white. The reason for this is not entirely clear but we have already mentioned the metabolic advantages of a black colour to Bedouin goats in the winter (Ch. 5), and it is possible that this advantage has ultimately dictated the colour of the Bedouins' robes and tents. Shkolnik *et al.* (1980b) have recently compared the heat exchange of a subject wearing white and black Bedouin robes when exposed to the desert sun. As expected, they found that the net radiation gain minus convective loss was two to three times greater on the surface of the black robes than on the white robes. Surprisingly, however, the temperature of the air space between the robes and skin did not differ between the two colours. This is ascribed by the authors to a greater convective loss of heat beneath the black robes brought about by a 'chimney effect' causing an upward movement of air between the robes and the skin, drawing cooler air in from the bottom of the robe (Fig. 10.2).

Fig. 10.2 Although black Bedouin robes gain more radiant energy from the sun than white robes, the temperature of the air space between the skin and robe was the same for both colours. Increased convection beneath the black robes may account for this unexpected result. See text for details. (From Shkolnik *et al.* 1980b.)

Alternatively, as the robes flow in the wind a 'bellows effect' could increase convective heat loss beneath the robes. In any event, whatever mechanism is responsible for the increased convective heat loss, the net gain of heat of the experimental subject did not differ when wearing either black or white robes.

In the same study the authors compared the net heat gain of a semi-nude subject wearing only shorts, with the same subject dressed in a standard military combat uniform or dressed in Bedouin robes. When semi-nude, the subject gained the most heat (208 W m^{-2}), less when wearing the tan-coloured army uniform (161 W m^{-2}), while in Bedouin robes he averaged a heat gain of 138 W m^{-2}. Naturally, thermoregulatory considerations are not always paramount when designing desert garments and combat uniforms must provide the wearer with camouflage and freedom of movement. Nevertheless, more research is required in this field and until

then the Bedouins' solution, which has evolved over millenia, seems to be the most practical compromise. Before leaving this subject perhaps we could pose the perennial question which is asked of all male Scots wearing kilts. The answer in the case of the Bedouins is that traditionally nothing is worn beneath the double-layered robe, which makes good sense from the physicist's point of view.

When considering a suitable diet in the desert environment, the basic nutritional requirements for high-quality protein, vitamins, minerals and sufficient energy naturally also apply. The high temperatures, particularly in the middle of the day, and the enormous loss of water through copious sweating do, however, require special consideration. We have already noted that the normal amount of salt used for flavouring food is more than sufficient to replace the small loss of electrolytes in the sweat and that additional salt will place additional stress on kidneys, which are already functioning maximally. The same would also be true for excessively large intakes of protein which would lead to excessive urea production, and ultimately require more water to pass through the kidneys. Very high protein intakes are also undesirable from the point of view of their high specific dynamic action. Everyone has experienced the sensation of warmth flooding through the body after eating a heavy meal, particularly in a hot environment. This is due to the specific dynamic action (SDA) of food, and protein has a higher SDA than both carbohydrates and fats. More important, however, is the consideration of SDA in relation to the time at which meals are taken. A heavy meal at midday in a hot desert climate can cause considerable discomfort and is not recommended. If breakfast is to be immediately followed by moderate or strenuous physical activity it should also not be a large meal. Ideally the main meal should be taken in the evening when temperatures are falling and no strenuous activity will follow the meal.

We have mentioned the great importance of fluid replacement in the desert environment and the rather poorly developed homoiostatic control over fluid balance in the human. Copious drinking of fluids is therefore recommended even when the person does not have a particularly strong sensation of thirst. In this connection it is of interest that in the early years of training in the Israeli Army, water was withheld from troops to 'accustom' them to water deprivation in the desert. This decision led in some instances to serious kidney damage and troops are now encouraged to drink as much fluid as possible. As we have seen, flavouring of water with suitable fruit juice concentrates increases voluntary fluid intakes and is recommended. Surprisingly, drinking of hot tea, apart from its action as a stimulant, also appears to be beneficial. Professor Duncan Mitchell and his colleagues at the Witwatersrand Medical School have recently shown that hot tea causes a massive peripheral heat-loss response which eventually leads to a drop in rectal temperature after 25 to 40 minutes (Fielding *et al.* 1980).

Although the above theoretical considerations are of interest, the actual diet of indigenous desert peoples, who are mostly poor, is dictated largely by availability, ease of preservation and by strong historical and cultural influences. The low-protein cereal grains used to make delicious pitta bread in the Middle East are supplemented with protein-rich leguminous seeds such as chick-peas ground into a paste (hoummous) and flavoured with hot peppers and olive oil. Goat cheese provides high-quality protein in small amounts but goats are too valuable to provide goat meat regularly. They are saved for special occasions such as feast days. The so-called holy foods of the Bible such as wheat, barley, grapes, figs, pomegranates, olives and dates, are still much in evidence. Alcohol, which can be particularly harmful under hot desert conditions, is forbidden to Muslims, while tea and coffee are highly prized and an important part of the ritualised greeting ceremony. In summary then, the

traditional diet of the Middle East fulfils most of our theoretical criteria, with perhaps the exception of vitamin C. This conclusion is, however, based on the assumption that sufficient quantities of the above foods are always available, which is naturally not the case in the unpredictable desert environment.

The physical principles governing the design of suitable desert dwellings and other buildings are well known. Penetration of heat into the building must be minimised by a highly reflective surface and good insulation of the walls. At night when temperatures fall, cool air should circulate through the dwelling both for the comfort of the inhabitants and to provide a thermal reserve against the heat of the next day. On first inspection the traditional dwellings of the Middle East and the south-western United States, with their thick walls and small windows, would seem to comply with most of the criteria. There are, however, certain obvious shortcomings. The small windows, although they reduce penetration of radiation during the day, do not allow free circulation of air at night. For this reason it is frequently customary to sleep out of doors or on the roof during particularly hot nights. Equally important, heating of the interior of the house by the sun during cold desert winters is not possible. It is therefore preferable by far to build a dwelling with well-insulated walls, using modern synthetic materials such as polyurethane foam, and to provide reasonably large windows with insulated shutters. The latter can be closed during the heat of the day and opened at night to allow free circulation of cool air, these convective currents across the surface of the skin being particularly important for thermal comfort. In addition, during sunny but cold winter days, the shutters are opened and the greenhouse effect through the window glass will keep the house comfortably warm. These principles have been incorporated, together with other imaginative innovations, in a design by Givoni (1978) of a solar-heated and night-radiation cooled dwelling using a roof radiation-trap (Fig. 10.3). From this design it is clear that imaginative planning can provide the desert inhabitant with considerable comfort without the use of fossil fuel energy, which introduces our next subject – the use of solar energy in the desert.

Solar energy

The technology required for the use of solar energy was developed many years ago but, apart from isolated examples, it is still not used extensively. The reasons for this are largely economic, but until recently the convenience of fossil fuels has also delayed applied research in this direction. The marked increase in the price of fossil fuels has now given new impetus to this field and significant new advances have been made. In making the following comments we have relied extensively on a recent review by Fiona Riddock and John Wilson (1980) on the application of solar energy in arid zones.

The amount of solar energy reaching the earth's surface, as well as its spectral characteristics, is affected by the amount of water vapour, dust and aerosols in the atmosphere. In temperate northern latitudes, because of the scattering effect of these particles, about 60 per cent of the annual insolation is received as diffuse radiation. This is an important consideration because, if optical concentrators are employed, the diffuse component of the solar radiation is not trapped. In these circumstances solar collectors, which approximate an ideal black body and which rely on the heating effect of the sun, will trap both diffuse and direct radiation. In any event it should be realised that even the most ideal localities only receive approximately $300 \text{ W m}^{-2} \text{ hr}^{-1}$ when averaged over 24 hr throughout the year. Moreover there is, as expected, considerable variation in the amount of insolation reaching various

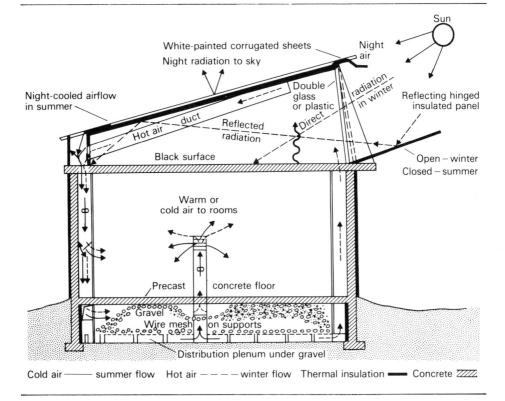

Fig. 10.3 A design for using a roof radiation-trap for solar heating and night-radiation cooling. See text for details. (From Givoni 1978.)

localities on the earth's surface. The mean daily insolation at London (England) is 2.5 k Wh m^{-2}, at Windhoek (Namibia) 3.1 kWh m^{-2}, Tucson (Arizona) 6.0 kWh m^{-2} and Alice Springs (Australia) 6.1 kWh m^{-2}. But, as Riddock and Wilson (1980) point out, these mean figures are not necessarily useful criteria in evaluating the suitability of a locality for the use of solar energy, as they conceal large diurnal and seasonal fluctuations. For example, on the above scale Windhoek in Namibia is rated only slightly higher than London while it is a far more favourable locality than London. A more useful criterion, which could be used in addition to mean daily insolation, is the ratio of the peak to average insolation. If this is applied, Alice Springs has a ratio of approximately 3 when compared with one of 12 for London.

To date the simplest applications of solar energy have been the most successful and these have usually been in a domestic environment. A discarded oil drum which has been blackened with fire can act as an inexpensive solar collector in the desert and provide a reasonable amount of warm water for domestic use on most days; so can a length of black plastic hose coiled on a roof. Both are inexpensive to replace but do, however, suffer from the obvious disadvantage of losing much heat via conduction and particularly via convection on windy days. To overcome these problems simple, flat-plate collectors have been developed which can heat either air or water. Insulation beneath the black absorber-plate and a transparent cover above reduce heat losses from conduction and convection very effectively (Fig. 10.4 (A)). In the previous section on housing we described an unusual design for heating and

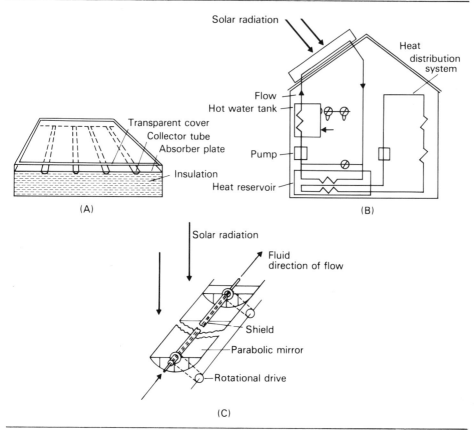

Fig. 10.4   (A) Flat-plate solar water heater; (B) installation of heater, omitting expansion tanks and valves; (C) schematic diagram of a parabolic trough collector used to produce very high fluid temperatures. The mirror is tracked to retain the sun's image on the absorber. (From Riddock and Wilson 1980.)

cooling a desert dwelling using solar energy. Figure 10.4(B) illustrates a more conventional use of the flat-plate collector to heat domestic water and the home.

If very high temperatures are required in the collector tubes, for example to produce high-pressure vapour from a liquid, the energy input into the system can be magnified some 10–100 times by the use of parabolic trough collectors, mounted on a rotational drive in order to track the sun (Fig. 10.4 (C)). It is also necessary, however, to reduce the radiant emission from the system, and at present research is directed towards developing transparent covers which would act as selective transmitters. Loss of heat to the atmosphere by conduction and convection can be eliminated by containing the tubular absorber in a vacuum jacket. The use of fields of parabolic mirrors, mounted on a computer-controlled mechanical driving system to track the sun, and focused on a single elevated water-tower is now under investigation in the United States. The radiant energy concentrated on the water-tower by the mirrors produces steam to drive a conventional steam turbine for electricity production. To date, however, there is doubt about the economic success of this venture.

A more efficient method of converting solar energy to electricity is through the

use of solar or photovoltaic cells. The most efficient of these have a power conversion efficiency as high as 26 per cent and are manufactured from alloys of gallium arsenide and aluminium arsenide. In contrast, the power conversion efficiency of the more familiar process of photosynthesis is only 14 per cent. But the cost of the above cells is still prohibitive and research is being directed towards developing inexpensive manufacturing methods for producing cheaper cells, such as single-crystal silicon cells, which have a power conversion ratio of 8–10 per cent. These are the only cells which have been used under practical conditions at present. According to Riddock and Wilson, they now cost 10–30 US dollars per watt of generating capacity in 1 kW m^{-2} sunlight and take approximately 12 years to repay the energy used in their production. The theoretical principles involved in the manufacture of photovoltaic cells are beyond the scope of this text and the interested reader is referred to a recent review by Perez-Albuerne and Yuan-Sheng Tyan (1980). Silicon cells have been used successfully on a small scale in many parts of the world and apparently also provide power to pump irrigation water in India. They are not suitable for large-scale electricity production and their future success depends largely on reducing manufacturing costs and developing more efficient storage methods for the electricity.

Another practical method of producing electricity on a small scale is by using wind-driven generators which derive their energy ultimately from the sun's influence on air movements across the earth's surface. They have been used successfully in rural areas in conjunction with lead storage batteries for many decades. Research at present is directed towards improving the aerodynamic design of the windmill blades and efficient storage of the electricity for windless days.

The exciting possibility of using solar energy to drive the photo-dissociation of water into hydrogen and oxygen is now receiving considerable attention. A sensitising dye is added to allow water to absorb sufficient energy from the sun to split the water molecule into its component parts. The advantage of this system is that it could be used on a large scale and the resultant fuel (hydrogen) could be stored efficiently.

None of the above electricity converters is yet suitable for large-scale application in industry but there is no reason to suppose that the solar heating of water for industrial use could not be developed economically. In arid zones the storage of hot water for industrial use is relatively easy in so-called solar ponds. These ponds have an inverted temperature gradient and the hot water in the bottom layer (100 °C) does not mix with the insulating upper layer because of its higher density, which is controlled by adding salt. Solar ponds have already been used successfully in Israel and at the time of writing an ambitious scheme has been announced to use the Dead Sea as a solar lake. Because both Israel and Jordan have diverted fresh water from the Jordan River on a large scale for irrigation purposes, the level of water in the Dead Sea is falling rapidly and it is becoming increasingly saline. The proposal to construct a large canal from the Mediterranean coast to allow water to flow from the Mediterranean Sea into the Dead Sea has now been accepted. As the Dead Sea is well below sea-level, hydroelectric power can be generated from the water flowing down the canal. In addition, the density gradient in the Dead Sea could theoretically be exploited for use as a solar lake.

The use of solar stills to desalinate drinking water holds great promise for desert areas where drinking water is frequently contaminated with dissolved salts. Riddock and Wilson (1980) report that 1 000–1 500 litres of pure water per year can be produced per square metre of collector. The required technology has been developed and large plants are in operation in Greece, Australia and the USSR.

To conclude then, solar technology is sufficiently advanced for immediate application on a small scale and especially in domestic systems in arid zones. This is particularly true for the conversion of solar energy into heat whereas the conversion of solar energy to electricity still requires further research to reduce manufacturing costs and improve storage techniques. Large-scale conversion of solar energy to electrical power still appears to be a remote possibility and efforts in this direction should plan for decentralised units, rather than for large centralised installations. In any event the increasing scarcity of both fossil fuels and particularly of natural 'biomass' fuels in arid zones makes it imperative that research on the application of solar energy be given very high priority.

Land use

Pastoral nomadism

As we have stressed in previous chapters, primary production in deserts is very low, unpredictable and, except during brief rainy spells, of poor quality. In addition to these factors, rainfall events are frequently very localised and it is therefore not surprising that an efficient nomadic pastoral system has developed over millennia in several deserts of the world. Domesticated ruminant animals are able to walk long distances efficiently and their ruminant micro-organisms degrade the cellulose-rich plant material to fatty acids while simultaneously synthesising B-vitamins as well as amino acids from recycled urea. The end result is the production of high quality foods in the form of meat and milk from low grade unusable roughage. The constraints are of course that the system can only support a small population and that over-exploitation can easily occur. Also free movement of nomads across political boundaries is no longer possible today.

It is in the Sahara, the deserts of the Middle East and in Central Asia that true pastoral nomadism is practised. This system developed in marginal desert areas where the soil became so impoverished that cultivation was no longer profitable, probably no earlier than 3 000 B.P. First cattle and sheep were raised but as conditions declined only camels and goats could survive. These days the nomadic system, in which stock owners wander freely in search of good pastures, is usually found in the most desertic areas (Cloudsley-Thompson 1977). Transhumance, wherein a permanent base is recognised but for part of each year grazing is obtained elsewhere, may occur where environmental conditions are somewhat more favourable (Wickens and White 1979). In the Negev, grazing by mobile herds of goats and sheep has been combined with cultivation of winter cereals, especially wheat and barley, for almost 5 000 years. The relative importance of the nomadic, grazing way of life depended on the amount of rainfall and on the current system of government in the area (Noy-Meir and Seligman 1979).

Black Bedouin goats provide one example of the stock used by semi-nomadic pastoralists in the Negev and we have already described their remarkable physiological adaptations (Ch. 5). These small animals are herded in the extreme deserts of the Middle East and are usually only watered once every 2–4 days. They are then able to replenish their entire water loss within several minutes, an amount which may exceed 40 per cent of their body weight. In contrast, sheep and other breeds of goats are watered once or twice a day and are thus less well adapted to efficient exploitation of the meagre desert pasture (Maltz and Shkolnik 1980) (Fig. 10.5). In Kenya Masai cattle may be watered only once every 3 days, thereby extending the grazing area (Barnes 1979); however it is presumed that under this system peak fitness is not maintained.

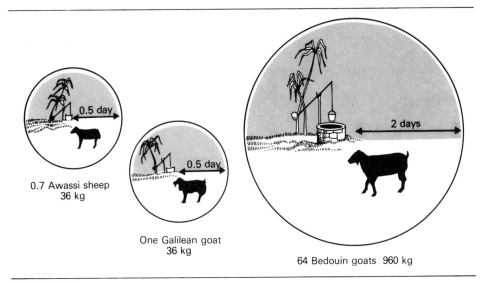

0.7 Awassi sheep
36 kg

0.5 day

One Galilean goat
36 kg

0.5 day

2 days

64 Bedouin goats 960 kg

Fig. 10.5   The time interval between drinking determines the foraging distance from the well. For this reason, and because of their ability to exist on a meagre food supply, 64 Bedouin goats can be grazed from a single well-point in contrast to one Galilean goat and 0.7 Awassi sheep. (From Shkolnik 1977.)

Even when lactating, black Bedouin goats drink only once every 2 days. Moreover, their milk production is the highest reported for any ruminant. In this way the fluids for the kids are supplied, despite the fact that under Bedouin husbandry the kids are kept far from water. Lactation doubles the water turnover in the black Bedouin goats and increases caloric demands, while the total body water of the lactating females is increased by 35 per cent. When dehydrated these goats have the capacity to rapidly rehydrate and to regain full milk yield (Maltz and Shkolnik 1980). Thus the black Bedouin goat is able to range successfully over vast distances, taking advantage of the minimal primary production in its desert habitat.

Nomads may also be hunters rather than primarily pastoralists and, until the arrival of mechanical transport, commercial nomadism was also important in Old World deserts (Cloudsley-Thompson 1977). Moreover, nomadism is not isolated from other forms of land use and nomads may exchange their produce with cultivators or even own land, employing others to cultivate it for them. In fact, the nomadic way of life probably represents the only way in which a maximum amount of food may be obtained from desert regions with a minimum of damage (Wickens and White 1979). If not used by nomads, vast areas which are now productive would become useless. In a recent book Cloudsley-Thompson (1977) suggests that the nomadic way of life should be modernised and encouraged to continue. However, the present trend of the governments concerned is towards settlement of the nomads and restriction of their movements. Noy-Meir and Seligman (1979) describe a temporarily successful compromise between cultivation and nomadic pastoralism in the semi-arid area of Israel. The future of this land use system is still uncertain however. We are not qualified to analyse the socio-political considerations, but an alternative to the nomadic use of the desert environment could be game ranching with oryx and gazelles either for viewing by tourists or for hunting by sportsmen.

Agriculture

In arid areas agriculture may, for the purposes of our discussion, be grouped in three major divisions: dry-land farming, irrigation farming and the use of greenhouses. Only a few of the possibilities under each heading will be touched upon. A variety of crops have been used for dry-land farming throughout the world. Cloudsley-Thompson (1977) summarises the main crops of desert regions under the headings of: grain cereals including wheat, barley, maize, sorghum, millet and rice; pulses or grain legumes including various types of peas and beans; sugar crops; oil crops including groundnuts, safflower and sunflower; and forage crops. Recently, particularly in North America, agriculturists have been considering introduction or reintroduction of suitable desert plants into general field cultivation. Food sources used by native American Indians, for example the tepary beans, *Phaseolus acutifolius* may prove to be valuable additions to the list of more traditional dry-land crops (Nabhan 1979). Another arid-adapted plant, the jojoba (*Simmondsia chinensis*), a native Sonoran Desert shrub, appears to be an economically viable crop with seeds yielding an unsaturated oil composed of non-glyceride esters, mainly straight-chain acids and alcohols (Foster and Wright 1980).

In the Sahara dry-land cropping is only viable along the southern fringe of the desert where rainfall is in excess of about 300 mm yr^{-1}. Varieties of millet and sorghum are the staple crops (Wickens and White 1979). In areas of sparse precipitation rain-fed crops are confined to 'favoured' sites having sufficient water run-on and soils with moisture-retention characteristics suitable for supporting a fast-maturing crop. The same sites are cultivated more or less continually although they may not be used in years of unusually low rainfall (Wickens and White 1979). Until recently land in the semi-arid Sahelian zone was left fallow for 15–20 years before recropping in a system of shifting agriculture (Cloudsley-Thompson 1977). In the Negev, all soils deeper than 50 mm in areas with an annual precipitation of more than 250 mm and most deep soils in wadi beds in areas with 150–250 mm have been cultivated and sown almost every year. In less favourable areas, with less rainfall or shallower soils, crop rotation may be practised or seeds sown only in the years with good early rains (Noy-Meir and Seligman 1979).

In the Sahara the introduction of cash crops has reduced the time that the land remains fallow and has caused marginal areas to be brought under cultivation. Productivity of dry-land farming can be improved to a limited extent by reducing water run-off and increasing infiltration. Plant breeding can lead to improved varieties, the water requirements of which fit the predicted rainfall closely. In addition, fertilizers and crop rotation can be used to improve soil fertility. However, dry-land cropping in arid and semi-arid areas can never be expected to produce extensive cash crops or food on a dependable basis (Cloudsley-Thompson 1977).

Irrigation may be an effective form of land use in deserts where water can be collected and used in terraced wadis or depressions. Evenari *et al.* (1971) describe such a system, constructed by the Nabateans at Avdat and Shivta in the Negev during the Roman–Byzantine period, that was recently reconstructed and is now in use. Various field crops, vegetables, medicinal and pasture plants as well as fruit trees have been successfully introduced and are currently in production. Irrigation may also be effectively employed where water is obtainable from rivers originating outside the desertic area. Egyptian civilisation has depended for millennia on the Nile for water and the rich soil necessary for plant growth (Cloudsley-Thompson 1977).

When water supplies are unlimited, rapid growth of plants occurs in the desert climate. Many types of systems, including cotton, tropical fruits and cut flowers, may

be supported through irrigation. However, pumping is required except, for example, where artesian water is available, and the cost of irrigation may be prohibitive. More often the energy required for pumping water, manufacturing fertiliser, herbicides and insecticides, and for agricultural machinery and harvesting is greater than the energy value of the produce grown. This is the case in the Negev where supplementary irrigation is used during critical times, particularly during establishment and early growth of the wheat crop. Although the cost of subsidised water makes the practice profitable to the farmer, the real costs are seldom covered by the increased wheat yield (Noy-Meir and Seligman 1979).

Water stored under the desert may be fossil water, as for example in the Sahara, or it may be very limited in amount and thus not be replenished. Ecological consequences of irrigation schemes involving dams may also be unfavourable. For example, the shoreline of the Nile delta has retreated, deposition of silt in the dam has made fertilisation necessary, mud is no longer available for bricks and the incidence of schistosomiasis has increased as a result of the Aswan dam (Cloudsley-Thompson 1977). Hence, with several notable exceptions, large-scale irrigation is usually an uneconomical undertaking.

Large-scale use of greenhouses and their equivalents is still in the experimental stage. However, if synthetic materials can provide cheaper methods of construction, there is great potential in the use of structures in which transpired water can be condensed and reapplied. Extensive experimental work is being carried out in Israel, Arizona and other desert areas to achieve this end.

Agricultural pests are relatively scarce in desert environments with the exception of locusts and termites. Locusts may reach plague proportions depending on a succession of meteorological events, but this pest, historically very significant, has largely been brought under control. Nevertheless, when exotic pests are introduced to irrigated areas or oases they tend to flourish. We have had personal experience in this regard with several common pests in the Namib.

Desert encroachment

Desert encroachment, or the degeneration of productive land into unusable wasteland, has been most spectacular in the southern Sahara in recent years. This area will serve as our main example. As the natural environmental situation is important, a brief description is warranted. Immediately south of the desert itself lies the 'Sahel savanna' where rain averages 250–500 mm and falls during 4–5 summer months. This, in turn, grades into the 'Sudan savanna' where mean rainfall is 500–1 000 mm. Further south rainfall averages more than 1 000 mm in the wooded 'Guinea savanna' but a severe dry season also occurs. The 'Guinea savanna' itself grades into tropical forest. The savanna areas are maintained and reforestation prevented by constant burning associated with a pattern of shifting cultivation (Cloudsley-Thompson 1977). In the drier areas transhumance and migration were practised in response to the natural climatic cycles. This mobility, combined with shorter human life expectancies and lower human and animal populations (Wickens and White 1979), meant that man was more or less in balance with his environment.

This relative stability, during which only a very gradual degradation of the environment occurred, was maintained from approximately 2 500 B.P., when the present climate of the Sahara was established, until the last few centuries. Before about 2 500 B.P., during portions of the Pleistocene and post-Pleistocene, the climate of the Sahara was much wetter, as evidenced by extensive fossil and historical data. Similar evidence comes from other areas. For example the present Thar Desert

of India was dense forest 4 000 years ago (Cloudsley-Thompson 1977).

Most of the degradation to more desertic conditions or even to wasteland has occurred in the last several hundred years in many parts of the world. For example the present shrubby Chihuahuan desert of the south-western United States supported a grassland until it was seriously overgrazed in the nineteenth century. In South Africa the semi-arid Karoo has increased by 50 per cent during the last century (Cloudsley-Thompson 1977). In the Negev most destruction has occurred during the twentieth century. The oak forests of Sharon disappeared when the Turkish railway was built to Suez. The introduction of modern fire-arms has resulted in a decrease of large wildlife species. Desert soil and vegetation have suffered with the continuous increase in the Bedouin population and livestock and consequently the area cultivated by them. Moreover, most of the overall deterioration has occurred in the Negev during the last 30–40 years (Noy-Meir and Seligman 1979). Cloudsley-Thompson (1977) quotes figures that indicate an increase in desert or wasteland of 9.4 per cent to 23.3 per cent of the earth's surface during the period from 1882 to 1952. However, he cautions that these figures may only be taken to indicate relative magnitude as an exact definition of a desert is not provided.

In the southern Sahara, particularly in the 'Sahel savanna', desert encroachment has recently been severe. One contributing factor is that the boundary of the zone where rain-based agriculture can be productive, at approximately 400 mm yr^{-1}, is not definite. During good years the human population builds up (Fig. 10.6), leading to overgrazing and the inability to continue shifting cultivation. This is aggravated by the provision of new watering-points and cessation of natural migrations. Hence during natural dry periods the environment suffers severe degradation which results in much suffering and death for man and his animals; further, there is no time for the land to recover (Wickens and White 1979). Although good agricultural practice could improve the situation slightly, this marginal area will never be able to support a dense population of man or his animals. Strong governmental action will be necessary even to return production to its recent relatively high levels.

Nature conservation and tourism

As we have repeatedly emphasised, primary production in desert areas is low because of the scarcity of water. This results in generally low densities of both plants and animals. Therefore, very large areas of desert are needed to preserve desert habitats adequately. In almost all desert areas today wildlife problems are acute. However, rocky, inaccessible desert habitats have survived better than the rolling hills and plains that are more easily occupied, used and travelled across (Mendelssohn 1980).

During the overall destruction of desert environments, the number of wild animals living in them has also decreased. Occupation by man of water-holes during times of drought has led directly to the extinction of two horse species in Asia within the last century (Mendelssohn 1980). Hunting has also contributed extensively to the decline in numbers of the larger mammal species. In addition to older influences of overgrazing, overbrowsing and hunting, the effects on wildlife of substrate destruction by motorised vehicles must also be considered (Mendelssohn 1980).

One way to protect desert wildlife from total destruction and to have it contribute to the overall economy is game ranching. However, only the Asian saiga antelope in Russia and the ostrich in southern Africa have been profitably managed to date. The indigenous fauna should be better adapted to desertic conditions but control of game would be very difficult over the necessarily large area in which they must range

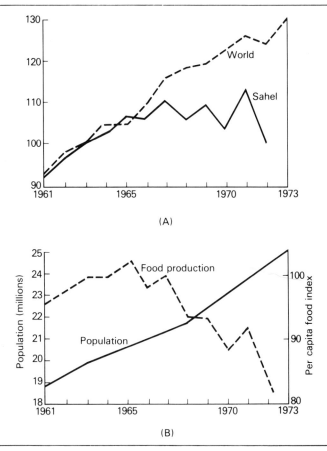

Fig. 10.6 Population and food production trends in six Sahelian countries. (A) Index of total food production (1963 = 100). (B) Population (millions) and index of per capita food production (1963 = 100) in the six Sahelian countries. (From Winstanley 1976.)

(Cloudsley-Thompson 1977). As suggested by Walker (1979) for the semi-arid zone, mixed game and cattle ranching may be a reasonable idea in those fringe areas where cattle can survive. Nevertheless, in the true desert areas where animals must be highly mobile and independent of free water, only indigenous game could survive in adequate numbers for cropping or recreational hunting.

Tourists are attracted to deserts and to semi-arid areas (Walker 1979) for some of the very characteristics which limit their usefulness to man as traditional food-producing areas. A sunny, dry climate, great expanses of space, comparative quiet and solitude and striking beauty are attracting more and more people to desert areas for tourism and recreation.

The number of people using the desert for these purposes must nevertheless, as in the semi-arid zones (Walker 1979), be kept well within the carrying capacity of the system. For the desert is as easily damaged by an excess of tourists as it is by overgrazing or bad agricultural practices. Studies carried out at camping sites in the southern California Desert indicate that recreational practices seriously affect the biotic and abiotic components of the environment (Davis 1974). For example compaction of the soil is increased by human activities, leading to increased water

run-off during rare showers. Increased compaction may also have a detrimental influence on growth of vegetation. Near campsites, direct damage to individual plants, as well as other more indirect but still harmful effects on the vegetation, were found to be high. In addition, the arthropod, reptile and mammal components of the ecosystem were also shown to be negatively affected. Hence any small disturbance to the soil–water–plant system, such as occurs at a desert campsite, may result in a significant loss of production affecting the entire ecosystem.

In addition to the possibilities for tourism and recreation in deserts, the general conditions for living in these areas attract many people. Although man has probably the most efficient physiological control over body temperature among all endotherms, the behavioural control of body temperature is also of great importance. There also appears to be a psychological component in this control system and many people take great pleasure in either sunbathing or merely warming themselves in the sun. This is particularly true for people living in cold northern latitudes, who flock in millions to the Mediterranean shores and other holiday resorts. Conversely, people who have lived most of their lives in a warm, sunny climate have great difficulty in adapting to cloudy cold conditions in the North and can become severely depressed. The desert environment therefore offers great scope for tourists seeking the sun and a good example in this context is the city of Phoenix in Arizona. This city was, until fairly recently, a mining and agricultural centre of only moderate size. Today it is a vast city and one of the swiftest-growing in the world. Thousands are arriving to retire there each year, financing themselves with wealth accumulated elsewhere. Their presence generates many complex commercial enterprises and the city continues to grow apace – a monument to behavioural thermoregulation!

Bibliography

Ahearn, G. A. (1970) The control of water loss in desert tenebrionid beetles. *J. Exp. Biol.*, **53**, 573–95.

Alexandrov, V. Ya., Lomagin, A. G. and Feldman, N. L. (1970) The responsive increase in thermostability of plant cells. *Protoplasma*, **69**, 417–58.

Arnon, I. (1972) *Crop Production in Dry Regions.* vol. 1. *Background and Principles.* Leonard Hill, London.

Baker, J. R. (1938) The evolution of breeding seasons. In *Evolution, Essays on Aspects of Evolutionary Biology* (ed. E. S. Goodrich), Clarendon, Oxford.

Baker, Mary Ann (1979) A brain cooling system in mammals. *Sci. Am.*, **240**, 114–22.

Baldwin, N. S. (1964) Sea lamprey in the Great Lakes. *Can. Audubon Mag.*, Nov.–Dec. 1964, 2–7. In Krebs, C. J. (1972).

Ballinger, R. E. (1977) Reproductive strategies: food availability as a source of proximal variation in a lizard. *Ecology*, **58**(3), 628–35.

Barnes, D. L. (1979) Cattle ranching in the semi-arid savannas of East and southern Africa. In *Management of Semi-arid Ecosystems* (ed. B. H. Walker). Elsevier, Amsterdam.

Bartholomew, G. A. (1977) Body temperature and energy metabolism. In *Animal Physiology, Principles and Adaptations.* 3rd edn (ed. M. S. Gordon), Ch. 8. Macmillan, New York.

Bartholomew, G. A., White, F. N. & Howell, T. R. (1976) The thermal significance of the nest of the sociable weaver *Philetairus socius:* summer observations. *Ibis*, **118**, 402–10.

Beatley, J. C. (1976) Rainfall and fluctuating plant populations in relation to distributions and numbers of desert rodents in southern Nevada. *Oecologia* (Berl.), **24**, 21–42

Belk, D. (1977) Zoogeography of the Arizona fairy shrimps (Crustacea: Anostraca). *J. Ariz. Acad. Sci.*, **12**, 70–8.

Belk, D. & Cole, G. A. (1975) Adaptational biology of desert temporary-pond inhabitants. In *Environmental Physiology of Desert Organisms* (ed. N. F. Hadley). Dowden, Hutchinson and Ross, Stroudsberg. Pa.

Bell, K. L., Hiatt, H. D. & Niles, W. E. (1979) Seasonal changes in biomass allocation in eight winter annuals of the Mojave Desert. *J. Ecol.*, **67**, 781–7.

Bentley, P. J. & Schmidt-Nielsen, K. (1966) Cutaneous water loss in reptiles. *Science*, **151**, 1547–9.

Bernstein, M. H. (1971) Cutaneous and respiratory evaporation in the painted quail, *Excalfactoria chinensis*, during ontogeny of thermoregulation. *Comp. Biochem. Physiol.*, **38A**, 611–17.

Berry, H. H., Millar, R. P. & Louw, G. N. (1979) Environmental cues influencing the breeding biology and circulating levels of various hormones and triglycerides in the Cape cormorant. *Comp. Biochem. Physiol.*, **62A**, 879–84.

Blair, W. F. (1976) Adaptation of anurans to equivalent desert scrub of North and South America. In *Evolution of Desert Biota* (ed. D. W. Goodall). University of Texas Press, Austin.

Bonsma, J. C. (1940) The influence of climatological factors on cattle. *Dept. Agric. and Forestry Bull., Union of S. Afr.*, No. 223.

Bonsma, J. C. & Pretorius, A. J. (1943) Influence of colour and coat colour on adaptability of cattle. *Farming S. Afr.*, **18**, 101–20.

Bourlière, F. (1973) The comparative ecology of rain forest mammals in Africa and tropical America: some introductory remarks. In *Tropical Forest Ecosystems in Africa and South America: A Comparative Review* (eds B. J. Meggus, E. S. Ayensu & W. D. Duckworth), Smithsonian Institution Press, Washington.

Bradshaw, S. D. & Shoemaker, V. H. (1967) Aspects of water and electrolyte changes in a field population of *Amphibolurus* lizards. *Comp. Biochem. Physiol.*, **20**, 855–65.

Bridges, K. W., Wilcott, C., Westoby, M., Kickert, R. & Wilkin, D. (1972) Nature: a guide to ecosystem modelling. Ecosystem Modelling Symposium, AIBS Meeting, Minneapolis. In Noy-Meir, I. (1973).

Brown, J. H. (1975) Geographical ecology of desert rodents. In *Ecology and Evolution of Communities* (eds M. L. Cody & J. M. Diamond). The Belknap Press of Harvard U. P., Cambridge, Mass.

174

Brown, J. H., Davidson, D. W. & Reichman, O. J. (1979a) An experimental study of competition between seed-eating desert rodents and ants. *Amer. Zoologist*, **19**, 1129–43.

Brown, J. H. & Lasiewski, R. C. (1972) Metabolism of weasels: the cost of being long and thin. *Ecology*, **53**, 939–43.

Brown, J. H., Reichman, O. J. & Davidson, D. W. (1979b) Granivory in desert ecosystems. *Annu. Rev. Ecol. Syst.*, **10**, 201–27.

Burrage, B. R. (1973) Comparative ecology and behaviour of *Chamaeleo pumilus pumilus* (Gmelin) and *C. namaquensis* A. Smith (Sauria: Chamaeleonidae). *Ann. S. Afr. Mus.*, **61**, 1–158.

Bustard, H. R. (1967) Gekkonid lizards adapt fat storage to desert environments. *Science*, **158**, 1197–8.

Buxton, P. A. (1923) *Animal Life in Deserts: A Study of the Fauna in Relation to the Environment.* Arnold, London.

Cade, T. T. & Maclean, G. L. (1976) Transport of water by adult sandgrouse to their young. *Condor*, **69**, 323–43.

Callow, P. (1978) *Life Cycles.* Chapman and Hall, London.

Carlisle, D. B. (1968) *Triops* (entomostraca) eggs killed by boiling. *Science*, **161**, 279

Cena, K. & Monteith, J. L. (1975a) Transfer processes in animal coats. I. Radiative transfer. *Proc. roy. Soc. Lond. B.*, **188**, 377–94.

Cena, K. & Monteith, J. L. (1975b) Transfer processes in animal coats. II. Conduction and convection. *Proc. roy. Soc. Lond. B.*, **188**, 395–411.

Chambers, A. B. (1970) A psychrometric chart for physiological research. *J. appl. Physiol.*, **29**, 406–12.

Charley, J. L. (1959) Soil salinity–vegetation patterns in western New South Wales and their modification by overgrazing. Ph.D. thesis, Univ. New England, Armidale. In Noy-Meir, I. (1973).

Charley, J. L. (1972) The role of shrubs in nutrient cycling. In *Wildland Shrubs – Their Biology and Utilization* (O. B. Williams, 1979). USDA Forest Service, General Technical Report. INT-1.

Charley, J. L. & Cowling, S. L. (1968) Changes in soil nutrient status resulting from overgrazing and their consequences in plant communities of semi-arid areas. *Proc. Ecol. Soc. Aust.*, **3**, 28–38.

Chew, R. M. & Chew A. E. (1970) Energy relationships of the mammals of a desert shrub (*Larrea tridentata*) community. *Ecol. Monogr.*, **40**, 1–21.

Chosniak, I. & Shkolnik, A. (1978) The rumen as a protective osmotic mechanism during rapid rehydration in the black Bedouin goat. In *Osmotic and Volume Regulation.* Alfred Benzon Symposium XI, Munksgaard.

Clegg, J. S. (1964) The control of emergence and metabolism by external osmotic pressure and the role of free glycerol in developing cysts of *Artemia salina. J. Exp. Biol.*, **41**, 879–92.

Cloudsley-Thompson, J. L. (1964) Terrestrial animals in dry heat: arthropods. In *Adaptation to the Environment. Handbook of Physiology* (ed. D. B. Dill), **4**, 451–65.

Cloudsley-Thompson, J. L. (1965) *Desert Life.* Pergamon, Oxford.

Cloudsley-Thompson, J. L. (1977) *Man and the Biology of Arid Zones.* Edward Arnold, London.

Cloudsley-Thompson, J. L. & Chadwick, M. J. (1964) *Life in Deserts.* G. T. Foulis, London.

Cole, G. A. (1968) Desert limnology. In *Desert Biology* (ed. G. W. Brown, Jr.). vol. 1. Academic Press, N.Y.

Congdon, J. D., Laurie, J. Vitt, & Hadley, N. F. (1978) Parental investment: comparative reproductive energetics in bisexual and unisexual lizards, genus *Cnemidophorus. Am. Nat.*, **112**, 509–21.

Connell, J. H. (1961a) The effects of competition, predation by *Thais lapillus*, and other factors on natural populations of the barnacle *Balanus balanoides. Ecol. Monogr.*, **31**, 61–104.

Connell, J. H. (1961b) The influence of interspecific competition and other factors on the distribution of the barnacle *Chthamalus stellatus. Ecology*, **42**, 710–23.

Connell, J. H. (1978) Diversity in tropical rain forests and coral reefs. *Science*, **199**, 1302–10.

Coutchié, P. A. & Crowe, J. H. (1979) Transport of water vapor by tenebrionid beetles. I. Kinetics. *Physiol. Zool.*, **52**, 67–87.

Crawford, C. S. (1976) Feeding-season production in the desert millipede *Orthoporus ornatus* (Girrard) (Diplopoda). *Oecologia* (Berl.), **24**, 265–76.

Crawford, C. S. (1979) Desert detritivores: a review of life history patterns and trophic roles. *J. Arid Environments*, **2**, 31–42.

Danin, A. (1978) Plant species diversity and plant succession in a sandy area in the northern Negev. *Flora*, **167**, 409–22. In Noy-Meir, I. (1979/80).

Dantzler, W. H. & Schmidt-Nielsen, B. (1966) Excretion in fresh-water turtle (*Pseudemys scripta*) and desert tortoise (*Gopherus agassizii*). *Am. J. Physiol.*, **210**, 198–210.

Davidson, D. W. (1977) Species diversity and community organization in desert seed-eating ants. *Ecology*, **58**, 711–24.

Davis, R. (ed.) (1974) Desert land use and management in California: Its ecological and sociological consequences. Unpublished report; University of California, Irvine.

Day, J. A. (1980) Zoology Department, University of Cape Town – unpublished data.

176 *Bibliography*

Dixon, J. E. W. & Louw, G. N. (1978) Seasonal effects on nutrition, reproduction and aspects of thermoregulation in the Namaqua sandgrouse (*Pterocles namaqua*). *Madoqua*, **11**, 19–29.

Dunham, A. E. (1978) Food availability as a proximate factor influencing individual growth rates in the iguanid lizard *Sceloporus merriami*. *Ecology*, **39**, 770–8.

Edholm, O. G. (1978) *Man – Hot and Cold.* Edward Arnold, London.

Edney, E. B. (1966) Absorption of water vapour from unsaturated air by *Arenivaga* (Polyphagidae, Dictyoptera). *Comp. Biochem. Physiol.*, **19**, 387–408.

Edney, E. B. (1977) *Water Balance in Land Arthropods.* Springer-Verlag, Berlin.

Edward, D. H. (1968) Chironomidae in temporary fresh waters. *Aust. Soc. Limnol. Newsletter*, **3**, 29–30.

Ellenberg, H. (1958) Uber den Wasserhaushalt Tropischer Nebeloasen in der Küstenwüste Perus. *Bericht Geobotanische Forschungsinstitut Rübel*, 47–74.

Elton, C. & Nicholson, M. (1942) The ten-year cycle in numbers of the lynx in Canada. *J. anim. Ecol.*, **11**, 215–44.

Evenari, M., Shanan, L. & Tadmor, N. H. (1971) *The Negev: The Challenge of a Desert.* Harvard U. P., Cambridge, Mass.

Fielding, K., Mitchell, D. & Laburn, H. P. (1980) Human responses to internal thermal load. *S. Afr. J. Sci.*, **76**, 326.

Finch, V. A., Dmi'el, R., Boxman, R., Shkolnik, A. & Taylor, C. R. (1980) Why black goats in hot deserts? Effects of coat color on heat exchanges of wild and domestic goats. *Physiol. Zool.*, **53**, 19–25.

Foin, T. C., Jr. (1977) Visitor impacts on National parks: the Yosemite ecological impact study. *Institute of Ecology Publication No. 10*, University of California, Davis.

Folk, G. E. (1974) *Textbook of Environmental Physiology.* 2nd edn Lea and Febiger, N.Y.

Fonteyn, P. J. & Mahall, B. E. (1978) Competition among desert plants. *Nature*, **275**, 544–5.

Foster, K. E. & Wright, N. G. (1980) Constraints to Arizona agriculture and possible alternatives. *J. Arid Environments*, **3**, 85–94.

Friedman, J., Orshan, G. & Ziger-Cfir, Y. (1977) Suppression of annuals by *Artemisia herba-alba* in the Negev Desert of Israel. *J. Ecol.*, **65**, 413–26.

Friedman, J. & Stein, Z. (1980) The influence of seed-dispersal mechanisms on the dispersal of *Anastratica hierochuntica* (Cruciferae) in the Negev Desert, Israel. *J. Ecol.*, **68**, 43–50.

Gates, D. M., Alderfer, R. & Taylor, E. (1968) Leaf temperatures of desert plants. *Science*, **159**, 994–5.

Gause, G. F. (1934) *The Struggle for Existence.* Hafner, N.Y.

Gibbs, J. G. & Patten, D. T. (1970) Plant temperatures and heat flux in a Sonoran Desert ecosystem. *Oecologia (Berl)*, **5**, 165–84.

Givoni, B. (1978) Solar heating and night radiation cooling by a roof radiation trap. First Annual Report, Institute for Desert Research, Ben-Gurion University, Sde Boger, 122–3.

Goodall, D. W. (1979) Animal Processes – Integration. In *Arid-land Ecosystems: Structure, Functioning and Management* (eds D. W. Goodall, R. A. Perry & K. M. W. Howes). Cambridge U.P.

Hadley, N. F. (1972) Desert species and adaptation. *Am. Sci.*, **60**, 338–47.

Hadley, N. F. (1977) Epicuticular lipids of the desert tenebrionid beetle, *Eleodes armata*: seasonal and acclimatory effects on composition. *Insect Biochem.*, **7**, 277–83.

Hadley, N. F. (1979a) Wax secretion and colour phases of the desert tenebrionid beetle *Cryptoglossa verrucosa* (Le Conte). *Science*, **203**, 367–9.

Hadley, N. F. (1979b) Adaptation of animals to desert environments. In *Research Handbook on the Deserts of North America* (ed. G. Bender). Greenwood Press, Westport, Conn. (in press).

Hadley, N. F. & Szarek, S. R. (1980) Productivity of desert ecosystems: producer, consumer and decomposer organisms. *Bioscience* (in press).

Hafner, M. S. (1977) Density and diversity in Mojave Desert rodent and shrub communities. *J. anim. Ecol.*, **46**, 925–38.

Haim, A. & Borut, A. (1976) Thermoregulation and non-shivering thermogenesis as factors limiting distribution of the golden spiny mouse (*Acomys russatus*). *Isr. J. Med. Sci.*, **12**, 896.

Hamilton, W. J. III. (1973) *Life's Color Code.* McGraw-Hill, N.Y.

Hamilton, W. J. III. (1975) Coloration and its thermal consequences for diurnal desert insects. In *Environmental Physiology of Desert Organisms* (ed. N. F. Hadley). Dowden, Hutchinson and Ross, Stroudsberg, Pa.

Hamilton, W. J. III., Buskirk, R. E. & Buskirk, W. H. (1977) Intersexual dominance and differential mortality of gemsbok *Oryx gazella* at Namib Desert waterholes. *Madoqua*, **10**, 5–19.

Hamilton, W. J. III., Buskirk, R. E. & Buskirk, W. H. (1978) Omnivory and utilization of food resources by chacma baboons, *Papio ursinus*. *Am. Nat.*, **112**, 911–24.

Hamilton, W. J. III. & Seely, M. K. (1976) Fog basking by the Namib Desert beetle, *Onymacris unguicularis*. *Nature*, **262**, 284–5.

Hattingh, J. (1972) A comparative study of transepidermal water loss through the skin of various animals. *Comp. Biochem. Physiol.*, **43A**, 715.

Heal, O. W. & Maclean, S. F., Jr. (1975) Comparative productivity in ecosystems – secondary productivity. In *Unifying Concepts in Ecology* (eds W. H. van Dobben & R. H. Lowe-McConnell). Dr W. Junk, B. V. Publishers, The Hague.

Heinrich, B. (1979) Keeping a cool head: honeybee thermoregulation. *Science*, **205**, 1269–71.

Heinrich, B. & Bartholomew, G. A. (1979) The ecology of the African dung beetle. *Sci. Am.*, **241**, 118–26.

Hemmingsen, A. M. (1960) Energy metabolism as related to body size and respiratory surfaces, and its evolution. *Reports of the Steno Memorial Hospital and the Nordisk Insulinlaboratorium*, **9**, 1–110.

Henderson, C. & Loveridge, J. P. (1980) Unpublished results, Zoology Department, University of Cape Town.

Henwood, K. (1975) A field-tested thermoregulation model for two diurnal Namib Desert tenebrionid beetles. *Ecology*, **56**, 1329–42.

Hochachka, P. W. & Somero, G. N. (1973) *Strategies of Biochemical Adaption*. Saunders, Phila.

Hofmeyr, M. D. (1980) Unpublished results, Zoology Department, University of the Western Cape.

Hofmeyr, M. D. & Louw, G. N. (1980) Unpublished results, Zoology Department, University of Cape Town.

Holling, C. S. (1959) The components of predation as revealed by a study of small-mammal predation of the European pine sawfly. *Can. Entomol.*, **91**, 293–320.

Hudson, J. W. (1962) The role of water in the biology of the antelope ground squirrel, *Citellus tereticaudus*. *Univ. Calif. Publs. Zool.*, **64**, 1–56.

Hudson, J. W., Deavers, D. R. & Bradley, S. R. (1972) A comparative study of temperature regulation in ground squirrels with special reference to the desert species. *Symp. zool. Soc. Lond.*, **31**, 191–213.

Hutchinson, G. E. (1957) Concluding remarks. *Cold Spring Harbour Symp. Quant. Biol.*, **22**, 415–29.

Hutchinson, J. C. D. & Brown, G. B. (1969) Penetrance of cattle coats by radiation. *J. appl. Physiol.*, **26**, 454–64.

Hutchinson, J. C. D., Brown, G. D. & Allen, T. E. (1976) Effects of solar radiation on the sensible heat exchange of mammals. In *Progress in Animal Biometeorology* (ed. H. D. Johnson). Swets and Zeitlinger, Amsterdam.

Immelmann, K. (1963) Drought adaptations in Australian desert birds *Proc. 13th Int. Ornithol. Congr.*, Ithaca, N.Y.

Jarvis, J. U. M. (1978) Energetics of survival in *Heterocephalus glaber* (Rüppel), the naked mole-rat (Rodentia: Bathyergidae). *Bull. Carnegie Mus. Nat. Hist.*, **6**, 81–7.

Johnson, D. R. & Schreiber, R. K. (1979) Assimilation, respiration and production: (b) vertebrates. In *Arid-land Ecosystems: Structure, Functioning and Management* (eds D. W. Goodall, R. A. Perry & K. M. W. Howes), vol. 1. Cambridge U.P.

Karr, J. R. & James, F. C. (1975) Ecomorphological configurations and convergent evolution. In *Ecology and Evolution of Communities* (eds M. L. Cody & J. M. Diamond). The Belknap Press of Harvard U.P., Cambridge, Mass.

Kassas, M. (1966) Plant life in deserts. In *Arid lands: A Geographical Appraisal* (ed. F. S. Hills), Methuen, London.

Keith, L. B. (1963) *Wildlife's Ten-year Cycle*. University of Wisconsin Press, Madison.

Khalil, F. & Abdel-Messeih, G. (1959) The storage of extra water by various tissues of *Varanus griseus* Daud. *Z. vergl. Physiol.*, **42**, 415–21.

Kislev, M. (1972) Pollination ecology of desert plants. Ph.D. thesis, Hebrew University, Jerusalem. In Noy-Meir, I. (1979/80)

Koller, D. (1972) Environmental control of seed germination. In *Seed Biology* (ed. T. T. Kozlowski), vol. 2. Academic Press, N.Y.

Krebs, C. J. (1972) *Ecology: The Experimental Analysis of Distribution and Abundance*. Harper and Row, N.Y.

Krutch, J. W. (1966) *The Voice of the Desert*. William Sloane Associates, N.Y.

Lack, D. (1948) The significance of litter size. *J. anim. Ecol.*, **17**, 45–50.

Lange, O. L., Schulze, E. D., Kappen, K., Buschbom, U. & Evenari, M. (1975) Adaptations of desert lichens to drought and extreme temperatures. In *Environmental Physiology of Desert Organisms* (ed. N. F. Hadley). Dowden, Hutchinson and Ross, Stroudsberg, Pa.

Larcher, W. (1975) *Physiological Plant Ecology*. Springer-Verlag, Berlin.

Lasiewski, R. C. (1969) Physiological responses to heat stress in the poorwill. *Am. J. Physiol.*, **217**, 1504–09.

Lavigne, D. M. & Øritsland, N. A. (1974) Black polar bears. *Nature*, **251**, 281.

Leigh, E. G. (1975) Population fluctuations, community stability and environmental variability. In *Ecology and Evolution of Communities* (eds M. L. Cody & J. M. Diamond). The Belknap Press of Harvard U.P. Cambridge, Mass.

le Houérou, H. N. (1979) Description and structure of arid ecosystems: North Africa. In *Arid-land Ecosystems: Structure, Functioning and Management* (eds D. W. Goodall, R. A. Perry & K. M. W.

Howes), vol. 1. Cambridge. U.P.

Leistner, O. A. (1979) Description and structure of arid ecosystems: southern Africa. In *Arid-land Ecosystems: Structure, Functioning and Management* (eds D. W. Goodall, R. A. Perry & K. M. W. Howes), vol. 1. Cambridge U.P.

Leopold, A. S. (1962) *The Desert.* Time Inc., N.Y.

le Roux, G. J. (1970) The microbiology of sand-dune ecosystems in the Namib Desert. M.Sc. thesis, University of Stellenbosch.

Levitt, J. (1972) *Responses of Plants to Environmental Stress.* Academic Press, N.Y.

Licht, P. (1964) The temperature dependence of myosine-adenosine-triphosphotase and alkaline phosphotase in lizards. *Comp. Biochem. Physiol.*, **12**, 331–40.

Litav, M. (1957) The influence of *Tamarix aphylla* on soil composition in the northern Negev of Israel. *Bull. Res. Counc. Isr.*, **D6**, 38–45. In Noy-Meir, I. (1973).

Lotka, A. J. (1925) *Elements of Physical Biology.* (Reprinted in 1956 by Dover Publications, N.Y.).

Louw, G. N. (1972) The role of advective fog in the water economy of certain Namib Desert animals. *Symp. zool. Soc. Lond.*, **31**, 297–314.

Louw, G. N., Belonje, P. C. & Coetzee, H. J. (1969) Renal function, respiration, heart rate and thermoregulation in the ostrich (*Struthio camelus*). *Scient. Pap. Namib Desert Res. Stat.*, **42**, 43–54.

Louw, G. N. & Hamilton, W. J. III., (1972) Physiological and behavioural ecology of the ultrapsammophilous Namib Desert tenebrionid *Lepidochora argentogrisea. Madogua*, **1**, 87–95.

Louw, G. N. & Holm, E. (1972) Physiological, morphological and behavioural adaptations in the ultrapsammophilous Namib Desert lizard, *Aporosaura anchietae. Madoqua*, **1**, 67–85.

Loveridge, J. P. (1970) Observations on nitrogenous excretion and water relations of *Chiromantis xerampelina* (Amphibia, Anura). *Arnoldia* (Rhodesia), **5**, 1–6.

Loveridge, J. P. (1976) Strategies of water conservation in southern African frogs. *Zool. Afr.*, **11**, 319–33.

Loveridge, J. P. & Bursell, E. (1975) Studies on the water relations of adult locusts (Orthoptera, Acrididae). 1. Respiration and the production of metabolic water. *Bull. Entomol. Res.*, **65**, 13–20.

Loveridge, J. P. & Withers, P. C. (1981) The metabolism and water balance of active and cocooned African bullfrogs, *Pyxicephalus adspersus. Physiol. Zool.* **54**, 203–214.

Low, B. S. (1976) The evolution of amphibian life histories in the desert. In *Evolution of Desert Biota* (ed. D. W. Goodall). University of Texas Press, Austin.

Low, B. S. (1979) The predictability of rain and the foraging patterns of the red kangaroo (*Megaleia rufa*) in central Australia. *J. Arid Environments*, **2**, 61–76.

Lyndolph, P. E. (1957) A comparative analysis of the dry western littorals. *Association of American Geographers, Annals*, **47**, 213–30.

MacArthur, R. H. & Wilson, E. O. (1967) *The Theory of Island Biogeography.* Princeton University Press, Princeton, N.J.

Macfarlane, W. V. (1964) Terrestrial animals in dry heat: ungulates. In *Adaptation to the Environment. Handbook of Physiology* (ed. D. B. Dill). American Physiological Society, Washington D.C.

Maclean, G. L. (1974) Arid-zone ornithology in Africa and South Africa. *Proc. 16th Int. Ornithol. Congr.*, 468–80.

MacMahon, J. A. (1979) Description and structure of arid ecosystems: North America. In *Arid-land Ecosystems: Structure, Functioning and Management* (eds D. W. Goodall, R. A. Perry & K. M. W. Howes), vol. 1. Cambridge U.P.

Macmillen, R. E. (1965) Aestivation in the cactus mouse, *Peromyscus eremicus. Comp. Biochem. Physiol.*, **16**, 227–48.

Macmillen, R. E. & Christopher, E. A. (1975) The water relations of two populations of noncaptive desert rodents. In *Environmental Physiology of Desert Organisms* (ed. N. F. Hadley). Ch. 8. Dowden, Hutchinson and Ross, Stroudsberg, Pa.

Macmillen, R. E. & Lee, A. K. (1967) Australian desert mice: independence of exogenous water. *Science*, **158**, 383–5.

McClanahan, L. L., Stinner, J. N. & Shoemaker, V. H. (1978) Skin lipids, water loss and energy metabolism in a South American tree frog (*Phyllomedusa sauvagei*). *Physiol. Zool.*, **51**, 179–87.

McCleary, J. A. (1968) The biology of desert plants. In *Desert Biology* (ed. G. W. Brown), vol. 1. Academic Press, N.Y.

McGinnies, W. G. (1979) Description and structure of arid ecosystems: general description of desert areas. In *Arid-land Ecosystems: Structure, Functioning and Management* (eds D. W. Goodall, R. A. Perry & K. M. W. Howes), vol. 1. Cambridge U.P.

McGinnies, W. G., Goldman, B. J. & Paylore, P. (1968) *Deserts of the World.* University of Arizona Press, Tucson.

McKee, E. D. (ed.) (1979) *A Study of Global Sand Seas.* Geological Survey Professional Paper 1052, US Government Printing Office, Washington, D.C.

McMahon, T. (1973) Size and shape in biology. *Science*, **179**, 1201–4.

Maloiy, G. M. O. (ed.) (1972) *Comparative Physiology of Desert Animals*. Academic Press, London.

Maltz, E. & Shkolnik, A. (1980) Milk production in the desert: lactation and water economy in the black Bedouin goat. *Physiol. Zool.*, **53**, 12–18.

Marder, J. (1973) Body temperature regulation in the brown-necked raven (*Corvus corax ruficollis*). II. Thermal changes in the plumage of ravens exposed to solar radiation. *Comp. Biochem. Physiol.*, **45A**, 431–40.

Mares, M. A. (1978) Convergent evolution in desert ecosystems (Abstract). *Proc. 2nd Int. Congr. of Ecol.*, Jerusalem, **I**, 225.

Marsh, A. C., Louw, G. & Berry, H. H. (1978) Aspects of renal physiology, nutrition and thermoregulation in the ground squirrel *Xerus inauris*. *Madoqua*, **II (2)**, 129–35.

Mayr, E. (1963) *Animal Species and Evolution*. The Belknap Press of Harvard U.P., Cambridge, Mass.

Meentemeyer, V. (1978) Macroclimate and lignin control of litter decomposition rates. *Ecology*, **59**, 465–72.

Meigs, P. (1953) World distribution of arid and semi-arid homoclimates. In *Reviews of Research on Arid Zone Hydrology*, Unesco, Paris, **1**, 203–10.

Mendelssohn, H. (1980) Conservation in desert ecosystems (Abstract). In *International Symposium on Habitats and their Influences on Wildlife*. Pretoria, 3–4 July 1980. The Endangered Wildlife Trust.

Menzel, D. W. & Ryther, J. H. (1961) Annual variations in primary production of the Sargasso Sea off Bermuda. *Deep Sea Res.*, **7**, 282–8.

Millar, R. P. (1972) Reproduction in the rock hyrax (*Procavia capensis*) with special reference to seasonal sexual activity in the male. Ph.D. thesis, University of Liverpool.

Miller, R. S. (1967) Pattern and process in competition. *Adv. Ecol. Res.*, **4**, 1–74.

Mispagel, M. E. (1978) The ecology and bioenergetics of the acridid grasshopper, *Bootettix puctatus* on creosote bush, *Larrea tridentata*, in the northern Mojave Desert. *Ecology*, **59**, 779–88.

Mitchell, D. (1977) Physical basis of thermoregulation. In *International Review of Physiology, Environmental Physiology II* (ed. D. Robertshaw), vol. 15. University Park Press, Baltimore.

Monod, T. (1954) Modes 'contracte' et 'diffus' de la végétation saharienne. In *Biology of Deserts* (ed. J. L. Cloudsley-Thompson). Proceedings: Symposium on the Biology of Hot and Cold Deserts, 1952, London. Institute of Biology, London.

Monteith, J. L. (1973) *Principles of Environmental Physics*. American Elsevier, N.Y.

Mooney, H. A. (1972) The carbon balance of plants. *Annu. Rev. Ecol. Syst.*, **3**, 315–46.

Moorehead, A. (1963) *Coopers Creek*. Hamish Hamilton, London.

Mott, J. J. (1972) Germination studies on some annual species from an arid region of Western Australia. *J. Ecol.*, **60**, 293–304.

Mulroy, T. W. & Rundel, P. W. (1977) Annual plants: adaptations to desert environments. *Bioscience*, **27**, 109–14.

Murphy, G. I. (1968) Pattern in life-history and the environment. *Am. Nat.*, **102**, 390–404.

Nabhan, G. P. (1979) Tepary beans: the effects of domestication on adaptations to arid environments. *Arid Lands Newsletter*, No. 10, University of Arizona, Tucson.

Naiman, R. J., Gerking, S. D. & Ratcliff, T. D. (1973) Thermal environment of a Death Valley pupfish. *Copeia*, **2**, 366–9.

Nicolson, S. W. (1980) Water balance and osmoregulation in *Onymacris plana*, a tenebrionid beetle from the Namib Desert. *J. Insect Physiol.*, **26**, 315–20.

Niering, W. A. Whittaker, R. H. & Lowe, C. H. (1963) The saguaro: a population in relation to environment. *Science*, **142**, 15–23.

Noy-Meir, I. (1973) Desert ecosystems: environment and producers. *Annu. Rev. Ecol. Syst.*, **4**, 25–51.

Noy-Meir, I. (1974) Desert ecosystems: higher trophic levels. *Annu. Rev. Ecol. Syst.*, **5**, 195–214.

Noy-Meir, I. (1978) Structure and function of desert ecosystems (Abstract). *Proc. 2nd Int. Congr. Ecol.*, Jerusalem, **1**, 265.

Noy-Meir, I. (1979/80) Structure and function of desert ecosystems. *Isr. J. Bot.*, **28**, 1–19.

Noy-Meir, I. & Seligman, N. G. (1979) Management of semi-arid ecosystems in Israel. In *Management of Semi-arid Ecosystems* (ed. B. H. Walker). Elsevier, Amsterdam.

Nutting, W. L., Haverty, M. I. & Le Fage, J. P. (1974) Colony characteristics of termites as related to population density and habitat. *US/IBP Desert Research Memorandum, RM 74-28*. Logan, Utah. In Crawford, C. S. (1979).

Odum, E. P. (1975) Diversity as a funtion of energy flow. In *Unifying Concepts in Ecology* (eds W. H. van Dobben & R. H. Lowe-McConnell). Dr W. Junk BV Publishers, The Hague.

Ohmart, R. D. & Lasiewski, R. C. (1971) Roadrunners: energy conservation by hypothermia and absorption of sunlight. *Science*, **172**, 67–9.

Orians, G. H. & Solbrig, O. T. (1977) *Convergent Evolution in Warm Deserts*. Dowden, Hutchinson and Ross, Stroudsburg, Pa.

Paine, R. T. (1966) Food web complexity and species diversity. *Am. Nat.*, **100**, 65–76.

Park, T. (1962) Beetles, competition and populations. *Science*, **138**, 1369–75.

Pearson, O. P. (1966) The prey of carnivores during one cycle of mouse abundance. *J. anim. Ecol.*, **35**, 217–33.

Pennycuick, L. (1975) Movements of the migratory wildebeest population in the Serengeti area between 1960 and 1973. *E. Afr. Wildl. J.*, **13**, 65–87.

Perez-Albuerne, E. A. & Yuan-Sheng, Tyan (1980) Photovoltaic materials. *Science*, **208**, 902–7.

Petrov, M. P. (1976) *Deserts of the World*. Halstead Press, N.Y.

Pianka, E. R. (1970) On *r*- and *k*-selection. *Am. Nat.*, **104**, 592–7.

Pianka, E. R. (1973) The structure of lizard communities. *Annu. Rev. Ecol. Syst.*, **4**, 53–74.

Pianka, E. R. (1974) *Evolutionary Ecology*. Harper and Row, N.Y.

Pianka, E. R. (1975) Niche relations of desert lizards. In *Ecology and Evolution of Communities* (eds M. L. Cody & J. M. Diamond). The Beiknap Press of Harvard U.P., Cambridge Mass.

Pielou, E. C. (1975) *Ecological Diversity*. Wiley, N.Y.

Pimentel, D., Nagel, W. P. & Madde, J. L. (1963) Space-time structure of the environment and the survival of parasite-host systems. *Am. Nat.*, **97**, 141–67.

Pitelka, L. F. (1977) Energy allocation in annual and perennial lupines (*Lupinus*: Leguminosae). *Ecology*, **58**, 1055–65.

Polis, G. A. & Farley, R. D. (1979) Characteristics and environmental determinants of natality, growth and maturity in a natural population of the desert scorpion, *Paruroctonus mesaensis* (Scorpionida: Vaejovidae). *J. Zool., Lond.*, **187**, 517–42.

Porter, W. P. (1967) Solar radiation through the living body walls of vetebrates with emphasis on desert reptiles. *Ecol. Monogr.*, **33**, 273–96.

Porter, W. P. & Gates, D. M. (1969) Thermodynamic equilibria of animals with environment. *Ecol. Monogr.*, **39**, 227–45.

Price, M. V. (1978) The role of microhabitat in structuring desert rodent communities. *Ecology*, **59(5)**, 910–21.

Prosser, C. L. & Brown, F. A. (1961) *Comparative Animal Physiology*. Saunders, Phila.

Reichman, O. J. & Brown, J. H. (1979) The use of torpor by *Perognathus amplus* in relation to resource distribution. *J. Mammal.*, **60**, 550–5.

Ricklefs, R. E. (1973) *Ecology*. Nelson, London.

Ricklefs, R. E. (1974) Energetics of reproduction in birds. In *Avian Energetics* (ed. R. A. Paynter). Nuttal Ornithological Club, Cambridge, Mass.

Riddle, W. A. (1979) Metabolic compensation for temperature change in the scorpion *Paruroctonus utahensis*. *J. thermal Biology*, **4**, 125–8.

Riddle, W. A., Crawford, C. S. & Zeitone, A. M. (1976) Patterns of haemolymph osmoregulation in three desert arthropods. *J. Comp. Physiol.*, **112**, 295–305.

Riddock, F. & Wilson, J. I. B. (1980) The application of solar energy in arid zones. *J. of Arid Environments*, **3**, 1–8.

Riemerschmid, G. & Elder, J. S. (1945) The absorptivity for solar radiation of different coloured hair coats of cattle. *Onderstepoort J. Vet. Sci.*, **20**, 223–34.

Rigler, F. H. (1975) The concept of energy flow and nutrient flow between trophic levels. In *Unifying Concepts in Ecology* (eds W. H. van Dobben & R. H. Lowe-McConnell). Dr W. Junk B. V. Publishers, The Hague.

Robinson, E. R. (1977) Phytosociology of the Namib Desert Park, South West Africa. M.Sc. thesis, University of Natal.

Robinson, M. D. (1980) Unpublished results. University Simon Bolivar, Caracas, Venezuela.

Robinson, M. D. & Cunningham, A. B. (1978) Comparative diet of two Namib Desert sand lizards (Lacertidae). *Madoqua*, **11**, 41–53.

Rosenzweig, M. L. & Winakur, J. (1969) Population ecology of desert rodent communities: habitats and environmental complexity. *Ecology*, **50**, 558–72.

Ruibal, R., Tevis, L. & Roig, V. (1969) The terrestrial ecology of the spadefoot toad *Scaphiopus hammondi*. *Copeia*, 571–84.

Rundel. P. W. (1976) Succulents in the coastal fog zone of northern Chile. *Cactus and Succulent Journal (US)*, **48**, 269–71.

Rundel, P. W. (1978) Ecological relationships of desert fog zone lichens. *Bryologist*, **81**, 277–93.

Rutherford, M. C. (1980) Annual plant production – precipitation relations in arid and semi-arid regions. *S. Afr. J. Sci.*, **76**, 53–6.

Rzóska, J. (1961) Observations on tropical rainpools and general remarks on temporary waters. *Hydrobiologia*, **17**, 265–86.

Sadlier, R. M. F. S. (1969) *The Ecology of Reproduction in Wild and Domestic Mammals*. Methuen, London.

Sanders, H. L. (1968) Marine benthic diversity: a comparative study. *Am. Nat.*, **102**, 243–83.

Schaffer, W. M. & Gadgil, M. D. (1975) Selection for optimal life histories in plants. In *Ecology and Evolution of Communities* (eds M. L. Cody & J. M. Diamond). Harvard U.P. Cambridge, Mass.

Schall, J. J. & Pianka, E. R. (1978) Geographical trends in numbers of species. *Science*, **201**, 679–86.

Schmidt-Nielsen, Bodil, Schmidt-Nielsen, K., Brokaw, Adelaide & Schneiderman, H. (1948) Water conservation in desert rodents. *J. cell. comp. Physiol.*, **32**, 331–60.

Schmidt-Nielsen, K. (1964) *Desert Animals: Physiological Problems of Heat and Water*. Oxford U.P. U.N.Y.

Schmidt-Nielsen, K. (1970) *Animal Physiology*, 3rd edn. Prentice-Hall, Engelwood Cliffs, N.J.

Schmidt-Nielsen, K., Schmidt-Nielsen, B. Jarnum, S. A. & Houpt, T. R. (1957) Body temperature of the camel and its relation to water economy. *Am. J. Physiol.*, **188**, 103–12.

Schmidt-Nielsen, K., Taylor, C. R. & Shkolnik, A. (1972) Desert snails: problems of survival. *Symp. zool. Soc. Lond.*, **31**, 1–13.

Schulze, E.-D., Ziegler, H. & Stichler, W. (1976) Environmental control of Crassulacean Acid Metabolism in *Welwitschia mirabilis* Hook fil. in its range of natural distribution in the Namib Desert. *Oecologia* (Berl.), **24**, 323–34.

Seely, M. K. (1976) Sand solidified by gemsbok urine as selected burrow sites by gerbils. *Zool. Afr.*, **12**, 246–8.

Seely, M. K. (1978a) The Namib Dune Desert: an unusual ecosystem. *J. Arid Environments*, **1**, 117–28.

Seely, M. K. (1978b) Grassland productivity: the desert end of the curve. *S. Afr. J. Sci.*, **74**, 295–7.

Seely, M. K., de Vos, M. P. & Louw, G. N. (1977) Fog imbibition, satellite fauna and unusual leaf structure in a Namib Desert dune plant, *Trianthema hereroensis*. *S. Afr. J. Sci.*, **73**, 169–72.

Seely, M. K. & Hamilton W. J. III. (1976) Fog catchment sand trenches constructed by tenebrionid beetles, *Lepidochora*, from the Namib Desert. *Science*, **193**, 484–6.

Seely, M. K. & Louw, G. N. (1980) First approximation of the effects of rainfall on the ecology and energetics of a Namib Desert dune ecosystem. *J. Arid Environments*, **3**, 25–54.

Serventy, D. L. (1971) Biology of desert birds. In *Avian Biology* (eds D. S. Farner, J. R. King & K. C. Parkes), vol. 1. Academic Press, N.Y.

Shkolnik, A. (1977) Physiological adaptations of mammals to life in the desert. In *The Desert, Past, Present, Future* (ed. Ezra Sohar), Ch. 3. (In Hebrew)

Shkolnik, A., Borut, A., Chosniak, I. & Maltz, E. (1975) Water economy and drinking regime of the Bedouin goat. *Symposium Israel–France*, Volcani Center, Bet-Dagan, Israel. pp. 79–90.

Shkolnik, A., Schroter, R. C. & Schmidt-Nielsen, K. (1980a) Exhalation of unsaturated air in camels (Abstract). *Proc. XXVIII Int. Congr. Phys. Sci., Budapest.*

Shkolnik, A., Taylor, C. R., Finch, V. & Borut, A. (1980b) Why do Bedouins wear black robes in hot deserts? *Nature*, **283**, 373–5.

Shoemaker, V. H. & Nagy, K. A. (1977) Osmoregulation in amphibians and reptiles. *Annu. Rev. Physiol.*, **39**, 449–71.

Sinclair, A. R. E. (1975) The resource limitation of trophic levels in tropical grassland ecosystems. *J. anim. Ecol.*, **44**, 497–520.

Soholt, L. F. (1973) Consumption of primary production by a population of kangaroo rats (*Dipodomys merriami*) in the Mojave Desert. *Ecol. Monogr.*, **43**, 357–76.

Solbrig, O. T. & Orians, G. H. (1977) The adaptive characteristics of desert plants. *Amer. Sci.*, **65**, 412–21.

Strydom, N. B. (1980) Textbook themes on thermal regulation. *S. Afr. J. Sci.*, **76**, 324.

Stuart, C. T. (1976) Diet of the black-backed jackal *Canis mesomelas* in the Central Namib Desert, South West Africa. *Zool. Afr.*, **11**, 193–205.

Syvertsen, J. P., Nickell, G. L., Spellenberg, R. W., & Cunningham, G. L. (1976) Carbon reduction pathways and standing crop in three Chihuahuan desert plant communities. *The Southwestern Naturalist*, **21**, 311–20.

Szarek, S. R. (1979) Primary production in four North American deserts: indices of efficiency. *J. Arid Environments*, **2**, 187–209.

Takahashi, F. (1977) Generation carryover of a fraction of population members as an animal adaptation to unstable environmental conditions. *Res. Popul. Ecol.*, **18**, 235–42.

Taylor, C. R. (1969) The eland and the oryx. *Sci. Amer.*, **220**, 88–95.

Taylor, C. R. (1972) The desert gazelle: a paradox resolved. *Symp. zool. Soc. Lond.*, **31**, 215–27.

Taylor, C. R. (1977) Exercise and environmental heat loads: different mechanisms for solving different problems? In *International Review of Physiology, Environmental Physiology II* (ed. D. Robertshaw), vol. 15. University Press, Baltimore.

Taylor, C. R., Schmidt-Nielsen, K. & Raab, J. L. (1970) Scaling of the energetic cost of running to body size in mammals. *Am. J. Physiol.*, **219**, 1104–7.

Ting, I. P., Johnson, H. & Szarek, S. (1972) Net CO_2 fixation in CAM plants. In *Net CO_2 Assimilation in Higher Plants* (ed. C. C. Black). Symposium of the southern section of the American Society of Plant

Physiologists, Cotton Inc., N.C.

Tinkle, D. W. (1967) Home range, density, dynamics and structure of a Texas population of the lizard *Uta stansburiana*. In *Lizard Ecology – A Symposium* (ed. W. M. Milstead). University of Missouri Press, Columbia.

Tinkle, D. W. (1969) The concept of reproductive effort and its relation to the evolution of life-histories of lizard. *Am. Nat.*, **103**, 501–16.

Treshaw, M. (1970) *Environment and Plant Response*. McGraw-Hill, N.Y.

Turner, R. M., Alcorn, S. M. & Olin, G. (1969) Mortality of transplanted saguaro seedlings. *Ecology*, **50**, 835–44.

Vinegar, M. B. (1975) Demography of the striped plateau lizard, *Sceloporus virgatus*. *Ecology*, **56**, 172–82.

Vogel, J. C., Fuls, A. & Ellis, R. P. (1978) The geographical distribution of Kranz grasses in South Africa. *S. Afr. J. Sci.*, **74**, 209–15.

Vogel, J. C. & Seely, M. K. (1977) Occurrence of C-4 plants in the central Namib Desert. *Madoqua*, **10**, 75–8.

Vogel, S. (1955) Niedere 'Fensterpflanzen' in der südafrikanischen Wüste. *Beitr. Biol. Pflanz.*, **31**, 45–135.

Volterra, V. (1926) Fluctuations in the abundance of a species considered mathematically. *Nature*, **118**, 558–60.

Vossbrink, C. R., Coleman, D. C. & Woolley, T. A. (1979) Abiotic and biotic factors in litter decomposition in a semi-arid grassland. *Ecology*, **60**, 265–71.

Walker, B. H. (1979) Management principles for semi-arid ecosystems. In *Management of Semi-arid Ecosystems* (ed. B. H. Walker). Elsevier, Amsterdam.

Wallace, A., Romney E. M. & Hunter, R. B. (1978) Nitrogen cycle in the northern Mojave Desert: implications and predictions. In *Nitrogen in Desert Ecosystems* (eds N. E. West & J. Skujins). US/IBP Synthesis Series 9. Dowden, Hutchinson and Ross, Stroudsberg, Pa.

Walsberg, G. E. (1977) Ecology and energetics of contrasting social systems in *Phainopepla nitens* (Aves: Ptilogonatidae). *Univ. Calif. Publs. Zool.*, **108**, 1–62.

Walsberg, G. E., Campbell, G. S. & King, J. R. (1978) Animal coat color and radiative heat gain: a re-evaluation. *J. comp. Physiol.*, **126**, 211–22.

Walter, H. (1939) Grasland, Savanne und Busch der ariden Teile Afrikas in ihrer ökologischen Bedingtheit. *Jahrb. Wiss. Bot.*, **87**, 750–860.

Walter, H. (1964) *Die Vegetation der Erde in öko-physiologischer Betrachtung*, vol. 1, 2nd edn, Fischer, Jena.

Walter, H. (1971) *Ecology of Tropical and Subtropical Vegetation*. Oliver and Boyd, Edinburgh.

Walter, H. (1976) Gibt es in der Namib Nebelpflanzen? *Namib und Meer*, **7**, 5–13.

Walter, H. & Stadelman, E. (1974) A new approach to the water relations of desert plants. In *Desert Biology* (ed. G. W. Brown), vol. II. Academic Press, N.Y.

Webb, W., Szarek, S., Lavenroth, W., Kinerson, R. & Smith, M. (1978) Primary productivity and water use in native forest, grassland and desert ecosystems. *Ecology*, **59**, 1239–47.

Weigert, R. C., Odum, E. P. & Schnell, J. H. (1967) Forb-arthropod food chains in a one-year experimental field. *Ecology*, **48**, 75–83.

Weisser, P., Weisser, J., Schreier, K. & Robres, L. (1975) Discovery of a subterranean species of *Neschilenia* (Chileorebutia, Thelocephala) in the Atacama Desert, Chile, and notes about its habitat. *Excelsa*, **5**, 97–9, 104.

West, N. E. & Skujins, J. (eds) (1978) *Nitrogen in Desert Ecosystems*. US/IBP Synthesis Series 9. Dowden, Hutchinson and Ross, Stroudsberg, Pa.

Westoby, M. (1972) Problem-oriented modelling: a conceptual framework. Presented at Desert Biome Information Meeting, Tempe, Ariz. In Noy-Meir, I. (1973).

White, L. P. (1969) Vegetation arcs in Jordan. *J. Ecol.*, **57**, 461–4.

White, T. C. R. (1978) The importance of relative shortage of food in animal ecology. *Oecologia* (Berl.), **33**, 71–86.

Whitford, W. G. & Bryant, M. (1979) Behaviour of a predator and its prey: the horned lizard (*Phrynosoma cornutum*) and harvester ants (*Pogonomyrmex* spp.). *Ecology*, **60**, 689–94.

Whitman, W. C. & Wolters, G. (1967) Microclimatic gradients in mixed grass prairie. In *Ground Level Climatology* (ed. R. H. Shaw). American Association for the Advancement of Science Publication No. 86, Washington, D.C.

Whittaker, R. H. (1975) *Communities and Ecosystems*. Macmillan, N. Y.

Wickens, G. E. & White, L. P. (1979) Land-use in the southern margins of the Sahara. In *Management of Semi-arid Ecosystems* (ed. B. H. Walker). Elsevier, Amsterdam.

Williams, O. B. (1979) Description and structure of arid ecosystems: Australia. In *Arid-land Ecosystems: Structure, Functioning and Management* (eds D. W. Goodall, R. A. Perry & K. M. W. Howes).

Cambridge U.P.

Winstanley, D. (1976) Climatic changes and the future of the Sahel. In *The Politics of a Natural Disaster: The Case of the Sahel* (ed. M. Glantz). Praeger, N.Y.

Withers, P. C., Louw, G. N. & Henschel, J. (1980) Energetics and water relations in Namib Desert rodents. *S. Afr. J. Zool.*, **15**, 131–7.

Withers, P. C., Louw, G. N. & Siegfried, W. R. (1981) Unpublished results, Zoology Department, University of Cape Town.

Yeaton, R. I. (1978) A cyclic relationship between *Larrea tridentata* and *Opuntia leptocaulis* in the northern Chihuahuan Desert. *J. Ecol.*, **66**, 651–6.

Yeaton, R. I. & Cody, M. L. (1976) Competition and spacing in plant communities: the northern Mojave Desert. *J. Ecol.*, **64**, 689–96.

Yeaton, R. I., Travis, J. & Gilinsky, E. (1977) Competition and spacing in plant communities: the Arizona upland association. *J. Ecol.*, **65**, 587–95.

Yom-Tov, Y. (1970) The effects of predation on population densities of some desert snails. *Ecology*, **51**, 907–11.

Yom-Tov, Y. (1971) The biology of two desert snails: *Trochoidea* (Xerocrassa) *seatzenii* and *Sphincterochila boissieri*. *Isr. J. Zool.*, **20**, 231–48.

Yousef, M. K., Horvath, S. M. & Bullard, R. W. (1972) *Physiological Adaptations: Desert and Mountain.* Academic Press, N.Y.

Zemach, J. (1974) Ecological research on *Salsola inermis* in Sde Fin. M.Sc. thesis, Hebrew University, Jerusalem. In Noy-Meir, I. (1979/80).

Zohary, M. (1973) *Geobotanical Foundations of the Middle East.* Gustav Fischer Verlag, Stuttgart.

Index